The
Supreme
Court,
Race,
and
Civil
Rights

To the memory of my parents,
the late Rev. and Mrs. Jordan Davis;
my sister, the late Alva Barnes;
and my brothers, the late Hillis and Elbert Davis,
for their genuine love.

Abraham L. Davis

To the memory of my parents,
Slade and Ruby Luck.

Barbara Luck Graham

The
Supreme Court, Race, *and* Civil Rights

Abraham L. Davis
Barbara Luck Graham

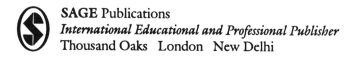
SAGE Publications
International Educational and Professional Publisher
Thousand Oaks   London   New Delhi

For information address:

SAGE Publications, Inc.
2455 Teller Road
Thousand Oaks, California 91320
E-mail: order@sagepub.com

SAGE Publications Ltd.
6 Bonhill Street
London EC2A 4PU
United Kingdom

SAGE Publications India Pvt. Ltd.
M-32 Market
Greater Kailash I
New Delhi 110048 India

Printed in the United States of America

Library of Congress Cataloging-in-Publication Data

Davis, Abraham L.
The Supreme Court, race, and civil rights/ Abraham L. Davis,
Barbara Luck Graham.
p. cm.
Includes bibliographical references and index.
ISBN 0-8039-7219-9.—ISBN 0-8039-7220-2
1. Race discrimination—Law and legislation—United States.
2. Civil rights—United States 3. United States—Supreme Court.
I. Graham, Barbara Luck. II. Title.
KF4755.D38   1995
342.73'085—dc20
[347.30285]   95-12923

This book is printed on acid-free paper.

00 01 02 03   10 9 8 7 6 5

Sage Production Editor: Diana E. Axelsen
Sage Typesetter: Danielle Dillahunt

Contents

Preface   **xiii**

**Introduction: The Supreme Court, Civil Rights,
and the Enduring Struggle for Equality**   **xvii**

1. **From Marshall to Fuller: The Era of White Supremacy
   and Second-Class Citizenship, 1801-1910**   **1**
   The Constitution and Slavery   1
   The Supreme Court and the Legitimization of Slavery:
       The Marshall and Taney Eras, 1801-1864   3
       Fugitive Slave Law   6
       Slavery in the Territories   7
   The Post-Civil War Era: Reconstruction and
       National Protection of Civil Rights   10
   The Supreme Court's Assault on Equality, 1864-1888   13
       The Chase Court, 1864-1873   13
       The Waite Court, 1874-1888   17
       The Equal Protection Clause and Chinese Ancestry   20
   The Fuller Court, 1888-1910:
       The Nadir in the Quest for Equality   20
       Separate but Equal in Law, Separate but Unequal in Fact   21
       The Thirteenth Amendment and the Peonage Cases   26
   Conclusion   27

CASES   28

Prigg v. The Commonwealth of Pennsylvania (1842)   28
Dred Scott v. Sandford (1857)   31
Slaughter-House Cases (1873)   35
United States v. Reese (1876)   38
Hall v. DeCuir (1878)   40
Strauder v. West Virginia (1880)   42
Pace v. Alabama (1883)   43
United States v. Harris (1883)   44
Civil Rights Cases (1883)   46
Yick Wo v. Hopkins (1886)   48
Plessy v. Ferguson (1896)   50
Berea College v. Commonwealth of Kentucky (1908)   53
Bailey v. Alabama (1911)   54

2. **From White to Vinson: The Campaign**
   for Racial Equality, 1910-1953   **57**
   The Supreme Court in Transition   57
   The Persistent Struggle for the Ballot:
       Blacks' Abiding Faith in Democracy   60
   Jim Crow Housing and the Emergence
       of Restrictive Covenants   66
   Race and the Administration of Justice:
       The Dawning of Hope   69
       The Right to Counsel: The Scottsboro Case   69
       Discrimination in the Selection of Juries   70
       Coerced Confessions and the Use of Excessive Force   72
       Blacks and the Death Penalty   73
   United States v. Carolene Products Co.
       and the Famous Footnote 4:
       The Birth of Discrete and Insular Minorities   75
       The Emergence of Strict Scrutiny and a Two-Tiered
           Approach to Equal Protection:
           The Japanese Internment Cases   77
   Equal Protection and Higher Education:
       The Beginning of the Demise of
       the Separate-but-Equal Doctrine   79
       The Introduction of Social Science Evidence:
           A First for an Education Case   80
   The Thrill of Victory Over Jim Crow in
       Interstate Travel and Public Accommodations   81
   Group Libel Laws:
       Protecting Racial and Religious
       Groups from Defamation   84
   Conclusion   85

CASES   86

Nixon v. Herndon (1927)   86
Grovey v. Townsend (1935)   87
Smith v. Allwright (1944)   89
Buchanan v. Warley (1917)   91
Shelley v. Kraemer (1948)   92
Powell v. Alabama (1932)   94
Screws v. United States (1945)   96
Louisiana ex rel. Francis v. Resweber (1947)   98
Korematsu v. United States (1944)   100
Missouri ex rel. Gaines v. Canada (1938)   103
McLaurin v. Oklahoma State Regents
      for Higher Education (1950)   105
Sweatt v. Painter (1950)   106
Mitchell v. United States (1941)   107
Morgan v. Virginia (1946)   108
Beauharnais v. Illinois (1952)   110

3. **The Warren Court: The Era of Rising**
   Expectations and Massive Resistance, 1953-1969   **115**
   The Warren Court and the Egalitarian Revolution
         in Constitutional Law   115
   Brown I and *II:* School Desegregation   117
         Brown I and the Use of Social Science Data   121
         Aftermath of *Brown I: Brown II,*
               Resistance, and More Litigation   125
   Interest Groups' Political Use of the Courts:
         The Attack on the NAACP   128
   The Persistent Struggle to Vote:
         From Litigation to Congressional Action   131
   Sit-Ins, Peaceful Demonstrations,
         and the Judicial Response   137
         Efforts to Desegregate Public Facilities:
               The Application of *Brown* in Other Contexts   138
         The Sit-In Cases   139
         Mass Demonstrations: Lawful and Unlawful Conduct   146
   Eradicating Racial Discrimination in Public Accommodations   149
   Equal Housing Opportunities   152
   Race and the Administration of Justice: Equal or Unequal?   153
         Private Interference With Constitutional Rights:
               Criminal and Civil Remedies   155
         Jury Discrimination: A Persistent Problem   158
   Wills, Segregation, and the Fourteenth Amendment   159
   Interracial Dating and Marriages: Constitutional Issues   160
   Conclusion   161

CASES   164

Brown v. Board of Education (Brown I) (1954)   164
Bolling v. Sharpe (1954)   166
Brown v. Board of Education (Brown II) (1955)   167
Green v. County School Board of New Kent County (1968)   168
NAACP v. Alabama ex rel. Patterson (1958)   169
Gomillion v. Lightfoot (1960)   172
South Carolina v. Katzenbach (1966)   173
Boynton v. Virginia (1960)   176
Burton v. Wilmington Parking Authority (1961)   179
Garner v. Louisiana (1961)   181
Hamm v. City of Rock Hill (1964)   184
Edwards v. South Carolina (1963)   186
Cox v. Louisiana (Cox I) (1965)   188
Cox v. Louisiana (Cox II) (1965)   190
Walker v. City of Birmingham (1967)   192
Heart of Atlanta Motel, Inc. v. United States (1964)   195
Jones v. Alfred H. Mayer Co. (1968)   197
Hunter v. Erickson (1969)   200
United States v. Guest (1966)   201
Griffin v. Breckenridge (1971)   204
Adickes v. S.H. Kress & Co. (1970)   206
Swain v. Alabama (1965)   210
Evans v. Newton (1966)   212
Loving v. Virginia (1967)   214

4. The Burger Court:
   The Era of Ambivalence and Uncertainty, 1969-1986   217
   Republican Conservatism Replaces the Liberal Warren Court   217
   School Desegregation Remedies   218
      The Furor Over Busing   219
      The Intractable Desegregation Problem Moves North and West   221
      The Struggle of Mexican Americans in the Educational Arena   223
      Discriminatory Practices in Private Institutions   226
   Second-Generation Voting Rights Litigation:
      The Problem of Minority Vote Dilution   228
      From *Whitcomb* to *Bolden:* The Evolution
         of Constitutional Standards   228
      Congressional Response to *Bolden:* Amending § 2
         of the Voting Rights Act of 1965   233
      The Significance of § 5 of the Voting Rights Act   234
   Fair Employment and the Emergence of Affirmative Action   238
      Title VII and the Elimination of Racial Bias in the Labor Market   240
      The Emergence of Affirmative Action   245
      The Legality of Preferential Admissions in Higher Education   246
      Race-Conscious Remedies in the Labor Market   248

Housing Discrimination: The Increasing
    Significance of Race and Class   250
    Public Housing Referendums as a Barrier to Fair Housing   252
    Access to the Courts: Fair Housing and Standing to Sue   252
    Site Selection and Rezoning   254
    Fair Housing Issues in the Contexts of
        Exclusionary Zoning and Street Closings   255
The Death Penalty and the Pervasive Influence of Race   257
Jury Discrimination: New Era, Old Practices   262
    Racial, Ethnic, and Gender Bias in Jury Selection   262
    Prosecutorial Peremptory Challenges and Juror Bias:
        Swain Revisited   267
Private Discrimination: Sophisticated Segregation   267
    Private Discrimination Versus Right of Association   269
Protest Rights and Activity   270
    The Constitutional Status of Economic Boycotts   270
    Vagrancy Laws and Minorities: Police Harassment
        or Protecting Society?   271
Conclusion   272
CASES   274
Swann v. Charlotte-Mecklenburg
    Board of Education (1971)   274
Milliken v. Bradley (*Milliken I*) (1974)   277
Keyes v. School District No. 1,
    Denver, Colorado (1973)   281
Runyon v. McCrary (1976)   284
Bob Jones University v. United States (1983)   287
City of Mobile v. Bolden (1980)   291
Thornburg v. Gingles (1986)   295
United Jewish Organizations, Inc. v. Carey (1977)   301
Griggs v. Duke Power Co. (1971)   304
Washington v. Davis (1976)   306
Regents of the University of California v. Bakke (1978)   309
United Steelworkers of America v. Weber (1979)   317
Fullilove v. Klutznick (1980)   320
Wygant v. Jackson Board of Education (1986)   324
Warth v. Seldin (1975)   328
Havens Realty Corp. v. Coleman (1982)   330
Moore v. City of East Cleveland (1977)   333
Memphis v. Greene (1981)   335
Furman v. Georgia (1972)   338
Batson v. Kentucky (1986)   346
NAACP v. Claiborne Hardware Co. (1982)   350

5. **The Rehnquist Court:**
   The Era of Retrenchment and Unpredictability, 1986-1995   **355**
   A More Conservative Policy Direction
      for Civil Rights   355
   School Desegregation:
      A Relaxation of Federal Court Supervision   359
      Dismantling De Jure Segregation in Higher Education   361
   Voting Rights and Race in the 1990s   362
      The Continuing Significance of §§ 2 and 5 of the Voting Rights Act   363
      Race-Conscious Remedies and Legislative Redistricting   366
   The Rehnquist Court's Assault on Affirmative Action
      and Employment Discrimination Jurisprudence   369
      The Continuing Confusion Over Affirmative Action Jurisprudence   369
      Employment Discrimination and the Rehnquist Court:
         A Cramped View of Title VII   373
      Narrowing the Scope of § 1981 of the Civil Rights Act of 1866   376
      Congress Reacts: The Civil Rights Acts of 1990 and 1991   376
      The Definition of Race and §§ 1981 and 1982   379
   Housing Discrimination:
      A Problem for the 21st Century   379
   The Death Penalty:
      Removing Barriers to Expeditious Executions   382
   Removing the Remaining Vestiges of the Discriminatory
      Use of Peremptory Challenges   385
   Hate Speech and Hate Crimes:
      The Clash Between Free Speech and Equality   386
      Hate Crimes   386
      Hate Speech in the University Setting   389
   The Second African American Supreme Court Justice:
      The Politics of Race and the Role of Ideology   392
   The Rodney King Tape: Race and the Criminal Justice System   397
      Police Officers and the Use of Excessive Force:
         A Nationwide Problem   403
   Conclusion   406
   CASES   412
   Board of Education of Oklahoma City Public Schools v.
      Dowell (1991)   412
   Freeman v. Pitts (1992)   414
   United States v. Fordice (1992)   418
   Presley v. Etowah County Commission (1992)   422
   Shaw v. Reno (1993)   425
   City of Richmond v. J. A. Croson Co. (1989)   430
   Metro Broadcasting, Inc. v. FCC (1990)   434
   Wards Cove Packing Co., Inc. v. Atonio (1989)   437
   Patterson v. McLean Credit Union (1989)   440
   Spallone v. United States (1990)   443

McCleskey v. Kemp (1987)   445

Powers v. Ohio (1991)   449

R.A.V. v. City of St. Paul, Minnesota (1992)   451

Wisconsin v. Mitchell (1993)   454

*UWM Post, Inc. v. Board of Regents of the
        University of Wisconsin System* (1991)   456

Suggested Readings   461

Index   465

Table of Cases   471

About the Authors   483

Preface

The issue of race and civil rights has been on the Supreme Court's agenda throughout American history and undoubtedly will continue to be an intractable problem facing the nation in the 21st century. Chief Justice Earl Warren, in his civil rights lecture at the University of Notre Dame, acknowledged this fact when he stated, "If there is one lesson to be learned from our tragic experience in the Civil War and its wake, it is that the question of racial discrimination is never settled until it is settled right. It is not yet rightly settled." We have tried earnestly to examine the landmark civil rights cases covering a broad range of issues over a time span of more than 194 years to give students a deeper appreciation of the persistent quest by black Americans and other ethnic groups to obtain equality under the law. We examine the struggle to eliminate the vestiges of discrimination in a number of policy contexts from the perspective of racial and ethnic groups—the politically disadvantaged groups in American society.

Many constitutional law casebooks devote a chapter to racial discrimination and include a few landmark cases on several significant issues, including desegregation, affirmative action, and access to public accommodations. Our book is more comprehensive and examines cases on the above issues plus landmark cases involving slavery, housing discrimination, interracial marriages, voting, wills with discriminatory provisions, group libel, hate speech policies, hate crime laws, sits-ins, and peaceful demonstrations. We also include a section on the trial of the police accused of beating Rodney King, because the issue of race reemerged and took center stage, as has been the case on so many occasions throughout American history. We emphasize the statutory foundation of civil rights law—an area of increasing importance for the contemporary Court and illustrative of the interaction between Congress and the Supreme Court in refining the meaning of equality. We highlight excerpts from civil rights statutes and other important background material in boxes in each chapter.

Our book is designed for upper-level undergraduates, graduate students, and law students. It can be used as a primary text for courses that emphasize civil rights or race and the law. The book is also designed to be used as a supplement for a one- or two-semester undergraduate- or graduate-level courses in constitutional law, civil liberties and civil rights, constitutional history, the U.S. Supreme Court, and for specialized courses on race and the law and those that deal with law and the social sciences.

Our organizational approach to understanding civil rights law employs three interdependent perspectives: legal, historical, and political. First, we analyze the problem through an examination of leading Supreme Court cases concerning antidiscrimination law. In each chapter, we trace the doctrinal developments of civil rights law in a straightforward manner, with minimal use of legal jargon and technical language. Our principle objective is to highlight legal principles and theories used by the Supreme Court in reaching its decisions. Following each of the chapters are case excerpts, 88 in total. Excerpted cases appear in capital letters in their respective chapter. Each excerpted case is preceded by a headnote that presents the factual background of the case, how the lower courts ruled, and how the Justices voted in the case. We provide ample excerpts from concurring and dissenting opinions in order to illustrate the conflict and disagreements among the Justices over the legal issues presented in the cases. In addition, we include in each chapter some tables that highlight the development of the law in most policy areas discussed in the chapter. To permit deeper exploration of civil rights law, minor cases that are not discussed in the chapters also appear in these tables.

Second, we present the discussion of civil rights cases from a historical perspective—that is, exploring the dynamics of Supreme Court behavior over time. The chapters are divided into the eras of tenure of the Chief Justices, beginning with Chief Justice John Marshall's tenure through the Rehnquist Court era. Beginning with the Warren Court (1953-1969), we devote a single chapter to subsequent Courts. We think it is important for students to examine the landmark civil rights cases within the context of the events that shaped that historical period. This chronological approach will allow students to see more clearly the changes as well as the continuities of judicial policies over time. This approach also allows us to address issues salient to particular eras that may not fit neatly into a categorical or doctrinal presentation of the cases.

Finally, we think it is very important for students to understand the public policy and political contexts of judicial decision making in civil rights law. We emphasize political factors, both internal and external to the Court, that shape the development of civil rights law. For example, because personnel change is a major source of policy change on the Court, we emphasize in each chapter how appointments to the Court affected policy outcomes. We also show how Congress, the president, interest groups, shifts in public opinion, and other topics emerge as significant political forces in contributing to our understanding of civil rights law. In sum, our book is intended to give professors the flexibility to pick and choose from among the chapter sections and cases for each historical period to fulfill their individual goals for their courses, and students will be afforded the freedom to explore beyond the required assignments for their courses to gain deeper insights concerning the quest for equality on a broad range of significant issues.

This book has been in the works for some time, and many individuals have played a variety of roles during its production. Although the supporters and contributors for this volume are too numerous to mention, they should know that their assistance is appreciated boundlessly. We are compelled, however, to make a few acknowledgments. Oronde Ollie, a student assistant whose untimely death touched the Morehouse College family deeply, always had words of encouragement concerning this volume and assisted us ably with a variety of tasks. The assistance of Troi Smith, DeWayne Martin, and Donald Pollard, Jr.—three student assistants at Morehouse—is also deeply appreciated. We also owe a debt of gratitude to Melvin Gardner for his invaluable assistance in providing us with a number of important resources. We would also like to thank staff members and their student assistants at the law libraries at the University of Wisconsin at Madison and Georgia State University for their untiring efforts in locating resources that were essential for the successful completion of this most challenging undertaking. We are indebted to colleagues in the Department of Political Science at the University of Wisconsin at Madison and the University of Missouri at St. Louis for their constructive criticisms and words of encouragement. We are also particularly grateful for the persistent encouragement that the students who were enrolled in our classes provided.

We also acknowledge the invaluable professional assistance of Carrie Mullen, Acquisitions Editor at Sage. We both are very appreciative of her patience and understanding during the various stages of the manuscript. We would also like to express our gratitude to our Production Editor, Diana Axelsen, and to Linda Poderski, Copy Editor, who provided us with outstanding proofreading and editorial suggestions.

Introduction

THE SUPREME COURT, CIVIL RIGHTS, AND THE ENDURING STRUGGLE FOR EQUALITY

The position of the Negro today in America is the tragic but inevitable consequence of centuries of unequal treatment. Measured by any benchmark of comfort or achievement, meaningful equality remains a distant dream for the Negro.

Justice Thurgood Marshall*

Education, employment, housing, political participation, and access to public accommodations are just a few of the major areas of American life that affect all segments of the society. But when we employ racial, national ancestry, or ethnic criteria to understanding whether and to what extent all groups are afforded the opportunity to enjoy these basic rights, a portrait of inequality and discriminatory treatment emerges. The struggle for politically disadvantaged groups in American society to obtain equality under the law has been an enduring one. Although attempts to combat various obstacles that impede equality have been fought in the political arena, the federal courts, especially during the modern era, have been special targets for the nation's politically powerless to obtain the promise of equality. The purpose of our book is to present an examination of the quest to obtain equality under the law through an examination of leading constitutional and statutory Supreme Court cases

---

*The quote is from Justice Thurgood Marshall's dissenting opinion in *Regents of the University of California v. Bakke,* 438 U.S. 265 (1978), p. 395.

from 1801-1995. Through a presentation of introductory essays and excerpted cases, our primary pedagogical goal is to introduce students to how the Supreme Court has both furthered and frustrated the quest for equality over time.

Our book concentrates on civil rights law that focuses on the substantive equality claims of racial and ethnic minorities. Jack Greenberg has defined civil rights as "freedom from racial discrimination."[1] Because many of the leading civil rights cases involve black citizens, our book focuses primarily on their struggle to eliminate vestiges of racial discrimination in a variety of contexts. It is important for students to understand, however, that the quest for equalitarianism is not limited to a single racial group in a multicultural society in which resources are limited. Other politically disadvantaged groups have used strategies similar to those of black Americans in their quest to be free from discriminatory practices. Although it is important to focus on all forms of inequality, we are unable to address them within the confines of this volume.

We have written a book that concentrates on the significant decisions that shape and influence the development of civil rights law. The constitutional foundation of civil rights law lies in the Civil War Amendments. The Thirteenth Amendment abolished slavery and authorized Congress to enact legislation to enforce the prohibition. After the ratification of the Thirteenth Amendment, the Supreme Court narrowly interpreted the amendment in a manner that prohibited Congress from addressing both private discrimination and racial discrimination in public accomodations. The Fourteenth Amendment prohibits the states from denying persons due process and equal protection of the laws. This amendment was rendered virtually meaningless for blacks during certain periods of the Court's history. In the modern era, however, the Fourteenth Amendment continues to be the bulwark against discrimination. Finally, the Fifteenth Amendment, together with the Fourteenth, protects the voting rights of black citizens. As our discussion of voting rights cases over time will illustrate, the Court was a major barrier to black voting, thus relegating the Fifteenth Amendment to only a paper guarantee. We also include a substantial discussion of the statutory foundation of civil rights—federal civil rights laws. Although antidiscrimination legislation has been enacted since the Civil War, the most significant civil rights legislation was not passed until the 1960s, with the enactment of the Civil Rights Act of 1964, the Voting Rights Act of 1965, and the Fair Housing Act of 1968. What our analysis amply illustrates is that federal protection of civil rights, encompassing both public and private forms of discrimination, has not eliminated all vestiges of discrimination. In some instances, antidiscrimination statutes, especially those that embrace affirmative action, have generated considerable controversy and have been met with vigorous opposition.

It must be emphasized that we analyze the leading civil rights cases from the politically disadvantaged groups' perspective. First, we think this approach offers students insights into the struggle for equality that might otherwise be overlooked if we adopted a purely doctrinal approach toward civil rights cases. There is hardly anything novel about analyzing civil rights law from the litigants' perspective—that is, winners and losers in our nation's civil and criminal courts. This approach, for example, is illustrative of the political jurisprudence conception of law and the legal process—how courts authoritatively allocate values or, as articulated somewhat differently, who gets what, when, and how. Laws, of course, are not neutral; that is, they benefit certain interests and disadvantage others. In the following chapters, we show how various laws and customs supported segregation in America at various points in this nation's history. Judicial interpretation of these laws often reinforced segregationist practices. The Justices' judicial philosophies and policy preferences affect the distribution of resources in civil rights cases. The Court's interpretation of Title VII of the Civil Rights Act of 1964, for example, determines whether employers' or employees' interests will prevail in litigation. By focusing on who wins and who loses, the reader is able to draw conclusions about the pattern of outcomes in civil rights cases and the Supreme Court's institutional commitment to equal rights under the law.

The quest for equality today is just as controversial and divisive as it was 100 years earlier in this nation's history. Demands by the politically disadvantaged to make equality a meaningful concept have been met with stiff opposition and resistance. It is often argued in many circles that the rights of minorities infringe on the rights of the majority. In addition to this debate, the struggle for civil rights has often cast equality claims against other competing principles. For example, Americans attach quite a bit of value to freedom, individualism, and property rights. Our book is replete with examples in which the Supreme Court subordinated the rights of blacks to property interest claims. The hate speech/hate crimes topic, discussed in Chapter 5, is illustrative of the clash between the competing values of equality and free speech. When fundamental principles inherent in the Bill of Rights clash with the principle of equality, which principle should take precedence and why? Our book highlights how the Supreme Court has responded to balancing competing interests inherent in our constitutional order.

Prior studies of interest-group litigation reveal why courts were especially attractive targets in the effort to undermine the system of racial subordination in America. Unresponsive political institutions were a primary factor for disadvantaged groups resorting to the judiciary to achieve their objectives. For example, prior to the passage of the Voting Rights Act of 1965, a substantial percentage of blacks were disfranchised throughout the South where de jure and de facto segregation prevented them from using conventional methods of political participation to bring pressure on state legislatures and executives to respond to their demands. With respect to Congress, the Southern coalition dominated many key committees that effectively prevented major civil rights legislation from ever becoming law until the 1960s. Early chief executives' efforts were mixed in their attempt to further the goals of the Fourteenth and Fifteenth Amendments. Because most Southern blacks were excluded from political society, the promise for full citizenship had to be pursued in nonelective forums.

The special role accorded to the federal courts in protecting minority rights and interests against majority tyranny is grounded in the theory of limited government. One of the themes that led the framers to construct the Constitution as they did was that government must protect various liberties, especially economic rights of minorities. Intermixed with this view was the idea that political majorities could not be trusted to achieve these objectives. The federalist vision of government—in its reliance on separation of powers and federalism in order to ensure that the majority faction could be constrained from impeding minority rights—saw the protection of individual rights against infringement by the government as one of its most important functions. Despite this role, our analysis reveals that the Supreme Court's behavioral propensities in civil rights cases have varied over time. For instance, from 1801 to 1910, the Supreme Court constitutionalized racism, subordinated blacks and women to second-class citizenship status, disfranchised blacks and women, and fostered segregation in public education, public accommodations, and housing. From 1910-1953, we identify a transitional shift in the Supreme Court's commitment to racial equality. The Supreme Court's institutional commitment to egalitarianism reached its peak during the Warren Court era (1953-1969), the period we refer to as the "modern era" with respect to civil rights. We also view the Burger Court (1969-1986) as a Court in transition, providing continuity with the Warren Court in some policy areas but becoming increasingly conservative in others. Finally, our analysis of the Rehnquist Court (1986-1995) indicates that it has substantially reduced its support for civil rights, compared with the previous Courts during the modern era.

Against this background, we assert that the civil rights of politically disadvantaged groups are often uncertain because of the absence of commitment by political elites, incoherent policy directives, and judicial indifference. An examination of Supreme Court behavior over time reveals that progress has been tenuous and unsteady, at best, historically. The struggle for equality by black Americans can be characterized as a cyclical pattern of winning and losing cases. Derrick Bell has expressed the core of this phenomenon in these words:

> The commonly-held view of civil rights as a long, unbroken line of precedents resulting in slow but steady progress is reassuring. Encouragement though, while welcome, is not actuality. And too often, what is denominated progress has been a cyclical phenomenon in which legal rights are gained, then lost, then gained in response to economic and political developments in the country over which blacks exercise little or no control. Constitutional law has always been part of rather than an exception to this cyclical phenomenon.[2]

Our 194-year examination of the role of the Supreme Court in civil rights policymaking indicates that politically disadvantaged groups such as blacks have to relitigate over and over again in their enduring struggle for equality. Our analysis of the Rehnquist Court in Chapter 5, for example, is illustrative of this pattern. In 1989 the Rehnquist Court rendered six rulings that effectively overturned or narrowed previous precedents in the area of employment and affirmative action rendered by the Burger Court. Congress quickly responded by overturning or modifying these rulings in the Civil Rights Act of 1991. In the area of voting rights, the Rehnquist Court narrowly construed § 5 of the Voting Rights Act in *Presley v. Etowah County Commission,* 502 U.S. 491 (1992), which had been given an expansive interpretation by the Warren Court in *Allen v. State Board of Elections,* 393 U.S. 544 (1969). Moreover, in the controversial ruling of *Shaw v. Reno,* 113 S.Ct. 2816 (1993), the Court established that white voters could challenge a majority black congressional district—a ruling that ran counter to a similar Burger Court decision, *United Jewish Organizations, Inc. v. Carey,* 430 U.S. 144 (1977). And in the area of school desegregation, the Rehnquist Court supported relaxed federal district court supervision of school districts in dismantling de jure segregation.

Our analysis shows that, during particular historical eras, the Supreme Court has both furthered equality and frustrated equality goals. The dominant theme of this book is that the Court's behavior reflects a dual character with respect to its role in bringing about legal equality for victims of discrimination. Moreover, incrementalism and the lack of enforcement have resulted in additional litigation to transform previously enunciated principles into concrete policy outcomes. We think this approach presents a historically accurate portrait of the Court's institutional commitment in safeguarding and protecting civil rights.

It is difficult to understand the politically disadvantaged groups' quest for equality without an appreciation of the blend of politics and law in evaluating significant pronouncements from the Supreme Court, Congress, and the executive branch of government. Civil rights issues occupy a significant place on not only the Supreme Court's agenda but also that of the political branches of government. To that end, it is important to emphasize various factors that illustrate the interaction between politics and law in the area of civil rights. Conventional thinking in the judicial politics and behavior literature posits that Supreme Court policymaking is not independent from the influences of its external environment. Perhaps one of the most important contextual factors is that of presidential appointments to the Court. Personnel changes on the Supreme Court are a major source of policy change because presidents appoint individuals to the Court who share their ideological views. As Dahl contended more than three decades ago, "the policy views dominant on the Court are never for long out of line with the policy views dominant among the lawmaking majorities of the United States."[3] Lawmaking majorities in this sense are properly understood as referring to the policy preferences of the appointing president. In short, membership change is a very important factor in accounting for the Supreme Court's shifts in direction on civil rights issues.

We are able to make the following observations about politically disadvantaged groups' struggle to obtain equality under the law. First, race continues to be on the forefront of the American legal and political agenda. The quest for racial equality has and continues to be controversial and divisive. Our analysis reveals that the Supreme Court's institutional role, consigned during the modern era as a protector of the politically powerless, is actually an aberration. Throughout much of its institutional history, the Supreme Court has been a conservative and reactionary institution even when compared to the political branches of government. Even when the Supreme Court rules in favor of the politically powerless, efforts to thwart or impede implementation by other institutions or policymakers often lead to additional litigation, and the win-lose cyclical pattern emerges.

The remainder of the book examines the institutional commitment of the Supreme Court in civil rights cases. Chapter 1 presents a discussion of the Marshall, Taney, Chase, Waite, and Fuller Courts for the 1801-1910 period. The underlying theme of this chapter is that through its rulings, the Supreme Court reinforced white supremacy and the second-class citizenship status of blacks. This historical era produced the most devastating blows to blacks' quest for equality despite national protection for civil rights. The principal cases of this era—*Dred Scott v. Sandford,* 60 U.S. (19 How.) 393 (1857), the *Slaughter-House Cases,* 83 U.S. (16 Wall.) 36 (1873), and *Plessy v. Ferguson,* 163 U.S. 537 (1896)—are illustrative of the nadir in the quest for equality under the law. Chapter 2 provides a discussion of the White, Taft, Hughes, Stone, and Vinson Courts for the 1910-1953 period. Here we trace the doctrinal transformation from separate but equal to its near demise by the mid-1950s. Blacks during this period experienced some victories in the judicial arena, and the NAACP launched its attack on Jim Crow segregation. The most significant doctrinal changes during this period included the acknowledgment of discrete and insular minorities in Footnote 4 in *United States v. Carolene Products Co.,* 304 U.S. 144 (1938) and the emergence of a two-tiered approach to the equal protection clause. President Franklin Delano Roosevelt's court-packing efforts resulted in nine appointments in the Supreme Court and accounted for some of the movement toward equality.

Beginning with 1953 (the modern era), we trace each Court's civil rights cases in separate chapters. Chapter 3 deals with the Warren Court era (1953-1969). We begin with a discussion of the Court's most significant decision during the modern era—*Brown v. Board of Education,* 347 U.S. 483 (1954)—and the remaining school desegregation cases. We trace the Warren Court's commitment to equality, unparalleled in other points in its history, in such areas as desegregating public accommodations, sit-in and peaceful demonstration cases, voting rights, race and the administration of justice and wills, and segregation. We also highlight the passage of the most significant pieces of civil rights legislation ever passed: the Civil Rights Act of 1964, the Voting Rights Act of 1965, and Title VIII of the Fair Housing Act of 1968. Chapter 4 discusses the transition from the liberal Warren Court to the more conservative Burger Court (1969-1986). The Burger Court's civil rights jurisprudence is especially significant because it grappled with such policy areas as minority vote dilution and affirmative action cases, not previously addressed by the Supreme Court. The book concludes with Chapter 5, on the Rehnquist Court era (1986-1995). As our cyclical framework amply demonstrates, the Rehnquist Court's revisiting of several landmark cases highlights its more conservative stance toward civil rights issues in voting, affirmative action, employment discrimination, and death penalty jurisprudence. We also present an analysis of the newer issues on the Rehnquist Court's agenda—hate speech and hate crimes cases. In this chapter, we also discuss two of the more controversial political events that occurred during the Rehnquist Court era— the nomination of Judge Clarence Thomas to the Supreme Court and the trial of the police accused of beating Rodney King.

NOTES

1. Greenberg, J. (1989). Civil rights. In L. W. Levy, K. L. Karst, & D. J. Mahoney (Eds.), *Civil rights and equality.* New York: Macmillan, p. 3.

2. Bell, D. (1987, May). *Victims as heroes: A minority perspective on constitutional law.* Paper delivered at the Smithsonian Institution's International Symposium, Constitutional Roots, Rights, and Responsibilities, p. 3.

3. Dahl, R. (1957). Decision-making in a democracy: The Supreme Court as a national policy-maker. *Journal of Public Law, 6,* p. 285.

1

From Marshall to Fuller

THE ERA OF WHITE SUPREMACY
AND SECOND-CLASS CITIZENSHIP,
1801-1910

The years of slavery did more than retard the progress of blacks. Even a greater
wrong was done to the whites by creating arrogance instead of humility and by
encouraging the growth of the fiction of a superior race.

Justice William O. Douglas*

THE CONSTITUTION AND SLAVERY

In the United States, slavery was part of the American ethos by the middle
of the 18th century, and slaves constituted approximately 40% of the Southern
colonial population. A. Leon Higginbotham's analysis of legislative and judicial pronouncements during the colonial era demonstrates how the law contributed to the legal subjugation and dehumanization of blacks.[1] The tension
between proslavery and antislavery forces over the institution of slavery was
evident during the drafting of the Declaration of Independence. A draft of the
document contained a provision condemning the international slave trade, but
it was deleted from the final version. Nor did the Declaration of Independence
contain any reference to slaves or slavery. The institution of slavery was

---

*The quote is from Justice William O. Douglas's dissenting opinion in *DeFunis v. Odegaard,*
416 U.S. 312 (1974), p. 336.

incompatible with Thomas Jefferson's powerful assertions that all men are created equal and are endowed by their Creator with the inalienable rights of life, liberty, and the pursuit of happiness. Despite these admirable proclamations in the Declaration of Independence, blacks were not entitled to the natural rights or equality promised to all. Jefferson and the other founders' property interests in slavery superseded any moral, religious, political, or legal justification for its abolishment.

African slavery was an important part of America's developing economic system, and indifference to the institution was widespread. John Hope Franklin observed:

> It was inevitable that slavery should have been an important consideration at the Constitutional Convention. At a time when slavery was waning in the North, the southern states saw in slavery an increasing source of wealth both in the market value of slaves and in what slaves could produce. An economic interest so important could not be ignored by a convention one of whose major concerns was to protect property and to advance the economic interests of those who were to live within the new frame of government.[2]

More than one fourth of the delegates to the constitutional convention, including George Washington and James Madison, owned slaves, and it was clear that the Southern states would not approve the Constitution if it in any way impeded the institution of slavery. The controversy over slavery thus intensified the debate between the proslavery and antislavery forces during the drafting of the Constitution. The words *slave* and *slavery* were not specifically mentioned in the Constitution until the passage of the Thirteenth Amendment. Slaves were referred to as "persons." Don E. Fehrenbacher described the contrast between text and purpose of the Constitution: "It is as though the framers were half-consciously trying to frame two constitutions, one for their own time and the other for the ages, with slavery viewed bifocally—that is, plainly visible at their feet, but disappearing when they lifted their eyes."[3]

Four provisions in the Constitution explicitly protected the institution of slavery. Article I, § 2, Clause 3—popularly known as the Three-Fifths Compromise—provided that each slave would be counted as three fifths of a free person for the purposes of direct taxation and apportionment of seats in the House of Representatives. Article I, § 9, Clause 1—known as the slave trade clause—prohibited Congress from restricting the slave trade for a period of 20 years. The slave trade clause also imposed an authority to tax the importation of each slave. Article IV, § 2, Clause 3—the fugitive slave clause—provided for the return of fugitive slaves. Finally, Article V, which addresses the amending power, prohibited any constitutional amendment involving the slave trade before 1808. Legal historians have noted that at least 10 other clauses in the Constitution were influenced by slavery.[4]

Property rights prevailed over the minimal legal rights that blacks possessed, and subservience to whites in every respect was the expected behavioral pattern. Prejudice and the double standard were the norm. C. Vann Woodward observed, "Slavery was only one of several ways by which the white man has sought to define the Negro's status, his 'place,' and to assure his subordination."[5]

THE SUPREME COURT AND
THE LEGITIMIZATION OF SLAVERY:
THE MARSHALL AND TANEY ERAS, 1801-1864

The Supreme Court under the leadership of the great Chief Justice John Marshall (1801-1835) was primarily preoccupied with constitutional issues concerning nationalism, property rights, and judicial power. The Court's progress in these areas, according to Robert McCloskey, was "aided by a basic disability of the localist movement—its very lack of unity."[6] According to McCloskey's analysis, the Court under Marshall's leadership left alone potentially unifying issues such as slavery. During its early years, the Marshall Court was confronted with petitions for freedom filed by slaves in *Scott v. Negro London,* 7 U.S. (3 Cranch) 324 (1806); *Scott v. Negro Ben,* 10 U.S. (6 Cranch) 3 (1810); *Wood v. Davis,* 11 U.S. (7 Cranch) 271 (1812); and *Queen v. Hepburn,* 11 U.S. (7 Cranch) 290 (1813). In each of these cases, the Court, in majority opinions written by Chief Justice Marshall, rejected the slaves' petitions on narrow grounds and sided in favor of the slave owner. During the final years of the Marshall Court era, the Court rejected the claims of slaves that they were free under provisions of a will in *M'Cutchen v. Marshall,* 33 U.S. (8 Pet.) 220 (1834).

The leading slavery cases during the Marshall Court era involved the African slave trade (see Table 1.1). In 1807 Congress enacted legislation prohibiting the slave trade after June 1, 1808. The slave trade continued, however, and Congress passed a law in 1820 that provided that anyone convicted of slave trading would be considered a pirate and put to death. In *The Antelope,* 23 U.S. (10 Wheat.) 66 (1825), a privateer sailing under a Venezuelan commission entered the port of Baltimore, Maryland, in 1819 and took an American crew. The ship, the *Arraganta,* captured an American and Portuguese vessel and took the Africans aboard. It also captured the *Antelope,* a Spanish vessel. Both ships sailed to Brazil, and the *Arraganta* was wrecked. The crew of the wrecked ship was transferred to the *Antelope,* and subsequently an American ship brought the *Antelope* (now named the *General Ramirez*) to the port of Savannah, Georgia, with 280 Africans aboard. The lower courts awarded the Africans to the Spanish and the Portuguese, and the federal government appealed to the Supreme Court, claiming that the Africans were free men under United States laws. In a 6-0 opinion (Justice Todd not participating), Chief Justice Marshall held that the international slave trade did not violate international law and that some slaves should be returned to their Spanish owners and the others turned over to the United States as a result of the illegal trade. Chief Justice Marshall acknowledged that the slave trade was contrary to the law of nature, but he also stated that slave trading could not be considered piracy under international law. Chief Justice Marshall's

Table 1.1 Slavery Cases During the Marshall and Taney Eras, 1801-1864

Case	Vote	Ruling
The Antelope, 23 U.S. (10 Wheat.) 66 (1825)	6-0	Chief Justice John Marshall held that the international slave trade did not violate international law despite the fact that the slave trade was contrary to the law of nature.
United States v. Gooding, 25 U.S. (12 Wheat.) 460 (1827)	7-0	Justice Story upheld an indictment against Gooding, who was illegally engaged in the slave trade, in violation of the Slave Trade Act of 1818.
LaGrange v. Chouteau, 29 U.S. (4 Pet.) 287 (1830) and *Menard v. Aspasia,* 30 U.S. (5 Pet.) 505 (1831)	7-0	The Supreme Court dismissed, for lack of jurisdiction, claims made by slaves who resided in the Northwest Territory that they were free.
United States v. The Amistad, 40 U.S. (15 Pet.) 518 (1841)	9-0	Justice Story ruled that the African trade was illegal under Spanish law and that a captured cargo of Africans were free men and should be returned to Africa.
Groves v. Slaughter, 40 U.S. (15 Pet.) 449 (1841)	5-2	Justice Thompson ruled that the commerce clause could not be used to interfere with slavery on the state level.
Prigg v. The Commonwealth of Pennsylvania, 41 U.S. (16 Pet.) 539 (1842)	8-1	Justice Story upheld the constitutionality of the Fugitive Slave Act of 1793.
Wharton Jones v. John Van Zandt, 46 U.S. (5 How.) 215 (1847)	9-0	Justice Woodbury declared that the Fugitive Slave Act of 1793 was a valid exercise of Congress' power under the slave trade clause.
Strader v. Graham, 51 U.S. (10 How.) 82 (1851)	9-0	Chief Justice Taney held that each state had a right to determine for itself the status of blacks within its jurisdiction.
Moore v. Illinois, 55 U.S. (14 How.) 13 (1852)	7-1	Justice Grier declared that a state could aid in the arrest and restraint of runaway slaves as it may do in cases of idlers, vagabonds, and paupers under its police powers and is valid under the fugitive slave clause.
Dred Scott v. Sandford, 60 U.S. (19 How.) 393 (1857)	7-2	Chief Justice Taney declared that blacks could not be considered citizens of the United States and that the Missouri Compromise was unconstitutional.
Ableman v. Booth, 62 U.S. (21 How.) 506 (1859)	9-0	Chief Justice Taney declared that the Fugitive Slave Act of 1850 was constitutional.

Table 1.1 *continued*

Case	Vote	Ruling
Kentucky v. Dennison, 65 U.S. (24 How.) 66 (1861)	8-0	Chief Justice Taney held that interstate extradition of a free black who had helped a slave escape was solely a matter of gubernatorial discretion and that no law of Congress can force the state official to act.
Ex parte Gordon, 66 U.S. (1 Black) 503 (1861)	9-0	Chief Justice Taney sustained Gordon's death sentence for piracy under congressional law prohibiting the African slave trade.
The Slavers, 69 U.S. 350 (2 Wall.) (1864)	10-0	The Supreme Court in four cases upheld the seizure of vessels illegally engaged in the slave trade.

opinion thus upheld the United States prohibition of the slave trade while at the same time it permitted international slave trading.

Toward the last years of the Marshall Court era, the Court began to adopt a more permissive attitude toward states' rights, thus providing the foundation for the Taney era. After several vacancies opened on the Supreme Court, President Andrew Jackson nominated Roger Brooke Taney in January 1835, but Jackson's political enemies managed to postpone the nomination. When Chief Justice John Marshall died on July 6, 1835, President Jackson submitted Taney's name for Marshall's replacement. He was confirmed in March 1836 by a 29-15 vote. Chief Justice Taney, an intensely partisan, proslavery Southerner, was also a staunch supporter of states' rights. A majority of the Justices on the Supreme Court from 1801 to 1864 were Southerners, and many Northerners on the Court were sympathetic to the proslavery views of their Southern colleagues.

In *United States v. The Amistad,* 40 U.S. (15 Pet.) 518 (1841), a Spanish schooner drifted into an American port near Long Island, New York, after a mutiny by the slaves on board that took place off the coast of Cuba. An American vessel seized the ship and brought it to the port of New London, Connecticut, charging the black mutineers with piracy. Meanwhile, the Spanish government demanded that the slaves be returned to their Spanish masters. The slaves, however, had been imported from Africa, in violation of treaties prohibiting the international slave trade. The issue finally reached the Taney Court, which ruled in an opinion written by Justice Story that the Africans were free men and should be returned to Africa.

The international slave trade also influenced the commerce clause (Article I, § 8, Clause 3) cases that came before the Court. *Groves v. Slaughter,* 40 U.S. (15 Pet.) 449 (1841) was the leading slavery case that directly addressed

Congress's commerce power. In *Groves,* Mississippi's constitution expressly prohibited the importation of slaves into the state as merchandise or for sale in order to reduce the flow of capital out of the state and to protect its slave-breeding industry. Robert Slaughter, a slave trader and resident of Louisiana, violated the constitutional provision by selling slaves in Mississippi and receiving promissory notes from the buyer, Moses Groves, who later defaulted on them. The issue before the Taney Court was whether the promissory notes were void under the Mississippi constitution. Justice Thompson, writing for the 5-2 plurality, avoided the constitutional issue raised by the case and held that the notes were legal because Mississippi had not enacted legislation implementing the constitutional provision. In a proslavery concurring opinion, Chief Justice Taney insisted that state control over slavery was exclusive of all federal power.

Fugitive Slave Law

As indicated in the previous section, Article IV, § 2, Clause 3 of the Constitution provided for the return of fugitive slaves. The fear of slave insurrections and the problem of criminal extradition of fugitive slaves led to the enactment of the Fugitive Slave Act of 1793. The law authorized masters or their agents to capture fugitive slaves across state lines and to bring them before a state or federal magistrate in order to obtain a certificate of removal, which would allow the return of the slave. Many Northern states passed personal liberty laws, or antikidnapping statutes, to protect the rights of free blacks. The personal liberty laws also included a procedure to facilitate the return of fugitive slaves and made it difficult for slaveholders to seize people who they claimed were runaway slaves. In the first Supreme Court decision on fugitive slaves, the Taney Court, in PRIGG V. THE COMMONWEALTH OF PENNSYLVANIA, 41 U.S. (16 Pet.) 539 (1842), invalidated Pennsylvania's personal liberty law (and all state laws that interfered with the enforcement of the Fugitive Slave Act). In an 8-1 opinion written by Justice Story, the Taney Court upheld the constitutionality of the Fugitive Slave Act of 1793. This ruling meant that the federal government had exclusive power over fugitive slaves and that sectional conflicts were inevitable because states were not given an opportunity to pass laws dealing with fugitive slaves. In his concurring opinion, Chief Justice Taney, in *Prigg,* argued that the states were not prohibited from enforcing the Fugitive Slave Act.

Wharton Jones v. John Van Zandt, 46 U.S. (5 How.) 215 (1847) provided an opportunity for abolitionists to challenge the constitutionality of the Fugitive Slave Act. Salmon P. Chase, who later became Chief Justice of the United States, argued on behalf of a conductor of the underground railroad who was accused of harboring and concealing slaves. Chase argued that the 1793 Act was unconstitutional because the federal government lacked power to support slaves and that Article IV, § 2, Clause 3 gave no enforcement power to Congress on the slavery issue. In a unanimous opinion written by Justice Woodbury, the Court declared that the 1793 Act was a valid exercise of

Congressional power under the slave trade clause and that it was not repugnant to the Northwest Ordinance of 1787, which outlawed slavery in the territories. Even when § 4 of the Fugitive Slave Act of 1793 was repealed by the Fugitive Slave Act of 1850, the protection of property rights in slaves was the major policy objective. For example, the 1793 law gave the master the right to seize a runaway slave and return him or her to the state from which he or she had fled, without a jury trial. The 1850 law simply authorized federal commissioners, on proof of ownership, to allow claimants to remove fugitive slaves without a jury trial. The Act did not even permit slaves to testify.[7]

Subsequent fugitive slave decisions by the Taney Court (see Table 1.1) reflected its proslavery behavioral propensities. In *Strader v. Graham,* 51 U.S. (10 How.) 82 (1851), Christopher Graham, a slaveowner and citizen of Kentucky, permitted three of his slaves who were musicians to make regular visits to other states, including Ohio, to work as entertainers. While in Louisville, the slaves were taken aboard a steamboat owned by Jacob Strader and were carried to Cincinnati, where they later escaped to Canada. Graham sued Strader and others for damages under a Kentucky law that allowed recovery of damages when a steamboat owner takes slaves out of the state without the master's permission. Strader claimed that because the Northwest Ordinance of 1787 prohibited slavery in the territories, including Ohio, the slaves were free men when they fled to Canada. The question before the Taney Court was whether slaves who had been permitted by their master to travel from Kentucky to Ohio acquired their freedom on returning to Kentucky. Chief Justice Taney held for a unanimous Court that the laws of Kentucky alone control the status of blacks when they return to the state. Chief Justice Taney also held that the federal courts lacked jurisdiction over the issue because the Northwest Ordinance was superseded by the adoption of the Constitution. According to Taney's reasoning, the Constitution placed the states of the Union in perfect equality; therefore, each state had a right to determine for itself the status of blacks within its jurisdiction.

Proslavery decisions supported white supremacy, as well as Southern economic and political power. John Arthur pointed out that "eleven of the first fifteen presidents were Southerners, as were seventeen of twenty-eight Supreme Court Justices and twenty-one of thirty-four speakers of the House."[8] Proslavery sentiment also received support from the presidents. For example, John Tyler, who became president after the death of William H. Harrison in 1841, supported slavery. Official support of the institution from the three branches of government intensified and prolonged the dehumanization that blacks experienced as slaves.

Slavery in the Territories

The hotly contested issue of slavery in the territories was on the forefront of the American political agenda by the 1800s. The broader question was whether slavery was an exclusively state institution (the prevalent view of that era) or whether the federal government had power to legislate on the issue of slavery in the territories. Antislavery forces asserted national authority to prohibit slavery in the territories. When Missouri sought admission into the Union in 1819 as a slave state, it engendered a bitter debate over congressional intervention of slavery in the territories and how new states would be brought into the Union. Under the Missouri Compromise of 1820, Missouri was admitted as a slave state, Maine was admitted as a free state, and Congress prohibited slavery in the Louisiana Purchase Territory north of the 36° 30′ line of latitude (the southern border of Missouri). Proslavery forces were alarmed by growing antislavery sentiment and congressional efforts to impede slavery's spread into the territories. The annexation of the territory of Texas in 1845 and the Mexican War of 1846 led to the possibility of additional slave territories. In response, Congress enacted the Wilmot Proviso of 1846, which prohibited slavery in any territory that might be acquired from Mexico as a result of the war. This proviso remained in force for 15 years. The sectional conflict over slavery in the territories, however, intensified by 1850 and led to another attempt by Congress to settle the slavery question and the admission of new states into the Union. The Missouri Compromise of 1850 admitted California as a free state; Texas, Utah, and the New Mexico territories were admitted without a slavery prescription; and slavery was abolished in the District of Columbia. By 1854 the slavery question was again on the national agenda in full force. The Kansas-Nebraska Act of 1854, which repealed the 36° 30′ line of the Missouri Compromise, provided for a policy of letting the residents vote on slavery under the doctrine of popular sovereignty. Once again, this Act provoked immediate political upheaval among the free states because it appeared to expand slavery in the two territories. In the meantime, the *Dred Scott* litigation had commenced in 1846 in a Missouri circuit court in St. Louis and was working its way though the state and federal court systems. It was obvious that the political branches were incapable of settling the slavery controversy, but what about the Supreme Court?

In the case of DRED SCOTT V. SANDFORD, 60 U.S. (19 How.) 393 (1857), Chief Justice Taney rendered the most infamous decision ever made by the Supreme Court (see Box 1.1). Dred Scott, a slave, was taken from Missouri by his master to Illinois, where slavery was forbidden by state law, and to the northern section of the Louisiana Purchase Territory, where slavery was forbidden by the Missouri Compromise of 1820. He was returned to Missouri by his owner, who later died. Title to Scott was passed to John Sanford (his name was misspelled in the official record), a New York citizen. In 1846 Scott sued for his freedom in the Missouri courts but was not successful. His attorney filed suit in the federal court in Missouri, and the case was heard in the U.S. Supreme Court in 1856. On March 6, 1857, Chief Justice Taney, in a 7-2 decision, held that Scott could not become a United States citizen because he was a slave and a Negro. Chief Justice Taney's conservative beliefs regarding slavery were reflected in the majority opinion. He pinpointed the constitutional status of blacks when he emphasized that they "had no rights which the white man was bound to respect." Congress had exceeded its powers in passing the Missouri Compromise of 1820, and Scott's status was deter-

---

BOX 1.1

Impact of *Dred Scott*

"In its primary effect, the decision meant the exclusion of Negroes from access to the federal courts in civil cases, but the potential ramifications were more numerous and complex than anyone realized at the time. For one thing, there was the problem of definition. Could an Ohio quadroon, white according to the law of his state, bring a federal suit against a white person in Tennessee, where quadroons were legally black? . . . The executive branch of the federal government . . . could now proceed with authority to deny blacks all privileges associated with United States citizenship, such as passports for travel abroad. . . . The decision likewise lent support to the discriminatory laws of state governments and encouraged further assaults upon the already limited freedom and security of the nonslave black population. . . . [T]he decision posed a threat to black suffrage in the few states allowing it; for the franchise was in each case limited to United States citizens. Had Taney's opinion, then, made Negro voting unconstitutional?"

SOURCE: From *Slavery, Law, and Politics: The* Dred Scott *Case in Historical Perspective* (pp. 236-237), by D. E. Fehrenbacher, 1981, New York: Oxford University Press.

---

mined by Missouri law on his return to Missouri, and not by his visit to free territory in Illinois. Justices Curtis and McLean, the two dissenters in *Dred Scott,* argued that free blacks had been accepted as citizens in 1787 and that Scott's status was determined by his residing in free territory. They also believed that the Missouri Compromise was constitutional. It had become abundantly clear that the highest court in the land was incapable of solving the slavery issue once and for all. According to McCloskey, Chief Justice Taney's "first and greatest [mistake] had been to imagine that a flaming political issue could be quenched by calling it a 'legal' issue and deciding it judicially."[9] The *Dred Scott* decision undoubtedly tarnished Chief Justice Taney's reputation and seriously tarnished the reputation, prestige, and legitimacy of the Supreme Court. Taney's 28 years on the Court are remembered primarily for the infamous *Dred Scott* decision.

Despite the infamy surrounding *Dred Scott,* the Taney Court continued to render proslavery decisions. Two years after *Dred Scott,* in *Ableman v. Booth,* 62 U.S. (21 How.) 506 (1859), Chief Justice Taney declared for a unanimous Court that the Fugitive Slave Act of 1850 was constitutional in all of its provisions. Taney also held that state courts had no authority to interfere with the conduct of federal laws and the U.S. Constitution in preventing the illegal detention of abolitionist Sherman Booth, who aided in the escape of a fugitive slave, in the hands of a federal marshal.

In the last major slavery case before the Supreme Court and decided after secession from the Union had begun, the Taney Court was confronted with the question whether it could force the governor of Ohio, William Dennison, to extradite a free black, Willis Lago, who had helped a slave escape from Kentucky. The governor of Kentucky, Beriah Magoffin, sought a writ of mandamus to compel Dennison to act under the Supreme Court's original jurisdiction. Without wanting to set precedent that would permit the federal government to force state officials to act, Chief Justice Taney, in *Kentucky v. Dennison*, 65 U.S. (24 How.) 66 (1861), refused to issue a mandamus against the Ohio governor on the ground that interstate extradition was a matter of gubernatorial discretion. Chief Justice Taney also argued that Congress could not force a state officer to perform any duty by act of Congress. If the officer refuses, no law of Congress can compel him.

The issue of slavery, however, raised such intense sectional feelings that it was settled on the battlefield, rather than by the Supreme Court. The proslavery decision divided the Democratic Party and allowed the Republican Party, determined to prevent the spread of slavery in the territories, and Abraham Lincoln to capture the White House in the 1860 presidential election. By the time of his inauguration in March 1861, seven states had seceded from the Union. Later that April, the Confederate attack on Fort Sumter took place, thus throwing the Union into a constitutional crisis that eventually was settled by the Civil War. On September 22, 1862, President Abraham Lincoln announced the Emancipation Proclamation (see Box 1.2), which would take effect in 100 days (January 1, 1863). Although the Emancipation Proclamation promised slaves their freedom and permitted them to serve in the Union forces, it applied only to those areas that were under Confederate control. As Union forces moved farther into the South, the Emancipation Proclamation became more meaningful. Edgar Toppin wrote, "Emancipation was also an important diplomatic weapon in that it won the Union the support of many Europeans who favored an end to slavery. Now they would pressure their governments not to aid the Confederacy since it was plain that the Civil War had become a war not only to save the Union but also to end slavery."[10] Despite the Emancipation Proclamation, indignities against blacks continued without interruption. Approximately 200,000 blacks were recruited by President Lincoln to save the Union and crush the rebellion, and in return they received "inequities in rank, pay, and dignity, compared with whites."[11]

THE POST-CIVIL WAR ERA: RECONSTRUCTION AND NATIONAL PROTECTION OF CIVIL RIGHTS

The Emancipation Proclamation, with its limited success, led to the introduction of constitutional amendments in Congress to destroy the institution of slavery. The Thirteenth Amendment was introduced in Congress in January 1865 and was ratified by the states on December 6, 1865. Section 1

BOX 1.2

The Emancipation Proclamation

January 1, 1863

. . . Now, therefore, I, Abraham Lincoln, President of the United States, by virtue of the power in me vested as Commander-in-Chief of the Army and Navy of the United States in time of actual armed rebellion against the authority and government of the United States, and as a fit and necessary war measure for suppressing said rebellion, do . . . order and declare that all persons held as slaves within said designated States and parts of States are, and henceforward shall be, free; and that the Executive Government of the United States, including the military and naval authorities thereof, will recognize and maintain the freedom of said persons.

And I hereby enjoin upon the people so declared to be free to abstain from all violence, unless in necessary self-defense; and I recommend to them that, in all cases when allowed, they labor faithfully for reasonable wages.

And I further declare and make known that such persons of suitable condition will be received into the armed service of the United States to garrison forts, positions, stations, and other places, and to man vessels of all sorts in said service.

And upon this act, sincerely believed to be an act of justice, warranted by the Constitution upon military necessity, I invoke the considerate judgment of mankind and the gracious favor of Almighty God.

SOURCE: 12 Stat. 68 (1863)

of the Thirteenth Amendment prohibits slavery in the United States. Between 1865 and 1877, the enormous task that faced the nation was the reconstruction of the Union. Equally important was the difficult task of determining the citizenship status of blacks that was stripped away by the *Dred Scott* decision. The Fourteenth Amendment, which was ratified on July 9, 1868, would become the chief legal weapon in black America's struggle for equality. Section 1 prohibits the states from (a) abridging the privileges or immunities of citizens of the United States; (b) depriving any person of life, liberty, or property without due process of law; and (c) denying to any person within its jurisdiction equal protection of the laws.

The 1868 presidential election, in which Republican candidate Ulysses S. Grant won with only 52% of the popular vote, signaled that something had to be done about the disfranchised black voter in the Southern states in order to counter possible Democratic victories in Congress and the states. Republicans also articulated the egalitarian sentiment of eradicating racial discrimination in voting. The Fifteenth Amendment was introduced on February 26, 1869, and became law on March 30, 1870. It provides in § 1 that the right of citizens

BOX 1.3

The Black Codes

. . . They defined racial status; forbade blacks from pursuing certain occupations or professions; prohibited blacks from owning firearms or other weapons; controlled the movement of blacks by systems of passes; required proof of residence; prohibited the congregation of groups of blacks; restricted blacks from residing in certain areas; and specified an etiquette of deference to whites, such as by prohibiting blacks from directing insulting words at whites. The Codes forbade racial intermarriage and provided the death penalty for blacks raping white women, while omitting special provisions for whites raping black women. . . . They excluded blacks from jury duty, public office, and voting. Some Black Codes required racial segregation in public transportation or created Jim Crow schools. Most Codes authorized whipping and the pillory as punishment for freedmen's offenses.

The Codes salvaged the labor-discipline elements of slave law in master-and-servant statutes, vagrancy and pauper provisions, apprenticeship regulations, and elaborate labor contract statutes, especially those pertaining to farm labor. Other provisions permitted magistrates to hire out offenders unable to pay fines. These statutes provided a basis for subsequent efforts, extending well into the twentieth century, to provide a legal and paralegal structure forcing blacks to work, restricting their occupational mobility, and providing harsh systems of forced black labor, sometimes verging on peonage.

SOURCE: From "Black Codes," by W. M. Wiecek, 1989, in L. W. Levy, K. L. Karst, and D. J. Mahoney (Eds.), *Civil Rights and Equality*, pp. 111-112, New York: Macmillan.

of the United States to vote shall not be denied or abridged by the United States or by any state on account of race, color, or previous condition of servitude.

Between 1865 and 1866, the former slave states enacted laws that were known as the Black Codes (see Box 1.3). Their primary purpose was to relegate blacks to a state of racial subordination and social inferiority and to render the progeny of emancipation meaningless. Coupled with the perpetration of violence against the newly freed blacks, a series of laws enacted by Congress were designed to enforce the Civil War Amendments and to strip the Black Codes of their raison d'être.[12] The Civil Rights Act of 1866, which was passed over President Andrew Johnson's veto, continues to be one of the nation's most important civil rights laws. Section 1 of the Act grants to blacks the same rights as whites possessed to make contracts, to sue, and to inherit, purchase, lease, sell, hold, and convey real and personal property. This Act also provides for the punishment of anyone acting "under color of law" who prevents individuals from enjoying these rights. Three other major civil rights laws were passed during the Reconstruction era. The First Enforcement Act of May 31, 1870, designed to enforce the Fifteenth Amendment, made it a federal crime for state officials to deny qualified blacks the right to vote. Under this Act, any person who hindered or obstructed qualified voters in the exercise of their franchise was subject to fines and imprisonment. The Second Enforcement Act of February 28, 1871, granted federal courts jurisdiction over supervisors of elections, and interference with their work was made a federal crime. The Ku Klux Klan Act of April 20, 1871, the Third Enforcement Act, was designed to stop private violence against blacks after the Civil War. This Act prohibited conspiracies to deprive persons of their civil rights. In its most far-reaching civil rights legislation at the time, Congress passed the Civil Rights Act of 1875, which prohibited discrimination in the enjoyment of accommodations, inns, public conveyances on land and water, and theaters and other places of public amusement. As we demonstrate in the next section, the civil rights acts that were passed between 1866 and 1875 were no more than cosmetic legal symbols not taken seriously by the populace or the Supreme Court.

THE SUPREME COURT'S
ASSAULT ON EQUALITY, 1864-1888

Racial attitudes had not changed much after the Civil War, and fewer than five million blacks (13% of the population) faced stiff white opposition in their quest for equalitarianism. Matters would get much worse before they got better. Because of conservative Republican and Southern Democratic support, the election of Rutherford B. Hayes in the presidential election of 1876 resulted in the famous Compromise of 1877. The Compromise led to a pledge against the resort to force to protect black civil rights. The Compromise in reality meant an end to Reconstruction and federal control of the Democratic Party in the South. The Democratic Party thus was able to put in full force its conservative philosophy on race. As the federal troops were withdrawn from the Southern states, the predicament facing blacks became more dismal. The Supreme Court vitiated the Civil War Amendments' potency through a series of decisions beginning in the 1870s (see Table 1.2).

The Chase Court, 1864-1873

Chief Justice Taney died on October 12, 1864, at the age of 87, as the Civil War was coming to an end. After President Lincoln's reelection in 1864, Salmon P. Chase was nominated to succeed Taney as the sixth Chief Justice of the United States on December 6, 1864. He was 56 years old and served as Chief Justice for only nine years. President Lincoln also appointed four other Justices: Noah H. Swayne, Samuel F. Miller, David Davis, and Stephen

Table 1.2 Major Cases During the Chase and Waite Courts, 1864-1888

Case	Vote	Ruling
Osborn v. Nicholson, 80 U.S. (13 Wall.) 654 (1872)	8-1	Justice Swayne upheld the validity of a prewar contract for the sale of a slave.
Blyew v. United States, 80 U.S. (13 Wall.) 581 (1872)	7-1	Justice Story ruled that the Civil Rights Act of 1866 did not permit the federal courts to take jurisdiction of a case in which blacks had been murdered in Kentucky and Kentucky law prohibited blacks from testifying unless they were parties in a case.
Slaughter-House Cases, 83 U.S. (16. Wall.) 36 (1873)	5-4	Justice Miller held that the privileges or immunities clause of the Fourteenth Amendment barred states from abridging only the privileges or immunities of the citizens of the United States.
Bradwell v. The State of Illinois, 83 U.S. (16. Wall.) 130 (1873)	9-0	The Supreme Court rejected the claim of Myra Bradwell that her right to practice law was protected by the privileges or immunities clause of the Fourteenth Amendment.
Minor v. Happersett, 88 U.S. (21 Wall.) 163 (1875)	9-0	Chief Justice Waite held that despite the fact that women were citizens of the United States, they had not been given the right to vote by the privileges or immunities clause of the Fourteenth Amendment.
United States v. Cruikshank, 92 U.S. (2 Otto) 542 (1876)	9-0	Chief Justice Waite declared that § 6 of the Enforcement Act of 1870, which prohibits conspiracies to deny citizens their constitutional rights, were rights of national citizenship and fell under the protection of the United States.
United States v. Reese, 92 U.S. (2 Otto) 214 (1876)	8-1	Chief Justice Waite declared two sections of the Enforcement Act of 1870 unconstitutional on the grounds that the statute was broad enough to cover any type of discrimination and that the legislation should have been limited to state interference on account of race or previous condition of servitude.
Hall v. DeCuir, 95 U.S. 485 (1878)	9-0	Chief Justice Waite struck down a Louisiana law guaranteeing equal rights on conveyances on the ground that it was an unconstitutional invasion by Louisiana on the national government's exclusive jurisdiction over interstate commerce.

Table 1.2 *continued*

Case	Vote	Ruling
Strauder v. West Virginia, 100 U.S. 303 (1880)	7-2	Justice Strong declared that excluding blacks from jury service was a denial of the equal protection of the laws.
Ex parte Virginia, 100 U.S. (10 Otto) 339 (1880)	7-2	Justice Strong upheld a section of the Civil Rights Act of 1875 that provided for the punishment of any officer or person who sought to prevent blacks from serving on juries.
Neal v. Delaware, 103 U.S. (13 Otto) 370 (1880)	7-2	Justice Harlan reaffirmed the principle enunciated in *Strauder* that excluding blacks from juries violates the Constitution.
Virginia v. Rives, 100 U.S. (13 Otto) 313 (1880)	9-0	Justice Strong undercut the force of *Strauder, Neal,* and *Ex parte Virginia* when he ruled that a mixed jury is not essential to the equal protection of the laws.
Pace v. Alabama, 106 U.S. 583 (1883)	9-0	Justice Field held that an Alabama law that permitted a more severe punishment for sexual activity between members of different races than for the same offense when both persons were of the same race did not violate the equal protection clause.
United States v. Harris, 106 U.S. 629 (1883)	8-1	Justice Woods concluded that the Ku Klux Klan Act of 1871 was invalid on the ground that protection of blacks from private conspiracies was a function of state government, not the federal government.
Civil Rights Cases, 109 U.S. 3 (1883)	8-1	Justice Bradley declared that the Thirteenth and Fourteenth Amendments did not empower Congress to pass the Civil Rights Act of 1875.
Ex parte Yarbrough, 110 U.S. 651 (1884)	9-0	Justice Miller concluded that Congress has the power to protect and enforce the right to vote under the Enforcement Act of 1870.
Yick Wo v. Hopkins, 118 U.S. 356 (1886)	9-0	Justice Matthews struck down, under the Fourteenth Amendment, a San Francisco ordinance that discriminated against individuals of Chinese ancestry.

J. Field. During the Chase Court era, the United States was still laboring under the intense sectional hostility that was brought about by the *Dred Scott* decision. A politically and ideologically divided Chase Court primarily addressed issues of Reconstruction and federal and state regulatory power, but it was the Chase Court's interpretation of the Fourteenth Amendment during its final term that undermined the ability of the national government to protect the civil rights of black citizens.

Despite the ratification of the Thirteenth Amendment in 1865, the Chase Court upheld the validity of a prewar contract for the sale of a slave. In *Osborn v. Nicholson,* 80 U.S. (13 Wall.) 654 (1872), an Arkansas slave owner sold a slave to the buyer, warranting him to be a slave for life. After the Thirteenth Amendment was ratified and the slave was liberated, the defendant sued to recover $1,300 plus interest that he paid for the slave. In an 8-1 opinion written by Justice Swayne, the Court held that because slavery was lawful at the time the contract was made, the right to sue was not taken away by the Thirteenth Amendment. According to Justice Swayne, to hold otherwise "would, in effect, take away one man's property and give it to another and the deprivation would be 'without due process of law.' " Chief Justice Chase, the sole dissenter in the case, argued that the Thirteenth Amendment nullified any slave contracts and that the Fourteenth Amendment forbids compensation for slaves emancipated by the Thirteenth Amendment.

The first cases in which the Supreme Court was afforded the opportunity to interpret the Fourteenth Amendment were the SLAUGHTER-HOUSE CASES, 83 U.S. (16 Wall.) 36 (1873). Louisiana enacted a statute that granted a monopoly to a livestock company to slaughter and butcher all animals in New Orleans. Butchers who were affected by the monopoly (many of them lost their jobs) brought lawsuits challenging the constitutionality of the Louisiana law. In a 5-4 opinion written by Justice Miller, the Court held that the Fourteenth Amendment's privileges or immunities clause did not protect the right to labor. Justice Miller reasoned that the privileges or immunities clause belonged to the citizens of the states and is to be protected by the states. For blacks, this interpretation of the Fourteenth Amendment meant that protection of their rights remained the responsibility of the states that were least likely to provide that protection.

Women, like blacks, were also consigned to second-class citizenship status in the white-male-dominated society. They could not vote, serve on juries, hold political office, or participate in a variety of professional opportunities that were considered the domain of white males. During this era, the Fourteenth Amendment was not very helpful in altering discriminatory practices against them. In the same year that the *Slaughter-House Cases* were decided, the Chase Court, in *Bradwell v. The State of Illinois,* 83 U.S. (16 Wall.) 130 (1873), unanimously declared that the states had the authority to regulate admissions to the bar and therefore rejected the claim of Myra Bradwell that her right to practice law was an attribute of United States citizenship and protected by the privileges or immunities clause of the Fourteenth Amendment. Two years later, in the case of *Minor v. Happersett,* 88 U.S. (21 Wall.) 163 (1875), the Waite Court unanimously ruled that despite the fact that women were citizens under the Constitution, women had not been given the right to vote by the Fourteenth Amendment's privileges or immunities clause. Forty-five years later, women finally were guaranteed the right to vote when the Nineteenth Amendment to the Constitution was ratified by the states. It would take another 51 years before the Burger Court declared legislative classifications based on gender invalid under the equal protection clause, in *Reed v. Reed,* 404 U.S. 71 (1971).

The Waite Court, 1874-1888

On May 7, 1873, Chief Justice Chase died of a stroke. On January 19, 1874, President Ulysses S. Grant nominated Morrison R. Waite as the seventh Chief Justice of the United States. Waite had very little experience, compared with many of the other Justices who served on the Supreme Court. It is important to note that Waite was the fourth choice of President Grant. His first choice, Senator Roscoe Conkling of New York, refused the job, and the next two controversial choices withdrew because of the real possibility of being rejected. Chief Justice Waite, described as a disciple of Roger B. Taney, articulated the states' rights position on constitutional questions involving civil rights. In addition, the Waite Court made it clear that the Fourteenth and Fifteenth Amendments had not bestowed on Congress plenary power to defend the civil rights of blacks. A series of landmark decisions by the Waite Court established its unwillingness to use judicial power to put the Court behind the struggle for racial equality.

In 1873 more than 100 whites attacked blacks who had gathered in front of a courthouse in Colfax, Louisiana, to discuss a contested gubernatorial election for governor. After the attack, during which more than 100 blacks were killed, William Cruikshank and two other whites were indicted and found guilty in federal court for violating § 6 of the Enforcement Act of 1870. Section 6 of the Act prohibited conspiracies to deny citizens their constitutional rights, including their right to vote. The conspirators appealed their conviction on the ground that the indictments were faulty. In a unanimous decision by Chief Justice Waite, the Court, in *United States v. Cruikshank,* 92 U.S. (2 Otto) 542 (1876), held that the conspirators' indictments were too vague and general and therefore not good and sufficient in law. Relying on the rationale of the *Slaughter-House Cases,* Chief Justice Waite reasoned that the charges against Cruikshank and the others in denying blacks specific rights, such as the right to bear arms and the right of assembly, were attributes of national citizenship and fell under the protection of the United States. Furthermore, the charges depriving blacks of their due process and equal protection rights, according to the Court, were covered only by state action, and not by actions of private individuals. On the charge of whether the conspirators sought to deprive blacks of their voting rights, Chief Justice Waite found that "it does not appear that it was their intent to interfere with any right granted or secured by the constitution or laws of the United States. We may suspect that race was the cause of the hostility; but it is not so averred." The Court concluded in *Cruikshank* that the state was responsible for punishing the defendants.

In the same year that *Cruikshank* was decided, the Waite Court severely restricted the scope of the Fifteenth Amendment and congressional authority to enforce it. In UNITED STATES V. REESE, 92 U.S. (2 Otto) 214 (1876), inspectors of a municipal election in Kentucky had refused to register a black citizen's vote. Indictments against the inspector were brought under the Enforcement Act of 1870. In an 8-1 ruling, Chief Justice Waite declared sections of the Act unconstitutional because they went beyond prohibiting interference with the right to vote under the Fifteenth Amendment. In addition, the Court held that the framers of the Fifteenth Amendment understood that it did not guarantee the right to vote but simply forbids the state and federal governments from excluding individuals from voting because of race or previous condition of servitude.

Two years later, the Waite Court, in HALL V. DeCUIR, 95 U.S. 485 (1878), made it abundantly clear that a Louisiana statute prohibiting racial discrimination in transportation interfered with interstate commerce. In a unanimous decision, the Waite Court found that the law was an unconstitutional invasion by Louisiana on the national government's exclusive jurisdiction over interstate commerce. Justice Clifford's concurring opinion in *DeCuir* presented a defense of what was later termed "separate-but-equal" in public accommodations.

Blacks were systematically denied service on juries throughout much of the South. The Black Codes often mandated all-white juries, and such systematic discrimination severely impeded blacks' ability to secure justice in the criminal process. In 1880 the Waite Court delivered four jury discrimination rulings that for decades would have a significant impact on their jury service. In STRAUDER V. WEST VIRGINIA, 100 U.S. 303 (1880), the Waite Court gave blacks a reason to have a modicum of faith in the equal protection clause of the Fourteenth Amendment. In *Strauder,* a West Virginia statute that limited jury service to white males was declared unconstitutional under the equal protection clause. In *Ex parte Virginia,* 100 U.S. (10 Otto) 339 (1880), Justice Strong held that a judge of a county court in Virginia who was charged with the selection of jurors and who had deliberately excluded blacks from grand and petit juror service was properly arrested for his actions and that the lower court was correct in denying him relief. The Court, in *Ex parte Virginia,* validated the Civil Rights Act of 1875, which provided punishment for any officer or person who sought to disqualify citizens to serve on grand or petit juries on account of race, color, or previous condition of servitude as being authorized by the Thirteenth and Fourteenth Amendments of the Constitution. In *Neal v. Delaware,* 103 U.S. (13 Otto) 370 (1880), the Waite Court, in a 7-2 opinion, invalidated Delaware's practice of excluding blacks from service on juries. Justice Harlan reaffirmed the doctrine announced in *Strauder* and held that the exclusion of blacks from juries violated the prisoners' rights under the Constitution and laws of the United States. In *Virginia v. Rives,* 100 U.S. (13 Otto) 313 (1880), however, the Waite Court undercut the force of *Strauder, Neal,* and *Ex parte Virginia* when it ruled that the fact that no blacks had served on the grand and petit juries in any case involving murder was not a violation of any civil rights and did not prove discrimination on the basis of race because there was no overt exclusion of blacks from jury service. In a unanimous opinion, Justice Strong pointed out that a mixed jury is not essential to the equal protection of the laws and that the black defendants had no right to a jury composed, in part, of blacks. Accordingly, the ruling in *Rives* meant that Southern states could deny blacks their rights to serve on juries.

In PACE V. ALABAMA, 106 U.S. 583 (1883), an Alabama law provided a more severe punishment for fornication and adultery between blacks and whites than for the same offense between individuals of the same race. The Waite Court, in a unanimous decision, rejected Pace's claim by emphasizing that the two sections of the code are consistent because the one prescribes a punishment for an offense between individuals of different sexes, whereas the other ordains punishment only if the two sexes are of different races. The Court had stretched logic to an unusual conclusion and provided for an "equal discrimination" exception to equal protection analysis.

In UNITED STATES V. HARRIS, 106 U.S. 629 (1883), the Waite Court substantially weakened the Ku Klux Klan Act of 1871 when it held that state action, and not the action of private individuals, is the focus of the Fourteenth Amendment. Blacks had to endure inhumane treatment because of the Waite Court's conclusion that the Ku Klux Klan Act of 1871 was invalid on the ground that protection of blacks from private conspiracies was a function for the state government, and not the federal government.

The prospect of legal equality was further frustrated by the Supreme Court in the CIVIL RIGHTS CASES, 109 U.S. 3 (1883). This adverse ruling was the most devastating one that blacks had experienced since *Dred Scott*. The Waite Court, in an 8-1 opinion written by Justice Bradley, declared that the Civil Rights Act of 1875 was unconstitutional because the Fourteenth Amendment is directed at state action of a particular character and that an "[i]ndividual invasion of individual rights is not the subject matter of the amendment." Justice Harlan dissented and held that Congress' intent was abundantly clear. The opinion was "too narrow and artificial," according to his analysis. Moreover, he pointed out that the language of the Fourteenth Amendment does not authorize prohibitions on state proceedings. After the Civil Rights Act of 1875, Congress did not enact another civil rights law until 1957. Institutional indifference toward genuine equalitarianism was the norm for the Waite Court. Leonard Levy described the Court's ruling in the *Civil Rights Cases* as "one of the most fateful decisions in American history. It had the effect of reinforcing racist attitudes and practices, while emasculating a heroic effort by Congress and the President to prevent the growth of a Jim Crow society."[13]

One year after the *Civil Rights Cases,* the Supreme Court ruled, in *Ex parte Yarbrough,* 110 U.S. 651 (1884), that Congress could protect the rights of blacks to vote in congressional elections from individual and state interference. In this case, Jasper Yarbrough and seven of his Ku Klux Klan friends were found guilty of violating the Enforcement Act of 1870 by using violence to discourage Berry Saunders from voting. Yarbrough appealed to the Supreme Court on the ground that Congress did not have the authority to regulate elections. Writing for a unanimous Court, Justice Miller disagreed with his argument and deviated from the norm of deciding against blacks in civil rights cases. The Waite Court ruled that to suggest that Congress "has no power by appropriate laws to secure this election from the influence of violence, of corruption, and of fraud, is a proposition so startling as to arrest attention and demand the gravest consideration." Because the government's very existence depends on elections, it must have the power to see to it that they are free from violence.

The Equal Protection Clause and Chinese Ancestry

Americans of Chinese ancestry were subjected to Jim Crow laws designed to segregate whites and Chinese by the Western states. The Supreme Court was provided the opportunity to interpret the meaning of the Fourteenth Amendment's equal protection clause in a case involving discrimination against individuals of Chinese ancestry. In YICK WO V. HOPKINS, 118 U.S. 356 (1886), a San Francisco ordinance required all persons operating a laundry in a building constructed of materials other than brick or stone to receive special permission from the board of supervisors. Yick Wo alleged that the ordinance was unconstitutional under the Fourteenth Amendment because of its illegal discrimination against the Chinese. Justice Matthews, writing for a unanimous Court, held that the ordinance denied the Chinese the equal protection of the laws. The Court acknowledged that the board of supervisors could use its police power to regulate laundries for health and safety reasons, but an underlying concern in *Yick Wo* was protection of property rights. The Court found that the board of supervisors arbitrarily exercised its police powers in refusing to grant licenses to Chinese persons to operate laundries, thus depriving them of their livelihood. Despite the potential of the Court's expansive interpretation of the equal protection clause in securing the civil rights of blacks, changes in the Court's personnel and the lack of private property rights in most Southern Jim Crow legislation rendered *Yick Wo* a dormant precedent until well into the next century.

THE FULLER COURT, 1888-1910: THE NADIR IN THE QUEST FOR EQUALITY

On April 30, 1888, President Grover Cleveland nominated Melville W. Fuller to replace Morrison Waite as the nation's eighth Chief Justice. On July 20, 1888, he was confirmed by a 41-20 vote. Like Chief Justice Waite, Fuller was not well known. Moreover, he had never held public office at the federal level and had no previous judicial experience. Nor was he considered a leader on the Court. From 1888 to 1910, five presidents filled 11 vacancies on the high court. President Cleveland, a Democrat, appointed Edward White and Rufus Peckham, in addition to Fuller's appointment to the position of Chief Justice. The remaining appointments were made by Republican presidents. President Benjamin Harrison appointed David Brewer, Henry Brown,

George Shiras, and Howell Jackson. President William McKinley appointed Joseph McKenna in 1897. President Theodore Roosevelt appointed Oliver Wendell Holmes, William Day, and William Moody to the Court. And President William Howard Taft appointed Horace Lurton in 1909, during the remaining few months of the Fuller Court. With the exception of the appointment of Holmes, Owen M. Fiss described the Fuller Court as "one of the most homogenous in the history of the Court."[14] Justices Brewer and Peckham emerged as the intellectual leaders of the Fuller Court.

During the Fuller Court era, the Supreme Court was largely preoccupied with governmental regulation of business (see Table 1.3), and it used the tool of substantive due process to promote economic freedom. After all, it was the Fuller Court that rendered the infamous *Lochner v. New York,* 198 U.S. 45 (1905) decision. In *Lochner,* the Fuller Court struck down a New York law prohibiting employees from working in bakeries more than 60 hours a week or 10 hours a day, under the liberty provision of the due process clause of the Fourteenth Amendment. The Court held that the statute "interfered with the right to contract between the employer and employees, concerning the number of hours in which the latter may labor in the bakery of the employer." The laissez faire rationale embraced by the Fuller Court in *Lochner* was used to strike down attempts to reform social and economic conditions.

By the 1890s, ideas of black intellectual, biological, and cultural inferiority dominated popular and scientific thought. During the Fuller Court era, the black vote in the South was largely ineffectual because of various methods of disfranchisement, including the imposition of poll taxes, literacy tests, and grandfather clauses. Meaningful economic opportunity for Southern blacks in particular was virtually nonexistent. Substantial inequalities in education were a serious problem. The lynching of blacks reached its peak in the 1890s. In addition to these setbacks, Booker T. Washington's 1895 Atlanta Exposition speech, which essentially urged Southern blacks to accept their subordinated status and Jim Crow segregation while proving themselves worthy of equality, catapulted him into the national limelight. Frederick Douglass, who had been at the forefront in pressing for full equality for blacks but whose influence waned in his later years, died months before the Washington speech. To be sure, scientific racism, disfranchisement, lynching, and Jim Crow segregation relegated blacks to their nadir—the lowest point in their elusive quest for equality.

Separate but Equal in Law,
Separate but Unequal in Fact

Charles A. Lofgren found that Southern states began passing mandatory Jim Crow laws around 1890 and a second wave of laws a decade later.[15] The main focus of these laws was railway travel, and Florida, Mississippi, Texas, Louisiana, Alabama, Arkansas, and Kentucky adopted separate-but-equal measures prior to 1896. According to Lofgren's analysis, political agrarianism, growing black assertiveness, and a more permissive environment pro-

Table 1.3 Major Cases During the Fuller Court, 1888-1910

Case	Vote	Ruling
Louisville, New Orleans & Texas Railway Co. v. Mississippi, 133 U.S. 587 (1890)	7-2	Justice Brewer held that a Mississippi law requiring segregated accommodations intrastate did not intrude on Congress' power to regulate commerce.
Chesapeake & Ohio Railway Company v. Kentucky, 179 U.S. 388 (1900)	8-1	Justice Brown ruled that Kentucky's separate coach law was not an infringement on Congress' power to regulate interstate commerce.
Plessy v. Ferguson, 163 U.S. 537 (1896)	7-1	Justice Brown upheld the separate-but-equal principle under the Fourteenth Amendment.
Williams v. Mississippi, 170 U.S. 213 (1898)	9-0	Justice McKenna upheld provisions of Mississippi's Constitution and laws that, in effect, denied blacks jury service because they were not qualified to vote due to restrictive voting qualifications that disfranchised blacks.
Cumming v. Richmond County Board of Education, 175 U.S. 528 (1899)	9-0	Justice Harlan held that providing a high school for whites but not for blacks did not violate the equal protection clause because black children would not benefit by closing the white high school.
Carter v. Texas, 177 U.S. 442 (1900)	9-0	Justice Gray ruled that the lower courts improperly denied a black defendant's motion to introduce witnesses and testimony regarding discrimination in jury selection.
James v. Bowman, 190 U.S. 127 (1903)	6-2	Justice Brewer concluded that, under a federal statute, Congress has the power to punish private action that hindered blacks' right to vote in federal elections only, thus applying the concept of state action to the Fifteenth Amendment.
Giles v. Harris, 189 U.S. 475 (1903)	6-3	Justice Holmes ruled that the federal courts lacked jurisdiction in a case to provide relief against massive disfranchisement of blacks in Alabama.
Rogers v. Alabama, 192 U.S. 226 (1904)	9-0	Justice Holmes, relying on *Carter v. Texas,* held that when the state excludes blacks from grand juries, equal protection has been denied to a black defendant.
Clyatt v. United States, 197 U.S. 207 (1905)	9-0	The Supreme Court upheld the constitutionality of the Peonage Act of 1867 under Congress' power to enforce the Thirteenth Amendment.

Table 1.3 *continued*

Case	Vote	Ruling
Hodges v. United States, 203 U.S. 1 (1906)	7-2	Justice Brewer held that the federal government lacked jurisdiction under the Thirteenth Amendment and federal statutes to prosecute a gang of whites who forced blacks off a job at an Arkansas lumber mill and that the remedy must be pursued through state courts.
Berea College v. Commonwealth of Kentucky, 211 U.S. 45 (1908)	7-2	Justice Brewer upheld a Kentucky statute that required segregation of private colleges.
Thomas v. Texas, 212 U.S. 278 (1909)	9-0	Chief Justice Fuller held that discrimination cannot be presumed from the mere fact that none of the jurors were black in a black defendant's attempt to quash his murder indictment on the ground of discrimination against blacks on grand and petit juries.
Chiles v. Chesapeake & Ohio Railway Company, 218 U.S. 71 (1910)	8-1	Justice McKenna upheld the segregation of whites and blacks on interstate trains in Kentucky.
Bailey v. Alabama, 219 U.S. 219 (1911)	7-2	Justice Hughes struck down an Alabama statute that compelled the service or labor by making it a crime to refuse or fail to perform under the Thirteenth Amendment and the Peonage Act of 1867.
United States v. Reynolds, 235 U.S. 133 (1914)	9-0	Justice Day struck down Alabama's criminal surety laws under the Thirteenth Amendment and the antipeonage provisions.

duced by urbanization contributed to the enactment of segregated transportation legislation.[16] The case of *Louisville, New Orleans & Texas Railway Co. v. Mississippi,* 133 U.S. 587 (1890) is illustrative of Lofgren's observations. A Mississippi law required segregated railroad accommodations for blacks and whites traveling through the state. The Fuller Court, in a 7-2 opinion written by Justice Brewer, held that the law did not intrude on Congress' power to regulate interstate commerce. In his dissent, Justice Harlan argued that the Mississippi statute was an unconstitutional regulation of interstate commerce. Twelve years earlier, in the *DeCuir* case, the Court had declared that a state law prohibiting discrimination on public transportation systems was unconstitutional because it was an invasion of the federal government's exclusive jurisdiction over interstate commerce.

A group of Louisiana blacks decided to test the constitutionality of the state's Separate Car Act, which required that all railway companies provide equal but separate accommodations for whites and blacks. Homer Plessy was chosen to break the law because he was only one eighth black and thus appeared to be white (it was known that Plessy had a black great-grandmother), in order to highlight the arbitrariness of the Act's racial classification. When Plessy attempted to take a seat on the coach reserved for whites, he was ejected and charged with violating the Louisiana statute. Plessy lost his case in the lower courts in Louisiana. In PLESSY V. FERGUSON, 163 U.S. 537 (1896), Justice Brown, writing for a 7-1 majority, found Louisiana's Separate Car Act constitutional. According to his reasoning, the Fourteenth Amendment "could not have been intended to abolish distinctions based upon color, or to enforce social, as distinguished from political equality, or a commingling of the two races upon terms unsatisfactory to either." The Fuller majority found that the statute was no more unreasonable than laws that required separate schools for black children. Only Justice John Marshall Harlan dissented in *Plessy*. By this time, he had secured a reputation as a defender of black civil rights, and he was chiefly known for his "great dissents" despite the fact that he was from a slave-owning family and was himself briefly a slave owner. For Justice Harlan, the Louisiana statute did, in fact, stamp a badge of inferiority on blacks. With respect to the Fourteenth Amendment analysis, he found the law unreasonable because separation of the races was not a legitimate legislative end. He observed in these often-quoted words, "But in view of the Constitution, in the eye of the law, there is in this country no superior, dominant, ruling class of citizens. There is no caste here. Our Constitution is color-blind, and neither knows nor tolerates classes among citizens. In respect of civil rights, all citizens are equal before the law." He argued that the *Plessy* ruling would be just as pernicious as the Taney Court's *Dred Scott* ruling. The separate-but-equal doctrine strengthened white supremacy and legalized Jim Crow segregation. The high court did not reverse the principle until 58 years later.

In *Williams v. Mississippi,* 170 U.S. 213 (1898), blacks were prevented from jury service in a case involving a black male, Henry Williams, indicted for murder. Williams's attorney argued that because blacks were stripped of their right to exercise the franchise by the Mississippi Constitution and laws, they were, in effect, denied the right to jury service because the law mandated that only qualified voters were eligible for jury service. The Fuller Court, in a unanimous opinion written by Justice McKenna, concluded that the Mississippi Constitution and laws were not discriminatory against blacks. Logic had been stretched to an ingenious level, and the Court's persistent behavioral propensity of indifference to the rights of blacks was a harsh reality.

In 1897 Seth Carter was convicted of murder. He sought to quash the indictment on the ground that blacks were excluded from the jury. Carter wanted to introduce witnesses and testimony regarding the discrimination, but the court refused to hear any evidence. In *Carter v. Texas,* 177 U.S. 442 (1900), Justice Gray, writing for the Court, ruled that the lower courts denied Carter the right to offer evidence of discrimination. However, in *Martin v. Texas,* 200 U.S. 316 (1906), a black man accused of murder moved to quash the indictment on the ground that blacks had been excluded from the grand jury on account of race. In a unanimous opinion by Justice Harlan, the Court found that the defendant offered no proof on the charge of discrimination.

In two cases decided in 1903, the Fuller Court essentially rendered the Fifteenth Amendment meaningless and expressed its unwillingness to allow federal courts to redress widespread disfranchisement against Southern blacks. The principle that was established 19 years earlier in *Ex parte Yarbrough* was completely ignored in *James v. Bowman,* 190 U.S. 127 (1903). In *Bowman,* a federal grand jury indicted Henry Bowman and Harry Weaver for bribery and for unlawfully intimidating blacks from exercising their right to vote in a congressional election held in Kentucky in 1898. In his petition for habeas corpus before the federal district court, Bowman challenged the indictment on the ground that § 5507 of the Revised Statutes, which provided for the punishment of individuals who prevented, hindered, controlled, or intimidated others from exercising their right to vote guaranteed by the Fifteenth Amendment was unconstitutional. The federal district judge granted the writ and, on appeal, the Fuller Court, in a 6-2 opinion written by Justice Brewer (Justice McKenna did not participate), agreed that § 5507 was unconstitutional. In *Bowman,* Justice Brewer reasoned that, on its face, § 5507 "purports to be an exercise of the power granted to Congress by the Fifteenth Amendment." Justice Brewer, relying on previous precedents—*Virginia v. Rives, United States v. Cruikshank,* and the *Civil Rights Cases*—reasoned that the Fifteenth Amendment "relates solely to action 'by the United States or by any State,' and does not contemplate wrongful individual acts." By applying the state action concept to the Fifteenth Amendment, the Fuller Court prohibited the federal government from controlling private action that thwarted blacks' right to vote. Justices Harlan and Brown dissented in *Bowman* without opinion.

A black man brought a class action suit on behalf of himself and more than 5,000 black citizens of Montgomery, Alabama, against the board of registrars in that county. He attempted to register to vote in March 1902 but was refused on account of color, as were other blacks statewide. He challenged the constitutional validity of several provisions of Alabama's Constitution that provided that persons who registered before January 1, 1903, remained electors for life unless disqualified by certain crimes. After January 1, 1903, persons attempting to register to vote had to undertake more severe tests for voting: good character tests, poll taxes, literacy tests, and various property qualifications. In a 6-3 ruling written by Justice Oliver Wendell Holmes, the Fuller Court declared, in *Giles v. Harris,* 189 U.S. 475 (1903), that the federal courts lacked jurisdiction to hear the case. According to Justice Holmes, § 1979 of the Revised Statutes, which provided that every person who, under color of a state statute, ordinance, regulation, or custom, causes citizens of the United States or of the jurisdiction to be deprived of any rights secured by the Constitution and laws should be liable to the party injured in a lawsuit in equity "does not extend the sphere of equitable jurisdiction in respect of what shall be held an appropriate subject matter for that kind of relief." Invoking the political question doctrine, Justice Holmes stated, "The traditional limits of proceedings in equity have not embraced a remedy for political wrongs." In their dissent, Justices Brewer and Harlan argued that sufficient Court precedents provided support for the position that the Court had jurisdiction in the case. The *Giles* decision legitimated the widespread disfranchisement of Southern blacks during this era.

Three years after *Plessy*, the separate-but-equal doctrine was extended to public schools in *Cumming v. Richmond County Board of Education*, 175 U.S. 528 (1899). In *Cumming*, black parents brought suit against the county board of education when the board stated it could not maintain a high school for black children for economic reasons. In a unanimous opinion written by Justice Harlan, the Fuller Court held that providing a high school for whites but not blacks did not violate the equal protection clause of the Fourteenth Amendment because black children would not benefit by closing the white high school. Justice Harlan's opinion in *Cumming* clearly ran counter to his egalitarian sentiment expressed in previous civil rights cases, especially *Plessy*. In BEREA COLLEGE V. COMMONWEALTH OF KENTUCKY, 211 U.S. 45 (1908), Justice Brewer, writing for a 7-2 majority, held that under the separate-but-equal doctrine the state could forbid even a private college from instructing blacks and whites together. In his dissent, Justice Harlan argued that the Kentucky statute was "an arbitrary invasion of the rights of liberty and property guaranteed by the Fourteenth Amendment against hostile state action and is, therefore void."

The Thirteenth Amendment and the Peonage Cases

In addition to its cramped interpretation of the Fourteenth and Fifteenth Amendments, the Fuller Court narrowly interpreted the Thirteenth Amendment in *Plessy* as abolishing involuntary servitude only and not putting an end to the incidents or badges of slavery. In *Hodges v. United States*, 203 U.S. 1 (1906), the Fuller Court held that the federal government lacked jurisdiction under the Thirteenth Amendment (§§ 1977, 1978, 1979, 5508, and 5510 of the Revised Statutes) to prosecute a gang of whites who forced blacks off a job at an Arkansas lumber mill. In a 7-2 opinion written by Justice Brewer, the Court declared that unless the Thirteenth Amendment vests jurisdiction in the federal government, the remedy for wrongs committed by individuals on blacks is through state action and state courts. According to Justice Brewer, "it was not the intent of the Amendment to denounce every act done to an individual which was wrong if done to a free man and yet justified in a condition of slavery, and to give authority to Congress to enforce such denunciation." Justice Harlan, joined by Justice Day, dissented. He argued, "It would seem impossible, under former decisions, to sustain the view that a combination or conspiracy of individuals, albeit acting without the sanction of the State, may not be reached and punished by the United States, if the combination and conspiracy has for its object, by force, to prevent or burden the free exercise or enjoyment of a right or privilege created or secured by the Constitution or laws of the United States."

Many blacks in the rural South continued to live under the shadow of slavery under the peonage system. Justice Brewer, in *Clyatt v. United States,* 197 U.S. 207 (1905), defined *peonage* as "a status or condition of compulsory service, based upon the indebtedness of the peon to the master." In *Clyatt* the Fuller Court, in a unanimous opinion, upheld the constitutionality of the Peonage Act of 1867 (§§ 1190 and 5526 of the Revised Statutes), which abolished peonage in the New Mexico territory and provided for punishment for persons holding another in peonage under Congress' power to enforce the Thirteenth Amendment. This case arose when Samuel Clyatt and other whites went to Florida, sought the arrest of two blacks, Will Gordon and Mose Ridley, and took them back to Georgia in order for them to work out a debt claimed to be owed the whites.

In BAILEY V. ALABAMA, 219 U.S. 219 (1911), the Court, in a 7-2 ruling, struck down, under the Thirteenth Amendment and the Peonage Act of 1867, an Alabama statute that provided punishment for an employee who failed to perform a service for an employer and who received money from the employer and left without paying it back. Justice Hughes reasoned that although the state's purpose was to punish fraud, its main objective was to punish employees for failing to perform their work and to prevent indebted employees from leaving their service. In his dissenting opinion, Justice Holmes, joined by Justice Lurton, argued that "the Thirteenth Amendment does not outlaw contracts for labor."

In *United States v. Reynolds,* 235 U.S. 133 (1914), the Court, in a unanimous decision, struck down Alabama's criminal surety laws. These laws provided that a convict could be released on the payment of a fine by a surety of an employer in order to avoid the chain gang and would be liable for separate punishment if he failed to carry out the terms of the contract. Justice Day stated that constant fear of punishment under the criminal law renders work compulsory and concluded that the surety system violated the Thirteenth Amendment and antipeonage provisions. The Court's peonage cases, although firmly establishing the unconstitutional nature of peonage, did not wipe out its existence, nor did these decisions affect threats, intimidation, and fear that supported its continued existence in the rural South. (The White Court decided the cases of *Bailey v. Alabama* and *United States v. Reynolds.*)

CONCLUSION

Before and after the Civil War, the Supreme Court of the United States restricted the scope of laws and the Constitution in ways that relegated blacks to second-class citizenship status. Our analysis in this chapter has shown that the legal guarantees of emancipation and the Thirteenth, Fourteenth, and Fifteenth Amendments were made a travesty by the Supreme Court through a series of decisions that refused to recognize equality for blacks. Intense opposition by Southern whites and violence by individual groups prevented blacks from exercising the franchise and seriously impeded civil rights enforcement. The decisions of the Waite and Fuller Courts illustrated their ultraconservative posture and outright hostility to civil rights. The separate-but-equal doctrine established in *Plessy* strengthened white supremacy and reinforced the prevailing view that blacks were inferior. Institutional indifference to the rights of blacks and overt acts of bigotry were interpreted as tacit approval of the double standard and explains why it took so long for black Americans to enjoy basic civil rights.

NOTES

1. Higginbotham, A. L., Jr. (1978). *In the matter of color: Race and the American legal process, the colonial period.* New York: Oxford University Press.

2. Franklin, J. H. (1989). Slavery and the Constitution. In L. Levy, K. L. Karst, & D. J. Mahoney (Eds.), *Civil rights and equality: Selections from the* Encyclopedia of the American Constitution. New York: Macmillan, p. 62. Also see Franklin, J. H. (1981). *From slavery to freedom: A history of Negro Americans* (4th ed.). New York: Oxford University Press.

3. Fehrenbacher, D. E. (1981). *Slavery, law, and politics: The* Dred Scott *case in historical perspective.* New York: Oxford University Press, p. 15.

4. Hall, K. L., Wiecek, W. M., & Finkelman, P. (1991). *American legal history: Cases and materials.* New York: Oxford University Press, p. 187.

5. Woodward, C. V. (1974). *The strange career of Jim Crow* (3rd rev. ed.). New York: Oxford University Press, p. 11.

6. McCloskey, R. G. (1960). *The American Supreme Court.* Chicago: University of Chicago Press, p. 59.

7. Kelly, A. H., Harbison, W. A., & Belz, H. (1991). *The American Constitution: Its origins and development* (Vol. 1, 7th ed.). New York: Norton, pp. 246-249.

8. Arthur, J. (1989). *The unfinished Constitution: Philosophy and constitutional practice.* Belmont, CA: Wadsworth, p. 213.

9. McCloskey, R. G. (1960). *The American Supreme Court.* Chicago: University of Chicago Press, p. 96.

10. Toppin, E. A. (1971). *A biographical history of blacks in America since 1528.* New York: David McKay, p. 117.

11. Hyman, H. M. (1989). Emancipation Proclamation. In L. W. Levy, K. L. Karst, & D. J. Mahoney (Eds.), *Civil rights and equality: Selections from the encyclopedia of the American Constitution.* New York: Macmillan, p. 100.

12. For a discussion of the laws passed during this period, see *Freedom to the free: Century of emancipation, 1863-1963, A report to the President by the U.S. Commission on Civil Rights* (1970). Washington, DC: Government Printing Office, pp. 35-50.

13. Levy, L. W. (1989). Civil rights cases. In L. W. Levy, K. L. Karst, & D. J. Mahoney (Eds.), *Civil rights and equality: Selections from the encyclopedia of the American Constitution.* New York: Macmillan, p. 163.

14. Fiss, O. M. (1989). Fuller Court. In L. W. Levy, K. L. Karst, & D. J. Mahoney (Eds.), *American constitutional history.* New York: Macmillan, p. 185.

15. Lofgren, C. A. (1987). *The* Plessy *case: A legal-historical interpretation.* New York: Oxford University Press, pp. 21-22.

16. Lofgren, C. A. (1987). *The* Plessy *case: A legal-historical interpretation.* New York: Oxford University Press, pp. 25-27.

CASES

PRIGG V. THE COMMONWEALTH OF PENNSYLVANIA
41 U.S. (16 PET.) 539 (1842)

Margaret Morgan, daughter of Maryland slaves, escaped to Pennsylvania in 1832 with her children. She had another child while living in Pennsylvania. After Morgan's owner died, Margaret Ashmore, the niece and heir, hired Edward Prigg, a slave catcher, to apprehend Morgan and her children as fugitive slaves. Prigg attempted to obtain from a Pennsylvania magistrate a certificate of removal, which would allow him to take Morgan under Pennsylvania's personal liberty law, but his request was refused. Prigg then captured Morgan and her children without legal authority and was convicted of kidnapping, in violation of the Pennsylvania law. The Supreme Court of Pennsylvania affirmed the judgment, and Prigg appealed to the U.S. Supreme Court, challenging the constitutionality of the Pennsylvania statute and the Fugitive Slave Law of 1793. *Vote: 8-1.*

* * *

MR. JUSTICE STORY delivered the opinion of the Court.

. . . There are two clauses in the Constitution upon the subject of fugitives, which stand in juxtaposition with each other, and have been thought mutually to illustrate each other. They are both contained in the second section of the fourth article, and are in the following words: "A person charged in any state with treason, felony, or other crime, who shall flee from justice, and be found in another state, shall, on demand of the executive authority of the state from which he fled, be delivered up, to be removed to the state having jurisdiction of the crime."

"No person held to service or labour in one state under the laws thereof, escaping into another, shall in consequence of any law or regulation therein, be discharged from such service or labour; but shall be delivered up, on claim of the party to whom such service or labour may be due."

The last clause is that, the true interpretation whereof is directly in judgment before us. Historically, it is well known, that the object of this clause was to secure to the citizens of the slaveholding states the complete right and title of ownership in their slaves, as property, in every state in the Union into which they might escape from the state where they are held in servitude. The full recognition of this right and title was indispensable to the security of this species of property in all the slaveholding states; and, indeed, was so vital to the preservation of their domestic interests and institutions, that it cannot be doubted that it constituted a fundamental article, without the adoption of which the Union could not have been formed. Its true design was to guard against the doctrines and principles prevalent in the non-slaveholding states, by preventing them from intermeddling with, or obstructing, or abolishing the rights of the owners of slaves.

. . . The state of slavery is deemed to be a mere municipal regulation, founded upon and limited to the range of the territorial laws. This was fully recognized in Somerset's Case, Lofft's Rep. 1 [1772] . . . which was decided before the American revolution. It is manifest from this consideration, that if the Constitution had not contained in this clause, every non-slaveholding state in the Union would have been at liberty to have declared free all runaway slaves coming within its limits, and to have given them entire immunity and protection against the claims of their masters; a course which would have created the most bitter animosities, and engendered perpetual strife between the different states. The clause was, therefore, of the last importance to the safety and security of the southern states; and could not have been surrendered by them without endangering their whole property in slaves. The clause was accordingly adopted into the Constitution by the unanimous consent of the framers of it; a proof at once of its intrinsic and practical necessity.

. . . We have said that the clause contains a positive and unqualified recognition of the right of the owner in the slave, unaffected by any state law or regulation whatsoever. . . . If this be so, then all the incidents to that right attach also; the owner must, therefore, have the right to seize and repossess the slave, which the local laws of his own state confer upon him as property; and we all know that his right of seizure and recaption is universally acknowledged in all the slaveholding states. . . . Upon this ground we have not the slightest hesitation in holding, that, under and in virtue of the Constitution, the owner of a slave is clothed with entire authority, in every state in the Union, to seize and recapture his slave, whenever he can do it without any breach of the peace, or any illegal violence. In this sense, and to this extent this clause of the Constitution may properly be said to execute itself; and to require no aid from legislation, state or national.

. . . If, therefore, the clause of the Constitution had stopped at the mere recognition of the right, without providing or contemplating any means by which it might be established and enforced in cases where it did not execute itself, it is plain that it would have, in a great variety of cases, a delusive and empty annunciation. . . .

. . . These, and many other questions, will readily occur upon the slightest attention to the clause; and it is obvious that they can receive but one satisfactory answer. They require the aid of legislation to protect the right, to enforce the delivery, and to secure the subsequent possession of the slave. If, indeed, the Constitution guarantees the right, and if it requires the delivery upon the claim of the owner, . . . the natural inference certainly is, that the national government is clothed with the appropriate authority and functions to enforce it. The fundamental principle applicable to all cases of this sort, would seem to be, that where the end is required, the means are given; and where the duty is enjoined, the ability to perform it is contemplated to exist on the part of the functionaries to whom it is entrusted. The clause is found in the national Constitution, and not in that of any state. It does not point out any state functionaries, or any state action to carry its provisions into effect. The states cannot, therefore, be compelled to enforce them; and it might well be deemed an unconstitutional exercise of the power of interpretation, to insist that the states are bound to provide means to carry into effect the duties of the national government, nowhere delegated or intrusted to them by the Constitution. On the contrary, the natural, if not the necessary conclusion is, that the national government, in the absence of all positive provisions to the contrary, is bound, through its own proper departments, legislative, judicial, or executive, as the case may require, to carry into effect all the rights and duties imposed upon it by the Constitution. . . .

It is plain, then, that where a claim is made by the owner, out of possession, for the delivery of a slave, it must be made, if at all, against some other person; and inasmuch as the right is a right of property capable of being recognised and asserted by proceedings before a Court of justice, between parties adverse to each other, it constitutes, in the strictest sense, a controversy between the parties, and a case "arising under the Constitution" of the United States; within the express delegation of judicial power given by that instrument. Congress, then, may call that power into activity for the very purpose of giving effect to that right; and if so, then it may prescribe the mode and extent in which it shall be applied, and how, and under what circumstances the proceedings shall afford a complete protection and guaranty to the right.

. . . But it has been argued, that the act of Congress is unconstitutional, because it does not fall within the scope of any of the enumerated powers of legislation confided to that body; and therefore it is void. . . . If this be the true interpretation of the Constitution, it must, in a great measure, fail to attain many of its avowed and positive objects as a security of rights, and a recognition of duties. Such a limited construction of the Constitution has never yet been adopted as correct, either in theory or practice. No one has ever supposed that Congress could, constitutionally, by its legislation, exercise powers, or enact laws beyond the powers delegated to it by the Constitution; but it has, on various occasions, exercised powers which were necessary and proper as means to carry into effect rights expressly given, and duties expressly enjoined thereby. . . .

. . . We hold the act to be clearly constitutional in all its leading provisions, and, indeed, with the exception of that part which confers authority upon state magistrates, to be free from reasonable doubt and difficulty upon the grounds already stated. As to the authority so conferred upon state magistrates, while a difference of opinion has existed, and may exist still on the point, in different states, whether state magistrates are bound to act under it; none is entertained by this Court that state magistrates may,

if they choose, exercise that authority, unless prohibited by state legislation.

The remaining question is, whether the power of legislation upon this subject is exclusive in the national government, or concurrent in the states, until it is exercised by Congress. In our opinion, it is exclusive. . . .

. . . It would be a strange anomaly, and forced construction, to suppose that the national government meant to rely for the due fulfillment of its own proper duties and the rights which it intended to secure, upon state legislation; and not upon that of the Union. A fortiori, it would be more objectionable to suppose that a power, which was to be the same throughout the Union, should be confided to state sovereignty, which could not rightfully act beyond its own territorial limits.

. . . It is scarcely conceivable that the slaveholding states would have been satisfied with leaving to the legislation of the non-slaveholding states, a power of regulation, in the absence of that of Congress, which would or might practically amount to a power to destroy the rights of the owner. . . .

These are some of the reasons . . . upon which we hold the power of legislation on this subject to be exclusive in Congress. To guard, however, against any possible misconstruction of our views, it is proper to state, that we are by no means to be understood in any manner whatsoever to doubt or to interfere with the police power belonging to the states in virtue of their general sovereignty. . . . We entertain no doubt whatsoever, that the states, in virtue of their general police power, possess full jurisdiction to arrest and restrain runaway slaves, and remove them from their borders, and otherwise to secure themselves against their depredations and evil example, as they certainly may do in cases of idlers, vagabonds, and paupers. . . .

Upon these grounds, we are of opinion that the act of Pennsylvania upon which this indictment is founded, is unconstitutional and void. It purports to punish as a public offence against that state, the every act of seizing and removing a slave by his master, which the Constitution of the United States was designed to justify and uphold. . . . That judgment must, therefore, be reversed, and the cause remanded to the Supreme Court of Pennsylvania.

[The concurring opinions of MR. CHIEF JUSTICE TANEY, MR. JUSTICE THOMPSON, MR. JUSTICE BALDWIN, MR. JUSTICE WAYNE, and MR. JUSTICE DANIEL are omitted.]

* * *

MR. JUSTICE McLEAN [dissenting].

. . . The important point is, shall the presumption of right set up by the master, unsustained by any proof, or the presumption which arises from the laws and institutions of the state, prevail. This is the true issue. The sovereignty of the state is on one side, and the asserted interest of the master on the other. That interest is protected by the paramount law, and a special, a summary, and an effectual mode of redress is given. But his mode is not pursued, and the remedy is taken into his own hands by the master.

. . . The coloured person is taken, and forcibly conveyed beyond the jurisdiction of the state. This force, not being authorized by the act of Congress nor by the Constitution, may be prohibited by the state. As the act covers the whole power in the Constitution, and carries out, by special enactments, its provisions, we are, in my judgment, bound by the act. We can no more, under such circumstances, administer a remedy under the Constitution, in disregard of the act, than we can exercise a commercial or other power in disregard of an act of Congress on the same subject.

This view respects the rights of the master and the rights of the state. It neither jeopards nor retards the reclamation of the slave. It removes all state action prejudicial to the rights of the master; and recognises in the state a power to guard and protect its own jurisdiction, and the peace of its citizens.

It appears, in the case under consideration, that the state magistrate before whom the fugitive was brought refused to act. In my judgment he was bound to perform the duty required of him by a law paramount to any act, on the same subject, in his own state. But this refusal does not justify the subsequent action of the claimant. He should have taken the fugitive before a judge of the United States, two of whom resided within the state.

DRED SCOTT V. SANDFORD
60 U.S. (19 HOW.) 393 (1857)

Dr. John Emerson, an army medical officer, owned Dred Scott, a Missouri slave. Emerson took Scott to military posts in Illinois and in federal territory where slavery had been prohibited by the Missouri Compromise. They returned to Missouri in 1838. Emerson died in 1843 and left his estate to his wife, Irene Emerson. John Emerson named his wife's brother, John Sanford, one of the executors of his will. In 1846 Dred and Harriet Scott filed a petition in Missouri circuit court in St. Louis to gain their freedom because they resided in a free state and in territory that was free under the Missouri Compromise. After two lawsuits (a suit for damages for alleged beatings by Irene Emerson and a suit for freedom), Scott won his freedom temporarily. Irene Emerson appealed to the Missouri Supreme Court, but the court dismissed the suit. After a retrial, the case reached the Missouri Supreme Court again in 1852. By this time, the political climate on the slavery issue had changed in Missouri, and the state supreme court found that Dred Scott was still a slave and ordered the judgment of the lower court reversed. Emerson had remarried and sold Scott to her brother, a New Yorker. Because of the diversity of jurisdiction issues involved in the case, Dred Scott brought a new suit for freedom in the federal courts in 1853. On the merits of the case, the district court ruled that Scott's legal status was correctly determined by the Missouri Supreme Court. Scott then appealed the case to the Supreme Court. Sanford's name was misspelled in the official record. *Vote: 7-2.*

* * *

MR. CHIEF JUSTICE TANEY delivered the opinion of the Court.

. . . The question is simply this: Can a negro, whose ancestors were imported into this country, and sold as slaves, become a member of the political community formed and brought into existence by the Constitution of the United States, and as such become entitled to all the rights, and privileges, and immunities, guarantied by that instrument to the citizen? One of which rights is the privilege of suing in a court of the United States in the cases specified in the Constitution.

. . . The words "people of the United States" and "citizens" are synonymous terms, and mean the same thing. They both describe the political body who, according to our republican institutions, form the sovereignty, and who hold the power and conduct the Government through their representatives. They are what we familiarly call the "sovereign people," and every citizen is one of this people, and a constituent member of this sovereignty. The question before us is, whether the class of persons described in the plea in abatement compose a portion of this people, and are constituent members of this sovereignty? We think they are not, and that they are not included, and were not intended to be included, under the word "citizens" in the Constitution, and can therefore claim none of the rights and privileges which that instrument provides for and secures to citizens of the United States. On the contrary, they were at that time considered as a subordinate and inferior class of beings, who had been subjugated by the dominant race, and, whether emancipated or not, yet remained subject to their authority, and had no rights or privileges but such as those who held the power and the Government might choose to grant them.

. . . The question then arises, whether the provisions of the Constitution, in relation to the personal rights and privileges to which the citizen of a State should be entitled, embraced the negro African race, at that time in this country, or who might afterwards be imported, who had then or should afterwards be made free in any State; and to put it in the power of a single State to make him a citizen of the United States, and endue him with the full rights of citizenship in every other State without their consent? Does the Constitution of the United States act upon him whenever he shall be made free under the laws of a State, and raised there to the rank of a citizen, and immediately clothe him with all the privileges of a citizen in every other State, and in its own courts?

The court think the affirmative of these propositions cannot be maintained. And if it cannot, the plaintiff in error could not be a citizen of the State of Missouri, within the meaning of the Constitution of the United States, and, consequently, was not entitled to sue in its courts.

. . . In the opinion of the court, the legislation and histories of the times, and the language used in the Declaration of Independence, show, that neither the class of persons who had been imported as slaves, nor their descendants, whether they had become free or not, were then acknowledged as part of the people, nor intended to be included in the general words used in that memorable instrument.

It is difficult at this day to realize the state of public opinion in relation to that unfortunate race, which prevailed in the civilized and enlightened portions of the world at the same time of the Declaration of Independence, and when the Constitution of the United States was framed and adopted. But the public history of every European nation displays it in a manner too plain to be mistaken.

They had for more than a century before been regarded as beings of an inferior order, and altogether unfit to associate with the white race, either in social or political relations; and so far inferior, that they had no rights which the white man was bound to respect; and that the negro might justly and lawfully be reduced to slavery for his benefit. He was bought and sold, and treated as an ordinary article of merchandise and traffic, whenever a profit could be made by it. This opinion was at that time fixed and universal in the civilized portion of the white race. It was regarded as an axiom in morals as well as in politics, which no one thought of disputing, or supposed to be open to dispute; and men in every grade and position in society daily and habitually acted upon it in their private pursuits, as well as in matters of public concern, without doubting for a moment the correctness of this opinion.

. . . [Colonial laws] show that a perpetual and impassable barrier was intended to be erected between the white race and the one which they had reduced to slavery, and governed as subjects with absolute and despotic power, and which they then looked upon as so far below them in the scale of created beings, that intermarriages between white persons and negroes or mulattoes were regarded as unnatural and immoral, and punished as crimes, not only in the parties, but in the person who joined them in marriage. And no distinction in this respect was made between the free negro or mulatto and the slave, but this stigma, of the deepest degradation, was fixed upon the whole race.

We refer to these historical facts for the purpose of showing the fixed opinions concerning that race, upon which the statesmen of that day spoke and acted. It is necessary to do this, in order to determine whether the general terms used in the Constitution of the United States, as to the rights of man and the rights of the people, was intended to include them, or to give to them or their posterity the benefit of any of its provisions.

. . . But there are two clauses in the Constitution which point directly and specifically to the negro race as a separate class of persons, and show clearly that they were not regarded as a portion of the people or citizens of the Government then formed.

One of these clauses reserves to each of the thirteen States the right to import slaves until the year 1808, if it thinks proper. And the importation which it thus sanctions was unquestionably of persons of the race of which we are speaking, as the traffic in slaves in the United States had always been confined to them. And by the other provision the States pledge themselves to each other to maintain the right of property of the master, by delivering up to him any slave who may have escaped from his service, and be found within their respective territories. . . .

No one of that race had ever migrated to the United States voluntarily; all of them had been brought here as articles of merchandise. The number that had been emancipated at that time were but few in comparison with those held in slavery; and they were identified in the public mind with the race to which they belonged, and regarded as a part of the slave population rather than the free. It is obvious that they were not even in the minds of the framers of the Constitution when they were conferring special rights and privileges upon the citizens of a State in every other part of the Union.

. . . The legislation of the States therefore shows, in a manner not to be mistaken, the inferior and subject condition of that race at the time the Constitution was adopted, and long afterwards, throughout the thirteen States by which that instrument was framed; and it is hardly consistent with the respect due to these States, to suppose that they regarded at that time, as fellow-citizens and members of the sovereignty, a class of beings whom they had thus stigmatized; whom, as we are bound, out of respect

[Handwritten margin notes:]

[Top margin] not necessarily the best arguments should be constitutionally based

[Left margin] establishing citizenship by residency of a single state — dred scott

[Left margin lower] history

[Center margin, vertical] Constitutional justification

to the State sovereignties, to assume they had deemed it just and necessary thus to stigmatize, and upon whom they had impressed such deep and enduring marks of inferiority and degradation; or, that when they met in convention to form the Constitution, they looked upon them as a portion of their constituents, or designed to include them in the provision so carefully inserted for the security and protection of the liberties and rights of their citizens. It cannot be supposed that they intended to secure to them rights, and privileges, and rank, in the new political body throughout the Union, which every one of them denied within the limits of its own dominion. More especially, it cannot be believed that the large slave-holding States regarded them as included in the word citizens, or would have consented to a Constitution which might compel them to receive them in that character from another State. For if they were so received, and entitled to the privileges and immunities of citizens, it would exempt them from the operation of the special laws and from the police regulations which they considered to be necessary for their own safety. It would give to persons of the negro race, who were recognised as citizens in any one State of the Union, the right to enter every other State whenever they pleased, singly or in companies, without pass or passport, and without obstruction, to sojourn there as long as they pleased, to go where they pleased at every hour of the day or night without molestation, unless they committed some violation of law for which a white man would be punished; and it would give them the full liberty of speech in public and in private upon all subjects upon which its own citizens might speak; to hold public meetings upon political affairs, and to keep and carry arms wherever they went. And all of this would be done in the face of the subject race of the same color, both free and slaves, inevitably producing discontent and insubordination among them, and endangering the peace and safety of the State.

. . . To all this mass of proof we have still to add, that Congress has repeatedly legislated upon the same construction of the Constitution that we have given. Three laws, two of which were passed almost immediately after the Government went into operation, will be abundantly sufficient to show this. The first two are particularly worthy of notice, because many of the men who assisted in framing the Constitution, and took an active part in procuring its adoption, were then in the halls of legislation, and certainly understood what they meant when they used the words "people of the United States" and "citizen" in that well-considered instrument.

The first of these acts is the naturalization law, which was passed at the second session of the first Congress, March 26, 1790, and confines the right of becoming citizens *to aliens being free white persons.*

. . . Another of the early laws of which we have spoken, is the first militia law, which was passed in 1792, at the first session of the second Congress. The language of this law is equally plain and significant with the one just mentioned. It directs that every "free able-bodied white male citizen" shall be enrolled in the militia. The word *white* is evidently used to exclude the African race, and the word "citizen" to exclude unnaturalized foreigners; the latter forming no part of the sovereignty; owing it no allegiance, and therefore under no obligation to defend it. The African race, however, born in the country, did owe allegiance to the Government, whether they were slave or free; but is repudiated, and rejected from the duties and obligations of citizenship in marked language.

The third Act to which we have alluded is even still more decisive; it was passed as late as 1813 . . . and it provides: "That from and after the termination of the war in which the United States are now engaged with Great Britain, it shall not be lawful to employ, on board of any public or private vessels of the United States, *or* persons of color, natives of the United States."

Here the line of distinction is drawn in express words. Persons of color, in the judgment of Congress, were not included in the word citizens, and they are described as another and different class of persons, and authorized to be employed, if born in the United States.

. . . The case of Legrand v. Darnall, (2 Peters, 664 [1829]) has been referred to for the purpose of showing that this court has decided that the descendant of a slave may sue as a citizen in a court of the United States; but the case itself shows that the question did not arise and could not have arisen in the case.

. . . And upon a full and careful consideration of the subject, the court is of opinion, that, upon the facts stated in the plea in abatement, Dred Scott was not a citizen of Missouri within the meaning of the Constitution of the United States, and not entitled as such to sue in its courts; and, consequently, that the Circuit Court had no jurisdiction of the case, and that the judgment on the plea in abatement is erroneous.

. . . In considering this part of the controversy, two questions arise: 1. Was he, together with his family, free in Missouri by reason of the stay in the territory of the United States hereinbefore mentioned? And 2. If they were not, is Scott himself free by reason of his removal to Rock Island, in the State of Illinois, as stated in the above admissions?

We proceed to examine the first question.

The Act of Congress, upon which the plaintiff relies, declares that slavery and involuntary servitude, except as a punishment for crime, shall be forever prohibited in all that part of that territory ceded by France, under the name of Louisiana, which lies north of thirty-six degrees thirty minutes north latitude, and not included within the limits of Missouri. And the difficulty which meets us at the threshold of this part of the inquiry is, whether *could Congress pass this law?.*

Congress was authorized to pass this law under any of the powers granted to it by the Constitution; for if the authority is not given by that instrument, it is the duty of this court to declare it void and inoperative, and incapable of conferring freedom upon one who is held as a slave under the laws of any one of the States.

. . . A brief summary of the history of the times, as well as the careful and measured terms in which the article is framed, will show the correctness of this proposition.

. . . [I]t may be safely assumed that citizens of the United States who migrate to a territory belonging to the people of the United States, cannot be ruled as mere colonists, dependent upon the will of the General Government, and to be governed by any laws it may think proper to impose. The principle upon which our Governments rest, and upon which alone they continue to exist, is the union of States, sovereign and independent within their own limits in their internal and domestic concerns, and bound together as one people by a General Government, possessing certain enumerated and restricted powers, delegated to it by the people of the several States, and exercising supreme authority within the scope of the powers granted to it, throughout the dominion of the United States. A power, therefore, in the General Government to obtain and hold Colonies and dependent Territories, over which they might legislate without restriction, would be inconsistent with its own existence in its present form. Whatever it acquires, it acquires for the benefit of the people of the several States who created it. It is their trustee acting for them, and charged with the duty of promoting the interest of the whole people of the Union in the exercise of the powers specifically granted.

. . . Upon these considerations, it is the opinion of the court that the act of Congress which prohibited a citizen from holding and owning property of this kind in the territory of the United States north of the line therein mentioned, is not warranted by the Constitution, and is therefore void; and that neither Dred Scott himself, nor any of his family, were made free by being carried into this territory; even if they had been carried there by the owner, with the intention of becoming a permanent resident.

Act is void

. . . But there is another point in the case which depends on State power and State law. And it is contended, on the part of the plaintiff, that he is made free by being taken to Rock Island, in the State of Illinois, independently of his residence in the territory of the United States; and being so made free, he was not again reduced to a state of slavery by being brought back to Missouri.

. Our notice of this part of the case will be very brief; for the principle on which it depends was decided in this court, upon much consideration, in the case of Strader et al. v. Graham reported in 10 Howard, 82 [1851]. In that case, the slaves had been taken from Kentucky to Ohio, with the consent of the owner, and afterwards brought back to Kentucky. And this court held that their *status* or condition, as free or slave, depended upon the laws of Kentucky, when they were brought back into that State, and not of Ohio; and that this court had not jurisdiction to revise the judgment of a State court upon its own laws. This was the point directly before the court, and the decision that this court had no jurisdiction, turned upon it, as will be seen by the report of the case.

So in this case. As Scott was a slave when taken into the State of Illinois by his owner, and was there held as such, and brought back in that character, his *status,* as free or slave, depended on the laws of Missouri, and not of Illinois.

. . . Upon the whole, therefore, it is the judgment of this court, that it appears by the record before us that the plaintiff in error is not a citizen of Missouri, in the sense in which that word is used in the Constitution; and that the Circuit Court of the United States, for that reason, had no jurisdiction in the case, and could give no judgment in it. Its judgment for the defendant must, consequently, be reversed, and a mandate issued, directing the suit to be dismissed for want of jurisdiction.

[The concurring opinions of MR. JUSTICE WAYNE, MR. JUSTICE NELSON, MR. JUSTICE GRIER, MR. JUSTICE DANIEL, MR. JUSTICE CAMPBELL, and MR. JUSTICE CATRON are omitted.]

* * *

MR. JUSTICE CURTIS dissenting.

. . . It has been often asserted that the Constitution was made exclusively by and for the white race. It has already been shown that in five of the thirteen original States, colored persons then possessed the elective franchise, and were among those by whom the Constitution was ordained and established. If so, it is not true, in point of fact, that the Constitution was made exclusively for the white race. And that it was made exclusively for the white race, is, in my opinion, not only an assumption not warranted by anything in the Constitution, but contradicted by its opening declaration, that it was ordained and established by the people of the United States, for themselves and their posterity. And as free colored persons were then citizens of at least five States, and so in every sense part of the people of the United States, they were among those for whom and whose posterity the Constitution was ordained and established.

. . . I dissent, therefore, from that part of the opinion of the majority of the court, in which it is held that a person of African descent cannot be a citizen of the United States; and I regret that I must go further, and dissent both from what I deem their assumption of authority to examine the constitutionality of the Act of Congress commonly called the Missouri compromise act, and the grounds and conclusions announced in their opinion.

Having first decided that they were bound to consider the sufficiency of the plea to the jurisdiction of the Circuit Court, and having decided that this plea showed that the Circuit Court had not jurisdiction, and consequently that this is a case to which the judicial power of the United States does not extend, they have gone on to examine the merits of the case as they appeared on the trial before the court and jury, on the issues joined on the pleas in bar, and so have reached the question of the power of Congress to pass the Act of 1820. On so grave a subject as this, I feel obliged to say that, in my opinion, such an exertion of judicial power transcends the limits of the authority of the court, as described by its repeated decisions, and, as I understand, acknowledged in this opinion of the majority of the court.

. . . Is it conceivable that the Constitution has conferred the right on every citizen to become a resident of the Territory of the United States with his slaves, and there to hold them as such, but has neither made nor provided for any municipal regulations which are essential to the existence of slavery?

It is not more rational to conclude that they who framed and adopted the Constitution were aware that persons held to service under the laws of a State are property only to the extent and under the conditions fixed by those laws; that they must cease to be available as property, when their owners voluntarily place them permanently within another jurisdiction, where no municipal laws on the subject of slavery exist; and that, being aware of these principles, and having said nothing to interfere with or displace them, or compel Congress to legislate in any particular manner on the subject, and having empowered Congress to make all needful rules and regulations respecting the Territory of the United States, it was their intention to leave to the discretion of Congress what regulations, if any, should be made concerning slavery therein? Moreover, if the right exists, what are its limits, and what are its conditions? If citizens of the United States have the right to take their slaves to a Territory, and hold them there as slaves, without regard to the laws of the Territory, I suppose this right is not to be restricted to the citizens of slaveholding States. A citizen of a State which does not tolerate slavery can hardly be denied the power of doing the same thing. And what law of slavery does either take with him to the Territory? If it be said to be those laws respecting slavery which existed in the particular State from which each slave last came, what an anomaly is this? Where else can we find, under the law of any civilized country, the power to introduce and permanently continue diverse systems of foreign municipal law, for holding persons in slavery? . . . Whatever theoretical importance may be now supposed to belong to the maintenance of such a right, I feel a perfect conviction that it would, if ever tried, prove to be as impracticable in fact, as it is, in my judgment, monstrous in theory.

[The dissenting opinion of MR. JUSTICE McLEAN is omitted.]

SLAUGHTER-HOUSE CASES
83 U.S. (16 WALL.) 36 (1873)

In an effort to control health risks posed by the slaughtering of animals and to centralize the slaughtering process, the Louisiana legislature enacted a statute in 1869 that prohibited the landing or slaughtering of livestock in the city of New Orleans and surrounding parishes except at the Crescent City Livestock Landing and Slaughter-House Company. The act granted the company a monopoly to slaughter livestock for a 25-year period. The legislation had the effect, however, of depriving 1,000 butchers of work. The Butcher's Benevolent Association of New Orleans brought suit, alleging that the act violated the Thirteenth and Fourteenth Amendments of the Constitution. The Louisiana Supreme Court upheld the state-created monopoly, and three separate cases involving the same circumstances, known as the Slaughter-House Cases, were appealed to the Supreme Court. *Vote: 5-4.*

* * *

MR. JUSTICE MILLER delivered the opinion of the Court.

. . . This statute is denounced not only as creating a monopoly and conferring odious and exclusive privileges upon a small number of persons at the expense of the great body of the community of New Orleans, but it is asserted that it deprives a large and meritorious class of citizens—the whole of the butchers of the city—of the right to exercise their trade, the business to which they have been trained and on which they depend for the support of themselves and their families; and that the unrestricted exercise of the business of butchering is necessary to the daily subsistence of the population of the city.

. . . The wisdom of the monopoly granted by the legislature may be open to question, but it is difficult to see a justification for the assertion that the butchers are deprived of the right to labor in their occupation, or the people of their daily service in preparing food, or how this statute, with the duties and guards imposed upon the company, can be said to destroy the business of the butcher, or seriously interfere with its pursuit.

The power here exercised by the legislature of Louisiana is, in its essential nature, one which has been, up to the present period in the constitutional history of this country, always conceded to belong to the States, however it may *now* be questioned in some of its details.

. . . The proposition is, therefore, reduced to these terms: Can any exclusive privileges be granted to any of its citizens, or to a corporation, by the legislature of a State?

. . . The plaintiffs in error . . . allege that the statute is a violation of the Constitution of the United States in these several particulars:

That it creates an involuntary servitude forbidden by the thirteenth article of amendment;

That it abridges the privileges and immunities of citizens of the United States;

That it denies to the plaintiffs the equal protection of the laws; and,

That it deprives them of their property without due process of law; contrary to the provisions of the first section of the fourteenth article of amendment.

This court is thus called upon for the first time to give construction to these articles.

. . . We repeat, then, in light of this recapitulation of events, almost too recent to be called history, but which are familiar to us all; and on the most casual examination of the language of these amendments, no one can fail to be impressed with the one pervading purpose found in them all, lying at the foundation of each, and without which none of them would have been even more suggested; we mean the freedom of the slave race, the security and firm establishment of that freedom, and the protection of the newly-made freeman and citizen from the oppressions of those who had formerly exercised unlimited dominion over him. It is true that only the fifteenth amendment, in terms, mentions the negro by speaking of his color and his slavery. But it is just as true that each of the other articles was addressed to the grievances of that race, and designed to remedy them as the fifteenth.

We do not say that no one else but the negro can share in this protection. Both the language and spirit of these articles are to have their fair and just weight in any question of construction. Undoubtedly while negro slavery alone was in the mind of the Congress which proposed the thirteenth article, it forbids any other kind of slavery, now or hereafter. . . . But what we do say, and what we wish to be understood is, that in any fair and just construction of any section or phrase of these amendments, it is necessary to look to the purpose which we have said was the

pervading spirit of them all, the evil which they were designed to remedy, and the process of continued addition to the Constitution, until that purpose was supposed to be accomplished, as far as constitutional law can accomplish it.

The first section of the fourteenth article, to which our attention is more specially invited, opens with a definition of citizenship—not only citizenship of the United States, but citizenship of the States. No such definition was previously found in the Constitution, nor had any attempt been made to define it by act of Congress. . . .

. . . The first observation we have to make on this clause is, that it puts at rest both the questions which we stated to have been the subject of differences of opinion. . . . That its main purpose was to establish the citizenship of the negro can admit of no doubt. . . .

The next observation is more important in view of the arguments of counsel in the present case. It is, that the distinction between citizenship of the United States and citizenship of a State is clearly recognized and established. Not only may a man be a citizen of the United States without being a citizen of a State, but an important element is necessary to convert the former into the latter. He must reside within the State to make him a citizen of it, but it is only necessary that he should be born or naturalized in the United States to be a citizen of the Union.

It is quite clear, then, that there is a citizenship of the United States, and a citizenship of a State, which are distinct from each other, and which depend upon different characteristics or circumstances in the individual.

We think this distinction and its explicit recognition in this amendment of great weight in this argument, because the next paragraph of this same section, which is the one mainly relied on by the plaintiffs in error, speaks only of privileges and immunities of citizens of the United States and does not speak of those citizens of the several States. The argument, however, in favor of the plaintiffs rests wholly on the assumption that the citizenship is the same, and the privileges and immunities guaranteed by the clause are the same.

The language is, "No State shall make or enforce any law which shall abridge the privileges or immunities of citizens of *the United States.*" It is a little remarkable, if this clause was intended as a protection to the citizen of a State against the legislative power of his own State, that the word citizen of the State should be left out when it is so carefully used, and used in contradistinction to citizens of the United States, in the very sentence which precedes it. It is too clear for argument that the change in phraseology was adopted understandingly and with a purpose.

Of the privileges and immunities of the citizen of the United States, and of the privileges and immunities of the citizen of the State, and what they respectively are, we will presently consider; but we wish to state here that it is only the former which are placed by this clause under the protection of the Federal Constitution, and that the latter, whatever they may be, are not intended to have any additional protection by this paragraph of the amendment.

If, then, there is a difference between the privileges and immunities belonging to a citizen of the United States as such, and those belonging to the citizen of the State as such, the latter must rest for their security and protection where they have heretofore rested; for they are not embraced by this paragraph of the amendment.

. . . [S]uch a construction followed by the reversal of the judgments of the Supreme Court of Louisiana in these cases, would constitute this court a perpetual censor upon all legislation of the States, on the civil rights of their own citizens, with authority to nullify such as it did not approve as consistent with those rights, as they existed at the time of the adoption of this amendment. The argument we admit is not always the most conclusive which is drawn from the consequences urged against the adoption of a particular construction of an instrument. But when, as in the case before us, these consequences are so serious, so far reaching and pervading, so great a departure from the structure and spirit of our institutions; when the effect is to fetter and degrade the State governments by subjecting them to the control of Congress, in the exercise of powers heretofore universally conceded to them of the most ordinary and fundamental character; when in fact it radically changes the whole theory of the relations of the State and Federal governments to each other and of both these governments to the people; the argument has a force that is irresistible, in the absence of language which expresses such a purpose too clearly to admit of doubt.

We are convinced that no such results were intended by the Congress which proposed these amendments, nor by the legislatures of the States which ratified them.

Having shown that the privileges and immunities relied on in the argument are those which belong to citizens of the States as such, and that they are left to the State governments for security and protection, and not by this article placed under the special care of the Federal government, we may hold ourselves excused from defining the privileges and immunities of citizens of the United States which no State can abridge, until some case involving those privileges may make it necessary to do so.

. . . In the light of the history of these amendments, and the pervading purpose of them, which we have already discussed, it is not difficult to give a meaning to this clause. The existence of laws in the States where the newly emancipated negroes resided, which discriminated with gross injustice and hardship against them as a class, was the evil to be remedied by this clause, and by it such laws are forbidden.

If, however, the States did not conform their laws to its requirements, then by the fifth section of the article of amendment Congress was authorized to enforce it by suitable legislation. We doubt very much whether any action of a State not directed by way of discrimination against the negroes as a class, or on account of their race, will ever be held to come within the purview of this provision. It is so clearly a provision for that race and that emergency, that a strong case would be necessary for its application to any other. But as it is a State that is to be dealt with, and not alone the validity of its laws, we may safely leave that matter until Congress shall have exercised its power, or some case of State oppression, by denial of equal justice in its courts, shall have claimed a decision at our hands. We find no such case in the one before us, and do not deem it necessary to go over the argument again, as it may have relation to this particular clause of the amendment.

. . . The judgments of the Supreme Court of Louisiana in these cases are

Affirmed.

* * *

MR. JUSTICE FIELD dissenting.

. . . The question presented is, therefore, one of the gravest importance, not merely to the parties here, but to the whole country. It is nothing less than the question whether the recent amendments to the Federal Constitution protect the citizens of the United States against the deprivation of their common rights by State legislation. In my judgment the fourteenth amendment does afford such protection, and was so intended by the Congress which framed and the States which adopted it.

. . . The amendment does not attempt to confer any new privileges or immunities upon citizens, or to enumerate or define those already existing. It assumes that there are such privileges and immunities which belong of right to citizens as such, and ordains that they shall not be abridged by State legislation. If this inhibition has no reference to privileges and immunities of this character, but only refers, as held by the majority of the court in their opinion, to such privileges and immunities as were before its adoption specially designated in the Constitution or necessarily implied as belonging to citizens of the United States, it was a vain and idle enactment, which accomplished nothing, and most unnecessarily excited Congress and the people on its passage. With privileges and immunities thus designated or implied no State could ever have interfered by its laws, and no new constitutional provision was required to inhibit such interference. The supremacy of the Constitution and the laws of the

United States always controlled any State legislation of that character. But if the amendment refers to the natural and inalienable rights which belong to all citizens, the inhibition has a profound significance and consequence.

What, then, are the privileges and immunities which are secured against abridgment by State legislation?

. . . The privileges and immunities designated are those *which of right belong to the citizens of all free governments.* Clearly among these must be placed the right to pursue a lawful employment in a lawful manner, without other restraint than such as equally affects all persons. . . .

. . . This equality of right, with exemption from all disparaging and partial enactments, in the lawful pursuits of life, throughout the whole country, is the distinguishing privilege of citizens of the United States. To them, everywhere, all pursuits, all professions, all avocations are open without other restrictions than such as are imposed equally upon all others of the same age, sex, and condition. The State may prescribe such regulations for every pursuit and calling of life as will promote the public health,

secure the good order and advance the general prosperity of society, but when once prescribed, the pursuit or calling must be free to be followed by every citizen who is within the conditions designated, and will conform to the regulations. This is the fundamental idea upon which our institutions rest, and unless adhered to in the legislation of the country our government will be a republic only in name. The fourteenth amendment, in my judgment, makes it essential to the validity of the legislation of every State that this equality of right should be respected. How widely this equality has been departed from, how entirely rejected and trampled upon by the act of Louisiana, I have already shown. And it is to me a matter of profound regret that its validity is recognized by a majority of this court, for by it the right of free labor, one of the most sacred and imprescriptible rights of man, is violated. . . .

. . . I am authorized by the CHIEF JUSTICE [CHASE], MR. JUSTICE SWAYNE, and MR. JUSTICE BRADLEY to state that they concur with me in this dissenting opinion.

[The dissenting opinions of MR. JUSTICE BRADLEY and MR. JUSTICE SWAYNE are omitted.]

UNITED STATES V. REESE
92 U.S. (2 OTTO) 214 (1876)

[handwritten: for constitutional guarantee against discrimination]

In 1873 two inspectors of a municipal election in Lexington, Kentucky, refused to register the vote of William Garner, a black man. Indictments were brought against the inspectors in federal court under the Enforcement Act of 1870. The circuit court discharged the indictments on the ground of their alleged insufficiency. *Vote: 8-1.*

* * *

MR. CHIEF JUSTICE WAITE delivered the opinion of the Court.

. . . Rights and immunities created by or dependent upon the Constitution of the United States can be protected by Congress. The form and the manner of the protection may be such as Congress, in the legitimate exercise of its legislative discretion, shall provide. These may be varied to meet the necessities of the particular right to be protected.

The Fifteenth Amendment does not confer the right of suffrage upon any one. It prevents the States, or the United States, however, from giving preference, in this particular, to one citizen of the United States over another on account of race, color, or previous condition of servitude. Before its adoption, this could be done. It was as much within the power of a State to exclude citizens of the United States

from voting on account of race, &c., as it was on account of age, property, or education. Now it is not. If citizens of one race having certain qualifications are permitted by law to vote, those of another having the same qualifications must be. Previous to this amendment, there was no constitutional guaranty against this discrimination: now there is. It follows that the amendment has invested the citizens of the United States with a new constitutional right which is within the protecting power of Congress. That right is exemption from discrimination in the exercise of the elective franchise on account of race, color, or previous condition of servitude. This, under the express provisions of the second section of the amendment, Congress may enforce by "appropriate legislation."

This leads us to inquire whether the act now under consideration is "appropriate legislation" for that purpose. . . .

The third section does not in express terms limit the offence of an inspector of elections, for which the punishment is provided, to a wrongful discrimination on account of race, &c. This is conceded; but it is urged, that when this section is construed with those which precede it, and to which, as is claimed, it refers, it is so limited. The argument is, that the only wrongful act, on the part of the officer whose duty it is to receive or permit the requisite qualification, which can dispense with actual qualification under the State laws, and substitute the prescribed affidavit therefor, is that mentioned and prohibited in sect. 2,—to wit, discrimination on account of race, &c.; and that, consequently, sect. 3 is confined in its operation to the same wrongful discrimination.

This is a penal statute, and must be construed strictly; not so strictly, indeed, as to defeat the clear intention of Congress, but the words employed must be understood in the sense they were obviously used. . . . If, taking the whole statute together, it is apparent that it was not the intention of Congress thus to limit the operation of the act, we cannot give it that effect.

The statute contemplates a most important change in the election laws. Previous to its adoption, the States, as a general rule, regulated in their own way all the details of all elections. They prescribed the qualifications of voters, and the manner in which those offering to vote at an election should make known their qualifications to the officers in charge. This act interferes with this practice, and prescribes rules not provided by the laws of the States. It substitutes, under certain circumstances, performance wrongfully prevented for performance itself. If the elector makes and presents his affidavit in the form and to the effect prescribed, the inspectors are to treat this as the equivalent of the specified requirement of the State law. This is a radical change in the practice, and the statute which creates it should be explicit in its terms. Nothing should be left to construction, if it can be avoided. The law ought not to be in such a condition that the elector may act upon one idea of its meaning, and the inspector upon another.

The elector, under the provisions of the statute, is only required to state in his affidavit that he has been wrongfully prevented by the officer from qualifying. There are no words of limitation in this part of the section. In a case like this, if an affidavit is in the language of the statute, it ought to be sufficient both for the voter and the inspector. Laws which prohibit the doing of things, and provide a punishment for their violation, should have no double meaning. . . .

But when we go beyond the third section, and read the fourth, we find there no words of limitation, or reference even, that can be construed as manifesting any intention to confine its provisions to the terms of the Fifteenth Amendment. That section has for its object the punishment of all persons, who, by force, bribery, &c., hinder, delay, &c., any person from qualifying or voting. In view of all these facts, we feel compelled to say, that, in our opinion, the language of the third and fourth sections does not confine their operation to unlawful discriminations on account of race, &c. If Congress had the power to provide generally for the punishment of those who unlawfully interfere to prevent the exercise of the elective franchise without regard to such dis-

crimination, the language of these sections would be broad enough for that purpose.

It remains now to consider whether a statute, so general as this in its provisions, can be made available for the punishment of those who may be guilty of unlawful discrimination against citizens of the United States, while exercising the elective franchise, on account of their race, &c.

. . . We are, therefore, directly called upon to decide whether a penal statute enacted by Congress, with its limited powers, which is in general language broad enough to cover wrongful acts without as well as within the constitutional jurisdiction, can be limited by judicial construction so as to make it operate only on that which Congress may rightfully prohibit and punish. For this purpose, we must take these sections of the statute as they are. We are not able to reject a part which is unconstitutional, and retain the remainder, because it is not possible to separate that which is unconstitutional, if there be any such, from that which is not. . . .

. . . To limit this statute in the manner now asked for would be to make a new law, not to enforce an old one. This is no part of our duty.

We must, therefore, decide that Congress has not as yet provided by "appropriate legislation" for the punishment of the offence charged in the indictment; and that the Circuit Court properly sustained the demurrers, and gave judgment for the defendants.

Judgment affirmed.

[The concurring opinion of MR. JUSTICE CLIFFORD is omitted.]

* * *

MR. JUSTICE HUNT dissenting.

. . . 1. That the intention of Congress on this subject is too plain to be discussed. The Fifteenth Amendment had just been adopted, the object of which was to secure to a lately enslaved population protection against violations of their right to vote on account of their color or previous condition. The act is entitled "An Act to enforce the right of citizens of the United States to vote in the several States of the Union, and for other purposes." The first section contains a general announcement that such right is not to be embarrassed by the fact of race, color, or previous condition. The second section requires that equal opportunity shall be given to the races in providing every prerequisite for voting, and that any officer who violates this provision shall be subject to civil damages to the extent of $500, and to fine and imprisonment. To suppose that Congress, in making these provisions, intended to impose no duty upon, and subject to no penalty, the very officers who were to perfect the exercise of the right to vote,—to wit, the inspectors who receive or reject the votes,—would be quite absurd.

2. Garner, a citizen of African descent, had offered to the collector of taxes to pay any capitation-tax existing or claimed to exist against him as a prerequisite to voting at an election to be held in the city of Lexington on the thirtieth day of January, 1873. The collector illegally refused to allow Garner, on account of his race and color, to make the payment. This brought Garner and his case within the terms of the third section of the statute, that "the person so offering and failing as aforesaid"—that is, who had made the offer which had been illegally rejected on account of his race and color—shall be entitled to vote "as if he had, in fact, performed such act." He then made an affidavit setting forth these facts stating, with the particularity required in the statute, that he was wrongfully prevented from paying the tax, and presented the same to the inspector, who wrongfully refused to receive the same, and to permit him to vote, on account of his race and color.

A wrongful refusal to receive a vote which was, in fact, incompetent only by reason of the act "aforesaid,"—that is, on account of his race and color,—brings the inspector within the statutory provisions respecting race and color. By the words "as aforesaid," the provisions respecting race and color of the first and second sections of the statute are incorporated into and made a part of the third and fourth sections.

. . . I hold, therefore, that the third and fourth sections of the statute we are considering do provide for the punishment of inspectors of elections who refuse the votes of qualified electors on account of their race or color. The indictment is sufficient, and the statute sufficiently describes the offence.

. . . The question of the constitutionality of the act of May 31, 1870 arises mainly upon the Fifteenth Amendment to the Constitution of the United States. . . .

I observe, in the first place, that the right here protected is in behalf of a particular class of persons; to wit, citizens of the United States. The limitation is to the persons concerned, and not to the class of cases in which the question shall arise. The right of citizens of the United States to vote, and not the right to vote at an election for United States officers, is the subject of the provision. The person protected must be a citizen of the United States; and, whenever a right to vote exists in such person, the case is within the amendment. This is the literal and grammatical construction of the language; and that such was the intention of Congress will appear from many considerations. . . .

. . . I hold therefore, that the Fifteenth Amendment embraces the case of elections held for state or municipal as well as for federal officers; and that the first section of the act of May 31, 1870, wherein the right to vote is freed from all restriction by reason of race, color, or condition, at all elections by the people,—state, county, town, municipal, or of other subdivision,—is justified by the Constitution.

HALL V. DeCUIR
95 U.S. 485 (1878)

A Louisiana statute required that all persons shall enjoy equal rights and privileges on any conveyance of a public character without discrimination on account of color. John Benson, the owner of a steamboat that traveled between New Orleans and Vicksburg, Mississippi, refused Josephine DeCuir, a prominent, educated black woman, accommodations in the white section of the cabin during her voyage between New Orleans and Hermitage, Louisiana on account of her color. DeCuir sued under the provision of the Louisiana statute to recover damages for her mental and physical suffering. Benson argued that the statute was void because it was an attempt to regulate commerce among the states, in conflict with the interstate commerce clause of the Constitution. The Supreme Court of Louisiana rejected Benson's claim. Benson died while the claim was before the Court, and Eliza Hall, his administratrix, was substituted as plaintiff in error. *Vote: 9-0.*

* * *

MR. CHIEF JUSTICE WAITE delivered the opinion of the Court.

For the purposes of this case, we must treat the act of Louisiana of Feb. 23, 1869, as requiring those engaged in inter-state commerce to give all persons travelling in that State, upon the public conveyances employed in such business, equal rights and privileges in all parts of the conveyance, without distinction or discrimination on account of race or color. Such was the construction given to that act in the courts below, and it is conclusive upon us as the construction of a State law by the State courts. It is with this provision of the statute alone that we have to deal. We have nothing whatever to do with it as a regulation of internal commerce, or as affecting anything else than commerce among the States.

There can be no doubt but that exclusive power has been conferred upon Congress in respect to the regulation of commerce among the several States. The difficulty has never been as to the existence of this power, but as to what is to be deemed an encroachment upon it; for, as has been often said, "legislation may in a great variety of ways affect commerce and persons engaged in it without constituting a regulation of it within the meaning of the Constitution." . . .

. . . But we think it may safely be said that State legislation which seeks to impose a direct burden upon inter-state commerce, or to interfere directly with its freedom, does encroach upon the exclusive power of Congress. The statute now under consideration, in our opinion, occupies that position. It does not act upon the business through the local instruments to be employed after coming within the State, but directly upon the business as it comes into the State from without or goes out from within. While it purports only to control the carrier when engaged within the State, it must necessarily influence his conduct to some extent in the management of his business throughout his entire voyage. His disposition of passengers taken up and put down within the State, or taken up within to be carried without, cannot but affect in a greater or less degree those taken up without and brought within, and sometimes those taken up and put down without. A passenger in the cabin set apart for the use of whites without the State must, when the boat comes within, share the accommodations of that cabin with such colored persons as may come on board afterwards, if the law is enforced.

. . . This power of regulation may be exercised without legislation as well as with it. By refraining from action, Congress, in effect, adopts as its own regulations those which the common law or the civil law, where that prevails, has provided for the government of such business, and those which the States, in the regulation of their domestic concerns, have established affecting commerce, but not regulating it within the meaning of the Constitution. In fact, congressional legislation is only necessary to cure defects in existing laws, as they are discovered, and to adapt such laws to new developments of trade. . . . Applying that principle to the circumstances of this case, congressional inaction left Benson at liberty to adopt such reasonable rules and regulations for the disposition of passengers upon his boat, while pursuing her voyage within Louisiana or without, as seemed to him most for the interest of all concerned. The statute under which this suit is brought, as construed by the State court, seeks to take away from him that power so long as he is within Louisiana; and while recognizing to the fullest extent the principle which sustains a statute, unless its unconstitutionality is clearly established, we think this statute, to the extent it requires those engaged in the transportation of passengers among the States to carry colored passengers in Louisiana in the same cabin with whites, is unconstitutional and void. If the public good requires such legislation, it must come from Congress and not the States.

We confine our decision to the statute in its effect upon foreign and inter-state commerce, expressing no opinion as to its validity in any other respect.

Judgment will be reversed and the cause remanded, with instructions to reverse the judgment of the District Court, and direct such further proceedings in conformity with this opinion as may appear to be necessary; and it is

So ordered.

* * *

MR. JUSTICE CLIFFORD concurring.

. . . Cases of like import are quite numerous, and the Supreme Court of Pennsylvania decided directly that a public carrier may separate passengers in his conveyance; and they deduce his power to do so from his right of private property in the means of conveyance, and the necessity which arises for such a regulation to promote the public interest. Speaking to that point, they say that the private means the carrier uses belong wholly to himself; and they held the right of control in that regard as necessary to enable the carrier to protect his own interests, and to perform his duty to the travelling public. His authority in that regard, as that court holds, arises from his ownership of the property, and his public duty to promote the comfort and enjoyment of those travelling in his conveyance. Guided by those views, the court held that it is not an unreasonable regulation to seat passengers so as to preserve order and decorum, and to prevent contacts and collisions arising from natural or well-known customary repugnancies which are likely to breed disturbances, where white and colored persons are huddled together without their consent. . . .

. . . Questions of a kindred character have arisen in several of the States, which support these views in a course of reasoning entirely satisfactory and conclusive. Boards of education were created by a law of the State of Ohio, and they were authorized to establish within their respective jurisdictions one or more separate schools for colored children when the whole number by enumeration exceeds twenty, and when such schools will afford them, as far as practicable, the advantages and privileges of a common-school education. Under that law, colored children were not admitted as a matter of right into the schools for white children, which gave rise to contest, in which the attempt was made to set aside the law as unconstitutional: but the Supreme Court of the State held that it worked no substantial inequality of school privileges between the children of the two classes in the locality of the parties; that equality of rights does not involve the necessity of educating white and colored persons in the same school any more than it does that of educating children of both sexes in the same school; and that any classification which preserves substantially equal school advantages is not prohibited by either the State or Federal Constitution, nor would it contravene the provisions of either.

STRAUDER V. WEST VIRGINIA
100 U.S. 303 (1880)

A West Virginia statute provided that all 21-year-old white male citizens of the state were eligible to serve as jurors. Taylor Strauder, a black male, was convicted of murder before an all-white jury. Strauder alleged that the law that made blacks ineligible to serve on petit juries was unconstitutional under the Fourteenth Amendment. He sought to have his murder trial removed to a federal court. *Vote: 7-2.*

* * *

MR. JUSTICE STRONG delivered the opinion of the Court.

. . . [The controlling question is] whether, by the Constitution and laws of the United States, every citizen of the United States has a right to a trial of an indictment against him by a jury selected and impanelled without discrimination against his race or color, because of race or color. . . .

It is to be observed that the [question] is not whether a colored man, when an indictment has been preferred against him, has a right to a grand or a petit jury composed in whole or in part of persons of his own race or color, but it is whether, in the composition or selection of jurors by whom he is to be indicted or tried, all persons of his race or color may be excluded by law, solely because of their race or color, so that by no possibility can any colored man sit upon the jury.

The [question is] important, for [it demands] a construction of the recent amendments of the Constitution. If the defendant has a right to have a jury selected for the trial of his case without discrimination against all persons of his race or color, because of their race or color, the right, if not created, is protected by those amendments, and the legislation of Congress under them. . . .

. . . [The Fourteenth Amendment] was designed to assure to the colored race the enjoyment of all the civil rights that under the law are enjoyed by white persons, and to give to that race the protection of the general government, in that enjoyment, whenever it should be denied by the States. . . .

. . . If this is the spirit and meaning of the amendment, whether it means more or not, it is to be construed liberally, to carry out the purposes of its framers. . . . What is this but declaring that the law in the States shall be the same for the black as for the white; that all persons, whether colored or white, shall stand equal before the laws of the States, and, in regard to the colored race, for whose protection the amendment was primarily designed, that no discrimination shall be made against them by law because of their color? The words of the amendment, it is true, are prohibitory, but they contain a necessary implication of a positive immunity, or right, most valuable to the colored race,—the right to exemption from unfriendly legislation against them distinctively as colored,—exemption from legal discriminations, implying inferiority in civil society, lessening the security of their enjoyment of the rights which others enjoy, and discriminations which are steps toward reducing them to the condition of a subject race.

That the West Virginia statute respecting juries—the statute that controlled the selection of the grand and petit jury in the case of [Strauder]—is such a discrimination ought not to be doubted. Nor would it be if the persons excluded were white men. . . . The very fact that colored people are singled out and expressly denied by a statute all right to participate in the administration of the law, as jurors, because of their color, though they are citizens, and may be in other respects fully qualified, is practically a brand upon them, affixed by the law, an assertion of their inferiority, and a stimulant to that race prejudice which is an impediment to securing to individuals of the race that equal justice which the law aims to secure to all others.

The right to a trial by jury is guaranteed to every citizen of West Virginia by the Constitution of that State, and the constitution of juries is a very essential part of the protection such a mode of trial is intended to secure. The very idea of a jury is a body of men composed of the peers or equals of the person whose rights it is selected or summoned to determine; that is, of his neighbors, fellows, associates, persons having the same legal status in society as that which he holds. . . . It is well known that prejudices often exist against particular classes in the community, which sway the judgment of jurors, and which, therefore, operate in some cases to deny to persons of those classes the full enjoyment of that protection which others enjoy. Prejudice in a local community is held to be a reason for a change of venue. The framers of the constitutional amendment must have known full well that the existence of such prejudice and its likelihood to continue against the manumitted slaves and their race, and that knowledge was doubtless a motive that led to the amendment. By their manumission and citizenship the colored race became entitled to the equal protection of the laws of the States in which they resided; and the apprehension that through prejudice they might be denied that equal protection, that is, that there might be discrimination against them, was the inducement to bestow upon the national government the power to enforce the provision that no State shall deny to them the equal protection of the laws. Without the apprehended existence of prejudice that portion of the amendment would have been unnecessary, and it might have been left to the States to extend equality of protection.

In view of these considerations, it is hard to see why the statute of West Virginia should not be regarded as discriminating against a colored man when he is put upon trial for an alleged criminal offence against the State. It is not easy to comprehend how it can be said that while every white man is entitled to a trial by a jury selected from persons of his own race or color, or, rather, selected without discrimination against his color, and a negro is not, the latter is equally protected by the law with the former. . . .

We do not say that within the limits from which it is not excluded by the amendment a State may not prescribe the qualifications of its jurors, and in so doing make discriminations. It may confine the selection to males, freeholders, to citizens, to persons within certain ages, or to persons having educational qualifications. We do not believe the Four-

teenth Amendment was ever intended to prohibit this. . . .

. . . Concluding, therefore, that the statute of West Virginia, discriminating in the selection of jurors, as it does, against negroes because of their color, amounts to a denial of the equal protection of the laws to a colored man when he is put upon trial for an alleged offence against the State. . . .

. . . The judgment of the Supreme Court of West Virginia will be reversed, and the case remitted with instructions to reverse the judgment of the Circuit Court of Ohio county; and it is

So ordered.

* * *

MR. JUSTICE FIELD dissenting.

I dissent from the judgment of the court in this case, on the grounds stated in my opinion in *Ex parte Virginia* [100 U.S. (10 Otto) 339 (1880)] and MR. JUSTICE CLIFFORD concurs with me.

PACE V. ALABAMA
106 U.S. 583 (1883)

Two sections of an Alabama law provided a harsher punishment for fornication and adultery between blacks and whites than for the same offense between persons of the same race. In 1881 Tony Pace, a black man, and Mary Cox, a white woman, were convicted under the law and sentenced to two years imprisonment in the state penitentiary. The Supreme Court of Alabama affirmed the convictions, and on appeal to the U.S. Supreme Court, Pace argued that the Alabama law denied him equal protection of the laws, in violation of the Fourteenth Amendment. *Vote: 9-0.*

* * *

MR. JUSTICE FIELD delivered the opinion of the Court.

The counsel of the plaintiff in error compares sects. 4184 and 4189 of the Code of Alabama, and assuming that the latter relates to the same offence as the former, and prescribes a greater punishment for it, because one of the parties is a negro, or of negro descent, claims that a discrimination is made against the colored person in the punishment designated, which conflicts with the clause of the Fourteenth Amendment prohibiting a State from denying to any person within its jurisdiction the equal protection of the laws.

The counsel is undoubtedly correct in his view of the purpose of the clause of the amendment in

question, that it was to prevent hostile and discriminating State legislation against any person or class of persons. Equality of protection under the laws implies not only accessibility by each one, whatever his race, on the same terms with others to the courts of the country for the security of his persons and property, but that in the administration of criminal justice he shall not be subjected, for the same offence, to any greater or different punishment. Such was the view of Congress in the enactment of the Civil Rights Act of May 31, 1870, c. 114, after the adoption of the amendment. That act, after providing that all persons within the jurisdiction of the United States shall have the same right, in every State and Territory, to make and enforce contracts, to sue, be parties, give evidence, and to the full and equal benefit of all laws and proceedings for the security of person and property as is enjoyed by white citizens, declares, in sect. 16, that they "shall be subject to like punishment, pains, penalties, taxes, licenses, and exactions of every kind and none other, any law, statute, ordinance, regulation, or custom to the contrary notwithstanding."

The defect in the argument of counsel consists in his assumption that any discrimination is made by the laws of Alabama in the punishment provided for the offence for which the plaintiff in error was indicted when committed by a person of the African race and when committed by a white person. The two sections of the code cited are entirely consistent. The one prescribes, generally, a punishment for an offence committed between persons of different sexes; the other prescribes a punishment for an offence which can only be committed where the two sexes are of different races. There is in neither section any discrimination against either race. Sect. 4184 equally includes the offence when the persons of the two sexes are both white and when they are both black. Sect. 4189 applies the same punishment to both offenders, the white and the black. Indeed, the offence against which this latter section is aimed cannot be committed without involving the persons of both races in the same punishment. Whatever discrimination is made in the punishment prescribed in the two sections is directed against the offence designated and not against the person of any particular color or race. The punishment of each offending person, whether white or black, is the same.

Judgment affirmed.

UNITED STATES V. HARRIS
106 U.S. 629 (1883)

In 1876 R. G. Harris and 19 members of a Tennessee lynch mob took four black prisoners from their cell while they were in the custody of the deputy sheriff and unlawfully beat, bruised, and wounded them. One of the prisoners, P. M. Wells, died from the beating. A federal grand jury returned an indictment against the defendants, charging them with unlawfully conspiring to violate the prisoners' due process and equal protection rights under § 5519 of the Ku Klux Klan Act of 1871. This section prohibited conspiracies for the purpose of depriving any person or class of persons of the equal protection of the laws or for hindering state officials from securing persons the equal protection of the laws. The defendants challenged the indictments on the ground that § 5519 was unconstitutional. The circuit court judges were divided on the question of the constitutionality of § 5519 and requested that this issue be certified to the Supreme Court. *Vote: 8-1.*

* * *

MR. JUSTICE WOODS delivered the opinion of the Court.

. . . The demurrer filed to the indictment in this case questions the power of Congress to pass the law under which the indictment was found. It is, therefore, necessary to search the Constitution to ascertain whether or not the power is conferred.

. . . Section 5519, according to the theory of the prosecution . . . was framed to protect from invasion by private persons, the equal privileges and immunities under the laws, of all persons and classes of persons. It requires no argument to show that such a law cannot be founded on a clause of the Constitution whose sole object is to protect from denial or abridgment, by the United States or States, on account of race, color, or previous condition of servitude, the right of citizens of the United States to vote.

It is, however, strenuously insisted that the legislation under consideration finds its warrant in the first and fifth sections of the Fourteenth Amendment. . . .

It is perfectly clear from the language of the first section that its purpose also was to place a restraint upon the action of the States. In *Slaughter-House Cases,* 16 Wall. 36 [1873], it was held by the majority of the court, speaking by Mr. Justice Miller, that the object of the second clause of the first section of the Fourteenth Amendment was to protect from the hostile legislation of the States the privileges and immunities of citizens of the United States; and this was conceded by Mr. Justice Field, who expressed the views of the dissenting justices in that case. . . .

The purpose and effect of the two sections of the Fourteenth Amendment above quoted were clearly defined by Mr. Justice Bradley in the case of *United States v. Cruikshank,* 1 Woods, 308 [1876]. . . .

. . . So in *Virginia v. Rives* [100 U.S. (13 Otto) 313 (1880)], it was declared by this court, speaking by Mr. Justice Strong, that "these provisions of the Fourteenth Amendment have reference to State action exclusively, and not to any action of private individuals."

These authorities show conclusively that the legislation under consideration finds no warrant for its enactment in the Fourteenth Amendment.

The language of the amendment does not leave this subject in doubt. When the State has been guilty of no violation of its provisions; when it has not made or enforced any law abridging the privileges or immunities of citizens of the United States; when no one of its departments has deprived any person of life, liberty, or property without due process of law, or denied to any person within its jurisdiction the equal protection of the laws; when, on the contrary, the laws of the State, as enacted by its legislative, and construed by its judicial, and administered by its executive departments, recognize and protect the rights of all persons, the amendment imposes no duty and confers no power upon Congress.

Section 5519 of the Revised Statutes is not limited to take effect only in case the State shall abridge the privileges or immunities of citizens of the United States, or deprive any person of life, liberty, or property without due process of law, or deny to any person the equal protection of the laws. It applies, no matter how well the State may have performed its duty. Under it private persons are liable to punishment for conspiring to deprive any one of the equal protection of the laws enacted by the State.

In the indictment in this case, for instance, which would be a good indictment under the law if the law itself were valid, there is no intimation that the State of Tennessee has passed any law or done any act forbidden by the Fourteenth Amendment. On the contrary, the *gravamen* of the charge against the accused is that they conspired to deprive certain citizens of the United States and of the State of Tennessee of the equal protection accorded them by the laws of Tennessee.

As, therefore, the section of the law under consideration is directed exclusively against the action of private persons, without reference to the laws of the State or their administration by her officers, we are clear in the opinion that it is not warranted by any clause in the Fourteenth Amendment to the Constitution.

. . . But the question with which we have to deal is, does the Thirteenth Amendment warrant the enactment of sect. 5519 of the Revised Statutes. We are of the opinion that it does not. Our conclusion is based on the fact that the provisions of that section are broader than the Thirteenth Amendment would justify. Under that section it would be an offence for two or more white persons to conspire, &c., for the purpose of depriving another white person of the equal protection of the laws. It would be an offence for two or more colored persons, enfranchised slaves, to conspire with the same purpose against a white citizen or against another colored citizen who had never been a slave. Even if the amendment is held to be directed against the action of private individuals, as well as against the action of the States and United States, the law under consideration covers cases both within and without the provisions of the amendment. It covers any conspiracy between two free white men against another free white man to deprive him of any right accorded him by the laws of the State or of the United States. A law under which two or more free white private citizens could be punished for conspiring or going in disguise for the purpose of depriving another free white citizen of a right accorded by the law of the State to all classes of persons—as, for instance, the right to make a contract, bring a suit, or give evidence—clearly cannot be authorized by the amendment which simply prohibits slavery and involuntary servitude.

Those provisions of the law, which are broader than is warranted by the article of the Constitution by which they are supposed to be authorized, cannot be sustained.

Upon this question, *United States v. Reese,* 92 U.S. 214 [1876] is in point. . . .

. . . There is another view which strengthens this conclusion. If Congress has constitutional authority under the Thirteenth Amendment to punish a conspiracy between two persons to do an unlawful act, it can punish the act itself, whether done by one or more persons.

A private person cannot make constitutions or laws, nor can he with authority construe them, nor can he administer or execute them. The only way, therefore, in which one private person can deprive another of the equal protection of the laws is by the commission of some offence against the laws which protect the rights of persons, as by theft, burglary, arson, libel, assault, or murder. If, therefore, we hold that sect. 5519 is warranted by the Thirteenth Amendment, we should, by virtue of that amendment, accord to Congress the power to punish every crime by which the right of any person to life, property, or reputation is invaded. Thus, under a provision of the Constitution which simply abolished slavery and involuntary servitude, we should, with few exceptions, invest Congress with power over the whole catalogue of crimes. A construction of the amendment which leads to such a result is clearly unsound.

There is only one other clause in the Constitution of the United States which can, in any degree, be supposed to sustain the section under consideration; namely, the second section of article 4, which declares that "the citizens of each State shall be entitled to all the privileges and immunities of citizens of the several States." But this section, like the Fourteenth Amendment, is directed against State action. Its object is to place the citizens of each State upon the same footing with citizens of other States, and inhibit discriminative legislation against them by other States. . . .

. . . It was never supposed that the section under consideration conferred on Congress the power to enact a law which would punish a private citizen for an invasion of the rights of his fellow citizen, conferred by the State of which they were both residents; on all its citizens alike.

We have, therefore, been unable to find any constitutional authority for the enactment of sect. 5519 of the Revised Statutes. The decisions of this court above referred to leave no constitutional ground for the act to stand on.

The point in reference to which the judges of the Circuit Court were divided in opinion must, therefore, be decided against the *constitutionality of the law.*

* * *

MR. JUSTICE HARLAN dissented on the question of jurisdiction. He expressed no opinion on the merits.

CIVIL RIGHTS CASES
109 U.S. 3 (1883)

Five cases, consolidated under the name of the Civil Rights Cases, addressed the issue of the constitutionality of the Civil Rights Act of 1875 (*United States v. Stanley, United States v. Ryan, United States v. Nichols, United States v. Singleton,* and *Robinson & Wife v. Memphis and Charleston Railroad Company*). This Act prohibited private persons from violating the rights of other persons to the full and equal enjoyment of public accommodations on the basis of race or color, regardless of previous condition of servitude. In each of these cases, persons of color were denied access to public facilities covered under the Act (inns, theaters, and a railway car). For the first time, the Supreme Court addressed the Fourteenth Amendment's state action requirement. *Vote: 8-1.*

* * *

MR. JUSTICE BRADLEY delivered the opinion of the Court.

It is obvious that the primary and important question in all the cases is the constitutionality of the law: for if the law is unconstitutional none of the prosecutions can stand.

. . . The essence of the [Civil Rights Act of 1875] is, not to declare broadly that all persons shall be entitled to the full and equal enjoyment of the accommodations, advantages, facilities, and privileges of inns, public conveyances, and theatres; but that such enjoyment shall not be subject to any conditions applicable only to citizens of a particular race or color, or who had been in a previous condition of servitude. In other words, it is the purpose of the law to declare that, in the enjoyment of the accommodations and privileges of inns, public conveyances, theatres, and other places of public amusement, no distinction shall be made between citizens of different race or color, or between those who have, and those who have not, been slaves. Its effect is to declare, that in all inns, public conveyances, and places of amusement, colored citizens, whether formerly slaves or not, and citizens of other races, shall have the same accommodations and privileges in all inns, public conveyances, and places of amusement as are enjoyed by white citizens, and *vice versa.* The second section makes it a penal offence in any person to deny to any citizen of any race or color, regardless of previous condition of servitude, any of the accommodations or privileges mentioned in the first section.

Has Congress constitutional power to make such a law? Of course, no one will contend that the power to pass it was contained in the Constitution before the adoption of the last three amendments. . . .

The first section of the Fourteenth Amendment (which is the one relied on), after declaring who shall be citizens of the United States, and of the several States, is prohibitory in its character, and prohibitory upon the States. . . .

It is State action of a particular character that is prohibited. Individual invasion of individual rights is not the subject-matter of the amendment. It has a deeper and broader scope. It nullifies and makes void all State legislation, and State action of every kind, which impairs the privileges and immunities of citizens of the United States, or which injures them in life, liberty or property without due process of law, or which denies to any of them the equal protection of the laws. It not only does this, but, in order that the national will, thus declared, may not be a mere *brutum fulmen,* the last section of the amendment invests Congress with power to enforce it by appropriate legislation. To enforce what? To enforce the prohibition. To adopt appropriate legislation for correcting the effects of such prohibited State laws and State acts, and thus to render them effectually null, void, and innocuous. This is the legislative power conferred upon Congress, and this is the whole of it. It does not invest Congress with the power to legislate upon subjects which are within the domain of State legislation; but to provide modes of relief against State legislation, or State action, of the kind referred to. It does not authorize Congress to create a code of municipal law for the regulation of private rights; but to provide modes of redress against the operation of State laws, and the action of State officers executive or judicial, when these are subversive of the fundamental rights specified in the amendment. . . .

. . . An inspection of the law shows that it makes no reference whatever to any supposed or apprehended violation of the Fourteenth Amendment on the part of the States. It is not predicated on any such view. It proceeds *ex directo* to declare that certain acts committed by individuals shall be deemed offences, and shall be prosecuted and punished by proceedings in the courts of the United States. It does not profess to be corrective of any constitutional wrong committed by the States; it does not make its operation to depend upon any such wrong committed. It applies equally to cases arising in States which have the justest laws respecting the personal rights of citizens, and whose authorities are ever ready to enforce such laws, as to those which arise in States that may have violated the prohibition of the amendment. In other words, it steps into the domain of local jurisprudence, and lays down rules for the conduct of individuals in society towards each other, and imposes sanctions for the enforcement of those rules, without referring in any manner to any supposed action of the State or its authorities.

If this legislation is appropriate for enforcing the prohibitions of the amendment, it is difficult to see where it is to stop. Why may not Congress with equal show of authority enact a code of laws for the enforcement and vindication of all rights of life, liberty, and property? If it is supposable that the States may deprive persons of life, liberty, and property without due process of law (and the amendment itself does suppose this), why should not Congress proceed at once to prescribe due process of law for the protection of every one of these fundamental rights, in every possible case, as well as to prescribe equal privileges in inns, public conveyances, and theatres? The truth is, that the implication of a power to legislate in this manner is based upon the assumption that if the States are forbidden to legislate or act in a particular way on a particular subject, and power is conferred upon Congress to enforce the prohibition, this gives Congress power to legislate generally upon that subject, and not merely power to provide modes of redress against such State legislation or action. The assumption is certainly unsound. It is repugnant to the Tenth Amendment of the Constitution, which declares that powers not delegated to the United States by the Constitution, nor prohibited by it to the States, are reserved to the States respectively or to the people.

. . . In this connection it is proper to state that civil rights, such as are guaranteed by the Constitution against State aggression, cannot be impaired by the wrongful acts of individuals, unsupported by State authority in the shape of laws, customs, or judicial or executive proceedings. The wrongful act of an individual, unsupported by any such authority, is simply a private wrong, or a crime of that individual; an invasion of the rights of the injured party, it is true, whether they affect his person, his property, or his reputation; but if not sanctioned in some way by the State, or not done under State authority, his rights remain in full force, and may presumably be vindicated by resort to the laws of the State for redress. . . .

. . . [I]t is clear that the law in question cannot be sustained by any grant of legislative power made to Congress by the Fourteenth Amendment. That amendment prohibits the States from denying to any person the equal protection of the laws, and declares that Congress shall have power to enforce, by appropriate legislation, the provisions of the amendment. The law in question, without any reference to adverse State legislation on the subject, declares that all persons shall be entitled to equal accommodations and privileges of inns, public conveyances, and places of public amusement, and imposes a penalty upon any individual who shall deny to any citizen such equal accommodations and privileges. This is not corrective legislation; it is primary and direct; it takes immediate and absolute possession of the subject of the right of admission to inns, public conveyances, and places of amusement. It supersedes and displaces State legislation on the same subject, or only allows it permissive force. It ignores such legislation, and assumes that the matter is one that belongs to the domain of national regulation. Whether it would not have been a more effective protection of the rights of citizens to have clothed Congress with plenary power over the whole subject, is not now the question. What we have to decide is, whether such plenary power has been conferred upon Congress by the Fourteenth Amendment; and, in our judgment, it has not.

. . . The only question under the present head, therefore, is, whether the refusal to any persons of the accommodations of an inn, or a public conveyance, or a place of public amusement, by an individual, and without any sanction or support from any State law or regulation, does inflict upon such persons any manner of servitude, or form of slavery, as those terms are understood in this country? Many wrongs may be obnoxious to the prohibitions of the Fourteenth Amendment which are not, in any just sense, incidents or elements of slavery. Such, for example, would be the taking of private property without due process of law. . . . What is called class legislation would belong to this category, and would be obnoxious to the prohibitions of the Fourteenth Amendment, but would not necessarily be so to the Thirteenth Amendment, when not involving the idea of any subjection of one man to another. . . .

. . . [W]e are forced to the conclusion that such an act of refusal has nothing to do with slavery or involuntary servitude, and that if it is violative of any right of the party, his redress is to be sought under the laws of the State; or if those laws are adverse to his rights and do not protect him, his remedy will be found in the corrective legislation which Congress has adopted, or may adopt, for counteracting the effect of State laws, or State action, prohibited by the Fourteenth Amendment. It would be running the slavery argument into the ground to make it apply to every act of discrimination which a person may see fit to make as to the guests he will entertain, or as to the people he will take into his coach or cab or car, or admit to his concert or theatre, or deal with in other matters of intercourse or business. . . .

When a man has emerged from slavery, and by the aid of beneficent legislation has shaken off the inseparable concomitants of that state, there must be some stage in the progress of his elevation when he takes the rank of a mere citizen, and ceases to be the special favorite of the laws, and when his rights as a citizen, or a man, are to be protected in the ordinary modes by which other men's rights are protected. . . . Mere discriminations on account of race or color were not regarded as badges of slavery. If, since that time, the enjoyment of equal rights in all these respects has become established by constitutional enactment, it is not by force of the Thirteenth Amendment (which merely abolishes slavery), but by force of the Thirteenth and Fifteenth Amendments.

On the whole we are of opinion, that no countenance of authority for the passage of the law in question can be found in either the Thirteenth or Fourteenth Amendment of the Constitution; and no other ground of authority for its passage being suggested, it must necessarily be declared void, at least so far as its operation in the several States is concerned.

And it is so ordered.

* * *

MR. JUSTICE HARLAN dissenting.

The opinion in these cases proceeds, it seems to me, upon grounds entirely too narrow and artificial. I cannot resist the conclusion that the substance and spirit of the recent amendments of the Constitution have been sacrificed by a subtle and ingenious verbal criticism. . . .

. . . I am of the opinion that such discrimination practised by corporations and individuals in the exercise of their public or quasi-public functions is a badge of servitude the imposition of which Congress may prevent under its power, by appropriate legislation, to enforce the Thirteenth Amendment; and, consequently, without reference to its enlarged power under the Fourteenth Amendment, the act of March 1, 1875, is not, in my judgment, repugnant to the Constitution.

. . . I agree that government has nothing to do with social, as distinguished from technically legal, rights of individuals. No government ever has brought, or ever can bring, its people into social intercourse against their wishes. Whether one person will permit or maintain social relations with another is a matter with which government has no concern. . . . What I affirm is that no State, nor the officers of any State, nor any corporation or individual wielding power under State authority for the public benefit or the public convenience, can, consistently either with the freedom established by the fundamental law, or with that equality of civil rights which now belongs to every citizen, discriminate against freemen or citizens, in those rights, because of their race, or because they once labored under the disabilities of slavery imposed upon them as a race. The rights which Congress, by the act of 1875, endeavored to secure and protect are legal, not social rights. . . .

. . . My brethren say, that when a man has emerged from slavery, and by the aid of beneficent legislation has shaken off the inseparable concomitants of that state, there must be some stage in the progress of his elevation when he takes the rank of a mere citizen, and ceases to be the special favorite of the laws, and when his rights as a citizen, or a man, are to be protected in the ordinary modes by which other men's rights are protected. It is, I submit, scarcely just to say that the colored race has been the special favorite of the laws. The statute of 1875, now adjudged to be unconstitutional, is for the benefit of citizens of every race and color. What the nation, through Congress, has sought to accomplish in reference to that race, is—what had already been done in every State of the Union for the white race—to secure and protect rights belonging to them as freemen and citizens; nothing more. It was not deemed enough "to help the feeble up, but to support him after." The one underlying purpose of congressional legislation has been to enable the black race to take the rank of mere citizens. The difficulty has been to compel a recognition of the legal right of the black race to take the rank of citizens, and to secure the enjoyment of privileges belonging, under the law, to them as a component part of the people for whose welfare and happiness government is ordained. . . . To-day, it is the colored race which is denied, by corporations and individuals wielding public authority, rights fundamental in their freedom and citizenship.

YICK WO V. HOPKINS
118 U.S. 356 (1886)

A San Francisco ordinance prohibited the operation of a laundry business within the corporate limits of the city and county in any building not made of brick or stone without having first obtained the consent of the board of supervisors. The ordinance was aimed at Chinese laundries because they operated in wooden buildings. Local officials used their discretion to deny licenses to approximately 200 applicants of Chinese ancestry but allowed 80 others (79 non-Chinese and 1 Chinese) to carry on the same business under similar conditions. Yick Wo violated the ordinance in or-

der to test its validity. He was found guilty, fined, and subsequently jailed for violating the ordinance. He alleged that he was deprived of his personal liberty by the defendant sheriff, Hopkins. The California Supreme Court affirmed the convictions. *Vote: 9-0.*

* * *

MR. JUSTICE MATTHEWS delivered the opinion of the Court.

... The rights of the petitioners, as affected by the proceedings of which they complain, are not less, because they are aliens and subjects of the Emperor of China. By the third article of the treaty between this Government and that of China, concluded November 17, 1880, 22 Stat. 827, it is stipulated: "If Chinese laborers, or Chinese of any other class, now either permanently or temporarily residing in the territory of the United States, meet with ill treatment at the hands of any other persons, the Government of the United States will exert all its powers to devise measures for their protection, and to secure to them the same rights, privileges, immunities and exemptions as may be enjoyed by the citizens or subjects of the most favored nation, and to which they are entitled by treaty."

The Fourteenth Amendment to the Constitution is not confined to the protection of citizens. It says: "Nor shall any State deprive any person of life, liberty, or property without due process of law; nor deny to any person within its jurisdiction the equal protection of the laws." These provisions are universal in their application, to all persons within the territorial jurisdiction, without regard to any differences of race, of color, or of nationality; and the equal protection of the laws is a pledge of the protection of equal laws. ... The questions we have to consider and decide in these cases, therefore, are to be treated as involving the rights of every citizen of the United States equally with those of the strangers and aliens who now invoke the jurisdiction of the court.

It is contended on the part of the petitioners, that the ordinances for violations of which they are severally sentenced to imprisonment, are void on their face, as being within the prohibitions of the Fourteenth Amendment; and, in the alternative if not so, that they are void by reason of their administration operating unequally, so as to punish in the present petitioners what is permitted to others as lawful, without any distinction of circumstances—an unjust and illegal discrimination, it is claimed, which, though not made expressly by the ordinances is made possible by them.

When we consider the nature and the theory of our institutions of government, the principles upon which they are supposed to rest, and review the history of their development, we are constrained to conclude that they do not mean to leave room for the play and action of purely personal and arbitrary power. ... But the fundamental rights to life, liberty, and the pursuit of happiness, considered as individual possessions, are secured by those maxims of constitutional law which are the monuments showing the victorious progress of the race in securing to men the blessings of civilization under the reign of just and equal laws. ... For, the very idea that one man may be compelled to hold his life, or the means of living, or any material right essential to the enjoyment of life, at the mere will of another, seems to be intolerable in any country where freedom prevails, as being the essence of slavery itself.

... For the cases present the ordinances in actual operation, and the facts shown establish an administration directed so exclusively against a particular class of persons as to warrant and require the conclusion, that, whatever may have been the intent of the ordinances as adopted, they are applied by the public authorities charged with their administration, and thus representing the State itself, with a mind so unequal and oppressive as to amount to a practical denial by the State of that equal protection of the laws which is secured to the petitioners, as to all other persons, by the broad and benign provisions of the Fourteenth Amendment to the Constitution of the United States. Though the law itself be fair on its face, and impartial in appearance, yet, if it is applied and administered by public authority with an evil eye and an unequal hand, so as practically to make unjust and illegal discriminations between persons in similar circumstances, material to their rights, the denial of equal justice is still within the prohibition of the Constitution. This principle of interpretation has been sanctioned by the court in *Henderson v. Mayor of New York*, 92 U.S. 259 [1876]; *Chy Lung v. Freeman*, 92 U.S. 275 [1876]; *Ex parte Virginia*, 100 U.S. 339 [1880]; *Neal v. Delaware*, 103 U.S. 370 [1880]; and *Soon Hing v. Crowley*, 113 U.S. 703 [1885].

The present cases, as shown by the facts disclosed in the record, are within this class. It appears that both petitioners have complied with every requisite, deemed by the law or by the public officers charged with its administration, necessary for the protection of neighboring property from fire, or as a precaution against injury to the public health. No reason whatever, except the will of the supervisors, is assigned why they should not be permitted to carry on, in the accustomed manner, their harmless and useful occupation, on which they depend for a livelihood. And while this consent of the supervisors is withheld from them and from two hundred others who have also petitioned, all of whom happen to be Chinese subjects, eighty others, not Chinese subjects, are permitted to carry on the same business under similar conditions. The fact of this discrimination is admitted. No reason for it is shown, and the conclusion cannot be resisted, that no reason for it exists except hostility to the race and nationality to which the petitioners belong, and which in the eye of the law is not justified. The discrimination is, therefore, illegal, and the public administration which enforces it is a denial of the equal protection of the laws and a violation of the Fourteenth Amendment of the Constitution. The imprisonment of the petitioners is, therefore, illegal, and they must be discharged. To this end, [the judgment of the Supreme Court of California in the cases of Yick Wo and Wo Lee are]

[Reversed and Remanded].

PLESSY V. FERGUSON
163 U.S. 537 (1896)

In 1890, Louisiana enacted the Separate Car Act, which required that all railway companies carrying passengers provide equal but separate accommodations for whites and blacks. A group of New Orleans blacks, known as the American Citizens' Equal Rights Association, and some railway companies that objected to the additional costs of providing separate cars decided to test the constitutionality of the Jim Crow statute. Homer Plessy, who described himself as seven eighths white and one eighth black and who appeared to be white, agreed to challenge the statute. Being careful to avoid the interstate commerce issue, Plessy made sure that his ticket was only for an intrastate journey. Having made known in advance to the conductor of his mixed race, Plessy took a vacant seat in a coach that was reserved for whites and was ordered by the conductor to take a seat assigned to blacks. When he refused to comply with the conductor's demand, he was forcibly ejected from the coach and imprisoned for violating the Louisiana statute. At the trial, Plessy argued that the Louisiana statute violated the Thirteenth and Fourteenth Amendments, but the court rejected his arguments. The Louisiana Supreme Court found the law constitutional. Plessy then appealed the case to the Supreme Court, with the Hon. John H. Ferguson, the judge of the criminal district court for the parish of Orleans, as respondent. *Vote: 7-1.*

* * *

MR. JUSTICE BROWN delivered the opinion of the Court.

This case turns upon the constitutionality of an act of the General Assembly of the State of Louisiana, passed in 1890, providing for separate railway carriages for the white and colored races. . . .

. . . The constitutionality of this act is attacked upon the ground that it conflicts both with the Thirteenth Amendment of the Constitution, abolishing slavery, and the Fourteenth Amendment, which prohibits certain restrictive legislation on the part of the States.

1. That it does not conflict with the Thirteenth Amendment, which abolished slavery and involuntary servitude, except as a punishment for crime, is too clear for argument. Slavery implies involuntary servitude—a state of bondage; the ownership of mankind as a chattel, or at least the control of the labor and services of one man for the benefit of another, and the absence of a legal right to the disposal of his own person, property and services. This amendment was said in the *Slaughter-house cases,* 16 Wall. 36 [1873], to have been intended primarily to abolish slavery. . . . It was intimated, however, in that case that this amendment was regarded by the statesmen of that day as insufficient to protect the colored race from certain laws which had been enacted in the Southern States, imposing upon the colored race onerous disabilities and burdens, and curtailing their rights in the pursuit of life, liberty and property to such an extent that their freedom was of little value; and that the Fourteenth Amendment was devised to meet this exigency.

So, too, in the *Civil Rights cases,* 109 U.S. 3, 24 [1883], it was said that the act of a mere individual, the owner of an inn, a public conveyance or place of amusement, refusing accommodations to colored people, cannot be justly regarded as imposing any badge of slavery or servitude upon the applicant, but only as involving an ordinary civil injury, properly cognizable by the laws of the State, and presumably subject to redress by those laws until the contrary appears. . . .

A statute which implies merely a legal distinction between the white and colored races—a distinction which is founded in the color of the two races, and which must always exist so long as white men are distinguished from the other race by color—has no tendency to destroy the legal equality of the two races, or reestablish a state of involuntary servitude. . . .

2. . . . The object of the [Fourteenth] amendment was undoubtedly to enforce the absolute equality of the two races before the law, but in the nature of things it could not have been intended to abolish distinctions based upon color, or to enforce social, as distinguished from political equality, or a commingling of the two races upon terms unsatisfactory to either. Laws permitting, and even requiring, their separation in places where they are liable to be brought into contact do not necessarily imply the inferiority of either race to the other, and have been generally, if not universally, recognized as within the competency of the state legislatures in the exercise of their police power. The most common instance of this is connected with the establishment of separate schools for white and colored children, which has been held to be a valid exercise of the legislative power even by courts of States where the political rights of the colored race have been longest and most earnestly enforced.

One of the earliest cases is that of *Roberts v. City of Boston,* 5 Cush. 198 [1849], in which the Supreme Judicial Court of Massachusetts held that the general school committee of Boston had power to make provision for the instruction of colored children in separate schools established exclusively for them, and to prohibit their attendance upon the other schools. . . . Similar laws have been enacted by Congress under its general power of legislation over the District of Columbia . . . as well as by the legislatures of many of the States, and have been generally, if not uniformly, sustained by the courts. . . .

Laws forbidding the intermarriage of the two races may be said in a technical sense to interfere with the freedom of contract, and yet have been universally recognized as within the police power of the State. . . .

The distinction between laws interfering with the political equality of the negro and those requiring the separation of the two races in schools, theatres and railway carriages has been frequently drawn by this court. . . .

. . . It is claimed by [Plessy] that, in any mixed community, the reputation of belonging to the dominant race, in this instance the white race, is *property*, in the same sense that a right of action, or of inheritance, is property. Conceding this to be so, for the purposes of this case, we are unable to see how this statute deprives him of, or in any way affects his right to, such property. If he be a white man and assigned to a colored coach, he may have his action for damages against the company for being deprived of his so called property. Upon the other hand, if he be a colored man and be so assigned, he has been deprived of no property, since he is not lawfully entitled to the reputation of being a white man.

[Counsel for Plessy suggests] that the same argument that will justify the state legislature in requiring railways to provide separate accommodations for the two races will also authorize them to require separate cars to be provided for people whose hair is of a certain color, or who are aliens, or who belong to certain nationalities, or to enact laws requiring colored people to walk upon one side of the street, and white people upon the other, or requiring white men's houses to be painted white, and colored men's black, or their vehicles or business signs to be of different colors, upon the theory that one side of the street is as good as the other, or that a house or vehicle of one color is as good as one of another color. The reply to all this is that every exercise of the police power must be reasonable, and extend only to such laws as are enacted in good faith for the promotion for the public good, and not for the annoyance or oppression of a particular class. . . .

So far, then, as a conflict with the Fourteenth Amendment is concerned, the case reduces itself to the question of whether the statute of Louisiana is a reasonable regulation, and with respect to this there must necessarily be a large discretion on the part of the legislature. In determining the question of reasonableness it is at liberty to act with reference to the established usages, customs and traditions of the people, and with a view to the promotion of their comfort, and the preservation of the public peace and good order. Gauged by this standard, we cannot say that a law which authorizes or even requires the separation of the two races in public conveyances is unreasonable, or more obnoxious to the Fourteenth Amendment than the acts of Congress requiring separate schools for colored children in the District of Columbia, the constitutionality of which does not seem to have been questioned, or the corresponding acts of state legislatures.

We consider the underlying fallacy of the plaintiff's argument to consist in the assumption that the enforced separation of the two races stamps the colored race with a badge of inferiority. If this be so, it is not by reason of anything found in the act, but solely because the colored race chooses to put that construction upon it. The argument necessarily assumes that if, as has been more than once the case, and is not unlikely to be so again, the colored race should become the dominant power in the state legislature, and should enact a law precisely similar in terms, it would thereby relegate the white race to an inferior position. We imagine that the white race, at least, would not acquiesce in this assumption. The argument also assumes that social prejudices may be overcome by legislation, and that equal rights cannot be secured to the negro except by an enforced commingling of the two races. We cannot accept this proposition. If the two races are to meet upon terms of social equality, it must be the result of natural affinities, a mutual appreciation of each other's merits and a voluntary consent of individuals. . . . Legislation is powerless to eradicate racial instincts or to abolish distinctions based upon physical differences, and the attempt to do so can only result in accentuating the difficulties of the present situation. If the civil and political rights of both races be equal one cannot be inferior to the other civilly or politically. If one race be inferior to the other socially, the Constitution of the United States cannot put them upon the same plane.

. . . The judgment of the court below is, therefore, *Affirmed*.

who decides this?

* * *

MR. JUSTICE HARLAN dissenting.

. . . In respect of civil rights, common to all citizens, the Constitution of the United States does not, I think, permit any public authority to know the race of those entitled to be protected in the enjoyment of such rights. Every true man has pride of race, and under appropriate circumstances when the rights of others, his equals before the law, are not to be affected, it is his privilege to express such pride and to take such action based upon it as to him seems proper. But I deny that any legislative body or judicial tribunal may have regard to the race of citizens when the civil rights of those citizens are involved. Indeed, such legislation, as that here in question, is inconsistent not only with that equality of rights which pertains to citizenship, National and State, but with the personal liberty enjoyed by every one within the United States.

The Thirteenth Amendment does not permit the withholding or the deprivation of any right necessarily inhering in freedom. It not only struck down the institution of slavery as previously existing in the United States, but it prevents the imposition of any burdens or disabilities that constitute badges of slavery or servitude. It decreed universal civil freedom in this country. This court has so adjudged. But that amendment having been found inadequate to the protection of the rights of those who had been in slavery, it was followed by the Fourteenth Amendment, which added greatly to the dignity and glory of American citizenship, and to the security of personal liberty, by declaring that "all persons born or naturalized in the United States, and subject to the jurisdiction thereof, are citizens of the United States and of the State wherein they reside," and that "no State shall make or enforce any law which shall abridge the privileges or immunities of citizens of the United States; nor shall any State deprive any person of life, liberty or property without due process of law, nor deny to any person within its jurisdiction the equal protection of the laws." These two amendments, if enforced according to their true intent and meaning, will protect all the civil rights that pertain to freedom and citizenship. Finally, and to the end that no citizen should be denied, on account of his race, the privilege of participating in the political control of his country, it was declared by the Fifteenth Amendment that "the right of citizens of the United States to vote shall not be denied or abridged by the United States or by any State on account of race, color or previous condition of servitude."

. . . It was said in argument that the statute of Louisiana does not discriminate against either race, but prescribes a rule applicable alike to white and colored citizens. But this argument does not meet the difficulty. Every one knows that the statute in question had its origin in the purpose, not so much to exclude white persons from railroad cars occupied by blacks, as to exclude colored people from coaches occupied by or assigned to white persons. Railroad corporations of Louisiana did not make discrimination among whites in the matter of accommodation for travellers. The thing to accomplish was, under the guise of giving equal accommodation for whites and blacks, to compel the latter to keep to themselves while travelling in railroad passenger coaches. . . .

. . . If a State can prescribe, as a rule of civil conduct, that whites and blacks shall not travel as passengers in the same railroad coach, why may it not so regulate the use of the streets of its cities and towns as to compel white citizens to keep on one side of a street and black citizens to keep on the other? Why may it not, upon like grounds, punish whites and blacks who ride together in street cars or

in open vehicles on a public road or street? Why may it not require sheriffs to assign whites to one side of a court-room and blacks to the other? And why may it not also prohibit the commingling of the two races in the galleries of legislative halls or in public assemblages convened for the consideration of the political questions of the day? Further, if this statute of Louisiana is consistent with the personal liberty of citizens, why may not the State require the separation in railroad coaches of native and naturalized citizens of the United States, or of Protestants and Roman Catholics?

The answer given at the argument to these questions was that regulations of the kind they suggest would be unreasonable, and could not, therefore, stand before the law. Is it meant that the determination of questions of legislative power depends upon the inquiry whether the statute whose validity is questioned is, in the judgment of the courts, a reasonable one, taking all the circumstances into consideration? . . .

. . . The white race deems itself to be the dominant race in this country. And so it is, in prestige, in achievements, in education, in wealth and in power. So, I doubt not, it will continue to be for all time, if it remains true to its great heritage and holds fast to the principles of constitutional liberty. But in view of the Constitution, in the eye of the law, there is in this country no superior, dominant, ruling class of citizens. There is no caste here. Our Constitution is color-blind, and neither knows nor tolerates classes among its citizens. In respect of civil rights, all citizens are equal before the law. The humblest is the peer of the most powerful. The law regards man as man, and takes no account of his surroundings or of his color when his civil rights as guaranteed by the supreme law of the land are involved. It is, therefore, to be regretted that this high tribunal, the final expositor of the fundamental law of the land, has reached the conclusion that it is competent for a State to regulate the enjoyment by citizens of their civil rights solely upon the basis of race.

In my opinion, the judgment this day rendered will, in time, prove to be quite as pernicious as the decision made by this tribunal in the *Dred Scott* case [60 U.S. 393 (1857)]. . . . The present decision, it may well be apprehended, will not only stimulate aggressions, more or less brutal and irritating, upon the admitted rights of colored citizens, but will encourage the belief that it is possible, by means of state enactments, to defeat the beneficent purposes which the people of the United States had in view when they adopted the recent amendments of the Constitution, by one of which the blacks of this country were made citizens of the United States and of the States in which they respectfully reside, and whose privileges and immunities, as citizens, the States are forbidden to abridge. Sixty millions of whites are in no danger from the presence here of eight millions of blacks. The destinies of the two races, in this country, are indissolubly linked together, and the interests of both require that the common government of all shall not permit the seeds of race hate to be planted under the sanction of law. What can more certainly arouse race hate, what more certainly create and perpetuate a feeling of distrust between these races, than state enactments, which, in fact, proceed on the ground that colored citizens are so inferior and degraded that they cannot be allowed to sit in public coaches occupied by white citizens? That, as all will admit, is the real meaning of such legislation as was enacted in Louisiana.

* * *

MR. JUSTICE BREWER did not hear the argument or participate in the decision of this case.

BEREA COLLEGE V. COMMONWEALTH OF KENTUCKY
211 U.S. 45 (1908)

In 1904, Kentucky enacted a statute that made it illegal "for any person, corporation or association of persons to maintain or operate any college, school or institution where persons of the white and negro races are both received as pupils for instruction." Berea College, a private institution and corporation under the laws of Kentucky, was found guilty of violating the statute and fined $1,000. The Kentucky Court of Appeals upheld the conviction, and the college appealed to the Supreme Court, arguing that the entire act was unconstitutional under the Fourteenth Amendment. *Vote:* 7-2.

* * *

MR. JUSTICE BREWER delivered the opinion of the Court.

There is no dispute as to the facts. That the act does not violate the constitution of Kentucky is settled by the decision of its highest court, and the single question for our consideration is whether it conflicts with the Federal Constitution. The Court of Appeals discussed at some length the general power of the State in respect to the separation of the two races. It also ruled that "the right to teach white and negro children in a private school at the same time and place is not a property right. Besides, appellant as a corporation created by this State has no natural right to teach at all. Its right to teach is such as the State sees fit to give to it. The State may withhold it altogether, or qualify it." *Allgeyer v. Louisiana,* 165 U.S. 578 [1897].

. . . Again, the decision by a state court of the extent and limitation of the powers conferred by the State upon one of its own corporations is of a purely local nature. In creating a corporation a State may withhold powers which may be exercised by and cannot be denied to an individual. It is under no obligation to treat both alike. In granting corporate powers the legislature may deem that the best interests of the State would be subserved by some restriction, and the corporation may not plead that in spite of the restriction it has more or greater powers because the citizen has. . . . [The act] may conflict with the Federal Constitution in denying to individuals powers which they may rightfully exercise, and yet, at the same time, be valid as to a corporation created by the State.

. . . The statute is clearly separable and may be valid as to one class while invalid as to another. Even if it were conceded that its assertion of power over individuals cannot be sustained, still it must be upheld so far as it restrains corporations.

There is no force in the suggestion that the statute, although clearly separable, must stand or fall as an entirety on the ground the legislature would not have enacted one part unless it could reach all. That the legislature of Kentucky desired to separate the teaching of white and colored children may be conceded, but it by no means follows that it would not have enforced the separation so far as it could do so, even though it could not make it effective under all circumstances. In other words, it is not at all unreasonable to believe that the legislature, although advised beforehand of the constitutional question, might have prohibited all organizations and corporations under its control from teaching white and colored children together, and thus made at least uniform official action. . . .

. . . Now, an amendment to the original charter, which does not destroy the power of the college to furnish education to all persons, but which simply separates them by time or place of instruction, cannot be said to "defeat or substantially impair the object of the grant." The language of the statute is not in terms an amendment, yet its effect is an amendment, and it would be resting too much on mere form to hold that a statute which in effect works a change in the terms of the charter is not to be considered as an amendment, because not so designated. The act itself, being separable, is to be read as though it in one section prohibited any person, in another section any corporation, and in a third any association of persons to do the acts named. Reading the statute as containing a separate prohibition on all corporations, at least, all state corporations, it substantially declares that any authority given by previous charters to instruct the two races at the same time and in the same place is forbidden, and that prohibition being a departure from the terms of the original charter in this case may properly be adjudged an amendment.

. . . We are of the opinion, for reasons stated, that it does come within that power, and on this ground the judgment of the Court of Appeals of Kentucky is

Affirmed.

MR. JUSTICE HOLMES and MR. JUSTICE MOODY concur.

* * *

MR. JUSTICE HARLAN dissenting.

. . . It is absolutely certain that the legislature had in mind to prohibit the teaching of the two races in the same private institution, at the same time by whomsoever that institution was conducted. It is a reflection upon the common sense of legislators to suppose that they might have prohibited a private *corporation* from teaching by its agents, and yet left individuals and unincorporated associations entirely at liberty, by the same instructors, to teach the two races in the same institution at the same time. It was the teaching of pupils of the two races *together,* or in the same school, no matter by whom or under whose authority, which the legislature sought to prevent. The manifest purpose was to prevent the association of white and colored persons in the same school. That such was its intention is evident from the title of the act, which, as we have seen, was "to prohibit white and colored persons from attending the same school." . . .

. . . Therefore, the court cannot, as I think, properly forbear to consider the validity of the provisions that refer to teachers who do not represent corporations. If those provisions constitute as, in my judgment, they do, an essential part of the legislative scheme or policy, and are invalid, then, under the authorities cited, the whole act must fall. The provision as to corporations may be valid, and yet the other clauses may be so inseparably connected with that provision and the policy underlying it, that the validity of all the clauses necessary to effectuate the legislative intent must be considered. There is no magic in the fact of incorporation which will so transform the act of teaching the two races in the same school at the same time that such teaching can be deemed lawful when conducted by private individuals, but unlawful when conducted by the representatives of corporations.

. . . In my judgment the court should directly meet and decide the broad question presented by the statute. It should adjudge whether the statute, as a whole, is or is not unconstitutional, in that it makes it a crime against the State to maintain or operate a private institution of learning where white and black pupils are received, at the same time, for instruction. In the view which I have as to my duty I feel obliged to express my opinion as to the validity of the act as a whole. I am of the opinion that in its essential parts the statute is an arbitrary invasion of the rights of liberty and property guaranteed by the Fourteenth Amendment against hostile state action and is, therefore, void.

MR. JUSTICE DAY also dissents.

BAILEY V. ALABAMA
219 U.S. 219 (1911)

Section 4730 of the Code of Alabama of 1896 (as amended in 1907) provided that any person, who with intent to injure or defraud his employer, enters into a written contract for service and thereby obtains money or property from the employer and fails to refund the money or pay for the property was subjected to criminal penalties. Alonzo Bailey, a black man, was convicted under the statute for obtaining $15 from the Riverside Corporation, which hired him as a farmhand, but refusing to perform the service and failing to refund the money. Bailey was found guilty under § 4730, and the Alabama Supreme Court affirmed his conviction. *Vote: 7-2.*

* * *

MR. JUSTICE HUGHES delivered the opinion of the Court.

. . . We at once dismiss from consideration the fact that the plaintiff in error is a black man. While the action of a State through its officers charged with the administration of a law, fair in appearance, may be of such a character as to constitute a denial of the equal protection of the laws (*Yick Wo v. Hopkins,* 118 U.S. 356, 373 [1886]), such a conclusion is here neither required nor justified. The statute, on its face, makes no racial discrimination, and the record fails to show its existence in fact. No question of a sectional character is presented, and we may view the legislation in the same manner as if it had been enacted in New York or in Idaho. Opportunities for coercion and oppression, in varying circumstances, exist in all parts of the Union, and the citizens of all the States are interested in the maintenance of the constitutional guarantees, the consideration of which is here involved.

Prior to the amendment of the year 1903, enlarged in 1907, the statute did not make the mere breach of the contract, under which the employee had obtained from his employer money which was not refunded or property which was not paid for, a crime. The essential ingredient of the offense was the intent of the accused to injure or defraud. To justify conviction, it was necessary that this intent should be established by competent evidence, aided only by such inferences as might logically be derived from the facts proved, and should not be the subject of mere surmise or arbitrary assumption.

. . . We cannot escape the conclusion that, although the statute in terms is to punish fraud, still its natural and inevitable effect is to expose to conviction for crime those who simply fail or refuse to perform contracts for personal service in liquidation of a debt, and judging its purpose by its effect that it seeks in this way to provide the means of compulsion through which performance of such service may be secured. The question is whether such a statute is constitutional.

. . . In the present case it is urged that the statute as amended, through the operation of the presumption for which it provides, violates the Thirteenth Amendment of the Constitution of the United States and the act of Congress passed for its enforcement.

The Thirteenth Amendment provides:

"SECTION 1. Neither slavery nor involuntary servitude, except as a punishment for crime whereof the party shall have been duly convicted, shall exist within the United States, or any place subject to their jurisdiction.

"SECTION 2. Congress shall have power to enforce this article by appropriate legislation."

Pursuant to the authority thus conferred, Congress passed the act of March 2, 1867, c. 187, 14 Stat. 546, the provisions of which are now found in §§ 1990 and 5526 of the Revised Statutes, as follows:

"SEC. 1990. The holding of any person to service or labor under the system known as peonage is abolished and forever prohibited in the Territory of New Mexico, or in any other Territory or State of the United States; and all acts, laws, resolutions, orders, regulations, or usages of the Territory of New Mexico, or of any other Territory or State, which have heretofore established, maintained, or enforced, or by virtue of which any attempt shall hereafter be made to establish, maintain, or enforce, directly or indirectly, the voluntary or involuntary service or labor of any persons as peons, in liquidation of any debt or obligation, or otherwise, are declared null and void."

"SEC. 5526. Every person who holds, arrests, returns, or causes to be held, arrested, or returned, or in any manner aids in the arrest or return of any person to a condition of peonage, shall be punished by a fine of not less than one thousand nor more than five thousand dollars, or by imprisonment not less than one year nor more than five years, or by both."

The language of the Thirteenth Amendment was not new. It reproduced the historic words of the ordinance of 1787 for the government of the Northwest Territory and gave them unrestricted application within the United States and all places subject to their jurisdiction. While the immediate concern was with African slavery, the Amendment was not limited to that. It was a charter of universal civil freedom for all persons, of whatever race, color or estate, under the flag.

The words involuntary servitude have a "larger meaning than slavery." . . . The plain intention was to abolish slavery of whatever name and form and all its badges and incidents; to render impossible any state of bondage; to make labor free, by prohibiting that control by which the personal service of one man is disposed of or coerced for another's benefit which is the essence of involuntary servitude.

While the Amendment was self-executing, so far as its terms were applicable to any existing condition, Congress was authorized to secure its complete enforcement by appropriate legislation. . . .

The act of March 2, 1867 . . . was a valid exercise of this express authority. *Clyatt v. United States,* 197 U.S. 207 [1905]. It declared that all laws of any State, by virtue of which any attempt should be made "to establish, maintain, or enforce, directly or indirectly, the voluntary or involuntary service or labor of any persons as peons, in liquidation of any debt or obligation, or otherwise," should be null and void.

Peonage is a term descriptive of a condition which has existed in Spanish America, and especially in Mexico. The essence of the thing is compulsory service in payment of a debt. A peon is one who is compelled to work for his creditor until his debt is paid. And in this explicit and comprehensive enactment, Congress was not concerned with mere names or manner of description, or with a particular place or section of the country. It was concerned with a fact, wherever it might exist; with a condition, however named and wherever it might be established, maintained or enforced.

The fact that the debtor contracted to perform the labor which is sought to be compelled does not withdraw the attempted enforcement from the condemnation of the statute. The full intent of the constitutional provision could be defeated with obvious facility if, through the guise of contracts under which advances had been made, debtors could be held to compulsory service. It is the compulsion of the service that the statute inhibits, for when that occurs the condition of servitude is created, which would be not less involuntary because of the original agreement to work out the indebtedness. The contract exposes the debtor to liability for the loss due to the breach, but not to enforced labor. This has been so clearly stated by this court in the case of *Clyatt* . . . that discussion is unnecessary. . . .

The act of Congress, nullifying all state laws by which it should be attempted to enforce the "service or labor of any persons as peons, in liquidation of any debt or obligation, or otherwise," necessarily embraces all legislation which seeks to compel the service or labor by making it a crime to refuse or fail to perform it. Such laws would furnish the readiest means of compulsion. The Thirteenth Amendment prohibits involuntary servitude except as punishment for crime. But the exception, allowing full latitude of the enforcement of penal laws, does not destroy the prohibition. It does not permit slavery or involuntary servitude to be established or maintained through the operation of the criminal law by making it a crime to refuse to submit to the one or to render the service which would constitute the other. The State may impose involuntary servitude as a punishment for crime, but it may not compel one man to labor for another in payment of a debt, by punishing him as a criminal if he does not perform the service or pay the debt.

If the statute in this case had authorized the employing company to seize the debtor and hold him to the service until he paid the fifteen dollars, or had furnished the equivalent in labor, its invalidity would not be questioned. It would be equally clear that the State could not authorize its constabulary to prevent the servant from escaping and to force him to work out his debt. But the State could not avail itself of the sanction of the criminal law to supply the compulsion any more than it could use or authorize the use of physical force. . . .

What the State may not do directly it may not do indirectly. If it cannot punish the servant as a criminal for the mere failure or refusal to serve without paying his debt, it is not permitted to accomplish the same result by creating a statutory presumption which upon proof of no other fact exposes him to conviction and punishment. Without imputing any actual motive to oppress, we must consider the natural operation of the statute here in question . . . and it is apparent that it furnishes a convenient instrument for the coercion which the Constitution and the act of Congress forbid; an instrument of compulsion peculiarly effective as against the poor and the ignorant, its most likely victims. There is no more important concern than to safeguard the freedom of labor upon which alone can enduring prosperity be based. The provisions designed to secure it would soon become a barren form if it were possible to establish a statutory presumption of this sort and to hold over the heads of laborers the threat of punishment for crime, under the name of fraud but merely upon evidence of failure to work out their debts. The act of Congress deprives of effect all legislative measures of any State through which directly or indirectly the prohibited thing, to wit, compulsory service to secure the payment of a debt may be established or maintained; and we conclude that § 4730, as amended, of the Code of Alabama, in so far as it makes the refusal or failure to perform the act or service, without refunding the money or paying for the property received, *prima facie* evidence of the commission of the crime which the section defines, is in conflict with the Thirteenth Amendment and the legislation authorized by that Amendment, and is therefore invalid. . . .

Reversed and cause remanded for further proceedings not inconsistent with this opinion.

* * *

MR. JUSTICE HOLMES, with whom MR. JUSTICE LURTON concurs, dissenting.

. . . I shall begin then by assuming for the moment what I think is not true and shall try to show not to be true, that this statute punishes the mere refusal to labor according to contract as a crime, and shall inquire whether there would be anything contrary to the Thirteenth Amendment or the statute if it did, supposing it to have been enacted in the State of New York. I cannot believe it. The Thirteenth Amendment does not outlaw contracts for labor. That would be at least as great a misfortune for the laborer as for the man that employed him. For it certainly would affect the terms of the bargain unfavorably for the laboring man if it were understood that the employer could do nothing in case the laborer saw fit to break his word. But any legal liability for breach of contract is a disagreeable consequence which tends to make the contractor do as he said he would. Liability to an action for damages has that tendency as well as a fine. If the mere imposition of such consequences as tend to make a man keep to his promise is the creation of peonage when the contract happens to be for labor, I do not see why the allowance of a civil action is not, as well as an indictment ending in fine. Peonage is service to a private master at which a man is kept by bodily compulsion against his will. But the creation of the ordinary legal motives for right conduct does not produce it. Breach of a legal contract without excuse is wrong conduct, even if the contract is for labor, and if a State adds to civil liability a criminal liability to fine, it simply intensifies the legal motive for doing right, it does not make the laborer a slave.

. . . To sum up, I think that obtaining money by fraud may be made a crime as well as murder or theft; that a false representation, expressed or implied, at the time of making a contract of labor that one intends to perform it and thereby obtaining an advance, may be declared a case of fraudulently obtaining money as well as any other; that if made a crime it may be punished like any other crime, and that an unjustified departure from the promised service without payment may be declared a sufficient case to go to the jury for their judgment; all without in any way infringing the Thirteenth Amendment or the statutes of the United States.

2

From White to Vinson

THE CAMPAIGN FOR
RACIAL EQUALITY, 1910-1953

The public symbols and constant reminders of his inferior position were the segregation statutes, or "Jim Crow" laws.
C. Vann Woodward*

THE SUPREME COURT IN TRANSITION

After the death of Chief Justice Fuller on July 4, 1910, President William Howard Taft nominated Associate Justice Edward D. White to replace Fuller on December 10, 1910. He was confirmed by a voice vote on the same day that he was nominated. White initially was appointed to the Court by President Grover Cleveland in 1894. White was raised in the South and had served as United States Senator from Louisiana. The year he became Chief Justice was also the year the National Association for the Advancement of Colored People (NAACP) was founded. At the time of White's appointment as Chief Justice, President Taft felt strongly that the Court was suffering because of the advanced age of some of the Justices. President Taft reinvigorated the Court, however, with five additional appointments: Howard Lurton, Charles Evans Hughes, Willis Van Devanter, Joseph R. Lemar, and Mahlon Pitney. President

---

*Woodward, C. Vann. (1974). *The Strange Career of Jim Crow.* New York: Oxford University Press, p. 17.

Woodrow Wilson made three appointments to the White Court: the ultra-conservative and anti-Semite James C. McReynolds; the liberal Louis D. Brandeis, the first Jewish Justice to the Court; and John H. Clarke, who often voted with Brandeis on a number of issues. During White's tenure as Chief Justice (1910-1921), several surprising decisions were rendered by the Supreme Court in the areas of voting, public accommodations, and residential segregation that were supportive of black civil rights. For the first time, favorable decisions for blacks were a fait accompli, but virtually nothing else changed. Blacks were still the recipients of the double standard where Jim Crow reigned supreme (see Box 2.1).

In May 1921, Chief Justice White died and President Warren G. Harding nominated William Howard Taft to replace White as Chief Justice. Taft was confirmed by a voice vote on June 30, 1921, and was the only person to serve as President of the United States and Chief Justice. This moment was the culmination of Taft's most coveted aspiration. President Harding also appointed George Sutherland, Pierce Butler, and Edward T. Sanford to the Court. The Taft Court (1921-1930) continued the conservative posture of the White Court. For example, the Tenth Amendment was used by the Taft Court to prevent federal power from intruding into those powers reserved for the states. Robert Cover observed that during the Taft Court, as with previous courts, "racist justice was a deeply rooted problem, not high on the conservative agenda for reform."[1]

On February 3, 1930, Chief Justice Taft resigned because of a serious illness. President Herbert Hoover nominated Charles Evans Hughes to replace Taft on the same day Taft resigned. Hughes was confirmed by the Senate on February 13, 1930, by a 52-26 vote. At the age of 67, Hughes became the 11th Chief Justice of the United States. Approximately 20 years earlier, President Taft had nominated Hughes to replaced Justice Brewer. President Hoover then nominated John J. Parker to replace Justice Sanford, who died on March 8; however, the Senate rejected the nomination, in part, because of the NAACP's opposition to Parker, because of his alleged views on black civil rights. Instead, the Senate confirmed President Hoover's second choice, Owen J. Roberts, to the Court. President Hoover also appointed Benjamin N. Cardozo, the second Jewish Justice, to the high court.

The Hughes Court (1930-1941) was marked by profound changes in personnel after the election of Franklin Delano Roosevelt in 1936. President Roosevelt's New Deal philosophy and his court-packing plan led to a clash between the President and the Court and eventually contributed to the famous "switch in time that saved nine" ruling in *West Coast Hotel Co. v. Parrish,* 300 U.S. 379 (1937). After Justice Owen Roberts's vote to uphold the minimum wage law at issue in *Parrish,* Justice Van Devanter retired. Prior to 1941, President Roosevelt appointed Hugo L. Black, Stanley F. Reed, Felix Frankfurter, William O. Douglas, and Frank Murphy to the Hughes Court. During the Hughes Court era, blacks won significant victories in the criminal justice area, interstate travel, and education. In general, the Hughes Court became more sympathetic to civil liberties and civil rights issues.

BOX 2.1

Jim Crow Segregation Practices

"The extremes to which caste penalties and separation were carried in parts of the South could hardly find a counterpart short of the latitudes of India and South Africa. In 1909 Mobile passed a curfew law applying exclusively to Negroes and requiring them to be off the streets by 10 p.m. The Oklahoma legislature in 1915 authorized its Corporation Commission to require telephone companies 'to maintain separate booths for white and colored patrons.' North Carolina and Florida required that textbooks used by the public-school children of one race be kept separate from those used by the other, and the Florida law specified separation even while the books were in storage. South Carolina for a time segregated a third caste by establishing separate schools for mulatto as well as for white and Negro children. A New Orleans ordinance segregated white and Negro prostitutes in separate districts. Ray Stannard Baker found Jim Crow Bibles for Negro witnesses in Atlanta courts and Jim Crow elevators for Negro passengers in Atlanta buildings.

"A search of the statute books fails to disclose any state law or city ordinance specifying separate Bibles and separate elevators. Right here it is well to admit, and even to emphasize, that *laws are not an adequate index of the extent and prevalence of segregation and discriminatory practices in the South.* The practices often anticipated and sometimes exceeded the laws. It may be confidently assumed—and it could be verified by present observation—that there is more Jim Crowism practiced in the South than there are Jim Crow laws on the books."

SOURCE: *The Strange Career of Jim Crow* (3rd rev. ed., pp. 101-102), by C. V. Woodward, 1974, New York: Oxford University Press.

Chief Justice Hughes retired in 1941, and President Roosevelt nominated Harlan Fiske Stone to replace him. Stone was President Roosevelt's sixth appointment to the Court. He later appointed James F. Byrnes, Robert H. Jackson, and Wiley B. Rutledge to the Supreme Court. In all, President Roosevelt made nine appointments to the Supreme Court during his lengthy tenure.

The Stone Court (1941-1946) must be examined in relationship to the Vinson Court (1946-1953) in order to understand the nature of the evolutionary expansion of civil rights and liberties. On June 6, 1946, President Harry S. Truman nominated Frederick M. Vinson to replace Stone. The Vinson Court's record was more impressive in rendering decisions favorable to blacks. However, the Stone Court deserves credit for laying the foundation on which the Vinson Court launched its attack on unequal facilities in graduate and professional schools.

As we indicated in the previous chapter, the Supreme Court's decision in *Plessy v. Ferguson,* 168 U.S. 537 (1896) legitimated Jim Crow segregation in the United States. The devastating effects of constitutionally sanctioned racism in the lives of blacks from the 1900s to the 1950s are vividly illustrated in C. Vann Woodward's landmark study of the history of segregation in the United States.[2] Woodward presents a description of the nature of Jim Crow laws and customs as practiced in the South. Although the tendency is to equate the rigid caste system of Jim Crow with the South, Woodward also points out that segregation had its impact in the North as well. Federal indifference and Congressional inability or unwillingness to fill the void in civil rights protection convinced many blacks that the chief weapon and best hope in securing legal and political equality before the law was the Fourteenth Amendment. The Supreme Court's early restrictive interpretations of the Fourteenth Amendment, however, proved to be blacks' worst enemy from 1896 to the mid-1930s. For example, Richard Bardolph found that, until 1938, the Fourteenth Amendment was meaningless as far as blacks were concerned. His study indicated that 604 decisions were rendered by the Supreme Court between 1868 and 1911 that involved the Fourteenth Amendment.[3] Of this number, only 28 involved black interests, and 22 of these were decided against the black litigant. These severe losses before the high court occurred despite the fact that the Fourteenth Amendment was adopted for the purpose of granting relief to blacks. In this chapter, we show how personnel changes on the Court, especially after 1935, led to the incremental abandonment of its restrictive interpretation of the Fourteenth Amendment in the areas of voting rights, housing segregation, the administration of justice, segregation in the higher education context, and segregated interstate travel.

THE PERSISTENT
STRUGGLE FOR THE BALLOT:
BLACKS' ABIDING FAITH IN DEMOCRACY

Voting constitutes the very essence of a democratic society. However, blacks had great difficulty obtaining this fundamental right for more than a century. Ward E. Y. Elliott pointed out, "From Reconstruction to World War I the Supreme Court showed more ingenuity in voiding voting rights actions than in upholding them."[4] If the Fourteenth Amendment was, for the most part, meaningless in protecting the constitutional rights of black Americans, the same can be said about the Fifteenth Amendment, which was ratified in 1870. Ingenious and devious schemes were developed by the power wielders to prevent blacks from voting. The grandfather clause was a clever legal device that many Southern states enacted to disfranchise blacks but not unqualified whites. In *Guinn v. United States,* 238 U.S. 347 (1915), the clause was challenged and met its waterloo. The cleverly disguised Oklahoma Constitution provided that no lineal descendant of a person who was entitled to vote on January 1, 1866, or prior thereto, shall be denied the right to vote because of the inability to read or write sections of such Constitution. *Guinn* was the first case in which the NAACP participated. Moorfield Storey, counsel for the NAACP, argued in an amicus curiae brief that the undoubted purpose and effect of Oklahoma's grandfather clause was to discriminate against black voters. In a unanimous opinion written by Chief Justice White, the Court declared the grandfather clause unconstitutional on Fifteenth Amendment grounds.

In 1916 the Oklahoma legislature, in response to the Court's decision in *Guinn,* enacted a new scheme for registration as a prerequisite to voting. The new scheme provided that all citizens who were qualified to vote in 1916 and who failed to register between April 30 and May 11, 1916, would be perpetually disfranchised except those who voted in 1914. The effect of the legislation was that whites who were on the voter lists in 1914 could vote, whereas blacks who were kept from registering because of the grandfather clause would remain forever disfranchised unless they registered during the 12-day period. In its second case before the high court, the NAACP challenged the constitutionality of the law. In *Lane v. Wilson,* 307 U.S. 268 (1939), the Court, in a 6-2 opinion (Justice Douglas did not participate), distinguished this case from *Giles v. Harris,* 189 U.S. 475 (1903) (discussed in the previous chapter) and held that the Court had jurisdiction in the case. On the merits, Justice Frankfurter found that the Fifteenth Amendment "nullifies sophisticated as well as simple-minded modes of discrimination. It hits onerous procedural requirements which effectively handicap exercise of the franchise by the colored race although the abstract right to vote may remain unrestricted as to race." The Court invalidated the scheme chosen as a substitute for the grandfather clause under the Fifteenth Amendment.

The victory in the grandfather clause case gave blacks some hope of full participation in the political arena, but other methods of preventing blacks from exercising the franchise persisted. The fight reverted to the white primary. The White Court made it difficult to attack the white primary in a case that had nothing to do with black voting rights. In *Newberry v. United States,* 256 U.S. 232 (1921), Truman Newberry and 15 other persons were found guilty of violating the Federal Corrupt Practices Act, which placed limits on how much money candidates could spend in final elections or primaries and conventions for U.S. Senate and U.S. House of Representative seats. In a unanimous opinion by Justice McReynolds, the Court declared the Act unconstitutional because Congress lacked authority under Article 1, § 4 of the Constitution to regulate primary elections. According to Justice McReynolds, primaries "are in no sense elections for an office, but merely methods by which party adherents agree upon candidates whom they intended to offer and support for ultimate choice by all qualified electors." Robert Brisbane observed, "The state of Texas, however, was interested only in the distinctions between a primary election and a regular election and the clear implication that primary elections were the business of the state and, hence, exempt from federal control. Texas enacted its first statewide white primary law in 1923."[5]

Brisbane's analysis of black politics and the white primary revealed that "contrary to what is generally thought, however, the *first* Texas white primary law as such was not inspired by the decision in the *Newberry* case nor was the *Nixon v. Herndon* case the first Texas white primary case to reach the United States Supreme Court."[6] His study revealed that the City Democratic Executive Committee of Houston, Texas, had published four months earlier a rule that blacks would not be permitted to vote in the February 9, 1921, Democratic primary election. Several black Democrats filed for an injunction to prohibit the committee from enforcing the rule. Their request was denied by the lower courts on the ground that the case was moot because the election had been held. The Taft Court, three years later in *Love v. Griffith,* 266 U.S. 32 (1924), affirmed the Texas court's ruling that Houston blacks' Fifteenth Amendment rights were not violated because the case was moot.

The white primary was a major obstacle to black voting because whoever won in the primary won in the general election. Coupled with the one-party (Democratic) dominance in the South, the imposition of the white primary was an effective tool to disfranchise blacks. In 1924 the NAACP decided to bring a test case to challenge the constitutionality of Texas' white primary law. In a unanimous Taft Court decision written by Justice Holmes, the Court held, in NIXON V. HERNDON, 273 U.S. 536 (1927), that the Texas statute was unconstitutional and constituted an obvious infringement of Nixon's rights under the Fourteenth Amendment and that it was therefore unnecessary to even consider the Fifteenth Amendment.

The first solid blow to the white primary had been thrown. Shortly after the Court's ruling in *Herndon,* the Texas legislature enacted a new statute that gave the State Executive Committee the power to proscribe voting qualifications of its own members. Under this new statute, the State Executive Committee of the Democratic Party adopted a resolution limiting participation in the primaries to white Democrats. Nixon was again refused the right to vote, and the NAACP challenged the constitutionality of the committee's action in a second suit. In a 5-4 opinion written by Justice Cardozo, the Hughes Court, in *Nixon v. Condon,* 286 U.S. 73 (1932), determined that the power exercised by the executive committee was not the power of the political party as a voluntary organization, but rather came from the statute that excluded Nixon on the basis of his race. The Court held that the case was ruled by *Herndon* and that the committee's action constituted discrimination under the Fourteenth Amendment. Justice McReynolds, writing for the dissenters (Van Devanter, Sutherland, and Butler), stated:

> Such authority as the State of Texas has to legislate concerning party primaries is derived in part from her duty to secure order, prevent fraud, etc., and in part from obligation to prescribe appropriate methods for selecting candidates whose names shall appear upon the official ballots used at regular elections.
>
> Political parties are fruits of voluntary action. Where there is no unlawful purpose, citizens may create them at will and limit their membership as seems wise. The State may not interfere. White men may organize; blacks may do

likewise. A women's party may exclude males. This much is essential to free government.

White officials in Texas refused to concede victory to blacks and devised a more sophisticated scheme to circumvent the decision. In 1932 the state convention of the Democratic Party passed a resolution that excluded blacks from participation in any of its activities. This scheme was different from what had occurred in *Nixon v. Condon* in that a state convention of the party had decided to exclude blacks; this constituted a significant change from a determination by the Executive Committee. When William Grovey was refused an absentee ballot by the county clerk on account of race, he brought suit with the assistance of NAACP lawyers. In GROVEY V. TOWNSEND, 295 U.S. 45 (1935), the Hughes Court, in a unanimous decision, declared that it was constitutional for a political party to restrict voting to whites in primaries as long as state law was not a requirement for such a restriction. The Court expressed the crux of its opinion in these words: "Here the qualifications of citizens to participate in party counsels and to vote at party primaries have been declared by the representatives of the party in convention assembled, and this action upon its face is not state action." Walter White, the NAACP's Executive Secretary from 1931 to 1955, expressed the feeling of black Americans about the *Grovey* decision:

> It should not be difficult to imagine the gloom we all felt. Years of hard work and heavy expense appeared to have gone for naught. But we could not afford to give up in despair. We had to continue the struggle, whatever the cost, to make effective what should have been settled for all time by the Fourteenth and Fifteenth Amendments—the right of every qualified citizen to vote regardless of race.[7]

The struggle for the ballot had become an enduring one. The *Grovey* decision had neutralized the significance of the Fifteenth Amendment, and blacks were effectively excluded from voting in primary elections in the South.

The Hughes Court made it clear in 1937 that the poll tax was constitutional. In *Breedlove v. Suttles,* 302 U.S. 277 (1937), a white male citizen of Georgia challenged the state requirement that citizens between ages 21 and 60 pay a poll tax of $1. Women were exempt from the poll tax requirement. He argued that the Georgia law violated the equal protection clause of the Fourteenth Amendment and the Nineteenth Amendment. In a unanimous opinion written by Justice Butler, the Court rejected his claims. He found that, "To make payment of poll taxes a prerequisite of voting is not to deny any privilege or immunity protected by the Fourteenth Amendment." The Court established that states may condition suffrage as they deemed appropriate. Justice Butler offered the following rationale in upholding the exemption for women:

> The tax being upon persons, women may be exempted on the basis of special considerations to which they are naturally entitled. In view of burdens necessarily borne by them for the preservation of the race, the State reasonably may

exempt them from poll taxes. . . . The laws of Georgia declare the husband to be the head of the family and the wife to be subject to him. . . . To subject her to the levy would be to add to his burden. Moreover, Georgia poll taxes are laid to raise money for educational purposes, and it is the father's duty to provide for education of the children.

In 1940 the newly created Civil Rights Division of the Department of Justice brought criminal charges against Louisiana officials for violating §§ 19 and 20 of the Criminal Code for falsely counting and certifying ballots in a Louisiana congressional primary election. The government argued that the right of qualified voters to have their votes counted as cast was secured by Article I, §§ 2 and 4 of the Constitution and that a conspiracy to deprive citizens of that right violated §§ 19 and 20 of the Criminal Code. The Hughes Court agreed with the government's position in a 5-3 opinion written by Justice Stone (Chief Justice Hughes did not participate). In *United States v. Classic,* 313 U.S. 299 (1941), the Court overruled *Newberry v. United States* when it stated that "the authority of Congress, given by § 4, includes the authority to regulate primary elections when, as in this case, they are a step in the exercise by the people of their choice of representatives in Congress." Justice Stone also acknowledged:

> Moreover, we cannot close our eyes to the fact . . . that the practical influence of the choice of candidates at the primary may be so great as to affect profoundly the choice at the general election, even though there is no effective legal prohibition upon the rejection at the election of the choice made at the primary, and may thus operate to deprive the voter of his constitutional right of that choice.

Interestingly, the Court did not mention the decision of *Grovey* in *Classic,* although the Court's ruling appeared to undercut much of the *Grovey* rationale.

In the late 1930s, Thurgood Marshall worked as special counsel for the NAACP. When the NAACP Legal Defense and Education Fund, Inc., was created in 1939 to handle the association's legal work, Walter White asked Marshall to become its director-counsel.[8] Commonly referred to as "The Fund" or "LDF," it "was established separately from the NAACP to take advantage of new federal laws granting tax-exempt status to nonprofit organizations that did not have lobbying as their principle function."[9] Michael D. Davis and Hunter R. Clark, in their biography of Marshall, indicated that the charter and purpose of The Fund was

> to render free legal aid to Negroes who suffer legal injustice because of their race or color and cannot afford to employ legal assistance. To seek and promote educational opportunities denied to Negroes because of their color. To conduct research and publish information on educational facilities and inequalities furnished for Negroes out of public funds and on the status of the Negro in American life.[10]

Thurgood Marshall served as director-counsel for The Fund for 21 years, until he was appointed by President John F. Kennedy in 1961 to serve as judge on the U.S. Court of Appeals for the Second Circuit. Thurgood Marshall, William Hastie, and other Fund lawyers saw the *Classic* ruling as an opportunity to attack the constitutionality of the white primary.

SMITH V. ALLWRIGHT, 321 U.S. 649 (1944) was the vehicle of attack. In *Smith,* the Democratic Party adopted a resolution on May 24, 1932, stating that all white citizens in Texas were qualified to vote under the Constitution and laws of the state and were eligible for membership in the party. In overruling *Grovey v. Townsend* and nullifying the white primary practices in Texas, the Stone Court, in an 8-1 opinion, held that "when convinced of former error, this Court has never felt constrained to follow precedent." Justice Reed emphasized for the majority that it is state action within the meaning of the Fifteenth Amendment when "the party takes its character as a state agency" and "when primaries become a part of the machinery for choosing officials, state and national." After a protracted legal battle, the white primary was declared unconstitutional. Brisbane pointed out that three years after *Smith v. Allwright* the number of black registered voters in the South increased from fewer than 100,000 to 645,000. By 1952 the number had increased to one million.[11] Black political empowerment that is visible today had its origins in what transpired in 1944.

Black Americans would have to resort to the Court once again because white officials in Texas had devised yet another scheme to avoid the principle established in *Smith v. Allwright.* In 1889 the Jaybird Association was organized, and its membership was limited to white voters. The association had operated like a regular political party, and its candidates had always won in the primary and general elections. The association's elections were not governed by state laws, nor did they use the state elective machinery or funds. Black voters of Fort Bend County brought suit, alleging that the association excluded blacks from its primaries on racial grounds. The Jaybird Association denied that their exclusion violated the Fifteenth Amendment because it was a self-governing voluntary club. In an 8-1 plurality decision written by Justice Black and joined by Justices Douglas and Burton, the Vinson Court, in *Terry v. Adams,* 345 U.S. 461 (1953), found that the association's overriding purpose was to get around the command of the Fifteenth Amendment and to deny blacks a voice in governmental affairs solely on the basis of race. Black wrote the following:

> The only election that has counted in this Texas county for more than fifty years has been that held by the Jaybirds from which Negroes were excluded. The Democratic primary and the general election have become no more than the perfunctory ratifiers of the choice that has already been made in Jaybird elections from which Negroes have been excluded. It is immaterial that the state does not control that part of this elective process which it leaves for the Jaybirds to manage. The Jaybird primary has become an integral part, indeed, the only effective part, of the elective process that determines who shall rule and govern in the county. The effect of the whole procedure, Jaybird primary plus Democratic primary plus general election, is to do precisely that which the Fifteenth Amendment forbids—strip Negroes of every vestige of influence in selecting the officials who control the local county matters that intimately touch the daily lives of citizens.

The struggle for the ballot was far from over. The Fifteenth Amendment, ratified in 1870, should have been adequate. However, the cyclical win-lose-win scenario that was prevalent in other policy areas was alive and well in black Americans' quest to vote (see Table 2.1).

JIM CROW HOUSING
AND THE EMERGENCE
OF RESTRICTIVE COVENANTS

One of the most persistent problems facing blacks has been residential segregation. In taking legal action to enable them to live in the residential area of their choice, blacks consistently relied on the Fourteenth Amendment before the passage of Title VIII of the Fair Housing Act of 1968 and before resorting to the Civil Rights Act of 1866, after the landmark case of *Jones v. Alfred H. Mayer Co.,* 392 U.S. 409 (1968). The NAACP turned its attention to the problem by mounting a legal attack against racial zoning laws (see Table 2.2). In BUCHANAN V. WARLEY, 245 U.S. 60 (1917), the city of Louisville, Kentucky, passed an ordinance that established exclusive residential zones for blacks and whites. The White Court, in a unanimous opinion by Justice Day, decided that such an ordinance was not a legitimate exercise of the police power of the state and that it violated the due process clause of the Fourteenth Amendment. The argument that segregated neighborhoods will promote the public peace by preventing race conflict cannot be accomplished by ordinances that deny rights protected by the Constitution. In reality, *Buchanan* permitted whites to sell their homes without restrictions or interference.

Because the *Buchanan* decision established that blacks could not be prohibited from living in white residential areas, whites resorted to restrictive covenants to reverse this policy. In many communities, private agreements, called restrictive covenants, contained contractual language that bound successive purchasers not to lease or sell their property to anyone but members of their own racial or ethnic group. They were more common in Northern states. In *Corrigan v. Buckley,* 271 U.S. 323 (1926), a restrictive covenant was challenged by the NAACP. In a unanimous decision, the Taft Court ruled that the covenant was valid. Justice Sanford, writing for the Court, held that the Fifth Amendment was only a limitation on the powers of the federal government and that the Fourteenth Amendment's state action requirement does not reach action of private individuals. Moreover, he indicated that the Thirteenth Amendment does not protect the individual rights of blacks. Justice Sanford's ruling legalized restrictive covenants for the next two decades.

After World War II, the NAACP and The Fund launched another legal attack against restrictive covenants.[12] In SHELLEY V. KRAEMER, 334 U.S. 1 (1948) and the companion case *McGhee v. Sipes,* 334 U.S. 1 (1948), the Court rendered restrictive covenants unenforceable. In these cases, blacks from Missouri and Michigan, respectively, had purchased houses from whites

Table 2.1 First-Generation Voting Rights Cases

Case	Vote	Ruling
Guinn v. United States, 238 U.S. 347 (1915)	9-0	Chief Justice White declared the grandfather clause unconstitutional on Fifteenth Amendment grounds.
Newberry v. United States, 256 U.S. 232 (1921)	9-0	Justice McReynolds declared that Congress lacked authority, under Article 1, § 4 of the Constitution, to regulate primary elections.
Love v. Griffith, 266 U.S. 32 (1924)	9-0	Justice Holmes upheld a Texas court ruling that blacks could not challenge a white primary law because the election had been held; therefore, blacks' Fifteenth Amendment rights were not violated.
Nixon v. Herndon, 273 U.S. 536 (1927)	9-0	Justice Holmes declared the Texas white primary law unconstitutional under the Fourteenth Amendment.
Nixon v. Condon, 286 U.S. 73 (1932)	5-4	Justice Cardozo struck down a Texas law that gave the State Executive Committee power to proscribe voting qualifications, which it limited to white Democrats under the Fourteenth Amendment.
Grovey v. Townsend, 295 U.S. 45 (1935)	9-0	Justice Roberts declared that it is constitutional for a political party to restrict voting to whites in primaries so long as state action was not present.
Breedlove v. Suttles, 302 U.S. 277 (1937)	9-0	Justice Butler upheld a Georgia poll tax requirement that exempted women under the Fourteenth Amendment.
Lane v. Wilson, 307 U.S. 268 (1939)	6-2	Justice Frankfurter invalidated a new scheme enacted by the Oklahoma legislature to disfranchise black voters under the Fifteenth Amendment.
United States v. Classic, 313 U.S. 299 (1941)	5-3	Justice Stone overruled *Newberry v. United States* (1921) and declared that Congress had the authority to regulate primary elections.
Smith v. Allwright, 321 U.S. 649 (1944)	8-1	Justice Reed overruled *Grovey v. Townsend* (1935) under the Fifteenth Amendment.
Terry v. Adams, 345 U.S. 461 (1953)	8-1	Justice Black held that the Jaybird Association, a voluntary club that limited its membership to white voters, violated blacks' Fifteenth Amendment rights by excluding their participation in primaries.

Table 2.2 Restrictive Covenant Cases

Case	Vote	Ruling
Buchanan v. Warley, 245 U.S. 60 (1917)	9-0	Justice Day struck down, on Fourteenth Amendment grounds, a Kentucky ordinance that established segregated neighborhoods for whites and blacks.
Corrigan v. Buckley, 271 U.S. 323 (1926)	9-0	Justice Sanford upheld the validity of a restrictive covenant in the District of Columbia.
Benjamin v. Tyler, 273 U.S. 668 (1927)	per curiam	The Supreme Court struck down restrictive covenants on the authority of *Buchanan v. Warley*.
City of Richmond v. Deans, 281 U.S. 704 (1930)	per curiam	The Supreme Court struck down restrictive covenants on the authority of *Buchanan v. Warley*.
Shelley v. Kraemer and *McGhee v. Sipes*, 334 U.S. 1 (1948)	9-0	Chief Justice Vinson rendered restrictive covenants unenforceable under the Fourteenth Amendment.
Hurd v. Hodge, 334 U.S. 24 (1948)	9-0	The Supreme Court declared that the judicial enforcement of restrictive covenants in the District of Columbia violated the Civil Rights Act of 1866 and was inconsistent with United States public policy.
Barrows v. Jackson, 346 U.S. 249 (1953)	6-1	Justice Minton ruled that an individual could not be sued for damages for failing to observe restrictive covenants.

whose properties were subject to restrictive covenants. The owners of other properties that were subject to the covenants sued to prevent the blacks from taking possession. In *Shelley* Chief Justice Vinson, writing for a unanimous Court, held that the state may not give discriminatory acts of private individuals the force of law. In his words, "The action of state courts and judicial officers in their official capacities is to be regarded as action of the State within the meaning of the Fourteenth Amendment." On the same day that *Shelley* was decided, the Court unanimously declared, in *Hurd v. Hodge*, 334 U.S. 24 (1948), that the judicial enforcement of restrictive covenants in the District of Columbia violated the Civil Rights Act of 1866 and was inconsistent with United States public policy.

The final blow to restrictive covenants came five years later, in *Barrows v. Jackson*, 346 U.S. 249 (1953). In *Barrows*, the Vinson Court, in a 6-1 opinion written by Justice Minton, made it clear that an individual could not be sued for damages for failing to observe restrictive covenants. The majority also emphasized that if damage judgments were allowed, prospective sellers would not sell their property to nonwhites. *Shelley* and *Barrows* removed the legal enforceability of restrictive covenants. These decisions, however, did not lessen discriminatory practices in the housing market in the North or the South. Eradicating these deeply entrenched practices was one of the major challenges facing the Warren Court.

RACE AND THE
ADMINISTRATION OF JUSTICE:
THE DAWNING OF HOPE

Violence and racial tension often resulted when blacks attempted to secure racial justice. Racial violence in the form of lynching thrived until the 1940s, although sporadic sensational incidents continued. Mary Frances Berry noted, "From 1901 to 1910, 846 persons were lynched in the United States. Of this number, 92 were white and 754 were black. Ninety percent of the lynchings took place in the South. Congress and the president took no action to prevent lynchings, and state governments did not prosecute the perpetrators, even when the event was publicized at least a day in advance."[13] Race riots, jailhouse riots, racial murder, and mob action erupted during the first two decades of the 20th century in Atlanta (1906); Brownsville, Texas (1906); Springfield, Illinois (1908); East St. Louis, Illinois (1917); Houston (1917); Charleston, South Carolina (1919); Chicago (1919); Knoxville, Tennessee (1919); Omaha (1919); Philips County, Arkansas (1919); Washington, D.C. (1919); New York (1943); Detroit (1943); and Los Angeles (1943). Antilynching legislation was never passed by Congress. During the 1930s, black Americans turned to the Fourteenth Amendment's due process clause, in several landmark criminal cases, in their quest for racial justice against official abuse. The pendulum began to swing painfully slowly toward "Equal Justice Under Law" for blacks who were caught up in the criminal justice system.

The Right to Counsel: The Scottsboro Case

In the celebrated case POWELL V. ALABAMA, 287 U.S. 45 (1932), the Court for the first time made it clear that the appointment of counsel by state courts is essential to due process of law in those cases where lack of representation would result in an unfair trial. In *Powell* nine black youths were accused of raping two white women in Scottsboro, Alabama. Because of the intense hostility by a crowd of whites, the sheriff called on the militia to safeguard the prisoners, who were not provided counsel in any real sense. All except one of the defendants received the death penalty. The Hughes Court, in a 7-2 opinion written by Justice Sutherland, held that the defendants' illiteracy, combined with their youthfulness, public hostility, and the fact that they were separated from their families and friends, made the assistance of counsel a necessity even if the accused had not requested it. The defendants therefore had been denied their rights, in violation of the due process clause of the Fourteenth Amendment, and a new trial was ordered. The defense team, made up of the NAACP, the ACLU, and the International Labor Defense, was successful in freeing most of the defendants in the case, which received worldwide attention.

Discrimination in the Selection of Juries

During the 1930s and 1940s, the Supreme Court addressed several cases involving the systematic and discriminatory exclusion of black grand and petit jurors in criminal cases, especially where the death sentence was involved. In each of these cases, the Court established that the exclusion of blacks from grand and petit juries violates the equal protection clause of the Fourteenth Amendment. In two cases brought to the Hughes Court by the NAACP, the Court, in a per curiam opinion in *Hollins v. Oklahoma,* 295 U.S. 394 (1935) and in *Hale v. Kentucky,* 303 U.S. 613 (1938), held that blacks had been excluded from jury service in violation of equal protection of the laws and reversed the black criminal defendants' convictions.

In the second Scottsboro case, *Norris v. Alabama,* 294 U.S. 587 (1935), the question before the Hughes Court was whether the systematic exclusion of blacks from jury service solely on the basis of race violated the Fourteenth Amendment's equal protection clause. Although some blacks were qualified for jury duty, for more than a generation none had served on any jury in Jackson County, where Clarence Norris had been indicted. In Morgan County, where the trial was held, no black had ever served on a jury within the memory of witnesses who were called to testify. Chief Justice Hughes, in an 8-0 opinion (Justice McReynolds did not participate), contended that the systematic and arbitrary exclusion of blacks from jury service was violative of the equal protection clause. For Chief Justice Hughes, the evidence was compelling:

> We think this evidence failed to rebut the strong *prima facie* case which defendant had made. That showing as to the long-continued exclusion of negroes from jury service, and as to the many negroes qualified for that service, could not be met by mere generalities. . . . The general attitude of the jury commissioner is shown by the following extract from his testimony: "I do not know of any negro in Morgan County over twenty-one and under sixty-five who is generally reputed to be honest and intelligent and who is esteemed in the community for his integrity, good character and sound judgment, who is not an habitual drunkard, who isn't afflicted with a permanent disease or physical weakness which would render him unfit to discharge the duties of a juror, and who can read English, and who has never been convicted of a crime involving moral turpitude." In the light of the testimony given by defendant's witnesses, we find it impossible to accept such a sweeping characterization of the lack of qualifications of negroes in Morgan County. It is so sweeping, and so contrary to the evidence as to the many qualified negroes, that it destroys the intended effect of the commissioner's testimony.

Approximately 18 years after the original Scottsboro trial, the last of the Scottsboro defendants had been released. Dan Carter, a history professor at Emory University, points out that Norris, the last surviving defendant, jumped parole twice between 1944 and 1946. He captures the crux of the final saga to the American tragedy in these words: "Clarence . . . Norris . . . was sitting in a Harlem bar when an excited friend burst in with the news that Governor George Wallace had signed a 'full and unconditional pardon' restoring his civil rights."[14]

In *Pierre v. Louisiana,* 306 U.S. 354 (1939), the Hughes Court overturned a conviction of a black man for the murder of a white man on the basis that between 1896 and 1936 no black had served on grand or petit juries in the parish of St. John and that only one had served in 1936. In a unanimous opinion, Justice Black stated, "Indictment by Grand Jury and trial by jury cease to harmonize with our traditional concepts of justice at the very moment particular groups, classes or races—otherwise qualified to serve as jurors in a community—are excluded as such from jury service." In another unanimous opinion written by Justice Black, the Hughes Court, in *Smith v. Texas,* 311 U.S. 128 (1940), struck down the rape conviction of a black man on Fourteenth Amendment grounds. The evidence indicated that between 1931 and 1938 only 5 black grand jurors out of 584 grand jurors had ever served, despite the fact that blacks in Harris County, Texas, constituted 20% of the population and that 3,000 to 6,000 were qualified for jury service. The Stone Court, in *Hill v. Texas,* 316 U.S. 400 (1942), relied on *Smith v. Texas* when it unanimously held that the jury commissioners failed to perform their constitutional duty under § 4 of the Civil Rights Act of 1875 and the command of *Neal v. Delaware,* 103 U.S. (13 Otto) 370 (1880) when it excluded jurors on racial grounds. And in *Patton v. Mississippi,* 332 U.S. 463 (1947), Justice Black, writing for a unanimous Court, overturned the conviction of a black man indicted by an all-white grand jury and convicted by an all-white petit jury on the basis of the evidence that no black had served on grand or petit juries in Lauderdale County, Mississippi, for 30 years. For Justice Black, this evidence created a strong presumption that blacks were systematically denied jury service, in violation of the equal protection clause.

In *Aldridge v. United States,* 238 U.S. 308 (1931), a black man was sentenced to death for murdering a white police officer in the District of Columbia. Aldridge's attorney was not permitted by the court to ask the jurors during the voir dire examination whether they had any racial prejudice against blacks. Chief Justice Hughes, in reversing the lower court's decision, held that the reality of racial prejudice cannot justify "forbidding the inquiry," especially "when the issue of life or death" is involved. He also contended that the justice system would fall into disrepute if persons with racial prejudice were allowed to serve on a jury.

Blatant discriminatory practices continued in other states as if the Supreme Court had not addressed the problem of jury discrimination. For example, the names of prospective white and black jurors in one Georgia county were printed on white and yellow tickets, respectively, and placed together in a jury box. A judge then drew a specified number of tickets from the box. Chief Justice Vinson, writing for the unanimous Court in *Avery v. Georgia,* 345 U.S. 559 (1953), declared that the use of white and yellow tickets made it very easy for individuals who were prone to discriminate to do so. Moreover, because no black had been chosen from a panel of 60, a prima facie case of discrimination in the selection of a jury had been made by the petitioner.

Coerced Confessions and the Use of Excessive Force

The NAACP also was active in securing racial justice for those blacks accused of crime. One example from 1919 involved mob action in Phillips County, Arkansas, where white landlords with guns attacked black sharecroppers who were meeting at a church to discuss allegations of peonage against the landlords. Several blacks and one white man were killed. A race riot then ensued, during which white residents killed more than 200 blacks. Although no whites were prosecuted, 12 blacks, after a trial that lasted less than an hour, were convicted and sentenced to death for murdering a white deputy. Frank Moore and five other blacks appealed their convictions to the Supreme Court. In *Moore v. Dempsey,* 261 U.S. 86 (1923), the Taft Court, in a 6-2 opinion written by Justice Holmes (Justice Clarke did not participate), ordered a habeas corpus hearing held because a mob-dominated trial violated the due process clause of the Fourteenth Amendment.

Thirteen years later, the Court for the first time decided that the due process clause of the Fourteenth Amendment prohibited states from using an accused's coerced confession against him. In *Brown v. Mississippi,* 297 U.S. 278 (1936), a black man was brutally beaten and hanged twice before he confessed to a crime. He had been informed that unless he confessed to the crime, the brutality would continue. The Hughes Court held that such revolting methods to obtain a confession were a clear denial of due process of law. Chief Justice Hughes, writing for the unanimous Court, stated, "The rack and torture chamber may not be substituted for the witness stand." Four years after *Brown v. Mississippi,* a second landmark decision involving coerced confessions was rendered by the Hughes Court in *Chambers v. Florida,* 309 U.S. 227 (1940). In this case, an elderly white man was robbed and murdered in Pompano, Florida, on May 13, 1933. Approximately 30 minutes after the murder, Charles Davis, a black man, was arrested, and during the next 24 hours another 30 to 40 blacks were arrested without warrants and carried to the county jail. They underwent persistent and repeated questioning for several days and nights before confessions were obtained. The last night was referred to as the "all night vigil." The defendants were not permitted to see relatives or counsel. The Court, in a unanimous opinion written by Justice Black, held that the dragnet methods of arrest and protracted questioning were "calculated to break the strongest nerves and the stoutest resistance" and were therefore a violation of the due process clause of the Fourteenth Amendment. Justice Black, who formerly had been a member of the Ku Klux Klan for three years, emphasized that the law enforcement methods that were employed were not necessary to uphold our laws.

One of the few cases that Thurgood Marshall lost before the high court involved a coerced confession. In *Lyons v. Oklahoma,* 322 U.S. 596 (1944), W. D. Lyons, a black man, was convicted and sentenced to life imprisonment for murdering a white family and setting their home afire to conceal the crime. Marshall, who argued the case at trial, sought to overturn the conviction on the grounds that the officials had beaten and coerced Lyons into signing a confession. In a 6-3 opinion written by Justice Reed, the Court affirmed Lyons's conviction on the ground that "the Fourteenth Amendment does not protect one who has admitted guilt because of forbidden inducements against the use at trial of his subsequent confessions under all possible circumstances." According to the majority, the evidence in the case indicated that the confession was voluntary and therefore not violative of due process.

The following year, the Stone Court was confronted with another case involving the use of excessive force and police brutality. In SCREWS V. UNITED STATES, 325 U.S. 91 (1945), Claude Screws, the sheriff of Baker County, Georgia, and another policeman arrested Robert Hall, a black man, for stealing a tire. He was brutally beaten for more than 20 minutes while handcuffed and died without regaining consciousness. The defendants were convicted under § 20 (now § 242 of § 18 U.S.C.) for violating Hall's federal due process rights by officials acting under color of law. The Court, in a 5-4 plurality opinion, interpreted § 20 narrowly to avoid the vagueness problem by requiring specific intent to deprive a person of a federal right. Five justices, however, decided that Screws should be granted a new trial because the question of intent was not submitted to the jury with the proper instructions. He was acquitted at the second trial.

Blacks and the Death Penalty

Two years after the *Screws* decision, the Court decided LOUISIANA EX REL. FRANCIS V. RESWEBER, 329 U.S. 459 (1947), a very unusual case. Willie Francis, a black man, was convicted of murder in Louisiana in 1945 and was sentenced to be electrocuted. The executioner flipped the switch, but death did not occur because of a mechanical failure. Francis was returned to prison, and the governor issued a new death warrant for execution on May 9, 1946. Counsel claimed that, under the circumstances, Francis was denied due process because of the Fifth Amendment's double jeopardy provision. Counsel also claimed that his Eighth Amendment's protection against cruel and unusual punishments had been denied because he had received a current of electricity. Justice Reed, writing for the 5-4 plurality, declared, "When an accident with no suggestion of malevolence, prevents the consummation of a sentence" the double jeopardy provision of the Fifth Amendment has not been violated. Moreover, the cruel and unusual punishments provision was not violated because there was no intent to inflict unnecessary pain. Justice Burton dissented: "While five applications would be more cruel and unusual than one, the uniqueness of the present case demonstrates that, today, two separated

Table 2.3 Discrimination and the Administration of Justice Cases

Case	Vote	Ruling
Moore v. Dempsey, 261 U.S. 86 (1923)	6-2	Justice Holmes ordered a habeas corpus hearing held because a mob-dominated trial violated the due process clause of the Fourteenth Amendment.
Aldridge v. United States, 283 U.S. 308 (1931)	8-1	Chief Justice Hughes reversed a lower court's ruling that prohibited counsel for a black defendant accused of murdering a white police officer from asking jurors during the voir dire examination whether they had any racial prejudice against blacks.
Powell v. Alabama, 287 U.S. 45 (1932)	7-2	Justice Sutherland held that the Scottsboro Boys' due process rights were violated when they were denied the appointment of counsel after being tried and convicted of raping two white women.
Norris v. Alabama, 294 U.S. 587 (1935)	8-0	Chief Justice Hughes held in the second Scottsboro Boys' case that the systematic and arbitrary exclusion of blacks from jury service violated the equal protection clause.
Hollins v. Oklahoma, 295 U.S. 394 (1935)	per curiam	The Supreme Court held that blacks had been excluded from jury service, in violation of the equal protection clause.
Brown v. Mississippi, 297 U.S. 278 (1936)	9-0	Chief Justice Hughes declared that the due process clause of the Fourteenth Amendment prohibited coerced confessions.
Hale v. Kentucky, 303 U.S. 613 (1938)	per curiam	The Supreme Court held that the exclusion of blacks from jury service violates the equal protection clause.
Pierre v. Louisiana, 306 U.S. 354 (1939)	9-0	Justice Black overturned the conviction of a black defendant on the ground that blacks had been excluded from service on grand and petit juries.
Chambers v. Florida, 309 U.S. 227 (1940)	9-0	Justice Black held that coerced confessions violated the due process clause of the Fourteenth Amendment.
Smith v. Texas, 311 U.S. 128 (1940)	9-0	Justice Black struck down the rape conviction of a black defendant on the ground that blacks were excluded from serving on grand juries.
Hill v. Texas, 316 U.S. 400 (1942)	9-0	The Supreme Court held that jury commissioners failed to perform their constitutional duty under § 4 of the Civil Rights Act of 1875 and the command of *Neal v. Delaware* (1880) when they excluded jurors on racial grounds.
Lyons v. Oklahoma, 322 U.S. 596 (1944)	6-3	Justice Reed upheld the conviction of a black man sentenced to life imprisonment for murdering a white family and setting fire to their home, on the ground that the confession was voluntary and not violative of due process.
Screws v. United States, 325 U.S. 91 (1945)	5-4	Justice Douglas interpreted §20 (now §242) that although police officers acted under color of law when they brutally beat a black man who died, they misused their power by using excessive force in making the arrest.

Table 2.3 *continued*

Case	Vote	Ruling
Akins v. Texas, 325 U.S. 398 (1945)	6-3	Justice Reed rejected claims by a black defendant who alleged arbitrary and purposeful discrimination by grand jury commissioners despite the fact that only one black had served on the grand jury.
Patton v. Mississippi, 332 U.S. 463 (1947)	9-0	Justice Black overturned the conviction of a black man indicted by an all-white grand jury and convicted by an all-white petit jury on the ground that no black had served on grand or petit juries in Lauderdale County for 30 years.
Louisiana ex rel. Francis v. Resweber, 329 U.S. 459 (1947)	5-4	Justice Reed held that the cruel and unusual punishments provision was not violated when, during the execution of a black man, death did not occur due to a mechanical failure and a new death warrant for execution was issued.
Cassell v. Texas, 339 U.S. 282 (1950)	7-1	The Supreme Court reversed the murder conviction of a black man on the ground that statements made by the jury commissioners that they chose only jurors whom they knew and that they knew no blacks in an area where blacks made up so large a proportion of the population proved intentional discrimination.
Avery v. Georgia, 345 U.S. 559 (1953)	9-0	Chief Justice Vinson declared that the practice of putting the names of prospective white and black jurors on white and yellow tickets, respectively, and placing them into a jury box constituted discrimination.

applications are sufficiently 'cruel and unusual' to be prohibited. If five attempts would be 'cruel and unusual,' it would be difficult to draw the line between two, three, four and five."

UNITED STATES V. CAROLENE PRODUCTS CO. AND THE FAMOUS FOOTNOTE 4: THE BIRTH OF DISCRETE AND INSULAR MINORITIES

Cases similar to *Screws v. United States* and *Brown v. Mississippi* sensitized the Justices of the Supreme Court to the senseless cruelty that blacks faced, especially in the South. Because Southern blacks, for the most part, were disfranchised, their chances of improving their dismal plight through electoral politics was out of the picture. Ultraconservative senators and even the executive branch of government were indifferent and, in many instances, hostile to their quest for racial equality. The answer to this seemingly intractable problem was to be found in the famous Footnote 4 that Justice Stone

BOX 2.2

United States v. Carolene Products Co.:
Footnote 4

There may be narrower scope for operation of the presumption of constitutionality when legislation appears on its face to be within a specific prohibition of the Constitution, such as those of the first ten amendments, which are deemed equally specific when held to be embraced within the Fourteenth. See *Stromberg v. California,* 283 U.S. 359, 369-370 [1931]; *Lovell v. Griffin,* 303 U.S. 444, 452 [1938].

It is unnecessary to consider now whether legislation which restricts those political processes which can ordinarily be expected to bring about repeal of undesirable legislation, is to be subjected to more exacting judicial scrutiny under the general prohibitions of the Fourteenth Amendment than are most other types of legislation. On restrictions upon the right to vote, see *Nixon v. Herndon,* 273 U.S. 536 [1927]; *Nixon v. Condon,* 286 U.S. 73 [1932]; on restraints upon the dissemination of information, see *Near v. Minnesota ex rel. Olson,* 283 U.S. 697, 713-714, 718-720, 722 [1931]; *Grosjean v. American Press Co.,* 297 U.S. 233 [1936]; *Lovell v. Griffin, supra;* on interferences with political organizations, see *Stromberg v. California, supra,* 369; *Fiske v. Kansas,* 274 U.S. 380 [1927]; *Whitney v. California,* 274 U.S. 357, 373-378 [1927]; *Herndon v. Lowry,* 301 U.S. 242 [1937]; and see Holmes, J., in *Gitlow v. New York,* 268 U.S. 652, 673 [1925]; as to prohibition of peaceable assembly, see *De Jonge v. Oregon,* 299 U.S. 353, 365 [1937].

Nor need we enquire whether similar considerations enter into the review of statutes directed at particular religious, *Pierce v. Society of Sisters,* 268 U.S. 510 [1925], or national, *Meyer v. Nebraska,* 262 U.S. 390 [1923]; *Bartels v. Iowa,* 262 U.S. 404 [1923]; *Farrington v. Tokushige,* 273 U.S. 284 [1927], or racial minorities, *Nixon v. Herndon, supra; Nixon v. Condon, supra:* whether prejudice against discrete and insular minorities may be a special condition, which tends seriously to curtail the operation of those political processes ordinarily to be relied upon to protect minorities, and which may call for a correspondingly more searching judicial inquiry. Compare *McCulloch v. Maryland,* 4 Wheat. 316, 428 [1819]; *South Carolina v. Barnwell Bros.,* 303 U.S. 177, 184, n. 2 [1938], and cases cited.

formulated in the well-known case of *United States v. Carolene Products Co.,* 304 U.S. 144 (1938) (see Box 2.2). This footnote has become the most important one even when compared with the landmark Footnote 11 in the *Brown v. Board of Education* (*Brown I*), 347 U.S. 483 (1954) decision. A novel jurisprudence was in its embryonic stage of development, and racial and ethnic minorities would be its recipients.[15] A legal weapon had been devised that would transform the constitutional order in the area of civil liberties.

In *Carolene Products,* the Filled Milk Act of 1923 forbade the shipment of skimmed milk compounded with fat or oils in interstate commerce. The Carolene Company was indicted for shipping filled milk, in violation of the Act. The Court upheld the Act under Congress' constitutional authority to regulate interstate commerce. Prior to Footnote 4, the Supreme Court had applied deferential scrutiny or the rational basis test to legislation. If the statutory classification was reasonably related to the legislature's purpose, the statute was upheld. There is a presumption of constitutionality behind such laws. The constitutional significance of Footnote 4 lies in its justification for a higher degree of scrutiny, or strict scrutiny, against legislation that discriminates against discrete and insular minorities. Each paragraph offers such a justification. For example, paragraph one suggests that legislation may be presumed unconstitutional if it conflicts with the Bill of Rights. Paragraph two suggests that greater scrutiny will be used against legislation that restricts the right to vote or restricts political organizations, the dissemination of information, and the right to assembly. Paragraph three suggests that greater scrutiny will be directed against legislation that discriminates against religious, national, and racial minorities because they are incapable of using the political process to their advantage. The double standard emerged from *Carolene Products;* that is, the Court signaled its willingness to employ deferential scrutiny in the economic realm and a greater degree of scrutiny in the areas of civil liberties and civil rights. A few months after *Carolene Products* was decided, the Hughes Court was presented with an opportunity to apply this approach in a case involving segregation in higher education. See *Missouri ex rel. Gaines v. Canada,* 305 U.S. 337 (1939), discussed below.

The Emergence of Strict Scrutiny and a Two-Tiered Approach to Equal Protection: The Japanese Internment Cases

In the cases of *Hirabayashi v. United States,* 320 U.S. 81 (1943) and KOREMATSU V. UNITED STATES, 323 U.S. 214 (1944), the Stone Court made it abundantly clear that racial distinctions were suspect classifications. The novel jurisprudence was indeed operational. In *Hirabayashi,* Executive Order 9066 required all persons of Japanese ancestry in specific military areas of the West Coast to remain in their residences from 8:00 p.m. to 6:00 a.m. The Court, in a unanimous decision, sustained Gordon Hirabayashi's conviction for violating the curfew. Chief Justice Stone, writing for the Court, stated, "Distinctions between citizens solely because of their ancestry are by their nature odious to a free people whose institutions are founded upon the doctrine of equality. For that reason, legislative classification or discrimination based on race alone" is a denial of equal protection. However, the Stone Court deferred to Congress and the executive's judgment that there were disloyal members within the Japanese American community and upheld their actions on the basis of national security reasons. Justice Murphy, in his concurring opinion, observed that the curfew order "bears a melancholy resemblance to the treatment accorded to members of the Jewish race in Germany and in other parts of Europe. The result is the creation in this country of two classes of citizens for the purposes of a critical and perilous hour—to sanction discrimination between groups of United States citizens on the basis of ancestry. In my opinion, this goes to the very brink of constitutional power."

One year later, in *Korematsu,* Fred Korematsu, an American citizen of Japanese ancestry, was convicted in a federal district court for remaining in a military area, in violation of Civilian Exclusion Order No. 34, which directed all Japanese to be excluded from such areas. This order resulted in the detention of 112,000 Americans of Japanese ancestry. Justice Black, writing for the 6-3 majority, delineated the standard to be used in cases involving the classification of racial minorities. He stated, "It should be noted, to begin with, that all legal restrictions which curtail the civil rights of a single racial group are immediately suspect. That is not to say that all such restrictions are unconstitutional. It is to say that courts must subject them to the most rigid scrutiny." Despite the enunciation of the strict scrutiny standard, Justice Black found that Civilian Exclusion Order No. 34 was constitutional when Fred Korematsu violated it. For Justice Black, the military urgency of the situation, and not racism, was the motivation behind the majority's decision. The dissenters—Justices Roberts, Murphy, and Jackson—argued that the curfew order at issue in *Hirabayashi* was quite different from the internment order presented in *Korematsu.* They all recognized that the deprivation of liberty in the *Korematsu* case was racist. Justice Murphy challenged the credibility of the military's evidence that suggested group disloyalty, as opposed to individual disloyalty. He also noted that similar disloyal activities were also engaged in by Americans of German and Italian descent but that they were not treated in the same manner as Japanese Americans.

The Stone Court broke new ground when it held, in *Hirabayashi* and *Korematsu,* that racial classifications must be subjected to the most rigid scrutiny and held unconstitutional unless they are narrowly tailored and are necessary to accomplish a compelling state interest or objective. The real tragedy of the rulings was that about 120,000 Japanese Americans on the West Coast lost their homes, their jobs, and their liberty and were ordered to internment camps in the interior of the country for an indefinite period and without evidence of individual disloyalty or other unlawful conduct. The sole basis for this action was race. Peter Irons uncovered federal records indicating that the federal government had suppressed evidence in the cases and had deliberately misled the Supreme Court on the issue of military necessity for the evacuation. The cases of Gordon Hirabayashi and Fred Korematsu were reopened through a little-used legal procedure, *coram nobis,* which is available to criminal defendants whose trials had been tainted by fundamental error or manifest injustice.[16] Federal courts vacated their convictions, and a court of appeals ruling held that General John L. DeWitt was a racist and that his military orders were based on racism.[17] The government lawyers declined to appeal the case to the Supreme Court.

EQUAL PROTECTION
AND HIGHER EDUCATION:
THE BEGINNING OF THE DEMISE OF
THE SEPARATE-BUT-EQUAL DOCTRINE

Thirty-one years after *Plessy,* the Taft Court reaffirmed the separate-but-equal principle in public education in a case involving Chinese ancestry. In *Gong Lum v. Rice,* 275 U.S. 78 (1927), the Court ruled, in a unanimous opinion, that a child of Chinese descent could be required to attend a black school in Mississippi under the separate-but-equal doctrine. "Colored" was interpreted by the Court to mean everyone except whites, and excluding Chinese students from white schools was not a violation of equal protection.

Thurgood Marshall, Charles H. Houston, William H. Hastie, and other NAACP legal staff members had mounted a campaign designed to chip away at the separate-but-equal principle in education, beginning with higher education.[18] In the 1930s, black Americans were seeking admission to graduate and professional schools, and the separate-but-equal doctrine was being tested time and time again. In MISSOURI EX REL. GAINES V. CANADA, 305 U.S. 337 (1938), the Hughes Court examined with care the "equal" part of the separate-but-equal formula and held that Lloyd Gaines must be admitted to the state university's law school because there was no separate law school for blacks. Cash grants from Missouri to black applicants to attend law school in one of the adjacent states was beside the point. The fundamental consideration boiled down to "what opportunities Missouri itself furnishes to white students and denies to negroes solely upon the ground of color." It should be noted that Lloyd Gaines disappeared mysteriously after his legal victory and was never found.

Ten years later, in *Sipuel v. Board of Regents of the University of Oklahoma,* 332 U.S. 631 (1948), the Vinson Court, in a per curiam opinion, reaffirmed *Gaines* and ordered that Ada Lois Sipuel be admitted to the University of Oklahoma School of Law because there was no separate law school for blacks. In later action, the Oklahoma Supreme Court directed officials to open a black law school in three rooms of the state capitol. Students had access to the state law library, and officials hired three white attorneys as faculty to the law school.[19] According to Tushnet's account, NAACP lawyers invoked a rarely used procedure to compel compliance with Supreme Court rulings. Thurgood Marshall "filed a motion for permission to file a petition for an order directing the Oklahoma courts to comply with the original decision by ordering Sipuel's admission to the white law school."[20] In *Fisher v. Hurst,* 333 U.S. 147 (1948), the Supreme Court, in a per curiam opinion, refused to grant the request on the grounds that *Sipuel* did not present the issue of whether a state might satisfy the Fourteenth Amendment by establishing a separate school for blacks. According to the Court, the Oklahoma courts had jurisdiction over the issue.

Two years later, the Vinson Court was confronted with a case involving a black male student, G. W. McLaurin, who was interested in working toward a Ph.D. in education. The Oklahoma legislature and the University of Oklahoma worked out a very peculiar arrangement whereby blacks could take courses on a segregated basis that were not available elsewhere in the state. However, McLaurin was admitted with certain restrictions. For example, he was required to sit at a designated desk in an anteroom that adjoined the classroom and at a designated desk in the library, and he had to eat at a designated table in the cafeteria at a different time from the other students. In the landmark case of McLAURIN V. OKLAHOMA STATE REGENTS FOR HIGHER EDUCATION, 339 U.S. 637 (1950), a unanimous Court held that the segregated graduate instruction deprived McLaurin of "his personal and present right to the equal protection of the laws."

In SWEATT V. PAINTER, 339 U.S. 629 (1950), which was decided on the same day as *McLaurin,* Heman Sweatt applied for admission to the University of Texas Law School because there was no separate law school for blacks in the state. The state took quick action to establish a law school for blacks in Houston and also worked diligently to set up a temporary law school in the basement of a building in Austin (the permanent law school was to be located in Houston). Sweatt refused to enroll in the makeshift law school on the ground that to do so would be a clear denial of equal protection. Chief Justice Vinson, writing for a unanimous Court, emphasized that intangibles that make for greatness in a law school were lacking in the law school for blacks. Such intangibles included the reputation of the faculty, the experience of the administration, and the influence of the alumni and traditions. The Chief Justice ordered that Sweatt be admitted to the University of Texas Law School because at the law school for blacks he could not receive a legal education equivalent to that offered to white students.

The Introduction of Social Science Evidence:
A First for an Education Case

Sweatt v. Painter was the first case involving education that contained testimony of a sociological nature. Professor Robert Redfield, Chairman of the Anthropology Department and former Dean of the Social Sciences at the University of Chicago, presented testimony in the lower court on behalf of the black plaintiff. This testimony became part of the record and centered around the question of whether there were differences between blacks and whites in the intellectual capacity to learn. His opinion was expressed in these words:

> The conclusion . . . to which I come, is differences in intellectual capacity or inability to learn have not been shown to exist as between Negroes and whites, and further, that the results make it very probable that if such differences are later shown to exist, they will not prove to be significant for any educational policy or practice.[21]

To the question regarding the effects of segregation on the student, a subject later amplified in the public school cases, Redfield replied:

> My opinion is that segregation has effects on the student which are unfavorable to the full realization of the objectives of education. First,—for a number of reasons, perhaps I will try to distinguish. Speaking first with regard to the student, I would say that in the first place it prevents the student from the full, effective and economical coming to understand the nature and capacity of the group from which he is segregated. My comment, therefore, applies to both whites and Negroes, and as one of the objectives of education is the full and sympathetic understanding of the principal groups in the system in which the individual is to function as a citizen, this result which I have just stated is unfortunate.
>
> In the second place I would say that segregation has an unfortunate effect on the student . . . [and] has an unfortunate effect on the general community, in that it intensifies suspicion and distrust between Negroes and whites, and suspicion and distrust are not favorable conditions either for the acquisition and conduct of an education, or for the discharge of the duties of a citizen.[22]

The Supreme Court had cleverly employed an incrementalist strategy in cases involving higher education. This ingenious approach would result in less overt white resistance to the decisions that favored black Americans. Moreover, the Court's legitimacy would remain intact. The separate-but-equal doctrine was crumbling under its own weight, and the fatal blow was just a matter of time (see Table 2.4). The Stone and Vinson Courts set the stage for the eventual attack on segregation in the nation's primary and secondary public schools. Legal scholars could not predict the date and year of the *Brown* decision, but they could predict its outcome.

THE THRILL OF VICTORY
OVER JIM CROW IN INTERSTATE
TRAVEL AND PUBLIC ACCOMMODATIONS

Prior to the 1940s, the separate-but-equal principle was alive and well in the area of public accommodations and interstate travel. Laws providing for separate accommodations often imposed a financial burden on railroad companies that were required to provide separate facilities for blacks and whites. In 1907, Oklahoma passed the Separate Coach Law, which provided that railroad companies maintain separate coaches for whites and blacks. Five black citizens sought an injunction against the railway company to prevent the law from taking effect. In *McCabe v. Atchison, Topeka & Santa Fe Railway Company,* 235 U.S. 151 (1914), the Court, in a unanimous opinion written by Justice Hughes, found that the Oklahoma law applied exclusively to intrastate commerce and did not violate the commerce clause. Nor did the law violate the Fourteenth Amendment under *Plessy v. Ferguson.* The Court did reject, however, the railroad's argument that it had to provide accommodations only for whites because of insufficient use by blacks.

Table 2.4 Equal Protection and the Beginning of the Demise of Separate-but-Equal: Cases

Case	Vote	Ruling
Gong Lum v. Rice, 275 U.S. 78 (1927)	9-0	The Supreme Court ruled that a child of Chinese descent could be required to attend a black school under the separate-but-equal doctrine.
United States v. Carolene Products Co., 304 U.S. 144 (1938)	4-3	The Supreme Court, in Footnote 4, signaled its willingness to apply a greater degree of scrutiny in the areas of civil liberties and civil rights.
Missouri ex rel. Gaines v. Canada, 305 U.S. 337 (1938)	6-2	The Supreme Court ruled, under the separate-but-equal doctrine, that Gaines must be admitted to the state university's law school because there was no separate law school for blacks.
Hirabayashi v. United States, 320 U.S. 81 (1943)	9-0	While sustaining Hirabayashi's conviction for violating a military curfew, the Supreme Court declared that legislative classification based on race is a denial of equal protection.
Korematsu v. United States, 323 U.S. 214 (1944)	6-3	While upholding Civilian Exclusion Order No. 34, Justice Black delineated the standard to be used in cases involving the classification of racial minorities—strict scrutiny.
Sipuel v. Board of Regents of the University of Oklahoma, 332 U.S. 631 (1948)	per curiam	The Supreme Court reaffirmed *Missouri ex rel. Canada v. Gaines* (1938) and ordered that Sipuel be admitted to the state's law school because there was no separate law school for blacks.
Fisher v. Hurst, 333 U.S. 147 (1948)	per curiam	The Supreme Court refused to grant the NAACP lawyers' request for an order directing the Oklahoma courts to comply with the *Sipuel* ruling on the ground that *Sipuel* did not present the issue of whether a state might satisfy the Fourteenth Amendment by establishing a separate school for blacks.
McLaurin v. Oklahoma State Regents for Higher Education, 339 U.S. 637 (1950)	9-0	Chief Justice Vinson held that separate-but-equal graduate instruction violated the equal protection clause.
Sweatt v. Painter, 339 U.S. 629 (1950)	9-0	Chief Justice Vinson held that a newly created all-black law school was not equal to the University of Texas Law School, and the Supreme Court ordered Sweatt admitted to the law school at the University of Texas because of intangibles that make for greatness in a law school.

Between 1940 and 1950, it had become clear that the Court would attack segregated interstate travel as it had attacked discrimination in higher education and in the voting booth in the white primary cases (see Table 2.5). Interestingly, segregated interstate travel was not struck down under the equal protection clause of the Fourteenth Amendment, but rather the Court relied on the commerce clause. In MITCHELL V. UNITED STATES, 313 U.S. 80 (1941), Arthur Mitchell, a black U.S. congressman from Chicago, was refused Pullman accommodations while traveling between Chicago and Hot Springs, Arkansas. The Hughes Court held, in a unanimous opinion, that the accommodations afforded black passengers violated the Interstate Commerce Act because they were not equal to those afforded white passengers. In the Court's words, "The discrimination shown was palpably unjust and forbidden by the Act."

Four years later, in the landmark case MORGAN V. VIRGINIA, 328 U.S. 373 (1946), the NAACP assisted Irene Morgan, a black woman who challenged a Virginia law that segregated passengers according to race while they traveled in the state. Virginia prevailed in the trial court by arguing that this law was a valid exercise of the police power. The Stone Court disagreed and held that a statute requiring segregation along racial lines on carriers in interstate commerce placed an undue burden on such commerce and "infringes the requirements of national uniformity" in the regulation of interstate travel.

Two years after the *Morgan* decision, the Court continued its attack on discriminatory practices in transportation on a local steamship line. In *Bob-Lo Excursion Co. v. Michigan,* 333 U.S. 28 (1948), a Michigan corporation was engaged in transporting passengers on a steamship between Detroit and Bois Blanc Island, Canada, in violation of Michigan's Civil Rights Act, which prohibited discrimination on public carriers. Sara Ray, a black girl, was refused transportation while her 12 white classmates boarded the ship with their teacher. Relying on *Cooley v. Board of Wardens of Port of Philadelphia,* 53 U.S. (12 How.) 229 (1851), the Court upheld the Michigan law. It held, "It is difficult to imagine what national interest or policy, whether of securing uniformity in regulating commerce . . . with foreign nations . . . could reasonably be found to be adversely affected by applying Michigan's statute to these facts or to outweigh her interest in doing so."

Two years after *Bob-Lo Excursion,* the Vinson Court, in *Henderson v. United States,* 339 U.S. 816 (1950), struck a lethal blow to segregation in railroad dining cars. Elmer Henderson, a black passenger traveling from Washington, D.C., to Atlanta, Georgia, was refused service in the diner on the basis of race. The Court held, in a unanimous opinion, that this case was similar to *Mitchell* and that to deny Henderson a seat constituted a violation of the Interstate Commerce Act of 1887. Moreover, the railroad rules subjected passengers "to undue or unreasonable prejudice or disadvantage in violation of § 3(1)" of the Act.

During the 1950s, racial segregation in the nation's capitol was prevalent in the areas of housing, education, federal employment, and public accommodations. In an attempt to desegregate eating establishments in Washington,

Table 2.5 Discrimination in Interstate Travel and Public Accommodations: Cases

Case	Vote	Ruling
McCabe v. Atchison, Topeka & Santa Fe Railway Company, 235 U.S. 151 (1914)	9-0	Justice Hughes held that Oklahoma's Separate Coach Law applied exclusively to intrastate commerce and did not violate the commerce clause or the Fourteenth Amendment.
Mitchell v. United States, 313 U.S. 80 (1941)	9-0	The Supreme Court held that segregated accommodations during interstate travel violated the Interstate Commerce Act.
Morgan v. Virginia, 328 U.S. 373 (1946)	7-1	The Supreme Court struck down a Virginia statute that required segregation while traveling in the state on the ground that it placed an undue burden on interstate travel.
Bob-Lo Excursion Co. v. Michigan, 333 U.S. 28 (1948)	7-2	Justice Rutledge upheld a Michigan law that prohibited discrimination on public carriers, as applied to a steamship.
Henderson v. United States, 339 U.S. 816 (1950)	9-0	The Supreme Court struck down segregation in railroad dining cars under the Interstate Commerce Act.
District of Columbia v. John R. Thompson Co., Inc., 346 U.S. 100 (1953)	8-0	Under laws passed in 1872 and 1873, Justice Douglas declared that they were enforceable against the practice of denying service to blacks at restaurants in the District of Columbia.

D.C., blacks who were denied service at a restaurant brought suit under the 1872 and 1873 acts of the Legislative Assembly of the District of Columbia, which made it a crime to refuse service to any person on account of race or color. In *District of Columbia v. John R. Thompson Co., Inc.,* 346 U.S. 100 (1953), Justice Douglas declared that the acts had survived changes in the government and were therefore enforceable. These laws had been on the books for 81 years but had never been enforced. After this decision, segregation in public accommodations in Washington, D.C., came to an end.

GROUP LIBEL LAWS: PROTECTING RACIAL AND RELIGIOUS GROUPS FROM DEFAMATION

Group libel laws came into existence to counter a vicious form of defamation aimed at minorities for the specific purpose of perpetuating hatred and conflict.[23] Several states enacted these laws. Illinois passed its law on June

29, 1917, at a time when it was attempting to assimilate large numbers of newcomers, including Southern blacks, seeking jobs and a better way of life. It is also important to emphasize that, in 1908, the state experienced the first Northern race riot, which resulted in the loss of six lives and homelessness for many blacks. The central thrust of the law in Illinois provided that it shall be unlawful for any person to publish or exhibit in public any "lithograph," "picture," or "sketch" that portrays "depravity," "criminality," or "lack of virtue" of a class of any race or religion that could result in riots or a breach of the peace. Joseph Beauharnais, a white man, was convicted for distributing leaflets that called on the mayor to prevent the white race from being mongrelized and their neighborhoods from being invaded by blacks.

In BEAUHARNAIS V. ILLINOIS, 343 U.S. 250 (1952), the Court was afforded the opportunity to decide whether group libel laws were constitutional. Justice Frankfurter, writing for the 5-4 majority, declared that the Illinois law was valid because "libelous utterances" were not protected by the First Amendment. He concluded that Illinois had experienced intense tension between the races that often led to violence. Moreover, it was self-evident that "wilful purveyors of falsehood concerning racial and religious groups promote strife and tend powerfully to obstruct the manifold adjustments required for free, ordered life in a metropolitan, polyglot community." Justices Black and Douglas dissented. They argued that the First and Fourteenth Amendments forbid such laws because they prohibit individuals from being able to petition their elected officials and also stifle speech and thought. Given the prevalence of racial tensions in the United States during the Vinson Court era, the zeitgeist as viewed by a narrow majority of the Court's members was captured in the *Beauharnais* decision.

CONCLUSION

It is fair to conclude that, from 1910 to 1953, blacks, with some exceptions, received a raw deal from the three branches of government at the state and national levels. Their valiant efforts outweighed by far the inconsequential support they received from those who authoritatively allocate values. Judicial indifference and the cyclical pattern of winning and losing are additional reasons why it took them so long to secure the most basic rights that whites took for granted. Although the Vinson Court cannot be categorized as activist on race-related issues, it must be given credit for laying the foundation for the activist Warren Court. On September 8, 1953, a fatal heart attack prevented Chief Justice Vinson from hearing oral argument in the *Brown* case, which was set for October 1953. His successor, Earl Warren, would deliver the opinion in this landmark case. Unlike previous Courts, the Vinson Court was not indifferent to the enduring issue of racial discrimination, and the Warren, Burger, and Rehnquist Courts would have to confront the issue of civil rights head-on as the Vinson Court had done. After all, the controversial issue of race had taken center stage on the nation's agenda, and the Supreme Court itself was on trial.

NOTES

1. Cover, R. (1989). Taft Court: 1921-1930. In L. W. Levy, K. L. Karst, & D. J. Mahoney (Eds.), *American constitutional history: Selections from the* Encyclopedia of the American Constitution. New York: Macmillan, p. 224.

2. Woodward, C. V. (1974). *The strange career of Jim Crow* (3rd rev. ed.). New York: Oxford University Press, pp. 101-102.

3. Bardolph, R. (1970). *The civil rights record: Black Americans and the law, 1849-1970.* New York: Thomas Y. Crowell, p. 199.

4. Elliott, W. E. Y. (1989). Fifteenth Amendment. In L. W. Levy, K. L. Karst, & D. J. Mahoney (Eds.), *Civil rights and equality: Selections from the* Encyclopedia of the American Constitution. New York: Macmillan, p. 129.

5. Brisbane, R. H. (1970). *The Black vanguard: Origins of the Negro social revolution, 1900-1960.* Valley Forge, PA: Judson, p. 128.

6. Brisbane, R. H. (1970). *The Black vanguard: Origins of the Negro social revolution, 1900-1960.* Valley Forge, PA: Judson, p. 128.

7. White, W. (1948). *A man called White: The autobiography of Walter White.* Bloomington: Indiana University Press, p. 88.

8. Davis, M. D., & Clark, H. R. (1992). *Thurgood Marshall: Warrior at the bar, rebel on the bench.* New York: Birch Lane, p. 108.

9. Davis, M. D., & Clark, H. R. (1992). *Thurgood Marshall: Warrior at the bar, rebel on the bench.* New York: Birch Lane, p. 108.

10. Davis, M. D., & Clark, H. R. (1992). *Thurgood Marshall: Warrior at the bar, rebel on the bench.* New York: Birch Lane, p. 108.

11. Brisbane, R. (1970). *The black vanguard: Origins of the Negro social revolution, 1900-1960.* Valley Forge, PA: Judson, p. 193.

12. Vose, C. (1959). *Caucasians only: The Supreme Court, the NAACP, and the restrictive covenant cases.* Berkeley: University of California Press.

13. Berry, M. F. (1994). *Black resistance, white law: A history of constitutional racism in America.* New York: Allen Lane, p. 98.

14. Carter, D. T. (1979). Scottsboro: *A tragedy of the American South* (rev. ed.). Baton Rouge: Louisiana State University Press, p. 425.

15. See Murphy, W., Fleming, J. E., & Harris, W. F., II. (1986). *American constitutional interpretation.* Mineola, NY: Foundation Press, pp. 748-751. Also see Erler, E. J. (1989). Discrete and insular minorities. In L. W. Levy, K. L. Karst, & D. J. Mahoney (Eds.), *Civil rights and equality: Selections from the* Encyclopedia of the American Constitution. New York: Macmillan, pp. 187-189.

16. Irons, P. (1990). *The courage of their convictions: Sixteen Americans who fought their way to the Supreme Court.* New York: Penguin, p. 47.

17. Irons, P. (1990). *The courage of their convictions: Sixteen Americans who fought their way to the Supreme Court.* New York: Penguin, p. 49.

18. See Kluger, R. (1977). *Simple justice: The history of* Brown v. Board of Education *and black America's struggle for equality.* New York: Vintage; and Tushnet, M. V. (1987). *The NAACP's legal strategy against segregated education, 1925-50.* Chapel Hill: University of North Carolina Press.

19. Tushnet, M. V. (1987). *The NAACP's legal strategy against segregated education, 1925-1950.* Chapel Hill: University of North Carolina Press, p. 122.

20. Tushnet, M. V. (1987). *The NAACP's legal strategy against segregated education, 1925-1950.* Chapel Hill: University of North Carolina Press, p. 122.

21. Verbatim record of the lower court testimony in *Sweatt v. Painter* (1950) (Microfilm, Main Library at The Ohio State University, Columbus, Ohio), pp. 193-194.

22. Verbatim record of the lower court testimony in *Sweatt v. Painter* (1950) (Microfilm, Main Library at The Ohio State University, Columbus, Ohio), p. 194.

23. Kalven, H., Jr., (1965). *The Negro and the first amendment.* Columbus: Ohio State University Press, pp. 7-8.

CASES

NIXON V. HERNDON
273 U.S. 536 (1927)

In 1923, Texas enacted a statute that stated, "In no event shall a negro be eligible to participate in a Democratic party primary election held in the State of Texas." Dr. L. A. Nixon, a black citizen of El Paso, Texas, sought to vote in the primary election in El Paso for senator and representatives in Congress and other state offices. Nixon was a member of the Democratic Party and in every way qualified to vote except for the Texas white primary law. He brought suit (sponsored by the NAACP), attacking the constitutionality of the white primary on Fourteenth and Fifteenth Amendment grounds. The district court dismissed the suit on the basis of the political question doctrine, and a writ of error was taken directly to the Supreme Court. *Vote: 9-0.*

* * *

MR. JUSTICE HOLMES delivered the opinion of the Court.

. . . The objection that the subject matter of the suit is political is little more than a play upon words. Of course the petition concerns political action but it alleges and seeks to recover for private damage. That private damage may be caused by such political action and may be recovered for in a suit at law hardly has been doubted for over two hundred years. . . . If the defendants' conduct was a wrong to the plaintiff the same reasons that allow a recovery for denying the plaintiff a vote at a final election allow it for denying a vote at the primary election that may determine the final result.

The important question is whether the statute can be sustained. But although we state it as a question the answer does not seem to us open to a doubt. We find it unnecessary to consider the Fif-

teenth Amendment, because it seems to us hard to imagine a more direct and obvious infringement of the Fourteenth. That Amendment, while it applies to all, was passed, as we know, with a special intent to protect the blacks from discrimination against them. *Slaughter House Cases,* 83 U.S. 16 Wall. 36 [1873]; *Strauder v. West Virginia,* 100 U.S. 303 [1880]. That Amendment "not only gave citizenship and the privileges of citizenship to persons of color, but it denied to any State the power to withhold from them the equal protection of the laws. . . . What is this but declaring that the law in the States shall be the same for the black as for the white; that all persons, whether colored or white, shall stand equal before the laws of the States, and, in regard to the colored race, for whose protection the amendment was primarily designed, that no discrimination shall be made against them by law because of their color?" . . . *Buchanan v. Warley,* 245 U.S. 60, 77 [1917]. See *Yick Wo v. Hopkins,* 118 U.S. 356, 374 [1886]. The statute of Texas in the teeth of the prohibitions referred to assumes to forbid negroes to take part in a primary election the importance of which we have indicated, discriminating against them by the distinction of color alone. States may do a good deal of classifying that it is difficult to believe rational, but there are limits, and it is too clear for extended argument that color cannot be made the basis of a statutory classification affecting the right set up in this case.

Judgment reversed.

GROVEY V. TOWNSEND
295 U.S. 45 (1935)

R. R. Grovey, a black resident of Texas, filed a complaint against Townsend, a county clerk who refused to give him an absentee ballot for a Democratic party primary election because of race. Townsend's refusal to issue the ballot was based on a resolution adopted by the State Democratic Convention of Texas on May 24, 1932: "Be it resolved, that all white citizens of the State of Texas who are qualified to vote under the Constitution and laws of the state shall be eligible to membership in the Democratic party and as such entitled to participate in its deliberations." Grovey alleged that Townsend's act constituted a violation of the Fourteenth and Fifteenth Amendments of the U.S. Constitution. The lower court dismissed the complaint. *Vote: 9-0.*

* * *

MR. JUSTICE ROBERTS delivered the opinion of the Court.

. . . *First.* An argument pressed upon us in *Nixon v. Condon,* 286 U.S. 73 [1932] which we found it unnecessary to consider, is again presented. It is that the primary election was held under statutory compulsion; is wholly statutory in origin and incidents; those charged with its management have been deprived by statute and judicial decision of all power to establish qualifications for participation therein inconsistent with those laid down by the laws of the state, save only that the managers of such elections have been given the power to deny negroes the vote. It is further urged that while the election is designated that of the Democratic party, the statutes not only require this method of selecting party nominees, but define the powers and duties of the party's representatives, and of those who are to conduct the election, so completely, and make them so thoroughly officers of the state, that any action taken by them in connection with the qualifications of members of the party is in fact state action and not party action.

In support of this view petitioner refers to Title 50 of the Revised Civil Statutes of Texas of 1925. ... A perusal of these provisions, so it is said, will convince that the state has prescribed and regulated party primaries as fully as general elections, and has made those who manage the primaries state officers subject to state direction and control.

While it is true that Texas has by its laws elaborately provided for the expression of party preference as to nominees, has required that preference to be expressed in a certain form of voting, and has attempted in minute detail to protect the suffrage of the members of the organization against fraud, it is equally true that the primary is a party primary; the expenses of it are not borne by the state, but by members of the party seeking nomination (Arts. 3108; 3116); the ballots are furnished not by the state, but by the agencies of the party (Arts. 3109; 3119); the votes are counted and the returns made by instrumentalities created by the party (Arts. 3123; 3124-5; 3127); and the state recognizes the state convention as the organ of the party for the declaration of principles and the formulation of policies (Arts. 3136; 3139).

... We cannot, as petitioner urges, give weight to earlier expressions of the state courts said to be inconsistent with this declaration of the law. The Supreme Court of the state has decided, in a case definitely involving the point, that the legislature of Texas has not essayed to interfere, and indeed may not interfere, with the constitutional liberty of citizens to organize a party and to determine the qualifications of its members. If in the past the legislature has attempted to infringe that right and such infringement has not been gainsaid by the courts, the fact constitutes no reason for our disregarding the considered decision of the state's highest court. The legislative assembly of the state, so far as we are advised, had never attempted to prescribe or to limit the membership of a political party, and it is now settled that it has no power so to do. The state, as its highest tribunal holds, though it has guaranteed the liberty to organize political parties, may legislate for their governance when formed and for the method whereby they may nominate candidates, but must do so with full recognition of the right of the party to exist, to define its membership, and to adopt such policies as to it shall seem wise. In the light of the principles so announced, we are unable to characterize the managers of the primary election as state officers in such sense that any action taken by them in obedience to the mandate of the state convention respecting eligibility to participate in the organization's deliberations, is state action.

Second. We are told that §§ 2 and 27 of the Bill of Rights of the Constitution of Texas as construed in *Bell v. Hill,* 74 S.W. (2d) 113 [1934], violate the Federal Constitution, for the reason that so construed they fail to forbid a classification based upon race and color, whereas in *Love v. Wilcox,* 119 Tex. 256; 28 S.W. (2d) [1930], they were not held to forbid classifications based upon party affiliations and membership or non-membership in organizations other than political parties, which classification were by Article 3107 of Revised Civil Statutes, 1925, prohibited. But, as above said, in *Love v. Wilcox* the court did not construe or apply any constitutional provision and expressly reserved the question as to the power of a party in convention assembled to specify the qualifications for membership therein.

Third. An alternative contention of petitioner is that the state Democratic convention which adopted the resolution here involved was a mere creature of the state and could not lawfully do what the Federal Constitution prohibits to its creator. The argument is based upon the fact that Article 3167 of the Revised Civil Statutes of Texas, 1925, requires a political party desiring to elect delegates to a national convention, to hold a state convention on the fourth Tuesday of May, 1928, and every four years thereafter; and provides for the election of delegates to that convention at primary conventions, the procedure of which is regulated by law. In *Bell v. Hill,* ... the Supreme Court of Texas held that Article 3167 does not prohibit declarations of policy by a state Democratic convention called for the purpose of electing delegates to a national convention. While it may be, as petitioner contends, that we are not bound by the state court's decision on the point, it is entitled to the highest respect, and petitioner points to nothing which in any wise impugns its accuracy. If, as seems to be conceded, the Democratic party in Texas held conventions many years before the adoption of Article 3167, nothing is shown to indicate that the regulation of the method of choosing delegates or fixing the times of their meetings, was intended to take away the plenary power of conventions in respect of matters as to which they would normally announce the party's will. Compare *Nixon v. Condon* [286 U.S. 73 (1932)]. We are not prepared to hold that in Texas the state convention of a party has become a mere instrumentality or agency for expressing the voice or will of the state.

Fourth. The complaint states that candidates for the offices of Senator and Representative in Congress were to be nominated at the primary election of July 9, 1934, and that in Texas nomination by the Democratic party is equivalent to election. These facts (the truth of which the demurrer assumes) the petitioner insists, without more, make out a forbidden discrimination. A similar situation may exist in other states where one or another party includes a great majority of the qualified electors. The argument is that as a negro may not be denied a ballot at a general election on account of his race or color, if exclusion from the primary renders his vote at the general election insignificant and useless, the result is to deny him the suffrage altogether. So to say is to confuse the privilege of membership in a party with the right to vote for one who is to hold a public office. With the former the state need have no concern, with the latter it is bound to concern itself, for the general election is a function of the state government and discrimination by the state as respects participation by negroes on account of their race or color is prohibited by the Federal Constitution.

Fifth. The complaint charges that the Democratic party has never declared a purpose to exclude negroes. The premise upon which this conclusion rests is that the party is not a state body but a national organization, whose representative is the national Democratic convention. No such convention, so it is said, has resolved to exclude negroes from membership. We have no occasion to determine the cor-

rectness of the position, since even if true it does not tend to prove that the petitioner was discriminated against or denied any right to vote by the State of Texas. Indeed, the contention contradicts any such conclusion, for it assumes merely that a state convention, the representative and agent of a state association, has usurped the rightful authority of a national convention which represents a larger and superior country-wide association.

We find no ground for holding that the respondent has in obedience to the mandate of the law of Texas discriminated against the petitioner or denied him any right guaranteed by the Fourteenth and Fifteenth Amendments.

Judgment affirmed.

SMITH V. ALLWRIGHT
321 U.S. 649 (1944)

In 1932 the Texas Democratic Party, in a state convention, adopted the following resolution: "Be it resolved that all white citizens of the State of Texas who are qualified to vote under the Constitution and laws of the State shall be eligible to membership in the Democratic party and, as such, entitled to participate in its deliberations." Lonnie Smith, a black citizen, brought suit against the election judge, S. C. Allwright, when the judge refused to allow him to vote in a Democratic Party primary for the nomination of candidates to national and state offices solely on account of race, in violation of the Fourteenth and Fifteenth Amendments. The district court and court of appeals dismissed the case on the authority of *Grovey v. Townsend* (1935). *Vote: 8-1.*

* * *

MR. JUSTICE REED delivered the opinion of the Court.

. . . Texas is free to conduct her elections and limit her electorate as she may deem wise, save only as her action may be affected by the prohibitions of the United States Constitution or in conflict with powers delegated to and exercised by the National Government. The Fourteenth Amendment forbids a State from making or enforcing any law which abridges the privileges or immunities of citizens of the United States and the Fifteenth Amendment specifically interdicts any denial or abridgement by a State of the right of citizens to vote on account of color. Respondents appeared in the District Court and the Circuit Court of Appeals and defended on the ground that the Democratic party of Texas is a voluntary organization with members banded together for the purpose of selecting individuals of the group representing the common political beliefs as

candidates in the general election. As such a voluntary organization, it was claimed, the Democratic party is free to select its own membership and limit to whites participation in the party primary. Such action, the answer asserted, does not violate the Fourteenth, Fifteenth or Seventeenth Amendment as officers of government cannot be chosen at primaries and the Amendments are applicable only to general elections where governmental officers are actually elected. Primaries, it is said, are political party affairs, handled by party, not governmental, officers. No appearance for respondents is made in this Court. Arguments presented here by the Attorney General of Texas and the Chairman of the State Democratic Executive Committee of Texas, as amici curiae, urged substantially the same grounds as those advanced by the respondents.

. . . It may now be taken as a postulate that the right to vote in such a primary for the nomination of candidates without discrimination by the State, like the right to vote in a general election, is a right secured by the Constitution. *United States v. Classic,* 313 U.S. at 314 [1941]; *Myers v. Anderson,* 238 U.S. 368 [1915]; *Ex parte Yarbrough,* 110 U.S. 651, 663 [1884]. By the terms of the Fifteenth Amendment that right may not be abridged by any State on account of race. Under our Constitution the great privilege of the ballot may not be denied a man by the State because of his color.

We are thus brought to an examination of the qualifications for Democratic primary electors in Texas, to determine whether state action or private action has excluded Negroes from participation. Despite Texas' decision that the exclusion is produced by private or party action, . . . federal courts must for themselves appraise the facts leading to that conclusion. It is only by the performance of this obligation that a final and uniform interpretation can be given to the Constitution, the "supreme Law of the Land." *Nixon v. Condon,* 286 U.S. 73, 88 [1932] . . . Texas requires electors in a primary to pay a poll tax. Every person who does so pay and who has the qualifications of age and residence is an acceptable voter for the primary. . . . As appears above in the summary of the statutory provisions set out in note 6, Texas requires by the law the election of the county officers of a party. These compose the county executive committee. The county chairmen so selected are members of the district executive committee and choose the chairman for the district. Precinct primary election officers are named by the county executive committee. Statutes provide for the election by the voters of precinct delegates to the county convention of a party and the selection of delegates to the district and state conventions by the county convention. The state convention selects the state executive committee. No convention may place in platform or resolution any demand for specific legislation without endorsement of such legislation by the voters in a primary. Texas thus directs the selection of all party officers.

Primary elections are conducted by the party under state statutory authority. The county executive committee selects precinct election officials and the county, district or state executive committees, respectively, canvass the returns. These party committees or the state convention certify the party's candidates to the appropriate officers for inclusion on the official ballot for the general election. No name which has not been so certified may appear upon the ballot for the general election as a candidate of a political party. No other name may be printed on the ballot which has not been placed in nomination by qualified voters who must take oath that they did not participate in a primary for the selection of a candidate for the office for which the nomination is made.

The state courts are given exclusive original jurisdiction of contested elections and of mandamus proceedings to compel officers to perform their statutory duties.

We think that this statutory system for the selection of party nominees for inclusion on the general election ballot makes the party which is required to follow these legislative directions an agency of the State in so far as it determines the participants in a primary election. The party takes its character as a state agency from the duties imposed upon it by state statutes; the duties do not become matters of private law because they are performed by a political party. The plan of the Texas primary follows substantially that of Louisiana, with the exception that in Louisiana the State pays the cost of the primary while Texas assesses the cost against candidates. In numerous instances, the Texas statutes fix or limit the fees to be charged. Whether paid directly by the State or through state requirements, it is state action which compels. When primaries become a part of the machinery for choosing officials, state and national, as they have here, the same tests to determine the character of discrimination or abridgement should be applied to the primary as are applied to the general election. If the State requires a certain electoral procedure, prescribes a general election ballot made up of party nominees so chosen and limits the choice of the electorate in general elections for state offices, practically speaking, to those whose names appear on such a ballot, it endorses, adopts and enforces the discrimination against Negroes, practiced by a party entrusted by Texas law with the determination of the qualifications of participants in the primary. This is state action within the meaning of the Fifteenth Amendment. *Guinn v. United States,* 238 U.S. 347, 362 [1915].

The United States is a constitutional democracy. Its organic law grants to all citizens a right to participate in the choice of elected officials without restriction by any State because of race. This grant to the people of the opportunity for choice is not to be nullified by a State through casting its electoral process in a form which permits a private organization to practice racial discrimination in the election. Constitutional rights would be of little value if they could be thus indirectly denied. *Lane v. Wilson,* 307 U.S. 268, 275 [1939].

The privilege of membership in a party may be, as this Court said in *Grovey v. Townsend,* 295 U.S. 45, 55 [1935] no concern of a State. But when, as here, that privilege is also the essential qualification for voting in a primary to select nominees for a general election, the State makes the action of the party the action of the State. In reaching this conclusion we are not unmindful of the desirability of continuity of decision in constitutional questions. However, when convinced of former error, this Court has never felt constrained to follow precedent. In constitutional questions, where correction depends upon amendment and not upon legislative action this Court throughout its history has freely exercised its power to reexamine the basis of its constitutional decisions. . . . Here we are applying, contrary to the recent decision in *Grovey v. Townsend,* the well-established principle of the Fifteenth Amendment, forbidding the abridgement by a State of a citizen's right to vote. *Grovey v. Townsend* is overruled.

Judgment reversed.
MR. JUSTICE FRANKFURTER concurs.

* * *

MR. JUSTICE ROBERTS dissenting.
. . . The reason for my concern is that the instant decision, overruling that announced about nine years ago, tends to bring adjudications of this tribunal into the same class as a restricted railroad ticket, good for this day and train only. I have no assurance, in view of current decisions, that the opinion an-

nounced today may not shortly be repudiated and overruled by justices who deem they have new light on the subject. In the present term the court has overruled three cases.

In the present case, . . . the court below relied, as it was bound to, upon our previous decision. As that court points out, the statutes of Texas have not been altered since *Grovey v. Townsend* was decided. The same resolution is involved as was drawn in question in *Grovey v. Townsend*. Not a fact differentiates that case from this except the names of the parties.

BUCHANAN V. WARLEY
245 U.S. 60 (1917)

A Louisville ordinance prohibited black persons from occupying houses in blocks where the greater number of houses were occupied by whites and vice versa. Buchanan, a white seller, brought suit to enforce the contract for the sale of property to a black man, alleging that the ordinance violated the Fourteenth Amendment. The Kentucky Court of Appeals upheld the validity of the ordinance. *Vote: 9-0.*

* * *

MR. JUSTICE DAY delivered the opinion of the Court.

. . . We pass then to a consideration of the case upon its merits. This ordinance prevents the occupancy of a lot in the City of Louisville by a person of color in a block where the greater number of residences are occupied by white persons; where such a majority exists colored persons are excluded. This interdiction is based wholly upon color; simply that and nothing more. In effect, premises situated as are those in question in the so-called white block are effectively debarred from sale to persons of color, because if sold they cannot be occupied by the purchaser nor by him sold to another of the same color.

This drastic measure is sought to be justified under the authority of the State in the exercise of the police power. It is said such legislation tends to promote the public peace by preventing racial conflicts; that it tends to maintain racial purity; that it prevents the deterioration of property owned and occupied by white people, which deterioration, it is contended, is sure to follow the occupancy of adjacent premises by persons of color.

. . . The concrete question here is: May the occupancy, and, necessarily, the purchase and sale of property of which occupancy is an incident, be inhibited by the States, or by one of its municipalities, solely because of the color of the proposed occupant of the premises? That one may dispose of his property, subject only to the control of lawful enactments curtailing that right in the public interest, must be conceded. The question now presented makes it pertinent to enquire into the constitutional right of the white man to sell his property to a colored man, having in view the legal status of the purchaser and occupant.

. . . In the face of these constitutional and statutory provisions [the Thirteenth and Fourteenth Amendments and the Civil Rights Acts of 1866 and 1870], can a white man be denied, consistently with due process of law, the right to dispose of his property to a purchaser by prohibiting the occupation of it for the sole reason that the purchaser is a person of color intending to occupy the premises as a place of residence?

The statute of 1866, originally passed under sanction of the Thirteenth Amendment, . . . and practically re-enacted after the adoption of the Fourteenth Amendment, . . . expressly provided that all citizens of the United States shall have the same right to purchase property as is enjoyed by white citizens. Colored persons are citizens of the United States and have the right to purchase property and enjoy and use the same without laws discriminating against them solely on account of color. *Hall v. DeCuir,* 95 U.S. 485, 508 [1878]. These enactments did not deal with the social rights of men, but with those fundamental rights in property which it was intended to secure upon the same terms to citizens of every race and color. *Civil Rights Cases,* 109 U.S. 3, 22 [1883]. The Fourteenth Amendment and these statutes enacted in furtherance of its purpose operate to qualify and entitle a colored man to acquire property without state legislation discriminating against him solely because of color.

The defendant in error insists that *Plessy v. Ferguson,* 163 U.S. 537 [1896] is controlling in principle in favor of the judgment of the court below. . . .

. . . That there exists a serious and difficult problem arising from a feeling of race hostility which the law is powerless to control, and to which it must give measure of consideration, may be freely admitted. But its solution cannot be promoted by depriving citizens of their constitutional rights and privileges.

As we have seen, this court has held laws valid which separated the races on the basis of equal accommodations in public conveyances, and courts of high authority have held enactments lawful which provide for separation in the public schools of white and colored pupils where equal privileges are given. But in view of the rights secured by the Fourteenth Amendment to the Federal Constitution such legislation must have its limitations, and cannot be sustained where the exercise of authority exceeds the restraints of the Constitution. We think these limitations are exceeded in laws and ordinances of the character now before us.

It is the purpose of such enactments, and, it is frankly avowed it will be their ultimate effect, to require by law, at least in residential districts, the compulsory separation of the races on account of color. Such action is said to be essential to the maintenance of the purity of the races, although it is to be noted in the ordinance under consideration that the employment of colored servants in white families is permitted, and nearby residences of colored persons not coming within the blocks, as defined in the ordinance, are not prohibited.

The case presented does not deal with an attempt to prohibit the amalgamation of the races. The right which the ordinance annulled was the civil right of a white man to dispose of his property if he saw fit to do so to a person of color and of a colored person to make such disposition to a white person.

It is urged that this proposed segregation will promote the public peace by preventing race conflicts. Desirable as this is, and important as is the preservation of the public peace, this aim cannot be accomplished by laws or ordinances which deny rights created or protected by the Federal Constitution.

It is said that such acquisitions by colored persons depreciate property owned in the neighborhood by white persons. But property may be acquired by undesirable white neighbors or put to disagreeable though lawful uses with like results.

We think this attempt to prevent the alienation of the property in question to a person of color was not a legitimate exercise of the police power of the State, and is in direct violation of the fundamental law enacted in the Fourteenth Amendment of the Constitution preventing state interference with property rights except by due process of law. That being the case the ordinance cannot stand. *Booth v. Illinois,* 184 U.S. 425, 429 [1902]. . . .

Reaching this conclusion it follows that the judgment of the Kentucky Court of Appeals must be reversed, and the cause remanded to that court for further proceedings not inconsistent with this opinion.
Reversed.

SHELLEY V. KRAEMER
334 U.S. 1 (1948)

Black families in St. Louis, Missouri; and Detroit, Michigan, purchased homes containing racial restrictive covenants in the deeds. White residents whose property was subject to the terms of the restrictive covenants sued to restrain the Shelley and Ferguson families from using or occupying the property. The state supreme courts, in *Shelley v. Kraemer* and the companion case *McGhee v. Sipes,* held that the enforcement of the restrictive covenants did not violate the Fourteenth Amendment. In *Hurd v. Hodge,* 334 U.S. 24 (1948), decided the same day as *Shelley,* the Court considered a similar issue involving the use of racial restrictive covenants in Washington, D.C. *Vote: 6-0.*

* * *

MR. CHIEF JUSTICE VINSON delivered the opinion of the Court.

. . . It is well, at the outset, to scrutinize the terms of the restrictive agreements involved in these cases. In the Missouri case, the covenant declares that no part of the affected property shall be "occupied by any person not of the Caucasian race, it being intended hereby to restrict the use of said property . . . against the occupancy as owners or tenants of any portion of said property for resident

or other purpose by people of the Negro or Mongolian Race." Not only does the restriction seek to proscribe use and occupancy of the affected properties by members of the excluded class, but as construed by the Missouri courts, the agreement requires that title of any person who uses his property in violation of the restriction shall be divested. The restriction of the covenant in the Michigan case seeks to bar occupancy by persons of the excluded class. It provides that "This property shall not be used or occupied by any person or persons except those of the Caucasian race."

. . . It cannot be doubted that among the civil rights intended to be protected from discriminatory state action by the Fourteenth Amendment are the rights to acquire, enjoy, own and dispose of property. Equality in the enjoyment of property rights was regarded by the framers of that Amendment as an essential pre-condition to the realization of other basic civil rights and liberties which the Amendment was intended to guarantee. Thus, § 1978 of the Revised Statutes, derived from § 1 of the Civil Rights Act of 1866 which was enacted by Congress while the Fourteenth Amendment was also under consideration, provides:

"All citizens of the United States shall have the same right, in every State and Territory, as is enjoyed by white citizens thereof to inherit, purchase, lease, sell, hold, and convey real and personal property."

This Court has given specific recognition to the same principle. *Buchanan v. Warley,* 245 U.S. 60 (1917).

It is likewise clear that restrictions on the right of occupancy of the sort sought to be created by the private agreements in these cases could not be squared with the requirements of the Fourteenth Amendment if imposed by state statute or local ordinance. . . .

. . . But the present cases . . . do not involve action by state legislatures or city councils. Here the particular patterns of discrimination and the areas in which the restrictions are to operate, are determined, in the first instance, by the terms of agreements among private individuals. Participation of the State consists in the enforcement of the restrictions so defined. The crucial issue with which we are here confronted is whether this distinction removes these cases from the operation of the prohibitory provisions of the Fourteenth Amendment.

Since the decision of this Court in the *Civil Rights Cases,* 109 U.S. 3 (1883), the principle has become firmly embedded in our constitutional law that the action inhibited by the first section of the Fourteenth Amendment is only such action as may fairly be said to be that of the States. That Amendment erects no shield against merely private conduct, however discriminatory or wrongful.

We concluded, therefore, that the restrictive agreements standing alone cannot be regarded as violative of any rights guaranteed to petitioners by the Fourteenth Amendment. So long as the purposes of those agreements are effectuated by voluntary adherence to their terms, it would appear clear that there has been no action by the State and the provisions of the Amendment have not been violated. Cf. *Corrigan v. Buckley,* [271 U.S. 323 (1926)].

But here there was more. These are cases in which the purposes of the agreements were secured only by judicial enforcement by state courts of the restrictive terms of the agreements. The respondents urge that judicial enforcement of private agreements does not amount to state action; or, in any event, the participation of the State is so attenuated in character as not to amount to state action within the meaning of the Fourteenth Amendment. Finally, it is suggested, even if the States in these cases may be deemed to have acted in the constitutional sense, their action did not deprive petitioners of the rights guaranteed by the Fourteenth Amendment. We move to a consideration of these matters.

That the action of state courts and judicial officers in their official capacities is to be regarded as action of the State within the meaning of the Fourteenth Amendment, is a proposition which has long been established by decisions of this Court. . . .

. . . But the examples of state judicial action which have been held by this Court to violate the Amendment's commands are not restricted to situations in which the judicial proceedings were found in some manner to be procedurally unfair. It has been recognized that the action of state courts in enforcing a substantive common-law rule formulated by those courts, may result in the denial of rights guaranteed by the Fourteenth Amendment, even though the judicial proceedings in such cases may have been in complete accord with the most rigorous conceptions of procedural due process. . . .

. . . The short of the matter is that from the time of the adoption of the Fourteenth Amendment until the present, it has been the consistent ruling of this Court that the action of the States to which the Amendment has reference includes action of state courts and state judicial officials. Although, in construing the terms of the Fourteenth Amendment, differences have from time to time been expressed as to whether particular types of state action may be said to offend the Amendment's prohibitory provisions, it has never been suggested that state court action is immunized from the operation of those provisions simply because the act is that of the judicial branch of the state government.

. . . We have no doubt that there has been state action in these cases in the full and complete sense of the phrase. The undisputed facts disclose that petitioners were willing purchasers of properties upon which they desired to establish homes. The owners of the properties were willing sellers; and contracts of sale were accordingly consummated. It is clear that but for the active intervention of the state courts, supported by the full panoply of state power, petitioners would have been free to occupy the properties in question without restraint.

These are not cases, as has been suggested, in which the States have merely abstained from action, leaving private individuals free to impose such discriminations as they see fit. Rather, these are cases in which the States have made available to such individuals the full coercive power of government to deny to petitioners, on the grounds of race or color, the enjoyment of property rights in premises which petitioners are willing and financially able to acquire and which the grantors are willing to sell. The difference between judicial enforcement and nonenforcement of the restrictive covenants is the difference to petitioners between being denied rights of property available to other members of the community and being accorded full enjoyment of those rights on an equal footing.

The enforcement of the restrictive agreements by the state courts in these cases was directed pursuant to the common-law policy of the States as formulated by those courts in earlier decisions. In the Missouri case, enforcement of the covenant was directed in the first instance by the highest court of the State after the trial court had determined the agreement to be invalid for want of the requisite number of signatures. In the Michigan case, the order of enforcement by the trial court was affirmed by the highest state court. The judicial action in each case bears the clear and unmistakable imprimatur of the State. . . .

We hold that in granting judicial enforcement of the restrictive agreements in these cases, the States have denied petitioners the equal protection of the laws and that, therefore, the action of the state courts cannot stand. We have noted that freedom from discrimination by the States in the enjoyment of property rights was among the basic objectives sought to be effec-

tuated by the framers of the Fourteenth Amendment. That such discrimination has occurred in these cases is clear. Because of the race or color of these petitioners they have been denied rights of ownership or occupancy enjoyed as a matter of course by other citizens of different race or color. . . .

. . . For the reasons stated, the judgment of the Supreme Court of Missouri and the judgment of the Supreme Court of Michigan must be reversed.

Reversed.

MR. JUSTICE REED, MR. JUSTICE JACKSON, and MR. JUSTICE RUTLEDGE took no part in the consideration or decision of these cases.

POWELL V. ALABAMA
287 U.S. 45 (1932)

In three cases, Ozie Powell and eight other black youths between the ages of 13 and 20 were convicted in Alabama for the rape of two white women on a freight train in 1931. As each of the three cases was called for trial, the defendants entered a plea of not guilty. The trials were completed within a single day. The jury found the defendants guilty and imposed the death penalty on all of them. The judgments were affirmed by the Alabama Supreme Court (except for the 13-year-old). On appeal to the U.S. Supreme Court, the defendants alleged that they had been denied due process and equal protection of the laws because they were denied the right to counsel for effective consultation and opportunity of preparation for trial. *Powell v. Alabama* (1932) was the first of the Scottsboro cases. *Vote: 7-2.*

* * *

MR. JUSTICE SUTHERLAND delivered the opinion of the Court.

. . . [W]e confine ourselves . . . to the inquiry whether the defendants were in substance denied the right of counsel, and if so, whether such denial infringes the due process clause of the Fourteenth Amendment.

First. The record shows that immediately upon the return of the indictment defendants were arraigned and pleaded not guilty. Apparently they were not asked whether they had, or were able to employ, counsel, or wished to have counsel appointed; or whether they had friends or relatives who might assist in that regard if communicated with. That it would not have been an idle ceremony to have given the defendants reasonable opportunity to communicate with their families and endeavor to obtain counsel is demonstrated by the fact that, very soon after conviction, able counsel appeared in their behalf. . . .

It is hardly necessary to say that, the right to counsel being conceded, a defendant should be afforded a fair opportunity to secure counsel of his own choice. Not only was that not done here, but such designation of counsel as was attempted was either so indefinite or so close upon the trial as to amount to a denial of effective and substantial aid in that regard. . . .

. . . It thus will be seen that until the very morning of the trial no lawyer had been named or definitely designated to represent the defendants. Prior to that time, the trial judge had "appointed all the members of the bar" for the limited "purpose of arraigning the defendants." Whether they would represent the defendants thereafter if no counsel appeared in their behalf, was a matter of speculation only, or, as the judge indicated, of mere anticipation on the part of the court. Such a designation, even if made for all purposes, would, in our opinion, have fallen far short of meeting, in any proper sense, a requirement for the appointment of counsel. How many lawyers were members of the bar does not appear; but, in the very nature of things, whether many or few, they would not, thus collectively named, have been given that clear appreciation of responsibility or impressed with that individual sense of duty which should and naturally would accompany the appointment of a selected member of the bar, specifically named and assigned.

That this action of the trial judge in respect of appointment of counsel was little more than an expansive gesture, imposing no substantial or definite obligation upon any one, is borne out by the fact that prior to the calling of the case for trial on April 6, a leading member of the local bar accepted employment on the side of the prosecution and actively participated in the trial. It is true that he said that before doing so he had understood Mr. Roddy would be employed as counsel for the defendants. This the lawyer in question, of his own accord, frankly stated to the court; and no doubt he acted with the utmost good faith. Probably other members of the bar had a like understanding. In any event, the circumstance lends emphasis to the conclusion that during perhaps the most critical period of the proceedings against these defendants, that is to say, from the time of their arraignment until the beginning of their trial, when consultation, thoroughgoing investigation and preparation were vitally important, the defendants did not have the aid of counsel in any real sense, although they were as much entitled to such aid during that period as at the trial itself. . . .

Nor do we think the situation was helped by what occurred on the morning of the trial. At that time, . . . Mr. Roddy stated to the court that he did not appear as counsel, but that he would like to appear along with counsel that the court might appoint; that he had not been given an opportunity to prepare the case; that he was not familiar with the procedure in Alabama, but merely came down as a friend of the people who were interested; that he thought the boys would be better off if he should step entirely out of the case. Mr. Moody, a member of the local bar, expressed a willingness to help Mr. Roddy in anything he could do under the circumstances. To this the court responded, "All right, all the lawyers that will; of course I would not require a lawyer to appear if—." And Mr. Moody continued, "I am willing to do that for him as a member of the bar; I will go ahead and help do anything I can do." With this dubious understanding, the trials immediately proceeded. The defendants, young, ignorant, illiterate, surrounded by hostile sentiment, haled back and forth under guard of soldiers, charged with an atrocious crime regarded with especial horror in the community where they were to be tried, were thus put in peril of their lives within a few moments after counsel for the first time charged with any degree of responsibility began to represent them.

It is not enough to assume that counsel thus precipitated into the case thought there was no defense, and exercised their best judgment in proceeding to trial without preparation. Neither they nor the court could say what a prompt and thoroughgoing investigation might disclose as to the facts. No attempt was made to investigate. No opportunity to do so was given. Defendants were immediately hurried to trial. . . . Under the circumstances disclosed, we hold that defendants were not accorded the right of counsel in any substantial sense. To decide otherwise, would simply be to ignore actualities. . . .

. . . *Second.* The Constitution of Alabama provides that in all criminal prosecutions the accused shall enjoy the right to have the assistance of counsel; and a state statute requires the court in a capital case, where the defendant is unable to employ counsel, to appoint counsel for him. The state supreme court held that these provisions had not been infringed, and with that holding we are powerless to interfere. The question, however, which it is our duty, and within our power, to decide, is whether the denial of the assistance of counsel contravenes the due process clause of the Fourteenth Amendment to the federal Constitution.

. . . In the light of the facts outlined in the forepart of this opinion—the ignorance and illiteracy of the defendants, their youth, the circumstances of public hostility, the imprisonment and the close surveillance of the defendants by the military forces, the fact that their friends and families were in other states and communication with them necessarily difficult, and above all that they stood in deadly peril of their lives—we think the failure of the trial court to give them reasonable time and opportunity to secure counsel was a clear denial of due process.

But passing that, and assuming their inability, even if opportunity had been given, to employ counsel, as the trial court evidently did assume, we are of the opinion that, under the circumstances just stated, the necessity of counsel was so vital and imperative that the failure of the trial court to make an effective appointment of counsel was likewise a denial of due process within the meaning of the Fourteenth Amendment. . . . All that is necessary now to decide, as we do decide, is that in a capital case, where the defendant is unable to employ counsel, and is incapable adequately of making his own defense because of ignorance, feeble mindedness, illiteracy, or the like, it is the duty of the court, whether requested or not, to assign counsel for him as a necessary requisite of due process of law; and that duty is not discharged by an assignment at such a time or under such circumstances as to preclude the giving of effective aid in the preparation and trial of the case. . . . In a case such as this . . . the right to have counsel appointed, when necessary, is a logical corollary from the constitutional right to be heard by counsel. . . .

. . . The judgments must be reversed and the causes remanded for further proceedings not inconsistent with this opinion.

Judgments reversed.

* * *

MR. JUSTICE BUTLER, with whom MR. JUSTICE McREYNOLDS concurs, dissenting.

. . . The informality disclosed by the colloquy between court and counsel, which is quoted in the opinion of this Court and so heavily leaned on, is not entitled to any weight. It must be inferred from the record that Mr. Roddy at all times was in touch with the defendants and the people who procured him to act for them. Mr. Moody and others of the local bar also acted for defendants at the time of the first arraignment and, as appears from the part of the record that is quoted in the opinion, thereafter proceeded in the discharge of their duty, including conferences with the defendants. There is not the slightest ground to suppose that Roddy or Moody were by fear or in any manner restrained from full performance of their duties. Indeed, it clearly appears that the State, by proper and adequate show of its purpose and power to preserve order, furnished adequate protection to them and the defendants.

SCREWS V. UNITED STATES
325 U.S. 91 (1945)

Sheriff Claude Screws and two police officers, Jones and Kelly, arrested a young black man, Robert Hall, late at night in Hall's home on the charge of theft of a tire in Georgia. As Hall alighted from the car at the courthouse, the police officers began beating him with their fists and a two-pound blackjack, claiming that Hall (who was handcuffed at the time) had reached for a gun and had used insulting language. On Hall's being thrown into jail, an ambulance was called, in which he died without regaining consciousness. An indictment was returned against the police officers for violating § 20 (now § 242) of the Criminal Code and conspiracy to violate § 20 (18 U.S.C. § 52), contrary to § 37 of the Criminal Code (18 U.S.C. § 88). The trial court found the defendants guilty, and a fine and imprisonment on each count were imposed. The court of appeals affirmed the conviction. *Vote: 5–4.*

* * *

MR. JUSTICE DOUGLAS announced the judgment of the Court and delivered the following opinion, in which the CHIEF JUSTICE, MR. JUSTICE BLACK, and MR. JUSTICE REED concur.
. . . We are met at the outset with the claim that § 20 is unconstitutional, insofar as it makes criminal acts in violation of the due process clause of the Fourteenth Amendment. The argument runs as follows: It is true that this Act as construed in *United States v. Classic,* 313 U.S. 299, 328 [1941] was upheld in its application to certain ballot box frauds committed by state officials. But in that case the constitutional rights protected were the rights to vote specifically guaranteed by Art. I, § 2 and § 4 of the Constitution. Here there is no ascertainable standard of guilt. There have been conflicting views in the Court as to the proper construction of the due process clause. The majority have quite consistently construed it in broad general terms. . . .
It is said that the Act must be read as if it contained those broad and fluid definitions of due process and that if it is so read it provides no ascertainable standard of guilt. . . .
. . . Sec. 20 was enacted to enforce the Fourteenth Amendment. It derives from § 2 of the Civil Rights Act of April 9, 1866. . . . In origin it was an antidiscrimination measure (as its language indicated), framed to protect Negroes in their newly won rights. . . . It was amended by § 17 of the Act of May 31, 1870 . . . and made applicable to "any inhabitant of any State or Territory." The prohibition against the "deprivation of any rights, privileges, or immunities, secured or protected by the Constitution and laws of the United States" was introduced by the revisers in 1874. . . . Those words were taken [from the so-called Ku-Klux Act] which provided civil suits for redress of such wrongs. . . . The requirement for a "willful" violation was introduced by the draftsmen of the Criminal Code of 1909. . . . And we are told "willfully" was added to § 20 in order to make the section "less severe." . . .
We hesitate to say that when Congress sought to enforce the Fourteenth Amendment in this fashion it did a vain thing. We hesitate to conclude that for 80 years this effort of Congress, renewed several times, to protect the important rights of the individual guaranteed by the Fourteenth Amendment has been an idle gesture. Yet if the Act fails by reason of vagueness so far as due process of law is concerned, there would seem to be a similar lack of specificity when the privileges and immunities clause . . . and the equal protection clause . . . of the Fourteenth Amendment are involved. Only if no construction can save the Act from this claim of unconstitutionality are we willing to reach that result. We do not reach it, for we are of the view that if § 20 is confined more narrowly than the lower courts confined it, it can be preserved as one of the sanctions to the great rights which the Fourteenth Amendment was designed to secure.
. . . Moreover, the history of § 20 affords some support for the narrower construction. . . . We think the inference is permissible that its severity was to be lessened by making it applicable only where the requisite bad purpose was present, thus requiring specific intent not only where discrimination is claimed but in other situations as well. We repeat that the presence of a bad purpose or evil intent alone may not be sufficient. We do say that a requirement of a specific intent to deprive a person of a federal right made definite by decision or other rule of law saves the Act from any charge of unconstitutionality on the grounds of vagueness.
Once the section is given that construction, we think that the claim that the section lacks an ascertainable standard of guilt must fail. The constitutional requirement that a criminal statute be definite serves a high function. It gives a person acting with

reference to the statute fair warning that his conduct is within its prohibition. This requirement is met when a statute prohibits only "willful" acts in the sense we have explained. One who does act with such specific intent is aware that what he does is precisely that which the statute forbids. He is under no necessity of guessing whether the statute applies to him . . . for he either knows or acts in reckless disregard of its prohibition of the deprivation of a defined constitutional or other federal right. . . . Nor is such an act beyond the understanding and comprehension of juries summoned to pass on them. The Act would then not become a trap for law enforcement agencies acting in good faith. . . .

. . . The difficulty here is that this question of intent was not submitted to the jury with the proper instructions. The court charged that petitioners acted illegally if they applied more force than was necessary to make the arrest effectual or to protect themselves from the prisoner's alleged assault. But in view of our construction of the word "willfully" the jury should have been further instructed that it was not sufficient that petitioners had a generally bad purpose. To convict it was necessary for them to find that petitioners had the purpose to deprive the prisoner of a constitutional right, e.g., the right to be tried by a court rather than by ordeal. And in determining whether that requisite bad purpose was present the jury would be entitled to consider all the attendant circumstances,—the malice of petitioners, the weapons used in the assault, its character and duration, the provocation, if any, and the like.

. . . It is said, however, that petitioners did not act "under color of any law" within the meaning of § 20 of the Criminal Code. We disagree. We are of the view that petitioners acted under "color" of law in making the arrest of Robert Hall and in assaulting him. They were officers of the law who made the arrest. By their own admissions they assaulted Hall in order to protect themselves and to keep their prisoner from escaping. It was their duty under Georgia law to make the arrest effective. Hence, their conduct comes within the statute.

Some of the arguments which have been advanced in support of the contrary conclusion suggest that the question under § 20 is whether Congress has made it a federal offense for a state officer to violate the law of his State. But there is no warrant for treating the question in state law terms. The problem is not whether state law has been violated but whether an inhabitant of a State has been deprived of a federal right by one who acts under "color of any law." He who acts under "color" of law may be a federal officer or a state officer. He may act under "color" of federal law or of a state law. The statute does not come into play merely because of the federal law or the state law under which the officer purports to act is violated. It is applicable when and only when someone is deprived of a federal right by that action. The fact that it is also a violation of state law does not make it any the less a federal offense punishable as such. Nor does its punishment by federal authority encroach on state authority or relieve the state from its responsibility for punishing state offenses.

We agree that when this statute is applied to the action of state officials, it should be construed so as to respect the proper balance between the States and the federal government in law enforcement. Violation of local law does not necessarily mean that federal rights have been invaded. The fact that a prisoner is assaulted, injured, or even murdered by state officials does not necessarily mean that he is deprived of any right protected or secured by the Constitution or laws of the United States. . . . The Fourteenth Amendment did not alter the basic relations between the States and the national government. . . . It is only state action of a "particular character" that is prohibited by the Fourteenth Amendment and against which the Amendment authorizes Congress to afford relief. *Civil Rights Cases*, 109 U.S. 3, 11, 13 [1883]. Thus Congress in § 20 of the Criminal Code did not undertake to make all torts of state officials federal crimes. It brought within § 20 only specified acts done "under color" of law and then only those acts which deprived a person of some right secured by the Constitution or laws of the United States.

. . . In the present case, as we have said, the defendants were officers of the law who had made an arrest and who by their own admissions made the assault in order to protect themselves and to keep the prisoner from escaping, i.e., to make the arrest effective. That was a duty they had under Georgia law. *United States v. Classic* is, therefore, indistinguishable from this case so far as "under color of" state law is concerned. In each officers of the State were performing official duties; in each the power which they were authorized to exercise was misused. We cannot draw upon a distinction between them unless we are to say that § 20 is not applicable to police officers. But the broad sweep of its language leaves no room for such an exception.

. . . Since there must be a new trial, the judgment below is

Reversed.

[The concurring opinion of MR. JUSTICE RUTLEDGE is omitted.]

* * *

MR. JUSTICE ROBERTS, MR. JUSTICE FRANKFURTER, and MR. JUSTICE JACKSON dissenting.

. . . So to read § 20 disregards not merely the normal function of language to express ideas appropriately. It fails not merely to leave the States the province of local crime enforcement, that the proper balance of political forces in our federalism requires. It does both, heedless of the Congressional purpose, clearly evinced even during the feverish Reconstruction days, to leave undisturbed the power and the duty of the States to enforce their criminal law by restricting federal authority to the punishment only of those persons who violate federal rights under claim of State authority and not by exerting federal authority against offenders of State authority. Such a distortion of federal power devised against recalcitrant State authority never entered the minds of the proponents of the legislation.

. . . In subjecting to punishment "deprivation of any rights, privileges, or immunities secured or protected by the Constitution and laws of the United States," § 20 on its face makes criminal deprivation of the whole range of undefined appeals to the Constitution. Such is the true scope of the forbidden conduct. Its domain is unbounded and therefore too indefinite. Criminal statutes must have more or less specific contours. This has none. . . .

. . . The complicated and subtle problems for law enforcement raised by the Court's decision emphasize the conclusion that § 20 was never designed for the use to which it has now been fashioned. The Government admits that it is appropriate to leave the punishment of such crimes as this to local authorities. Regard for this wisdom in federal-State relations was not left by Congress to executive discretion. It is, we are convinced, embodied in the statute itself.

[The dissenting opinion of MR. JUSTICE MURPHY is omitted.]

LOUISIANA EX REL. FRANCIS V. RESWEBER
329 U.S. 459 (1947)

In September 1945, Willie Francis, a black citizen of Louisiana, was convicted of murdering a white man and was sentenced to be electrocuted. On May 3, 1946, Francis was prepared for electrocution and placed in the electric chair. The executioner threw the switch, but because of some mechanical difficulty, death did not result. Francis was removed from the chair, and another death warrant for his execution was issued for a later date. Francis appealed to the Louisiana Supreme Court to prevent a second attempt to execute him for murder. The Louisiana Supreme Court denied his application, and Francis appealed to the U.S. Supreme Court, claiming that a second execution would deny him due process because of the double jeopardy provision of the Fifth Amendment and the cruel and unusual punishment provision of the Eighth Amendment. *Vote: 5-4.*

* * *

MR. JUSTICE REED announced the judgment of the Court in an opinion in which THE CHIEF JUSTICE, MR. JUSTICE BLACK, and MR. JUSTICE JACKSON join.

. . . To determine whether or not the execution of the petitioner may fairly take place after the experience through which he passed, we shall examine the circumstances under the assumption, but without so deciding, that violation of the principles of the Fifth and Eighth Amendments, as to double jeopardy and cruel and unusual punishment, would be violative of the due process clause of the Fourteenth Amendment. As nothing has been brought to our attention to suggest the contrary, we must and do assume that the state officials carried out their duties under the death warrant in a careful and humane manner. Accidents happen for which no man is to blame. We turn to the question as to whether the proposed enforcement of the criminal law of the state is offensive to any constitutional requirements to which reference has been made.

First. Our minds rebel against permitting the same sovereignty to punish an accused twice for the same offense. . . . But where the accused successfully seeks review of a conviction, there is no double jeopardy upon a new trial. . . . Even where a state obtains a new trial after conviction because of errors, while an accused may be placed on trial a second time, it is not the sort of hardship to the accused that is forbidden by the Fourteenth Amendment. *Palko v. Connecticut,* 302 U.S. 319, 328 [1937]. As this is a prosecution under state law, so far as double jeopardy is concerned, the *Palko* case is decisive. For we see no difference from a constitutional point of view between a new trial for error of law at the instance of the state that results in a death sentence instead of imprisonment for life and an execution that follows a failure of equipment. When an accident, with no suggestion of malevolence, prevents the consummation of a sentence, the state's subsequent course in the administration of its criminal law is not affected on that account by any requirement of due process under the Fourteenth Amendment. We find no double jeopardy here which can be said to amount to a denial of federal due process in the proposed execution.

Second. We find nothing in what took place here which amounts to cruel and unusual punishment in the constitutional sense. The case before us does not call for an examination into any punishments except that of death. See *Weems v. United States,* 217 U.S. 349 [1910]. The traditional humanity of modern Anglo-American law forbids the infliction of unnecessary pain in the execution of the death sentence. Prohibition against the wanton infliction of pain has come into our law from the Bill of Rights of 1688. The identical words appear in our Eighth Amendment. The Fourteenth would prohibit by its due process clause execution by a state in a cruel manner.

Petitioner's suggestion is that because he once underwent the psychological strain of preparation for electrocution, now to require him to undergo this preparation again subjects him to a lingering or cruel and unusual punishment. Even the fact that petitioner has already been subjected to a current of electricity does not make his subsequent execution any more cruel in the constitutional sense than any other execution. The cruelty against which the Constitution protects a convicted man is cruelty inherent in the method of punishment, not the necessary suffering involved in any method employed to extinguish life humanely. The fact that an unforeseeable accident prevented the prompt consummation of the sentence cannot, it seems to us, add an element of cruelty to a subsequent execution. There is no purpose to inflict unnecessary pain nor any unnecessary pain involved in the proposed execution. The situation of the unfortunate victim of this accident is just as though he had suffered the identical amount of mental anguish and physical pain any other occurrence, such as, for example, a fire in the cell block. We cannot agree that the hardship imposed upon the petitioner rises to that level of hardship denounced as denial of due process because of cruelty.

Third. The Supreme Court of Louisiana also rejected petitioner's contention that death inflicted after his prior sufferings would deny him the equal protection of the laws, guaranteed by the Fourteenth Amendment. This suggestion in so far as it differs from the due process argument is based on the idea that execution, after an attempt at execution has failed, would be a more severe punishment than is imposed upon others guilty of a like offense. That is, since others do not go through the strain of preparation for execution a second time or have not experienced a nonlethal current in a prior attempt at execution, as petitioner did, to compel petitioner to submit to execution after these prior experiences denies to him equal protection. Equal protection does not protect a prisoner against even illegal acts of officers in charge of him, much less against accidents during his detention for execution. See *Lisenba v. California,* 314 U.S. 219, 226 [1942]. Laws cannot prevent accidents nor can a law equally protect all against them. So long as the law applies to all alike, the requirements of equal protection are met. We have no right to assume that Louisiana singled out Francis for a treatment other than that which has been or would generally be applied.

Fourth. There is suggestion in the brief that the original trial itself was so unfair to the petitioner as to justify a reversal of the judgment of conviction and a new trial. Petitioner's claim in his brief is that he was inadequately represented by counsel. The record of the original trial presented to us shows the warrant for arrest, the indictment, the appointment of counsel and the minute entries of trial, selection of jury, verdict and sentence. There is nothing in any of these papers to show any violation of petitioner's constitutional rights. See *Carter v. Illinois,* 329 U.S. 173 [1946]. Review is sought here because of a denial of due process of law that would be brought about by execution of petitioner after failure of the first effort to electrocute him. Nothing is before us upon which a ruling can be predicated as to alleged denial of federal constitutional rights during petitioner's trial. On this record, we see nothing upon which we could conclude that the constitutional rights of petitioner were infringed.

Affirmed.

[The concurring opinion of MR. JUSTICE FRANKFURTER is omitted.]

* * *

MR. JUSTICE BURTON, with whom MR. JUSTICE DOUGLAS, MR. JUSTICE MURPHY, and MR. JUSTICE RUTLEDGE concur, dissenting.

. . . In determining whether the proposed procedure is unconstitutional, we must measure it against a lawful electrocution. The contrast is that between instantaneous death and death by installments—caused by electric shocks administered after one or more intervening periods of complete consciousness of the victim. Electrocution, when instantaneous, *can* be inflicted by a state in conformity with due process of law. *In re Kemmler,* 136 U.S. 436 [1890]. The Supreme Court of Louisiana has held that electrocution, in the manner prescribed in its statute, is more humane than hanging. . . .

The all-important consideration is that the execution shall be so instantaneous and substantially painless that the punishment shall be reduced, as nearly as possible, to no more than that of death itself. Electrocution has been approved only in a form that eliminates suffering.

. . . [The Louisiana statute] does not provide for electrocution by interrupted or repeated applications of electric current at intervals of several days or even minutes. It does not provide for the application of electric current of an intensity less than that sufficient to cause death. It prescribes expressly and solely for the application of a current of sufficient intensity to cause death and for the *continuance* of that application until death results. Prescribing capital punishment, it should be construed strictly. There can be no implied provision for a second, third or multiple application of the current. There is no statutory or judicial precedent upholding a delayed process of electrocution. . . .

If the state officials deliberately and intentionally had placed the relator in the electric chair five times and, each time, had applied electric current to his body in such a manner not sufficient, until the final time, to kill him, such a form of torture would rival that of burning at the stake. Although the failure of the first attempt, in the present case, was unintended, the reapplication of the electric current will be intentional. How many deliberate and intentional reapplications of electric current does it take to produce a cruel, unusual and unconstitutional punishment? While five applications would be more cruel and unusual than one, the uniqueness of the present case demonstrates that, today, two separated applications are sufficiently "cruel and unusual" to be prohibited. If five attempts would be "cruel and unusual," it would be difficult to draw the line between two, three, four and five. It is not difficult, however, as we here contend, to draw the line between the one continuous application prescribed by statute and any other application of the current.

Lack of intent that the first application be less than fatal is not material. The intent of the executioner cannot lessen the torture or excuse the result. It was the statutory duty of the state officials to make sure that there was no failure. The procedure in this case contrasts with common knowledge of precautions generally taken elsewhere to insure against failure of electrocutions. The high standard of care generally taken evidences the significance properly attached to the unconditional requirement of a single continued application of the current until death results. In our view of this case, we are giving careful recognition to the law of Louisiana. Neither the Legislature nor the Supreme Court of Louisiana has expressed approval of electrocution other than by one continuous application of a lethal current.

Executive clemency provides a common means of avoiding unconstitutional or otherwise questionable executions. When, however, the unconstitutionality of proposed executive procedure is brought before this Court, as in this case, we should apply the constitutional protection. In this case, final recourse is had to the high trusteeship vested in this Court by the people of the United States over the constitutional process by which their own lives may be taken.

KOREMATSU V. UNITED STATES
323 U.S. 214 (1944)

Fred Korematsu, an American citizen of Japanese descent, was convicted in federal district court for violating Civilian Exclusion Order No. 34 when he remained in San Leandro, California. This order directed that, after May 9, 1942, all persons of Japanese ancestry should be excluded from that West Coast military area. Korematsu challenged the constitutionality of the exclusion and detention program. The court of appeals affirmed his conviction. *Vote: 6-3.*

* * *

MR. JUSTICE BLACK delivered the opinion of the Court.

. . . It should be noted, to begin with, that all legal restrictions which curtail the civil rights of a single racial group are immediately suspect. That is not to say that all such restrictions are unconstitutional. It is to say that courts must subject them to the most rigid scrutiny. Pressing public necessity may sometimes justify the existence of such restrictions; racial antagonism never can.

. . . In the light of the principles we announced in the *Hirabayashi* [*v. United States,* 320 U.S. 81 (1943)] case, we are unable to conclude that it was beyond the war power of Congress and the Executive to exclude those of Japanese ancestry from the West Coast war area at the time they did. True, exclusion from the area in which one's home is located is a far greater deprivation than constant confinement to the home from 8 p.m. to 6 a.m. Nothing short of apprehension by the proper military authorities of the gravest imminent danger to the public safety can constitutionally justify either. But exclusion from a threatened area, no less than curfew, has a definite and close relationship to the prevention of espionage and sabotage. The military authorities, charged with the primary responsibility of defending our shores, concluded that curfew provided inadequate protection and ordered exclusion. They did so, as pointed out in our *Hirabayashi* opinion, in accordance with Congressional authority to the military to say who should, and who should not, remain in the threatened areas.

In this case the petitioner challenges the assumptions upon which we rested our conclusions in the *Hirabayashi* case. He also urges that by May 1942, when Order No. 34 was promulgated, all danger of Japanese invasion of the West Coast had disappeared. After careful consideration of these contentions we are compelled to reject them.

Here, as in the *Hirabayashi* case, . . . "we . . . cannot reject as unfounded the judgment of the military authorities and of Congress that there were disloyal members of that population, whose number and strength could not be precisely and quickly ascertained. We cannot say that the war-making branches of the Government did not have ground for believing that in a critical hour such persons could not readily be isolated and separately dealt with, and constituted a menace to the national defense and safety, which demanded that prompt and adequate measures be taken to guard against it."

Like curfew, exclusion of those of Japanese origin was deemed necessary because of the presence of an unascertained number of disloyal members of the group, most of whom we have no doubt were loyal to this country. It was because we could not reject the finding of the military authorities that it was impossible to bring about an immediate segregation of the disloyal from the loyal that we sustained the validity of the curfew as applying to the whole group. In the instant case, temporary exclusion of the entire group was rested by the military on the same ground. The judgment that exclusion of the whole group was for the same reason a military imperative answers the contention that the exclusion was in the nature of group punishment based on antagonism to those of Japanese origin. That there were members of the group who retained loyalties to Japan has been confirmed by investigations made subsequent to the exclusion. Approximately five thousand American citizens of Japanese ancestry refused to swear unqualified allegiance to the United States and to renounce allegiance to the Japanese Emperor, and several thousand evacuees requested repatriation to Japan.

We uphold the exclusion order as of the time it was made and when the petitioner violated it. . . . In doing so, we are not unmindful of the hardships imposed by it upon a large group of American citizens. . . . But hardships are a part of war, and war is an aggregation of hardships. All citizens alike, both in and out of uniform, feel the impact of war in greater or lesser measure. Citizenship has its responsibilities as well as its privileges, and in time of war the burden is always heavier. Compulsory exclusion of large groups of citizens from their homes, except under circumstances of direst emergency and peril, is inconsistent with our basic governmental institutions. But when under conditions of modern warfare our shores are threatened by hostile forces, the power to protect must be commensurate with the threatened danger.

It is argued that on May 30, 1942, the date the petitioner was charged with remaining in the prohibited area, there were conflicting orders outstanding, forbidding him both to leave the area and to remain there. Of course, a person cannot be convicted for doing the very thing which it is a crime to fail to do. But the outstanding orders here contained no such contradictory commands.

. . . Since the petitioner has not been convicted of failing to report or to remain in an assembly or relocation center, we cannot in this case determine the validity of those separate provisions of the order. It is sufficient here for us to pass upon the order which the petitioner violated. To do more would be to go beyond the issues raised, and to decide momentous questions not contained within the framework of the pleadings or the evidence within this case. It will be time enough to decide the serious constitutional issues which petitioner seeks to raise when an assembly or relocation order is applied or is certain to be applied to him, and we have its terms before us.

Some of the members of the Court are of the view that evacuation and detention in an Assembly Center were inseparable. After May 3, 1942, the date of the Exclusion Order No. 34, Korematsu was under compulsion to leave the area not as he would choose but via an Assembly Center. The Assembly Center was conceived as a part of the machinery for group evacuation. The power to exclude includes the power to do it by force if necessary. And any forcible measure must necessarily entail some degree of detention or restraint whatever method of removal is selected. But whichever view is taken, it results in holding that the order under which petitioner was convicted was valid.

It is said that we are dealing here with the case of imprisonment of a citizen in a concentration camp solely because of his ancestry, without evidence or inquiry concerning his loyalty and good disposition towards the United States. Our task would be simple, our duty clear, were this a case involving the imprisonment of a loyal citizen in a concentration camp because of racial prejudice. Regardless of the true nature of the assembly and relocation centers— and we deem it unjustifiable to call them concentration camps with all the ugly connotations that term implies—we are dealing specifically with nothing but an exclusion order. To cast this case into outlines of racial prejudice, without reference to the real military dangers which were presented, merely confuses the issue. Korematsu was not excluded from the Military Area because of hostility to him or his race. He *was* excluded because we are at war with the Japanese Empire, because the properly constituted military authorities feared an invasion of our West Coast and felt constrained to take proper security measures, because they decided that the military urgency of the situation demanded that all citizens of Japanese ancestry be segregated from the West Coast temporarily, and finally, because Congress, reposing its confidence in this time of war in our military leaders—as inevitably it must—determined that they should have the power to do just this. There was evidence of disloyalty on the part of some, the military authorities considered that the need for action was great, and time was short. We cannot—by availing ourselves of the calm perspective of hindsight—now say that at that time these actions were unjustified.

Affirmed.
[The concurring opinion of MR. JUSTICE FRANKFURTER is omitted.]

* * *

MR. JUSTICE MURPHY dissenting.

This exclusion of "all persons of Japanese ancestry, both alien and non-alien," from the Pacific Coast area on a plea of military necessity in the absence of martial law ought not to be approved. Such exclusion goes over "the very brink of constitutional power" and falls into the ugly abyss of racism.

In dealing with matters relating to the prosecution and progress of a war, we must accord great respect and consideration to the judgments of the military authorities who are on the scene and who have full knowledge of the military facts. The scope of their discretion must, as a matter of necessity and common sense, be wide. And their judgments ought not to be overruled lightly by those whose training and duties ill-equip them to deal intelligently with matters so vital to the physical security of the nation.

At the same time, however, it is essential that there be definite limits to military discretion, especially where martial law has not been declared. Individuals must not be left impoverished of their constitutional rights on a plea of military necessity that has neither substance nor support. Thus, like other claims conflicting with the asserted constitutional rights of the individual, the military claim must subject itself to the judicial process of having its reasonableness determined and its conflicts with other interests reconciled. . . .

The judicial test of whether the Government, on a plea of military necessity, can validly deprive an individual of any of his constitutional rights is whether the deprivation is reasonably related to a public danger that is so "immediate, imminent, and impending" as not to admit of delay and not to permit the intervention of ordinary constitutional processes to alleviate the danger. . . . Civilian Exclusion Order No. 34 . . . clearly does not meet that test. Being an obvious racial discrimination, the order deprives all those within its scope of the equal protection of the laws as guaranteed by the Fifth Amendment. It further deprives these individuals of their constitutional rights to live and work where they will, to establish a home where they choose and to move about freely. In excommunicating them without benefit of hearings, this order also deprives them of all their constitutional rights to procedural due process. Yet no reasonable relation to an "immediate, imminent, and impending" public danger is evident to support this racial restriction which is one of the most sweeping and complete deprivations of constitutional rights in the history of this nation in the absence of martial law.

. . . That this forced exclusion was the result in good measure of this erroneous assumption of racial guilt rather than bona fide military necessity is evidenced by the Commanding General's Final Report on the evacuation from the Pacific Coast area. In it he refers to all individuals of Japanese descent as "subversive," as belonging to "an enemy race" whose "racial strains are undiluted," and as constituting "over 112,000 potential enemies . . . at large today" along the Pacific Coast. In support of this blanket condemnation of all persons of Japanese descent, however, no reliable evidence is cited to show that such individuals were generally disloyal, or had generally so conducted themselves in this area as to constitute a special menace to defense installations or war industries, or had otherwise by their behavior furnished reasonable ground for their exclusion as a group.

Justification for the exclusion is sought, instead, mainly upon questionable racial and sociological grounds not ordinarily within the realm of expert military judgment, supplemented by certain semi-military conclusions drawn from an unwarranted use of circumstantial evidence. Individuals of Japanese ancestry are condemned because they are said to be "a large unassimilated, tightly knit racial group, bound to an enemy nation by strong ties of race, culture, custom and religion." They are claimed to be given to "emperor worshipping ceremonies" and to "dual citizenship." Japanese language schools and allegedly pro-Japanese organizations are cited as evidence of possible group disloyalty, together with facts as to certain persons being educated and residing at length in Japan. It is intimated that many of these individuals deliberately resided "adjacent to strategic points," thus enabling them "to carry into execution a tremendous program of sabotage on a mass scale should any considerable number of them have been inclined to do so." The need for protective custody is also asserted. The report refers without identity to "numerous incidents of violence" as well as to other admittedly unverified or cumulative incidents. From this, plus certain other events not shown to have been connected with the Japanese Americans, it is concluded that the "situation was fraught with danger to the Japanese population itself" and that the general public "was ready to take matters into its own hands." Finally, it is intimated, though not directly charged or proved, that persons of Japanese ancestry were responsible for three minor isolated shellings and bombings of the Pacific Coast area, as well as for unidentified radio transmissions and night signalling.

The main reasons relied upon by those responsible for the forced evacuation, therefore, do not prove a reasonable relation between the group characteristics of Japanese Americans and the dangers of invasion, sabotage and espionage. The reasons appear, instead, to be largely an accumulation of much of the misinformation, half-truths and insinuations that for years have been directed against Japanese Americans by people with racial and economic prejudices—the same people who have been among the foremost advocates of the evacuation. A military judgment based upon such racial and sociological considerations is not entitled to the great weight ordinarily given the judgments based upon strictly military considerations. Especially is this so when every charge relative to race, religion, culture, geographical location, and legal and economic status has been substantially discredited by independent studies made by experts in these matters.

The military necessity which is essential to the validity of the evacuation order thus resolves itself into a few intimations that certain individuals actively aided the enemy, from which it is inferred that the entire group of Japanese Americans could not be trusted to be or remain loyal to the United States. No one denies, of course, that there were some disloyal persons of Japanese descent on the Pacific Coast who did all in their power to aid their ancestral land. Similar disloyal activities have been engaged in by many persons of German, Italian and even more pioneer stock in our country. But to infer that examples of individual disloyalty prove group disloyalty and justify discriminatory action against the entire group is to deny that under our system of law individual guilt is the sole basis for deprivation of rights. Moreover, this inference, which is at the very heart of the evacuation orders, has been used in support of the abhorrent and despicable treatment of minority groups by the dictatorial tyrannies which this nation is now pledged to destroy. To give constitutional sanction to that inference in this case, however well-intentioned may have been the military command on the Pacific Coast, is to adopt one of the cruelest of the rationales used by our enemies to destroy the dignity of the individual and to encourage and open the door to discriminatory actions against other minority groups in the passions of tomorrow.

[The dissenting opinions of MR. JUSTICE JACKSON and MR. JUSTICE ROBERTS are omitted.]

MISSOURI EX REL. GAINES V. CANADA
305 U.S. 337 (1938)

Lloyd Gaines was refused admission to the University of Missouri Law School under Missouri law that required separate schools and universities for whites and blacks. Under Missouri law, the board of curators was required to arrange for the attendance and payment of tuition and fees of black residents of Missouri to a university of any adjacent state in order to pursue studies that were not taught at Lincoln University (a black university). Gaines brought suit against Canada, the registrar of the University of Missouri, to compel the curators to admit him. He asserted that this refusal constituted a denial by the state of equal protection of the laws. The Missouri Supreme Court refused to grant Gaines the mandamus because he failed to apply for aid to attend an out-of-state law school. *Vote: 7-2.*

* * *

MR. CHIEF JUSTICE HUGHES delivered the opinion of the Court.

. . . The state court stresses the advantages that are afforded by the law schools of the adjacent States,—Kansas, Nebraska, Iowa and Illinois,— which admit non-resident negroes. The court considered that these were schools of high standing where one desiring to practice law in Missouri can get "as sound, comprehensive, valuable legal education" as in the University of Missouri; that the system of education in the former is the same as that in the latter and is designed to give the students a basis for the practice of law in any State where the Anglo-American system of law obtains; that the law school of the University of Missouri does not specialize in Missouri law and that the course of study and the case books used in the five schools are substantially identical. Petitioner insists that for one intending to practice in Missouri there are special advantages in attending a law school there, both in relation to the opportunities for the particular study of Missouri law and for the observation of the local courts, and also in view of the prestige of the Missouri law school among the citizens of the State, his prospective clients. Proceeding with its examination of relative advantages, the state court found that the difference in distances to be traveled afforded no substantial ground of complaint and that there was an adequate appropriation to meet the full tuition fees which petitioner would have to pay.

We think that these matters are beside the point. The basic consideration is not as to what sort of opportunities other States provide, or whether they are as good as those in Missouri, but as to what opportunities Missouri itself furnishes to white students and denies to negroes solely upon the ground of color. The admissibility of laws separating the races in the enjoyment of privileges afforded by the State rests wholly upon the equality of the privileges which the laws give to the separated groups within the State. The question here is not of a duty of the State to supply legal training, or of the quality of the training which it does supply, but of its duty when it provides such training to furnish it to the residents of the State upon the basis of an equality of right. By the operation of the laws of Missouri a privilege has been created for white students which is denied to negroes by reason of their race. The white resident is afforded legal education within the State; the negro resident having the same qualifications is refused it there and must go outside the State to obtain it. That is a denial of the equality of legal right to the enjoyment of the privilege which the State has set up, and the provision for the payment of tuition fees in another State does not remove the discrimination.

The equal protection of the laws is a "pledge of the protection of equal laws." *Yick Wo v. Hopkins,* 118 U.S. 356, 369 [1886]. Manifestly, the obligation of the State to give the protection of equal laws can be performed only where its laws operate, that is, within its own jurisdiction. It is there that the equality of legal right must be maintained. That obligation is imposed by the Constitution upon the States severally as governmental entities,—each responsible for its own laws establishing the rights and duties of persons within its borders. It is an obligation the burden of which cannot be cast by one State upon another, and no State can be excused from performance by what another State may do or fail to do. That separate responsibility of each State within its own sphere is of the essence of statehood maintained under our dual system. It seems to be implicit in respondents' argument that if other States did not provide courses for legal education, it would nevertheless be the constitutional duty of Missouri when it supplied such courses for white students to make equivalent provision for negroes. But that plain duty would exist because it rested upon the State independently of the action of other States. We find it impossible to conclude that what otherwise would be an unconstitutional discrimination, with respect to the legal right to the enjoyment of opportunities within the State, can be justified by requiring resort to opportunities elsewhere. That resort may mitigate the inconvenience of the discrimination but cannot serve to validate it.

Nor can we regard the fact that there is but a limited demand in Missouri for the legal education of negroes as excusing the discrimination in favor of whites. . . .

Here, petitioner's right was a personal one. It was as an individual that he was entitled to the equal protection of the laws, and the State was bound to furnish him within its borders facilities for legal education substantially equal to those which the State there afforded for persons of the white race, whether or not other negroes sought the same opportunity.

It is urged, however, that the provision for tuition outside the State is a temporary one,—that it is intended to operate merely pending the establishment of a law department for negroes at Lincoln University. While in that sense the discrimination may be termed temporary, it may nevertheless continue for an indefinite period by reason of the discretion given to the curators of Lincoln University and the alternative of arranging for tuition in other States, as permitted by the state law as construed by the state court, so long as the curators find it unnecessary and impracticable to provide facilities for the legal instruction of negroes within the State. In that view, we cannot regard the discrimination as excused by what is called its temporary character.

. . . We are of the opinion that the [state court] ruling was error, and that petitioner was entitled to be admitted to the law school of the State University in the absence of other and proper provision for his legal training within the State.

The judgment of the Supreme Court of Missouri is reversed and the cause is remanded for further proceedings not inconsistent with this opinion.

Reversed.

* * *

MR. JUSTICE McREYNOLDS, with whom MR. JUSTICE BUTLER concurs, dissenting.

Considering the disclosures of the record, the Supreme Court of Missouri arrived at a tenable conclusion and its judgment should be affirmed. That court well understood the grave difficulties of the situation and rightly refused to upset the settled legislative policy of the State by directing a mandamus.

. . . For a long time Missouri has acted upon the view that the best interest of her people demands separation of whites and negroes in schools. Under the opinion just announced, I presume she may abandon her law school and thereby disadvantage her white citizens without improving petitioner's opportunities for legal instruction; or she may break down the settled practice concerning separate schools and thereby, as indicated by experience, damnify both races. Whether by some other course it may be possible for her to avoid condemnation is [a] matter for conjecture.

The State has offered to provide the negro petitioner opportunity for study of the law—if perchance that is the thing really desired—by paying his tuition at some nearby school of good standing. This is far from unmistakable disregard of his rights and in the circumstances is enough to satisfy any reasonable demand for specialized training. It appears that never before has a negro applied for admission to the Law School and none has ever asked that Lincoln University provide legal instruction.

The problem presented obviously is a difficult and highly practical one. A fair effort to solve it has been made by offering adequate opportunity for study when sought in good faith. The State should not be unduly hampered through theorization inadequately restrained by experience.

McLAURIN V. OKLAHOMA STATE REGENTS FOR HIGHER EDUCATION
339 U.S. 637 (1950)

Under Oklahoma's laws requiring segregated higher education, G. W. McLaurin, a black man who sought to pursue doctoral study in education at the University of Oklahoma, was denied admission because of his race. McLaurin sought injunctive relief, alleging that the state's laws deprived him of the equal protection of the laws. A three-judge district court, citing *Missouri ex rel. Gaines v. Canada* (1938) and *Sipuel v. Board of Regents* (1948), held that the state had a duty to provide McLaurin with the education he sought. Under the pressure of litigation, the Oklahoma legislature amended these statutes to permit blacks to the university but on a segregated basis. McLaurin was assigned to special seating for black students in the classroom, library, and cafeteria. The district court held that McLaurin's treatment did not violate the Fourteenth Amendment. In the interval between the district court's decision and the Supreme Court hearing, the university removed the Reserved for Colored sign in the classroom, but McLaurin was assigned to seats in the classroom, library, and cafeteria on a segregated basis. *Vote: 9-0.*

* * *

MR. CHIEF JUSTICE VINSON delivered the opinion of the Court.

In this case, we are faced with the question of whether a state may, after admitting a student to graduate instruction in its state university, afford him different treatment from other students solely because of his race. We decide only this issue. . . .

. . . It is said that the separations imposed by the State in this case are in form merely nominal. McLaurin uses the same classroom, library and cafeteria as students of other races; there is no indication that the seats to which he is assigned in these rooms have any disadvantage of location. He may wait in line in the cafeteria and there stand and talk with his fellow students, but while he eats he must remain apart.

These restrictions were obviously imposed in order to comply, as nearly as could be, with the statutory requirements of Oklahoma. But they signify that the State, in administering the facilities it affords for professional and graduate study, sets McLaurin apart from the other students. The result is that appellant is handicapped in his pursuit of effective graduate instruction. Such restrictions impair and inhibit his ability to study, to engage in discussions and exchange views with other students, and, in general, to learn his profession.

Our society grows increasingly complex, and our need for trained leaders increases correspondingly. Appellant's case represents, perhaps, the epitome of that need, for he is attempting to obtain an advanced degree in education, to become, by definition, a leader and trainer of others. Those who will come under his guidance and influence must be directly affected by the education he receives. Their own education and development will necessarily suffer to the extent that his training is unequal to that of his classmates. State-imposed restrictions which produce such inequalities cannot be sustained.

It may be argued that appellant will be in no better position when these restrictions are removed, for he may still be set apart by his fellow students. This we think irrelevant. There is a vast difference—a Constitutional difference—between restrictions imposed by the state which prohibit the intellectual commingling of students, and the refusal of individuals to commingle where the state presents no such bar. *Shelley v. Kraemer,* 334 U.S. 1, 13-14 (1948). The removal of the state restrictions will not necessarily abate individual and group predilections, prejudices and choices. But at the very least, the state will not be depriving appellant of the opportunity to secure acceptance by his fellow students on his own merits.

We conclude that the conditions under which this appellant is required to receive his education deprive him of his personal and present right to the equal protection of the laws. See *Sweatt v. Painter,* [339 U.S. 629 (1950)]. We hold that under these circumstances the Fourteenth Amendment precludes differences in treatment by the state based upon race. Appellant, having been admitted to a state-supported graduate school, must receive the same treatment at the hands of the state as students of the other races. The judgment is

Reversed.

SWEATT V. PAINTER
339 U.S. 629 (1950)

Heman Sweatt, a black Houston letter carrier who wanted to become a lawyer, applied to the University of Texas Law School but was denied admission on account of his race under Texas law. At the time, no law school in Texas admitted blacks. While Sweatt brought suit to compel his admission to the University of Texas law school, the state established a law school for blacks at Texas State University for Negroes. Sweatt refused to register at the new school, asserting that the educational facilities at Texas State were substantially unequal to those at the University of Texas Law School. The lower courts held that the law school for blacks was substantially equal to the University of Texas Law School. *Vote: 9-0.*

* * *

MR. CHIEF JUSTICE VINSON delivered the opinion of the Court.

This case and *McLaurin v. Oklahoma State Regents,* [339 U.S. 637 (1950)] present different aspects of this general question: To what extent does the Equal Protection Clause of the Fourteenth Amendment limit the power of a state to distinguish between students of different races in professional and graduate education in a state university? . . .

. . . The University of Texas Law School, from which petitioner was excluded, was staffed by a faculty of sixteen full-time and three part-time professors, some of whom are nationally recognized authorities in their field. Its student body numbered 850. The library contained over 65,000 volumes. Among the other facilities available to the students were a law review, moot court facilities, scholarship funds, and Order of the Coif affiliation. The school's alumni occupy the most distinguished positions in the private practice of law and in the public life of the State. It may properly be considered one of the nation's ranking law schools.

The law school for Negroes which was to have opened in February, 1947, would have had no independent faculty or library. The teaching was to be carried on by four members of the University of Texas Law School Faculty, who were to maintain their offices at the University of Texas while teaching at both institutions. Few of the 10,000 volumes ordered for the library had arrived; nor was there any full-time librarian. The school lacked accreditation.

Since the trial of this case, respondents report the opening of a law school at the Texas State University for Negroes. It is apparently on the road to full accreditation. It has a faculty of five full-time professors; a student body of 23; a library of some 16,500 volumes serviced by a full-time staff; a practice court and legal aid association; and one alumnus who has become a member of the Texas Bar.

Whether the University of Texas Law School is compared with the original or the new law school for Negroes, we cannot find substantial equality in the educational opportunities offered white and Negro law students by the State. In terms of number of the faculty, variety of courses and opportunity for specialization, size of the student body, scope of the library, availability of law review and similar activities, the University of Texas Law School is superior. What is more important, the University of Texas Law School possesses to a far greater degree those qualities which are incapable of objective measurement but which make for greatness in a law school. Such qualities, to name but a few, include reputation of the faculty, experience of the administration, position and influence of the alumni, standing in the community, traditions and prestige. It is difficult to believe that one who had a free choice between these law schools would consider the question close.

Moreover, although the law is a highly learned profession, we are well aware that it is an intensely practical one. The law school, the proving ground for legal learning and practice, cannot be effective in isolation from the individuals and institutions with which the law interacts. Few students and no one who has practiced law would choose to study in an academic vacuum, removed from the interplay of ideas and the exchange of views with which the law is concerned. The law school to which Texas is willing to admit petitioner excludes from its student body members of the racial groups which number 85% of the population of the State and include most of the lawyers, witnesses, jurors, judges and other officials with whom petitioner will inevitably be dealing when he becomes a member of the Texas Bar. With such a substantial and significant segment of society excluded, we cannot conclude that the education offered petitioner is substantially equal to that which he would receive if admitted to the University of Texas Law School.

It may be argued that excluding petitioner from that school is no different from excluding white students from the new law school. This contention overlooks realities. It is unlikely that a member of a group so decisively in the majority, attending a school with rich traditions and prestige which only a history of consistently maintained excellence could command, would claim that the opportunities afforded him for legal education were unequal to those held open to petitioner. That such a claim, if made, would be dishonored by the State, is no answer. . . .

It is fundamental that these cases concern rights which are personal and present. This Court has stated unanimously that "The State must provide [legal education] for [petitioner] in conformity with the equal protection clause of the Fourteenth Amendment and provide it as soon as it does for applicants of any other group." *Sipuel v. Board of Regents,* 332 U.S. 631, 633 (1948). That case "did not present the issue whether a state might not satisfy the equal protection clause of the Fourteenth Amendment by establishing a separate law school for Negroes." *Fisher v. Hurst,* 333 U.S. 147, 150 (1948). In *Missouri ex rel. Gaines v. Canada,* 305 U.S. 337, 351 (1938), the Court, speaking through Chief Justice Hughes, declared that "petitioner's right was a personal one. It was as an individual that he was entitled to the equal protection of the laws, and the State was bound to furnish him within its borders facilities for legal education substantially equal to those which the State there afforded for persons of the white race, whether or not other negroes sought the same opportunity." These are the only cases in this Court which present the issue of the constitutional validity of race distinctions in state-supported graduate and professional education.

In accordance with these cases, petitioner may claim his full constitutional right: legal education equivalent to that offered by the State to students of other races. Such education is not available to him in a separate law school as offered by the State. We cannot, therefore, agree with respondents that the doctrine of *Plessy v. Ferguson,* 163 U.S. 537 (1896), requires affirmance of the judgment below. Nor need we reach petitioner's contention that *Plessy v. Ferguson* should be reexamined in the light of contemporary knowledge respecting the purposes of the Fourteenth Amendment and the effects of racial segregation. . . .

We hold that the Equal Protection Clause of the Fourteenth Amendment requires that petitioner be admitted to the University of Texas Law School. . . .
Reversed.

MITCHELL V. UNITED STATES
313 U.S. 80 (1941)

Representative Arthur W. Mitchell, a black resident of Chicago and a member of the U.S. House of Representatives, paid a round-trip fare for a trip from Chicago to Hot Springs, Arkansas, on the line of the Chicago, Rock Island & Pacific Railway Company. Representative Mitchell filed a complaint with the Interstate Commerce Commission (ICC), alleging unjust discrimination in the furnishing of accommodations to black passengers when the train conductor, shortly after leaving Memphis, took the Memphis-Hot Springs portion of the ticket but refused to accept payment for the Pullman seat from Memphis. Just before the train reached Memphis, he had a Pullman porter transfer Mitchell to the Chicago-Hot Springs sleeper on the same train. The conductor's action was in purported compliance with an Arkansas statute requiring segregation of black from white persons. The ICC dismissed Mitchell's complaint, and he brought suit to set aside the commission's order. A three-judge district court upheld the ICC's order. *Vote: 9-0.*

* * *

MR. CHIEF JUSTICE HUGHES delivered the opinion of the Court.

. . . The case was submitted to the District Court upon the evidence taken before the Commission. The undisputed facts showed conclusively that, having paid a first-class fare for the entire journey from Chicago to Hot Springs, and having offered to pay the proper charge for a seat which was available in the Pullman car for the trip from Memphis to Hot Springs, he was compelled, in accordance with custom, to leave that car and to ride in a second-class car and was thus denied the standard conveniences and privileges afforded to first-class passengers. This was manifestly a discrimination against him in the course of his interstate journey and admittedly that discrimination was based solely upon the fact that he was a Negro. The question whether this was a discrimination forbidden by the Interstate Commerce Act is not a question of segregation but one of equality of treatment. The denial to appellant of equality of accommodations because of his race would be an invasion of a fundamental individual right which is guaranteed against state action by the Fourteenth Amendment (*McCabe v. Atchison, T.& S.F. Ry. Co.,* 235 U.S. 151, 160-162 (1914); *Missouri ex rel. Gaines v. Canada,* 305 U.S. 337, 344, 345 [1938] and in view of the nature of the right and of our constitutional policy it cannot be maintained that the discrimination as it was alleged was not essentially unjust. In that aspect it could not be deemed to lie outside the purview of the sweeping prohibitions of the Interstate Commerce Act.

We have repeatedly said that it is apparent from the legislative history of the Act that not only was the evil of discrimination the principal thing aimed at, but that there is no basis for the contention that Congress intended to exempt any discriminatory action or practice of interstate carriers affecting interstate commerce which it had to reach. . . . Paragraph 1 of § 3 of the Act says explicitly that it shall be unlawful for any common carrier subject to the Act "to subject any particular person . . . to any undue or unreasonable prejudice or disadvantage in any respect whatsoever." . . . From the inception of its administration the Interstate Commerce Commission has recognized the applicability of this provision to discrimination against colored passengers because of their race and the duty of carriers to provide equality of treatment with respect to transportation facilities; that is, that colored persons who buy first-class tickets must be furnished with accommodations equal in comforts and conveniences to those afforded to first-class white passengers. . . .

. . . We find no sound reason for the failure to apply this principle by holding the discrimination from which the appellant suffered to be unlawful and by forbidding it in the future.

That there was but a single instance was not a justification of the treatment of the appellant. Moreover, the Commission thought it plain that "the incident was mentioned as representative of an alleged practice that was expected to continue." And the Commission found that the ejection of appellant from the Pullman car and the requirement that he should continue his journey in a second-class car was "in accordance with custom," that is, as we understand it, according to the custom which obtained in similar circumstances.

Nor does the change in the carrier's practice avail. That did not alter the discrimination to which appellant had been subjected, and as to the future the change was not adequate. It appears that since July, 1937, the carrier has put in service a coach for colored passengers which is of equal quality with that used by second-class white passengers. But, as the Government well observes, the question does not end with travel on second-class tickets. It does not appear that colored passengers who have bought first-class tickets for transportation by the carrier are given accommodations which are substantially equal to those afforded to white passengers. . . . And the Commission has recognized that inequality persists with respect to certain other facilities such as dining-car and observation-parlor car accommodations.

We take it that the chief reason for the Commission's action was the "comparatively little colored traffic." But the comparative volume of traffic cannot justify the denial of a fundamental right of equality of treatment, a right specifically safeguarded by the provisions of the Interstate Commerce Act. We thought a similar argument with respect to volume of traffic to be untenable in the application of the Fourteenth Amendment. We said that it made the constitutional right depend upon the number of persons who may be discriminated against, whereas the essence of that right is that it is a personal one. . . . While the supply of particular facilities may be conditioned upon there being a reasonable demand therefor, if facilities are provided, substantial equality of treatment of persons traveling under like conditions cannot be refused. It is the individual, we said, who is entitled to the equal protection of the laws,—not merely a group of individuals, or a body of persons according to their numbers. . . . And the Interstate Commerce Act expressly extends its prohibitions to the subjecting of "any particular person" to unreasonable discriminations.

On the facts here presented, there is no room, as the Government properly says, for administrative or expert judgment with respect to practical difficulties. It is enough that the discrimination shown was palpably unjust and forbidden by the Act.

The decree of the District Court is reversed and the cause is remanded with directions to set aside the order of the Commission and to remand the case to the Commission for further proceedings in conformity with this opinion.

Reversed.

MORGAN V. VIRGINIA
328 U.S. 373 (1946)

Irene Morgan, a black passenger traveling on a Greyhound bus from Gloucester County, Virginia, to Baltimore, Maryland, refused to sit at the back of the bus at the request of the driver. Morgan was convicted of violating a Virginia act "which requires all passenger motor vehicle carriers, both interstate and intrastate, to separate without discrimination the white and colored passengers in their motor buses so that contiguous seats will not be occupied by persons of different races at the same time." The Supreme Court of Appeals of Virginia affirmed her conviction. *Vote: 7-1.*

* * *

MR. JUSTICE REED delivered the opinion of the Court.

. . . The precise degree of a permissible restriction on state power cannot be fixed generally or indeed not even for one kind of state legislation, such as taxation or health or safety. There is a recognized abstract principle, however, that may be taken as a postulate for testing whether particular state legislation in the absence of action by Congress is beyond state power. This is that the state legislation is invalid if it unduly burdens that commerce in matters where uniformity is necessary—necessary in the constitutional sense of useful in accomplishing a permitted purpose. Where uniformity is essential for the functioning of commerce, a state may not interpose its local regulation. Too true it is that the principle lacks in precision. Although the quality of such a principle is abstract, its application to the facts of a situation created by the attempted enforcement of a statute brings about a specific determination as to whether or not the statute in question is a burden on commerce. Within the broad limits of the principle, the cases turn on their own facts.

In the field of transportation, there has been a series of decisions which hold that where Congress has not acted and although the state statute affects interstate commerce, a state may validly enact legislation which has predominantly only a local influence on the course of commerce. It is equally settled that, even where Congress has not acted, state legislation or a final court order is invalid which materially affects interstate commerce. Because the Constitution puts the ultimate power to regulate commerce in Congress, rather than the states, the degree of state legislation's interference with that commerce may be weighed by federal courts to determine whether the burden makes the statute unconstitutional. The courts could not invalidate federal legislation for the same reason because Congress, within the limits of the Fifth Amendment, has authority to burden commerce if that seems to it a desirable means of accomplishing a permitted end.

This statute is attacked on the ground that it imposes undue burdens on interstate commerce. It is said by the Court of Appeals to have been passed in the exercise of the state's police power to avoid friction between the races. But this Court pointed out years ago "that a State cannot avoid the operation of this rule by simply invoking the convenient apologetics of the police power." Burdens upon commerce are those actions of a state which directly "impair the usefulness of its facilities for such traffic." That impairment, we think, may arise from other causes than costs or long delays. A burden may arise from a state statute which requires interstate passengers to order their movements on the vehicle in accordance with local rather than national requirements.

On appellant's journey, this statute required that she sit in designated seats in Virginia. Changes in seat designation might be made "at any time" during the journey when "necessary or proper for the comfort and convenience of passengers." This occurred in this instance. Upon such change of designation, the statute authorizes the operator of the vehicle to require, as he did here, "any passenger to change his or her seat as it may be necessary or proper." An interstate passenger must if necessary repeatedly shift seats while moving in Virginia to meet the seating requirements of the changing passenger group. On arrival at the District of Columbia line, the appellant would have had freedom to occupy any available seat and so to the end of her journey.

Interstate passengers traveling via motor buses between the north and south or the east and west may pass through Virginia on through lines in the day or in the night. The large buses approach the comfort of pullmans and have seats convenient for rest. On such interstate journeys the enforcement of the requirements for reseating would be disturbing.

Appellant's argument, properly we think, include facts bearing on interstate motor transportation beyond those immediately involved in this journey under the Virginia statutory regulations. To appraise the weight of the burden of the Virginia statute on interstate commerce, related statutes of other states are important to show whether there are cumulative effects which may make local regulation impracticable. Eighteen states, it appears, prohibit racial separation on public carriers. Ten require separation on motor carriers. Of these, Alabama applies specifically to interstate passengers with an exception for interstate passengers with through tickets from states without laws on separation of passengers. The language of the other acts, like this Virginia statute before the Court of Appeals' decision in this case, may be said to be susceptible to an interpretation that they do or do not apply to interstate passengers.

In states where separation of races is required in motor vehicles, a method of identification as white or colored must be employed. This may be done by definition. Any ascertainable Negro blood identifies a person as colored for purposes of separation in some states. In the other states which require the separation of the races in motor carriers, apparently no definition generally applicable or made for the purposes of the statute is given. Court definition or further legislative enactments would be required to clarify the line between the races. Obviously there may be changes by legislation in the definition.

The interferences to interstate commerce which arise from state regulation of racial association on interstate vehicles has long been recognized. Such regulation hampers freedom of choice in selecting accommodations. The recent changes in transportation brought about by the coming of automobiles does not seem of great significance in the problem. People of all races travel today more extensively than in 1878 when this Court first passed upon state regulation on racial segregation in commerce. The factual situation set out in preceding paragraphs emphasizes the soundness of this Court's early conclusion in *Hall v. DeCuir,* 95 U.S. 485 [1878].

. . . In weighing the factors that enter into our conclusion as to whether this statute so burdens interstate commerce or so infringes the requirements of national uniformity as to be invalid, we are mindful of the fact that conditions vary between northern or western states such as Maine or Montana, with practically no colored population; industrial states such as Illinois, Ohio, New Jersey and Pennsylvania with a small, although appreciable, percentage of colored citizens; and the states of the deep south with percentages of from twenty-five to nearly fifty per cent colored, all with varying densities of the white and colored races in certain localities. Local efforts to promote amicable relations in difficult areas by legislative segregation in interstate transportation emerge from the latter racial distribution. As no state law can reach beyond its own border nor bar transportation of passengers across its boundaries, diverse seating requirements for the races in interstate journeys result. As there is no federal act dealing with the separation of the races in interstate transportation, we must decide the validity of this Virginia statute on the challenge that it interferes with commerce, as a matter of balance between the exercise of the local police power and the need for national uniformity in the regulations for interstate travel. It seems clear to us that seating arrangements for the different races in interstate motor travel require a single, uniform rule to promote and protect national travel. Consequently, we hold the Virginia statute in controversy invalid.

Reversed.

MR. JUSTICE RUTLEDGE concurs in the result.

[The concurring opinions of MR. JUSTICE BLACK and MR. JUSTICE FRANKFURTER are omitted.]

* * *

MR. JUSTICE BURTON dissenting.

. . . The basic weakness in the appellant's case is the lack of facts and findings essential to demonstrate the existence of such a serious and major burden upon the national interest in interstate commerce as to outweigh whatever state or local benefits are attributable to the statute and which would be lost by its invalidation. The Court recognizes that it serves as "the final arbiter of the competing demands of state and national interest" and that it must fairly determine, in the absence of congressional action, whether the state statute actually imposes such an undue burden upon interstate commerce as to invalidate that statute. In weighing these competing demands, if this Court is to justify the invalidation of this statute, it must, first of all, be satisfied that the many years of experience of the state and the carrier that are reflected in this state law should be set aside. It represents the tested public policy of Virginia regularly enacted, long maintained and currently observed. The officially declared state interests, even when affecting interstate commerce, should not be laid aside summarily by this Court in the absence of congressional action. It is only Congress that can supply affirmative national uniformity of action.

* * *

MR. JUSTICE JACKSON took no part in the consideration or decision of this case.

BEAUHARNAIS V. ILLINOIS
343 U.S. 250 (1952)

Joseph Beauharnais was the president of the White Circle League, a group of whites who advocated racial segregation. At a meeting on January 6, 1950, he handed out literature to volunteers for distribution in downtown Chicago the next day. Among the literature was a leaflet entitled "Preserve and Protect White Neighborhoods" in the form of a petition addressed to the mayor and the city council of Chicago. Among other things, the leaflet stated that the white population of Chicago "are seething, nervous and agitated because of the constant and continuous invasion, harassment and encroachment by the Negroes upon them" and that there was "great danger to the Government from communism which is rife among Negroes." The leaflet also claimed that "we are not against the Negro; we are for the white

people and the white people are entitled to protection" and called for a single national organization to work for white interests. The following statement was also contained in the leaflet: "THE WHITE CIRCLE LEAGUE OF AMERICA is the only articulate white voice in America being raised in protest against negro aggressions and infiltrations into all white neighborhoods. The white people of Chicago MUST take advantage of this opportunity to become UNITED. If persuasion and the need to prevent the white race from becoming mongrelized by the negro will not unite us, then the aggressions . . . rapes, robberies, knives, guns and marijuana of the negro, SURELY WILL." The leaflet concluded by stating, "IT WILL BE EASIER TO REVERSE THE CURRENT OF THE ATLANTIC OCEAN THAN TO

DEGRADE THE WHITE RACE AND ITS NATU-
RAL LAWS BY FORCED MONGRELIZATION.
THE HOUR HAS STRUCK FOR ALL NORMAL
WHITE PEOPLE TO STAND UP AND FIGHT FOR
OUR RIGHTS TO LIFE, LIBERTY AND THE
PURSUIT OF HAPPINESS." Beauharnais was convicted of violating § 471 of the Illinois Criminal
Code, which makes it a crime for any person, firm,
or corporation to exhibit in any public place any publication that "portrays depravity, criminality, unchas-
tity, or lack of virtue of a class of citizens, of any
race, color, creed or religion" that "exposes the
citizens of any race, color, creed or religion to contempt, derision, or obloquy." The Illinois Supreme
Court rejected Beauharnais' contention that the statute violated the free speech and press guarantees of
the First and Fourteenth Amendments. *Vote: 5-4.*

* * *

MR. JUSTICE FRANKFURTER delivered the
opinion of the Court.
. . . Libel of an individual was a common-law
crime, and thus criminal in the colonies. Indeed, at
common law, truth or good motives was no defense.
In the first decades after the adoption of the Constitution, this was changed by judicial decision, statute
or constitution in most States, but nowhere was there
any suggestion that the crime of libel be abolished.
Today, every American jurisdiction—the forty-eight
States, the District of Columbia, Alaska, Hawaii and
Puerto Rico—punish libels directed at individuals.
"There are certain well-defined and narrowly limited classes of speech, the prevention and punishment of which have never been thought to raise any
Constitutional problem. These include the lewd and
obscene, the profane, the libelous, and the insulting
or 'fighting' words—those which by their very utterance inflict injury or tend to incite an immediate
breach of the peace. It has been well observed that
such utterances are no essential part of any exposi
tion of ideas, and are of such slight social value as
a step to truth that any benefit that may be derived
from them is clearly outweighed by the social interest in order and morality. 'Resort to epithets or
personal abuse is not in any proper sense communication of information or opinion safeguarded by the
Constitution, and its punishment as a criminal act
would raise no question under that instrument.'
Cantwell v. Connecticut, 301 U.S. 296, 309-310
[1940]." Such were the views of a unanimous Court
in *Chaplinsky v. New Hampshire,* [315 U.S. 568,
571-572 (1942)].
No one will gainsay that it is libelous falsely to
charge another with being a rapist, robber, carrier of
knives and guns, and user of marijuana. The precise
question before us, then, is whether the protection of
"liberty" in the Due Process Clause of the Fourteenth
Amendment prevents a State from punishing such

libels—as criminal libel has been defined, limited
and constitutionally recognized time out of mind—
directed at designated collectivities and flagrantly
disseminated. There is even authority, however dubious, that such utterances were also crimes at common law. It is certainly clear that some American
jurisdictions have sanctioned their punishment under ordinary criminal libel statutes. We cannot say,
however, that the question is concluded by history
and practice. But if an utterance directed at an individual may be the object of criminal sanctions, we
cannot deny to a State power to punish the same
utterance directed at a defined group, unless we can
say that this is a wilful and purposeless restriction
unrelated to the peace and well-being of the State.
Illinois did not have to look beyond her own
borders or await the tragic experience of the last
three decades to conclude that wilful purveyors of
falsehood concerning racial and religious groups
promote strife and tend powerfully to obstruct the
manifold adjustments required for free, ordered life
in a metropolitan, polyglot community. From the
murder of the abolitionist Lovejoy in 1837 to the
Cicero riots of 1951, Illinois has been the scene of
exacerbated tension between the races, often flaring
into violence and destruction. In many of these
outbreaks, utterances of the character here in question, so the Illinois legislature could conclude, played
a significant part. The law was passed on June 29,
1917, at a time when the State was struggling to
assimilate vast numbers of new inhabitants, as yet
concentrated in discrete racial or national or religious groups—foreign-born brought to it by the
crest of the great wave of immigration, and Negroes
attracted by jobs in war plants and the allurements
of northern claims. Nine year earlier, in the very city
where the legislature sat, what is said to be the first
northern race riot had cost the lives of six people,
left hundreds of Negroes homeless and shocked
citizens into action far beyond the borders of the
State. Less than a month before the bill was enacted,
East St. Louis had seen a day's rioting, prelude to an
outbreak, only four days after the bill became law,
so bloody that it led to Congressional investigation.
A series of bombings had begun which was to cul-
minate two years later in the awful race riot which
held Chicago in its grip for seven days in the summer
of 1919. Nor has tension and violence between the
groups defined in the statute been limited in Illinois
to clashes between whites and Negroes.
In the face of this history and its frequent obli-
gato of extreme racial and religious propaganda, we
would deny experience to say that the Illinois legislature was without reason in seeking ways to curb
false or malicious defamation of racial and religious
groups, made in public places and by means calculated to have a powerful emotional impact on those
to whom it was presented. . . .
It may be argued, and weightily, that this legislation will not help matters; that tension and on occasion

violence between racial and religious groups must be traced to causes more deeply embedded in our society than the rantings of modern Know-Nothings. Only those lacking responsible humility will have a confident solution for problems as intractable as the frictions attributable to differences of race, color, or religion. This being so, it would be out of bounds for the judiciary to deny the legislature a choice of policy, provided it is not unrelated to the problem and not forbidden by some explicit limitation on the State's power. That the legislative remedy might not in practice mitigate the evil, or might itself raise new problems, would only manifest once more the paradox of reform. It is the price to be paid for the trial-and-error inherent in legislative efforts to deal with obstinate social issues. . . .

Long ago this Court recognized that the economic rights of an individual may depend for the effectiveness of their enforcement on rights in the group, even though not formally corporate, to which he belongs. *American Foundries v. Tri-City Council,* 257 U.S. 184 [1921]. Such group-protection on behalf of the individual may, for all we know, be a need not confined to the part that a trade union plays in effectuating rights abstractly recognized as belonging to its members. It is not within our competence to confirm or deny claims of social scientists as to the dependence of the individual on the position of his racial or religious group in the community. It would, however, be arrant dogmatism, quite outside the scope of our authority in passing on the powers of a State, for us to deny that the Illinois legislature may warrantably believe that a man's job and his educational opportunities and the dignity accorded him may depend as much on the reputation of the racial and religious group to which he willy-nilly belongs, as on his own merits. This being so, we are precluded from saying that speech concededly punishable when immediately directed at individuals cannot be outlawed if directed at groups with whose position and esteem in society the affiliated individual may be inextricably involved.

We are warned that the choice open to the Illinois legislature here may be abused, that the law may be discriminatorily enforced; prohibiting libel of a creed or of a racial group, we are told, is but a step from prohibiting libel of a political party. Every power may be abused, but the possibility of abuse is a poor reason for denying Illinois the power to adopt measures against criminal libels sanctioned by centuries of Anglo-American law. . . .

. . . It is suggested that while it was clearly within the constitutional power of Illinois to punish this utterance if the proceeding were properly safeguarded, in this particular case Illinois denied the defendant rights which the Due Process Clause commands. Specifically, it is argued that the defendant was not permitted to raise at the trial defenses constitutionally guaranteed in a criminal libel prosecution: (1) the defense of truth; (2) justification of the utterance as "fair comment"; and (3) its privilege as means for redressing grievances.

Neither by proffer of evidence, requests for instructions, nor motion before or after verdict did the defendant seek to justify his utterance as "fair comment" or as privileged. Nor has the defendant urged as a ground for reversing his conviction in this Court that his opportunity to make those defenses was denied below. And so, whether a prosecution for libel of a racial or religious group is unconstitutionally invalid where the State did deny the defendant such opportunities is not before us. Certainly the State may cast the burden of justifying what is patent defamation upon the defamer. The benefits of hypothetical defenses, never raised below or pressed upon us, are not to be invoked in the abstract.

As to the defense of truth, Illinois in common with many States requires a showing not only that the utterance state the facts, but also that the publication be made "with good motives and for justifiable ends." . . . Both elements are necessary if the defense is to prevail. What has been called "the common sense of American criminal law," as formulated, with regard to necessary safeguards in criminal libel prosecutions, in the New York Constitution of 1821, . . . has been adopted in terms by Illinois. The teaching of a century and a half of criminal libel prosecutions in this country would go by the board if we were to hold that Illinois was not within her rights in making this combined requirement. Assuming that defendant's offer of proof directed to a part of the defense was adequate, it did not satisfy the entire requirement which Illinois could exact.

. . . We find no warrant in the Constitution for denying to Illinois the power to pass the law here under attack. But it bears repeating—although it should not—that our finding that the law is not constitutionally objectionable carries no implication of approval of the wisdom of the legislation or of its efficacy. These questions may raise doubts in our minds as well as in others. It is not for us, however, to make the legislative judgment. We are not at liberty to erect those doubts into fundamental law.

Affirmed.

* * *

MR. JUSTICE BLACK, with whom MR. JUSTICE DOUGLAS concurs, dissenting.

. . . The Court condones this expansive state censorship by painstakingly analogizing it to the law of criminal libel. As a result of this refined analysis, the Illinois statute emerges labeled a "group libel law." This label may make the Court's holding more palatable for those who sustain it, but the sugar-coating does not make the censorship less deadly. However tagged, the Illinois law is not that criminal libel which has been "defined, limited and constitutionally recognized time out of mind." For as "constitutionally recognized" that crime has provided for punishment of false, malicious, scurrilous charges against individuals, not against huge groups. This limited scope of the law of criminal libel is of no small importance. It has confined state punishment of speech and expression to the narrowest of areas involving nothing more than purely private feuds. Every expansion of the law of criminal libel so as to punish discussions of matters of public concern means a corresponding invasion of the area dedicated to free expression by the First Amendment.

Prior efforts to expand the scope of criminal libel beyond its traditional boundaries have not usually met with widespread popular acclaim. "Seditious libel" was such an expansion and it did have its day, particularly in the English Court of Star Chamber. But the First Amendment repudiated seditious libel for this country. . . .

The Court's reliance on *Chaplinsky v. New Hampshire* . . . is also misplaced. New Hampshire had a state law making it an offense to direct insulting words at an *individual* on a public street. Chaplinsky had violated that law by calling a man vile names "face-to-face." We pointed out in that context that the use of such "fighting" words was not an essential part of exposition of ideas. Whether the words used in their context here are "fighting" words in the same sense is doubtful, but whether so or not they are not addressed to or about individuals. Moreover, the leaflet used here was also the means adopted by an assembled group to enlist interest in their efforts to have legislation enacted. And the fighting words were but a part of arguments on questions of wide public interest and importance. Freedom of petition, assembly, speech and press could be greatly abridged by a practice of meticulously scrutinizing every editorial, speech, sermon or other printed matter to extract two or three naughty words on which to hang charges of "group libel." The Chaplinsky case makes no such broad inroads on the First Amendment freedoms. Nothing MR. JUSTICE MURPHY wrote for the Court in that case or in any other case justifies any such inference.

Unless I misread history the majority is giving libel a more expansive scope and more respectable status than it was ever accorded even in the Star Chamber. For here it is held to be punishable to give publicity to any picture, moving picture, play, drama or sketch, or any printed matter which a judge may find unduly offensive to any race, color, creed or religion. In other words, in arguing for or against the enactment of laws that may differently affect huge groups, it is now very dangerous indeed to say something critical of one of the groups. And any "person, firm or corporation" can be tried for this crime. "Person, firm or corporation" certainly includes a book publisher, newspaper, radio or television station, candidate or even a preacher.

It is easy enough to say that none of this latter group have been proceeded against under the Illinois Act. And they have not—yet. But emotions bubble and tempers flare in racial and religious controversies, the kind here involved. It would not be easy for any court, in good conscience, to narrow this Act so as to exclude from it any of those I have mentioned. Furthermore, persons tried under the Act could not even get a jury trial except as to the bare fact of publication. Here, the court simply charged the jury that Beauharnais was guilty if he had caused distribution of the leaflet. Such trial by judge rather than by jury was outlawed in England in 1792 by Fox's Libel Law.

. . . No rationalization on a purely legal level can conceal the fact that state laws like this one present a constant overhanging threat to freedom of speech, press and religion. Today Beauharnais is punished for publicly expressing strong views in favor of segregation. Ironically enough, Beauharnais, convicted of crime in Chicago, would probably be given a hero's reception in many other localities, if not in some parts of Chicago itself. Moreover, the same kind of state law that makes Beauharnais a criminal for advocating segregation in Illinois can be utilized to send people to jail in other states for advocating equality and nonsegregation. What Beauharnais said in his leaflet is mild compared with usual arguments on both sides of racial controversies.

. . . If there be minority groups who hail this holding as their victory, they might consider the possible relevancy of this ancient remark:

"Another such victory and I am undone."

* * *

MR. JUSTICE DOUGLAS dissenting.

. . . The Court in this and in other cases places speech under an expanding legislative control. Today a white man stands convicted for protesting in unseemly language against our decisions invalidating restrictive covenants. Tomorrow a Negro will be haled before a court for denouncing lynch law in heated terms. Farm laborers in the West who compete with field hands drifting up from Mexico; whites who feel the pressure of orientals; a minority which finds employment going to members of the dominant religious group—all of these are caught in the mesh of today's decision. Debate and argument even in the courtroom are not always calm and dispassionate. Emotions sway speakers and audiences alike. Intemperate speech is a distinctive characteristic of man. Hotheads blow off and release destructive energy in the process. They shout and rave, exaggerating weaknesses, magnifying error, viewing with alarm. So it has been from the beginning; and so it will be throughout time. The Framers of the Constitution knew human nature as well as we do. They too had lived in dangerous days; they too knew the suffocating influence of orthodoxy and standardized thought. They weighed the compulsions for restrained speech and thought against the abuses of liberty. They chose liberty. That should be our choice today no matter how distasteful to us the pamphlet of Beauharnais may be. It is true that this is only one decision which may later be distinguished or confined to narrow limits. But it represents a philosophy at war with the First Amendment—a constitu- tional interpretation which puts free speech under the legislative thumb. It reflects an influence moving ever deeper into our society. It is notice to the legislatures that they have the power to control unpopular blocs. It is a warning to every minority that when the Constitution guarantees free speech it does not mean what it says.

[The dissenting opinion of MR. JUSTICE JACKSON is omitted.]

[The dissenting opinion of MR. JUSTICE REED, with whom MR. JUSTICE DOUGLAS joins, is omitted.]

3

The Warren Court

THE ERA OF RISING EXPECTATIONS
AND MASSIVE RESISTANCE,
1953-1969

Thus, in the long effort to gain equality through integration, blacks have learned that white America will accommodate the interests of blacks and other racial minorities in achieving racial equality when and only when those interests converge with the interests of whites.

Derrick Bell*

THE WARREN COURT AND THE
EGALITARIAN REVOLUTION
IN CONSTITUTIONAL LAW

The Warren Court, which lasted for 16 years (1953-1969), articulated an egalitarian judicial philosophy in the areas of racial discrimination, reapportionment, criminal procedure, and separation of church and state. Thirteen months before his death, Chief Justice Warren delivered the commencement address at the University of San Diego School of Law. He stated:

I do not feel a need to defend any decision the Court made during my years as Chief Justice. Only history will tell whether they were good or bad. . . . But, I

---

*The quote is from Derrick Bell's paper, *Victims as Heroes: A Minority Perspective on Constitutional Law,* presented at the Smithsonian Institution's International Symposium "Constitutional Roots, Rights, and Responsibilities," May 21, 1987, p. 14.

do deplore any effort made to change the institutions of the country because they have not failed us in any respect. The failure to follow the constitutional provisions and the wisdom of the Founding Fathers—not the failure of our institutions themselves—is responsible for our shortcomings.[1]

His comments are a partial response to the many critics of several landmark cases that were rendered during his tenure on the Court. The nation witnessed bold and progressive changes in constitutional development, especially in the area of race relations, during a turbulent era in our nation's history. President Dwight D. Eisenhower was indebted to Warren for his crucial support during the 1952 Republican convention and appointed him Chief Justice in 1953.[2] At the age of 62, he became the fourteenth Chief Justice of the United States.

President Eisenhower made four additional appointments to the Supreme Court. In 1955 he appointed John Marshall Harlan II, the grandson of the first Justice John Marshall Harlan and an ardent defender of the doctrine of judicial self-restraint. The following year, President Eisenhower appointed William J. Brennan, Jr., who emerged as a prominent defender of liberty and equality and one of the Court's most influential members besides Warren. President Eisenhower lived to regret having appointed the liberals Warren and Brennan, but their genuine commitment to equalitarianism and racial justice is a fait accompli.[3] In 1957 and 1958, respectively, President Eisenhower appointed Charles Whittaker and Potter Stewart to the high court. President John F. Kennedy made two appointments during his tenure as president: In 1962 he appointed Byron R. White and Arthur J. Goldberg to the Court. President Lyndon Johnson had the opportunity to make two appointments: Abe Fortas and the historic appointment of Thurgood Marshall, the first African American Justice to serve on the Court, in 1967. President Johnson had previously appointed Marshall to the position of Solicitor General of the United States in 1965.

Our analysis of the Warren Court shows that its support for civil rights was more consistent and its policy directions more clear-cut than any previous Court (see Table 3.1). It is no coincidence that Chief Justice Warren said that the most important decisions rendered during his tenure were *Baker v. Carr,* 369 U.S. 186 (1962), *Brown v. Board of Education* (*Brown I*), 347 U.S. 483 (1954), and *Gideon v. Wainwright,* 372 U.S. 335 (1963).[4] Significant changes in criminal procedure emerged in a consistent pattern, and poor criminal defendants, who were disproportionately black, were the recipients of long-overdue constitutional protection. The Warren Court's venture into the area of reapportionment provides one of the best examples of its egalitarian posture toward the preservation of political rights under the Fourteenth Amendment. The Warren Court undoubtedly will be remembered for its remarkable commitment to democratic principles, individual liberties, justice, and equality.

BROWN I AND II:
SCHOOL DESEGREGATION

Fifty-eight years after *Plessy v. Ferguson,* 163 U.S. 537 (1896), the Supreme Court was afforded yet another opportunity to revisit the separate-but-equal doctrine. The NAACP spent many hours planning the strongest attack possible against segregated schools. The groundwork for the *Brown* decision had been laid with the legal principles examined in the professional education cases, beginning with *Missouri ex rel. Gaines v. Canada,* 305 U.S. 337 (1938), discussed in the previous chapter. The decision was made to present the strongest legal argument and available social science evidence against segregated schools. Thurgood Marshall, Robert L. Carter, Spottswood Robinson, III, Jack Greenberg, Constance Baker Motley, William Coleman, and James M. Nabrit, Jr. were among the lawyers who worked on the case. In addition, Kenneth Clark, a social scientist from City College in New York, was asked to provide the NAACP with his expertise.

The *Brown* case was a joinder of four cases arising in Kansas, Virginia, Delaware, and South Carolina.[5] The fifth case involved segregation of the public schools in the District of Columbia.[6] These cases initially reached the Supreme Court during its 1952 term. Just before the Eisenhower inauguration, President Harry S. Truman's support for equality goals was demonstrated by his decision to permit the Justice Department to file an amicus curiae brief in the *Brown* litigation. The administration had previously submitted amicus briefs in *Sweatt v. Painter,* 339 U.S. 629 (1950) and *McLaurin v. Oklahoma State Regents for Higher Education,* 339 U.S. 637 (1950), arguing that it was constitutionally impermissible for colleges and universities to discriminate against black students. In its amicus curiae brief in the *Brown* litigation, the federal government called for an end to racial segregation in the nation's public school system. The Truman administration emphasized the foreign policy implications of segregation in the United States in that it furnished "grist for the Communist propaganda mills" and described how dark-skinned foreign visitors "are often mistaken for American Negroes and refused food, lodging and entertainment."[7] The government summed up its position in the following manner:

> [T]he doctrine of "separate-but-equal" is an unwarranted departure, based upon dubious assumptions of fact combined with a disregard of the basic purposes of the Fourteenth Amendment, from the fundamental principle that all Americans, whatever their race or color, stand equal and alike before the law. The rule of *stare decisis* does not give it immunity from reexamination and rejection.[8]

Oral arguments began on December 9, 1952. However, a philosophically divided Vinson Court was unable to reach a consensus on the cases. According to Richard Kluger's account, Justice Frankfurter suggested that the Court

Table 3.1 The Warren Court and School Desegregation: Cases

Case	Vote	Ruling
Brown v. Board of Education (*Brown I*), 347 U.S. 483 (1954)	9-0	Chief Justice Warren overturned *Plessy v. Ferguson* (1896) and declared that separate-but-equal has no place in the field of public education.
Bolling v. Sharpe, 347 U.S. 497 (1954)	9-0	The Supreme Court declared that segregated public schools in the District of Columbia violate the concepts of equal protection inherent in the due process clause of the Fifth Amendment.
Florida ex rel. Hawkins v. Board of Control of Florida, 347 U.S. 971 (1954)	per curiam	The Supreme Court vacated and remanded a lower court's ruling that refused to admit Virgil Hawkins to the University of Florida on the authority of *Brown I.*
Tureaud v. Board of Supervisors of Louisiana State University, 347 U.S. 971 (1954)	per curiam	The Supreme Court set aside the lower court's refusal to admit a black student to Louisiana State University on the authority of *Brown I.*
Brown v. Board of Education (*Brown II*), 349 U.S. 294 (1955)	9-0	In its implementation ruling, the Supreme Court declared that desegregation should begin "with all deliberate speed."
Lucy v. Adams, 350 U.S. 1 (1955)	per curiam	The Supreme Court reinstated the injunction that enjoined and restrained university officials from denying Autherine Lucy and Polly Myers's right to enroll in the University of Alabama.
Board of Trustees of University of North Carolina v. Frazier, 350 U.S. 979 (1956)	per curiam	The Supreme Court affirmed a lower court's ruling that issued an injunction restraining the University of North Carolina from denying students admission to the undergraduate schools on account of race.
Cooper v. Aaron, 358 U.S. 1 (1958)	9-0	The Supreme Court declared that governors and state legislatures could not postpone the desegregation of its public schools under the Supremacy Clause of the Constitution, which made *Brown* binding on the states.

prepare questions for reargument so that the cases could be held over until the next term.[9] On June 8, 1953, all five cases were unanimously restored to the Court's docket, and the parties to the litigation were asked to discuss the five questions on the history and purpose of the Fourteenth Amendment (see Box 3.1) and whether Congress and the state legislatures intended to abolish

Table 3.1 *continued*

Case	Vote	Ruling
Goss v. Board of Education, 373 U.S. 683 (1963)	9-0	Justice Clark struck down a desegregation plan in which students would be permitted to transfer from a school in which their race was in a minority to one in which their race would constitute majority status on the ground that, in practice, the intent of the plan was to maintain segregation.
Griffin v. Prince Edward County School Board, 377 U.S. 218 (1964)	9-0	The Supreme Court declared that the closing of the public schools in Prince Edward County, Virginia, was a denial of equal protection.
Green v. County School Board of New Kent County, 391 U.S. 430 (1968)	9-0	The Supreme Court struck down a freedom of choice plan and ordered the school board to desegregate "now" by implementing a plan that promised to work.

segregated schools. The Court also invited the Attorney General of the United States to take part in the oral argument and to file an additional brief.

Prior to reargument, Chief Justice Vinson died of a heart attack on September 8, 1953. President Eisenhower's choice to replace Vinson was Earl Warren. Oral arguments were heard on December 7, 1953. The evidence that the lawyers were able to assemble after months of painstaking research led the Warren Court to conclude that the historical evidence was too inconclusive to allow for a clear-cut answer. Some scholars, however, disagree with the Court's opinion on this matter. Although very little was said about segregation during the debates in Congress, Alexander Bickel, a legal scholar and former law clerk to Justice Frankfurter, argued that § 1 of the Fourteenth Amendment was written in broad language so that individuals in the future would be able "to interpret it as prohibiting the practice of segregation."[10]

Unlike President Truman, President Eisenhower offered limited support for school desegregation. He initially opposed the Justice Department's filing of a brief in the *Brown* case.[11] Attorney General Herbert Brownell Jr. convinced President Eisenhower that it would be difficult for the administration to dodge the school segregation controversy because the Truman administration in 1952 had filed a brief in support of the black plaintiffs. The administration failed to take a clear stance on the crucial issue before the Court—whether the framers of the Fourteenth Amendment intended to abolish racial segregation in education. According to Robert Burk's account, the 180-page brief was so vague that members of the Supreme Court complained they did not understand the federal government's position and thus requested that Justice Department officials make clear what stance they were adopting in *Brown*.[12] Burk suggested that the Eisenhower administration submitted a

BOX 3.1

**Five Questions of the
Brown (1953) Litigation**

1. What evidence is there that the Congress that submitted and the state legislatures and conventions that ratified the Fourteenth Amendment contemplated or did not contemplate, understood or did not understand, that it would abolish segregation in the public schools?

2. If neither the Congress in submitting nor the states in ratifying the Fourteenth Amendment understood that compliance with it would require the immediate abolition of segregation in public schools, was it nevertheless the understanding of the framers of the Amendment

    (a) that future Congresses might in the exercise of their power under section 5 of the Amendment, abolish segregation, or

    (b) that it would be within the judicial power, in light of future conditions, to construe the Amendment as abolishing such segregation of its own force?

3. On the assumption that the answers to questions 2(a) and (b) do not dispose of the issue, is it within the judicial power, in construing the Amendment, to abolish segregation in public schools?

4. Assuming it is decided that segregation in public schools violates the Fourteenth Amendment

    (a) would a decree necessarily follow providing that, within the limits set by normal geographical school districting, Negro children should forthwith be admitted to schools of their choice, or

    (b) may this Court, in the exercise of its equity powers, permit an effective gradual adjustment to be brought about from existing segregated systems to a system not based on color distinctions?

5. On the assumption on which questions 4(a) and (b) are based, and assuming further that this Court will exercise its equity powers to the end described in question 4(b),

    (a) should this Court formulate detailed decrees in these cases;

    (b) if so, what specific issues should the decrees reach;

    (c) should this Court appoint a special master to hear evidence with a view to recommending specific terms for such decrees;

    (d) should this Court remand to the courts of first instance with directions to frame decrees in these cases, and if so, what general directions should the decrees of this Court include and what procedures should the courts of first instance follow in arriving at the specific terms of more detailed decrees?

SOURCE: *Brown v. Board of Education*, 345 U.S. 972, 972-973 (1953).

nebulous brief because it wanted to avoid the political pitfall of aggressively taking a pro-civil rights stance as Truman did—which resulted in Southerners walking out of the 1948 Democratic convention. Nor did President Eisenhower want to take the political risk of coming out against *Brown* and appearing to be anti-civil rights. A strong pro-*Brown* stance would have jeopardized his stature among Southern voters and damaged his chances of building a strong Republican Party in the South.

On May 17, 1954, the Warren Court relied on legal and nonlegal materials to support its decision in *BROWN V. BOARD OF EDUCATION* (1954) (*Brown I*). The Fourteenth Amendment was the legal basis for the decision. Chief Justice Warren, writing for a unanimous Court, declared, "We conclude that in the field of public education the doctrine of 'separate but equal' has no place. . . . Therefore, we hold that the plaintiffs . . . are . . . deprived of the equal protection of the laws guaranteed by the Fourteenth Amendment." The Court then turned to nonlegal or social science materials. The Court quoted the findings that were presented in the district court in the Kansas case that coincided with the opinion of Dr. Kenneth Clark. Chief Justice Earl Warren observed:

> Segregation of white and colored children in public schools has a detrimental effect upon the colored children. The impact is greater when it has the sanction of the law; for the policy of separating the races is usually interpreted as denoting the inferiority of the negro group. A sense of inferiority affects the motivation of a child to learn.

An important factor in the opinion was the famous Footnote 11 (see Box 3.2), which referred to studies made by various sociologists and psychologists who had written about the detrimental effects of segregation on black children. The Court then restored the cases to its docket for the following term in order to formulate the appropriate remedy.

Brown I and the Use of Social Science Data

The Court's use of social science data became the focal point of heated controversy in the *Congressional Record,* scholarly journals, law books, classrooms, and at public lectures.[13] Several Southern members of Congress questioned the Court's use of social science data. Senator James Eastland of Mississippi referred to the day that the *Brown* decision was rendered as "black Monday" and argued that it was completely unjustifiable for the Court to cite sociological and psychological authorities and to depart from legal precedents.[14] Going further, Senator Eastland introduced a resolution in the U.S. Senate in 1955 that gave the Senate Judiciary Committee the power to investigate those who were cited by the Court, as well as those who assisted in organizing the "modern scientific authority" in order to determine whether they could be identified with Communist-front organizations or alien ideologies.[15] This resolution was approved by the Senate on March 12, 1957. Congressman James Davis of Georgia introduced an article in the *Congressional Record* by Robert Pittman, whom he described as a lawyer of unusual ability. In this article, Pittman stated:

BOX 3.2

Brown I and Footnote 11

K. B. Clark, Effect of Prejudice and Discrimination on Personality Development (Midcentury White House Conference on Children and Youth, 1950); Witmer and Kotinsky, Personality in the Making (1952), c. VI; Deutscher and Chein, The Psychological Effects of Enforced Segregation: A Survey of Social Science Opinion, 26 J. Psychol. 259 (1948); Chein, What are the Psychological Effects of Segregation Under Conditions of Equal Facilities?, 3 Int. J. Opinion and Attitude Res. 229 (1949); Brameld, Educational Costs, in Discrimination and National Welfare (MacIver, ed., 1949), 44-48; Frazier, The Negro in the United States (1949), 674-681. And see generally Myrdal, An American Dilemma (1944).

SOURCE: *Brown v. Board of Education*, 347 U.S. 483, 494-495 (1954).

The doctrine that all men are created equal is the scrubbrush that is to brainwash the unstable intelligence of America. The Supreme Court of the United States has been thoroughly brainwashed with that brush. . . . In its decision, the Court held in effect that it could find no basis for integration in the Constitution or the law and therefore it turned to psychology and sociology. It cited Myrdal's *American Dilemma* as the "modern authority" for its decision.[16]

Other congressional critics who agreed with Eastland and Pittman were Senator Richard Russell of Georgia and Representatives Henderson Lanham, John Flynt, and James Davis of Georgia.[17]

A scholarly criticism of the Supreme Court's use of social science data in the *Brown* case was presented by Edmond Cahn, a law professor at New York University. In a highly publicized law review article, he stated that the impression had arisen that a major factor influencing the outcome of the *Brown* case was the data presented to the Court by social scientists who played the role of factfinders. He argued that the constitutional rights of blacks or other ethnic groups should not rest on flimsy scientific foundations. He expressed his position succinctly:

Today the social psychologists—at least the leaders of the discipline—are liberal and egalitarian in basic approach. Suppose, a generation hence, some of their successors were to revert to the ethnic mysticism of the very recent past; suppose they were to present us with a collection of racist notions and label them "science." What then would be the state of our constitutional rights?[18]

He was particularly critical of the testimony presented by Kenneth Clark in *Briggs v. Elliott* (1951), the Clarendon County, South Carolina, case. He emphasized that Clark had spoken more as an advocate for the black plaintiffs than as an objective professional witness and therefore had exaggerated the experts' contribution to the *Brown* case. Moreover, Cahn thought the social science statements had failed to convey any new information. Because Clark had used only 16 children for the doll test in Clarendon County, Cahn argued it was highly possible that some of the children tested had "untypical private experiences" and that the result could easily mislead because of the very small sample. Moreover, several of the interpretations drawn by Clark were predetermined, according to Cahn: For example, "If Negro children say a *brown* doll is like themselves, he infers that segregation had made them conscious of race; yet if they say a *white* doll is like themselves, he infers that segregation has forced them to evade reality."[19] Finding it difficult to understand how Clark had inferred that the black children were evading reality because 7 out of 10 picked the white doll when asked to choose the doll that resembled themselves, Cahn noted:

> I gather that these seven children were among the ten who had previously chosen the white doll as "nice." Were they wrong, then, to claim that the white doll was very much "like themselves" because they too were "nice"? No one can state positively what these children were thinking at the time; but if they did have perception enough to insist to themselves that the "*niceness*" was decisive and not the color, lo and behold! [T]his would be wisdom indeed![20]

Cahn believed that the test did not actually demonstrate the social and psychological effects of school segregation per se because the experiences of the children at school were neither isolated nor differentiated from the general effects of minority group status.[21]

Another criticism of Clark's testimony was presented by Richard D. Schwartz, a sociology and law professor at Yale University. He asserted that Clark had observed that the testimony presented in the South Carolina case was consistent with previous findings in 1947, which resulted from testing more than 300 children. In this study, black children in the integrated schools of Springfield, Massachusetts, were compared with black children in the segregated schools of Hot Springs, Pine Bluff, and Little Rock, Arkansas. They were given the same test that was administered in Clarendon County, South Carolina. Schwartz observed that the test results of 1947 revealed a preference for the white doll by more Northern than Southern blacks. According to Schwartz, "The children in integrated schools showed a higher incidence of the very reactions which Clark cited in his testimony as evidence of harmful effects on segregated children."[22] Schwartz thought the Court's opinion would have been freer of criticism had it included this observation. A. James Gregor, a professor of psychology at Columbia University, made similar observations to that of Schwartz.[23] Ernest Van Den Haag, a professor in the Department of Social Philosophy at New York University, also emphasized that Clark's testimony actually misled the Court.[24] He expressed his disappointment with Clark's conclusions in these provocative words: "From Professor Clark's experiments, his testimony and, finally, the essay to which

I am replying, the best conclusion that can be drawn is that he did not know what he was doing; and the worst, that he did."[25]

It is important to note that Clark responded strongly to these criticisms, especially the allegation that he was an advocate for the desegregation interests rather than an objective scientist. For example, he made it clear that it was not his decision, but the decision of the NAACP lawyers, to introduce social science data in the *Brown* case. Moreover, Clark addressed Cahn's allegation that he was a partisan advocate rather than an objective scientist in these words:

> The primary research studies were conducted ten years before these cases were heard on the trial court level. Professor Cahn's allegation that the writer served in the role of advocate rather than of an objective scientist in his participation in these cases seems difficult to sustain in the face of testimony given on the basis of research conducted ten years before these cases were heard. One would have to be gifted with the power of a seer in order to prepare himself for the role of advocate in these specific cases ten years in advance.[26]

He also pointed out that the White House Conference manuscript cited by the Supreme Court in the famous Footnote 11 in the *Brown* case was prepared months before he was aware that the NAACP had plans to challenge segregated public schools in federal courts.[27]

Some legal scholars were not critical of the judicial use of social science data in the *Brown* case. They emphasized that it was decided primarily on the equal protection clause of the Fourteenth Amendment. For example, Mitchell Franklin observed that the decision "was decided exclusively under the text of the Fourteenth Amendment and was justified by it as an historical text formulating American social morality."[28] Herbert Hill and Jack Greenberg asserted that the *Brown* case was decided within the purview of the legal tradition.[29]

Professor Paul Freund, in an article reprinted in the *Congressional Record* at the request of Representative John Walter Heselton of Massachusetts, addressed those who have argued that the decision was not justified by the history or language of the Fourteenth Amendment. He concluded that the silence of the United States Constitution actually proves too much because the doctrine of separate-but-equal would be ruled out from its silence. The Constitution fails to mention agriculture, but this does not mean that Congress is helpless to debate "price supports for agricultural commodities."[30] Freund also argued that the *Brown* case had not been hastily decided and that every conceivable argument against the decision had already been presented by interested parties. If the Court had held that separate public schooling failed to violate the Fourteenth Amendment, this would have been equivalent to saying that the American people do not recognize equality of educational opportunity to be a minimum standard for government to observe and enforce.

Arnold M. Rose, a professor of sociology at the University of Minnesota and a participant in the preparation of briefs in the *Brown* case, observed that the question of whether segregation involves discrimination is a question of social fact and that social scientists will more than likely appear in a great variety of cases in the future.[31] Finally, Jack Greenberg wrote, "Social scientists' testimony is playing a role in the shaping of judge-made law and in helping find relevant facts which must be proved under existing rules of law."[32]

A strong case can be made that the Court would have reached the same result in the *Brown* case if social science data had never been introduced. In *Briggs v. Elliott,* 103 F. Supp. 920 (1952) and *Davis v. County School Board of Prince Edward County,* 103 F. Supp. 337 (1952), the district courts in South Carolina and Virginia, respectively, held that the social science testimony was irrelevant and unproven. Moreover, in BOLLING V. SHARPE, 347 U.S. 497 (1954), the District of Columbia case, social science evidence was not presented and the Supreme Court still held that segregation was unconstitutional. *Bolling* addressed the constitutionality of segregated schools in Washington, D.C., under the due process clause of the Fifth Amendment. Because the *Brown* decision relied on the equal protection clause of the Fourteenth Amendment, Chief Justice Warren, in a unanimous opinion, held that "the concepts of equal protection and due process, both stemming from our American ideal of fairness, are not mutually exclusive." Thus, *Bolling* is significant for imposing the same constitutional duty to desegregate on the federal government.

It is reasonable to suggest that logic, history, precedents, the Constitution, the spirit of the times, prevailing concepts of justice, and the ideological orientations of the Justices were important factors in the outcome of the *Brown* case. Thomas F. Pettigrew, a social psychologist, expressed the view of many of his colleagues when he said, "Our influence on the 1954 ruling was actually of only footnote importance."[33]

Aftermath of *Brown I:*
Brown II, Resistance, and More Litigation

After *Brown I* the Court, in BROWN V. BOARD OF EDUCATION (*Brown II*), 349 U.S. 294 (1955), had to decide the manner in which relief was to be granted. Chief Justice Earl Warren expressed the crux of the decision when he declared that the desegregation process should proceed with "all deliberate speed." "With all deliberate speed" resulted in all deliberate delay in carrying out school desegregation. It was actually a weapon that worked to the advantage of white Southerners who were not in favor of the policy pronouncement in *Brown I.* Some legal scholars believed that *Brown II* was a mistake that simply placated whites and encouraged noncompliance. According to Philip Elman, a former clerk to Justice Frankfurter, the phrase was used to obtain a majority in the *Brown* litigation. He argued, "Without 'all deliberate speed' in the remedy, the Court could never have decided the constitutional issue in the strong, forthright unanimous way that it did; and it was essential for the Court to do so if its decision was to be accepted and followed throughout the country."[34] Incrementalism and stubborn resistance were the norm. For example, 10 years after *Brown I,* 1.2% of black children attended schools with whites in the South.[35]

A number of strategies were employed to thwart, evade, and defy compliance with the mandate enunciated in *Brown I*.[36] The Southern Manifesto was a statement signed by 19 senators and 77 members of the House of Representatives. It charged the Supreme Court with abusing its power and encroaching on the rights reserved to the states. In addition, the Southern Manifesto requested that the people in the affected states use all lawful means at their disposal to oppose integration.[37] Official resistance to genuine desegregation took the forms of pupil placement laws, freedom of choice plans, school closing laws, whites transferring to private schools, anti-barretry laws, and very weak enforcement efforts.

Implementing *Brown* was also delayed by the appointment of federal judges who were racists. When John F. Kennedy appointed several racists from Louisiana, Georgia, and Mississippi, blacks who had overwhelmingly supported him for president in 1960 were dismayed and found it difficult to make sense of these appointments. President Kennedy's appointment of William Harold Cox to the district court in Mississippi was a huge step backward for the federal judiciary. Widely regarded as the worst of several racist judges appointed by President Kennedy, Cox referred to blacks as "chimpanzees."[38] Judge Cox also delayed handling voting discrimination cases, and the Fifth Circuit Court of Appeals criticized him for his behavior. In one case that involved six freedom riders who sought to remove their case to a federal district court, Judge Cox wrote, "This Court may not be regarded as any haven for any such counterfeit citizens from other states deliberately seeking to cause trouble here among its people."[39]

Judge E. Gordon West, a Kennedy appointee from Louisiana, had the following to say after ordering the city of Baton Rouge to devise a school desegregation plan: "I personally regard the 1954 holding of the Supreme Court in the now famous *Brown* . . . case as one of the truly regrettable decisions of all time."[40] J. Robert Elliott, another Kennedy appointee from Georgia, opposed efforts to end rural domination in Georgia. He observed, "I don't want these pinks, radicals and black voters to outvote those who are trying to preserve segregation laws and other traditions."[41]

Two years after the *Brown* decision, C. Vann Woodward counted 106 evasive legal measures enacted by Southern states to prevent blacks from attending integrated schools.[42] When Congress passed the Civil Rights Act of 1964, Title VI of the Act mandated that federal funds would be terminated to any program or activity in which there had been a finding of discrimination. Movement to comply with *Brown I* was slight and very slow. A judicial victory had turned into a loss, and intense pressure by whites to preserve the status quo forced blacks to return to the courts to recapture what had been previously granted and to transform previously enunciated judicial principles into workable outcomes. Given this cyclical pattern, genuine progress was tenuous at best.

Three years after *Brown II*, the Supreme Court decided *Cooper v. Aaron*, 358 U.S. 1 (1958). Governor Orval Faubus and the legislature of Arkansas had worked enthusiastically to frustrate compliance with *Brown I* and *II*. The school board's decision to comply was short-lived. On February 20, 1958, it requested permission to postpone implementation of the desegregation plan for 2½ years because of intense public hostility against integrated schools. In *Cooper v. Aaron,* the Warren Court emphasized that Article VI makes the Constitution the "supreme law of the land" and that, therefore, the *Brown* decision was binding on the states. It concluded that "law and order are not here to be preserved by depriving the Negro children of their constitutional rights." Despite the fact that President Eisenhower sent federal troops to Little Rock to ensure that the desegregation order would be implemented, he did not use the dramatic confrontation at Little Rock to say that lawlessness would not be tolerated in America any longer; nor did he follow up and call on the country to move ahead with school desegregation. Rather, the president, in his address to the nation, intimated that he might not be in favor of the *Brown* decree. The president stated the Supreme Court had decided that separate schools for the races was unconstitutional; however, he also implied that he differed with the opinion by stating that although we disagree with the opinion, we must comply with it.[43]

In *Goss v. Board of Education,* 373 U.S. 683 (1963), an ingenious scheme was adopted whereby students would be permitted to transfer from a school in which their race was in a minority to one in which their race would constitute majority status. The Court held this plan unacceptable because, although it appeared to be neutral, in reality its intent was to maintain segregation. In 1959, Prince Edward County, Virginia, closed its schools to avoid desegregation, and white students began to attend private schools with tuition grants from public funds. Black students, with some exceptions, were not afforded the opportunity to attend public schools until 1963. In *Griffin v. Prince Edward County School Board,* 377 U.S. 218 (1964), the Supreme Court held that closing the schools in Prince Edward County while the public schools were operating in all other counties was a denial of equal protection of the laws.

In the same year that *Griffin* was decided, the Court of Appeals for the Fifth Circuit decided an important case that never reached the Supreme Court. In *Stell v. Savannah-Chatham County Board of Education,* 333 F.2d 55 (1964), the appeals court, speaking through Judge Griffin Bell, ruled that the Fourteenth Amendment prohibits classifying children in schools on the basis of achievement and "psychometric intelligence tests" "because the difference in aptitude is also a racial characteristic." He also contended that many of the black students would be segregated on the basis of race even when their achievements measured up to their white counterparts because of differences in test averages between blacks and whites. "Therein is the discrimination." In another important lower court case, attorney William Kunstler brought a class action suit on behalf of black and poor children in the public schools of the District of Columbia that tested the principles of *Bolling v. Sharpe.* In *Hobsen v. Hansen,* 269 F. Supp. 401 (1967),[44] the question before the district court was whether the school board unconstitutionally deprived black and poor public school children of the right to equal educational opportunities with the District's white and more affluent public school children. The court, in an opinion written by Judge J. Skelley Wright, concluded that it did. Among the several issues addressed in *Hobsen* was the tracking system—a form of ability grouping in which standardized tests determined whether children would be assigned to the basic or "slow track" or to the honors or "gifted" curriculum. Judge Wright found that the tracking system relegated black and disadvantaged children to the lower tracks, where chances of escape were remote, and therefore, they were being denied an equal educational opportunity.

The Court, in GREEN V. COUNTY SCHOOL BOARD OF NEW KENT COUNTY, 391 U.S. 430 (1968), announced that the freedom of choice plan failed to comply with the mandate in the *Brown* decision and ordered the school board to desegregate "now" by implementing a plan that promised to work. The Court's patience with cleverly designed delaying tactics was growing thin, and the Warren Court was rapidly coming to an end. It would be left to the Burger Court to grapple with the problem of implementation of school desegregation decrees.

INTEREST GROUPS' POLITICAL USE OF THE COURTS: THE ATTACK ON THE NAACP

As noted in the previous section, resistance and evasive schemes continued after *Brown II*. An all-out assault on the NAACP and the LDF by a number of Southern states emerged. After all, they deeply resented these groups' successful efforts in *Brown I* and their commitment to enforce its mandate. The assault to harass and destroy the nation's oldest civil rights organization began when the Alabama legislature attempted to prevent it from operating in the state. The NAACP was held in contempt and fined $100,000 for failing to disclose its membership to state authorities. The Alabama Supreme Court refused to overturn the contempt citation. The Warren Court declared, in NAACP V. ALABAMA EX REL. PATTERSON, 357 U.S. 449 (1958), that the order would infringe on the NAACP's freedom of association. Justice Harlan, writing for the unanimous Court, held that "Alabama has fallen short of showing a controlling justification for the deterrent effect on the free enjoyment of the right to associate which disclosure of membership lists is likely to have." This decision was the first time the Supreme Court formally proclaimed a right of association under the First Amendment.

Approximately one year later, in *Harrison v. NAACP*, 360 U.S. 167 (1959), the NAACP sought declaratory and injunctive relief with respect to three Virginia statutes that were enacted to cripple the NAACP in Virginia. The statutes sought to regulate registration, activities relating to the passage of racial legislation, advocacy of racial integration or segregation, and fundraising in connection with litigation and barretry statutes. Justice Harlan, writing for the 6-3 majority, held that "[a]ll we hold is that these enactments should be exposed to state construction or limiting interpretation before the federal courts are asked to decide upon their constitutionality." Justices Douglas and Brennan and Chief Justice Warren dissented and expressed their displeasure with the majority opinion in these words: "We need not—we should not—give deference to a state policy that seeks to undermine paramount federal law. We fail to perform the duty expressly enjoined by Congress on the federal judiciary in the Civil Rights Acts when we do so."

In *Louisiana ex rel. Gremillion v. NAACP,* 366 U.S. 293 (1961), Louisiana sued the NAACP in state court to prevent the organization from doing business in the state because of its failure to comply with state laws requiring certain types of organizations to file annually with the secretary of state a list of their officers and members. The case was moved to federal court, where the NAACP sued Louisiana and sought a declaratory judgment that the Louisiana laws were unconstitutional. The district court entered a temporary injunction that denied relief to the state and enjoined it from enforcing the two statutes in question. The Supreme Court affirmed. Justice Douglas, writing for the Court, concluded, "At one extreme is criminal conduct which cannot have shelter in the First Amendment. At the other extreme are regulatory measures which, no matter how sophisticated, cannot be employed in purpose or effect to stifle, penalize, or curb the exercise of First Amendment rights."

In *Gibson v. Florida Legislative Investigation Committee,* 372 U.S. 539 (1963), the president of the Miami branch of the NAACP was found in contempt, fined, and imprisoned for refusing to divulge contents of the membership records of that branch to a Florida legislative investigative committee that was investigating the infiltration of Communists into various organizations. The committee wanted to determine whether 14 persons previously identified as Communists were members of the Miami branch of the NAACP. The Court held, in a 5-4 opinion written by Justice Goldberg, that groups that are neither subversive nor engaged in illegal activity must be protected in their rights of free and private association guaranteed by the First and Fourteenth Amendments. The dissenters argued that the majority's ruling placed a serious limitation on the right of the legislature to investigate the Communist Party and its activities.

In *NAACP v. Alabama ex rel. Flowers,* 377 U.S. 288 (1964), an Alabama court permanently enjoined the NAACP from operating in the state for failing to comply with Alabama's corporate regulations and business qualification laws. Justice Harlan, writing for the unanimous Court, struck down the decree. For the Court, "This case, in truth, involves not the privilege of a corporation to do business in a state, but rather the freedom of individuals to associate for the collective advocacy of ideas."

Local branches of the NAACP were tried, convicted, and fined for violating occupational tax ordinances of two Arkansas cities for refusing to furnish the membership lists of the local branches to city officials. In *Bates v. Little Rock,* 361 U.S. 516 (1964), the Court unanimously reversed the convictions and declared that forcing the NAACP to disclose its membership list would constitute interference with its freedom of association, which is safeguarded by the due process clause of the Fourteenth Amendment. A similar law was struck down in *Shelton v. Tucker,* 364 U.S. 479 (1964). In *Shelton,* an Arkansas statute required every public school and college teacher to file annually affidavits listing without limitation every organization to which they belonged or regularly contributed within the preceding five years. Teacher contracts were not renewed if they failed to file the affidavits. B. T. Shelton, a member of the NAACP, brought a class action suit challenging the constitutionality of the statute. The Court, in a 5-4 opinion written by Justice Stewart, found that the statute deprived teachers of the right of associational freedom protected by the due process clause of the Fourteenth Amendment. In his dissent, Justice Frankfurter argued that the disclosure of teacher association was not a restriction on their liberty and that it was a reasonable way for the state to assess professional fitness.

In *NAACP v. Button,* 371 U.S. 415 (1963), the NAACP sought to restrain the enforcement of several Virginia laws that regulated the improper solicitation of legal business. The Court, in a 5-4 opinion written by Justice Brennan, held that the NAACP's activities, affiliates, and legal staff were modes of expression and association protected by the First and Fourteenth Amendments. *Button's* significance also lies in its endorsement of litigation as a legitimate way for interest groups to seek equality of treatment. Writing for the dissenters, Justice Harlan argued that the litigation activities of the NAACP fell within an area of activity, speech plus, in which a state may constitutionally regulate.

In *NAACP v. Overstreet,* 384 U.S. 118 (1966), a 14-year-old black boy complained that he had been kicked by the white owner of a market and accused of stealing. The local chapter of the NAACP organized a picket of the establishment. The evidence showed that some customers had been intimidated, sidewalks had been blocked, and some violence had occurred. The trial judge instructed the jury that the local branch could be held responsible for the respondent's economic losses if it found that the misconduct of others was caused by the picketing. He further instructed the jury that if the local branch was liable, it might also hold the national branch of the NAACP liable if the local branch turned out to be its agent. The Court, in a 5-4 per curiam ruling, granted certiorari on the question of whether holding the national NAACP liable for acts performed without its knowledge and by persons beyond its control denied the national NAACP rights secured by the Fourteenth Amendment. The Court dismissed the writ of certiorari, however, as improvidently granted. In his dissent, Justice Douglas, joined by Chief Justice Warren and Justices Brennan and Fortas, argued that the national branch could literally be destroyed if it could be held liable for the misconduct of the local branch without having authorized it. After concluding there was only a loose relationship between the two branches, Douglas said, "Today a judgment of more than $80,000 is fastened on the national NAACP. Juries hostile to the aims of an organization . . . can deliver crushing verdicts that may stifle organized dissent from the views and policies accepted by the majority."

THE PERSISTENT STRUGGLE TO VOTE:
FROM LITIGATION TO
CONGRESSIONAL ACTION

The struggle for racial equality was not limited to litigation. Blacks saw the necessity to employ several strategies because it had become abundantly clear that litigation alone would not transform judicial principles into substantive equalitarian outcomes. Many scholars have argued that the civil rights movement began when Rosa Parks refused to give up her bus seat in Montgomery, Alabama, to a white passenger on December 5, 1955. After her arrest, Martin Luther King, Jr. and Ralph David Abernathy, two ministers who were not well known at the time, worked untiringly to support her by organizing a one-day boycott that eventually lasted for 382 days. Taylor Branch described the success of the first day of the bus boycott:

> The bus was empty! The early morning special on the South Jackson line, which was normally full of Negro maids on their way to work, still had its groaning engine and squeaky brakes, but it was an empty shell. So was the next bus, and the next. In spite of the bitter morning cold, their fear of white people and their desperate need for wages, Montgomery Negroes were turning the City Bus Lines into a ghost fleet.[45]

In 1955 Martin Luther King, Jr., who was then 25 years old, made a clarion call for nonviolence as the chief strategic weapon of the civil rights movement. At the age of 27, he organized the Southern Christian Leadership Conference (SCLC) in 1957 to carry out peaceful sit-ins and demonstrations. Blacks had the same problems that confronted them 100 years earlier: inequality in education, housing, jobs, access to public accommodations, the administration of justice, and voting. In January 1965, King organized peaceful demonstrations in Selma, Alabama, to focus attention on the insistence of Southern states to deny the right to vote to blacks because only 335 blacks were registered out of 9,877 registered voters.[46] Moreover, Selma required an excessively complicated registration procedure that required an applicant not only to read and answer questions concerning passages of the Constitution but also "to fill in more than 50 blanks."[47] This state of affairs and highly publicized demonstrations provided Congress with justifiable reasons to pass a series of laws to grant once again what had been granted by the Fifteenth Amendment in 1870. The Civil Rights Act of 1957 created the U.S. Commission on Civil Rights and granted it the power to investigate allegations of voting rights violations in federal elections. The federal government was authorized to sue anyone who violated the voting rights of any individual; however, the law was extremely weak. Three years later, Congress passed the Civil Rights Act of 1960, which required local registrars to preserve all federal election records for a minimum of 22 months. This authorization made it possible for the federal government to refer to the records when allegations of racial discrimination were made. When discrimination constituted a "pattern or practice," federal referees were authorized to register the voters who met all of the requirements.

One strategy that was employed to dilute the voting strength of blacks who were exercising the franchise was the racial gerrymander. In 1957, the Alabama legislature diluted the voting strength of blacks in Tuskegee, Alabama, by drawing the boundary lines in the shape of an unusual "twenty-eight sided figure." The effect was to remove nearly all blacks from the city while leaving all white persons in it. The Court, in GOMILLION V. LIGHTFOOT, 364 U.S. 339 (1960), invalidated the law and declared that the sole purpose for redrawing the boundaries was to disfranchise black voters, in violation of the Fifteenth Amendment. Four years after the *Gomillion* decision, the Court decided *Wright v. Rockefeller,* 376 U.S. 52 (1964). The issue in this case involved the drawing of congressional district lines to minimize black voting strength. The appellants contended that Chapter 980 of New York's 1961 congressional apportionment statute concentrated the vast majority of blacks and Puerto Ricans (86.3%) in Congressman Adam Clayton Powell's Eighteenth Congressional District but minimized the voting strength of blacks and Puerto Ricans to 28.5%, 27.5%, and 5.1% in the Nineteenth, Twentieth, and Seventeenth Districts, respectively, solely on the basis of racial considerations. Justice Black, writing for the majority, held that the minority voters had not proven that the legislature, in drawing the districts, was motivated by racial considerations. Justice Douglas was very forceful in his dissenting opinion. He emphasized that the "11-sided, step-shaped boundary between the Seventeenth and Eighteenth Districts" was designed to concentrate blacks and Puerto Ricans in the Eighteenth District while virtually excluding them from the Seventeenth District.

In addition to drawing district lines to dilute voting strength, states passed laws to encourage racial prejudice at the polls. In *Anderson v. Martin,* 375 U.S. 399 (1964), Louisiana passed a law requiring that the race of the candidate be designated on all ballots in all primary, general, and special elections. Justice Clark declared that such a scheme placed the state behind a racial classification that "furnishes a vehicle by which racial prejudice may . . . operate against one group because of race and for another" and promotes discrimination, in violation of the equal protection clause. In *Tancil v. Woolls,* 379 U.S. 19 (1964) and the companion case *Virginia Board of Elections v. Hamm,* 379 U.S. 19 (1964), the Supreme Court, without opinion, invalidated a Virginia statute requiring that lists of qualified voters and residence certificates be maintained according to race. Classifying records on the basis of race is violative of the equal protection clause. The Court upheld, however, the section of the Virginia statute that required the denotation in divorce decrees of the race of the husband and wife because "vital statistics, obviously, are aided by denotation in the divorce decrees of the race of the parties."[48]

Among other issues, the Civil Rights Act of 1964 addressed voting rights. The Voting Rights title of the Act required that blacks be registered under the same standards applicable to whites and prohibited the use of immaterial

---

BOX 3.3

**Summary of the Main Provisions
of the Voting Rights Act of 1965**

§ 2 [1973]. Section 2, which applies nationwide, prohibits the denial or abridgement of the right to vote on account of race or color through voting qualifications or prerequisites to voting or standard, practice or procedure.

§ 4 [1973b]. Section 4 prohibits the use of any test or device in any federal, state, or local election in determining eligibility to vote. It establishes the jurisdiction of three-judge district courts to hear allegations of voting rights violations under the Act. Congress also banned voting discrimination against citizens of language minorities in § 4.

§ 5 [1973c]. Section 5 establishes a preclearance provision whereby covered states and political subdivisions must obtain permission from the U.S. District Court for the District of Columbia or the Attorney General before enacting or administering any change in voting qualification or prerequisite to voting, or standard, practice, or procedure that was different from that in force or effect on November 1, 1968.

SOURCE: Voting Rights Act of 1965, Pub. L. 89-110, Title I, § 2 et seq., 79 Stat. 437.

---

errors to disqualify individuals. Literacy tests must be given in writing, and completion of the sixth grade was rebuttable evidence of literacy for persons voting in federal elections. These laws were the precursor to the Voting Rights Act of 1965, which was signed by President Johnson on August 6, 1965, and is the most significant federal measure ever passed by Congress in the area of voting. The purpose of the Voting Rights Act is to prohibit racial discrimination in voting and to enforce the Fourteenth and Fifteenth Amendments. The major provisions of the Act (see Box 3.3) are 2, 4, and 5. A more extensive treatment of the provisions of the Voting Rights Act is presented in Chapters 4 and 5.

Registered voters in Georgia brought an action challenging the countywide voting requirement for electing some of the state's 54 senators. This would be the first case to reach the U.S. Supreme Court involving allegations of vote dilution resulting from countywide voting requirements in multidistrict counties. Justice Brennan held, in *Fortson v. Dorsey,* 379 U.S. 433 (1965), that the equal protection clause does not require that a state's apportionment scheme consist of only single-member districts as long as "substantial equality of population among the various districts" is achieved and one citizen's vote is approximately equal to that of any other of the state's citizens. He then emphasized that appellees offered no proof that the voting strength of racial minorities is minimized by using the countywide election method. Justice Douglas dissented because he thought the two types of senatorial districts produced different results. He cautioned that "to allow some candidates to be chosen by the electors in their districts and others to be defeated by the voters of foreign districts" is "the test of unequal protection under the Fourteenth Amendment."

In *Burns v. Richardson,* 384 U.S. 73 (1966), the Court, in a unanimous opinion, rejected a challenge to the presence of multimember districts in a 1965 interim reapportionment plan adopted by the Hawaii legislature. The district court disapproved of the plan because of the failure to create single-member districts. Justice Brennan, writing for the Court, declared, "Where the requirements of *Reynolds v. Sims* are met, apportionment schemes including multi-member districts will constitute an invidious discrimination only if it can be shown that 'designedly or otherwise, a multi-member constituency apportionment scheme . . . would operate to minimize or cancel out the voting strength of racial or political elements of the voting population.' " In *Fortson* and *Burns,* the Warren Court required the showing of discriminatory purpose or effect in determining whether multimember districts unconstitutionally diluted the voting strength of the political elements of the voting population. Although these cases did not directly address the question of racial vote dilution, they were important precedents for the subsequent vote dilution cases examined by the Burger Court.

The Voting Rights Act of 1965 was challenged in the original jurisdiction case of SOUTH CAROLINA V. KATZENBACH, 383 U.S. 301 (1966) within one year of its passage on the ground that it constituted an unconstitutional infringement on the rights of the states. In declaring the Act constitutional, the Court determined that Congress had the power to pass the Act under § 2 of the Fifteenth Amendment, which authorizes Congress to enforce the Amendment by appropriate legislation. Chief Justice Warren, in a 8-1 decision, declared, "The Act creates stringent new remedies for voting discrimination where it persists on a pervasive scale. . . . After enduring nearly a century of systematic resistance to the Fifteenth Amendment, Congress might well decide to shift the advantage of time and inertia from the perpetrators of the evil to its victims."

Literacy tests were also used in many Southern states to prevent blacks from voting and withstood constitutional muster before being suspended by the Voting Rights Act of 1965. For example, in *Lassiter v. Northampton County Board of Elections,* 360 U.S. 45 (1959), a provision in North Carolina's Constitution provided that members of all races who presented themselves for registration were required to be able to read or write any section of the state's constitution. Justice Douglas, writing for a unanimous Court, held that the requirement did not violate the Fifteenth Amendment because it was applicable to all races and was a fair method of deciding whether an individual was literate. He also noted that the states have broad powers to set the conditions for voting. Moreover, North Carolina was interested only in raising the standards of all individuals who desired to exercise the franchise.

By 1965 the Warren Court had become less sympathetic to the imposition of literacy requirements to voting. For example, *Louisiana v. United States,* 380 U.S. 145 (1965), invalidated Louisiana's "interpretation test," which required voting applicants to interpret a section of the federal or state constitution to the registrar's satisfaction. Justice Black pointed out that the registrar was given unbridled discretion to deny the vote to a significant number of blacks in 21 parishes while allowing virtually all whites the right to exercise the franchise.

During the same year that *South Carolina v. Katzenbach* was decided, § 4(e) of the Voting Rights Act was challenged. This section stated, in part, that no person who had completed the sixth grade in a public or private school accredited by the Commonwealth of Puerto Rico in which the language of instruction was other than English shall be denied the right to vote if he or she is unable to read or write English. The election laws of New York mandated that a condition of voting was the ability to read and write English. Several hundred thousand residents of New York City who had come from Puerto Rico had therefore been denied the right to vote. Justice Brennan, writing for the 7-2 majority in *Katzenbach v. Morgan,* 384 U.S. 641 (1966), upheld the validity of § 4(e) of the Voting Rights Act of 1965 as a proper exercise of Congress' power under § 5 of the Fourteenth Amendment.

Blacks in Gaston County, North Carolina, challenged a literacy test that had been reinstated on August 18, 1966, after the passage of the Voting Rights Act. In *Gaston County, North Carolina v. United States,* 395 U.S. 285 (1969), the Court emphasized that Congress had decided to suspend the literacy test because Congress was cognizant of the relationship between the inferior education that blacks were receiving in segregated schools and the level of literacy. It concluded that the " '[i]mpartial' administration of the literacy test today would serve only to perpetuate these inequities in a different form."

In 1962 President Kennedy supported the Twenty-Fourth Amendment to the Constitution, which outlawed the poll tax as a prerequisite for voting in federal elections and primaries. This Amendment was ratified on January 24, 1964. Approximately two years after the Twenty-Fourth Amendment was ratified, the Court, in *Harper v. Virginia Board of Elections,* 383 U.S. 663 (1966), overruled *Breedlove v. Suttles,* 302 U.S. 277 (1937) and declared that the equal protection clause precludes a state from imposing a poll tax as a requirement for voting in state elections.

In three cases from Mississippi and one case from Virginia, the Warren Court, during its final term, was afforded the opportunity to construe § 5 of the Voting Rights Act. In *Allen v. State Board of Elections,* 393 U.S. 544 (1969), the Court had to determine whether the changes from district to at-large elections, electing of officers to the appointment of them, and relocation of polling places fall under the approval requirements of § 5. According to the majority's expansive interpretation of § 5, "the legislative history on the whole supports the view that Congress intended to reach any state enactment which altered the election law of a covered State in even a minor way."

The first-generation voting rights cases in which the Warren Court removed the remaining obstacles to racial and ethnic voting were won only after a protracted legal and political struggle (see Table 3.2). As we demonstrate in the next chapter, on the Burger Court, the struggle for minority voting rights

Table 3.2 Discrimination in Voting Rights: Cases

Case	Vote	Ruling
Lassiter v. Northhampton County Board of Elections, 360 U.S. 45 (1959)	9-0	Justice Douglas upheld North Carolina's literacy requirement for registration under the Fifteenth Amendment because it was applicable to all races and because states have broad powers to set conditions for voting.
Gomillion v. Lightfoot, 364 U.S. 339 (1960)	9-0	The Supreme Court declared that the racial gerrymander violates the Fifteenth Amendment.
Wright v. Rockefeller, 376 U.S. 52 (1964)	7-2	Justice Black upheld a congressional apportionment statute that minimized the voting strength of blacks and Puerto Ricans in three districts on the grounds that minority voters had not proven that the legislation was motivated by race.
Anderson v. Martin, 375 U.S. 399 (1964)	9-0	Justice Clark struck down a Louisiana law stating that the race of the candidate be required on all ballots in all elections under the equal protection clause.
Tancil v. Woolls and *Virginia Board of Elections v. Hamm,* 379 U.S. 19 (1964)	9-0	The Supreme Court, without opinion, invalidated a Virginia statute that required lists of qualified voters and residence certificates be maintained by race.
Fortson v. Dorsey, 379 U.S. 433 (1965)	8-1	In reversing a lower court's ruling that found invidious discrimination in a Georgia senatorial reapportionment plan, Justice Brennan devised the rule that, designedly or otherwise, a multimember apportionment scheme that operates to minimize or cancel out the voting strength of racial or political elements of the voting population would violate the equal protection clause.
Louisiana v. United States, 380 U.S. 145 (1965)	9-0	Justice Black invalidated Louisiana's interpretation test, which required voting applicants to interpret a section of the federal or state constitution to the registrar's satisfaction.
South Carolina v. Katzenbach, 383 U.S. 301 (1966)	8-1	Chief Justice Warren upheld the constitutionality of the Voting Rights Act of 1965 under § 2 of the Fifteenth Amendment, which authorizes Congress to enforce the Amendment by appropriate legislation.

Table 3.2 *continued*

Case	Vote	Ruling
Burns v. Richardson, 384 U.S. 73 (1966)	9-0	Justice Brennan held that although the equal protection clause does not require at least one house of a bicameral state legislature to consist of a single-member district, apportionment schemes that include multimember districts may constitute invidious discrimination if discriminatory purpose or impact is shown.
Harper v. Virginia Board of Elections, 383 U.S. 663 (1966)	6-3	The Supreme Court declared that the equal protection clause prohibits a state from imposing a poll tax as a requirement for voting in state elections.
Katzenbach v. Morgan, 384 U.S. 641 (1966)	7-2	Justice Brennan upheld the validity of § 4(e) of the Voting Rights Act of 1965, which prohibits the denial of the right to vote if persons are unable to read or write English, against a New York requirement that mandated the ability to read or write English and had discriminated against Puerto Ricans.
Allen v. State Board of Elections, 393 U.S. 544 (1969)	5-4	The Supreme Court construed § 5 of the Voting Rights Act for the first time and held that changes from district to at-large elections, changes from the election to the appointment of officers, and the relocation of polling places fell under the ambit of § 5.
Gaston County, North Carolina v. United States, 395 U.S. 285 (1969)	8-1	Justice Harlan struck down North Carolina's reinstatement of the literacy test under the Voting Rights Act of 1965.

continued in a series of second-generation voting rights cases involving the problem of minority vote dilution.

SIT-INS, PEACEFUL DEMONSTRATIONS, AND THE JUDICIAL RESPONSE

From the *Brown* decision until the 1960s, the response to institutionalized discrimination was litigation, for the most part. The successful one-year bus boycott in Montgomery was followed by a series of creative strategies to destroy all vestiges of Jim Crow segregation. The civil rights struggle had moved from the courts to the streets. Blacks expressed a view similar to that of Frederick Douglass when he observed that "power concedes nothing without a demand."[49] Martin Luther King, Jr. believed that highly publicized peaceful demonstrations that focused on the denial of basic rights would appeal to the conscience of whites "to do the right thing."

Efforts to Desegregate Public Facilities: The Application of *Brown* in Other Contexts

Black Americans were elated with the *Brown* decision but soon discovered that its mandate was being ignored. Many public officials were deeply involved in perpetuating segregation in virtually every facet of American life. Racial segregation was held invalid when instituted by private parties if state authority was in the picture. In BOYNTON V. VIRGINIA, 364 U.S. 454 (1960), a restaurant located in a Trailways bus terminal serving interstate passengers could not refuse service to a black law student traveling from Washington, D.C., to Montgomery, Alabama. Justice Black, writing for the 7-2 majority, relied on prior decisions involving segregation in public transportation (discussed in the previous chapter) and concluded that discrimination in transportation services against interstate passengers in terminals and terminal restaurants owned and operated by terminal carriers violated the Interstate Commerce Act.

Using the state action theory, blacks were successful in outlawing segregation on city-owned buses, in courtrooms, on city-owned golf courses, public beaches, and bathhouses and in other areas (see Table 3.3). For example, in BURTON V. WILMINGTON PARKING AUTHORITY, 365 U.S. 715 (1961), the Court held that a private restaurant located in a publicly owned automobile parking building could not refuse service to blacks because "when a State leases public property in the manner . . . shown . . . here, the proscriptions of the Fourteenth Amendment must be complied with by the lessee as certainly as though they were binding covenants written into the agreement itself." Approximately one year later, in *Turner v. City of Memphis,* 369 U.S. 350 (1962), a black male was refused service in a municipal airport restaurant leased from the city. The Court, in a per curiam opinion, cited the *Burton* case and declared that the "restaurant was subject to the strictures of the Fourteenth Amendment."

A highly publicized Burger Court decision, *Palmer v. Thompson,* 403 U.S. 217 (1971), addressed the constitutionality of segregated swimming facilities. The city council of Jackson, Mississippi, decided to desegregate all of its recreational facilities except its swimming pools. Blacks brought action on equal protection grounds to force the city to reopen the pools to blacks and whites. Writing for the majority, Justice Black asserted there was substantial evidence in the record to support the view that integrated pools could not be operated safely and economically; therefore, closing the pools to both blacks and whites was not a denial of equal protection of the laws. Justices Douglas and Marshall dissented. Justice Douglas thought that city officials should not abolish municipal services to encourage apartheid "because it finds life in a multi-racial community difficult or unpleasant." Justice Marshall asserted that when officials in Jackson, Mississippi, denied any black child the opportunity to swim in a public facility, they were denying that child rights guaranteed by the Fourteenth Amendment.

The Sit-In Cases

The Congress of Racial Equality (CORE) organized "freedom rides" throughout the South to protest segregation. The Student Nonviolent Coordinating Committee (SNCC), formed in 1960, also was responsible for mass demonstrations against segregation. On February 1, 1960, Ezell Blair, David Richmond, Joseph McNeil, and Franklin McCain, four black freshmen at North Carolina Agricultural and Technical College, organized a sit-in at the Woolworth store in Greensboro, North Carolina. This event was the spark that ignited the era of civil disobedience and other direct action techniques against Jim Crow segregation. Nonviolent sit-ins and demonstrations spread like wildfire, especially in a number of Southern states. Many black students and white students were arrested and convicted of state breach of the peace and trespass charges. The Warren Court had the difficult task of devising a rule that could bridge the state-private action dichotomy. Whether the principle established in *Shelley v. Kraemer*, 344 U.S. 1 (1948) could extend to prosecution of sit-in demonstrators was an approach that never gained majority support from the Court. Instead, the Court decided many of the sit-in cases on narrow grounds (see Table 3.4) and later relied on Title II of the Civil Rights Act of 1964, the public accommodations provision.

The first sit-in case decided by the Supreme Court was GARNER V. LOUISIANA, 368 U.S. 157 (1961). A group of black demonstrators were arrested for disturbing the peace in Baton Rouge, Louisiana, for refusing to give up their seats at whites-only lunch counters. They made no speeches and were very orderly. Chief Justice Warren held there was no evidence to support a finding that the demonstrators had disturbed the peace. His opinion emphasized that the police "were left with nothing to support their actions except their own opinions that it was a breach of the peace . . . to sit peacefully in a place where custom decreed they should not sit." Justice Douglas, in a concurring opinion, concluded that the majority opinion should have held that the state of Louisiana was supporting a discriminatory policy.

In *Peterson v. City of Greenville,* 373 U.S. 244 (1963), the Court decided that it was unconstitutional under the equal protection clause for a city ordinance to prohibit service to blacks at lunch counters at a Kress store but to allow them to shop freely throughout the store. Chief Justice Warren held, "When the State has commanded a particular result, it has . . . removed that decision from the sphere of private choice." In *Lombard v. Louisiana,* 373 U.S. 267 (1963), four students (three blacks and one white) were arrested in the McCrory store in New Orleans and convicted for refusing to leave the

Table 3.3 Efforts to Desegregate Other Public Facilities: Cases

Case	Vote	Ruling
Muir v. Louisville Park Theatrical Association, 347 U.S. 971 (1954)	per curiam	The Supreme Court struck down the refusal of the Louisville Park Theatrical Association, a privately owned enterprise, in its refusal to admit blacks to its operatic performances during the summer.
Mayor and City Council of Baltimore City v. Dawson, 350 U.S. 877 (1955)	per curiam	The Supreme Court struck down segregated public beaches and bathhouses that were maintained by the city and state under the Fourteenth Amendment.
Holmes v. City of Atlanta, 350 U.S. 879 (1955)	per curiam	The Supreme Court struck down segregated municipal golf courses under the Fourteenth Amendment.
Gayle v. Browder, 352 U.S. 903 (1956)	per curiam	The Supreme Court struck down Alabama statutes and city ordinances that required segregation on motor buses under the Fourteenth Amendment.
Derrington v. Plummer, 240 F.2d 922 (1957); *cert. denied sub nom., Casey v. Plummer*, 353 U.S. 924 (1957)	cert. denied	The Supreme Court denied certiorari in a lower court case that declared that a private cafeteria located in the basement of a new county courthouse could not exclude blacks.
New Orleans City Park Improvement Association v. Ditiege, 358 U.S. 54 (1958)	per curiam	The Supreme Court affirmed a lower court's ruling that prohibited segregated golf course facilities at the New Orleans City Park on equal protection grounds.
Boynton v. Virginia, 364 U.S. 454 (1960)	7-2	Justice Black held that a restaurant located in a Trailways bus terminal serving interstate passengers could not refuse service to blacks under the Interstate Commerce Act.
Burton v. Wilmington Parking Authority, 365 U.S. 715 (1961)	6-3	The Supreme Court held that a private restaurant located in a publicly owned automobile parking building could not refuse blacks service under the Fourteenth Amendment.
Turner v. City of Memphis, 369 U.S. 350 (1962)	per curiam	Relying on *Burton*, the Supreme Court ruled that refusing to serve blacks in a municipal airport restaurant violated the Fourteenth Amendment.

whites-only lunch counter when ordered to do so by the person in charge. The city had no local segregation law, but the mayor had issued a statement, published in the *New Orleans Times-Picayune:* "I have today directed the

Table 3.3 *continued*

Case	Vote	Ruling
Watson v. City of Memphis, 373 U.S. 526 (1963)	9-0	The Supreme Court struck down the denial of the use of public parks and other publicly owned recreational facilities in Memphis, Tennessee.
Wright v. Georgia, 373 U.S. 284 (1963)	9-0	The Supreme Court reversed the breach of peace convictions of six blacks who were peacefully playing basketball in a segregated public park in Savannah, Georgia, and did not disperse when ordered to do so by police.
Johnson v. Virginia, 373 U.S. 61 (1963)	per curiam	The Supreme Court reversed the conviction of Ford Johnson when he was convicted of contempt for refusing to sit in the section of the courtroom reserved for blacks.
Palmer v. Thompson, 403 U.S. 217 (1971)	5-4	The Burger Court upheld the closing of public swimming pools under the Fourteenth Amendment.

superintendent of police that no additional sit-in demonstrations . . . will be permitted . . . regardless of the avowed purpose or intent of the participants." The Court, in a unanimous opinion written by Chief Justice Warren, held that state action was apparent because the public statement by the mayor was equivalent to a city ordinance, and the Court reversed the convictions.

In *Gober v. City of Birmingham*, 373 U.S. 374 (1963) and *Avent v. North Carolina*, 373 U.S. 375 (1963), black students in Birmingham, Alabama, and Durham, North Carolina, were convicted for criminal trespass for refusing to leave whites-only lunch counters. In per curiam opinions, the Court reversed their convictions in the light of the *Peterson* decision. In *Shuttlesworth v. City of Birmingham*, 373 U.S. 262 (1963), the Court reversed the conviction of two black ministers for aiding a violation of a Birmingham criminal trespass ordinance. They had been charged with inciting 10 blacks to participate in a sit-in at a whites-only lunch counter. The convictions were set aside on the authority of *Gober*. In the opinion, Chief Justice Warren declared, "It is generally recognized that there can be no conviction for aiding and abetting someone to do an innocent act."

In *Bell v. Maryland*, 378 U.S. 226 (1964), 12 black students were convicted of a Maryland trespass statute for engaging in a sit-in protest at the whites-only Hooper's restaurant. Their convictions were upheld by the highest state court in Maryland. Before the case reached the Supreme Court, the city of Baltimore and the Maryland legislature enacted a public accommodations statute that abolished the crime for which the demonstrators had been convicted. Justice Brennan, writing for a 6-3 majority, refused to address the questions raised in the case under the equal protection and due process clauses

Table 3.4 The Sit-Ins and Peaceful Demonstration: Cases

Case	Vote	Ruling
Garner v. Louisiana, 368 U.S. 157 (1961)	9-0	Chief Justice Warren held there was no evidence to support a finding that black demonstrators arrested in Baton Rouge, Louisiana, in protest of segregated lunch counters were lawfully convicted of disturbing the peace.
Taylor v. Louisiana, 370 U.S. 154 (1962)	per curiam	Relying on *Garner,* the Court declared that blacks traveling by bus from Shreveport, Louisiana, to Jackson, Mississippi, were within their rights to use the waiting room customarily reserved for whites and that there was no evidence of violence.
Peterson v. City of Greenville, 373 U.S. 244 (1963)	9-0	Chief Justice Warren reversed the convictions of 10 blacks protesting whites-only lunch counters at a Kress store under a trespass ordinance on the ground that a city ordinance could not prohibit service to blacks in a restaurant under the equal protection clause.
Lombard v. Louisiana, 373 U.S. 267 (1963)	9-0	Chief Justice Warren reversed the convictions of three black students and one white student for refusing to leave a whites-only lunch counter despite no local segregation law, but the Court found state action in the mayor's public statement directing police to arrest sit-in demonstrators.
Gober v. City of Birmingham, 373 U.S. 374 (1963)	per curiam	The Supreme Court reversed the convictions of black students for criminal trespass for refusing to leave whites-only lunch counters in Birmingham, Alabama.
Avent v. North Carolina, 373 U.S. 375 (1963)	per curiam	The Supreme Court reversed the criminal trespass conviction of black students for refusing to leave whites-only lunch counters in Durham, North Carolina.
Shuttlesworth v. City of Birmingham, 373 U.S. 262 (1963)	8-1	Chief Justice Warren reversed the convictions of two black ministers for aiding a violation of a Birmingham, Alabama, criminal trespass ordinance for inciting 10 blacks to participate in a sit-in at a whites-only lunch counter on the authority of *Gober v. City of Birmingham.*

Table 3.4 *continued*

Case	Vote	Ruling
Edwards v. South Carolina, 372 U.S. 229 (1963)	8-1	Justice Stewart struck down a South Carolina breach of the peace statute that was used to convict 187 black high school and college students when they peacefully assembled at the South Carolina capitol to protest segregation on vagueness grounds.
Griffin v. Maryland, 378 U.S. 130 (1964)	6-3	Chief Justice Warren reversed the criminal trespass convictions of blacks who entered a privately owned amusement park that excluded blacks on the ground that a deputy sheriff who was an employee of the park arrested them and his action constituted state action.
Barr v. City of Columbia, 378 U.S. 146 (1964)	6-3	Justice Black reversed the criminal trespass and breach of the peace convictions of five black college students who were arrested for refusing to leave a whites-only drugstore lunch counter after having been refused service on the ground that there was no evidence to support the charges.
Robinson v. Florida, 378 U.S. 153 (1964)	9-0	Justice Black reversed the convictions of 18 blacks and whites who were arrested under a state misdemeanor statute that prohibited persons from remaining at a restaurant after having been asked to leave on the ground that when state policy discourages blacks and whites from being together, it is state action within the proscription of the Fourteenth Amendment.
Hamm v. City of Rock Hill and *Lupper v. Arkansas*, 379 U.S. 306 (1964)	5-4	Justice Clark reversed the convictions of sit-in demonstrators at whites-only lunch counters in South Carolina and Arkansas on the ground that Title II of the Civil Rights Act of 1964 prohibited discrimination in public accommodations.
Bell v. Maryland, 378 U.S. 226 (1964)	6-3	Justice Brennan reversed the criminal trespass convictions of 12 black students on the ground that Maryland had enacted laws that abolished the crime for which the students were convicted.
Bouie v. City of Columbia, 378 U.S. 347 (1964)	6-3	Justice Brennan reversed the convictions of two black sit-in demonstrators on the ground that they had no notice that the restaurant was barred to them.

continued

Table 3.4 *continued*

Case	Vote	Ruling
Cox v. Louisiana (*Cox I*), 379 U.S. 536 (1965)	7-2	Justice Goldberg reversed Rev. Cox's conviction for breach of the peace for leading a demonstration of 2,000 students who were protesting segregation and the jailing of students on overbreadth grounds.
Cox v. Louisiana (*Cox II*), 379 U.S. 559 (1965)	5-4	Justice Goldberg reversed Rev. Cox's obstructing the sidewalk conviction because police never suggested that the demonstration be held farther away from the courthouse than it actually was.
Adderley v. Florida, 385 U.S. 39 (1966)	5-4	Justice Black upheld the trespass conviction of black students who assembled on the premises of a county jail to protest the segregation and the arrest of other students on the ground that jails are not open to the public.
Brown v. Louisiana, 383 U.S. 131 (1966)	5-4	Justice Fortas reversed the sit-in convictions of five blacks who entered a library to protest its segregated operation on the ground that the protesters had been peaceful and unprovocative.
Walker v. City of Birmingham, 388 U.S. 307 (1967)	5-4	Justice Stewart upheld the contempt of court convictions of Reverend Martin Luther King Jr. and other civil rights demonstrators for having violated an injunction prohibiting marches on Easter weekend to protest segregation on the ground that they were not constitutionally free to ignore the procedures of law and carry their battle to the streets.
Cameron v. Johnson, 390 U.S. 611 (1968)	6-2	Justice Brennan upheld the convictions of black demonstrators under an antipicketing law prohibiting picketing that interfered with ingress or egress to any courthouse on the ground that officials never intended to interfere with picketers' rights to free expression.
Gregory v. City of Chicago, 394 U.S. 111 (1969)	9-0	Chief Justice Warren overturned the conviction of peaceful civil rights demonstrators who were arrested and convicted for disorderly conduct when they marched to the mayor's home to press their claims for desegregation of the public schools on First Amendment grounds.

of the Fourteenth Amendment. According to Justice Brennan, "The question of Maryland law raised here by the supervening enactment of the city and state public accommodations laws cleverly falls within the rule requiring us to vacate and reverse the judgment." Justice Douglas argued in his concurring opinion that the issue of the right of public accommodation under the Fourteenth Amendment was ripe for adjudication and that the demonstrators were entitled to an answer "here and now." Moreover, Justice Douglas acknowledged that the case was decided during the time the Civil Rights Act of 1964 was about to be passed and that the act contained a public accommodations provision. Justice Black, joined by Justices Harlan and White, dissented from the majority's refusal to decide the question "whether the Fourteenth Amendment forbids a state to enforce its trespass laws to convict a person who comes into a privately owned restaurant, is told that because of his color he will not be served, and over the owner's protest to leave." According to Justice Black, the Fourteenth Amendment does not forbid this application of a state's trespass laws.

In HAMM V. CITY OF ROCK HILL, 379 U.S. 306 (1964) and the companion case *Lupper v. Arkansas,* 379 U.S. 306 (1964), the Court was confronted with convictions of sit-in demonstrators at lunch counters in South Carolina and Arkansas shortly before the enactment of the historic Civil Rights Act of 1964. Title II of the Act outlawed discrimination in any inn, motel, hotel, restaurant, soda fountain, motion picture house, theater, and so on, on the basis of race, color, religion, or national origin if the operation affects commerce or is supported by state action (see the discussion of Title II and Box 3.4, below). The proponents of this Act wanted to move the civil rights movement from the streets to the judiciary. Justice Clark noted that the Act made it clear that the nation's public policy is to prohibit discrimination in public accommodations. Therefore, prosecuting the demonstrators would not serve the public interest. Because the conduct in the *Hamm* and *Lupper* cases occurred prior to the passage of the Act, "the still-pending convictions are abated by its passage." Justice Douglas contended that when the state courts prosecuted the demonstrators, they were in effect enforcing the discriminatory practices of the private owners of these businesses, in violation of the equal protection clause of the Fourteenth Amendment. Justice Black dissented because he thought the threat of violence increases when property owners believe that their property has been invaded by force.

In 1964 the nation experienced a series of demonstrations against segregation in a number of areas. On June 24, 1964, the Supreme Court announced decisions in four sit-in cases. In *Griffin v. Maryland,* 378 U.S. 130 (1964), several blacks entered a privately owned amusement park that had a policy of excluding blacks. When they refused to leave, a deputy sheriff who was an employee at the park arrested them. They were convicted of criminal trespass in a Maryland state court. Chief Justice Warren, in a 6-3 ruling, reversed the lower court's decision by holding that the deputy sheriff's action was prohibited by the Fourteenth Amendment because "if an individual is possessed of state authority and purports to act under that authority, his action is state action." In *Barr v. City of Columbia,* 378 U.S. 146 (1964), five black college students were arrested for criminal trespass and breach of the peace for refusing to leave a whites-only drugstore lunch counter in Columbia, South Carolina. They were allowed to make some purchases in another section of the store before proceeding to the lunch counter. In reversing the convictions, Justice Black, in a 6-3 opinion, held that the convictions for breach of the peace cannot stand because there was no evidence to support them. In *Bouie v. City of Columbia,* 378 U.S. 347 (1964), two black sit-in demonstrators refused to leave a restaurant in a Columbia, South Carolina, drugstore, claiming they had no notice that the restaurant was barred to them. In reversing the convictions, Justice Brennan held, in a 6-3 opinion, that "the South Carolina Code did not give them fair warning, at the time of their conduct . . . that the act for which they now stand convicted was rendered criminal by the statute." After all, the statute prohibited only entry on the premises of another and did not prohibit the act of remaining after having been asked to leave. Finally, in *Robinson v. Florida,* 378 U.S. 153 (1964), the Florida State Health Board required segregated rest rooms, and a manual based on state regulations also required segregated facilities. These regulations had been adopted under the legislature's authority. Eighteen blacks and whites were arrested and convicted under a state misdemeanor statute that prohibited persons from remaining at a restaurant after having been asked to leave. Justice Black, in a unanimous opinion, argued that when a state policy discourages serving blacks and whites together it is "state action, of the kind that falls within the proscription of the Equal Protection Clause."

Blacks found themselves unable to enter and enjoy the serenity of some public libraries 12 years after the *Brown* decision. In *Brown v. Louisiana,* 383 U.S. 131 (1966), five blacks entered a regional library to protest its operation on a segregated basis. They sat quietly after being informed to leave and were arrested and convicted for violating a breach of the peace statute. Justice Fortas, writing for the 5-4 plurality, noted that there was no evidence of a breach of the peace because the protesters had been very peaceful and unprovocative. Going further, he observed, "It is an unhappy circumstance that the locus of these events was a public library—a place dedicated to quiet, to knowledge, and to beauty. It is a sad commentary that this hallowed place . . . bore the ugly stamp of racism."

Mass Demonstrations: Lawful and Unlawful Conduct

In addition to sit-ins, mass street demonstrations were popular in the 1960s. The goal was to bring attention to segregation, which permeated nearly every facet of American life, and to prick the conscience of a nation that had become desensitized to racial injustice. The Court was inundated with cases during this period (see Table 3.4) raising "speech plus" issues—that is, speech plus conduct. In EDWARDS V. SOUTH CAROLINA, 372 U.S. 229 (1963), 187 black high school and college students peacefully assembled at the South Carolina capitol to protest segregation. After 15 minutes, instead of dispersing, as instructed by the police, they sang several patriotic and religious songs. Although there was no violence, they were arrested and convicted of the common law crime of breach of the peace. Writing for the majority, Justice Stewart held that the statute was so vague and indefinite that it was repugnant to the Fourteenth Amendment's guarantee of liberty.

Two years after the *Edwards* decision, the Court decided COX V. LOUISIANA (*Cox I*), 379 U.S. 536 (1965) and COX V. LOUISIANA (*Cox II*), 379 U.S. 559 (1965). In these cases, 23 students from Southern University were arrested in Baton Rouge, Louisiana, for picketing stores that had segregated lunch counters; they were convicted for disturbing the peace and obstructing the sidewalk. The next day, to protest the jailing, Reverend Cox led approximately 2,000 students to the courthouse that housed the jailed students. He was arrested and convicted for disturbing the peace. Justice Goldberg declared, in *Cox I,* that the breach of peace statute was overly broad and that the authorities permitted or prohibited parades in their uncontrolled discretion and are allowed to "act as a censor." *Cox II* arose out of the demonstration in *Cox I.* When Reverend Cox arrived in close proximity to the courthouse with the 2,000 students, the police chief told Cox that the demonstration would be permitted but that it should be confined to the west side of the street, which was across from the courthouse. Reverend Cox was arrested for breach of the peace and obstructing the sidewalk and for failure to disperse. In *Cox II* Justice Goldberg held that the Louisiana statute was narrowly drawn but that because the police never suggested the demonstration be held farther away from the courthouse than was actually the case, "it is clear that the dispersal order did not remove the protection accorded by the original grant of permission."

One year later, in *Adderley v. Florida,* 385 U.S. 39 (1966), the Court decided a case that was similar to *Edwards v. South Carolina* (1963). The basic difference was that, in *Adderley,* the demonstrators held their protest on the premises of the county jail, rather than on the statehouse grounds. Black students from Florida A&M University in Tallahassee assembled on a nonpublic jail driveway to demonstrate against the earlier arrest of their schoolmates and to protest against segregation in the jail and other facilities. While singing and dancing, they were advised by the jail's custodian, the sheriff, that they were trespassing on county property and would be arrested if they did not leave. Refusing to leave, approximately 107 of the demonstrators were arrested and convicted for violating a Florida trespass statute. The black students claimed that their case was controlled by *Edwards* and *Cox I* and that their convictions deprived them of their rights of free speech, assembly, petition, due process of law, and equal protection. In rejecting their claims, Justice Black emphasized that the statehouse grounds, unlike jails, are open to the public. After rejecting the students' claim that the Florida trespass statute was unconstitutionally vague, Justice Black noted that the entrance to the jail had not been used by the public but had been used to transport prisoners to and from the courts. Moreover, the state, like the owner of private property, is empowered to use the property for the purposes for which it is lawfully dedicated. Justice Douglas dissented in these words:

The jailhouse, like an executive mansion, a legislative chamber, a courthouse, or the statehouse itself . . . is one of the seats of government, whether it be the Tower of London, the Bastille, or a small county jail. And when it houses political prisoners or those who many think are unjustly held, it is an obvious center for protest.

Approximately one year before Dr. Martin Luther King Jr., was assassinated, the Court decided the case of WALKER V. CITY OF BIRMINGHAM, 388 U.S. 307 (1967). On April 10, 1963, a judge in Alabama issued a temporary injunction that enjoined Dr. King and other demonstrators from participating in mass demonstrations without a permit. The demonstrators held a news conference and made it clear that they intended to disobey the injunction. Street parades were held on Good Friday and Easter Sunday. In upholding the contempt convictions of Dr. King and the other demonstrators, Justice Stewart contended that the petitioners could not circumvent "orderly judicial review of the injunction before disobeying it." Justice Stewart was emphatic when he argued, "One may sympathize with the petitioners' impatient commitment to their cause. But respect for judicial process is a small price to pay for the civilizing hand of law."

One year later, in the case of *Cameron v. Johnson,* 390 U.S. 611 (1968), black demonstrators received another setback. They picketed the voting registration office located in the Forrest County, Mississippi, courthouse to protest voting discrimination. The sheriff laid out a route for the pickets with barricades so that citizens would have access to the courthouse. An antipicketing law that prohibited picketing from interfering with ingress or egress to any of the courthouses was violated by the demonstrators. Justice Brennan, in a 6-2 opinion, disagreed with the demonstrators' contentions that the law was overly broad because it prohibits picketing only if it "interferes with ingress or egress to or from the courthouse." He also argued that the officials had not acted in bad faith and never intended to interfere with the picketers' right to free expression by harassing them.

In *Gregory v. City of Chicago,* 394 U.S. 111 (1969), the Court was confronted with a problem it had failed to address earlier in *Feiner v. New York,* 340 U.S. 315 (1951) and the *Edwards* case. The issue before the Court involved the extent to which street demonstrations could be restrained because of the threat of violence by enraged bystanders. The demonstrators were engaged in a peaceful march to the mayor's home in Chicago to push for the desegregation of the public schools. Fearing disorderly conduct because the crowd had become unruly, the police ordered the demonstrators to disperse. The demonstrators were arrested for disorderly conduct for refusing to disperse. Their convictions were reversed on the basis of the *Edwards* decision because there was no evidence that their conduct had been disorderly.

After the violence that erupted in many American cities in the late 1960s, militancy and defiance replaced the sit-ins. An example of this change in tactics can be seen by examining *Street v. New York,* 394 U.S. 576 (1969). A black male learned from a news report on the radio that James Meredith had been shot in Mississippi. The man was so enraged that he grabbed an American flag and burned it at a street corner near his home. He told the group of approximately 35 persons, "If they let that happen to Meredith, we don't need an American flag." He was arrested and convicted. Justice Harlan, writing for the Court, relied on *Stromberg v. California,* 283 U.S. 359 (1931) and concluded that the evidence was insufficient to determine with certainty that Street was not convicted for his words. On remand of the case to the lower court, Street was retried and convicted for burning the American flag.

ERADICATING RACIAL DISCRIMINATION IN PUBLIC ACCOMMODATIONS

Before Congress enacted Title II, black Americans challenged discrimination in public accommodations by resorting to the equal protection clause. The Court had little difficulty invalidating state-supported discrimination in public facilities; however, racial discrimination in public facilities that are privately owned was more difficult to attack despite the fact that access to such facilities was a serious national problem for black Americans. Congress responded with Title II of the Civil Rights Act of 1964, which prohibits racial discrimination in public accommodations that serve or offer to serve interstate travelers (see Box 3.4). Some legal scholars have argued that this Act should have been grounded on § 5 of the Fourteenth Amendment, rather than on the commerce clause (Article I, § 8, Clause 3).

After the enactment of Title II, it was no longer necessary to determine whether the prosecution of sit-in demonstrators for criminal trespass was impermissible state action. Title II was upheld in HEART OF ATLANTA MOTEL, INC. V. UNITED STATES, 379 U.S. 241 (1964) and *Katzenbach v. McClung,* 379 U.S. 294 (1964). In *Heart of Atlanta,* a motel in Atlanta, Georgia, refused to rent rooms to blacks although it solicited patronage from other states through several national advertising media, and approximately 75% of its guests lived outside the state. The owners sought to enjoin enforcement of the Act by contending that Congress had exceeded its authority to regulate commerce in passing Title II. Writing for a unanimous Court, Justice Clark upheld the constitutionality of Title II of the Civil Rights Act. He noted that Congress could prevent, under its power to regulate commerce, any obstructions in interstate commerce that are caused by racial discrimination. Moreover, he stated that "[i]f it is interstate commerce that feels the pinch, it does not matter how local the operation which applies the squeeze."

On the same day that *Heart of Atlanta* was decided, the Court also rendered its decision in *Katzenbach v. McClung* (1964). A restaurant—Ollie's Barbecue, which had been in business since 1927—in Birmingham, Alabama, refused to serve blacks in its dining accommodations but did permit take-out service for them. A substantial portion of the food that was served had moved in interstate commerce. Justice Clark held that the power of Congress over

---

BOX 3.4

Title II of the Civil Rights Act of 1964:
Main Provisions

Title 42, U.S.C., § 201(a) [§ 2000a]. All persons shall be entitled to the full and equal enjoyment of the goods, services, facilities, privileges, advantages, and accommodations of any place of public accommodation . . . without discrimination or segregation on the ground of race, color, religion, or national origin.

   (b) Each of the following establishments which serves the public is a place of public accommodation within the meaning of this title if its operations affect commerce, or if discrimination or segregation by it is supported by State action:

     (1) any inn, hotel, motel, or other establishment which provides lodging to transient guests, other than an establishment located within a building which contains not more than five rooms for rent or hire and which is actually occupied by the proprietor of such establishment as his residence;

     (2) any restaurant, cafeteria, lunchroom, lunch counter, soda fountain, or other facility principally engaged in selling food for consumption on the premises, including, but not limited to, any such facility located on the premises of any retail establishment; or any gasoline station;

     (3) any motion picture house, theater, concert hall, sports arena, stadium or other place of exhibition or entertainment . . .

   (e) The provisions of this title shall not apply to a private club or other establishment not in fact open to the public, except to the extent that the facilities of such establishment are made available to the customers or patrons of an establishment within the scope of subsection (b).

   § 202 [§ 2000a-1]. All persons shall be entitled to be free, at any establishment or place, from discrimination or segregation of any kind on the ground of race, color, religion, or national origin, if such discrimination or segregation is or purports to be required by any law, statute, ordinance, regulation, rule, or order of a State or any agency or political subdivision thereof.

---

interstate commerce is very broad and that the Civil Rights Act of 1964 is appropriate to resolve this commercial problem, which is national in scope. Therefore, restaurants that discriminate on the basis of race impose an adverse effect on interstate commerce because a substantial portion of the food served had been received from outside the state.

Four years later, in *Newman v. Piggie Park Enterprises, Inc.,* 390 U.S. 400 (1968), the Court declared that Title II applied to drive-in restaurants. In the per curiam decision, the Court also emphasized that a litigant that is successful in obtaining an injunction under § 204(b) of Title II should recover attorneys' fees. The Court noted that the provision for attorneys' fees was enacted to encourage judicial relief to victims who are injured by racial discrimination

---

BOX 3.4

Title II of the Civil Rights Act of 1964:
Main Provisions (*continued*)

§ 203 [§ 2000a-2]. No person shall (a) withhold, deny, or attempt to withhold or deny, or deprive . . . any person of any right or privilege secured by section 201 or 202, or (b) intimidate, threaten, or coerce . . . any person with the purpose of interfering with any right or privilege secured by section 201 or 202, or (c) punish or attempt to punish any person for exercising . . . any right or privilege secured by section 201 or 202.

§ 204(a) [§ 2000a-3]. Whenever any person has engaged or there are reasonable grounds to believe that any person is about to engage in any act or practice prohibited by section 203, a civil action for preventive relief, including an application for a permanent or temporary injunction, restraining order or other order, may be instituted by the person aggrieved and, . . . the court may, in its discretion, permit the Attorney General to intervene in such civil action if he certifies that the case is of general public importance. . . .

(b) In any action commenced pursuant to this title, the court, in its discretion, may allow the prevailing party, other than the United States, a reasonable attorney's fee as part of the costs, and the United States should be liable for costs the same as a private person.

---

and to penalize individuals who advance arguments they know are untenable. One year later, in *Daniel v. Paul,* 395 U.S. 298 (1969), the Court had to decide whether Title II covered an amusement park located approximately 12 miles from Little Rock, Arkansas, that advertised over two radio stations and distributed a monthly magazine to Little Rock hotels but refused admission to blacks. Justice Brennan noted that the park was a public accommodation under § 201(c)(2) of the Act because a substantial amount of food that was served had moved in interstate commerce. Moreover, because the snack bar served all persons in the facility, it was reasonable to conclude that it offered service to out-of-state persons. Justice Black dissented because he thought that the Civil Rights Act of 1964 should have been based on § 5 of the Fourteenth Amendment, rather than on the power of Congress to regulate commerce. He also thought that it is "stretching the Commerce Clause . . . to give the Federal Government complete control over every little remote country place of recreation in every nook and cranny of every precinct and county."

In a number of lower court decisions, "place of entertainment" and "establishment" have been interpreted very broadly. In *Fazzio Real Estate Co., Inc. v. Adams,* 396 F.2d 146 (1968), the Court of Appeals for the Fifth Circuit declared that Title II covers a snack bar located in close proximity to the bowling lanes. Judge Johnson observed, "Fazzio's invites and encourages its bowling customers to make purchases from the refreshment counter." In *Rousseve v. Shape Spa for Health and Beauty, Inc.,* 516 F.2d 64 (1975), Judge

Gewin, in a decision from the Court of Appeals for the Fifth Circuit, ruled that a spa that offered "curative or rehabilitative treatment" was a "place of entertainment" and was covered under Title II.

Decisions upholding the rights of black Americans under Title II did not prevent covered establishments from discriminating against racial and ethnic minorities. Exclusive private clubs began to form from previously established places of public accommodation because they were not covered by Title II. This trend necessitated even more litigation and complicated the enforcement of previously established legal mandates. These decisions are examined in the next chapter.

EQUAL HOUSING OPPORTUNITIES

The federal government did very little to ensure equal housing opportunities before the 1960s. It was a part of the problem by allowing segregated housing to flourish during the 1950s. The 1960s saw a great increase of whites moving to the suburbs and blacks settling in the central cities. In 1966 the nation was experiencing increased white hostility, riots in a number of cities, and the shooting of James Meredith in Mississippi. In addition, Willie Ricks and Stokely Carmichael popularized the slogan "black power," which was intimidating to whites, including officials at the national, state, and local levels. The Johnson administration was unsuccessful in its efforts to pass a civil rights bill in 1966 that contained an open housing provision (Title IV). The measure prevailed in the House but was killed in the Senate. The Congress that had passed the Voting Rights Act of 1965 was unwilling to pass this bill because open housing was extremely controversial in 1966.[50]

Approximately one year before Congress enacted a fair housing law, the Court decided whether the states could encourage private discrimination in the sale, lease, or rental of property. In *Reitman v. Mulkey,* 387 U.S. 369 (1967), the voters in California approved Proposition 14, which provided, "Neither the State nor any subdivision or agency thereof shall deny, limit or abridge . . . the right of any person, who is willing or desires to sell, lease or rent any part or all of his real property, to decline to sell, lease or rent such property to such person or persons as he, in his absolute discretion, chooses." The Mulkeys, a black couple, sued the petitioners, alleging that they refused to rent to them solely on the basis of race. Justice White, in a 5-4 opinion, contended that Proposition 14 nullified California's Rumford and Unruh Acts, which prohibited discrimination in the housing market and "significantly encourage and involve the State in private discriminations." He also argued that upholding Proposition 14 was tantamount to endorsing the state's right to discriminate. Justice Harlan, writing for the dissenters, argued, "The Four-teenth Amendment does not reach such state constitutional action any more than it does a simple legislative repeal of legislation forbidding private discrimination."

On April 4, 1968, Dr. Martin Luther King, Jr. was assassinated in Memphis, Tennessee. He had gone there to support the black sanitation employees, who were working under deplorable conditions. The chaos and rioting that erupted in many of the nation's cities after his assassination prodded Congress to pass the Fair Housing Act of 1968 one week after his death. The most important section of the Act was Title VIII (see Box 3.5), which was a national fair housing law. Its purpose was to prohibit discrimination based on race, color, religion, gender, and familial status.

Several weeks after the passage of the Civil Rights Act of 1968, the Court decided the landmark case of JONES V. ALFRED H. MAYER CO., 392 U.S. 409 (1968). This case involved § 1982 of the Civil Rights Act of 1866, which provides that "all citizens of the United States shall have the same right, in every State and Territory, as is enjoyed by white citizens thereof to inherit, purchase, lease, sell, hold, and convey real and personal property." This case involved an interracial couple who alleged that the real estate company refused to sell them a home on account of race. Justice Stewart made it clear that the Civil Rights Act of 1968 (Title VIII) had no effect on this particular case. He argued that if a dollar could not buy for a black man what it could buy for a white man, then the Thirteenth Amendment is "a mere paper guarantee" and that the exclusion of blacks from white communities was simply "a substitute for the Black Codes." Within a year of the *Jones* decision, the Court decided *Sullivan v. Little Hunting Park, Inc.,* 396 U.S. 229 (1969), which held that whites could sue under § 1982 of the 1866 Civil Rights Act to exculpate the rights of blacks who have been the recipients of housing discrimination.

After the *Jones* case, the Court had to decide whether an amendment to a city charter in Akron, Ohio, that required a majority of the electors to approve any law pertaining to the sale or rental of property that involved race, religion, or national origin was constitutional. The Court invalidated the amendment in HUNTER V. ERICKSON, 393 U.S. 385 (1969) because the city of Akron had not presented any sufficient reasons to justify the racial classification. Moreover, Justice White, in writing for the 8-1 majority, reasoned that laws concerning racial matters could take effect contingent on the outcome of a referendum, whereas other housing ordinances become effective without a special election. In addition, the amendment had devised a novel procedure for lawmaking and made it exceedingly difficult for racial minorities to secure favorable legislation.

RACE AND THE ADMINISTRATION OF JUSTICE: EQUAL OR UNEQUAL?

Historically, race and class have been major determinants of who receives equal justice under the law. In some cases, blacks were treated in a disparaging manner by the courts. A. Leon Higginbotham, Jr., pinpointed what has occurred in some appellate courts:

BOX 3.5

Title VIII of the Fair Housing Act of 1968: Main Provisions

Title 42, U.S.C., § 804 [§ 3604]. *Discrimination in the sale or rental of housing and other prohibited practices.* As made applicable by 803 and except as exempted by §§ 803(b) and 807, it shall be unlawful—

(a) To refuse to sell or rent after the making of a bona fide offer, or to refuse to negotiate for the sale or rental of, or otherwise make unavailable or deny, a dwelling to any person because of race, color, religion, sex, familial status, or national origin.

(b) To discriminate against any person in the terms, conditions, or privileges of sale or rental of a dwelling, or in the provision of services or facilities in connection therewith, because of race, color, religion, sex, familial status, or national origin.

(c) To make, print, or publish, or cause to be made, printed, or published any notice, statement, or advertisement, with respect to the sale or rental of a dwelling that indicates any preference, limitation, or discrimination based on race, color, religion, sex, handicap, familial status, or national origin, or an intention to make any such preference, limitation, or discrimination.

(d) To represent to any person because of race, color, religion, sex, handicap, familial status, or national origin that any dwelling is not available for inspection, sale, or rental when such dwelling is in fact so available.

(e) For profit, to induce or attempt to induce any person to sell or rent any dwelling by presentations regarding the entry or prospective entry into the neighborhood of a person or persons of a particular race, color, religion, sex, handicap, familial status, or national origin.

§ 805(a) [§ 3605]. *Discrimination in residential real-estate transactions.* It shall be unlawful for any person or other entity whose business includes engaging in residential real estate-related transactions to discriminate against any person in making available such transaction, or in the terms or conditions of such a transaction, because of race, color, religion, sex, handicap, familial status, or national origin.

§ 806 [§ 3606]. *Discrimination in the provision of brokerage services.* After December 31, 1968, it shall be unlawful to deny any person access to or membership or participation in any multiple-listing service, real estate brokers' organization or other service, organization, or facility relating to the business of selling or renting dwellings, or to discriminate against him in the terms or conditions of such access, membership, or participation, on account of race, color, religion, sex, handicap, familial status, or national origin.

NOTE: § 3603(b)(1) exempts any single-family house sold or rented by an owner. Section 3603(b)(2) exempts rooms or units in dwellings containing living quarters occupied or intended to be occupied by no more than four families living independently of each other, if the owner actually maintains and occupies one of such living quarters as his residence.

In many other cases, appellate courts have upheld convictions despite prosecutors' references to black defendants and witnesses in such racist terms as "black rascal," "burr-headed nigger," "mean negro," "big nigger," "pickaninny," "mean nigger," "three nigger men," "niggers," and "nothing but just a common Negro, [a] black whore."[51]

In other cases, blacks were treated unjustly and disrespectfully by judges. In *Johnson v. Virginia*, 373 U.S. 61 (1963), the Supreme Court overturned a contempt conviction imposed on a black man, Ford Johnson, who refused to sit in a section of the courtroom reserved for blacks. One year later, in *Hamilton v. Alabama*, 376 U.S. 650 (1964), a trial court judge ruled that a black woman was in contempt of court for refusing to answer questions during cross examination when she was addressed repeatedly by her first name after requesting to be addressed as Miss Mary Hamilton. Hamilton was sentenced to five days in jail and fined $50. The Supreme Court, in a per curiam ruling, reversed the lower court, citing *Johnson* as authority.

Private Interference With Constitutional Rights: Criminal and Civil Remedies

In addition to the Fourteenth Amendment, black Americans have resorted to federal civil rights statutes designed to prohibit private conduct that interferes with federal constitutional rights. Many of these statutes have as their origin civil rights laws of the Reconstruction era that were passed by Congress to enforce the Civil War Amendments (see Chapter 2). For example, in the previous section we discussed § 1982, which originally was based on §1 of the Civil Rights Act of 1866. We explore the modern counterparts to these laws in this section.

Sections 241 and 242 are the federal criminal statutes that address private interferences with federal civil rights (see Box 3.6). The Warren Court addressed the scope of § 241 in UNITED STATES V. GUEST, 383 U.S. 745 (1966). In *Guest* six whites were accused of conspiring to deprive some black citizens of rights secured by the Constitution and federal laws. Specifically, the defendants conspired to deprive black citizens from using state facilities in Athens, Georgia, and from engaging freely in interstate travel, in violation of § 241. Justice Stewart held that arresting blacks on the basis of false reports by the cooperative action of state officials is sufficient to constitute a denial of those rights guaranteed by the equal protection clause.

On the same day that *Guest* was decided, the Warren Court addressed the legality of indictments based on §§ 241 and 242 to deprive three civil rights workers of their rights under the Fourteenth Amendment. In *United States v. Price*, 383 U.S. 787 (1966), indictments were brought against Sheriff Cecil Ray Price and two other law enforcement officers and 15 private individuals for the widely publicized murder of three civil rights workers—Michael Schwerner, James Chaney, and Andrew Goodman—near Philadelphia, Mississippi, in 1964. The first indictment charged the defendants with a conspir-

---

BOX 3.6

Federal Criminal Statutes

Title 18, U.S.C. § 241. *Conspiracy against rights.*

If two or more persons conspire to injure, oppress, threaten, or
intimidate any inhabitant of any State, Territory, or District in the
free exercise or enjoyment of any right or privilege secured to him
by the Constitution or laws of the United States, or because of his
having so exercised the same; or
  If two or more persons go in disguise on the highway, or on the
premises of another, with intent to prevent or hinder his free exercise
or enjoyment of any right or privilege so secured—
  They shall be fined not more than $10,000 or imprisoned not
more than ten years, or both; and if death results, they shall be subject
to imprisonment for any term of years or for life.

Title 18, U.S.C., § 242. *Deprivation of rights under color of law.*

Whoever, under color of any law, statute, ordinance, regulation, or
custom, willfully subjects any inhabitant of any State, Territory, or
District to the deprivation of any rights, privileges, or immunities
secured or protected by the Constitution or laws of the United States,
or to different punishments, pains or penalties, on account of such
inhabitant being an alien, or by reason of his color, or race, than are
prescribed for the punishment of citizens, shall be fined not more
than $1,000 or imprisoned not more than one year, or both; and if
bodily injury results shall be fined under this title or imprisoned not
more than ten years, or both; and if death results shall be subject to
imprisonment for any term of years or for life.

---

acy to violate § 242, which made it a misdemeanor to willfully and under color
of law subject a person to the deprivation of any rights secured or protected
by the Constitution. The other indictment charged the defendants with a
conspiracy to violate § 241, which makes it a felony to conspire to interfere
with a citizen in the free exercise or enjoyment of any right secured or
protected by the Constitution or laws of the United States. The district court
dismissed most of the charges. In reversing the dismissal of the charges against
the private defendants, Justice Fortas held that private persons jointly engaged
with state officials in the prohibited action are acting under color of law under
§ 242. The Court also found that § 241 includes rights and privileges protected
by the Fourteenth Amendment and extends to conspiracies within the scope
of the section.

  In *United States v. Johnson,* 390 U.S. 563 (1968), whites assaulted three
blacks for exercising their right to equal treatment in public accommodations

BOX 3.7

Federal Civil Statutes

Title 42 U.S.C., § 1983. *Civil action for deprivation of rights.*

Every person who, under color of any statute, ordinance, regulation, custom, or usage, of any State or Territory or the District of Columbia, subjects, or causes to be subjected, any citizen of the United States or other person within the jurisdiction thereof to the deprivation of any rights, privileges, or immunities secured by the Constitution and laws, shall be liable to the party injured in an action at law, suit in equity, or other proper proceeding for redress. For the purposes of this section, any Act of Congress applicable exclusively to the District of Columbia shall be considered to be a statute of the District of Columbia.

Title 42, U.S.C. § 1985. *Conspiracy to interfere with civil rights.*

(3) *Depriving persons of rights or privileges.* If two or more persons in any State or Territory conspire, or go in disguise on the highway or on the premises of another, for the purpose of depriving, either directly or indirectly, any person or class of persons of the equal protection of the laws, or of equal privileges and immunities under the laws, or for the purpose of preventing or hindering the constituted authorities of any State or Territory from giving or securing to all persons within such State or Territory the equal protection of the laws; or if two or more persons conspire to prevent by force, intimidation, or threat, any citizen who is lawfully entitled to vote, . . . the party so injured or deprived may have an action for the recovery of damages, occasioned by such injury or deprivation, against any one or more of the conspirators.

under § 201(a) of Title II. Their goal was to discourage the blacks from seeking service at the restaurant. Justice Douglas asserted that the defendants were subject to criminal prosecution under § 241, which provides fines and imprisonment for conspiring "to injure, oppress, threaten, or intimidate any citizen in the . . . enjoyment of any right or privilege secured to him by the Constitution or laws of the United States." Emphasizing that § 241 should be at least as broad as its language, he concluded his opinion in these words: "We refuse to believe that hoodlums operating in the fashion of the Ku Klux Klan, were given protection by the 1964 Act for violating those 'rights' of the citizen that § 241 was designed to protect."

Section 1985(e) provides for civil remedies against private interferences with federal civil rights. In GRIFFIN V. BRECKENRIDGE, 403 U.S. 88 (1971), an early Burger Court decision, several white men blocked a car occupied by several black men on a public highway and severely beat each of them with a blackjack and pipes because they believed the black men were civil rights workers. Their goal was to prevent the black men from enjoying the rights of U.S. citizens, including the rights of free speech, assembly, and movement. A damage suit was filed under § 1985(3) (see Box 3.7). Justice Stewart construed the statute as prohibiting private conspiracies that deprive petitioners of their legal rights for racial reasons.

In another early Burger Court decision, the Court was afforded an opportunity to construe § 1983, which provides civil remedies against actions under color of law (see Box 3.7). In ADICKES V. S. H. KRESS & CO., 398 U.S. 144 (1970), a white schoolteacher was refused service in one of the Kress restaurant facilities in Hattiesburg, Mississippi, because she was accompanied by six of her students who were black. She filed suit under § 1983 to recover damages for an alleged violation of her rights under the equal protection clause. Justice Harlan held that Adickes's claim was established under § 1983 if she proved that the custom of segregation in Hattiesburg restaurants was enforced by state officials. He also argued that the district court had erred when it concluded that only those customs enforced by state statutes can have the force of law. It should be noted that injunctive relief was available to Adickes under Title II, but she sought damages and therefore sued under § 1983.

Jury Discrimination: A Persistent Problem

Racial discrimination in the formation of juries has been a persistent problem in the United States. In 1968, Congress passed the Federal Jury Selection and Service Act, which prohibits discrimination in the selection of jurors for the federal judicial system (28 U.S.C. § 1861). The Warren Court decided a number of cases involving allegations of discrimination in the jury selection process. The general trend was for the state to show that the selection procedures were racially neutral once a prima facie case of discrimination was established by the plaintiff. In *Eubanks v. Louisiana,* 356 U.S. 584 (1958), a black male was indicted by an all-white jury for murdering a white woman and was tried and sentenced to death. Although blacks in the parish comprised one third of the population, only one had been picked for grand jury service out of 432 jurors between 1936 and 1954. Justice Black declared that local tradition that resulted in the exclusion of blacks from grand juries consistently was a denial of equal protection of the laws.

Six years later, in *Arnold v. North Carolina,* 376 U.S. 773 (1964), only one black had served on the grand jury in 24 years despite the fact that blacks comprised 28% of the county's tax records and 30% of its poll tax list from which jurors were drawn. In a per curiam decision, the Court relied on the *Eubanks* and *Norris v. Alabama,* 294 U.S. 587 (1935) decisions and held that blacks had been systematically excluded from grand jury duty, in violation of the equal protection clause. In *Whitus v. Georgia,* 385 U.S. 545 (1967), the Court decided that the great disparity between the percentage of blacks on the county tax digest (21.1%) and the number who served on the grand jury (7 of 90) was proof of purposeful discrimination.

The Warren Court made it difficult for black criminal defendants to challenge the alleged discriminatory use of the state's peremptory challenge— that is, removing jurors without cause. In SWAIN V. ALABAMA, 380 U.S. 202 (1965), a black male was sentenced to death for raping a white woman in Talladega, Alabama. He sought to quash the indictment on the grounds of racial discrimination in the selection of grand and petit juries and because the prosecutor used his peremptory challenge to exclude blacks. *Swain's* significance for jury discrimination cases is found in Justice White's ruling on the peremptory challenge question. Here, the majority held that the prosecutor's striking of blacks from the jury panel under the peremptory challenge system does not constitute a denial of equal protection of the laws. Justice White went on to state that even if the state's use of peremptory strikes raised a prima facie case of discrimination under the Fourteenth Amendment, the defendant failed to meet the burden of proof.

WILLS, SEGREGATION, AND THE FOURTEENTH AMENDMENT

Two years after *Brown II* was decided, the Warren Court was confronted with a restrictive provision in a will. Stephen Girard stated in his 1831 will that a trust should be established for a school for "poor white male orphans." The city of Philadelphia was named as trustee, and later city officials were named to administer the trust. Blacks were denied admission pursuant to Girard's will on account of race. The state court refused to admit them, but this decision was reversed by the Supreme Court in *Pennsylvania v. Board of Directors of City Trusts of the City of Philadelphia*, 353 U.S. 230 (1957). The central thrust of the opinion was expressed in these words: "The Board which operates Girard College is an agency of the State of Pennsylvania. Therefore, even though the Board was acting as a trustee, its refusal to admit Foust and Felder to the college because they were Negroes was discrimination by the State. Such discrimination is forbidden by the Fourteenth Amendment." After the decision, private trustees replaced the city officials. In 1968 an appeals court held that replacing city officials with private trustees constituted unconstitutional state action in *Commonwealth of Pennsylvania v. Brown*, 392 F.2d 120, *cert. denied*, 391 U.S. 921 (1968).

In 1966 the Court had to decide whether discrimination was permissible because of a provision in a will. Senator Augustus Bacon, in his 1911 will, left a tract of land to the city of Macon, Georgia, for the purpose of creating a park for whites only. Originally, the city served as trustee and enforced the whites-only intentions expressed in the will. The city realized that it could not continue to enforce the racial exclusion after *Brown I*, and therefore the state court accepted the resignation of the city as trustee and appointed private individuals to replace them. In EVANS V. NEWTON, 382 U.S. 296 (1966), the Court held that the Fourteenth Amendment prohibits operation of the park on a discriminatory basis because of its unmistakable public nature.

After the decision, the Georgia Supreme Court decided that it had become virtually impossible to accomplish Senator Bacon's intention and terminated the will and remanded the case to the trial court. It concluded that the trust had failed and ordered that the property be reverted to the senator's heirs. This decision was confirmed by the Georgia Supreme Court. Justice Black, writing for the majority in *Evans v. Abney,* 396 U.S. 435 (1970), affirmed the decision of the Georgia Supreme Court. He emphasized that the state courts had simply applied the "principles of Georgia law to determine the meaning and effect of a Georgia will." He also noted that eliminating the park meant eliminating discrimination against blacks. Thus, the loss was shared equally by blacks and whites, and the senator would have preferred that the intent of the will fail rather than integrate the park. Dissenting, Justice Brennan asserted that "it is a *public* park that is being closed for a discriminatory reason after having been operated for nearly half a century as a segregated *public* facility; and it is a state court that . . . keeps apparently willing parties of different races from coming together in the park. That is state action in overwhelming abundance."

INTERRACIAL DATING AND MARRIAGES: CONSTITUTIONAL ISSUES

Interracial dating and marriage, especially between black men and white women, have been unpopular and controversial since colonial times. Feelings were so strong against miscegenation that statutes prohibiting interracial marriages were enacted by some of the colonies as early as the 1660s. Although English common law did not ban miscegenation, many English strongly believed that blacks were an inferior species. The Supreme Court never ruled on the constitutionality of laws prohibiting miscegenation prior to the mid-1960s. In *Naim v. Naim,* 197 Va. 80 (1955), the Virginia Court of Appeals upheld the state's antimiscegenation statute. The majority thought that marriage was left to the exclusive control of the state by virtue of the Tenth Amendment and that one of the state's responsibilities was to prevent "the corruption of blood" and the mongrelization of the state's citizens.

Nine years later, in *McLaughlin v. Florida,* 379 U.S. 184 (1964), the Warren Court had to decide whether a Florida criminal statute that prohibited unmarried interracial couples from habitually cohabiting in the same room at night was constitutional. Florida did not have a law penalizing the same conduct by members of the same race. Justice White, in invalidating the statute, rejected the state's reliance on *Pace v. Alabama,* 106 U.S. 583 (1883) because it offered a narrow construction of the equal protection clause. Nor did Justice White find the state's purpose behind the statute—to prevent illicit extramarital and premarital promiscuity—justifiable under the equal protection clause. The Court, in *McLaughlin,* emphasized, however, that it expressed no view on the state's prohibition against miscegenation.

Three years later, the Court had to decide whether a Virginia antimiscegenation statute was constitutional. Sixteen states had laws prohibiting interracial marriages. In LOVING V. VIRGINIA, 388 U.S. 1 (1967), a white man married a black woman in Washington, D.C., in 1958 and returned to Virginia to live, in violation of the state's antimiscegenation statute. They were sentenced to one year in jail. Chief Justice Warren invoked strict scrutiny in striking down the statute and declared that the state cannot interfere with the right of an individual to marry a person from another race because the right to marry is a fundamental right. Because marriage is essential to the pursuit of happiness, restricting this freedom violates the very heart of the equal protection clause.

Seventeen years after the *Loving* decision, the effects of racial prejudice were at issue in *Palmore v. Sidote,* 466 U.S. 429 (1984). After the divorce of a white couple in Florida, the mother was awarded custody of their three-year-old daughter. Approximately one year later, the husband filed a petition to gain custody of his daughter because his former wife was cohabiting with a black man. The Florida courts awarded custody to the father because they concluded that the child would be damaged if she remained in a racially mixed environment. Chief Justice Burger, writing for the majority, reversed the lower court's decision. The crux of his opinion was expressed succinctly: "The Constitution cannot control such prejudices but neither can it tolerate them. . . . The effects of racial prejudice, however real, cannot justify a racial classification removing an infant child from the custody of its natural mother found to be an appropriate person to have such custody."

CONCLUSION

Although President Eisenhower lived to regret having appointed Earl Warren as Chief Justice, the Warren Court's profound impact on civil rights and civil liberties is a fait accompli. Some of the landmark cases rendered during his 16-year tenure as Chief Justice epitomize an earnest attempt to close the gap between American ideals and American reality. His extraordinary vision resulted in evolutionary changes in constitutional development in the volatile area of race relations. His leadership of the liberal wing of the Court resulted in the emergence of an unusually activist Court. This chapter has shown that support for civil rights during the Warren Court was more consistent, compared with previous Courts. The rising expectations that emanated from *Brown I* made business as usual a thing of the past, and the strategy of massive nonviolent protests resulted in a series of federal laws and high court decisions that would profoundly change American mores and folkways. Many serious challenges confronted black Americans in their struggle for equality, however, and they would press these claims, many involving novel legal questions, before the Burger Court.

NOTES

1. Warren, E. (1973-74). Address. Excerpts from an extemporaneous speech delivered at the commencement exercises of the University of San Diego School of Law on June 2, 1973. *San Diego Law Review, 11,* 295.

2. Because Congress was not in session, Warren was given a recess appointment. Attacks by Southern Democrats on Warren's so-called left-wing politics prevented his confirmation until March 1, 1954. See Abraham, H. J. (1985). *Justices and presidents: A political history of appointments to the Supreme Court* (2nd ed.). New York: Oxford University Press.

3. See Abraham, H. J. (1985). *Justices and presidents: A political history of appointments to the Supreme Court* (2nd ed.). New York: Oxford University Press, p. 7.

4. See White, G. E. (1982). *Earl Warren: A public life.* New York: Oxford University Press; and Pye, A. K. (1968-69). The Warren Court and criminal procedure. *Michigan Law Review, 67,* 249-268.

5. See *Brown v. Board of Education,* 98 F. Supp. 797 (1951) (Kansas); *Davis v. County School Board of Prince Edward County,* 103 F. Supp. 337 (1952) (Virginia); and *Belton v. Gebhart,* 87 A. 2d 862 (1952) (Delaware). In *Briggs v. Elliott,* 98 F. Supp. 529 (1951) (South Carolina), the three-judge district court found that the black schools were inferior to the white schools and ordered the defendants to begin immediately to equalize the facilities, but the court denied the plaintiffs' admission to the white schools during the equalization process. On remand, in *Briggs v. Elliott,* 103 F. Supp. 920 (1952), the district court found that substantial equality had been achieved except for buildings and that the defendants were proceeding to rectify this inequality as well. See *Brown I* (1954), pp. 486-487, footnote 1.

6. *Bolling V. Sharpe,* 347 U.S. 497 (1954).

7. Kurland, P., & Casper, G. (Eds.). (1975). *Landmark briefs and arguments of the Supreme Court of the United States* (Vol. 49). Arlington, VA: University Publications of America, pp. 120-121.

8. Kurland, P., & Casper, G. (Eds.). (1975). *Landmark briefs and arguments of the Supreme Court of the United States* (Vol. 49). Arlington, VA: University Publications of America, pp. 140-141.

9. Kluger, R. (1977). *Simple justice: The history of* Brown v. Board of Education *and black America's struggle for equality.* New York: Vintage, pp. 614-615.

10. Bickel, A. M. (1955). The original understanding and the segregation decision. *Harvard Law Review, 69,* 1-65.

11. Burk, R. F. (1984). *The Eisenhower administration and black civil rights.* Knoxville: University of Tennessee Press, p. 134.

12. Shortly thereafter, the Justice Department filed a brief stating that although it was impossible to draw a definitive conclusion regarding the framers' intention of the Fourteenth Amendment and racial discrimination in education, the legislative history of the Fourteenth Amendment suggested that the Congress that proposed it understood, not that the Fourteenth Amendment would abolish segregated schools, but that it forbade all legal distinctions based on color. See Burk, R. F. (1984). *The Eisenhower administration and black civil rights.* Knoxville: University of Tennessee Press.

13. For an overview of the use of social science data in the judicial decision-making process, see Davis, A. L. (1973). *The United States Supreme Court and the use of social science data.* New York: Irvington; Greenberg, J. (1955-56). Social scientists take the stand: A review and appraisal of their testimony in litigation. *Michigan Law Review, 54,* 953-970; Levin, B. (1978). School desegregation remedies and the role of social science research. *Law and Contemporary Problems, 42,* 1-36; Levin, B., & Moise, P. (1975). School desegregation litigation in the seventies and the use of social evidence: An annotated guide. *Law and Contemporary Problems, 39,* 50-133; and Rosen, P. L. (1972). *The Supreme Court and social science.* Urbana: University of Illinois.

14. *Congressional Record,* 83rd Congress, 2nd Session, 1954, vol. 100, Part 9, pp. 11522-11523. Senator Eastland pointed out that the entire basis of American jurisprudence had been destroyed as a result of the *Brown* decision. Senator Stennis of Mississippi agreed with Senator Eastland.

15. *Congressional Record,* 84th Congress, 1st Session, 1955, vol. 101, Part 5, pp. 6963-6964.

16. *Congressional Record,* 84th Congress, 2nd Session, 1956, vol. 102, Part 11E, p. A4667.

17. *Congressional Record,* 83rd Congress, 2nd Session, 1954, vol. 100, Part 5, p. 6750; *Congressional Record,* 84th Congress, 2nd Session, 1956, vol. 102, Part 7, p. 8757; *Congressional Record,* 84th Congress, 2nd Session, 1956, vol. 102, Part 3, pp. 3213-3214; and *Congressional Record,* 85th Congress, 1957, vol. 103, Part 7, p. 9887.

18. Cahn, E. (1955). Jurisprudence. *New York University Law Review, 30,* 167.

19. Cahn, E. (1955). Jurisprudence. *New York University Law Review, 30,* 163.

20. Cahn, E. (1955). Jurisprudence. *New York University Law Review, 30,* 164-165.

21. For viewpoints in agreement with Cahn's conclusions, see Garfinkel, H. (1959). Social science evidence and the school segregation cases. *Journal of Politics, 21,* 37-59. See also Note, Grade school segregation: The latest attack on racial discrimination. (1952). *Yale Law Journal, 61,* 737; this note made the following observation: "The unhealthy symptoms re-

vealed by the doll tests cannot, however, be traced with certainty to educational segregation."

22. Schwartz, R. D. (1959). The law and behavioral science program at Yale: A sociologist's account of some experiences. *Journal of Legal Education, 12,* 95. Also see Note, Grade school segregation: The latest attack on racial discrimination. (1952). *Yale Law Journal, 61,* 730-744; Clark, K. B., & Clark, M. K. (1940). Skin color as a factor in racial identification of Negro preschool children. *Journal of Social Psychology, 11,* 159-169.

23. Gregor, A. J. (1962-63). The law, social science, and school segregation: An assessment. *Western Reserve Law Review, 14,* 627.

24. Van Den Haag, E. (1960-61). Social science testimony in the desegregation cases: A reply to Professor Kenneth Clark. *Villanova Law Review, 6,* 77.

25. Van Den Haag, E. (1960-61). Social science testimony in the desegregation cases: A reply to Professor Kenneth Clark. *Villanova Law Review, 6,* 79.

26. Clark, K. B. (1959-60). The desegregation cases: Criticism of the social scientist's role. *Villanova Law Review, 5,* 229.

27. Clark, K. B. (1959-60). The desegregation cases: Criticism of the social scientist's role. *Villanova Law Review, 5,* 229.

28. Franklin, M. (1956-57). Law, morals, and social life. *Tulane Law Review, 31,* 471.

29. Hill, H., & Greenberg, J. (1955). *Citizen's guide to desegregation: A study of social and legal change in American life.* Boston: Beacon. Also see Kadish, S. H. (1956-57). Methodology and criteria in due process adjudication: A survey and criticism. *Yale Law Journal, 66,* 359. Kadish has observed that social science and economic data have a role to play in the adjudicatory process.

30. *Congressional Record,* 84th Congress, 2nd Session, 1956, vol. 102, Part 6, p. 7991.

31. Rose, A. M. (1955-56). The social scientist as an expert witness. *Minnesota Law Review, 40,* 205-218.

32. Greenberg, J. (1955-56). Social scientists take the stand: A review and appraisal of their testimony in litigation. *Michigan Law Review, 54,* 953.

33. Pettigrew, T. F. (1961). Social psychology and desegregation research. *American Psychologist, 16,* 106.

34. Silver, N. (1987). The Solicitor General's Office, Justice Frankfurter, and civil rights litigation, 1946-1960: An oral history (Philip Elman interviewed by Normal Silver). *Harvard Law Review, 100*(2), 830.

35. Rosenberg, G. N. (1991). *The hollow hope: Can courts bring about social change?* Chicago: University of Chicago Press, p. 52.

36. See Peltason, J. (1971). *Fifty-eight lonely men.* Urbana: University of Illinois Press.

37. Murphy, P. (1989). Southern Manifesto. In L. W. Levy, K. L. Karst, & D. J. Mahoney (Eds.), *Civil rights and equality: Selections from the* Encyclopedia of the American Constitution. New York: Macmillan, p. 223. See also Hyneman, C. S. (1963). *The Supreme Court on trial.* New York: Atherton, pp. 19-20.

38. Jackson, D. D. (1974). *Judges.* New York: Atheneum, p. 122. Also see Notes and Comments in Judicial performance in the fifth circuit. (1963-1964). *Yale Law Journal, 73,* 90-133.

39. The case was *Brown v. State of Mississippi,* 6 *Race Relations Law Reporter,* 780, (1961).

40. Lewis, A. (1963, July 19). Federal judges in South scared. *The New York Times,* p. 8, Copyright © 1963 by The New York Times Company. Reprinted by permission. Also see Sitton, C. (1963, June 9). Not taken freedom, full freedom. *The New York Times Magazine,* (Sec. 6, col. 4), p. 80.

41. Lewis, A. (1963, July 19). Federal judges in South scared. *The New York Times,* p. 8, Copyright © 1963 by The New York Times Company. Reprinted by permission.

42. Woodward, C. V. (1974). *The strange career of Jim Crow* (3rd rev. ed.). New York: Oxford University Press, p. 162.

43. Kluger, R. (1976). *Simple justice: The history of* Brown v. Board of Education *and black America's struggle for equality.* New York: Knopf, p. 754.

44. *Hobsen v. Hansen,* 269 F. Supp. 401 (1967); aff'd sub nom. *Smuck v. Hansen,* 408 F.2d 175 (1969); appeal dismissed, 393 U.S. 801 (1968).

45. Branch, T. (1988). *Parting the waters: America in the King years, 1954-63.* New York: Simon & Schuster, p. 135.

46. See Congressional Quarterly Service. (1969). *Congress and the nation: 1965-1968* (Vol. 2). Washington, DC: Author, p. 357.

47. Congressional Quarterly Service. (1969). *Congress and the nation: 1965-1968* (Vol. 2). Washington, DC: Author, p. 357.

48. *Hamm v. Virginia State Board of Elections,* 230 F. Supp. 156 (1964).

49. Blassingame, J. W. (1979). *The Frederick Douglass papers: Vol. 3., 1855-63.* New Haven, CT: Yale University Press. Frederick Douglass made this statement in a speech in Canandaqua, New York, on August 3, 1857, entitled, "The Significance of Emancipation in the West Indies."

50. For an account of the passage of the Civil Rights Act of 1968, see Congressional Quarterly Service. (1969). *Congress and the nation: 1965-1968* (Vol. 2). Washington, DC: Author, pp. 365-373.

51. Higginbotham, A. L., Jr. (1990). Racism in American and South African courts: Similarities and differences. *New York University Law Review, 65,* 542-543.

CASES

BROWN V. BOARD OF EDUCATION (BROWN I)
347 U.S. 483 (1954)

Brown I was a consolidation of four lawsuits challenging segregated public education in Topeka, Kansas (*Brown v. Board of Education*), Virginia (*Davis v. County School Board of Prince Edward County*), South Carolina (*Briggs v. Elliott*), and Delaware (*Belton v. Gebhart*). The fifth case, *Bolling v. Sharpe,* attacked the federal government's practice of segregated schools in Washington, D.C., and therefore was addressed in a separate opinion. In the lead case, *Brown,* Oliver Brown sued on behalf of his daughter, Linda, to challenge Topeka's segregated public schools. The U.S. Supreme Court accepted these cases for review for the 1952 term, and oral arguments initially were heard on December 9, 1952. The cases were restored to the Court's docket for reargument on October 12, 1953, and all parties were required to address five questions on the historical events surrounding the adoption of the Fourteenth Amendment. In the meantime, Chief Justice Vinson died of a heart attack on September 8, 1953, and President Eisenhower nominated Earl Warren, governor of California, as his successor. Reargument then was rescheduled for December 7. The opinion of the Court in *Brown* was announced on May 17, 1954. *Vote: 9-0.*

* * *

MR. CHIEF JUSTICE WARREN delivered the opinion of the Court.

These cases come to us from the States of Kansas, South Carolina, Virginia and Delaware. They are premised on different facts and different local conditions, but a common legal question justifies their consideration together in this consolidated opinion.

In each of the cases, minors of the Negro race, through their legal representatives, seek the aid of the courts in obtaining admission to the public schools of their community on a nonsegregated basis. In each instance, they had been denied admission to schools attended by white children under laws requiring or permitting segregation according to race. This segregation was alleged to deprive the plaintiffs of the equal protection of the laws under the Fourteenth Amendment. In each of the cases other than the Delaware case, a three-judge federal district court denied relief to the plaintiffs on the so-called "separate but equal" doctrine announced by this Court in *Plessy v. Ferguson,* 163 U.S. 537 [1896]. Under that doctrine, equality of treatment is ac-corded when the races are provided substantially equal facilities, even though these facilities be separate. In the Delaware case, the Supreme Court of Delaware adhered to that doctrine, but ordered that the plaintiffs be admitted to the white schools because of their superiority to the Negro schools.

The plaintiffs contend that segregated public schools are not "equal" and cannot be made "equal," and that hence they are deprived of the equal protection of the laws. Because of the obvious importance of the question presented, the Court took jurisdiction. Argument was heard in the 1952 Term, and reargument was heard this Term on certain questions propounded by the Court.

Reargument was largely devoted to the circumstances surrounding the adoption of the Fourteenth Amendment in 1868. It covered exhaustively consideration of the Amendment in Congress, ratification by the states, then existing practices in racial segregation, and the views of proponents and opponents of the Amendment. This discussion and our own investigation convince us that, although these sources cast some light, it is not enough to resolve the problem with which we are faced. At best, they are inconclusive. The most avid proponents of the post-War Amendments undoubtedly intended them to remove all legal distinctions among "all persons born or naturalized in the United States." Their opponents, just as certainly, were antagonistic to both the letter and the spirit of the Amendments and wished them to have the most limited effect. What others in Congress and the state legislatures had in mind cannot be determined with any degree of certainty.

An additional reason for the inconclusive nature of the Amendment's history, with respect to segregated schools, is the status of public education at that time. In the South, the movement toward free common schools, supported by general taxation, had not yet taken hold. Education of white children was largely in the hands of private groups. Education of Negroes was almost nonexistent, and practically all of the race were illiterate. In fact, any education of Negroes was forbidden by law in some states. Today, in contrast, many Negroes have achieved outstanding success in the arts and sciences as well as in the business and professional world. It is true that public school education at the time of the Amendment had advanced further in the North, but the effect of the Amendment on Northern States was generally ignored in the congressional debates. Even in the North, the conditions of public education did not approximate those existing today.

The curriculum was usually rudimentary; upgraded schools were common in rural areas; the school term was but three months a year in many states; and compulsory school attendance was virtually unknown. As a consequence, it is not surprising that there should be so little in the history of the Fourteenth Amendment relating to its intended effect on public education.

In the first cases in this Court construing the Fourteenth Amendment, decided shortly after its adoption, the Court interpreted it as proscribing all state-imposed discriminations against the Negro race. The doctrine of "separate but equal" did not make its appearance in this Court until 1896 in the case of *Plessy v. Ferguson,* . . . involving not education but transportation. American courts have since labored with the doctrine for over half a century. In this Court, there have been six cases involving the "separate but equal" doctrine in the field of public education. In *Cumming v. County Board of Education,* 175 U.S. 528 [1899], and *Gong Lum v. Rice,* 275 U.S. 78 [1927], the validity of the doctrine itself was not challenged. In more recent cases, all on the graduate school level, inequality was found in that specific benefits enjoyed by white students were denied to Negro students of the same educational qualifications. *Missouri ex rel. Gaines v. Canada,* 305 U.S. 337 [1938]; *Sipuel v. Oklahoma,* 332 U.S. 631 [1948]; *Sweatt v. Painter,* 339 U.S. 629 [1950]; *McLaurin v. Oklahoma State Regents,* 339 U.S. 637 [1950]. In none of these cases was it necessary to re-examine the doctrine to grant relief to the Negro plaintiff. And in *Sweatt v. Painter, supra,* the Court expressly reserved decision on the question whether *Plessy v. Ferguson* should be held inapplicable to public education.

In the instant cases, that question is directly presented. Here, unlike *Sweatt v. Painter,* there are findings below that the Negro and white schools involved have been equalized, or are being equalized, with respect to buildings, curricula, qualifications and salaries of teachers, and other "tangible" factors. Our decision, therefore, cannot turn on merely a comparison of these tangible factors in the Negro and white schools involved in each of the cases. We must look instead to the effect of segregation itself on public education.

In approaching this problem, we cannot turn the clock back to 1868 when the Amendment was adopted, or even to 1896 when *Plessy v. Ferguson* was written. We must consider public education in the light of its full development and its present place in American life throughout the Nation. Only in this way can it be determined if segregation in public schools deprives these plaintiffs of the equal protection of the laws.

Today, education is perhaps the most important function of state and local governments. Compulsory school attendance laws and the great expenditures for education both demonstrate our recognition of the importance of education to our democratic society. It is required in the performance of our most basic public responsibilities, even service in the armed forces. It is the very foundation of good citizenship. Today it is a principal instrument in awakening the child to cultural values, in preparing him for later professional training, and in helping him to adjust normally to his environment. In these days, it is doubtful that any child may reasonably be expected to succeed in life if he is denied the opportunity of an education. Such an opportunity, where the state has undertaken to provide it, is a right which must be made available to all on equal terms.

We come then to the question presented: Does segregation of children in public schools solely on the basis of race, even though the physical facilities and other "tangible" factors may be equal, deprive the children of the minority group of equal educational opportunities? We believe that it does.

In *Sweatt v. Painter,* . . . in finding that a segregated law school for Negroes could not provide them equal educational opportunities, this Court relied in large part on "those qualities which are incapable of objective measurement but which make for greatness in a law school." In *McLaurin v. Oklahoma State Regents,* . . . the Court, in requiring that a Negro admitted to a white graduate school be treated like all other students, again resorted to intangible considerations: ". . . his ability to study, to engage in discussions and exchange views with other students, and, in general, to learn his profession." Such considerations apply with added force to children in grade and high schools. To separate them from others of similar age and qualifications solely because of their race generates a feeling of inferiority as to their status in the community that may affect their hearts and minds in a way unlikely ever to be undone. The effect of this separation on their educational opportunities was well stated by a finding in the Kansas case by a court which nevertheless felt compelled to rule against the Negro plaintiffs:

"Segregation of white and colored children in public schools has a detrimental effect upon the colored children. The impact is greater when it has the sanction of the law; for the policy of separating the races is usually interpreted as denoting the inferiority of the negro group. A sense of inferiority affects the motivation of a child to learn. Segregation with the sanction of law, therefore, has a tendency to [retard] the educational and mental development of negro children and to deprive them of some of the benefits they would receive in a racial[ly] integrated school system."

Whatever may have been the extent of psychological knowledge at the time of *Plessy v. Ferguson,* this finding is amply supported by modern authority.

Any language in *Plessy v. Ferguson* contrary to this finding is rejected.

We conclude that in the field of public education the doctrine of "separate but equal" has no place. Separate educational facilities are inherently unequal. Therefore, we hold that the plaintiffs and others similarly situated for whom the actions have been brought are, by reason of the segregation complained of, deprived of the equal protection of the laws guaranteed by the Fourteenth Amendment. This disposition makes unnecessary any discussion whether such segregation also violates the Due Process Clause of the Fourteenth Amendment.

Because these are class actions, because of the wide applicability of this decision, and because of the great variety of local conditions, the formulation of decrees in these cases presents problems of considerable complexity. On reargument, the consideration of appropriate relief was necessarily subordinated to the primary question—the constitutionality of segregation in public education. We have now announced that such segregation is a denial of equal protection of the laws. In order that we may have the full assistance of the parties in formulating decrees, the cases will be restored to the docket, and the parties are requested to present further argument on Questions 4 and 5 previously propounded by the Court for the reargument this Term. The Attorney General of the United States is again invited to participate. The Attorneys General of the states requiring or permitting segregation in public education will also be permitted to appear as *amici curiae* upon request to do so by September 15, 1954, and submission of briefs by October 1, 1954.

It is so ordered.

BOLLING V. SHARPE
347 U.S. 497 (1954)

In 1950 Spottswood Thomas Bolling, Jr., a black youngster, and seven other black students were refused admission on account of race to John Philip Sousa Junior High School in Southeast Washington, D.C. A member of the NAACP Legal Defense Fund, James M. Nabrit, Jr., filed a class action suit against the president of the Board of Education of the District of Columbia, C. Melvin Sharpe, in 1951. *Vote: 9-0.*

* * *

MR. CHIEF JUSTICE WARREN delivered the opinion of the Court.

This case challenges the validity of segregation in the public schools of the District of Columbia. The petitioners, minors of the Negro race, allege that such segregation deprives them of the due process of law under the Fifth Amendment. They were refused admission to a public school attended by white children solely because of their race. They sought the aid of the district Court for the District of Columbia in obtaining admission. That court dismissed their complaint. The Court granted a writ of certiorari before judgment in the Court of Appeals because of the importance of the constitutional question presented.

We have this day held that the Equal Protection Clause of the Fourteenth Amendment prohibits the states from maintaining racially segregated schools. The legal problem in the District of Columbia is somewhat different, however. The Fifth Amendment, which is applicable in the District of Columbia, does not contain an equal protection clause as does the Fourteenth Amendment which applies only to the states. But the concepts of equal protection and due process, both stemming from our American ideal of fairness, are not mutually exclusive. The "equal protection of the laws" is a more explicit safeguard of prohibited unfairness than "due process of law," and, therefore, we do not imply that the two are always interchangeable phrases. But, as this Court has recognized, discrimination may be so unjustifiable as to be violative of due process.

Classifications based solely upon race must be scrutinized with particular care, since they are contrary to our traditions and hence constitutionally suspect. As long ago as 1896, this Court declared the principle "that the Constitution of the United States, in its present form, forbids, so far as civil and political rights are concerned, discrimination by the General Government, or by the States, against any citizen because of his race." And in *Buchanan v. Warley*, 245 U.S. 60 [1917], the Court held that a statute which limited the right of a property owner to convey his property to a person of another race was, as an unreasonable discrimination, a denial of due process of law.

Although the Court has not assumed to define "liberty" with any great precision, that term is not confined to mere freedom from bodily restraint. Liberty under law extends to the full range of conduct which the individual is free to pursue, and it cannot be restricted except for a proper governmental objective. Segregation in public education is not reasonably related to any proper governmental objective, and thus it imposes on Negro children of the

District of Columbia a burden that constitutes an arbitrary deprivation of their liberty in violation of the Due Process Clause.

In view of our decision that the Constitution prohibits the states from maintaining racially segregated public schools, it would be unthinkable that the same Constitution would impose a lesser duty on the Federal Government. We hold that racial segregation in the public schools of the District of Columbia is a denial of the due process of law guaranteed by the Fifth Amendment to the Constitution.

For the reasons set out in *Brown v. Board of Education*, [347 U.S. 483 (1954)], this case will be restored to the docket for reargument on Questions 4 and 5 previously propounded by the Court.

It is so ordered.

BROWN V. BOARD OF EDUCATION (BROWN II)
349 U.S. 294 (1955)

The Warren Court did not address the issue of remedies in *Brown I* because of the nature of the cases (class action lawsuits), varied local conditions, and the problem of formulation of decrees. The Court ordered that the cases be restored on its docket for the following term to address the question of appropriate relief. On May 31, 1955, the Supreme Court delivered its opinion on how to proceed with the desegregation mandate of *Brown I* in a unanimous, seven-paragraph opinion. *Vote: 9-0.*

* * *

MR. CHIEF JUSTICE WARREN delivered the opinion of the Court.

These cases were decided on May 17, 1954. The opinions of that date, declaring the fundamental principle that racial discrimination in public education is unconstitutional, are incorporated herein by reference. All provisions of federal, state, or local law requiring or permitting such discrimination must yield to this principle. There remains for consideration the manner in which relief is to be accorded.

Because these cases arose under different local conditions and their disposition will involve a variety of local problems, we requested further argument on the question of relief. In view of the nationwide importance of the decision, we invited the Attorney General of the United States and the Attorneys General of all states requiring or permitting racial discrimination in public education to present their views on that question. The parties, the United States, and the States of Florida, North Carolina, Arkansas, Oklahoma, Maryland, and Texas filed briefs and participated in the oral argument.

These presentations were informative and helpful to the Court in its consideration of the complexities arising from the transition to a system of public education freed of racial discrimination. The presentations also demonstrated that substantial steps to eliminate racial discrimination in public schools have already been taken, not only in some of the communities in which these cases arose, but in some of the states appearing as *amici curiae,* and in other states as well. Substantial progress has been made in the District of Columbia and in the communities in Kansas and Delaware involved in this litigation. The defendants in the cases coming to us from South Carolina and Virginia are awaiting the decision of this Court concerning relief.

Full implementation of these constitutional principles may require solution of varied local school problems. School authorities have the primary responsibility for elucidating, assessing, and solving these problems; courts will have to consider whether the action of school authorities constitutes good faith implementation of the governing constitutional principles. Because of their proximity to local conditions and the possible need for further hearings, the courts which originally heard these cases can best perform this judicial appraisal. Accordingly, we believe it appropriate to remand the cases to those courts.

In fashioning and effectuating the decrees, the courts will be guided by equitable principles. Traditionally, equity has been characterized by a practical flexibility in shaping its remedies and by a facility for adjusting and reconciling public and private needs. These cases call for the exercise of these traditional attributes of equity power. At stake is the personal interest of the plaintiffs in admission to public schools as soon as practicable on a nondiscriminatory basis. To effectuate this interest may call for elimination of a variety of obstacles in making the transition to school systems operated in accordance with the constitutional principles set forth in our May 17, 1954, decision. Courts of equity may properly take into account the public interest in the elimination of such obstacles in a systematic and effective manner. But it should go without saying that the vitality of these constitutional principles cannot be allowed to yield simply because of disagreement with them.

While giving weight to these public and private considerations, the courts will require that the defendants make a prompt and reasonable start toward full compliance with our May 17, 1954, ruling. Once such a start has been made, the courts may find that additional time is necessary to carry out the ruling in an effective manner. The burden rests upon the defendants to establish that such time is necessary in the public interest and is consistent with good faith compliance at the earliest practicable date. To that end, the courts may consider problems related to administration, arising from the physical condition of the school plant, the school transportation system, personnel, revision of school districts and attendance areas into compact units to achieve a system of determining admission to the public schools on a nonracial basis, and revision of local laws and regulations which may be necessary in solving the foregoing problems. They will also consider the adequacy of any plans the defendants may propose to meet these problems and to effectuate a transition to a racially nondiscriminatory school system. Dur-

ing this period of transition, the courts will retain jurisdiction of these cases.

The judgments below, except that in the Delaware case, are accordingly reversed and the cases are remanded to the District Courts to take such proceedings and enter such orders and decrees consistent with this opinion as are necessary and proper to admit to public schools on a racially nondiscriminatory basis with all deliberate speed the parties to these cases. The judgment in the Delaware case—ordering the immediate admission of the plaintiffs to schools previously attended only by white children—is affirmed on the basis of the principles stated in our May 17, 1954, opinion, but the case is remanded to the Supreme Court of Delaware for such further proceedings as that Court may deem necessary in light of this opinion.

It is so ordered.

GREEN V. COUNTY SCHOOL BOARD
OF NEW KENT COUNTY
391 U.S. 430 (1968)

The School Board in New Kent County, Virginia, operated a racially segregated school system after the *Brown* decisions as part of Virginia's massive resistance efforts. After a lawsuit was filed in 1965, challenging the board's practice, the school board adopted a freedom of choice plan for desegregating the schools. The plan permitted students, except those entering the first and eighth grades, to choose between the New Kent (all white) and Watkins (all black) Schools. Students not making a choice were assigned to the school previously attended, although it was mandatory that first- and eighth-grade students choose a school. During the freedom of choice plan's three years of operation, no white student chose to attend Watkins School and only 15% of the black students chose to attend New Kent School. The district court and the court of appeals upheld the freedom of choice plan. The Supreme Court had to consider whether the freedom of choice plan provided prompt assurance of disestablishing a dual school system. *Vote: 9-0.*

* * *

MR. JUSTICE BRENNAN delivered the opinion of the Court.

The question for decision is whether, under all the circumstances here, respondent School Board's adoption of a "freedom-of-choice" plan which allows a pupil to choose his own public school constitutes adequate compliance with the Board's responsibility "to achieve a system of determining admission to the public schools on a nonracial basis. . . ."

Brown v. Board of Education, 349 U.S. 294, 300-301 (*Brown II*) [1955] . . .

. . . It is against this background that 13 years after *Brown II* commanded the abolition of dual systems we must measure the effectiveness of respondent School Board's "freedom of choice" plan to achieve that end. The School Board contends that it has fully discharged its obligation by adopting a plan by which every student, regardless of race, may "freely" choose the school he will attend. The Board attempts to cast the issue in its broadest form by arguing that its "freedom-of-choice" plan may be faulted only by reading the Fourteenth Amendment as universally requiring "compulsory integration," a reading it insists the wording of the Amendment will not support. But that argument ignores the thrust of *Brown II.* In the light of the command of that case, what is involved here is the question whether the Board has achieved the "racially nondiscriminatory school system" *Brown II* held must be effectuated in order to remedy the established unconstitutional deficiencies of its segregated system. In the context of the state-imposed segregated pattern of long standing, the fact that in 1965 the Board opened the doors of the former "white" school to Negro children and of the "Negro" school to white children merely begins, not ends, our inquiry whether the Board has taken steps adequate to abolish its dual, segregated system. *Brown II* was a call for the dismantling of well-entrenched dual systems tempered by an awareness that complex and multifaceted problems would arise which would require time and flexibility for a successful resolution. School boards such as the respondent then operating state-compelled dual systems were nevertheless clearly charged with the affirmative duty to take whatever steps might be necessary to convert to a unitary system in which racial discrimination would be eliminated root and branch. . . . The constitutional rights of Negro school children articulated in *Brown I* permit no less than this; and it was to this end that *Brown II* commanded school boards to bend their efforts.

In determining whether respondent School Board met that command by adopting its "freedom-of-choice" plan, it is relevant that this first step did not come until some 11 years after *Brown I* was decided and 10 years after *Brown II* directed the making of a "prompt and reasonable start." This deliberate perpetuation of the unconstitutional dual system can only have compounded the harm of such a system. Such delays are no longer tolerable, for "the governing constitutional principles no longer bear the imprint of newly enunciated doctrine." . . . Moreover, a plan that at this late date fails to provide meaningful assurance of prompt and effective disestablishment of a dual system is also intolerable. . . . The burden on a school board today is to come forward with a plan that promises realistically to work, and promises realistically to work *now*.

The obligation of the district courts, as it always has been, is to assess the effectiveness of a proposed plan in achieving desegregation. There is no universal answer to complex problems of desegregation; there is obviously no one plan that will do the job in every case. The matter must be assessed in light of the circumstances present and the options available in each instance. It is incumbent upon the school board to establish that its proposed plan promises meaningful and immediate progress toward disestablishing state-imposed segregation. It is incumbent upon the district court to weigh that claim in light of the facts at hand and in light of any alternatives which may be shown as feasible and more promising in their effectiveness. Where the court finds the board to be acting in good faith and the proposed plan to have real prospects for dismantling the state-imposed dual system "at the earliest practicable date," then the plan may be said to provide effective relief. Of course, the availability to the board of other more promising courses of action may indicate a lack of good faith; and at the least it places a heavy burden upon the board to explain its preference for an apparently less effective method.

Moreover, whatever plan is adopted will require evaluation in practice, and the court should retain jurisdiction until it is clear that state-imposed segregation has been completely removed. . . .

We do not hold that "freedom of choice" can have no place in such a plan. We do not hold that a "freedom-of-choice" plan might of itself be unconstitutional, although that argument has been urged upon us. Rather, all we decide today is that in desegregating a dual system a plan utilizing "freedom of choice" is not an end in itself. . . .

. . . Although the general experience under "freedom of choice" to date has been such as to indicate its ineffectiveness as a tool of desegregation, there may well be instances in which it can serve as an effective device. Where it offers real promise of aiding a desegregation program to effectuate conversion of a state-imposed dual system to a unitary, nonracial system there might be no objection to allowing such a device to prove itself in operation. On the other hand, if there are reasonably available other ways, such for illustration as zoning, promising speedier and more effective conversion to a unitary, nonracial school system, "freedom of choice" must be held unacceptable.

The New Kent School Board's "freedom-of-choice" plan cannot be accepted as a sufficient step to "effectuate a transition" to a unitary system. In three years of operation not a single white child has chosen to attend Watkins school and although 115 Negro children enrolled in New Kent school in 1967 (up from 35 in 1965 and 111 in 1966) 85% of the Negro children in the system still attend the all-Negro Watkins school. In other words, the school system remains a dual system. Rather than further the dismantling of the dual system, the plan has operated simply to burden children and their parents with a responsibility which *Brown II* placed squarely on the School Board. The Board must be required to formulate a new plan and, in light of other courses which appear open to the Board, such as zoning, fashion steps which promise realistically to convert promptly to a system without a "white" school and a "Negro" school, but just schools.

The judgment of the Court of Appeals is vacated insofar as it affirmed the District Court and the case is remanded to the District Court for further proceedings consistent with this opinion.

It is so ordered.

**NAACP V.
ALABAMA EX REL. PATTERSON**
357 U.S. 449 (1958)

An Alabama statute required foreign corporations to qualify before doing business in the state (except as exempted) by filing its corporate charter with the secretary of state and designating a place of business and an agent to receive service of process (Ala. Code, 1940, Tit. 10, § 192-198). The statute imposed a fine on corporations transacting intrastate business before qualifying and provided for criminal prosecution of the corporations' officers. Hostility directed toward the NAACP's activities to desegregate public institutions and facilities resulted in state efforts to curtail its activities and to prevent additional litigation. In 1956 the Alabama Attorney General, John Patterson, brought suit against the NAACP, alleging that the group failed to comply with the foreign corporation statute. A regional Alabama affiliate of the NAACP, chartered in 1951, contended that it was exempt from the statute and never complied with it. At the state's request, the circuit court ordered the NAACP to produce many of its records, including the membership lists. The NAACP produced all of the records except its membership lists, and the circuit court subsequently imposed a fine of $100,000 for contempt of court. The state supreme court refused to review the contempt judgment. As a threshold question, the U.S. Supreme Court, on granting certiorari in the case, held that it had jurisdiction to consider the NAACP's claims. The Court also held that the NAACP had standing to assert the constitutional rights of its members. *Vote: 9-0.*

* * *

MR. JUSTICE HARLAN delivered the opinion of the Court.

We review from the standpoint of its validity under the Federal Constitution a judgment of civil contempt entered against petitioner, the National Association for the Advancement of Colored People, in the courts of Alabama. The question presented is whether Alabama, consistently with the Due Process Clause of the Fourteenth Amendment, can compel petitioner to reveal to the State's Attorney General the names and addresses of all its Alabama members and agents, without regard to their positions or functions in the Association. The judgment of contempt was based upon petitioner's refusal to comply fully with a court order requiring in part the production of membership lists. Petitioner's claim is that the order, in the circumstances shown by this record, violated rights assured to petitioner and its members under the Constitution.

. . . We thus reach petitioner's claim that the production order in the state litigation trespasses upon fundamental freedoms protected by the Due Process Clause of the Fourteenth Amendment. Petitioner argues that in view of the facts and circumstances shown in the record, the effect of compelled disclosure of the membership lists will be to abridge the rights of its rank-and-file members to engage in lawful association in support of their common beliefs. It contends that governmental action which,

although not directly suppressing association, nevertheless carries this consequence, can be justified only upon some overriding valid interest of the State.

Effective advocacy of both public and private points of view, particularly controversial ones, is undeniably enhanced by group association, as this Court has more than once recognized by remarking upon the close nexus between the freedoms of speech and assembly. *De Jonge v. Oregon,* 299 U.S. 353, 364 [1937]; *Thomas v. Collins,* 323 U.S. 516, 530 [1945]. It is beyond debate that freedom to engage in association for the advancement of beliefs and ideas is an inseparable aspect of the "liberty" assured by the Due Process Clause of the Fourteenth Amendment, which embraces freedom of speech. See *Gitlow v. New York,* 268 U.S. 652, 666 [1925]; *Palko v. Connecticut,* 302 U.S. 319, 324 [1937]; *Cantwell v. Connecticut,* 310 U.S. 296, 303 [1940]. Of course, it is immaterial whether the beliefs sought to be advanced by association pertain to political, economic, religious or cultural matters, and state action which may have the effect of curtailing the freedom to associate is subject to the closest scrutiny.

The fact that Alabama, so far as is relevant to the validity of the contempt judgment presently under review, has taken no direct action . . . to restrict the right of petitioner's members to associate freely, does not end inquiry into the effect of the production order. . . . In the domain of these indispensable liberties, whether of speech, press, or association, the decisions of this Court recognize that abridgment of such rights, even though unintended, may inevitably follow from varied forms of governmental action. . . . Similar recognition of possible unconstitutional intimidation of the free exercise of the right to advocate underlay this Court's narrow construction of the authority of a congressional committee investigating lobbying and of an Act regulating lobbying, although in neither case was there an effort to suppress speech. . . . The governmental action challenged may appear to be totally unrelated to protected liberties. Statutes imposing taxes upon rather than prohibiting particular activity have been struck down when perceived to have the consequence of unduly curtailing the liberty of freedom of press assured under the Fourteenth Amendment. . . .

It is hardly a novel perception that compelled disclosure of affiliation with groups engaged in advocacy may constitute as effective a restraint on freedom of association as the forms of governmental action in the cases above were thought likely to produce upon the particular constitutional rights there involved. This Court has recognized the vital relationship between freedom to associate and privacy in one's associations. When referring to the varied forms of governmental action which might interfere with freedom of assembly, it said in *Ameri-*

can Communications Assn. v. Douds, [339 U.S. 382 (1950)] at 402: "A requirement that adherents of particular religious faiths or political parties wear identifying arm-bands, for example, is obviously of this nature." Compelled disclosure of membership in an organization engaged in advocacy of particular beliefs is of the same order. Inviolability of privacy in group association may in many circumstances be indispensable to preservation of freedom of association, particularly where a group espouses dissident beliefs. . . .

We think that the production order, in the respects here drawn in question, must be regarded as entailing the likelihood of a substantial restraint upon the exercise by petitioner's members of their right to freedom of association. Petitioner has made an uncontroverted showing that on past occasions revelation of the identity of its rank-and-file members has exposed these members to economic reprisal, loss of employment, threat of physical coercion, and other manifestations of public hostility. Under these circumstances, we think it apparent that compelled disclosure of petitioner's Alabama membership is likely to affect adversely the ability of petitioner and its members to pursue their collective effort to foster beliefs which they admittedly have the right to advocate, in that it may induce members to withdraw from the Association and dissuade others from joining it because of fear of exposure of their beliefs shown through their associations and of the consequences of this exposure.

It is not sufficient to answer, as the State does here, that whatever repressive effect compulsory disclosure of names of petitioner's members may have upon participation by Alabama citizens in petitioner's activities follows not from *state* action but from *private* community pressures. The crucial factor is the interplay of governmental and private action, for it is only after the initial exertion of state power represented by the production order that private action takes hold.

We turn to the final question whether Alabama has demonstrated an interest in obtaining the disclosures it seeks from petitioner which is sufficient to justify the deterrent effect which we have concluded these disclosures may well have on the free exercise by petitioner's members of their constitutionally protected right of association. . . . It is not of moment that the State has here acted solely through its judicial branch, for whether legislative or judicial, it is still the application of state power which we are asked to scrutinize.

It is important to bear in mind that petitioner asserts no right to absolute immunity from state investigation, and no right to disregard Alabama's laws. As shown by its substantial compliance with the production order, petitioner does not deny Alabama's right to obtain from it such information as the State desires concerning the purposes of the Association and its activities within the State. Peti-

tioner has not objected to divulging the identity of its members who are employed by or hold official positions with it. It has urged the rights solely of its ordinary rank-and-file members. This is therefore not analogous to a case involving the interest of a State in protecting its citizens in their dealings with paid solicitors or agents of foreign corporations by requiring identification. . . .

Whether there was "justification" in this instance turns solely on the substantiality of Alabama's interest in obtaining the membership lists. During the course of a hearing before the Alabama Circuit Court on a motion of petitioner to set aside the production order, the State Attorney General presented at length, under examination by petitioner, the State's reason for requesting the membership lists. The exclusive purpose was to determine whether petitioner was conducting intrastate business in violation of the Alabama foreign corporation registration statute, and the membership lists were expected to help resolve this question. The issues in the litigation commenced by Alabama by its bill in equity were whether the character of petitioner and its activities in Alabama had been such as to make petitioner subject to the registration statute, and whether the extent of petitioner's activities without qualifying suggested its permanent ouster from the State. Without intimating the slightest view upon the merits of these issues, we are unable to perceive that the disclosure of the names of petitioner's rank-and-file members has a substantial bearing on either of them. . . .

From what has already been said, we think it apparent that *Bryant v. Zimmerman,* 278 U.S. 63 [1928], cannot be relied on in support of the State's position, for that case involved markedly different considerations in terms of the interest of the State in obtaining disclosure. There, this Court upheld, as applied to a member of a local chapter of the Ku Klux Klan, a New York statute requiring any unincorporated association which demanded an oath as a condition to membership to file with state officials copies of its ". . . constitution, by-laws, rules, regulations and oath of membership, together with a roster of its membership and a list of its officers for the current year." . . . In its opinion, the Court took care to emphasize the nature of the organization which New York sought to regulate. The decision was based on the particular character of the Klan's activities, involving acts of unlawful intimidation and violence, which the Court assumed was before the state legislature when it enacted the statute, and of which the Court itself took judicial notice. Furthermore, the situation before us is significantly different from that in *Bryant,* because the organization there had made no effort to comply with any of the requirements of New York's statute but rather had refused to furnish the State with *any* information as to its local activities.

We hold that the immunity from state scrutiny of membership lists which the Association claims on behalf of its members is here so related to the right of the members to pursue their lawful private interests privately and to associate freely with others in so doing as to come within the protection of the Fourteenth Amendment. And we conclude that Alabama has fallen short of showing a controlling justification for the deterrent effect on the free enjoyment of the right to associate which disclosure of membership lists is likely to have. Accordingly, the judgment of civil contempt and the $100,000 fine which resulted from petitioner's refusal to comply with the production order in this respect must fall.

. . . For the reasons stated, the judgment of the Supreme Court of Alabama must be reversed and the case remanded for proceedings not inconsistent with this opinion.

Reversed.

GOMILLION V. LIGHTFOOT
364 U.S. 339 (1960)

In 1957, Alabama passed Local Act No. 140, which redefined the boundaries of the city of Tuskegee. The Act altered the shape of the city from a square to an irregular, 28-sided figure that, in effect, removed from the city all but 4 or 5 of its 400 black voters while not removing a single white voter. Charles Gomillion and other black voters sued Phil Lightfoot, the mayor of Tuskegee, and other officials, alleging that the racial gerrymander deprived them of their right to vote in municipal elections. The district court dismissed the complaint on the basis that it lacked jurisdiction to hear the case, and the court of appeals affirmed the ruling. *Vote: 9-0.*

* * *

MR. JUSTICE FRANKFURTER delivered the opinion of the Court.

. . . In short, the cases that have come before this Court regarding legislation by States dealing with their political subdivisions fall into two classes: (1) those in which it is claimed that the State, by virtue of the prohibition against impairment of the obligation of contract (Art. I. § 10) and of the Due Process Clause of the Fourteenth Amendment, is without power to extinguish, or alter the boundaries of, an existing municipality; and (2) in which it is claimed that the State has no power to change the identity of a municipality whereby citizens of a pre-existing municipality suffer serious economic disadvantage.

Neither of these claims is supported by such a specific limitation upon State power as confines the States under the Fifteenth Amendment. As to the first category, it is obvious that the creation of municipalities—clearly a political act—does not come within the conception of a contract under the *Dartmouth College* [v. *Woodward*] case. 4 Wheat. 518 [1819]. As to the second, if one principle clearly emerges from the numerous decisions of this Court dealing with taxation it is that the Due Process Clause affords no immunity against mere inequalities in tax burdens, nor does it afford protection against their increase as an indirect consequence of a State's exercise of its political powers.

Particularly in dealing with claims under broad provisions of the Constitution, which derive content by an interpretive process of inclusion and exclusion, it is imperative that generalizations, based on and qualified by the concrete situations that gave rise to them, must not be applied out of context in disregard of variant controlling facts. Thus, a correct reading of the seemingly unconfined dicta of *Hunter* [v. *Pittsburgh,* 207 U.S. 161 (1907)] and kindred cases is not that the State has plenary power to manipulate in every conceivable way, for every conceivable purpose, the affairs of its municipal corporations, but rather that the State's authority is unrestrained by the particular prohibitions of the Constitution considered in those cases.

. . . If all this is so in regard to the constitutional protection of contracts, it should be equally true that, to paraphrase, such power, extensive though it is, is met and overcome by the Fifteenth Amendment to the Constitution of the United States, which forbids a State from passing any law which deprives a citizen of his vote because of his race. The opposite conclusion, urged upon us by respondents, would sanction the achievement by a State of any impairment of voting rights whatever so long as it was cloaked in the garb of the realignment of political subdivisions. "It is inconceivable that guaranties embedded in the Constitution of the United States may thus be manipulated out of existence." *Frost & Frost Trucking Co. v. Railroad Commission of California,* 271 U.S. 583, 594 [1926].

The respondents find another barrier to the trial of this case in *Colegrove v. Green,* 328 U.S. 549 [1946]. In that case the Court passed on an Illinois law governing the arrangement of congressional districts within that State. . . .

That case involved a complaint of discriminatory apportionment of congressional districts. The appellants in *Colegrove* complained only of a dilution of the strength of their votes as a result of legislative inaction over a course of many years. The petitioners here complain that affirmative legislative action deprives them of their votes and the consequent advantages that the ballot affords. When a legislature thus singles out a readily isolated segment of a racial minority for special discriminatory treatment, it violates the Fifteenth Amendment. In no case involving unequal weight in voting distribution that has come before the Court did the decision sanction a differentiation on racial lines whereby approval was given to unequivocal withdrawal of the vote solely from colored citizens. Apart from all else, these considerations lift this controversy out of the so-called "political" arena and into the conventional sphere of constitutional litigation.

. . . A statute which is alleged to have worked unconstitutional deprivations of petitioners' rights is not immune to attack simply because the mechanism employed by the legislature is a redefinition of municipal boundaries. According to the allegations here made, the Alabama Legislature has not merely redrawn the Tuskegee city limits with incidental inconvenience to the petitioners; it is more accurate to say that it has deprived the petitioners of the municipal franchise and consequent rights and to that end it has incidentally changed the city's boundaries. While in form this is merely an act redefining metes and bounds, if the allegations are established, the inescapable human effect of this essay in geometry and geography is to despoil colored citizens, and only colored citizens, of their theretofore enjoyed voting rights. That was not *Colegrove v. Green.*

When a State exercises power wholly within the domain of state interest, it is insulated from federal judicial review. But such insulation is not carried over when state power is used as an instrument for circumventing a federally protected right. This principle has had many applications. It has long been recognized in cases which have prohibited a State from exploiting a power acknowledged to be absolute in an isolated context to justify the imposition of an "unconstitutional condition." What the Court has said in those cases is equally applicable here, *viz.,* that "Acts generally lawful may become unlawful when done to accomplish an unlawful end . . . and a constitutional power cannot be used by way of condition to attain an unconstitutional result." . . . The petitioners are entitled to prove their allegations at trial.

For these reasons, the principal conclusions of the District Court and the Court of Appeals are clearly erroneous and the decision below must be *Reversed.*

* * *

MR. JUSTICE DOUGLAS, while joining the opinion of the Court, adheres to the dissents in *Colegrove v. Green,* 328 U.S. 549 [1946], and *South v. Peters,* 339 U.S. 276 [1950].

* * *

MR. JUSTICE WHITTAKER concurring.

I concur in the Court's judgment, but not in the whole of its opinion. It seems to me that the decision should be rested not on the Fifteenth Amendment, but rather on the Equal Protection Clause of the Fourteenth Amendment to the Constitution. . . .

SOUTH CAROLINA V. KATZENBACH
383 U.S. 301 (1966)

The voting rights provisions of the 1957, 1960, and 1964 Civil Rights Acts proved to be inadequate against the pervasive voting discrimination throughout the South and other parts of the country. In 1965 President Lyndon Johnson responded to significant political pressure urging the passage of new legislation that would remedy widespread discriminatory practices in voting. In August 1965, the president signed the Voting Rights Act into law. The following year, South Carolina filed a bill of complaint under the U.S. Supreme Court's original jurisdiction to have declared certain provisions of the Act unconstitutional and sought an injunction to prevent their enforcement by the defendant, Nicholas Katzenbach, the U.S. Attorney General. *Vote: 8-1.*

* * *

MR. CHIEF JUSTICE WARREN delivered the opinion of the Court.

. . . The constitutional propriety of the Voting Rights Act of 1965 must be judged with reference to the historical experience which it reflects. Before enacting the measure, Congress explored with great care the problem of racial discrimination in voting. . . .

Two points emerge vividly from the voluminous legislative history of the Act contained in the committee hearings and floor debates. First: Congress felt itself confronted by an insidious and pervasive evil which had been perpetrated in certain parts of our country through unremitting and ingenious defiance of the Constitution. Second: Congress concluded that the unsuccessful remedies which it had prescribed in the past would have to be replaced by sterner and more elaborate measures in order to satisfy the clear commands of the Fifteenth Amendment....

... At the outset, we emphasize that only some of the many portions of the Act are properly before us. South Carolina has not challenged §§ 2, 3, 4(e), 6(a), 8, 10, 12(d) and (e), 13(b), and other miscellaneous provisions having nothing to do with this lawsuit. Judicial review of these sections must await subsequent litigation. In addition, we find that South Carolina's attack on §§ 11 and 12(a)-(c) is premature. No person has yet been subjected to, or even threatened with, the criminal sanctions which these sections of the Act authorize.... Consequently, the only sections of the Act to be reviewed at this time are §§ 4(a)-(d), 5, 6(b), 7, 9, 13(a), and certain procedural portions of § 14, all of which are presently in actual operation in South Carolina....

... These provisions of the Voting Rights Act of 1965 are challenged on the fundamental ground that they exceed the powers of Congress and encroach on an area reserved to the States by the Constitution. South Carolina and certain of the *amici curiae* also attack specific sections of the Act for more particular reasons. They argue that the coverage formula prescribed in § 4(a)-(d) violates the principle of the equality of States, denies due process by employing an invalid presumption and by barring judicial review of administrative findings, constitutes a forbidden bill of attainder, and impairs the separation of powers by adjudicating guilt through legislation. They claim that the review of new voting rules required in § 5 infringes Article III by directing the District Court to issue advisory opinions. They contend that the assignment of federal examiners authorized in § 6(b) abridges due process by precluding judicial review of administrative findings and impairs the separation of powers by giving the Attorney General judicial functions; also that the challenge procedure prescribed in § 9 denies due process on account of its speed. Finally, South Carolina and certain of the *amici curiae* maintain that §§ 4(a) and 5, buttressed by § 14(b) of the Act, abridge due process by limiting litigation to a distant forum.

Some of these contentions may be dismissed at the outset. The word "person" in the context of the Due Process Clause of the Fifth Amendment cannot, by any reasonable mode of interpretation, be expanded to encompass the States of the Union, and to our knowledge this has never been done by any court.
... Likewise, courts have consistently regarded the Bill of Attainder Clause of Article I and the principle of the separation of powers only as protections for individual persons and private groups, those who are peculiarly vulnerable to nonjudicial determinations of guilt. ... The objections to the Act which are raised under these provisions may therefore be considered only as additional aspects of the basic question presented by the case: Has Congress exercised its powers under the Fifteenth Amendment in an appropriate manner with relation to the States?

The ground rules for resolving this question are clear. The language and purpose of the Fifteenth Amendment, the prior decisions construing its several provisions, and the general doctrines of constitutional interpretation all point to one fundamental principle. As against the reserved powers of the States, Congress may use any rational means to effectuate the constitutional prohibition of racial discrimination in voting....

Section 1 of the Fifteenth Amendment declares that "[t]he right of citizens of the United States to vote shall not be denied or abridged by the United States or by any State on account of race, color, or previous condition of servitude." This declaration has always been treated as self-executing and has repeatedly been construed, without further legislative specification, to invalidate state voting qualifications or procedures which are discriminatory on their face or in practice....

... Accordingly, in addition to the courts, Congress has full remedial powers to effectuate the constitutional prohibition against racial discrimination in voting.

... We therefore reject South Carolina's argument that Congress may appropriately do no more than to forbid violations of the Fifteenth Amendment in general terms—that the task of fashioning specific remedies or of applying them to particular localities must necessarily be left entirely to the courts. Congress is not circumscribed by any such artificial rules under § 2 of the Fifteenth Amendment. In the oft-repeated words of Chief Justice Marshall, referring to another specific legislative authorization in the Constitution, "This power, like all others vested in Congress, is complete in itself, may be exercised to its utmost extent, and acknowledges no limitations, other than are prescribed in the constitution." *Gibbons v. Ogden,* 9 Wheat. 1, 196 [1824].

Congress exercised its authority under the Fifteenth Amendment in an inventive manner when it enacted the Voting Rights Act of 1965. First: The measure prescribes remedies for voting discrimination which go into effect without any need for prior adjudication. This was clearly a legitimate response to the problem, for which there is ample precedent under other constitutional provisions. See *Katzenbach v. McClung,* 379 U.S. 294, 302-304 [1964] ... Congress had found that case-by-case litigation was inadequate to combat widespread and persistent discrimination in voting, because of the inordinate amount of time and energy required to overcome the obstructionist tactics invariably encountered in these lawsuits. After enduring nearly a century of systematic resistance to the Fifteenth Amendment, Congress might well decide to shift the advantage of time and inertia from the perpetrators of the evil to its victims. The question remains, of course, whether the specific remedies prescribed in the Act were an appropriate means of combatting the evil, and to this question we shall presently address ourselves.

Second: The Act intentionally confines these remedies to a small number of States and political subdivisions which in most instances were familiar to Congress by name. This, too, was a permissible method of dealing with the problem. Congress had learned that substantial voting discrimination presently occurs in certain sections of the country, and it knew no way of accurately forecasting whether the evil might spread elsewhere in the future. In acceptable legislative fashion, Congress chose to limit its attention to the geographic areas where immediate action seemed necessary. . . . The doctrine of the equality of States, invoked by South Carolina, does not bar this approach, for that doctrine applies only to the terms upon which States are admitted to the Union, and not to the remedies for local evils which have subsequently appeared. . . .

Coverage Formula

We now consider the related question of whether the specific States and political subdivisions within § 4(b) of the Act were an appropriate target for the new remedies. South Carolina contends that the coverage formula is awkwardly designed in a number of respects and that it disregards various local conditions which have nothing to do with racial discrimination. These arguments, however, are largely beside the point. Congress began work with reliable evidence of actual voting discrimination in a great majority of the States and political subdivisions affected by the new remedies of the Act. The formula eventually evolved to describe these areas was relevant to the problem of voting discrimination, and Congress was therefore entitled to infer a significant danger of the evil in the few remaining States and political subdivisions covered by § 4(b) of the Act. No more was required to justify the application to these areas of Congress' express powers under the Fifteenth Amendment. . . .

Suspension of Tests

We now arrive at consideration of the specified remedies prescribed by the Act for areas included within the coverage formula. South Carolina assails the temporary suspension of existing voting qualifications, reciting the rule laid down by *Lassiter v. Northampton County Bd. of Elections*, 360 U.S. 45 [1959], that literacy tests and related devices are not in themselves contrary to the Fifteenth Amendment. In that very case, however, the Court went on to say, "Of course a literacy test, fair on its face, may be employed to perpetuate that discrimination which the Fifteenth Amendment was designed to uproot." *Id.*, at 53. The record shows that in most of the States covered by the Act, including South Carolina, various tests and devices have been instituted with the purpose of disenfranchising Negroes, have been framed in such a way as to facilitate this aim, and

have been administered in a discriminatory fashion for many years. Under these circumstances, the Fifteenth Amendment has clearly been violated. . . .

The Act suspends literacy tests and similar devices for a period of five years from the last occurrence of substantial voting discrimination. This was a legitimate response to the problem, for which there is ample precedent in Fifteenth Amendment cases. . . . Underlying the response was the feeling that States and political subdivisions which had been allowing white illiterates to vote for years could not sincerely complain about "dilution" of their electorates through the registration of Negro illiterates. Congress knew that continuance of the tests and devices in use at the present time, no matter how fairly administered in the future, would freeze the effect of past discrimination in favor of unqualified white registrants. Congress permissibly rejected the alternative of requiring a complete re-registration of all voters, believing that this would be too harsh on many whites who had enjoyed the franchise for their entire adult lives.

Review of New Rules

The Act suspends new voting regulations pending scrutiny by federal authorities to determine whether their use would violate the Fifteenth Amendment. This may have been an uncommon exercise of congressional power, as South Carolina contends, but the Court has recognized that exceptional conditions can justify legislative measures not otherwise appropriate. . . . Congress knew that some of the States covered by § 4(b) of the Act had resorted to the extraordinary stratagem of contriving new rules of various kinds for the sole purpose of perpetuating voting discrimination in the face of adverse federal court decrees. Congress had reason to suppose that these States might try similar maneuvers in the future in order to evade the remedies for voting discrimination contained in the Act itself. Under the compulsion of these unique circumstances, Congress responded in a permissibly decisive manner.

Federal Examiners

The Act authorizes the appointment of federal examiners to list qualified applicants who are thereafter entitled to vote, subject to an expeditious challenge procedure. This was clearly an appropriate response to the problem, closely related to remedies authorized in prior cases. . . . In many of the political subdivisions covered by § 4(b) of the Act, voting officials have persistently employed a variety of procedural tactics to deny Negroes the franchise, often in direct defiance or evasion of federal court decrees. Congress realized that merely to suspend voting rules which have been misused or are subject to misuse might leave this localized evil undisturbed. As for the briskness of the challenge procedure, Congress knew that in some of the areas affected, challenges had been persistently employed to harass registered Negroes. It chose to forestall this abuse, at the same time providing alternative ways for removing persons listed through error or fraud. In addition to the judicial challenge procedure, § 7(d) allows for the removal of names by the examiner himself, and § 11(c) makes it a crime to obtain a listing through fraud.

In recognition of the fact that there were political subdivisions covered by § 4(b) of the Act in which the appointment of federal examiners might be unnecessary, Congress assigned the Attorney General the task of determining the localities to which examiners should be sent. There is no warrant for the claim, asserted by Georgia as *amicus curiae,* that the Attorney General is free to use this power in an arbitrary fashion, without regard to the purposes of the Act. Section 6(b) sets adequate standards to guide the exercise of his discretion, by directing him to calculate the registration ratio of nonwhites to whites, and to weigh evidence of good-faith efforts to avoid possible voting discrimination. At the same time, the special termination procedures of § 13(a) provide indirect judicial review for the political subdivisions affected, assuring the withdrawal of federal examiners from areas where they are clearly not needed. . . .

After enduring nearly a century of widespread resistance to the Fifteenth Amendment, Congress has marshalled an array of potent weapons against the evil, with authority in the Attorney General to employ them effectively. Many of the areas directly affected by this development have indicated their willingness to abide by any restraints legitimately imposed upon them. We here hold that the portions of the Voting Rights Act properly before us are a valid means for carrying out the commands of the Fifteenth Amendment. Hopefully, millions of nonwhite Americans will now be able to participate for the first time on an equal basis in the government under which they live. We may finally look forward to the day when truly "[t]he right to citizens of the United States to vote shall not be denied or abridged by the United States or by any State on account of race, color, or previous condition of servitude."

The bill of complaint is
Dismissed.

* * *

MR. JUSTICE BLACK concurring and dissenting.

. . . My . . . more basic objection to § 5 is that Congress has here exercised its power under § 2 of the Fifteenth Amendment through the adoption of means that conflict with the most basic principles of the Constitution. As the Court says the limitations of the power granted under § 2 are the same as the limitations imposed on the exercise of any of the powers expressly granted Congress by the Constitution. . . . Section 5, by providing that some of the States cannot pass state laws or adopt state constitutional amendments without first being compelled to beg federal authorities to approve their policies, so distorts our constitutional structure of government as to render any distinction drawn in the Constitution between state and federal power almost meaningless. One of the most basic premises upon which our structure of government was founded was that the Federal Government was to have certain specific and limited powers and no others, and all other power was to be reserved either "to the States respectively, or to the people." Certainly if all the provisions of our Constitution which limit the power of the Federal Government and reserve other power to the States are to mean anything, they mean at least that the States have power to pass laws and amend their constitutions without first sending their officials hundreds of miles away to beg federal authorities to approve them. Moreover, it seems to me that § 5 which gives federal officials power to veto state laws they do not like is in direct conflict with the clear command of our Constitution that "the United States shall guarantee to every State in this Union a Republican Form of Government." I cannot help but believe that the inevitable effect of any such law which forces any one of the States to entreat federal authorities in far-away places for approval of local laws before they can become effective is to create the impression that the State or States treated in this way are little more than conquered provinces. And if one law concerning voting can make the States plead for this approval by a distant federal court or the United States Attorney General, other laws on different subjects can force the States to seek the advance approval not only of the Attorney General but of the President himself or any other chosen members of his staff. It is inconceivable to me that such a radical degradation of state power was intended in any of the provisions of our Constitution or its Amendments. . . .

BOYNTON V. VIRGINIA
364 U.S. 454 (1960)

Bruce Boynton, a black law student at Howard University, bought a Trailways bus ticket from Washington, D.C., to Montgomery, Alabama. When the bus pulled up at the Richmond, Virginia, Trailways bus terminal, Boynton got off and went into the bus terminal to get something to eat. He sat down in the white section of the restaurant after finding the black section crowded and was asked by the waitress to move to the "colored section." He refused, and the assistant manager of the restaurant called the police. Boynton later was arrested, tried, and convicted of violating a statute making it a misdemeanor for any person to remain on the premises of another after having been forbidden to do so. On appeal, Boynton argued that his conviction violated the Interstate Commerce Act, the equal protection clause, and the commerce clause. The Virginia Supreme Court upheld the conviction. *Vote: 7-2.*

* * *

MR. JUSTICE BLACK delivered the opinion of the Court.

The basic question presented in this case is whether an interstate bus passenger is denied a federal statutory or constitutional right when a restaurant in a bus terminal used by the carrier along its route discriminates in serving food to the passenger solely because of his color.

. . . The petition for certiorari we granted presented only two questions: first, whether the conviction of petitioner is invalid as a burden on commerce in violation of Art. I. § 8, cl. 3 of the Constitution; and second, whether the conviction violates the Due Process and Equal Protection Clauses of the Fourteenth Amendment. Ordinarily we limit our review to the questions presented in an application for certiorari. We think there are persuasive reasons, however, why this case should be decided, if it can, on the Interstate Commerce Act contention raised in the Virginia courts. Discrimination because of color is the core of the two broad constitutional questions presented to us by petitioner, just as it is the core of the Interstate Commerce Act question presented to the Virginia courts. Under these circumstances we think it appropriate not to reach the constitutional questions but to proceed at once to the statutory issue.

The Interstate Commerce Act, . . . uses language of the broadest type to bar discriminations of all kinds. *United States v. Baltimore & Ohio R. Co.,* 333 U.S. 169, 175 [1948], and cases cited. We have held that the Act forbids railroad dining cars to discriminate in service to passengers on account of their color. *Henderson v. United States,* 339 U.S. 816 [1950]; see also *Mitchell v. United States,* 313 U.S. 80, 97 [1941].

Section 216(d) of Part II of the Interstate Commerce Act, . . . which applies to motor carriers, provides in part:

"It shall be unlawful for any common carrier by motor vehicle engaged in interstate or foreign commerce to make, give, or cause any undue or unreasonable preference or advantage to any particular person . . . in any respect whatsoever; or to subject any particular person

. . . to any unjust discrimination or any unjust or unreasonable prejudice or disadvantage in any respect whatsoever. . . ."

So far as relevant to our problem, the provisions of § 216(d) quoted are the same as those in § 3(1) of the Act, . . . except that the latter refers to railroads as defined in Part I of the Act instead of motor carriers as defined in Part II. Section 3(1) was the basis for this Court's holding in *Henderson v. United States,* . . . that it was an "undue or unreasonable prejudice" under that section for a railroad to divide its dining car by curtains, partitions and signs in order to separate passengers according to race. The Court said that under § 3(1) "[w]here a dining car is available to passengers holding tickets entitling them to use it, each such passenger is equally entitled to its facilities in accordance with reasonable regulations." . . . The *Henderson* case largely rested on *Mitchell v. United States* . . . which pointed out that while the railroads might not be required by law to furnish dining car facilities, yet if they did, substantial equality of treatment of persons traveling under like conditions could not be refused consistently with § 3(1). It is also of relevance that both cases upset Interstate Commerce Commission holdings, the Court stating in *Mitchell* that since the "discrimination shown was palpably unjust and forbidden by the Act" no room was left for administrative or expert judgment with reference to practical difficulties. . . .

It follows from the *Mitchell* and *Henderson* cases as a matter of course that should buses in transit decide to supply dining service, discrimination of the kind shown here would violate § 216(d). . . . Although this Court has not decided whether the same result would follow from a similar discrimination in service by a restaurant in a railroad or bus terminal, we have no doubt that the reasoning underlying the *Mitchell* and *Henderson* cases would compel the same decision as to the unlawfulness of discrimination in transportation services against interstate passengers in terminals and terminal restaurants owned or operated or controlled by interstate carriers. . . .

Respondent correctly points out, however, that, whatever may be the facts, the evidence in this record does not show that the bus company owns or actively operates or directly controls the bus terminal or the restaurant in it. But the fact that § 203(a)(19) says that the protections of the motor carrier provisions of the act extend to "include" facilities so operated or controlled by no means should be interpreted to exempt motor carriers from their statutory duty under § 216(d) not to discriminate should they choose to provide their interstate passengers with services that are an integral part of transportation through the use of facilities they neither own, control nor operate. The protections afforded by the Act against discriminatory transportation services are not so narrowly limited. We have held that a railroad cannot escape its statutory duty to treat its shippers alike either by use of facilities it does not own or by contractual arrangement with the owner of those facilities. *United States v. Baltimore & Ohio R. Co.* . . . And so here, without regard to contracts, if the bus carrier has volunteered to make terminal and restaurant facilities and services available to its interstate passengers as a regular part of their transportation, and the terminal and restaurant have acquiesced and cooperated in this undertaking, the terminal and restaurant must perform these services without discriminations prohibited by the Act. In the performance of these services under such conditions the terminal and restaurant stand in the place of the bus company in the performance of its transportation obligations. Cf. *Derrington v. Plummer,* 240 F. 2d 922, 925-926, cert. denied, 353 U.S. 924 [1957]. Although the courts below made no findings of fact, we think the evidence in this case shows such a relationship and situation here.

The manager of the restaurant testified that it was not affiliated in any way with the Trailways Bus Company and that the bus company had no control over the operation of the restaurant, but that while the restaurant had "quite a bit of business" from local people, it was primarily or partly for the service of the passengers on the Trailways bus. This last statement was perhaps much of an understatement, as shown by the lease agreement executed in writing and signed both by the "Trailways Bus Terminal, Inc.," as lessor, and the "Bus Terminal restaurant of Richmond, Inc.," as lessee. The first part of the document showed that Trailways Terminal was then constructing a "bus station" with built-in facilities "for the operation of a restaurant, soda fountain, and news stand." Terminal covenanted to lease this space to Restaurant for its use; to grant Restaurant the exclusive right to sell foods and other things usually sold in restaurants, newsstands, soda fountains and lunch counters; to keep the terminal building in good repair and to furnish certain utilities. Restaurant on its part agreed to use its space for the sale of commodities agreed on at prices that are "just and reasonable"; to sell no commodities not usually sold or installed in a bus terminal concession without Terminal's permission; to discontinue the sale of any commodity objectionable to Terminal; to buy, maintain, and replace equipment subject to Terminal's approval in writing as to its quality; to make alterations and additions only after Terminal's written consent and approval; to make no "sales on buses operating in and out of said bus station" but only "through the windows of said buses"; to keep its employees neat and clean; to perform no terminal service other than that pertaining to the operation of its restaurant as agreed on; and that neither Restaurant nor its employees were to "sell transportation of any kind or give information pertaining to schedules, rates or transportation matters, but shall refer all such inquiries to the proper agents of" Terminal. In short, as Terminal and Restaurant agreed, "the operation of the restaurant and the said stands shall be in keeping with the character of service maintained in an up-to-date, modern bus terminal."

All of these things show that this terminal building, with its grounds, constituted one project for a single purpose, and that was to serve passengers of one or more bus companies—certainly Trailways' passengers. The restaurant area was specifically designed and built into the structure from the beginning to fill the needs of bus passengers in this "up-to-date, modern bus terminal." Whoever may have had technical title or immediate control of the details of the various activities in the terminal, such as waiting-room seating, furnishing of schedule information, ticket sales, and restaurant service, they were all geared to the service of bus companies and their passengers, even though local people who might happen to come into the terminal or its restaurant might also be accommodated. Thus we have a well-coordinated and smoothly functioning plan for continuous cooperative transportation services between the terminal, the restaurant and buses like Trailways that made stopovers there. All of this evidence plus Trailways' use on this occasion shows that Trailways was not utilizing the terminal and restaurant services merely on a sporadic or occasional basis. This bus terminal plainly was just as essential and necessary, and as available for that matter, to passengers and carriers like Trailways that used it, as though such carriers had legal title and complete control over all of its activities. Interstate passengers have to eat, and the very terms of the lease of the built-in restaurant space in this terminal constitute a recognition of the essential need of interstate passengers to be able to get food conveniently on their journey and an undertaking by the restaurant to fulfill that need. Such passengers in transit on a paid interstate Trailways journey had a right to expect that this essential transportation food service voluntarily provided for them under such circumstances would be rendered without discrimination prohibited by the Interstate Commerce Act. Under the circumstances of this case, therefore, petitioner had a federal right to remain in the white portion of the restaurant. He was there under "authority of law"—the Interstate Commerce Act—and it was error for the Supreme Court of Virginia to affirm his conviction.

Because of some of the arguments made here it is necessary to say a word about what we are not deciding. We are not holding that every time a bus stops at a wholly independent roadside restaurant the Interstate Commerce Act requires that restaurant service be supplied in harmony with the provisions of that Act. We decide only this case, on its facts, where circumstances show that the terminal and restaurant operate as an integral part of the bus carrier's transportation service for interstate passengers. Under such circumstances, an interstate passenger need not inquire into documents of title or contractual arrangements in order to determine whether he has a right to be served without discrimination.

The judgment of the Supreme Court of Virginia is reversed and the cause is remanded to that Court for proceedings not inconsistent with this opinion.

Reversed and remanded.

* * *

MR. JUSTICE WHITTAKER dissenting.

. . . For me, the decisive question in this case is whether petitioner had a legal right to remain in the restaurant involved after being ordered to leave it by the proprietor. If he did not have that legal right, however arising, he was guilty of trespass and, unless proscribed by some federal law, his conviction therefor was legally adjudged under § 18-225 of the Code of Virginia.

If the facts in this record could fairly be said to show that the restaurant was a facility "operated or controlled by any [motor] carrier or carriers, and used in the transportation of passengers or property in interstate or foreign commerce," § 203(a)(19) of Part II of the Interstate Commerce Act, . . . I would agree that petitioner had a legal right to remain in and to insist on service by that restaurant and, hence, was not guilty of trespass in so remaining and insisting though in defiance of the manager's order to leave, for § 216(d) of the Act . . . makes it unlawful for a motor carrier while engaged in interstate commerce "to subject any particular person . . . to any unjust discrimination," and this Court has held that any discrimination by a carrier against its interstate passenger on account of his color in the use of its dining facilities is an unjust discrimination. . . .

But I respectfully submit that those are not the facts shown by this record. As I read it, there is no evidence in this record tending to show that the restaurant was "operated or controlled by any such carrier," directly or indirectly. Instead, all of the relevant evidence, none of which was contradicted, shows that the restaurant was owned and controlled by a noncarrier who alone operated it as a local and private enterprise. . . .

MR. JUSTICE CLARK concurs.

BURTON V.
WILMINGTON PARKING AUTHORITY
365 U.S. 715 (1961)

The Eagle Coffee Shoppe restaurant was located within an off-street automobile parking building in Wilmington, Delaware. The parking building was owned and operated by the Wilmington Parking Authority, an agency of the state of Delaware. Before actual construction of the parking facility, the authority realized the need for additional revenue to finance construction costs; therefore, it entered long-term leases with commercial tenants. In 1957 the authority leased space to the Eagle Coffee Shoppe. In August 1958, William Burton, a black man, parked his car in the building and walked around to enter the restaurant by its front door on Ninth Street. Restaurant personnel, however, refused to serve Burton because of his race. Burton brought suit, claiming that the refusal of service violated the equal protection clause of the Fourteenth Amendment. The chancellor of the trial court proceedings concluded that the lease would not serve to insulate the parking authority from the force and effect of the Fourteenth Amendment. The Supreme Court of Delaware held that Burton was not entitled to relief on the ground that action by the restaurant's personnel was not state action within the meaning of the Fourteenth Amendment and that the restaurant personnel were not required by a Delaware statute to serve all persons entering the place of business. *Vote: 6-3.*

* * *

MR. JUSTICE CLARK delivered the opinion of the Court.

. . . The *Civil Rights Cases,* 109 U.S. 3 (1883), "embedded in our constitutional law" the principle "that the action inhibited by the first section [Equal Protection Clause] of the Fourteenth Amendment is only such action as may fairly be said to be that of the States. That Amendment erects no shield against merely private conduct, however discriminatory or wrongful." Chief Justice Vinson in *Shelley v. Kraemer,* 334 U.S. 1, 13 (1948). It was language in the opinion in the *Civil Rights Cases* . . . that phrased the broad test of state responsibility under the Fourteenth Amendment, predicting its consequence upon "State action of every kind . . . which denies . . . the equal protection of the laws." . . . And only two Terms ago, some 75 years later, the same concept of state responsibility was interpreted as necessarily following upon "state participation through any arrangement, management, funds or property." *Cooper v. Aaron,* 358 U.S. 1, 4 (1958). It is clear, as it always has been since the *Civil Rights Cases,* . . . that "Individual invasion of individual rights is not the subject-matter of the amendment" . . . and that private conduct abridging individual rights does no violence to the Equal Protection Clause unless to some significant extent the State in any of its manifestations has been found to have become involved in it. Because the virtue of the right to equal protection of the laws could lie only in the breadth of its application, its constitutional assurance was reserved in terms whose imprecision was necessary if the right were to be enjoyed in the variety of individual-state relationships which the Amendment was designed to embrace. For the same reason, to fashion and apply a precise formula for recognition of state responsibility under the Equal Protection Clause is an "impossible task" which "This Court has never attempted." . . . Only by sifting facts and weighing circumstances can the nonobvious involvement of the State in private conduct be attributed its true significance.

The trial court's disposal of the issues on summary judgment has resulted in a rather incomplete record, but the opinion of the Supreme Court as well as that of the Chancellor presents the facts in sufficient detail for us to determine the degree of state participation in Eagle's refusal to serve petitioner. In this connection the Delaware Supreme Court seems to have placed controlling emphasis on its conclusion, as to the accuracy of which there is doubt, that only some 15% of the total cost of the facility was "advanced" from public funds; that the cost of the entire facility was allocated three-fifths to the space for commercial leasing and two-fifths to parking space; that anticipated revenue from parking was only some 30.5% of the total income, the balance of which was expected to be earned by the leasing; that the Authority had no original intent to place a restaurant in the building, it being only a happenstance resulting from the bidding; that Eagle expended considerable moneys on furnishings; that the restaurant's main and marked public entrance is on Ninth Street without any public entrance direct from the parking area; that "the only connection Eagle has with the public facility . . . is the furnishing of the sum of $28,700 annually in the form of rent which is used by the Authority to defray a portion of the operating expenses of an otherwise unprofitable enterprise." . . . While these factual considerations are indeed validly accountable aspects of the enterprise upon which the State has embarked, we cannot say that they lead inescapably to the conclusion that state action is not present. Their persuasiveness is diminished when evaluated in the context of other factors which must be acknowledged.

The land and building were publicly owned. As an entity, the building was dedicated to "public uses" in performance of the Authority's "essential governmental functions." . . . The costs of land acquisition, construction, and maintenance are defrayed entirely from donations by the City of Wilmington, from loans and revenue bonds and from the proceeds of rentals and parking services out of which the loans and bonds were payable. Assuming that the distinction would be significant, cf. *Derrington v. Plummer,* 240 F. 2d 922, 925 [1957], the commercially leased areas were not surplus state property, but constituted a physically and financially integral and, indeed, indispensable part of the State's plan to operate its project as a self-sustaining unit. Upkeep and maintenance of the building, including necessary repairs, were responsibilities of the Authority and were payable out of public funds. It cannot be doubted that the peculiar relationship of the restaurant to the parking facility in which it is located confers on each an incidental variety of mutual benefits. Guests of the restaurant are afforded a convenient place to park their automobiles, even if they cannot enter the restaurant directly from the parking area. Similarly, its convenience for diners may well provide additional demand for the Authority's parking facilities. Should any improvements effected in the leasehold by Eagle become part of the realty, there is no possibility of increased taxes being passed on to it since the fee is held by a tax-exempt government agency. Neither can it be ignored, especially in view of Eagle's affirmative allegation that for it to serve Negroes would injure its business, that profits earned by discrimination not only contribute to, but also are indispensable elements in, the financial success of a governmental agency.

Addition of all these activities, obligations and responsibilities of the Authority, the benefits mutually conferred, together with the obvious fact that the restaurant is operated as an integral part of a public building devoted to a public parking service, indicates that degree of state participation and involvement in discriminatory action which it was the design of the Fourteenth Amendment to condemn. It is irony amounting to grave injustice that in one part of a single building, erected and maintained with public funds by an agency of the State to serve a public purpose, all persons have equal rights, while in another portion, also serving the public, a Negro is a second-class citizen, offensive because of his race, without rights and unentitled to service, but at the same time fully enjoys equal access to nearby restaurants in wholly privately owned buildings. As the Chancellor pointed out, in its lease with Eagle the Authority could have affirmatively required Eagle to discharge the responsibilities under the Fourteenth Amendment imposed upon the private enterprise as a consequence of state participation. But no State may effectively abdicate its responsibilities by either ignoring them or by merely failing to discharge them whatever the motive may be. It is of no consolation to an individual denied the equal protection of the laws that it was done in good faith. Certainly the conclusions drawn in similar cases by the various Courts of Appeals do not depend upon such a distinction. By its inaction, the

Authority, and through it the State, has not only made itself a party to the refusal of service, but has elected to place its power, property and prestige behind the admitted discrimination. The State has so far insinuated itself into a position of interdependence with Eagle that it must be recognized as a joint participant in the challenged activity, which, on that account, cannot be considered to have been so "purely private" as to fall without the scope of the Fourteenth Amendment.

Because readily applicable formulae may not be fashioned, the conclusions drawn from the facts and circumstances of this record are by no means declared as universal truths on the basis of which every state leasing agreement is to be tested. Owning to the very "largeness" of government, a multitude of relationships might appear to some to fall within the Amendment's embrace, but that, it must be remembered, can be determined only in the framework of the peculiar facts or circumstances present. Therefore respondents' prophecy of nigh universal application of a constitutional precept so peculiarly dependent for its invocation upon appropriate facts fails to take into account "Differences in circumstances [which] beget appropriate differences in law." . . . Specifically defining the limits of our inquiry, what we hold today is that when a State leases public property in the manner and for the purpose shown to have been the case here, the proscriptions of the Fourteenth Amendment must be complied with by the lessee as certainly as though they were binding covenants written into the agreement itself.

The judgment of the Supreme Court of Delaware is reversed and the cause remanded for further proceedings consistent with this opinion.

Reversed and remanded.

* * *

MR. JUSTICE STEWART concurring.

I agree that the judgment must be reversed, but I reach that conclusion by a route much more direct than the one traveled by the Court. In upholding Eagle's right to deny service to the appellant solely because of his race, the Supreme Court of Delaware relied upon a statute which permits the proprietor of a restaurant to refuse to serve "persons whose reception or entertainment by him would be offensive to the major part of his customers." . . . There is no suggestion in the record that the appellant as an individual was such a person. The highest court of Delaware has thus construed this legislative enactment as authorizing discriminatory classification based exclusively on color. Such a law seems to me clearly violative of the Fourteenth Amendment. I think, therefore, that the appeal was properly taken, and that the statute, as authoritatively construed by the Supreme Court of Delaware, is constitutionally invalid.

* * *

MR. JUSTICE HARLAN, with whom MR. JUSTICE WHITTAKER joins, dissenting.

The Court's opinion, by a process of first undiscriminatingly throwing together various factual bits and pieces and then undermining the resulting structure by an equally vague disclaimer, seems to me to leave completely at sea just what it is in this record that satisfies the requirement of "state action."

I find it unnecessary, however, to inquire into the matter at this stage, for it seems to me apparent that before passing on the far-reaching constitutional questions that may, or may not, be lurking in this judgment, the case should first be sent back to the state court for clarification as to the precise basis of its decision. . . .

[The dissenting opinion of MR. JUSTICE FRANKFURTER is omitted.]

GARNER V. LOUISIANA
368 U.S. 157 (1961)

In the lead case of *Garner v. Louisiana* (No. 26), together with *Briscoe v. Louisiana* (No. 27) and *Hoston v. Louisiana* (No. 28), the Supreme Court considered the constitutionality of breach of the peace convictions for sit-ins at lunch counters in Baton Rouge, Louisiana. In *Garner* two black Southern University students took seats at the lunch counter of Sitman's drugstore. In *Briscoe* seven black students sought service at the lunch counter in the restaurant section of the Greyhound bus terminal. In *Hoston* seven Southern University students took seats at a lunch counter in Kress' department store. The students remained quietly in their seats after being told they could not be served there. They made no speeches, carried no placards, and did nothing to attract attention to themselves, except to sit at the lunch counters. The students were not asked to leave by the manager or their agents, but they were asked to leave by police officers. They were arrested and convicted of disturbing the peace when they failed to leave the premises. The students were denied relief by the Louisiana Supreme Court. *Vote: 9-0.*

* * *

MR. CHIEF JUSTICE WARREN delivered the opinion of the Court.

. . . In the view we take of the cases we find it unnecessary to reach the broader constitutional questions presented, and in accordance with our practice not to formulate a rule of constitutional law broader than is required by the precise facts presented in the record, . . . we hold that the convictions in these cases are so totally devoid of evidentiary support as to render them unconstitutional under the Due Process Clause of the Fourteenth Amendment. As in *Thompson v. City of Louisville,* [362 U.S. 199 (1960)] our inquiry does not turn on a question of sufficiency of evidence to support a conviction, but on whether these convictions rest upon any evidence which would support a finding that the petitioners' acts caused a disturbance of the peace. In addition, we cannot be concerned with whether the evidence proves the commission of some other crime, for it is as much a denial of due process to send an accused to prison following a conviction for a charge that was never made as it is to convict him upon a charge for which there is no evidence to support that conviction.

. . . Under our view of these cases, our task is to determine whether there is any evidence in the records to show that the petitioners, by their actions at the lunch counters in the business establishments involved, violated Title 14, Article 103(7), of the Louisiana Criminal Code. At the time of petitioners' acts, Article 103 provided:

"Disturbing the peace is the doing of any of the following in such a manner as would foreseeably disturb or alarm the public:

"(1) Engaging in a fistic encounter; or
"(2) Using of any unnecessarily loud, offensive, or insulting language; or
"(3) Appearing in an intoxicated condition; or
"(4) Engaging in any act in a violent and tumultuous manner by any three or more persons; or
"(5) Holding of an unlawful assembly; or
"(6) Interruption of any lawful assembly of people; or
"(7) Commission of any other act in such a manner as to unreasonably disturb or alarm the public."

. . . We think that the above discussion would give ample support to a conclusion that Louisiana law requires a finding of outwardly boisterous or unruly conduct in order to charge a defendant with "foreseeably" disturbing or alarming the public. However, because this case comes to us from a state court and necessitates a delicate involvement in federal-state relations, we are willing to assume with the respondent that the Louisiana courts might construe the statute more broadly to encompass the traditional common-law concept of disturbing the peace. Thus construed, it might permit the police to prevent an imminent public commotion even though caused by peaceful and orderly conduct on the part of the accused. . . . We therefore treat these cases as though evidence of such imminent danger, as well as evidence of a defendant's active conduct which is outwardly provocative, could support a finding that the acts might "foreseeably disturb or alarm the public" under the Louisiana statute.

Having determined what evidence is necessary to support a finding of disturbing the peace under Louisiana law, the ultimate question, as in *Thompson v. City of Louisville* . . . is whether the records in these cases contain any such evidence. With appropriate notations to the slight differences in testimony in the other two cases, we again turn to the record in No. 28. The manager of the department store in which the lunch counter was located testified that after the students had taken their seats at the "white lunch counter" where he was also occupying a seat, he advised the waitress on duty to offer the petitioners service at the counter across the aisle which served Negroes. The petitioners, however, after being "advised that they would be served at the other counter," remained in their seats, and the manager continued eating his lunch at the same counter. In No. 26, where there were no facilities to serve colored persons, the petitioners were merely told that they couldn't be served, but were never even asked to move. In No. 27, a waitress testified that the petitioners were merely told that they would have to go "to the other side to be served." The petitioners not only made no speeches, they did not even speak to anyone except to order food; they carried no placards, and did nothing, beyond their mere presence at the lunch counter, to attract attention to themselves or to others. In none of these cases was there any testimony that the petitioners were told that their mere presence was causing, or was likely to cause, a disturbance of the peace, nor that the petitioners were ever asked to leave the counters or the establishments by anyone connected with the stores.

The manager in No. 28 testified that after finishing his meal he went to the telephone and called the police department, advising them that Negroes were in his store sitting at the lunch counter reserved for whites. This is the only case in which "the owner or his agent" notified the police of the petitioners' presence at the lunch counter, and even here the manager gave no indication to the officers that he feared any disturbance or that he had received any complaint concerning the petitioners' presence. In No. 27, a waitress testified that a bus driver sitting in the restaurant notified the police that "there were several colored people sitting at the lunch counter."

In No. 26, the arresting officers were not summoned to the drugstore by anyone even remotely connected with Sitman's but, rather, by a call from an officer on his "beat" who had observed the petitioners sitting quietly at the lunch counter.

Although the manager of Kress' Department Store testified that the only conduct which he considered disruptive was the petitioners' mere presence at the counter, he did state that he called the police because he "feared that some disturbance might occur." However, his fear is completely unsubstantiated by the record. The manager continued eating his lunch in an apparently leisurely manner at the same counter at which the petitioners were sitting before calling the police. Moreover, not only did he fail to give the petitioners any warning of his alleged "fear," but he specifically testified to the fact that the petitioners were never asked to move or to leave the store. Nor did the witness elaborate on the basis of his fear except to state that "it isn't customary for the two races to sit together and eat together." In addition, there is no evidence that this alleged fear was ever communicated to the arresting officers, either at the time the manager made the initial call to police headquarters or when the police arrived at the store. Under these circumstances, the manager's general statement gives no support for the convictions within the meaning of *Thompson v. City of Louisville*. . . .

Subsequent to the manager's notification, the police arrived at the store and, without consulting the manager or anyone else on the premises, went directly to confront the petitioners. An officer asked the petitioners to leave the counter because "they were disturbing the peace and violating the law by sitting there." One of the students stated that she wished to get a glass of iced tea, but she and her friends were told, again by the police, they were disturbing the peace by sitting at a counter reserved for whites and that they would have to leave. When the petitioners continued to occupy the seats, they were arrested, as the officer testified, for disturbing the peace "[b]y sitting there" "because that place was reserved for white people." The same officer testified that the petitioners had done nothing other than take seats at that particular lunch counter which he considered to be a breach of the peace.

The respondent discusses at length the history of race relations and the high degree of racial segregation which exists throughout the South. Although there is no reference to such facts in the records, the respondent argues that the trial court took judicial notice of the general situation, as he may do under Louisiana law, and that it therefore became apparent to the court that the petitioners' presence at the lunch counters might cause a disturbance which it was the duty of the police to prevent. There is nothing in the records to indicate that the trial judge did in fact take judicial notice of anything. To extend the doctrine of judicial notice to the length pressed by the respon-dent would require us to allow the prosecution to do through argument to this Court what it is required by due process to do at the trial, and would be "to turn the doctrine into a pretext for dispensing with a trial." . . . Furthermore, unless an accused is informed at the trial of the facts of which the court is taking judicial notice, not only does he not know upon what evidence he is being convicted, but, in addition, he is deprived of any opportunity to challenge the deductions drawn from such notice or to dispute the notoriety or truth of the facts allegedly relied upon. Moreover, there is no way by which an appellate court may review the facts and law of a case and intelligently decide whether the findings of the lower court are supported by the evidence where that evidence is unknown. Such an assumption would be a denial of due process. . . .

Thus, having shown that these records contain no evidence to support a finding that petitioners disturbed the peace, either by outwardly boisterous conduct or by passive conduct likely to cause a public disturbance, we hold that these convictions violated petitioners' rights to due process of law guaranteed them by the Fourteenth Amendment to the United States Constitution. The undisputed evidence shows that the police who arrested the petitioners were left with nothing to support their actions except their own opinions that it was a breach of the peace for the petitioners to sit peacefully in a place where custom decreed they should not sit. Such activity, in the circumstances of these cases, is not evidence of any crime and cannot be so considered either by the police or by the courts.

The judgments are reversed.

* * *

MR. JUSTICE DOUGLAS concurring.

. . . There is a deep-seated pattern of segregation of the races in Louisiana, going back at least to *Plessy v. Ferguson*. . . . It was restated in 1960—the year in which petitioners were arrested and charged for sitting in white restaurants—by Act No. 630, which in its preamble states:

"WHEREAS, Louisiana has always maintained a policy of segregation of the races, and WHEREAS, it is the intention of the citizens of this sovereign state that such a policy be continued." La. Acts 1960, p. 1200

Louisiana requires that all circuses, shows, and tent exhibitions to which the public is invited have one entrance for whites and one for Negroes. La. Rev. Stat., 1950, § 4:5. No dancing, social functions, entertainment, athletic training, games, sports, contests "and other such activities involving personal and social contracts" may be open to both races. § 4:451 (1960 Supp.). Any public entertainment or athletic contest must provide separate seating arrangements and separate sanitary drinking water and "any other facilities" for the two races. § 4:452 (1960 Supp.). Marriage between members of the two races is banned. § 14:79. Segregation by race is required in prisons. § 15:752. The blind must be segregated. § 17.10. Teachers in public schools are barred from advocating desegregation of the races in the public school system. §§ 17:443, 17:462. So are other state employees. § 17:523. Segregation on trains is required. §§ 45:528-45:532. Common carriers of passengers must provide separate waiting rooms and reception room facilities for the two races (§ 45:1301 (1960 Supp.)) and separate toilets and separate facilities for drinking water as well. § 45:1303 (1960 Supp.) Employers must provide separate sanitary facilities for the two races. § 23:971 (1960 Supp.). Employers must also provide separate eating places in separate rooms and separate eating and drinking utensils for members of the two races. § 23.972 (1960 Supp.) Persons of one race may not establish their residence in a community of another race without approval of the majority of the other race. § 33:5066. Court dockets must reveal the race of the parties in divorce actions. § 13:917. And all public parks, recreation centers, playgrounds, community centers and "other such facilities at which swimming, dancing, golfing, skating or other recreational activities are conducted" must be segregated. § 33:4558.1 (1960 Supp.).

Though there may have been no state law or municipal ordinance that *in terms* required segregation of the races in restaurants, it is plain that the proprietors in the instant cases were segregating blacks from whites pursuant to Louisiana's custom. Segregation is basic to the structure of Louisiana as a community; the custom that maintains it is at least as powerful as any law. If these proprietors also choose segregation, their preference does not make the action "private," rather than "state," action. If it did, a minuscule of private prejudice would convert state into private action. Moreover, where the segregation policy is the policy of a State, it matters not that the agency to enforce it is a private enterprise. . . .

It is my view that a State may not constitutionally enforce a policy of segregation in restaurant facilities. Some of the argument assumed that restaurants are "private" property in the sense that one's home is "private" property. They are, of course, "private" property for many purposes of the Constitution. Yet so are street railways, power plants, warehouses, and other types of enterprises which have long been held to be affected with a public interest. Where constitutional rights are involved, the proprietary interests of individuals must give way. . . .

[The concurring opinions of MR. JUSTICE HARLAN and MR. JUSTICE FRANKFURTER are omitted.]

HAMM V. CITY OF ROCK HILL
379 U.S. 306 (1964)

In *Hamm* two blacks were refused service at the McCrory store lunch counter after making purchases in other parts of the store. The manager called the police when they refused to leave the lunch counter, and they were later convicted under § 16-388 of the South Carolina Code of Laws, which made it an offense for anyone to enter a place of business after having been warned not to do so. In the companion case, *Lupper v. Arkansas,* a group of blacks were refused service at the tearoom of a department store in Little Rock. They were arrested for refusing to leave and were convicted under § 41-1433 of an Arkansas statute that prohibited a person from remaining after having been requested to leave by the owner or manager. Their convictions in *Hamm* and *Lupper* were upheld by the Supreme Court of South Carolina and Alabama, respectively. *Vote: 5-4.*

* * *

MR. JUSTICE CLARK delivered the opinion of the Court.

These are "sit-in" cases that came here from the highest courts of South Carolina and Arkansas, respectively. . . . The petitioners asserted both in the state courts and here the denial of rights, privileges, and immunities secured by the Fourteenth Amendment; in addition, they claim here that the Civil Rights Act of 1964 . . . passed subsequent to their convictions and the affirmances thereof in the state courts, abated these actions.

. . . We hold that the convictions must be vacated and the prosecutions dismissed. The Civil Rights Act of 1964 forbids discrimination in places of public accommodation and removes peaceful attempts to be served on an equal basis from the category of punishable activities. Although the conduct in the present cases occurred prior to enactment of the Act, the still-pending convictions are abated by its passage.

. . . We treat these cases as involving places of public accommodation covered by the Civil Rights Act of 1964. Under that statute, a place of public accommodation is defined to include one which serves or offers to serve interstate travelers. Applying the rules of §§ 201(b)(2), (c) we find that each of them offers to serve interstate travelers. . . .

. . . Under the Civil Rights Act, petitioners' conduct could not be the subject of trespass prosecutions, federal or state, if it had occurred after the enactment of the statute.

Title II includes several sections, some of which are relevant here, that create federal statutory rights. The first is § 201(a) declaring that "[a]ll persons shall be entitled to the full and equal enjoyment of the goods, services, facilities, privileges, advantages, and accommodations of any place of public accommodation," which as we have found includes the establishments here involved. Next, § 203 provides:

> "No person shall (a) withhold, deny, or attempt to withhold or deny, or deprive or attempt to deprive, any person of any right or privilege secured by section 201 or 202, or (b) intimidate, threaten or coerce, or attempt to intimidate, threaten, or coerce any person with the purpose of interfering with any right or privilege secured by section 201 or 202, or (c) *punish or attempt to punish any person for exercising or attempting to exercise any right or privilege secured by section 201 or 202.*"

On its face, this language prohibits prosecution of any person for seeking service in a covered establishment, because of his race or color. It has been argued, however, that victims of discrimination must make use of the exclusive statutory mechanisms for the redress of grievances, and not resort to extralegal means. Although we agree that the law generally condemns self-help, the language of § 203(c) supports a conclusion that nonforcible attempts to gain admittance to or remain in establishments covered by the Act, are immunized from prosecution, for the statute speaks of exercising or attempting to exercise a "right or privilege" secured by its earlier provisions. The availability of the Act as a defense against punishment is not limited solely to those who pursue the statutory remedies. The legislative history specifically notes that the Act would be a defense to criminal trespass, breach of the peace and similar prosecutions. . . . In effect the Act prohibits the application of state laws in a way that would deprive any person of the rights granted under the Act. The Supremacy Clause, Art. VI, cl. 2, requires this result where "there is a clear collision" between state and federal law . . . or a conflict between federal law, and the application of an otherwise valid state enactment. . . . There can be no question that this was the intended result here in light of § 203(c). The present convictions and the command of the Civil Rights Act of 1964 are clearly in direct conflict. The only remaining question is the effect of the Act on judgments rendered, but not finalized, before its passage.

. . . Last Term, in *Bell v. Maryland,* 378 U.S. 226 [1964], we noted the existence of a body of federal and state law to the effect that convictions on direct review at the time the conduct in question is rendered no longer unlawful by statute, must abate. We consider first the effect the Civil Rights Act would have on petitioners' convictions if they had been federal convictions, and then the import of the fact that these are state and not federal convictions. We think it is clear that the convictions, if federal, would abate.

. . . We cannot believe that Congress, in enacting such a far-reaching and comprehensive scheme, intended the Act to operate less effectively than the run-of-the-mill repealer. Since the provisions of the Act would abate all federal prosecutions it follows that the same rule must prevail under the Supremacy Clause which requires that a contrary state practice or state statute must give way. Here the Act intervened before either of the judgments under attack was finalized. Just as in federal cases abatement must follow in these state prosecutions. Rather than a retroactive intrusion into state criminal law this is but the application of a long-standing federal rule, namely, that since the Civil Rights Act substitutes a right for a crime any state statute, or its application, to the contrary must by virtue of the Supremacy Clause give way under the normal abatement rule covering pending convictions arising out of a pre-enactment activity. The great purpose of the civil rights legislation was to obliterate the effect of a distressing chapter of our history. This demands no less than the application of a normal rule of statutory construction to strike down pending convictions inconsistent with the purposes of the Act.

Far from finding a bar to the application of the rule where a state statute is involved, we find that our construction of the effect of the Civil Rights Act is more than statutory. It is required by the Supremacy Clause of the Constitution. . . . Future state prosecutions under the Act being unconstitutional and there being no saving clause in the Act itself, convictions for pre-enactment violations would be equally unconstitutional and abatement necessarily follows.

Nor do we find persuasive reasons for imputing to the Congress an intent to insulate such prosecutions. As we have said, Congress, as well as the two Presidents who recommended the legislation, clearly intended to eradicate an unhappy chapter in our history. The peaceful conduct for which petitioners were prosecuted was on behalf of a principle since embodied in the law of the land. The convictions were based on the theory that the rights of a property owner had been violated. However, the supposed right to discriminate on the basis of race, at least in covered establishments, was nullified by the statute. Under such circumstances the actionable nature of the acts in question must be viewed in the light of the statute and its legislative purpose.

... In our view Congress clearly had the power to extend immunity to pending prosecutions. Some might say that to permit these convictions to stand would have no effect on interstate commerce which we have held justified the adoption of the Act. But even if this be true, the principle of abatement is so firmly imbedded in our jurisprudence as to be a necessary and proper part of every statute working a repealer of criminal legislation. Where Congress sets out to regulate a situation within its power, the Constitution affords it a wide choice of remedies. This being true, the only question remaining is whether Congress exercised its power in the Act to abate the prosecutions here. If we held that it did not we would then have to pass on the constitutional question of whether the Fourteenth Amendment, without the benefit of the Civil Rights Act, operates of its own force to bar criminal trespass convictions, where, as here, they are used to enforce a pattern of racial discrimination. As we have noted, some of the Justices joining this opinion believe that the Fourteenth Amendment does so operate; others are of the contrary opinion. Since this point is not free from doubt, and since as we have found Congress has ample power to extend the statute to pending convictions we avoid that question by favoring an interpretation of the statute which renders a constitutional decision unnecessary.

In short, now that Congress has exercised its constitutional power in enacting the Civil Rights Act of 1964 and declared that the public policy of our country is to prohibit discrimination in public accommodations as therein defined, there is no public interest to be served in the further prosecution of the petitioners. And in accordance with the long-established rule of our cases they must be abated and the judgment in each is therefore vacated and the charges are ordered dismissed.

It is so ordered.

[The concurring opinion of MR. JUSTICE DOUGLAS, with whom MR. JUSTICE GOLDBERG joins, is omitted.]

* * *

MR. JUSTICE BLACK dissenting.

... The record shows that the two petitioners in *Lupper* ... were part of a group of persons who went to a department store tearoom, seated themselves at tables and at the counter as part of a "sit-in" demonstration, and refused to leave when asked to do so. The Court says that this conduct "could not be the subject of trespass prosecutions, federal or state, if it had occurred after the enactment of the statute." I do not understand from what the Court says that it interprets those provisions of the Civil Rights Act which give a right to be served without discrimination in an establishment which the Act covers as also authorizing persons who are unlawfully refused service a "right" to take the new law into their own hands by sitting down and occupying the premises for as long as they choose to stay. I think one of the chief purposes of the 1964 Civil Rights Act was to take such disputes out of the streets and restaurants and into the courts, which Congress has granted power to provide an adequate and orderly judicial remedy.

Even assuming, however, that the Civil Rights Act was intended to let people who enter restaurants take the law into their own hands by forcibly remaining when service is refused them, this would be no basis for holding that Congress also meant to compel States to abate convictions like these for lawless conduct occurring before the Act was passed.... The judge-made "common law rule" of construction on which the Court relies has been applied heretofore only where there was a repeal of one statute by another—not, as my Brother HARLAN points out, where as here a later law passed by Congress places certain restrictions on the operation of the still valid law of a State. But even if the old common-law rule of construction taken alone would otherwise have abated these convictions, Congress nearly a century ago passed a "saving statute," 1 U.S.C. § 109 (1958 ed.), to keep courts from imputing to it an intent to abate cases retroactively, unless such an intent was expressly stated in the law it passed.... The purpose of this statute is plain on its face—it was to prevent courts from imputing to Congress an intent which Congress never entertained.... By today's discovery of a "long-established rule of our cases," the Court has now put back on Congress the burden of spelling out expressly, statute by statute, in laws passed hereafter that it does not want to upset convictions for past crimes, a burden which Congress renounced nearly 100 years ago and which it did not know it had when it passed the 1964 Act.

[The dissenting opinions of MR. JUSTICE HARLAN, MR. JUSTICE STEWART, and MR. JUSTICE WHITE are omitted.]

EDWARDS V. SOUTH CAROLINA
372 U.S. 229 (1963)

In expressing their dissatisfaction with the discriminatory treatment against blacks in South Carolina and in general, 187 black high school and college students peacefully assembled at the state house grounds of the South Carolina legislature. After a crowd of some 200 to 300 onlookers had collected in the area, police advised the black students that they would be arrested if they did not disperse within 15 minutes. No evidence was presented at the trial that violence or a threat of violence existed on the part of any member of the crowd. The students responded to the police by singing patriotic and religious songs while stamping their feet and clapping their hands. The police arrested the students, and they were convicted of a South Carolina breach of peace offense. The sentences ranged from a $10 fine or five days in jail to a $100 fine or 30 days in jail. The South Carolina Supreme Court affirmed the judgments of the trial court. *Vote: 8-1.*

* * *

MR. JUSTICE STEWART delivered the opinion of the Court.

. . . The petitioners contend that there was a complete absence of any evidence of the commission of [the breach of the peace] offense and that they were thus denied one of the most basic elements of due process of law. . . . Whatever the merits of this contention, we need not pass upon it in the present case. The state courts have held that the petitioners' conduct constituted breach of peace under state law, and we may accept their decision as binding upon us to that extent. But it nevertheless remains our duty in a case such as this to make an independent examination of the whole record. . . . And it is clear to us that in arresting, convicting, and punishing the petitioners under the circumstances disclosed by this record, South Carolina infringed the petitioners' constitutionally protected rights of free speech, free assembly, and freedom to petition for redress of their grievances.

It has long been established that these First Amendment freedoms are protected by the Fourteenth Amendment from invasion by the States. *Gitlow v. New York,* 268 U.S. 652 [1925] . . . The circumstances in this case reflect an exercise of these basic constitutional rights in their most pristine and classic form. The petitioners felt aggrieved by laws of South Carolina which allegedly "prohibited Negro privileges in this State." They peaceably assembled at the site of the State Government and there peaceably expressed their grievances "to the citizens of South Carolina, along with the Legislative Bodies of South Carolina." Not until they were told by police officials that they must disperse on pain of arrest did they do more. Even then, they but sang patriotic and religious songs after one of their leaders had delivered a "religious harangue." There was no violence or threat of violence on their part, or on the part of any member of the crowd watching them. Police protection was "ample."

This, therefore, was a far cry from the situation in *Feiner v. New York,* 340 U.S. 315 [at 317, 318, 321 (1951)], where two policemen were faced with a crowd which was "pushing, shoving and milling around," . . . where at least one member of the crowd "threatened violence if the police did not act," . . . where "the crowd was pressing closer around petitioner and the officer," . . . and where "the speaker passes the bounds of argument or persuasion and undertakes incitement to riot." . . . And the record is barren of any evidence of "fighting words." See *Chaplinsky v. New Hampshire,* 315 U.S. 568 [1942].

We do not review in this case criminal convictions resulting from the evenhanded application of a precise and narrowly drawn regulatory statute evincing a legislative judgment that certain specific conduct be limited or prescribed. If, for example, the petitioners had been convicted upon evidence that they had violated a law regulating traffic, or had disobeyed a law reasonably limiting the periods during which the State House grounds were open to the public, this would be a different case. . . . These petitioners were convicted of an offense so generalized as to be, in the words of the South Carolina Supreme Court, "not susceptible to exact definition." And they were convicted upon evidence which showed no more than the opinions which they were peaceably expressing were sufficiently opposed to the views of the majority of the community to attract a crowd and necessitate police protection.

The Fourteenth Amendment does not permit a State to make criminal the peaceful expression of unpopular views. "[A] function of free speech under our system of government is to invite dispute. It may indeed best serve its high purpose when it induces a condition of unrest, creates dissatisfaction with conditions as they are, or even stirs people to anger. Speech is often provocative and challenging. It may strike at prejudices and preconceptions and have profound unsettling effects as it presses for acceptance of an idea. That is why freedom of speech . . . is . . . protected against censorship or punishment, unless shown likely to produce a clear and present danger of a serious substantive evil that rises far above public inconvenience, annoyance, or unrest. . . . There is no room under our Constitution for a more restrictive view. For the alternative would lead to a standardization of ideas either by legislatures, courts, or dominant political or community groups." *Terminiello v. Chicago,* 337 U.S. 1, 4-5 [1949]. As in the *Terminiello* case, the courts of South Carolina have defined a criminal offense so as to permit conviction of the petitioners if their speech "stirred people to anger, invited public dispute, or brought about a condition of unrest. A conviction resting on any of these grounds may not stand." *Id.,* at 5.

. . . For these reasons we conclude that these criminal convictions cannot stand.

Reversed.

* * *

MR. JUSTICE CLARK dissenting.

. . . Petitioners . . . had a right to peaceable assembly, to espouse their cause and to petition, but in my view the manner in which they exercised those rights was by no means the passive demonstration which this Court relates; rather, as the City Manager of Columbia testified, "a dangerous situation was really building up" which South Carolina's courts expressly found had created "an actual interference with traffic and an imminently threatened disturbance of the peace of the community." Since the Court does not attack the state courts' findings and accepts the convictions as "binding" to the extent that the petitioners' conduct constituted a breach of the peace, it is difficult for me to understand its understatement of the facts and reversal of the convictions.

COX V. LOUISIANA (COX I)
379 U.S. 536 (1965)

In December 1961, Reverend B. Elton Cox, a CORE field secretary, was the leader of a civil rights demonstration of approximately 2,000 students who assembled at the site of the Old State Capitol building in Baton Rouge, Louisiana. The demonstration was in response to the arrest of 23 students from Southern University for picketing segregated lunch counters in downtown Baton Rouge. The demonstration was also part of a general protest movement against racial segregation. After Cox led the group to the site of the courthouse where the 23 students were jailed, they sang songs and displayed signs. Cox then addressed the group, telling the students to eat at segregated lunch counters. After observing "muttering" and "grumbling" by white onlookers, the sheriff construed Cox's remarks as inflammatory and ordered the dispersal of the group. When they refused to leave, the police used tear gas to break up the demonstrations. The next day, Cox was arrested and charged with four Louisiana offenses: criminal conspiracy, disturbing the peace, obstructing public passages, and picketing before a courthouse. He was convicted on the charges of peace disturbance, obstructing public passages, and courthouse picketing and was sentenced to 21 months in jail and fined $5,700. The Louisiana Supreme Court affirmed the conviction. *Cox I* addressed the appeal of the peace disturbance and obstructing public passages convictions. *Vote: 7-2.*

* * *

MR. JUSTICE GOLDBERG delivered the opinion of the Court.

. . . Appellant was convicted of violating a Louisiana "disturbing the peace" statute, which provides:

"Whoever with intent to provoke a breach of the peace, or under circumstances such that a breach of the peace may be occasioned thereby . . . crowds or congregates with others . . . in or upon . . . a public street or public highway, or upon a public sidewalk, or any other public place or building . . . and who fails or refuses to disperse and move on . . . when ordered so to do by any law enforcement officer of any municipality, or parish, in which such act or acts are committed, or by any law enforcement officer of the state of Louisiana, or any other authorized person . . . shall be guilty of disturbing the peace." La. Rev. Stat. § 14:103.1 (Cum. Supp. 1962)

It is clear to us that on the facts of this case, which are strikingly similar to those present in *Edwards v. South Carolina,* 372 U.S. 229 [1963] . . . Louisiana infringed upon appellant's rights of free speech and free assembly by convicting him under this statute. As in *Edwards,* we do not find it necessary to pass upon appellant's contention that there was a complete absence of evidence so that his conviction deprived him of liberty without due process of law. . . . We hold that Louisiana may not constitutionally punish appellant under this statute for engaging in the type of conduct which this record reveals, and also that the statute as authoritatively interpreted by the Louisiana Supreme Court is unconstitutionally broad in scope.

The Louisiana courts have held that appellant's conduct constituted a breach of the peace under state law, and, as in *Edwards,* "we may accept their decision as binding upon us to that extent," . . . but our independent examination of the record, which we are required to make, shows no conduct which the State had a right to prohibit as a breach of the peace.

. . . We now turn to the issue of the validity of appellant's conviction for violating the Louisiana statute, La. Rev. Stat. § 14:100.1 (Cum. Supp. 1962), which provides:

"No person shall wilfully obstruct the free, convenient and normal use of any public sidewalk, street, highway, bridge, alley, road, or other passageway, or the entrance, corridor or passage of any public building, structure, watercraft or ferry, by impeding, hindering, stifling, retarding or restraining traffic or passage thereon or therein.

"Providing however nothing herein contained shall apply to a bona fide legitimate labor organization or to any of its legal activities such as picketing, lawful assembly or concerted activity in the interest of its members for the purpose of accomplishing or securing more favorable wage standards, hours of employment and working conditions."

Appellant was convicted under this statute, not for leading the march to the vicinity of the courthouse, which the Louisiana Supreme Court stated to have been "orderly," . . . but for leading the meeting on the sidewalk across the street from the courthouse. . . . In upholding appellant's conviction under this statute, the Louisiana Supreme Court thus construed the statute so as to apply to public assemblies which do not have as their specific purpose the obstruction of traffic. There is no doubt from the record in this case that this far sidewalk was obstructed, and thus, as so construed, appellant violated the statute.

Appellant, however, contends that as so construed and applied in this case, the statute is an unconstitutional infringement on freedom of speech and assembly. This contention on the facts here presented raises an issue with which this Court has dealt in many decisions, that is, the right of a State or municipality to regulate the use of city streets and other facilities to assure the safety and convenience of the people in their use and the concomitant right of the people of free speech and assembly. . . .

. . . The rights of free speech and assembly, while fundamental in our democratic society, still do not mean that everyone with opinions or beliefs to express may address a group at any public place at any time. The constitutional guarantee of liberty implies the existence of an organized society maintaining public order, without which liberty itself would be lost in the excesses of anarchy. . . .

. . . We emphatically reject the notion urged by appellant that the First and Fourteenth Amendments afford the same kind of freedom to those who would communicate ideas by conduct such as patrolling, marching, and picketing on streets and highways, as these amendments afford to those who communicate ideas by pure speech. . . .

We have no occasion in this case to consider the constitutionality of the uniform, consistent, and nondiscriminatory application of a statute forbidding all access to streets and other public facilities for parades and meetings. Although the statute here involved on its face precludes all street assemblies and parades, it has not been so applied and enforced by the Baton Rouge authorities. City officials who testified for the State clearly indicated that certain meetings and parades are permitted in Baton Rouge, even though they have the effect of obstructing traffic, provided prior approval is obtained. This was confirmed in oral argument before this Court by counsel for the State. . . . From all the evidence before us it appears that the authorities in Baton Rouge permit or prohibit parades or street meetings in their completely uncontrolled discretion.

. . . This Court has recognized that the lodging of such broad discretion in a public official allows him to determine which expressions of view will be permitted and which will not. This thus sanctions a device for the suppression of the communication of ideas and permits the official to act as a censor. . . . Also inherent in such a system allowing parades or meetings only with the prior permission of an official is the obvious danger to the right of a person or group not to be denied equal protection of the laws. . . . It is clearly unconstitutional to enable a public official to determine which expressions of view will be permitted and which will not or to engage in invidious discrimination among persons or groups either by use of a statute providing a system of broad discretionary licensing power or, as in this case, the equivalent of such a system by selective enforcement of an extremely broad prohibitory statute.

. . . [I]t is clear that the practice in Baton Rouge allowing unfettered discretion in local officials in the regulation of the use of the streets for peaceful parades and meetings is an unwarranted abridgment of appellant's freedom of speech and assembly secured to him by the First Amendment, as applied to the States by the Fourteenth Amendment. It follows, therefore, that appellant's conviction for violating the statute as so applied and enforced must be reversed.

For the reasons discussed above the judgment of the Supreme Court of Louisiana is reversed.

Reversed.

[The concurring opinions of MR. JUSTICE BLACK and MR. JUSTICE CLARK are found in *Cox II.*]

[The opinion of MR. JUSTICE WHITE, joined by MR. JUSTICE HARLAN, concurring in part and dissenting in part, is found in *Cox II.*]

COX V. LOUISIANA (COX II)
379 U.S. 559 (1965)

Cox II grew out of the circumstances surrounding *Cox I. Cox II* involved the appeal of Rev. Cox's third conviction, courthouse picketing. *Vote: 5-4.*

* * *

MR. JUSTICE GOLDBERG delivered the opinion of the Court.

. . . We shall first consider appellant's contention that this statute must be declared invalid on its face as an unjustified restriction upon freedoms guaranteed by the First and Fourteenth Amendments to the United States Constitution.

. . . [The Louisiana] statute, unlike the two previously considered, is a precise, narrowly drawn regulatory statute which proscribes certain specific behavior. . . . It prohibits a particular type of conduct, namely, picketing and parading, in a few specified locations, in or near courthouses.

There can be no question that a State has a legitimate interest in protecting its judicial system from the pressures which picketing near a courthouse might create. Since we are committed to a government of laws and not of men, it is of the utmost importance that the administration of justice be absolutely fair and orderly. This Court has recognized that the unhindered and untrammeled functioning of our courts is part of the very foundation of our constitutional democracy. . . .

Nor does such a statute infringe upon the constitutionally protected rights of free speech and free assembly. The conduct which is the subject of this statute—picketing and parading—is subject to regulation even though intertwined with expression and association. The examples are many of the application by this Court of the principle that certain forms of conduct mixed with speech may be regulated or prohibited. . . .

. . . We hold that this statute on its face is a valid law dealing with conduct subject to regulation so as to vindicate important interests of society and that the fact that free speech is intermingled with such conduct does not bring with it constitutional protection.

We now deal with the Louisiana statute as applied to the conduct in this case. The group of 2,000, led by appellant, paraded and demonstrated before the courthouse. Judges and court officers were in attendance to discharge their respective functions. It is undisputed that a major purpose of the demonstration was to protest what the demonstrators considered an "illegal" arrest of 23 students the previous day. While the students had not been arraigned or their trial set for any day certain, they were charged with violation of the law, and the judges responsible for trying them and passing upon the legality of their arrest were then in the building.

It is, of course, true that most judges will be influenced only by what they see and hear in court. However, judges are human; and the legislature has the right to recognize the danger that some judges, jurors, and other court officials, will be consciously or unconsciously influenced by demonstrations in or near their courtrooms both prior to and at the time of the trial. A State may also properly protect the judicial process from being misjudged in the minds of the public. Suppose demonstrators paraded and picketed for weeks with signs asking that indictments be dismissed, and that a judge, completely uninfluenced by these demonstrations, dismissed the indictments. A State may protect against the possibility of a conclusion by the public under these circumstances that the judge's action was in part a product of intimidation and did not flow only from the fair and orderly working of the judicial process. . . .

. . . There are, however, more substantial constitutional objections arising from appellant's conviction on the particular facts of this case. Appellant was convicted for demonstrating not "in," but "near" the courthouse. It is undisputed that the demonstration took place on the west sidewalk, the far side of the street, exactly 101 feet from the courthouse steps and, judging from the pictures in the record, approximately 125 feet from the courthouse itself. The question is raised as to whether the failure of the statute to define the word "near" renders it unconstitutionally vague. . . . It is clear that there is some lack of specificity in a word such as "near." While this lack of specificity may not render the statute unconstitutionally vague, at least as applied to a demonstration within the sight and hearing of those in the courthouse, it is clear that the statute, with respect to the determination of how near the courthouse a particular demonstration can be, foresees a degree of on-the-spot administrative interpretation by officials charged with responsibility for administering and enforcing it. It is apparent that demonstrators, such as those involved here, would justifiably tend to rely on this administrative interpretation of how "near" the courthouse a particular demonstration might take place. Louisiana's statutory policy of preserving order around the courthouse would counsel encouragement of just such reliance. This administrative discretion to construe the term "near" concerns a limited control of the streets and other areas in the immediate vicinity of the courthouse and is the type of narrow discretion which this Court has recognized as the proper role of responsible officials in making determinations concerning the time, place, duration, and manner of demonstrations. . . . It is not the type of unbridled discretion which would allow an official to pick and choose among expressions of view the ones he will permit to use the streets and other public facilities, which we have invalidated in the obstruction of public passages statute as applied in [*Cox I*]. . . . Nor does this limited administrative regulation of traffic which the Court has consistently recognized as necessary and permissible, constitute a waiver of law which is beyond the power of the police. Obviously telling demonstrators how far from the courthouse steps is "near" the courthouse for purposes of a permissible peaceful demonstration is a far cry from allowing one to commit, for example, murder, or robbery.

The record here clearly shows that the officials present gave permission for the demonstration to take place across the street from the courthouse. . . .

. . . Thus, the highest police officials of the city, in the presence of the Sheriff and Mayor, in effect told the demonstrators that they could meet where they did, 101 feet from the courthouse steps, but could not meet closer to the courthouse. In effect, appellant was advised that a demonstration at the place it was held would not be one "near" the courthouse within the terms of the statute.

. . . There remains just one final point: the effect of the Sheriff's order to disperse. The State in effect argued that this order somehow removed the prior grant of permission and reliance on the officials' construction that the demonstration on the far side of the street was not illegal as being "near" the courthouse. This, however, we cannot accept. Appellant was led to believe that his demonstration on the far side of the street violated no statute. He was expressly ordered to leave, not because he was peacefully demonstrating too near the courthouse, nor because a time limit originally set had expired, but because officials erroneously concluded that what he said threatened a breach of the peace. . . . [E]ven if we were to accept the State's version that the sole reason for terminating the demonstration was that appellant exceeded the narrow time limits set by the police, his conviction could not be sustained. Assuming the place of the meeting was appropriate—as appellant justifiably concluded from the official grant of permission—nothing in this courthouse statute, nor in the breach of the peace or obstruction of public passages statutes with their broad sweep and application that we have condemned in [*Cox I*], authorizes the police to draw the narrow time line, unrelated to any policy of these statutes, that would be approved if we were to sustain appellant's conviction on this ground. Indeed, the allowance of such unfettered discretion in the police would itself constitute a procedure such as that condemned in [*Cox I*]. In any event . . . it is our conclusion from the record that the dispersal order had nothing to do with any time or place limitation, and thus, on this ground alone, it is clear that the dispersal order did not remove the protection accorded appellant by the original grant of permission.

. . . The application of these principles requires us to reverse the judgment of the Supreme Court of Louisiana.

Reversed.

* * *

MR. JUSTICE BLACK concurring in [*Cox I*] and dissenting in [*Cox II*].

. . . I agree with that part of the Court's opinion holding that the Louisiana breach-of-the-peace statute on its face and as construed by the State Supreme Court is so broad as to be unconstitutionally vague under the First and Fourteenth Amendments. . . . The statute does not itself define the conditions upon which people who want to express views may be allowed to use the public streets and highways, but leaves this to be defined by law enforcement officers. The statute therefore neither forbids all crowds to congregate and picket on streets, nor is it narrowly drawn to prohibit congregating or patrolling under certain clearly defined conditions while preserving the freedom to speak of those who are using the streets as streets in the ordinary way that the State permits. A state statute of either of the two types just mentioned, regulating *conduct*—patrolling and marching—as distinguished from *speech,* would in my judgment be constitutional, subject only to the condition that if such a law had the effect of indirectly impinging on freedom of speech, press, or religion, it would be unconstitutional if under the circumstances it appeared that the State's interest in suppressing the conduct was not sufficient to outweigh the individual's interest in engaging in conduct closely involving his First Amendment freedoms. . . .

. . . The Louisiana law against obstructing the streets and sidewalks, while applied here so as to convict Negroes for assembling and picketing on streets and sidewalks for the purpose of publicly protesting racial discrimination, expressly provides that the statute shall not bar picketing and assembly by labor unions protesting unfair treatment of union members. I believe that the First and Fourteenth Amendments require that if the streets of a town are open to some views, they must be open to all. It is worth noting in passing that the objectives of labor unions and of the group led by Cox here may have much in common. . . . [B]y specifically permitting picketing for the publication of labor union views, Louisiana is attempting to pick and choose among the views it is willing to have discussed on its streets. It thus is trying to prescribe by law what matters of public interest people whom it allows to assemble on its streets may and may not discuss. This seems to me to be censorship in a most odious form, unconstitutional under the First and Fourteenth Amendments. And to deny this appellant and his group use of the streets because of their views against racial discrimination, while allowing other groups to use the streets to voice opinions on other subjects, also amounts, I think, to an invidious discrimination forbidden by the Equal Protection Clause of the Fourteenth Amendment. . . . For these reasons I concur in reversing the conviction based on this law.

I would sustain the conviction of appellant for violation of Louisiana's [obstructing of public passages statute]. . . . While I agree that the record does not show boisterous or violent conduct or indecent language on the part of the "demonstrators," the ample evidence that this group planned the march on the courthouse and carried it out for the express purpose of influencing the courthouse officials in the performance of their official duties brings this case squarely within the prohibitions of the Louisiana statute and I think leaves us with no alternative but to sustain the conviction unless the statute itself is unconstitutional, and I do not believe that this statute is unconstitutional, either on its face or as applied.

This statute, like the federal one which it closely resembles, was enacted to protect courts and court officials from the intimidation and dangers that inhere in huge gatherings at courthouse doors and jail doors to protest arrests and to influence court officials in performing their duties. The very purpose of a court system is to adjudicate controversies, both criminal and civil, in the calmness and solemnity of the courtroom according to legal procedures. Justice cannot be rightly administered, nor are the lives and safety of prisoners secure, where throngs of people clamor against the processes of justice right outside the courthouse or jailhouse doors. The streets are not now and never have been the proper place to administer justice. Use of the streets for such purposes has always proved disastrous to individual liberty in the long run, whatever fleeting benefits may have appeared to have been achieved. And minority groups, I venture to suggest, are the ones who always have suffered and always will suffer most when street multitudes are allowed to substitute their pressures for the less glamorous but more dependable and temperate processes of the law. Experience demonstrates that it is not a far step from what to many seems the earnest, honest, patriotic, kind-spirited multitude of today, to the fanatical, threatening, lawless mob of tomorrow. And the crowds that press in the streets for noble goals today can be supplanted tomorrow by street mobs pressuring the courts for precisely opposite ends.

[The opinion of MR. JUSTICE CLARK, concurring in *Cox I* and dissenting in *Cox II*, is omitted.]

[The opinion of MR. JUSTICE WHITE, with whom MR. JUSTICE HARLAN joins, concurring in part and dissenting in part, is omitted.]

WALKER V. CITY OF BIRMINGHAM
388 U.S. 307 (1967)

In April 1963, the Southern Christian Leadership Conference (SCLC) and the Alabama Christian Movement for Human Rights made plans to demonstrate during the week preceding Easter Sunday in Birmingham, Alabama, to peacefully protest segregated practices. A representative of the organization, Lola Hendricks, went to the commissioner's office at city hall to apply for a permit to picket and parade and was refused by Commissioner Eugene "Bull" Connor. Subsequent attempts to secure a permit were unsuccessful. Pickets and sit-ins took place April 8-10 at various Birmingham stores and lunch counters. On April 10, the city sought an ex parte injunction directing the leaders of the demonstrations to refrain from their activities. The leaders—Rev. Wyatt T. Walker, Rev. Martin Luther King Jr., and Rev. Ralph Abernathy—were served with copies of the injunction on Thursday and on Good Friday. Because they believed that the injunction was unconstitutional, they disobeyed it and planned to continue the peaceful demonstrations on Easter weekend. The Birmingham police arrested King and Abernathy on Good Friday. Walker organized the Easter Sunday demonstration. On Monday the civil rights leaders sought to dissolve the injunction on the grounds that it was overbroad, vague, and restrained free speech, but the court, pointing out that there had been neither a motion to dissolve the injunction nor an effort to comply with it by applying for a permit, found them in contempt of court. The petitioners were given a sentence of five days in jail and a $50 fine. The Supreme Court of Alabama affirmed the convictions. *Vote: 5-4.*

* * *

MR. JUSTICE STEWART delivered the opinion of the Court.

. . . *Howat v. Kansas,* 258 U.S. 181 [1922], was decided by this Court almost 50 years ago. That was a case in which people had been punished by a Kansas trial court for refusing to obey an antistrike injunction issued under the state industrial relations act. They had claimed a right to disobey the court's order upon the ground that the state statute and the injunction based upon it were invalid under the Federal Constitution. . . .

This Court, in dismissing the writ of error, not only unanimously accepted but fully approved the validity of the rule of state law upon which the judgment of the Kansas court was grounded:

> "An injunction duly issuing out of a court of general jurisdiction with equity powers upon pleadings invoking its action, and served upon persons made parties therein and within the jurisdiction, must be obeyed by them however erroneous the action of the court may be, even if the error be in the assumption of the validity of a seeming but void law going to the merits of the case. It is for the court of first instance to determine the question of the validity of the law, and until its decision is reversed for error by orderly review, either by itself or by a higher court, its orders based on its decision are to be respected, and disobedience of them is contempt of its lawful authority, to be punished." 258 U.S., at 189-190

The rule of state law accepted and approved in *Howat v. Kansas* is consistent with the rule of law followed by the federal courts.

In the present case, however, we are asked to hold that this rule of law, upon which the Alabama courts relied, was constitutionally impermissible. We are asked to say that the Constitution compelled Alabama to allow the petitioners to violate this injunction, to organize and engage in these mass street parades and demonstrations, without any previous effort on their part to have the injunction dissolved or modified, or any attempt to secure a parade permit in accordance with its terms. Whatever the limits of *Howat v. Kansas,* we cannot accept the petitioners' contentions in the circumstances of this case.

Without question the state court that issued the injunction had, as a court of equity, jurisdiction over the petitioners and over the subject matter of the controversy. And this is not a case where the injunction was transparently invalid or had only a frivolous pretense to validity. We have consistently recognized the strong interest of state and local governments in regulating the use of their streets and other public places. . . . When protest takes the form of mass demonstrations, parades, or picketing on public streets and sidewalks, the free passage of traffic and the prevention of public disorder and violence become important objects of legitimate state concern. . . .

The generality of the language contained in the Birmingham parade ordinance upon which the injunction was based would unquestionably raise substantial constitutional issues concerning some of its provisions. . . . The petitioners, however, did not even attempt to apply to the Alabama courts for an authoritative construction of the ordinance. Had they

done so, those courts might have given the licensing authority granted in the ordinance a narrow and precise scope, as did the New Hampshire courts in *Cox v. New Hampshire,* [312 U.S. 569 (1941)] and *Poulos v. New Hampshire,* [345 U.S. 395 (1953)]. Here, just as in *Cox* and *Poulos,* it could not be assumed that this ordinance was void on its face.

The breadth and vagueness of the injunction itself would also unquestionably be subject to substantial constitutional question. But the way to raise that question was to apply to the Alabama courts to have the injunction modified or dissolved. The injunction in all events clearly prohibited mass parading without a permit, and the evidence shows that the petitioners fully understood that prohibition when they violated it.

The petitioners also claim that they were free to disobey the injunction because the parade ordinance on which it was based had been administered in the past in an arbitrary and discriminatory fashion. In support of this claim they sought to introduce evidence that, a few days before the injunction issued, requests for permits to picket had been made to a member of the city commission. One request had been rudely rebuffed, and this same official had later made clear that he was without power to grant the permit alone since the issuance of such permits was the responsibility of the entire city commission. Assuming the truth of this proffered evidence, it does not follow that the parade ordinance was void on its face. The petitioners, moreover, did not apply for a permit either to the commission itself or to any commissioner after the injunction was issued. Had they done so, and had the permit been refused, it is clear that their claim of arbitrary or discriminatory administration of the ordinance would have been considered by the state circuit court upon a motion to dissolve the injunction.

This case would arise in quite a different constitutional posture if the petitioners, before disobeying the injunction, had challenged it in the Alabama courts, and had been met with delay or frustration of their constitutional claims. But there is no showing that such would have been the fate of a timely motion to modify or dissolve the injunction. There was an interim of two days between the issuance of the injunction and the Good Friday march. The petitioners give absolutely no explanation of why they did not make some application to the state court during that period. The injunction had issued *ex parte;* if the court had been presented with the petitioners' contentions, it might well have dissolved or at least modified its order in some respects. If it had not done so, Alabama procedure would have provided for an expedited process of appellate review. It cannot be presumed that the Alabama courts would have ignored the petitioners' constitutional claims. Indeed, these contentions were accepted in another case by an Alabama appellate court that struck down on direct review the conviction under this very ordinance of one of these same petitioners.

. . . The rule of law that Alabama followed in this case reflects a belief that in the fair administration of justice no man can be judge in his own case, however exalted his station, however righteous his motives, and irrespective of his race, color, politics, or religion. This Court cannot hold that the petitioners were constitutionally free to ignore all the procedures of the law and carry their battle to the streets. One may sympathize with the petitioners' impatient commitment to their cause. But respect for judicial process is a small price to pay for the civilizing hand of law, which alone can give abiding meaning to constitutional freedom.

Affirmed.

* * *

MR. CHIEF JUSTICE WARREN dissenting.

Petitioners in this case contend that they were convicted under an ordinance that is unconstitutional on its face because it submits their First and Fourteenth Amendment rights to free speech and peaceful assembly to the unfettered discretion of local officials. They further contend that the ordinance was unconstitutionally applied to them because the local officials used their discretion to prohibit peaceful demonstrations by a group whose political viewpoint the officials opposed. The Court does not dispute these contentions, but holds that petitioners may nonetheless be convicted and sent to jail because the patently unconstitutional ordinance was copied into an injunction—issued *ex parte* without prior notice or hearing on the request of the Commissioner of Public Safety—forbidding all persons having notice of the injunction to violate the ordinance without any limitation of time. I dissent because I do not believe that the fundamental protections of the Constitution were meant to be so easily evaded, or that "the civilizing hand of the law" would be hampered in the slightest by enforcing the First Amendment in this case.

. . . These facts lend no support to the court's charges that petitioners were presuming to act as judges in their own case, or that they had a disregard for the judicial process. They did not flee the jurisdiction or refuse to appear in the Alabama courts. Having violated the injunction, they promptly submitted themselves to the courts to test the constitutionality of the injunction and the ordinance it parroted. They were in essentially the same position as persons who challenge the constitutionality of a statute by violating it, and then defend the ensuing criminal prosecution on constitutional grounds. It has never been thought that violation of a statute indicated such a disrespect for the legislature that the violator always must be punished even if the statute was unconstitutional. On the contrary, some cases have required that persons seeking to challenge the constitutionality of a statute first violate it to establish their standing to sue. Indeed, it shows no disrespect for law to violate a statute on the ground that it is unconstitutional and then to submit one's case to the courts with the willingness to accept the penalty if the statute is held to be valid.

. . . The unconstitutionality of the ordinance is compounded . . . when there is convincing evidence that the officials have in fact used their power to deny permits to organizations whose views they dislike. The record in this case hardly suggests that Commissioner Connor and the other city officials were motivated in prohibiting civil rights picketing only by their overwhelming concern for particular traffic problems. Petitioners were given to understand that under no circumstances would they be permitted to demonstrate in Birmingham, not that a demonstration would be approved if a time and place were selected that would minimize the traffic difficulties. The only circumstance that the court can find to justify anything other than a *per curiam* reversal is that Commission Connor had the foresight to have the unconstitutional ordinance included in an *ex parte* injunction, issued without notice or hearing or any showing that it was impossible to have notice or a hearing, forbidding the world at large (insofar as it knew of the order) to conduct demonstrations in Birmingham without the consent of the city officials. This injunction was such potent magic that it transformed the command of an unconstitutional statute into an impregnable barrier, challengeable only in what likely would have been protracted legal proceedings and entirely superior in the meantime even to the United States Constitution.

I do not believe that giving this Court's seal of approval to such a gross misuse of the judicial process is likely to lead to greater respect for the law any more than it is likely to lead to greater protection for First Amendment freedoms. The *ex parte* temporary injunction has a long and odious history in this country, and its susceptibility to misuse is all too apparent from the facts of the case. As a weapon against strikes, it proved so effective in the hands of judges friendly to employers that Congress was forced to take the drastic step of removing from federal district courts the jurisdiction to issue injunctions in labor disputes. . . .

Nothing in our prior decisions, or in the doctrine that a party subject to a temporary injunction issued by a court of competent jurisdiction with power to decide a dispute properly before it must normally challenge the injunction in the courts rather than by violating it, requires that we affirm the convictions in this case. The majority opinion in this case rests essentially on a single precedent, and that a case the authority of which has clearly been undermined by subsequent decisions. . . .

MR. JUSTICE BRENNAN and MR. JUSTICE FORTAS concur.

[The dissenting opinion of MR. JUSTICE DOUGLAS, with whom THE CHIEF JUSTICE, MR. JUSTICE BRENNAN, and MR. JUSTICE FORTAS join, is omitted.]

[The dissenting opinion of MR. JUSTICE BRENNAN, with whom THE CHIEF JUSTICE, MR. JUSTICE DOUGLAS, and MR. JUSTICE FORTAS join, is omitted.]

HEART OF ATLANTA MOTEL, INC.
V. UNITED STATES
379 U.S. 241 (1964)

The owner of a large motel in Atlanta, Heart of Atlanta Motel, solicited patronage from outside the state of Georgia through various national advertising media, and the motel was readily accessible to two interstate highways and state highways. Prior to the passage of the Civil Rights Act of 1964, the motel owner refused to rent rooms to blacks and alleged that the policy would continue after the Act's passage. The motel owner attacked the constitutionality of Title II of the Act and sought an injunction restraining its enforcement. In the companion case, *Katzenbach v. McClung,* 379 U.S. 294 (1964), Ollie's Barbecue, located in Birmingham, Alabama, also refused to serve blacks. Although few of the restaurant's patrons were out-of-state travelers, 46% of the restaurant's food supply was shipped into Alabama from out of state. Owner Ollie McClung also attacked the constitutionality of Title II as applied against his restaurant. In *Heart of Atlanta Motel,* a three-judge district court upheld the constitutionality of Title II; however, in *McClung* a three-judge court held that Title II cannot be constitutionally applied to the restaurant. *Vote: 9-0.*

* * *

MR. JUSTICE CLARK delivered the opinion of the Court.

. . . The appellant contends that Congress in passing this Act exceeded its power to regulate commerce under Art. I, § 8, cl. 3, of the Constitution of the United States; that the Act violates the Fifth Amendment because appellant is deprived of the right to choose its customers and operate its business as it wishes, resulting in a taking of its liberty and property without due process of law and a taking of its property without just compensation; and, finally, that by requiring appellant to rent available rooms to Negroes against its will, Congress is subjecting it to involuntary servitude in contravention of the Thirteenth Amendment.

The appellees counter that the unavailability to Negroes of adequate accommodations interferes significantly with interstate travel, and that Congress, under the Commerce Clause, has power to remove such obstructions and restraints; that the Fifth Amendment does not forbid reasonable regulation and that consequential damage does not constitute a "taking" within the meaning of that amendment; that the Thirteenth Amendment claim fails because it is entirely frivolous to say that an amendment directed to the abolition of human bondage and the removal of widespread disabilities associated with slavery places discrimination in public accommodations beyond the reach of both federal and state law.

. . . It is admitted that the operation of the motel brings it within the provisions of § 201(a) of the Act and that appellant refused to provide lodging for transient Negroes because of their race or color and that it intends to continue that policy unless restrained.

The sole question posed is, therefore, the constitutionality of the Civil Rights Act of 1964 as applied to these facts. The legislative history of the Act indicates that Congress based the Act on § 5 and the Equal Protection Clause of the Fourteenth Amendment as well as its power to regulate interstate commerce under Art. I, § 8, cl. 3, of the Constitution.

The Senate Commerce Committee made it quite clear that the fundamental object of Title II was to vindicate "the deprivation of personal dignity that surely accompanies denials of equal access to public establishments." At the same time, however, it noted that such an objective has been and could be readily achieved "by congressional action based on the commerce power of the Constitution." . . . Our study of the legislative record, made in the light of prior cases, has brought us to the conclusion that Congress possessed ample power in this regard, and we have therefore not considered the other grounds relied upon. This is not to say that the remaining authority upon which it acted was not adequate, a question upon which we do not pass, but merely that since the commerce power is sufficient for our decision here we have considered it alone. Nor is § 201(d) or § 202, having to do with state action, involved here and we do not pass upon either of those sections.

In light of our ground for decision, it might be well at the outset to discuss the *Civil Rights Cases,* [109 U.S. 3 (1883)] which declared provisions of the Civil Rights Act of 1875 unconstitutional. . . . We think that decision inapposite, and without precedential value in determining the constitutionality of the present Act. Unlike Title II of the present legislation, the 1875 Act broadly proscribed discrimination in "inns, public conveyances on land or water, theaters, and other places of public amusement," without limiting the categories of affected businesses to those impinging upon interstate commerce. In contrast, the applicability of Title II is carefully limited to enterprises having a direct and substantial relation to the interstate flow of goods and people, except where state action is involved. Further, the fact that certain kinds of businesses may not in 1875 have been sufficiently involved in interstate commerce to warrant bringing them within the ambit of the commerce power is not necessarily dispositive of the same question today. Our populace had not reached its present mobility, nor were facilities, goods and services circulating as readily in interstate commerce as they are today. . . . Finally, there is language in the *Civil Rights Cases* which indicates that the Court did not fully consider whether the 1875 Act could be sustained as an exercise of the commerce power. . . . Since the commerce power was not relied on by the Government and was without support in the record it is understandable that the Court narrowed its inquiry and excluded the Commerce Clause as a possible source of power. In any event, it is clear that such a limitation renders the opinion devoid of authority for the proposition that the Commerce Clause gives no power to Congress to regulate discriminatory practices now found substantially to affect interstate commerce. We, therefore, conclude that the *Civil Rights Cases* have no relevance to the basis of decision here where the Act explicitly relies upon the commerce power, and where the record is filled with testimony of obstructions and restraints resulting from the discriminations found to be existing. We now pass to that phase of the case.

While the Act as adopted carried no congressional findings the record of its passage through each house is replete with evidence of the burdens that discrimination by race or color places upon interstate commerce. . . . This testimony included the fact that our people have become increasingly mobile with millions of people of all races traveling from State to State; that Negroes in particular have been the subject of discrimination in transient accommodations, having to travel great distances to secure the same; that often they have been unable to obtain accommodations and have had to call upon friends to put them up overnight, . . . and that these conditions had become so acute as to require the listing of available lodging for Negroes in a special guidebook which was itself "dramatic testimony to the difficulties" Negroes encounter in travel. . . . These exclusionary practices were found to be nationwide, the Under Secretary of Commerce testifying that there is "no question that this discrimination

in the North still exists to a large degree" and in the West and Midwest as well. . . . This testimony indicated a qualitative as well as quantitative effect on interstate travel by Negroes. The former was the obvious impairment of the Negro traveler's pleasure and convenience that resulted when he continually was uncertain of finding lodging. As for the latter, there was evidence that this uncertainty stemming from racial discrimination had the effect of discouraging travel on the part of a substantial portion of the Negro community. . . . This was the conclusion not only of the Under Secretary of Commerce but also of the Administrator of the Federal Aviation Agency who wrote the Chairman of the Senate Commerce Committee that it was his "belief that air commerce is adversely affected by the denial to a substantial segment of the traveling public of adequate and desegregated public accommodations." . . .

The power of Congress to deal with these obstructions depends on the meaning of the Commerce Clause. Its meaning was first enunciated 140 years ago by the great Chief Justice John Marshall in *Gibbons v. Ogden,* 9 Wheat. 1 (1824). . . . In short, the determinative test of the exercise of power by the Congress under the Commerce Clause is simply whether the activity sought to be regulated is "commerce which concerns more States than one" and has a real and substantial relation to the national interest. Let us now turn to this facet of the problem.

That the "intercourse" of which the Chief Justice spoke included the movement of persons through more States than one was settled as early as 1849 in the *Passenger Cases,* 7 How. 283. . . . Nor does it make any difference whether the transportation is commercial in character. . . .

. . . It is said that the operation of the motel here is of a purely local character. But, assuming this to be true, "[i]f it is interstate commerce that feels the pinch, it does not matter how local the operation which applies the squeeze." *United States v. Women's Sportswear Mfrs. Assn.,* 336 U.S. 460, 464 (1949). . . . Thus the power of Congress to promote interstate commerce also includes the power to regulate the local incidents thereof, including local activities in both the States of origin and destination, which might have a substantial and harmful effect upon that commerce. One need only examine the evidence which we have discussed above to see that Congress may—as it has—prohibit racial discrimination by motels serving travelers, however "local" their operations may appear.

Nor does the Act deprive appellant of liberty or property under the Fifth Amendment. The commerce power invoked here by the Congress is a specific and plenary one authorized by the Constitution itself. The only questions are: (1) whether Congress had a rational basis for finding that racial discrimination by motels affected commerce, and (2) if it had such a basis, whether the means it selected to eliminate that evil are reasonable and appropriate. If they are, appellant has no "right" to select its guests as it sees fit, free from governmental regulation.

There is nothing novel about such legislation. Thirty-two States now have it on their books either by statute or executive order and many cities provide such regulation. Some of these Acts go back four-score years. It has been repeatedly held by this Court that such laws do not violate the Due Process Clause of the Fourteenth Amendment. . . .

. . . We find no merit in the remainder of appellant's contentions, including that of "involuntary servitude." As we have seen, 32 States prohibit racial discrimination in public accommodations. These laws but codify the common-law innkeeper rule which long predated the Thirteenth Amendment. It is difficult to believe that the Amendment was intended to abrogate this principle. . . .

We, therefore, conclude that the action of the Congress in the adoption of the Act as applied here to a motel which concededly serves interstate travelers is within the power granted it by the Commerce Clause of the Constitution, as interpreted by this Court for 140 years. It may be argued that Congress could have pursued other methods to eliminate the obstructions it found in interstate commerce caused by racial discrimination. But this is a matter of policy that rests entirely with the Congress, not with the courts. How obstructions in commerce may be removed—what means are to be employed—is within the sound and exclusive discretion of the Congress. It is subject only to one caveat—that the means chosen by it must be reasonably adapted to the end permitted by the Constitution. We cannot say that its choice here was not so adapted. The Constitution requires no more.

Affirmed.

[The concurring opinion of MR. JUSTICE BLACK is omitted.]

* * *

MR. JUSTICE DOUGLAS concurring.*

Though I join the Court's opinions, I am somewhat reluctant here, as I was in *Edwards v. California,* 314 U.S. 160, 177 [1941], to rest solely on the Commerce Clause. My reluctance is not due to any conviction that Congress lacks power to regulate commerce in the interests of human rights. It is rather my belief that the right of people to be free of state action that discriminates against them because of race, like the "right of persons to move freely from State to State" (*Edwards v. California* . . .), "occupies a more protected position in our constitutional system than does the movement of cattle, fruit, steel and coal across state lines." . . .

Hence I would prefer to rest on the assertion of legislative power contained in § 5 of the Fourteenth Amendment which states: "The Congress shall have power to enforce, by appropriate legislation, the provisions of this article"—a power which the Court concedes was exercised at least in part in this Act.

A decision based on the Fourteenth Amendment would have a more settling effect, thus making unnecessary litigation over whether a particular restaurant or inn is within the commerce definitions of the Act or whether a particular customer is an interstate traveler. Under my construction, the Act would apply to all customers in all the enumerated places of public accommodations. And that construction would put an end to all obstructionist strategies and finally close one door on a bitter chapter in American history.

*[This opinion applies to *Katzenbach v. McClung.*]

[The concurring opinion of MR. JUSTICE GOLDBERG is omitted.]

JONES V. ALFRED H. MAYER CO.
392 U.S. 409 (1968)

Joseph Lee Jones sued the Alfred H. Mayer Company when it refused to sell him a home in the Paddock Woods community of St. Louis County, Missouri, on account of race. Relying on § 1982, Jones sought injunctions and other relief in district court. The district court dismissed the complaint, and the court of appeals affirmed, concluding that § 1982 applies only to state action and does not reach private refusals to sell. *Vote: 7-2.*

* * *

MR. JUSTICE STEWART delivered the opinion of the Court.

In this case we are called upon to determine the scope and the constitutionality of an Act of Congress, 42 U.S.C. § 1982, which provides that:

"All citizens of the United States shall have the same right, in every State and Territory, as is enjoyed by white citizens thereof to inherit, purchase, lease, sell, hold, and convey real and personal property."

... We hold that § 1982 bars *all* racial discrimination, private as well as public, in the sale or rental of property, and that the statute, thus construed, is a valid exercise of the power of Congress to enforce the Thirteenth Amendment.

At the outset, it is important to make clear precisely what this case does *not* involve. Whatever else it may be, ... § 1982 is not a comprehensive open housing law. In sharp contrast to the Fair Housing Title (Title VIII) of the Civil Rights Act of 1968, ... the statute in this case deals only with racial discrimination and does not address itself to discrimination on grounds of religion or national origin. It does not deal specifically with discrimination in the provision of services or facilities in connection with the sale or rental of a dwelling. It does not prohibit advertising or other representations that indicate discriminatory preferences. It does not refer explicitly to discrimination in financing arrangements or in the provision of brokerage services. It does not empower a federal administrative agency to assist aggrieved parties. It makes no provision for intervention by the Attorney General. And, although it can be enforced by injunction, it contains no provision expressly authorizing a federal court to order the payment of damages.

Thus, although § 1982 contains none of the exemptions that Congress included in the Civil Rights Act of 1968, it would be a serious mistake to suppose that § 1982 in any way diminishes the significance of the law recently enacted by Congress. Indeed, the Senate Subcommittee on Housing and Urban Affairs was informed in hearings held after the Court of Appeals had rendered its decision in this case that § 1982 might well be "a presently valid federal statutory ban against discrimination by private persons in the sale or lease of real property." The Subcommittee was told, however, that even if this Court should so construe § 1982, the existence of that statute would not "eliminate the need for congressional action" to spell out "responsibility on the part of the federal government to enforce the rights it protects." The point was made that, in light of many difficulties confronted by private litigants seeking to enforce such rights on their own, "legislation is needed to establish federal machinery for enforcement of the rights guaranteed under Section 1982 of Title 42 even if the plaintiffs in *Jones v. Alfred H. Mayer Company* should prevail in the United States Supreme Court."

... This Court has had occasion to consider the scope of ... § 1982 in 1948, in *Hurd v. Hodge,* 334 U.S. 24. ...

... *Hurd v. Hodge* ... squarely held ... that a Negro citizen who is denied the opportunity to purchase the home he wants "[s]olely because of [his] race and color," has suffered the kind of injury that § 1982 was designed to prevent. ... The basic source of injury in *Hurd* was, of course, the action of private individuals—white citizens who had agreed to exclude Negroes from a residential area. But an arm of the Government—in that case, a federal court—had assisted in the enforcement of that agreement. Thus *Hurd v. Hodge* ... did not present the question whether *purely* private discrimination, unaided by any action on the part of government, would violate § 1982 if its effect were to deny a citizen the right to rent or buy property solely because of his race or color.

... Today we face that issue for the first time.

... On its face, therefore, § 1982 appears to prohibit *all* discrimination against Negroes in the sale or rental of property—discrimination by private owners as well as discrimination by public authorities. Indeed, even the respondents seem to concede that, if § 1982 "means what it says"—to use the words of the respondents' brief—then it must encompass every racially motivated refusal to sell or rent and cannot be confined to officially sanctioned segregation in housing. Stressing what they consider to be the revolutionary implications of so literal a reading of § 1982, the respondents argue that Congress cannot possibly have intended any such result. Our examination of the relevant history, however, persuades us that Congress meant exactly what it said.

In its original form, ... § 1982 was part of § 1 of the Civil Rights Act of 1866. ... The crucial language for our purposes was that which guaranteed all citizens "the same right, in every State and Territory in the United States, ... to inherit, purchase, lease, sell, hold, and convey real and personal property ... as is enjoyed by white citizens ..." To the Congress that passed the Civil Rights Act of 1866, it was clear that the right to do these things might be infringed not only by "State or local law" but also by "custom, or prejudice." Thus, when Congress provided in § 1 of the Civil Rights Act that the right to purchase and lease property was to be enjoyed equally throughout the United States by Negro and white citizens alike, it plainly meant to secure that right against interference from any source whatever, whether governmental or private.

Indeed, if § 1 had been intended to grant nothing more than an immunity from *governmental* interference, then much of § 2 would have made no sense at all. For that section, which provided fines and prison terms for certain individuals who deprived others of rights "secured or protected" by § 1, was carefully drafted to exempt private violations of § 1 from the criminal sanctions it imposed. There would, of course, have been no private violations to exempt if the only "right" granted by § 1 had been a right to be free of discrimination by public officials. Hence the structure of the 1866 Act, as well as its language, points to the conclusion urged by the petitioners in this case—that § 1 was meant to prohibit *all* racially motivated deprivations of the rights enumerated in the statute, although only those deprivations perpetrated "under color of law" were to be criminally punishable under § 2.

In attempting to demonstrate the contrary, the respondents rely heavily upon the fact that the Congress which approved the 1866 statute wished to eradicate the recently enacted Black Codes—laws which had saddled Negroes with "onerous disabilities and burdens, and curtailed their rights . . . to such an extent that their freedom was of little value . . ." *Slaughter-House Cases,* 16 Wall. 36, 70 [1873]. The respondents suggest that the only evil Congress sought to eliminate was that of racially discriminatory laws in the former Confederate States. But the Civil Rights Act was drafted to apply throughout the country, and its language was far broader than would have been necessary to strike down discriminatory statutes.

That broad language, we are asked to believe, was a mere slip of the legislative pen. We disagree. For the same Congress that wanted to do away with the Black Codes *also* had before it an imposing body of evidence pointing to the mistreatment of Negroes by private individuals and unofficial groups, mistreatment unrelated to any hostile state legislation. "Accounts in newspapers North and South, Freedmen's Bureau and other official documents, private reports and correspondence were all adduced" to show that "private outrage and atrocity" were "daily inflicted on freedmen . . ." The congressional debates are replete with references to private injustices against Negroes—references to white employers who refused to pay their Negro workers, white planters who agreed among themselves not to hire freed slaves without the permission of their former masters, white citizens who assaulted Negroes or who combined to drive them out of their communities.

. . . In light of the concerns that led Congress to adopt it and the contents of the debates that preceded its passage, it is clear that the Act was designed to do just what its terms suggest: to prohibit all racial discrimination, whether or not under color of law, with respect to the rights enumerated therein—including the right to purchase or lease property.

Nor was the scope of the 1866 Act altered when it was re-enacted in 1870, some two years after the ratification of the Fourteenth Amendment. It is quite true that some members of Congress supported the Fourteenth Amendment "in order to eliminate doubt as to the constitutional validity of the Civil Rights Act as applied to the States." . . . But it certainly does not follow that the adoption of the Fourteenth Amendment or the subsequent readoption of the Civil Rights Act was meant somehow to *limit* its application to state action. The legislative history furnishes not the slightest factual basis for any such speculation, and the conditions prevailing in 1870 make it highly implausible. For by that time most, if not all, of the former Confederate States, then under the control of "reconstructed" legislatures,

had formally repudiated racial discrimination, and the focus of congressional concern had clearly shifted from hostile statutes to the activities of groups like the Ku Klux Klan, operating wholly outside of the law.

Against this background, it would obviously make no sense to assume, without any historical support whatever, that Congress made a silent decision in 1870 to exempt private discrimination from the operation of the Civil Rights Act of 1866. "The cardinal rule is that repeals by implication are not favored." . . . All Congress said in 1870 was that the 1866 law "is hereby re-enacted." That is all Congress meant.

. . . The remaining question is whether Congress has power under the Constitution to do what § 1982 purports to do: to prohibit all racial discrimination, private and public, in the sale and rental of property. Our starting point is the Thirteenth Amendment, for it was pursuant to that constitutional provision that Congress originally enacted what is now § 1982. . . .

As its text reveals, the Thirteenth Amendment "is not a mere prohibition of State laws establishing or upholding slavery, but an absolute declaration that slavery or involuntary servitude shall not exist in any part of the United States." . . . It has never been doubted, therefore, "that the power vested in Congress to enforce the article by appropriate legislation," . . . includes the power to enact laws "direct and primary, operating upon the acts of individuals, whether sanctioned by State legislation or not." . . .

Thus, the fact that § 1982 operates upon the unofficial acts of private individuals, whether or not sanctioned by state law, presents no constitutional problem. If Congress has power under the Thirteenth Amendment to eradicate conditions that prevent Negroes from buying and renting property because of their race or color, then no federal statute calculated to achieve that objective can be thought to exceed the constitutional power of Congress simply because it reaches beyond state action to regulate the conduct of private individuals. The constitutional question in this case, therefore, comes to this: Does the authority of Congress to enforce the Thirteenth Amendment "by appropriate legislation" include the power to eliminate all racial barriers to the acquisition of real and personal property? We think the answer to that question is plainly yes.

. . . The judgment is

Reversed.

[The concurring opinion of MR. JUSTICE DOUGLAS is omitted.]

* * *

MR. JUSTICE HARLAN, with whom MR. JUSTICE WHITE joins, dissenting.

. . . For reasons which follow, I believe that the Court's construction of § 1982 as applying to purely private action is almost surely wrong, and at the least is open to serious doubt. The issues of the constitutionality of § 1982, as construed by the Court, and of liability under the Fourteenth Amendment alone, also present formidable difficulties. Moreover, the political processes of our own era have, since the date of oral argument in this case, given birth to a civil rights statute embodying "fair housing" provisions which would at the end of this year make available to others, though apparently not to the petitioners themselves, the type of relief which the petitioner now seeks. It seems to me that this latter factor so diminishes the public importance of this case that by far the wisest course would be for this Court to refrain from decision and to dismiss the writ as improvidently granted.

. . . In sum, the most which can be said with assurance about the intended impact of the 1866 Civil Rights Act upon purely private discrimination is that the Act probably was envisioned by most members of Congress as prohibiting official, community-sanctioned discrimination in the South, engaged in pursuant to local "customs" which in the recent time of slavery probably were embodied in laws or regulations. Acts done under the color of such "customs" were, of course, said by the Court in the *Civil Rights Cases,* 109 U.S. 3 [1883], to constitute "state action" prohibited by the Fourteenth Amendment. . . . Adoption of a "state action" construction of the Civil Rights Act would therefore have the additional merit of bringing its interpretation into line with that of the Fourteenth Amendment, which this Court has consistently held to reach only "state action." This seems especially desirable in light of the wide agreement that a major purpose of the Fourteenth Amendment, at least in the minds of its congressional proponents, was to assure that the rights conferred by the then recently enacted Civil Rights Act could not be taken away by a subsequent Congress.

HUNTER V. ERICKSON
393 U.S. 385 (1969)

In 1964 the Akron, Ohio, City Council enacted a fair housing ordinance, No. 873-1964 § 1, designed to "assure equal opportunity to all persons to live in decent housing facilities regardless of race, color, religion, ancestry, or national origin." The ordinance established a Commission on Equal Opportunity in Housing to enforce the antidiscrimination section through conciliation or persuasion or through judicial enforcement if necessary. A proposal to amend the city charter had been placed on the ballot at a general election on petition of more than 10% of Akron's voters, and the amendment passed with a majority vote. The charter amendment provided that any city council ordinance that regulates the use, sale, advertisement, transfer, listing assignment, lease, sublease, or financing of real property on the basis of race, color, religion, national origin, or ancestry must first be approved by a majority of the voters before becoming effective. When Nellie Hunter, a black citizen, addressed to the commission a complaint asserting that a real estate agent could not show her houses because the owners specified they did not want to sell their homes to blacks, she was informed that the fair housing ordinance was unavailable to her because of the city charter amendment. Hunter then brought a class action suit against Erickson, the mayor of Akron, and other officials to enforce the fair housing ordinance and to process her complaint. The Supreme Court of Ohio, in affirming the ruling of the trial court, held that the charter amendment did not violate the equal protection clause of the Constitution. The U.S. Supreme Court rejected Akron's threshold contention that an Ohio statute mooted the case. *Vote: 8-1.*

* * *

MR. JUSTICE WHITE delivered the opinion of the Court.

The question in this case is whether the City of Akron, Ohio, has denied a Negro citizen, Nellie Hunter, the equal protection of its laws by amending the city charter to prevent the city council from implementing any ordinance dealing with racial, religious, or ancestral discrimination in housing without the approval of the majority of voters in Akron.

. . . Akron argues that this case is unlike *Reitman v. Mulkey,* 387 U.S. 369 (1967) in that here the city charter declares no right to discriminate in housing, authorizes and encourages no housing discrimination, and places no ban on the enactment of fair housing ordinances. But we need not rest on *Reitman* to decide this case. Here, unlike *Reitman,* there was an explicitly racial classification treating racial housing matters differently from other racial and housing matters.

. . . Only laws to end housing discrimination based on "race, color, religion, national origin or ancestry" must run § 137's gauntlet. It is true that the section draws no distinctions among racial and religious groups. Negroes and whites, Jews and Catholics are all subject to the same requirements if there is housing discrimination against them which they wish to end. But § 137 nevertheless disadvantages those who would benefit from laws barring racial, religious, or ancestral discriminations as against those who would bar other discriminations or who would otherwise regulate the real estate market in their favor. The automatic referendum system does not reach housing discrimination on sexual or political grounds, or against those with children or dogs, nor does it affect tenants seeking more heat or better maintenance from landlords, nor those seeking rent control, urban renewal, public housing, or new building codes.

Moreover, although the law on its face treats Negro and white, Jew and gentile in an identical manner, the reality is that the law's impact falls on the minority. The majority needs no protection against discrimination and if it did, a referendum might be bothersome but no more than that. Like the law requiring specification of candidates' race on the ballot, *Anderson v. Martin,* 375 U.S. 399 (1964), § 137 places special burdens on racial minorities within the governmental process. This is no more permissible than denying them the vote, on an equal basis with others. . . . The preamble to the open housing ordinance which was suspended by § 137 recited that the population of Akron consists of "people of different race, color, religion, ancestry or national origin, many of whom live in circumscribed and segregated areas, under sub-standard, unhealthful, unsafe, unsanitary and overcrowded conditions, because of discrimination in the sale, lease, rental and financing of housing." Such was the situation in Akron. It is against this background that the referendum required by § 137 must be assessed.

Because the core of the Fourteenth Amendment is the prevention of meaningful and unjustified official distinctions based on race, . . . racial classifications are "constitutionally suspect," . . . and subject to the "most rigid scrutiny." . . . They "bear a far heavier burden of justification" than other classifications. . . .

We are unimpressed with any of Akron's justifications for its discrimination. Characterizing it simply as a public decision to move slowly in the delicate area of race relations emphasizes the impact and burden of § 137, but does not justify it. The amendment was unnecessary either to implement a decision to go slowly, or to allow the people of Akron to participate in that decision. Likewise, insisting that a State may distribute legislative power as it desires and that the people may retain for themselves the power over certain subjects may

generally be true, but these principles furnish no justification for a legislative structure which otherwise would violate the Fourteenth Amendment. Nor does the implementation of this change through popular referendum immunize it. . . . The sovereignty of the people is itself subject to those constitutional limitations which have been duly adopted and remain unrepealed. Even though Akron might have proceeded by majority vote at town meeting on all its municipal legislation, it has instead chosen a more complex system. Having done so, the State may no more disadvantage any particular group by making it more difficult to enact legislation in its behalf than it may dilute any person's vote or give any group a smaller representation than another of comparable size. . . .

We hold that § 137 discriminates against minorities, and constitutes a real, substantial, and invidious denial of the equal protection of the laws.

Reversed.

[The concurring opinion of MR. JUSTICE HARLAN, with whom MR. JUSTICE STEWART joins, is omitted.]

* * *

MR. JUSTICE BLACK dissenting.

. . . The Court purports to find its power to forbid the city to repeal its laws in the provision of the Fourteenth Amendment forbidding a State to "deny to any person within its jurisdiction the equal protection of the laws." For some time I have been filing my protests against the Court's use of the Due Process Clause to strike down state laws that shock the Court's conscience or offend the Court's sense of what it considers to be "fair" or "fundamental" or "arbitrary" or "contrary to the beliefs of the English-speaking people." I now protest just as vigorously against the use of the Equal Protection Clause to bar States from repealing laws that the Court wants the States to retain. Of course the Court under the ruling of *Marbury v. Madison,* 1 Cranch 137 (1803), has the power to invalidate state laws that discriminate on account of race. But it does not have the power to put roadblocks to prevent States from repealing these laws. Here, I think the Court needs to control itself, and not, as it is doing, encroach on a State's powers to repeal its old laws when it decides to do so.

UNITED STATES V. GUEST
383 U.S. 745 (1966)

Herbert Guest and five other whites were convicted of criminal conspiracy, in violation of § 241, to deprive black citizens of the free exercise and enjoyment of rights secured to them by the Constitution and laws of the United States. The indictment specified various means by which the objects of the conspiracy were achieved, including shooting, beating, and killing blacks; damaging and destroying property of blacks; pursuing blacks in automobiles and threatening them with guns; and causing the arrest of blacks by means of false reports of their criminal acts. This case involved the murder of Lemuel Penn, a black educator in Georgia. The district court dismissed the indictment on the ground that it did not charge an offense under the laws of the United States. The United States appealed directly to the Supreme Court under the Criminal Appeals Act, 18 U.S.C. § 3731. *Vote: 6-3.*

* * *

MR. JUSTICE STEWART delivered the opinion of the Court.

. . . The second numbered paragraph of the indictment alleged that the defendants conspired to injure, oppress, threaten, and intimidate Negro citizens of the United States in the free exercise and enjoyment of:

"The right to the equal utilization, without discrimination upon the basis of race, of public facilities in the vicinity of Athens, Georgia, owned, operated or managed by or on behalf of the State of Georgia or any subdivision thereof."

Correctly characterizing this paragraph as embracing rights protected by the Equal Protection Clause of the Fourteenth Amendment, the District Court held as a matter of statutory construction that 18 U.S.C. § 241 does not encompass any Fourteenth Amendment rights, and further held as a matter of constitutional law that "any broader construction of § 241 . . . would render it void for indefiniteness." . . . In so holding, the District Court was in error, as our opinion in *United States v. Price*, [383 U.S. 787 (1966)], decided today, makes abundantly clear.

To be sure, *Price* involves rights under the Due Process Clause, whereas the present case involves rights under the Equal Protection Clause. But no possible reason suggests itself for concluding that § 241—if it protects Fourteenth Amendment rights—protects rights secured by the one Clause but not those secured by the other. We have made clear in *Price* that when § 241 speaks of "any right or privilege secured . . . by the Constitution or laws of the United States," it means precisely that.

Moreover, inclusion of the Fourteenth Amendment rights within the compass of . . . § 241 does not render the statute unconstitutionally vague. Since the gravamen of the offense is conspiracy, the requirement that the offender must act with a specific intent to interfere with the federal rights in question is satisfied. *Screws v. United States*, 325 U.S. 91 [1945]. And the rights under the Equal Protection Clause described by this paragraph of the indictment have been so firmly and precisely established by a consistent line of decisions in this Court, that the lack of specification of these rights in the language of § 241 itself can raise no serious constitutional question on the ground of vagueness or indefiniteness.

Unlike the indictment in *Price*, however, the indictment in the present case names no person alleged to have acted in any way under color of state law. The argument is therefore made that, since there exist no Equal Protection Clause rights against wholly private action, the judgment of the District Court on this branch of the case must be affirmed. On its face, the argument is unexceptionable. The Equal Protection Clause speaks to the State or to those acting under the color of its authority.

In this connection, we emphasize that § 241 by its clear language incorporates no more than the Equal Protection Clause itself; the statute does not purport to give substantive, as opposed to remedial implementation to any rights secured by that Clause. Since we therefore deal here only with the bare terms of the Equal Protection Clause itself, nothing said in this opinion goes to the question of what kinds of other and broader legislation Congress might constitutionally enact under § 5 of the Fourteenth Amendment to implement that Clause or any other provision of the Amendment.

It is commonplace that rights under the Equal Protection Clause itself arise only where there has been involvement of the State or of one acting under the color of its authority. The Equal Protection Clause "does not . . . add any thing to the rights which one citizen has under the Constitution against another." . . . As MR. JUSTICE DOUGLAS more recently put it, "The Fourteenth Amendment protects the individual against state action, not against wrongs done by individuals." . . . This has been the view of the Court from the beginning. . . . It remains the Court's view today. . . .

This is not to say, however, that the involvement of the State need be either exclusive or direct. In a variety of situations the Court has found state action of a nature sufficient to create rights under the Equal Protection Clause even though the participation of the State was peripheral, or its action was only one of several co-operative forces leading to the constitutional violation. . . .

This case, however, requires no determination of the threshold level that state action must attain in order to create rights under the Equal Protection Clause. This is so because, contrary to the argument of the litigants, the indictment in fact contains an express allegation of state involvement sufficient at least to require the denial of a motion to dismiss. One of the means of accomplishing the object of the conspiracy, according to the indictment, was "By causing the arrest of Negroes by means of false reports that such Negroes had committed criminal acts.". . .

The fourth numbered paragraph of the indictment alleged that the defendants conspired to injure, oppress, threaten, and intimidate Negro citizens of the United States in the free exercise and enjoyment of:

"The right to travel freely to and from the State of Georgia and to use highway facilities and other instrumentalities of interstate commerce within the State of Georgia."

The District Court was in error in dismissing the indictment as to this paragraph. The constitutional right to travel from one State to another, and necessarily to use the highways and other instrumentalities of interstate commerce in doing so, occupies a position fundamental to the concept of our Federal Union. It is a right that has been firmly established and repeatedly recognized. . . .

Although there have been recurring differences in emphasis within the Court as to the source of the constitutional right of interstate travel, there is no need here to canvass those differences further. All have agreed that the right exists. Its explicit recognition as one of the federal rights protected by what is now . . . § 241 goes back at least as far as 1904. . . . We reaffirm it now.

This does not mean, of course, that every criminal conspiracy affecting an individual's right of free interstate passage is within the sanction of . . . § 241. A specific intent to interfere with the federal right must be proved, and at a trial the defendants are entitled to a jury instruction phrased in those terms. . . . Thus, for example, a conspiracy to rob an interstate traveler would not, of itself, violate § 241. But if the predominant purpose of the conspiracy is to impede or prevent the exercise of the right of interstate travel, or to oppress a person because of his exercise of that right, then, whether or not motivated by racial discrimination, the conspiracy becomes a proper object of the federal law under which the indictment in this case was brought. Accordingly, it was error to grant the motion to dismiss on this branch of the indictment.

For these reasons, the judgment of the District Court is reversed and the case is remanded to that court for further proceedings consistent with this opinion.

It is so ordered.

[The concurring opinion of MR. JUSTICE CLARK, with whom MR. JUSTICE BLACK and MR. JUSTICE FORTAS join, is omitted.]

[The opinion of MR. JUSTICE HARLAN, concurring in part and dissenting in part, is omitted.]

* * *

MR. JUSTICE BRENNAN, with whom THE CHIEF JUSTICE [WARREN] and MR. JUSTICE DOUGLAS join, concurring in part and dissenting in part.

. . . I do not agree [with that part of the Court's opinion] which holds, as I read the opinion, that a conspiracy to interfere with the exercise of the right to equal utilization of state facilities is not, within the meaning of § 241, a conspiracy to interfere with the exercise of a "right . . . secured . . . by the Constitution" unless discriminatory conduct by state officers is involved in the alleged conspiracy.

. . . Hence, while the order dismissing the second numbered paragraph of the indictment is reversed, severe limitations on the prosecution of that branch of the indictment are implicitly imposed. These limitations could only stem from an acceptance of appellees' contention that, because there exist no Equal Protection Clause rights against wholly private action, a conspiracy of private persons to interfere with the right to equal utilization of state facilities described in the second numbered paragraph is not a conspiracy to interfere with a "right . . . secured . . . by the Constitution" within the meaning of § 241. In other words, in the Court's view the only right referred to in the second numbered paragraph that is, for purposes of § 241, "secured . . . by the Constitution" is a right to be free— when seeking access to state facilities—from discriminatory conduct by state officers or by persons acting in concert with state officers.

I cannot agree with that construction of § 241. I am of the opinion that a conspiracy to interfere with the right to equal utilization of state facilities described in the second numbered paragraph of the indictment is a conspiracy to interfere with a "right . . . secured . . . by the Constitution" without regard to whether state officers participated in the alleged conspiracy. I believe that § 241 reaches such a private conspiracy, not because the Fourteenth Amendment of its own force prohibits such a conspiracy, but because § 241, as an exercise of congressional power under § 5 of the Fourteenth Amendment, prohibits *all* conspiracies to interfere with the exercise of a "right . . . secured . . . by the Constitution" and because the right to equal utilization of state facilities is a "right . . . secured . . . by the Constitution" within the meaning of that phrase as used in § 241.

My difference with the Court stems from its construction of the term "secured" as used in § 241 in the phrase a "right . . . secured by the Constitution or laws of the United States." The Court tacitly construes the term "secured" so as to restrict the coverage of § 241 to those rights that are "fully protected" by the Constitution or another federal law. Unless private interferences with the exercise of the right in question are prohibited by the Constitution itself or another federal law, the right cannot, in the Court's view, be deemed "secured . . . by the Constitution or laws of the United States" so as to make § 241 applicable to a private conspiracy to interfere with the exercise of that right. The Court then premises that neither the Fourteenth Amendment nor any other federal law prohibits private interferences with the exercise of the right to equal utilization of state facilities.

In my view, however, a right can be deemed "secured . . . by the Constitution or laws of the United States," within the meaning of § 241, even though only governmental interferences with the exercise of the right are prohibited by the Constitution itself (or another federal law). The term "secured" means "created by, arising under or dependent upon,". . . rather than "fully protected." A right is "secured . . . by the Constitution" within the meaning of § 241 if it emanates from the Constitution, if it finds its source in the Constitution. Section 241 must thus be viewed, in this context, as an exercise of congressional power to amplify prohibitions of the Constitution addressed, as is invariably the case, to government officers; contrary to the view of the Court, I think we are dealing here with a statute that seeks to implement the Constitution, not with the "bare terms" of the Constitution. Section 241 is not confined to protecting rights against private conspiracies that the Constitution or another federal law also protects against private interferences. No such duplicative function was envisioned in its enactment. . . . Nor has this Court construed § 241 in such a restrictive manner in other contexts. Many of the rights that have been held to be encompassed within § 241 are not additionally the subject of protection of specific federal legislation or of any provision of the Constitution addressed to private individuals. . . . The reach of § 241 should not vary with the particular constitutional provision that is the source of the right. For purposes of applying § 241 to a private conspiracy, the standard used to determine whether, for example, the right to discuss public affairs or the right to vote in a federal election is a "right . . . secured . . . by the Constitution" is the very same standard to be used to determine whether the right to equal utilization of state facilities is a "right . . . secured . . . by the Constitution."

GRIFFIN V. BRECKENRIDGE
403 U.S. 88 (1971)

On July 2, 1966, Lavon Breckenridge and James Calvin Breckenridge, white residents of DeKalb, Kemper County, Mississippi, drove their truck into the path of R. G. Grady's automobile and blocked its passage over a public road. They forced Grady and the other passengers out of the car, clubbed Grady with a blackjack, and threatened to injure and kill all of them. The defendants were acting under a mistaken belief that Grady was a civil rights worker. Grady filed a damage action under § 1985(3), charging that the Breckenridges, by their conspiracy, deprived them of their equal protection of the laws. The district court dismissed the complaint for failure to state a cause of action under *Collins v. Hardyman*, 341 U.S. 651 (1951). The district court interpreted § 1985(3) to reach only conspiracies under color of state law. The court of appeals affirmed. *Vote: 9-0.*

* * *

MR. JUSTICE STEWART delivered the opinion of the Court.

. . . We turn, then, to an examination of the meaning of § 1985(3). On their face, the words of the statute fully encompass the conduct of private persons. The provision speaks simply of "two or more persons in any State or Territory" who "conspire or go in disguise on the highway or on the premises of another." Going in disguise, in particular, is in this context an activity so little associated with official action and so commonly connected with private marauders that this clause could almost never be applicable under the artificially restrictive construction of *Collins*. And since the "going in disguise" aspect must include private action, it is hard to see how the conspiracy aspect, joined by a disjunctive, could be read to require the involvement of state officers.

The provision continues, specifying the motivation required "for the purpose of depriving, either directly or indirectly, any person or class of persons of the equal protection of the laws, or of equal privileges and immunities under the laws." This language is, of course, similar to that of § 1 of the Fourteenth Amendment, which in terms speaks only to the States, and judicial thinking about what can constitute an equal protection deprivation has, because of the Amendment's wording, focused almost entirely upon identifying the requisite "state action" and defining the offending forms of state law and official conduct. A century of Fourteenth Amendment adjudication has, in other words, made it understandably difficult to conceive of what might constitute a deprivation of the equal protection of the laws by private persons. Yet there is nothing inherent in the phrase that requires the action working the deprivation to come from the State. . . . Indeed, the failure to mention any such requisite can be viewed as an important indication of congressional intent to speak in § 1985(3) of *all* deprivations of "equal protection of the laws" and "equal privileges and immunities under the laws," whatever their source.

... It is thus evident that all indicators—text, companion, provisions, and legislative history—point unwaveringly to § 1985(3)'s coverage of private conspiracies. That the statute was meant to reach private action does not, however, mean that it was intended to apply to all tortious, conspiratorial interferences with the rights of others. For, though the supporters of the legislation insisted on coverage of private conspiracies, they were equally emphatic that they did not believe, in the words of Representative Cook, "that Congress has a right to punish an assault and battery when committed by two or more persons within a State." ... The constitutional shoals that would lie in the path of interpreting § 1985(3) as a general federal tort law can be avoided by giving full effect to the congressional purpose—by requiring, as an element of the cause of action, the kind of invidiously discriminatory motivation stressed by the sponsors of the limiting amendment. ... The language requiring intent to deprive of *equal* protection, or *equal* privileges and immunities, means that there must be some racial, or perhaps otherwise class-based, invidiously discriminatory animus behind the conspirators' action. The conspiracy, in other words, must aim at a deprivation of the equal enjoyment of rights secured by the law to all.

We return to the petitioners' complaint to determine whether it states a cause of action under § 1985(3) as so construed. To come within the legislation a complaint must allege that the defendants did (1) "conspire or go in disguise on the highway or on the premises of another" (2) "for the purpose of depriving, either directly or indirectly, any person or class of persons of the equal protection of the laws, or of equal privileges and immunities under the laws." It must then assert that one or more of the conspirators (3) did, or caused to be done, "any act in furtherance of the object of [the] conspiracy," whereby another was (4a) "injured in his person or property" or (4b) "deprived of having and exercising any right or privilege of a citizen of the United States."

The complaint fully alleges, with particulars, that the respondents conspired to carry out the assault. It further asserts that "[t]heir purpose was to prevent [the] plaintiffs and other Negro-Americans, through ... force, violence and intimidation, from seeking the equal protection of the laws and from enjoying the equal rights, privileges and immunities of citizens under the laws of the United States and the State of Mississippi," including a long list of enumerated rights such as free speech, assembly, association, and movement. The complaint further alleges that the respondents were "acting under mistaken belief that R. G. Grady was a worker for Civil Rights for Negroes." These allegations clearly support the requisite animus to deprive the petitioners of the equal enjoyment of legal rights because of their race. The claims of detention, threats, and battery amply satisfy the requirement of acts done in furtherance of the conspiracy. Finally, the petitioners—whether or not the nonparty Grady was the main or only target of the conspiracy—allege personal injury resulting from those acts. The complaint, then, states a cause of action under § 1985 (3). Indeed, the conduct here alleged lies so close to the core of the coverage intended by Congress that it is hard to conceive of wholly private conduct that would come within the statute if this does not. We must, accordingly, consider whether Congress had constitutional power to enact a statute that imposes liability under federal law for the conduct alleged in this complaint.

... That § 1985(3) reaches private conspiracies to deprive others of legal rights can, of itself, cause no doubts of its constitutionality. It has long been settled that ... § 241, a criminal statute of far broader phrasing ... reaches wholly private conspiracies and is constitutional. ... Our inquiry, therefore, need go only to identifying a source of congressional power to reach the private conspiracy alleged by the complaint in this case.

Even as it struck down Rev. Stat. § 5519 in *United States v. Harris* [106 U.S. 629 (1883)], the Court indicated that parts of its coverage would, if severable, be constitutional under the Thirteenth Amendment. ... And surely there has never been any doubt of the power of Congress to impose liability on private persons under § 2 of that amendment, "for the amendment is not a mere prohibition of State laws establishing or upholding slavery, but an absolute declaration that slavery or involuntary servitude shall not exist in any part of the United States." ... Not only may Congress impose such liability, but the varieties of private conduct that it may make criminally punishable or civilly remediable extend far beyond the actual imposition of slavery or involuntary servitude. ... We can only conclude that Congress was wholly within its powers under § 2 of the Thirteenth Amendment in creating a statutory cause of action for Negro citizens who have been the victims of conspiracies, racially discriminatory private action aimed at depriving them of the basic rights that the law secures to all free men.

Our cases have firmly established that the right of interstate travel is constitutionally protected, does not necessarily rest on the Fourteenth Amendment, and is assertable against private as well as governmental interference. *Shapiro v. Thompson,* 394 U.S. 618, 629-631 [1969] ...

The complaint in this case alleged that the petitioners "were travelling upon the federal, state and local highways in and about" DeKalb, Kemper County, Mississippi. Kemper County is on the Mississippi-Alabama border. One of the results of the conspiracy, according to the complaint, was to prevent the petitioners and other Negroes from exercising their "rights to travel the public highways without restraint in the same terms as white citizens in Kemper County, Mississippi." Finally, the conspiracy was alleged to have been inspired by the respondents' erroneous belief that Grady, a Tennessean, was a worker for Negro civil rights. Under these allegations it is open to the petitioners to prove at trial that they had been engaging in interstate travel or intended to do so, that their federal right to travel interstate was one of the rights meant to be discriminatorily impaired by the conspiracy, that the conspirators intended to drive out-of-state civil rights workers from the State, or that they meant to deter the petitioners from associating with such persons. This and other evidence could make it clear that the petitioners had suffered from conduct that Congress may reach under its power to protect the right of interstate travel.

. . . The judgment is reversed, and the case is remanded to the United States District for the Southern District of Mississippi for further proceedings consistent with this opinion.

It is so ordered.

* * *

MR. JUSTICE HARLAN concurring.

I agree with the Court's opinion, except that I find it unnecessary to rely on the "right of interstate travel" as a premise for justifying federal jurisdiction under § 1985(3). With that reservation, I join the opinion and judgment of the Court.

ADICKES v. S. H. KRESS & CO.
398 U.S. 144 (1970)

Sandra Adickes, a white school teacher from New York, accompanied six black students from a Mississippi "freedom school" where she was teaching that summer to a Kress store in Hattiesburg, Mississippi. The Kress' restaurant personnel refused to serve lunch to Adickes, but the students were offered service. On her departure from the store, she was arrested by the Hattiesburg police for vagrancy. Adickes brought a § 1983 suit alleging that (a) Kress had deprived her right under the equal protection clause not to be discriminated against on the basis of race and (b) both the refusal of service and her subsequent arrest were the product of a conspiracy between Kress and Hattiesburg police. On the first count, the district court and the court of appeals held that § 1983 required the discriminatory custom be proven to exist in the locale where the discrimination took place. The court of appeals also upheld the district court's dismissal of the second count on the ground that Adickes had failed to allege any facts from which a conspiracy might be inferred. *Vote: 6-2.*

* * *

MR. JUSTICE HARLAN delivered the opinion of the Court.

. . . [B]ecause respondent failed to show the absence of any disputed material fact, we think the District Court erred in granting summary judgment. With respect to the substantive count . . . we think petitioner will have made out a claim under § 1983 for violation of her equal protection rights if she proves that she was refused service by Kress because of a state-enforced custom requiring racial segregation in Hattiesburg restaurants. We think the courts below erred (1) in assuming that

the only proof relevant to showing that a custom was state-enforced related to the Mississippi criminal trespass statute; (2) in defining the relevant state-enforced custom as requiring proof of a practice both in Hattiesburg and throughout Mississippi, of refusing to serve white persons in the company of Negroes rather than simply proof of state-enforced segregation of the races in Hattiesburg restaurants.

. . . The terms of § 1983 make plain two elements that are necessary for recovery. First, the plaintiff must prove that the defendant has deprived him of a right secured by the "Constitution and laws" of the United States. Second, the plaintiff must show that the defendant deprived him of this constitutional right "under color of any statute, ordinance, regulation, custom, or usage, of any State or Territory." This second element requires that the plaintiff show that the defendant acted "under color of law."

[W]e read both counts of petitioner's complaint to allege discrimination based on race in violation of petitioner's equal protection rights. Few principles of law are more firmly stitched into our constitutional fabric than the proposition that a State must not discriminate against a person because of his race or the race of his companions, or in any way act to compel or encourage racial segregation. Although this is a lawsuit against a private party, not the State or one of its officials, our cases make clear that petitioner will have made out a violation of her Fourteenth Amendment rights and will be entitled to relief under § 1983 if she can prove that a Kress employee, in the course of employment, and a Hattiesburg policeman somehow reached an understanding to deny Miss Adickes service in the Kress store, or to cause her subsequent arrest because she was a white person in the company of Negroes.

The involvement of a state official in such a conspiracy plainly involves the state action essential to show a direct violation of petitioner's Fourteenth Amendment equal protection rights, whether or not the actions of the police were officially authorized or lawful. . . . Moreover, a private party involved in such a conspiracy, even though not an official of the State, can be liable under § 1983. "Private persons, jointly engaged with state officials in the prohibited action, are acting 'under color' of law for purposes of the statute. To act 'under color' of law does not require that the accused be an officer of the State. It is enough that he is a willful participant in joint activity with the State or its agents," *United States v. Price,* 383 U.S. 787, 794 (1966).

We now proceed to consider whether the District Court erred in granting summary judgment on the conspiracy count. In granting respondent's motion, the District Court simply stated that there was "no evidence in the complaint or in the affidavits and other papers from which a 'reasonably-minded person' might draw an inference of conspiracy." . . . Our own scrutiny of the factual allegations of petitioner's complaint, as well as the material found in the affidavits and depositions presented by Kress to the District Court, however, convinces us that summary judgment was improper here, for we think respondent failed to carry its burden of showing the absence of any genuine issue of fact. Before explaining why this is so, it is useful to state the factual arguments, made by the parties concerning summary judgment, and the reasoning of the courts below.

In moving for summary judgment, Kress argued that "uncontested facts" established that no conspiracy existed between any Kress employee and the police. To support this assertion, Kress pointed first to the statements in the deposition of the store manager (Mr. Powell) that (a) he had not communicated with the police, and that (b) he had, by a prearranged tacit signal, ordered the food counter supervisor to see that Miss Adickes was refused service only because he was fearful of a riot in the store by customers angered at seeing a "mixed group" of whites and blacks eating together. Kress also relied on affidavits from the Hattiesburg chief of police, and the two arresting officers, to the effect that store manager Powell had not requested that petitioner be arrested. Finally, Kress pointed to the statements in petitioner's own deposition that she had no knowledge of any communication between any Kress employee and any member of the Hattiesburg police, and was relying on circumstantial evidence to support her contention that there was an arrangement between Kress and the police.

Petitioner, in opposing summary judgment, pointed out that respondent had failed in its moving papers to dispute the allegation in petitioner's complaint, a statement at her deposition, and an unsworn statement by a Kress employee, all to the effect that there was a policeman in the store at the time of the refusal to serve her, and that this was the policeman who subsequently arrested her. Petitioner argued that although she had no knowledge of an agreement between Kress and the police, the sequence of events created a substantial enough possibility of a conspiracy to allow her to proceed to trial, especially given the fact that the noncircumstantial evidence of the conspiracy could only come from adverse witnesses. Further, she submitted an affidavit specifically disputing the manager's assertion that the situation in the store at the time of the refusal was "explosive," thus creating an issue of fact as to what his motives might have been in ordering the refusal of service.

We think that on the basis of this record, it was error to grant summary judgment. As the moving party, respondent had the burden of showing the absence of a genuine issue as to any material fact, and for these purposes the material it lodged must be viewed in the light most favorable to the opposing party. Respondent here did not carry its burden because of its failure to foreclose the possibility that there was a policeman in the Kress store while petitioner was awaiting service, and that this policeman reached an understanding with some Kress employee that petitioner not be served.

It is true that Mr. Powell, the store manager, claimed in his deposition that he had not seen or communicated with a policeman prior to his tacit signal to Miss Baggett, the supervisor of the food counter. But respondent did not submit any affidavits from Miss Baggett, or from Miss Freeman, the waitress who actually refused petitioner service, either of whom might well have seen and communicated with a policeman in the store. Further, we find it particularly noteworthy that the two officers involved in the arrest each failed in his affidavit to foreclose the possibility (1) that he was in the store while petitioner was there; and (2) that, upon seeing petitioner with Negroes, he communicated his disapproval to a Kress employee, thereby influencing the decision not to serve petitioner.

Given these unexplained gaps in the materials submitted by respondent, we conclude that respondent failed to fulfill its initial burden of demonstrating what is a critical element in this aspect of the case—that there was no policeman in the store. If a policeman were present, we think it would be open to a jury, in light of the sequence that followed, to infer from the circumstances that the policeman and a Kress employee had a "meeting of the minds" and thus reached an understanding that petitioner should be refused service. Because "[o]n summary judgment the inferences to be drawn from the underlying facts contained in [the moving party's] materials must be viewed in the light most favorable to the party opposing the motion," . . . we think respondent's failure to show there was no policeman in the store requires reversal.

. . . There remains to be discussed the substantive count of petitioner's complaint, and the showing necessary for petitioner to prove that respondent refused her service "under color of any . . . custom, or usage, of [the] State" in violation of her rights under the Equal Protection Clause of the Fourteenth Amendment.

We are first confronted with the issue of whether a "custom" for purposes of § 1983 must have the force of law, or whether, as argued in dissent, no state involvement is required. Although this Court has never explicitly decided this question, we do not interpret the statute against an amorphous backdrop.

What is now 42 U.S.C. § 1983 came into existence as § 1 of the Ku Klux Klan Act of April 20, 1871, 17 Stat. 13. The Chairman of the House Select Committee which drafted this legislation described § 1 as modeled after § 2 of the Civil Rights Act of 1866—a criminal provision that also contained language that forbade certain acts by any persons "under color of any law, statute, ordinance, regulation, or custom," 14 Stat. 27. In the *Civil Rights Cases,* 109 U.S. 3, 16 (1883), the Court said of this 1866 statute: "This law is clearly corrective in its character, intended to counteract and furnish redress against State laws and proceedings, and *customs having the force of law,* which sanction the wrongful acts specified." (Emphasis added.) Moreover, after an exhaustive examination of the legislative history of the 1866 Act, both the majority and dissenting opinions in *Jones v. Alfred H. Mayer Co.,* 392 U.S. 409 (1968), concluded that § 2 of the 1866 Civil Rights Act was intended to be limited to "deprivations perpetrated 'under color of *law.'* " (Emphasis added.)

Quite apart from this Court's construction of the identical "under color of" provision of § 2 of the 1866 Act, the legislative history of § 1 of the 1871 Act, the lineal ancestor of § 1983, also indicates that the provision in question here was intended to encompass only conduct supported by state action. That such a limitation was intended for § 1 can be seen from an examination of the statements and actions of both the supporters and opponents of the Ku Klux Klan Act.

. . . In addition to the legislative history, there exists an unbroken line of decisions, extending back many years, in which this Court has declared that action "under color of *law*" is a predicate for a cause of action under § 1983, or its criminal counterpart, 18 U.S.C. § 242. Moreover, with the possible exception of an exceedingly opaque district court opinion, every lower court opinion of which we are aware that has considered the issue, has concluded that a "custom or usage" for purposes of § 1983 requires state involvement and is not simply a practice that reflects longstanding social habits, generally observed by the people in a locality. Finally, the language of the statute itself points in the same direction for it expressly requires that the "custom or

usage" be that "of any *State,*" not simply of the people living in a state. In sum, against this background, we think it is clear that a "custom, or usage, of [a] State" for purposes of § 1983 must have the force of law by virtue of the persistent practices of state officials.

Congress included customs and usages within its definition of law in § 1983 because of the persistent and widespread discriminatory practices of state officials in some areas of the post-bellum South. As Representative Garfield said: "[E]ven where the laws are just and equal on their face, yet, by a systematic maladministration of them, or a neglect or refusal to enforce their provisions, a portion of the people are denied equal protection under them." Although not authorized by written law, such practices of state officials could well be so permanent and well settled as to constitute a "custom or usage" with the force of law.

This interpretation of custom recognizes that settled practices of state officials may, by imposing sanctions or withholding benefits, transform private predilections into compulsory rules of behavior no less than legislative pronouncements. . . .

. . . For petitioner to recover under the substantive count of her complaint, she must show a deprivation of a right guaranteed to her by the Equal Protection Clause of the Fourteenth Amendment. Since the "action inhibited by the first section of the Fourteenth Amendment is only such action as may fairly said to be that of the States," *Shelley v. Kraemer,* 334 U.S. 1, 13 (1948), we must decide, for purposes of this case, the following "state action" issue: Is there sufficient state action to prove a violation of petitioner's Fourteenth Amendment rights if she shows that Kress refused her service because of a state-enforced custom compelling segregation of the races in Hattiesburg restaurants?

In analyzing this problem, it is useful to state two polar propositions, each of which is easily identified and resolved. On the one hand, the Fourteenth Amendment plainly prohibits a State itself from discriminating because of race. On the other hand, § 1 of the Fourteenth Amendment does not forbid a private party, not acting against a backdrop of state compulsion or involvement, to discriminate on the basis of race in his personal affairs as an expression of his own personal predilections. As was said in *Shelley v. Kraemer, supra,* § 1 of "[t]hat Amendment erects no shield against merely private conduct, however discriminatory or wrongful." 334 U.S., at 13.

. . . The question most relevant for this case, however, is a slightly different one. It is whether the decision of an owner of a restaurant to discriminate on the basis of race under the compulsion of state law offends the Fourteenth Amendment. Although this Court has not explicitly decided the Fourteenth Amendment state action issue implicit in this question, underlying the Court's decisions in the sit-in cases is the notion that a State is responsible for the discriminatory act of a private party when the State, by its law, has compelled the act. . . . Moreover, there is much support in lower court opinions for the conclusion that discriminatory acts by private parties done under the compulsion of state law offend the Fourteenth Amendment. . . .

For state action purposes it makes no difference of course whether the racially discriminatory act by the private party is compelled by a statutory provision or by a custom having the force of law—in either case it is the State that has commanded the result by its law. Without deciding whether less substantial involvement of a State might satisfy the state action requirement of the Fourteenth Amendment, we conclude that petitioner would show an abridgment of her equal protection right, if she proves that Kress refused her service because of a state-enforced custom of segregating the races in public restaurants.

. . . In summary, if petitioner can show (1) the existence of a state-enforced custom of segregating the races in public eating places in Hattiesburg at the time of the incident in question; and (2) that Kress' refusal to serve her was motivated by that state-enforced custom, she will have made out a claim under § 1983.

For the foregoing reasons we think petitioner is entitled to a new trial on the substantive count of her complaint.

The judgment of the Court of Appeals is reversed and the case is remanded to that court for further proceedings consistent with this opinion.

It is so ordered.

MR. JUSTICE MARSHALL took no part in the decision of this case.

[The concurring opinion of MR. JUSTICE BLACK is omitted.]

* * *

MR. JUSTICE DOUGLAS dissenting in part.

The statutory words "under color of any statute, ordinance, regulation, custom, or usage, of any State," 42 U.S.C. § 1983, are seriously emasculated by today's ruling. Custom, it is said, must have "the force of law"; and "law," as I read the opinion, is used in the Hamiltonian sense.

The Court requires state involvement in the enforcement of a "custom" before that "custom" can be actionable under 42 U.S.C. § 1983. That means, according to the Court, that "custom" for the purposes of § 1983 "must have the force of law by virtue of the persistent practices of state officials." That construc-

tion of § 1983 is, to borrow a phrase from the first Mr. Justice Harlan, "too narrow and artificial." . . .

Section 1983 by its terms protects all "rights" that are "secured by the Constitution and laws" of the United States. There is no more basic "right" than the exemption from discrimination on account of race—an exemption that stems not only from the Equal Protection Clause of the Fourteenth Amendment but also from the Thirteenth Amendment and from a myriad of "laws" enacted by Congress. And so far as § 1983 is concerned it is sufficient that the deprivation of that right be "under color" of "any . . . custom . . . of any State." The "custom" to be actionable must obviously reflect more than the prejudices of a few; it must reflect the dominant communal sentiment.

. . . The "custom . . . of any State," however, can be much more pervasive. It includes the unwritten commitment, stronger than ordinances, statutes, and regulations, by which men live and arrange their lives. . . .

. . . The philosophy of the Black Codes reached much further than the sanctions actually prescribed in them. Federal judges, who entered the early school desegregation decrees, often felt the ostracism of the community, though the local "law" never even purported to place penalties on judges for doing such acts. Forty years ago in Washington, D.C., a black who was found after the sun set in the northwest section of the District on or above Chevy Chase Circle was arrested, though his only "crime" was waiting for a bus to take him home after caddying at a plush golf course in the environs. There was no "law" sanctioning such an arrest. It was done "under color" of a "custom" of the Nation's Capitol.

. . . If the wrong done to the individual was under "color" of "custom" alone, the ingredients of the cause of action were satisfied. The adoption of the Fourteenth Amendment expanded the substantive rights covered by § 1 of the 1871 Act *vis-à-vis* those covered by § 2 of the 1866 Act. But that expanded coverage did not make "state action" a necessary ingredient in all of the remedial provisions of § 1 of the 1871 Act. Neither all of § 1 of the 1871 Act nor all of its successor, § 1983, was intended to be conditioned by the need for "state" complicity.

. . . It is time we stopped being niggardly in construing civil rights legislation. It is time we kept up with Congress and construed its laws in the full amplitude needed to rid their enforcement of the lingering tolerance for racial discrimination that we sanction today.

[The opinion of MR. JUSTICE BRENNAN, concurring in part and dissenting in part, is omitted.]

SWAIN V. ALABAMA
380 U.S. 202 (1965)

Robert Swain, a 19-year-old black male, was indicted, convicted, and sentenced to death in Talladega County, Alabama, for the rape of a 17-year-old white female. He entered motions to quash the indictment on the ground of invidious discrimination in the selection of jurors. The motions were denied, and his conviction was affirmed by the Alabama Supreme Court. *Vote: 6-3.*

* * *

MR. JUSTICE WHITE delivered the opinion of the Court.

. . . We consider first petitioner's claims concerning the selection of grand jurors and the petit jury venire. The evidence was that while Negro males over 21 constitute 26% of all males in the county in this age group, only 10% to 15% of the grand and petit jury panels drawn from the jury box since 1953 have been Negroes, there having been only one case in which the percentage was as high as 23%. In this period of time, Negroes served on 80% of the grand juries selected, the number ranging from one to three. There were four or five Negroes on the grand jury panel of about 33 in this case, out of which two served on the grand jury which indicted petitioner. Although there has been an average of six to seven Negroes on petit jury venires in criminal cases, no Negro has actually served on a petit jury since about 1950. In this case there were eight Negroes on the petit jury venire but none actually served, two being exempt and six being struck by the prosecutor in the process of selecting the jury.

. . . Alabama law requires that the three jury commissioners in Talladega County place on the jury roll all male citizens in the community over 21 who are reputed to be honest, intelligent men and are esteemed for their integrity, good character and sound judgment. . . . In practice, however, the commissioners do not place on the roll all such citizens, either white or colored. A typical jury roll at best contains about 2,500 names, out of a total male population over 21, according to the latest census, of 16,406 persons. Each commissioner, with the clerk's assistance, produces for the jury list names of persons who in his judgment are qualified. The sources are city directories, registration lists, club and church lists, conversations with other persons in the community, both white and colored, and personal and business acquaintances.

Venires drawn from the jury box made up in this manner unquestionably contained a smaller proportion of the Negro community than of the white community. But a defendant in a criminal case is not constitutionally entitled to demand a proportionate number of his race on the jury which tries him nor on the venire or jury roll from which petit jurors are drawn. *Virginia v. Rives,* 100 U.S. 313, 322-323 [1880]; *Gibson v. Mississippi,* 162 U.S. 565 [1896]; *Thomas v. Texas,* 212 U.S. 278, 282 [1909]; *Cassell v. Texas,* 339 U.S. 282 [1950]. Neither the jury roll nor the venire need be a perfect mirror of the community or accurately reflect the proportionate strength of every identifiable group. . . . We cannot say that purposeful discrimination based on race alone is satisfactorily proved by showing that an identifiable group in a community is underrepresented by as much as 10%. . . . We do not think that the burden of proof was carried by petitioner in this case.

Petitioner makes a further claim relating to the exercise of peremptory challenges to exclude Negroes from serving on petit juries.

. . . The function of the challenge is not only to eliminate extremes of partiality on both sides, but to assure the parties that the jurors before whom they try the case will decide on the basis of the evidence placed before them, and not otherwise. In this way the peremptory satisfies the rule that "to perform its high function in the best way 'justice must satisfy the appearance of justice.' " . . . Indeed the very availability of peremptories allows counsel to ascertain the possibility of bias through probing questions on the *voir dire* and facilitates the exercise of challenges for cause by removing the fear of incurring a juror's hostility through examination and challenge for cause. Although historically the incidence of the prosecutor's challenge has differed from that of the accused, the view in this country has been that the system should guarantee "not only freedom from any bias against the accused, but also from any prejudice against his prosecution. Between him and the state the scales are to be evenly held." . . .

. . . With these considerations in mind, we cannot hold that the striking of Negroes in a particular case is a denial of equal protection of the laws. In the quest for an impartial and qualified jury, Negro and white, Protestant and Catholic, are alike subject to being challenged without cause. To subject the prosecutor's challenge in any particular case to the demands and traditional standards of the Equal Protection Clause would entail a radical change in the nature and operation of the challenge. The challenge, *pro tanto,* would no longer be peremptory, each and every challenge being open to examination, either at the time of the challenge or at a hearing afterwards. The prosecutor's judgment underlying each challenge would be subject to scrutiny for reasonableness and sincerity. And a great many uses of the challenge would be banned.

. . . [*Part III*] Petitioner, however, presses a broader claim in this Court. His argument is that not only were the Negroes removed by the prosecutor in this case but that there never has been a Negro on a petit jury in either a civil or criminal case in Talladega County and that in criminal cases prosecutors have consistently and systematically exercised their strikes to prevent any and all Negroes on petit jury venires from serving on the petit jury itself. This systematic practice, it is claimed, is invidious discrimination for which the peremptory system is insufficient justification.

We agree that this claim raises a different issue and it may well require a different answer. We have decided that it is permissible to insulate from inquiry the removal of Negroes from a particular jury on the assumption that the prosecutor is acting on acceptable considerations related to the case he is trying, the particular defendant involved and the particular crime charged. But when the prosecutor in a county, in case after case, whatever the circumstances, whatever the crime and whoever the defendant or the victim may be, is responsible for the removal of Negroes who have been selected as qualified jurors by the jury commissioners and who have survived challenges for cause, with the result that no Negroes ever serve on petit juries, the Fourteenth Amendment claim takes on added significance. . . . In these circumstances, giving even the widest leeway to the operation of irrational but trial-related suspicions and antagonisms, it would appear that the purposes of the peremptory challenge are being perverted. If the State has not seen fit to leave a single Negro on any jury in a criminal case, the presumption protecting the prosecutor may well be overcome. Such proof might support a reasonable inference that Negroes are excluded from juries for reasons wholly unrelated to the outcome of the particular case on trial and that the peremptory system is being used to deny the Negro the same right and opportunity to participate in the administration of justice enjoyed by the white population. These ends the peremptory challenge is not designed to facilitate or justify.

We need pursue this matter no further, however, for even if a State's systematic striking of Negroes in the selection of petit juries raises a prima facie case under the Fourteenth Amendment, we think it is readily apparent that the record in this case is not sufficient to demonstrate that the rule has been violated by the peremptory system as it operates in Talladega County. . . .

. . . Unlike the selection process, which is wholly in the hands of state officers, defense counsel participate in the peremptory challenge system, and indeed generally have a far greater role than any officers of the State. It is for this reason that a showing that Negroes have not served during a specified period of time does not, absent a sufficient showing of the prosecutor's participation, give rise to the inference of systematic discrimination on the part of the State. The ordinary exercise of challenges by defense counsel does not, of course, imply purposeful discrimination by state officials. This is not to say that a defendant attacking the prosecutor's use of peremptory challenges over a period of time need elicit an admission from the prosecutor that discrimination accounted for his rejection of Negroes, any more than a defendant attacking jury selection need obtain such an admission from the jury commissioners. But the defendant must, to pose the issue, show the prosecutor's systematic use of peremptory challenges against Negroes over a period of time. This is the teaching of *Hernandez v. Texas,* [347 U.S. 475 (1954)] . . . *Norris v. Alabama,* [294 U.S. 587 1935)], . . . and *Patton v. Mississippi,* [332 U.S. 463 (1947)]. We see no reason, except for blind application of a proof standard developed in a context where there is no question of state responsibility for the alleged exclusion, why the defendant attacking the prosecutor's systematic use of challenges against Negroes should not be required to establish on the record the prosecutor's conduct in this regard, especially where the same prosecutor for many years is said to be responsible for this practice and is quite available for questioning on this matter. Accordingly the judgment is

Affirmed.

MR. JUSTICE BLACK concurs in the result.

[The concurring opinion of MR. JUSTICE HARLAN is omitted.]

* * *

MR. JUSTICE GOLDBERG, with whom THE CHIEF JUSTICE [WARREN] and JUSTICE DOUGLAS join, dissenting.

. . . Alabama here does not deny Negroes as a race are excluded from serving on juries in Talladega County. The State seeks to justify this admitted exclusion of Negroes from jury service by contending that the fact that no Negro has ever served on a petit jury in Talladega County has resulted from use of the jury-striking system, which is a form of peremptory challenge. While recognizing that no Negro has ever served on any petit jury in Talladega County, that the method of venire selection was inadequate, that the prosecutor in this case used the peremptory challenge system to exclude all Negroes as a class, and that the systematic misuse by the State of a peremptory challenge system to exclude all Negroes from all juries is prohibited by the Fourteenth Amendment, the Court affirms petitioner's conviction on the ground that petitioner has "failed to carry" his burden of proof. The court holds this because it believes the record is silent as to whether the State participated in this total exclusion of all Negroes in previous cases; it would require petitioner specifically to negative the possibility that total exclusion of Negroes from jury service in all other cases was produced solely by the action of defense attorneys.

I cannot agree that the record is silent as to the State's involvement in the total exclusion of Negroes from jury service in Talladega County. The Alabama Supreme Court found that "Negroes are commonly on trial venires but are always struck by attorneys in selecting the trial jury." . . .

. . . Finally, it is clear that Negroes were removed from the venire and excluded from service by the prosecutor's use of the peremptory challenge system in this case and that they have never served on the jury in any case in the history of the county. On these facts, and the inferences reasonably drawn from them, it seems clear that petitioner has affirmatively proved a pattern of racial discrimination in which the State is significantly involved. . . . As this Court held in *Strauder* [*v. West Virginia,* 100 U.S. 303 (1880)], systematic exclusion of Negroes from jury service constitutes a brand of inferiority affixed upon them and state involvement in affixing such a brand is forbidden by the Fourteenth Amendment.

There is, however, a more fundamental defect in the Court's holding. Even if the Court were correct that the record is silent as to state involvement in previous cases in which Negroes have been systematically excluded from jury service, nevertheless, it is undisputed that no Negro has ever served on any petit jury in the history of Talladega County. Under *Norris, Patton* and the other cases discussed above, it is clear that petitioner by proving this made out a prima facie case of unlawful jury exclusion. The burden of proof then shifted to the State to prove, if it could, that this exclusion was brought about for some reason other than racial discrimination in which the State participated.

. . . Finally, the Court's reasoning on this point completely overlooks the fact that the total exclusion of Negroes from juries in Talladega County results from the interlocking of an inadequate venire selection system, for which the State concededly is responsible, and the use of peremptory challenges. All of these factors confirm my view that no good reason exists to fashion a new rule of burden of proof, which will make it more difficult to put an end to discriminatory selection of juries on racial

grounds and will thereby impair the constitutional promise of "Equal Protection of the Laws," made effective by *Strauder* and the cases which follow it. By undermining the doctrine of the prima facie case while paying lip service to *Strauder* the Court today allies itself with those "that keep the word of promise to our ear and break it to our hope."

. . . Were it necessary to make an absolute choice between the right of a defendant to have a jury chosen in conformity with the requirements of the Fourteenth Amendment and the right to challenge peremptorily, the Constitution compels a choice of the former. . . . But no such choice is compelled in this situation. The holding called for by this case, is that where, as here, a Negro defendant proves that Negroes constitute a substantial segment of the population, that Negroes are qualified to serve as jurors, and that none or only a token number has served on juries over an extended period of time, a prima facie case of the exclusion of Negroes from juries is then made out; that the State, under our settled decisions, is then called upon to show that such exclusion has been brought about "for some reason other than racial discrimination," . . . and that the State wholly fails to meet the prima facie case of systematic and purposeful racial discrimination by showing that it has been accomplished by the use of a peremptory challenge system unless the State also shows that it is not involved in the misuse of such a system to prevent all Negroes from ever sitting on any jury. Such a holding would not interfere with the rights of *defendants* to use peremptories, nor the right of the State to use peremptories as they normally and traditionally have been used.

It would not mean, as the Court's prior decisions, to which I would adhere, make clear, that Negroes are entitled to proportionate representation on a jury. . . . Nor would it mean that where systematic exclusion of Negroes from jury service has not always been shown, a prosecutor's motives are subject to question or judicial inquiry when he excludes Negroes or any other group from sitting on a jury in a particular case. Only where systematic exclusion has been shown, would the State be called upon to justify its use of peremptories or to negative the State's involvement in discriminatory jury selection.

EVANS V. NEWTON
382 U.S. 296 (1966)

In 1911 U.S. Senator Augustus Bacon willed a tract of land to the mayor and city council of Macon, Georgia, that was to be used as a park for white people only. The senator stated in the will that although he had only the kindest feeling for blacks, he was of the opinion that "in their social relations the

two races (white and negro) should be forever separate." The will provided that the park be controlled by a seven-member all-white board of managers. After the city desegregated the park, individual members of the board of managers sued the city of Macon and others, arguing that the city be removed as trustee and that the court appoint new trustees to the park. Black citizens of Macon intervened in the case, alleging that the racial limitation violated federal law. The city, which had alleged that it could not legally enforce segregation, asked to resign as trustee. Senator Bacon's heirs also intervened in the case, asking for reversion of the trust property to the Bacon estate if the petition was denied. The Georgia Supreme Court held that Senator Bacon had the right to leave his property to a limited class and that charitable trusts are subject to supervision of an equity court, which could appoint new trustees to avoid failure of the trust. *Vote: 6-3.*

* * *

MR. JUSTICE DOUGLAS delivered the opinion of the Court.

. . . There are two complementary principles to be reconciled in this case. One is the right of the individual to pick his own associates so as to express his preferences and dislikes, and to fashion his private life by joining such clubs and groups as he chooses. The other is the constitutional ban in the Equal Protection Clause of the Fourteenth Amendment against state-sponsored racial inequality, which of course bars a city from acting as trustee under a private will that serves the racial segregation cause. *Pennsylvania v. Board of Trusts,* 353 U.S. 230 [1957]. A private golf club, however, restricted to either Negro or white membership is one expression of freedom of association. But a municipal golf course that serves only one race is state activity indicating a preference on a matter as to which the State must be neutral. What is "private" action and what is "state" action is not always easy to determine. See *Burton v. Wilmington Parking Authority,* 365 U.S. 715 [1961]. Conduct that is formally "private" may become so entwined with governmental policies or so impregnated with a governmental character as to become subject to the constitutional limitations placed upon state action. The action of a city in serving as trustee of property under a private will serving the segregated cause is an obvious example. . . . A town may be privately owned and managed, but that does not necessarily allow the company to treat it as if it were wholly in the private sector. [*Marsh v. Alabama,* 326 U.S. 501 (1946)] . . . We have also held that where a State delegates an aspect of the elective process to private groups, they become subject to the same restraints as the State. *Terry v. Adams,* 345 U.S. 461 [1953]. That is to say, when private individuals or groups are endowed by the State with powers or functions governmental in nature, they become agencies or instrumentalities of the State and subject to its constitutional limitations.

. . . If a testator wanted to leave a school or center for the use of one race only and in no way implicated

the State in the supervision, control, or management of that facility, we assume arguendo that no constitutional difficulty would be encountered.

This park, however, is in a different posture. For years it was an integral part of the City of Macon's activities. From the pleadings we assume it was swept, manicured, watered, patrolled, and maintained by the city as a public facility for whites only, as well as granted tax exemption under Ga. Code Ann. § 92-201. The momentum it acquired as a public facility is certainly not dissipated *ipso facto* by the appointment of "private" trustees. So far as this record shows, there has been no change in municipal maintenance and concern over this facility. Whether these public characteristics will in time be dissipated is wholly conjectural. If the municipality remains entwined in the management or control of the park, it remains subject to the restraints of the Fourteenth Amendment just as the private utility in *Public Utilities Comm'n v. Pollak,* 343 U.S. 451, 462, [1952], remained subject to the Fifth Amendment because of the surveillance which federal agencies had over its affairs. We only hold that where the tradition of municipal control had become firmly established, we cannot take judicial notice that the mere substitution of trustees instantly transferred this park from the public to the private sector.

This conclusion is buttressed by the nature of the service rendered the community by a park. The service rendered even by a private park of this character is municipal in nature. It is open to every white person, there being no selective element other than race. Golf clubs, social centers, luncheon clubs, schools such as Tuskegee was at least in origin, and other like organizations in the private sector are often racially oriented. A park, on the other hand, is more like a fire department or police department that traditionally serves the community. Mass recreation through the use of parks is plainly in the public domain . . . and state courts that aid private parties to perform that public function on a segregated basis implicate the State in conduct proscribed by the Fourteenth Amendment. Like the streets of the company town in *Marsh v. Alabama,* . . . the elective process of *Terry v. Adams,* . . . and the transit system of *Public Utilities Comm'n v. Pollak,* . . . the predominant character and purpose of this park are municipal.

Under the circumstances of this case, we cannot but conclude that the public character of this park requires that it be treated as a public institution subject to the command of the Fourteenth Amendment, regardless of who now has title under state law. We may fairly assume that had the Georgia courts been of the view that even in private hands the park may not be operated for the public on a segregated basis, the resignation would not have been approved and private trustees appointed. We put the matter that way because on this record we cannot say that the transfer of title *per se* disentangled the park from segregation under the municipal regime that long controlled it.

Since the judgment below gives effect to that purpose, it must be and is

Reversed.

[The concurring opinion of MR. JUSTICE WHITE is omitted.]

* * *

MR. JUSTICE BLACK dissenting.

I find nothing in the United States Constitution that compels any city or other state subdivision to hold title to property it does not want or to act as trustee under a will when it chooses not to do so. And I had supposed until now that the narrow question of whether a city could resign such a trusteeship and whether a state court could appoint successor trustees depended entirely on state law. Here, however, the Court assumes that federal power exists to reverse the Supreme Court of Georgia for affirming a Georgia trial court's decree which, as the State Supreme Court held, did only these "two things: (1) Accepted the resignation of the City of Macon as trustee of Baconsfield; and (2) appointed new trustees." . . .

The State Supreme Court's interpretation of the scope and effect of this Georgia decree should be binding upon us unless the State Supreme Court has somehow lost its power to control and limit the scope and effect of Georgia trial court decrees relating to Georgia wills creating Georgia trusts of Georgia property. A holding that ignores this state power would be so destructive of our state judicial systems that it could find no support, I think, in our Federal Constitution or in any of this Court's prior decisions. For myself, I therefore accept the decision of the Georgia Supreme Court as holding only what it declared it held, namely, that the trial court committed no error under Georgia law in accepting the City of Macon's resignation as trustee and in appointing successor trustees to execute the Bacon trust.

I am not sure that the Court is passing at all on the only two questions the Georgia Supreme Court decided in approving the city's resignation as trustee and the appointment of successors. If the Court is holding that a State is without these powers, it is certainly a drastic departure from settled constitutional doctrine and a vastly important one which, I cannot refrain from saying, deserves a clearer explication than it is given. Ambiguity cannot, however, conceal the revolutionary nature of such a holding, if this is the Court's holding, nor successfully obscure the tremendous lopping off of power heretofore uniformly conceded by all to belong to the States. This ambiguous and confusing disposition of such highly important questions is particularly disturbing to me because the Court's discussion of the constitutional status of the park comes in the nature of an advisory opinion on federal constitutional questions the Georgia Supreme Court did not decide. Consequently, for all the foregoing reasons and particularly since the Georgia courts decided no federal constitutional question, I agree with my Brother HARLAN that the writ of certiorari should have been dismissed as improvidently granted.

[The dissenting opinion of MR. JUSTICE HARLAN, whom MR. JUSTICE STEWART joins, is omitted.]

LOVING V. VIRGINIA
388 U.S. 1 (1967)

In June 1958, Mildred Jeter Loving, a black woman, and Richard Loving, a white man, were married in Washington, D.C. Shortly after their marriage, they returned to Virginia and established residence in Caroline County. A grand jury issued an indictment charging the Lovings with violating Virginia's ban on interracial marriages (§§ 20-58 and 20-59 of the Virginia Code). On June 6, 1959, the Lovings pleaded guilty and were sentenced to one year in jail. The trial judge suspended the sentence for a period of 25 years on the condition that the Lovings leave the state and not return together for 25 years. After residing in Washington, D.C., for several years, the Lovings challenged their conviction on the ground that the Virginia statute violated the Fourteenth Amendment. The Virginia Supreme Court of Appeals upheld the constitutionality of the antimiscegenation statute. *Vote: 9-0.*

* * *

MR. CHIEF JUSTICE WARREN delivered the opinion of the Court.

This case presents a constitutional question never addressed by this Court: whether a statutory scheme adopted by the State of Virginia to prevent marriages between persons solely on the basis of racial classifications violates the Equal Protection and Due Process Clauses of the Fourteenth Amendment. For reasons which seem to us to reflect the central meaning of those constitutional commands, we conclude that these statutes cannot stand consistently with the Fourteenth Amendment.

. . . Virginia is now one of 16 States which prohibit and punish marriages on the basis of racial classifications. Penalties for miscegenation arose as an incident to slavery and have been common in Virginia since the colonial period. The present statutory scheme dates from the adoption of the Racial Integrity Act of 1924, passed during the period of extreme nativism which followed the end of the First World War. The central features of the Act, and current Virginia law, are the absolute prohibition of a "white person" marrying other than another "white person," a prohibition against issuing marriage licenses until the issuing official is satisfied that the applicants' statements as to their race are correct, certificates of "racial composition" to be kept by both local and state registrars, and the carrying forward of earlier prohibitions against racial intermarriage.

In upholding the constitutionality of these provisions in the decision below, the Supreme Court of Appeals of Virginia referred to its 1955 decision in *Naim v. Naim,* 197 Va. 80 [1955], as stating the reasons supporting the validity of these laws. In *Naim,* the state court concluded that the State's legitimate purposes were "to preserve the racial integrity of its citizens," and to prevent "the corruption of blood," "a mongrel breed of citizens," and "the obliteration of racial pride," obviously an endorsement of the doctrine of White Supremacy. . . . The court also reasoned that marriage has traditionally been subject to state regulation without federal intervention, and, consequently, the regulation of marriage should be left to exclusive state control by the Tenth Amendment.

While the state court is no doubt correct in asserting that marriage is a social relation subject to the State's police power, . . . the State does not contend in its argument before this Court that its powers to regulate marriage are unlimited notwithstanding the commands of the Fourteenth Amendment. Nor could it do so in light of *Meyer v. Nebraska,* 262 U.S. 390 (1923), and *Skinner v. Oklahoma,* 316 U.S. 535 (1942). Instead, the State argues that the meaning of the Equal Protection Clause, as illuminated by the statements of the Framers, is only that state penal laws containing an interracial element as part of the definition of the offense must apply equally to whites and Negroes in the same sense that members of each race are punished to the same degree. Thus, the State contends that, because its miscegenation statutes punish equally both the white and the Negro participants in an interracial marriage, these statutes, despite their reliance on racial classifications, do not constitute an invidious discrimination based upon race. The second argument advanced by the State assumes the validity of its equal application theory. The argument is that, if the Equal Protection Clause does not outlaw miscegenation statutes because of their reliance on racial classifications, the question of constitutionality would thus become whether there was any rational basis for a State to treat interracial marriages differently from other marriages. On this question, the State argues, the scientific evidence is substantially in doubt and, consequently, this Court should defer to the wisdom of the state legislature in adopting its policy of discouraging interracial marriages.

Because we reject the notion that the mere "equal application" of a statute containing racial classifications is enough to remove the classifications from the Fourteenth Amendment's proscription of all invidious racial discriminations, we do not accept the State's contention that these statutes should be upheld if there is any possible basis for concluding that they serve a rational purpose. The mere fact of equal application does not mean that our analysis of these statutes should follow the approach we have taken in cases involving no racial discrimination where the Equal Protection Clause has been arrayed against a statute discriminating between the kinds of advertising which may be displayed on trucks in New York City, . . . or an exemption in Ohio's ad valorem tax for merchandise owned by a nonresident in a storage warehouse. . . . In these cases, involving distinctions not drawn according to race, the Court has merely asked whether there is any rational foundation for the discriminations, and has deferred to the wisdom of the state legislatures. In the case at bar, however, we deal with statutes containing racial classifications, and the fact of equal application does not immunize the statute from the very heavy burden of justification which the Fourteenth Amendment has traditionally required of state statutes drawn according to race.

The State argues that statements in the Thirty-ninth Congress about the time of the passage of the Fourteenth Amendment indicate that the Framers did not intend the Amendment to make unconstitutional state miscegenation laws. Many of the statements alluded to by the State concern the debates over the Freedmen's Bureau Bill, which President Johnson vetoed, and the Civil Rights Act of 1866, . . . enacted over his veto. While these statements have some relevance to the intention of Congress in submitting the Fourteenth Amendment, it must be understood that they pertained to the passage of specific statutes and not to the broader, organic purpose of a constitutional amendment. . . . We have rejected the proposition that the debates in the Thirty-ninth Congress or in the state legislatures which ratified the Fourteenth Amendment supported the theory advanced by the State, that the requirement of equal protection of the laws is satisfied by penal laws defining offenses based on racial classifications so long as white and Negro participants in the offense were similarly punished. . . .

The State finds support for its "equal protection" theory in the decision of the Court in *Pace v. Alabama,* 106 U.S. 583 (1883). In that case, the Court upheld a conviction under an Alabama statute forbidding adultery or fornication between a white person and a Negro which imposed a greater penalty than that of a statute proscribing similar conduct by members of the same race. The Court reasoned that the statute could not be said to discriminate against Negroes because the punishment for each participant in the offense was the same. However, as recently as the 1964 Term, in rejecting the reasoning of that case, we stated "*Pace* represents a limited view of the Equal Protection Clause which has not withstood analysis in the subsequent decisions of this Court." *McLaughlin v. Florida* [379 U.S. 184 (1964)] at 188. As we there demonstrated, the Equal Protection Clause requires the consideration of whether the classifications drawn by any statute constitute an arbitrary and invidious discrimination. The clear and central purpose of the Fourteenth Amendment was to eliminate all official state sources of invidious racial discrimination in the States. . . .

There can be no question but that Virginia's miscegenation statutes rest solely upon distinctions drawn according to race. The statutes proscribe generally accepted conduct if engaged in by members of different races. Over the years, this Court has consistently repudiated "[d]istinctions between citizens solely because of their ancestry" as being "odious to a free people whose institutions are founded upon the doctrine of equality." *Hirabayashi v. United States,* 320 U.S. 81, 100 (1943). At the very least, the Equal Protection Clause demands that racial classifications, especially suspect in criminal statutes, be subjected to the "most rigid scrutiny," *Korematsu v. United States,* 323 U.S. 214, 216 (1944), and, if they are ever to be upheld, they must be shown to be necessary to the accomplishment of some permissible state objective, independent of the racial discrimination which it was the object of the Fourteenth Amendment to eliminate. . . .

There is patently no legitimate overriding purpose independent of invidious racial discrimination which justifies this classification. The fact that Virginia prohibits only interracial marriages involving white persons demonstrates that the racial classifi-cations must stand on their own justification, as measures designed to maintain White Supremacy. We have consistently denied the constitutionality of measures which restrict the rights of citizens on account of race. There can be no doubt that restricting the freedom to marry solely because of racial classifications violates the central meaning of the Equal Protection Clause.

These statutes also deprive the Lovings of liberty without due process of law in violation of the Due Process Clause of the Fourteenth Amendment. The freedom to marry has long been recognized as one of the vital personal rights essential to the orderly pursuit of happiness by free men.

Marriage is one of the "basic civil rights of man," fundamental to our very existence and survival. *Skinner v. Oklahoma* . . . See also *Maynard v. Hill,* 125 U.S. 190 (1888). To deny this fundamental freedom on so unsupportable a basis as the racial classifications embodied in these statutes, classifications so directly subversive of the principle of equality at the heart of the Fourteenth Amendment, is surely to deprive all the State's citizens of liberty without due process of law. The Fourteenth Amendment requires that the freedom of choice to marry not be restricted by invidious racial discriminations. Under our Constitution, the freedom to marry, or not marry, a person of another race resides with the individual and cannot be infringed by the State.

These convictions must be reversed.

It is so ordered.

* * *

MR. JUSTICE STEWART concurring.

I have previously expressed the belief that "it is simply not possible for a state law to be valid under our Constitution which makes the criminality of an act depend upon the race of an actor." *McLaughlin v. Florida* . . . Because I adhere to that belief, I concur in the judgment of the Court.

4

The Burger Court

THE ERA OF AMBIVALENCE
AND UNCERTAINTY, 1969-1986

*In many instances where the struggle for racial equality
has made limited progress, that progress has been perceived
as a threat and has been met with fear, hate and racism.*

Karen Blum*

REPUBLICAN CONSERVATISM
REPLACES THE LIBERAL WARREN COURT

After Chief Justice Earl Warren's retirement from the Supreme Court in 1969, President Richard Nixon nominated Warren Earl Burger to replace him on May 21, 1969, with almost no political opposition. On June 9, 1969, he was confirmed by the U.S. Senate by a 74-3 vote. Although Warren Burger was not well known outside the legal community, President Nixon was extremely impressed with his conservatism in criminal jurisprudence and with his behavioral propensity to narrowly construe the Constitution. In addition to Warren, President Nixon replaced Justices Fortas, Harlan, and Black with Justices Blackmun, Rehnquist, and Powell, respectively, within a four-year period. President Gerald Ford appointed Justice John Paul Stevens to replace Justice William O. Douglas in 1975. President Jimmy Carter did not have the

---

*The quote is from Karen Blum (1989), "Section 1981 Revisited: Looking Beyond *Runyon* and *Patterson.*" *Howard Law Journal, 32,* 37.

opportunity to appoint any Justice to the Supreme Court during his one term in office. These personnel changes on the Court were sufficient to establish an ideological shift away from the liberal activism of the Warren Court to a more conservative jurisprudence.

Two competing perspectives have emerged from the scholarly attempts assessing the doctrinal developments and change during the Burger Court era. Vincent Blasi concluded that no Burger Court counterrevolution occurred by undoing major elements of the Warren Court's jurisprudence.[1] Ronald Kahn argued that previous assessments of the Burger Court ignored the complexity of the equal protection clause before the Court and "the increased complexity of constitutional theory and the changing public expectations about political institutions and fundamental rights in the 1970s and 1980s."[2] Our analysis reveals that the Burger Court's jurisprudence on equality issues in a wide variety of contexts was mixed; that is, in some respects, there were important continuities with Warren Court precedents (e.g., school desegregation).[3] In contrast, the Burger Court made it more difficult for minorities to participate in the electoral process, unlike the Warren Court, which had shown a keen sensitivity to the principle of equality vis-à-vis political participation. In understanding our evaluation of the Burger Court, it must be remembered that the Court addressed controversial equal protection issues, such as busing and affirmative action, that were not previously considered by the Warren Court. In this chapter, we demonstrate that although the Burger Court "did not launch a full-scale, frontal attack on the civil rights gains made under the Warren Court," it did set a more conservative and reactionary tone toward civil rights for racial and ethnic minorities and the poor.[4] Consequently, the win-lose-win cyclical pattern was operative and in full force for 17 years during the Burger Court era. David O'Brien characterized the Burger Court as a "troubled and fragmented Court. Its legacy was that of a 'transitional Court': a Court divided between what the Warren Court accomplished and what the Rehnquist Court achieves and leaves behind."[5] This chapter reinforces the transitional character of the Burger Court in the area of equality.

SCHOOL DESEGREGATION REMEDIES

The landmark desegregation precedents established during the Warren Court were sustained by the Burger Court. In less than five months after Warren Burger was confirmed as the 15th Chief Justice, the Burger Court was confronted with a case in which the Court of Appeals for the Fifth Circuit had ordered a three-month delay in integrating 33 school districts in Mississippi. In a per curiam opinion, the Court, in *Alexander v. Holmes County Board of Education,* 396 U.S. 19 (1969), held that all dual school systems must be eliminated at once because "all deliberate speed" resulted in "deliberate delay" and therefore was no longer constitutionally permissible. The Court also emphasized that dual school systems should terminate at once. Resistance to the Burger Court's mandate in *Alexander* continued, especially because busing could be used as one of several methods of dismantling dual school systems.

As late as 1969, approximately two thirds of all black students in Charlotte, North Carolina, remained in schools that were virtually all black. The district court accepted a plan that involved the busing of white and black elementary students to achieve school desegregation. In SWANN V. CHARLOTTE-MECKLENBURG BOARD OF EDUCATION, 402 U.S. 1 (1971), Chief Justice Burger, writing for a unanimous Court, held that busing students was one tool that could be employed to achieve school desegregation if it was established that existing segregation resulted from a school district's history of deliberately segregating students along racial lines. He pointed out, however, that a few "one-race, or virtually one-race, schools within a district is not in and of itself the mark of a system that still practices segregation by law." This controversial decision drew stiff opposition.

Approximately one year after *Swann* was decided, the Court failed for the first time to achieve consensus on desegregation remedies, and Chief Justice Burger filed a dissenting opinion in which Justices Blackmun, Powell, and Rehnquist joined. In *Wright v. Council of Emporia,* 407 U.S. 451 (1972), Emporia, Virginia, had attempted to escape the impact of *Brown I* by creating a new school district from the existing one that had failed to eliminate the dual school system. Writing for a sharply divided Court, Justice Stewart held that Emporia's withdrawal of students from the county schools would simply increase the number of white students attending the school in Emporia and decrease their numbers in the county schools. He also pointed out that this approach would allow whites to attend the schools that are better equipped and "impede the process of dismantling a dual system." Chief Justice Burger, in his dissenting opinion, argued that it was mere speculation that Emporia's operation of a separate system would result in a continuation of racial segregation. He also contended that a separate school system should not be viewed as a manifestation of a discriminatory purpose.

The Furor Over Busing

After the unanimous *Swann* decision in 1971, the number of proposals seeking congressional approval to curb busing increased dramatically. Opposition, however, was not limited to Congress. President Nixon condemned court-ordered busing by referring to it as "forced busing." The legality of busing quickened the pace with which whites left the cities for the suburbs or enrolled their children in private schools. In MILLIKEN V. BRADLEY (*Milliken I*), 418 U.S. 717 (1974), the Court had to decide whether multidistrict remedies were permissible where de jure segregation existed in only one of the districts (the city of Detroit). Chief Justice Burger reversed the lower court's order that mandated a multidistrict remedy, which included busing, in the three-county metropolitan area of Detroit. He declared that because no evidence showed that the discrimination that existed in the Detroit schools was due to the actions of the outlying districts, a federal court could not impose an interdistrict remedy for de jure school segregation. Justice Marshall, in a sharply worded dissent, argued that the majority's view provided no remedy at all for the violation proved in this case. *Milliken I* signaled the Burger Court's reluctance to move too fast with school desegregation.

Antibusing sentiment intensified in the 1970s, but President Jimmy Carter vetoed a law that would have prohibited the Justice Department from initiating desegregation suits against school systems in which busing was mandated.[6] After President Carter's defeat for a second term, the Reagan administration echoed the antibusing sentiment that had engulfed the nation. The mood in the country encouraged states to enact measures that would curb busing remedies for de facto segregation, and these efforts were welcomed by the antibusing forces. In *Washington v. Seattle School District No. 1,* 458 U.S. 457 (1982), a statewide initiative (Initiative 350) was passed that prohibited the busing of children for the purpose of bringing about integration in the public schools. It also mandated that students be assigned to the school nearest or next nearest their home. Writing for a sharply divided Court, Justice Blackmun declared that Initiative 350 was a violation of the equal protection clause. The Court's opinion emphasized that it was impermissible for the state to use the racial nature of a decision to unduly burden racial minorities and to remove the power over busing to achieve desegregation from the local to the state level. Justice Powell, in a forceful dissent, argued that the Court had made an unprecedented intrusion into a matter in which the state had authority to handle and that the school districts were not under any federal constitutional obligation to bus any students.

In *Crawford v. Board of Education of the City of Los Angeles,* 458 U.S. 527 (1982), the Court sustained Proposition I, which prohibited busing ordered by state courts to alleviate de facto segregation unless a federal court would be permitted to do so to remedy a violation under the Fourteenth Amendment's equal protection clause. Justice Powell, who dissented in *Washington v. Seattle School District No. I,* delivered the opinion of the Court, with only Justice Marshall dissenting. Justice Powell argued that Proposition I did not violate the Fourteenth Amendment because it was not enacted with a discriminatory purpose. He also contended that it was constitutionally permissible for the people of California to decide that the Fourteenth Amendment's standard was more appropriate for the state courts to apply than the more exacting state standards. Dissenting, Justice Marshall observed that blacks who have sought diligently to counter centuries of racial discrimination are denied "the full remedial powers of the state judiciary." Going further, he argued that the rules of the game had been changed and that the Court's opinion was not justified by its prior decisions, including *Washington v. Seattle School District No. I.*

The antibusing forces continued to pressure the Reagan administration to curb busing, and the Justice Department's actions made it clear that busing was not on its list of priorities. Antibusing forces' efforts to counteract the *Swann* decision, however, were not successful. For example, in *Metropolitan County Board of Education of Nashville and Davidson County v. Kelley,* 459

U.S. 1183 (1983), the Court refused to grant a writ of certiorari to hear a desegregation case in which the sixth circuit had ruled that busing was necessary to desegregate the schools in Davidson County, because Nashville had a number of advantages, such as compactness, that would enhance solving the problem with few difficulties.

The Intractable Desegregation
Problem Moves North and West

After *Brown I* the focus of attention was on de jure segregation in the South. Northern school districts argued that predominantly black schools in their region were the result of de facto segregation and had nothing to do with official discriminatory practices, despite the fact that segregated neighborhoods emerged from the cooperative efforts of private and public ingenuity. During the 1970s, blacks challenged segregated schools in the North and West. The first school desegregation decision rendered by the Burger Court in the North was KEYES V. SCHOOL DISTRICT NO. 1, DENVER, COLORADO, 413 U.S. 189 (1973). The de jure/de facto distinction was before the Court, and it had its first opportunity to decide a desegregation case in a school system that did not have a history of segregating the races statutorily. Justice Brennan's majority opinion made it clear that purposeful discrimination that is a significant part of a school system is adequate for an inferential finding that de jure segregation is systemwide unless the board is able to rebut such a finding. He announced further that what distinguishes de jure from de facto segregation is the intent to segregate and that it was therefore unnecessary to consider the de facto "neighborhood school policy" due to the existence of de jure segregation.

Some school boards sought to terminate federal court supervision because they thought they had complied with *Brown I* and were operating a unitary school system. The NAACP and the Legal Defense Fund were suspicious of efforts to terminate supervision because they were well aware of the resolve of the opposition forces to obstruct and frustrate the desegregation process. In *Pasadena City Board of Education v. Spangler,* 427 U.S. 424 (1976), the public schools resegregated because of the movement of people in and out of the school system that previously had been desegregated by an order of the court. The district court ordered that the schools be desegregated so that no school would have a majority of any minority students. It retained jurisdiction until full compliance was accomplished. Justice Rehnquist, writing for a 6-2 majority, held that the district court had exceeded its authority in enforcing its order because school officials are not required to make yearly adjustments to fulfill the no majority of any minority mandate once the segregative practices were eliminated by the appropriate school officials. Justice Marshall, joined by Justice Brennan, dissented. He believed that the refusal of the district court to modify the no majority of any minority provision was not erroneous because the dual school system had not been eliminated.

The Court expressed its willingness to order systemwide remedies for Northern school districts but emphasized that the constitutional violations must be sufficient to justify such remedies. In *Dayton Board of Education v. Brinkman (Dayton I)*, 433 U.S. 406 (1977), which was decided approximately one year after Washington v. Davis, 426 U.S. 229 (1976), a court of appeals' systemwide remedy was set aside because of the lack of findings in the record that addressed specifically the scope of the remedy. Justice Rehnquist stated that unless it could be shown that the conditions resulted from intentional segregative action by the school board, the district court was in error in ordering a systemwide remedy. Going further, he pointed out that "the disparity between the evidence of constitutional violations and the sweeping remedy finally decreed requires supplementation of the record and additional findings addressed specifically to the scope of the remedy." However, in *Dayton Board of Education v. Brinkman (Dayton II)*, 443 U.S. 526 (1979) and the companion case, *Columbus Board of Education v. Penick,* 443 U.S. 449 (1979), the Court affirmed the court of appeals' decisions that ordered systemwide desegregation. In *Dayton II,* 51 of the 69 schools in the system were either virtually all white or all black. The evidence also showed that the schools that were 90% or more black in the 1951-52 school year remained the same in the 1971-72 year. Justice White declared that the Dayton Board was intentionally and purposefully operating a dual school system in violation of the equal protection clause. A systemwide remedy was in order because segregation in a significant part of the district warranted an inference that segregation in other parts was also intentional and therefore had a systemwide effect. In a dissenting opinion, Justice Rehnquist argued that the majority could not justify the perceived inequity of finding no violation in the *Dayton* case while imposing a systemwide remedy in the *Columbus* case. The Court did not clearly delineate the distinction between de jure and de facto segregation. In addition, Justice Rehnquist argued that these two cases clearly show the "hazards presented by the laissez-faire theory of appellate review in school desegregation cases."

The *Columbus* case relied on *Dayton II.* Black students charged the Columbus Board of Education with perpetuating purposeful segregative practices in the public schools. The evidence revealed that (a) black teachers and administrators were assigned to black schools for the most part; (b) as late as 1976, 70% of all students attended schools that were 80% black or 80% white; and (c) approximately half of the 172 schools were either 90% black or 90% white. Justice White, writing for the majority, declared the importance of fashioning a remedy commensurate with the alleged violation. Justice Rehnquist, in his dissenting opinion, argued that the sweeping remedy was not justified by the record and that it "is as complete and dramatic a displacement of local authority by the federal judiciary as is possible in our federal system."

After *Milliken I,* the district court ordered the submission of desegregation plans for the victims of Detroit's de jure segregated system. Hearings were held, and the court included in its order both a student assignment plan and several educational components in the area of testing, counseling, reading, and in-service teacher training. In upholding the lower court's decree in *Milliken v. Bradley (Milliken II)*, 433 U.S. 267 (1977), Chief Justice Burger held that remedies that do not exceed the violation and are tailored to correct the condition that offends the Constitution are constitutionally permissible. This is the only way the victims can be assisted in overcoming the effects of past acts of misconduct. In a concurring opinion, Justice Marshall argued that remediation was not only necessary but also inevitable because of intentional discrimination that had contributed greatly to the academic deficiencies adversely affecting many black youngsters.

In his 37-page opinion concurring in part and dissenting in part in *Keyes,* Justice Powell addressed the crux of the problem in fashioning judicial remedies in school desegregation cases. In *Keyes* Justice Powell argued that the Court should abandon the de facto/de jure distinction, "which long since has outlived its time, and formulate constitutional principles of a national rather than merely regional application." For Justice Powell, "the history of state-imposed segregation is more widespread in our country than the *de jure/de facto* distinction has traditionally cared to recognize." The failure of the Burger Court to grapple with this distinction contributed to its inability to formulate a coherent set of judicial principles in school desegregation jurisprudence (see Table 4.1).

The Struggle of Mexican Americans in the Educational Arena

The Burger Court addressed cases brought by Mexican Americans that involved financial inequities and the lack of access to public educational institutions. Mexican Americans, like blacks, were subject to the cyclical pattern of winning and losing before the Court. In *San Antonio Independent School District v. Rodriguez,* 411 U.S. 1 (1973), Demetrio Rodriguez brought a class action suit on behalf of Mexican American children, claiming that differences in the value of assessed property were the cause of interdistrict disparities in per pupil expenditures, in violation of the equal protection clause. Justice Powell, writing for a sharply divided Court, declared that wealth was not a suspect classification. Because Texas provides each student with some identifiable quantum of education, the system, although imperfect, is rationally related to a legitimate governmental purpose. In a 64-page dissenting opinion, Justice Marshall expressed the view that the Texas financing scheme violated the equal protection clause and that "discrimination on the basis of group wealth calls for careful judicial scrutiny."

Nine years later, in *Plyler v. Doe,* 457 U.S. 202 (1982), the Court applied the intermediate scrutiny standard when it invalidated a Texas statute that barred children of undocumented workers from enrolling in the public schools. A Texas statute authorized local school districts to deny enrollment to students who had not been legally admitted to the United States and to withhold state funds from school districts for the education of such students. A class action

Table 4.1 The Burger Court and School Desegregation: Major Cases

Case	Vote	Ruling
Alexander v. Holmes County Board of Education, 396 U.S. 19 (1969)	per curiam	The Supreme Court held that all dual school systems must be eliminated at once.
Dowell v. Board of Education of Oklahoma City Public Schools, 396 U.S. 269 (1969)	per curiam	Relying on *Alexander*, the Supreme Court held that the Oklahoma City school board must desegregate at once.
Carter v. West Feliciana Parish School Board, 396 U.S. 290 (1970)	per curiam	The Supreme Court emphasized that the lower court's deferral of school desegregation beyond February 1, 1970, was unacceptable.
Swann v. Charlotte-Mecklenburg Board of Education, 402 U.S. 1 (1971)	9-0	Among other remedies, Chief Justice Burger upheld the use of busing to achieve school desegregation under a de jure segregated system.
Davis v. Board of School Commissioners of Mobile County, 402 U.S. 33 (1971)	9-0	The Supreme Court held that all techniques, including the restructuring of attendance zones, would be considered to achieve a maximum level of desegregation.
McDaniel v. Barresi, 402 U.S. 39 (1971)	9-0	The Court concluded that a school board could take race into account in fulfilling its responsibility of converting to a unitary school district.
North Carolina State Board of Education v. Swann, 402 U.S. 43 (1971)	9-0	The Supreme Court struck down a North Carolina law that prohibited busing and assigning students to schools for the purpose of racial balance under the Fourteenth Amendment.
Wright v. Council of Emporia, 407 U.S. 451 (1972)	5-4	Justice Stewart struck down the creation of a new school district from an existing one on the ground that it would impede the process of dismantling a dual system.
Keyes v. School District No. I, Denver, Colorado, 413 U.S. 189 (1973)	7-1	Justice Brennan held, in the first desegregation case outside the South, that purposeful discrimination is adequate for an inferential finding that de jure segregation is systemwide.
Milliken v. Bradley (Milliken I), 418 U.S. 717 (1974)	5-4	Chief Justice Burger held that a multidistrict remedy could not be imposed on the metropolitan area of Detroit because there was no evidence that the outlying districts contributed to the segregation of the city of Detroit.

Table 4.1 *continued*

Case	Vote	Ruling
Pasadena City Board of Education v. *Spangler*, 427 U.S. 424 (1976)	6-2	Justice Rehnquist ruled that a district court had exceeded its authority in enforcing its no majority of any minority requirement once segregative practices were eliminated by the school officials.
Austin Independent School District v. United States, 429 U.S. 990 (1976)	7-2	The Supreme Court set aside and remanded a lower court's remedy that exceeded the constitutional violation in the light of *Washington v. Davis* (1976).
Metropolitan School District v. Buckley, 429 U.S. 1068 (1977)	6-3	The Supreme Court vacated a lower court's finding of a constitutional violation for housing segregation and segregated schools because the court had failed to make specific findings of discriminatory intent.
Milliken v. Bradley (*Milliken II*), 433 U.S. 267 (1977)	9-0	Chief Justice Burger held that remedies that do not exceed the violation and that are tailored to correct the condition that offends the Constitution are permissible.
Dayton Board of Education v. Brinkman (*Dayton I*), 433 U.S. 406 (1977)	8-0	Justice Rehnquist set aside a court of appeals' systemwide remedy because of the lack of intentional segregative action by the school board.
Columbus Board of Education v. Penick, 443 U.S. 449 (1979)	7-2	Justice White held that a systemwide remedy was permissible.
Dayton Board of Education v. Brinkman (*Dayton II*), 443 U.S. 526 (1979)	5-4	Justice White declared that a systemwide remedy was permissible because the Dayton board was intentionally and purposefully operating a dual school system, in violation of the equal protection clause.
Washington v. Seattle School District No. 1, 458 U.S. 457 (1982)	5-4	Justice Blackmun struck down Initiative 350, which prohibited the busing of children for the purpose of school desegregation, under the equal protection clause.
Crawford v. Board of Education of the City of Los Angeles, 458 U.S. 527 (1982)	6-3	Justice Powell upheld Proposition I, which prohibited busing ordered by state courts to alleviate de facto segregation unless a federal court would be permitted to do so to remedy a violation under the equal protection clause.

suit was brought on behalf of school-age children of Mexican origin, who challenged the state statute as violative of the equal protection clause. In the majority opinion, Justice Brennan noted that the Fourteenth Amendment extends to all persons within a state's boundaries and that denying these school children a basic education would surely mark them with the stigma of illiteracy and lessen their chances of making any worthwhile contributions to society. He concluded, "Section 21.031 imposes a lifetime hardship on a discrete class of children not accountable for their disabling status." Chief Justice Burger, joined by Justices White, Rehnquist, and O'Connor, dissented. Chief Justice Burger emphasized that the Constitution did not make judges platonic guardians or policymakers and that the courts should defer to the political processes for a solution to the complex problems of undocumented workers.

One year later, in *Martinez v. Bynum,* 461 U.S. 321 (1983), the Court refused to invalidate a Texas statute that denied tuition-free admission to minors who were living apart from their parents or guardians, if the primary purpose for living apart was to enable that minor to attend free public schools. Writing for an 8-1 majority, Justice Powell stressed the fact that a bona fide residence requirement satisfies constitutional standards by furthering the substantial state interest of providing services only to its residents. He also pointed out that a school district was justified in requiring parents and their school-age children to fulfill the residential requirement before it treated them as bona fide residents. Justice Marshall, the lone dissenter, argued that a child's education is fundamental and that therefore statutory classification that creates class distinctions by impeding educational access to some while providing it to others should be subjected to careful scrutiny.

Discriminatory Practices in Private Institutions

Discrimination against black Americans was not limited to the public schools. Invidious discriminatory practices in private schools forced blacks to resort to § 1981. In the well-publicized case of RUNYON V. McCRARY, 427 U.S. 160 (1976), black children in Northern Virginia were denied admission to a private school on racial grounds and sought relief under § 1981. In the majority opinion, Justice Stewart declared that the school was engaged in commercial, contractual relations and that § 1981 prohibits discrimination in making and enforcing private contracts. He also noted that although private discrimination might be viewed as a form of freedom of association protected by the First Amendment, it has not been granted constitutional protection. In their dissent, Justices White and Rehnquist disagreed strongly with the majority's interpretation of the legislative history of § 1981 and the statute. They thought that the "legislative history of § 1981 unequivocally confirms that Congress' purpose in enacting that statute was solely to grant to all persons equal capacity to contract as is enjoyed by whites and included no purpose to prevent private refusals to contract, however motivated."

A unanimous Court, in *Norwood v. Harrison,* 413 U.S. 455 (1973), reversed a decision that sustained Mississippi's statutory program of lending textbooks to private schools that discriminated against students on the basis of race. Chief Justice Burger observed that free textbooks are a form of financial assistance that benefits private schools and that when the state pays for these books, it gives support to the discriminatory policies. To perpetuate discriminatory practices against blacks, sophisticated schemes were devised to serve as a subterfuge, but they failed to withstand constitutional muster. For example, in *Gilmore v. City of Montgomery, Alabama,* 417 U.S. 556 (1974), the city of Montgomery provided segregated schools and segregated private clubs with football fields and recreational facilities after a successful challenge to segregated municipal parks. Justice Blackmun declared that the city's actions operated to contravene a school desegregation order and had "a significant tendency to facilitate, reinforce, and support private discrimination."

The Reagan administration was unsuccessful in its attempt to challenge the Internal Revenue Service's (IRS) denial of tax-exempt status to two private educational institutions in North Carolina and South Carolina that had racially discriminatory admissions policies. In BOB JONES UNIVERSITY V. UNITED STATES, 461 U.S. 574 (1983) and the companion case, *Goldsboro Christian Schools, Inc. v. United States,* 461 U.S. 574 (1983), blacks were excluded from a university and high school, respectively, based on the sponsors' interpretation of the Bible. Bob Jones University refused to admit any blacks until 1971. In that year, it accepted applications from blacks who had married other blacks. The Goldsboro Christian School had accepted children from marriages in which one parent was white. Chief Justice Burger, writing for an 8-1 majority, characterized the racially discriminatory practices in private schools as contrary to national public policy and, in addition, held that the governmental interest of eradicating such discrimination was compelling. In his dissent, Justice Rehnquist pointed out that although he agreed with the national policy that opposes racial discrimination, Congress had not denied tax-exempt status to institutions that practice discrimination on racial grounds. Thus, it was not the responsibility of the Court to legislate for Congress on this issue.

One year later, the Court declared, in *Allen v. Wright,* 468 U.S. 737 (1984), that black parents of public school children in a nationwide class action suit had no standing to sue the IRS because of its failure to adopt sufficient standards to deny tax-exempt status to private schools that practiced discrimination. Writing for the 5-4 majority, Justice O'Connor noted that the plaintiffs had not and did not intend to enroll their children in private schools and that therefore the line of causation between the IRS's grant of tax-exempt status to some private schools that have discriminatory policies and "the diminished ability of respondents' children to receive a desegregated education" is tenuous at best. In his dissent, Justice Brennan forcefully argued that the majority opinion represented a grave insensitivity to the role the federal courts have played historically in eliminating discriminatory practices from American schools. He concluded that the IRS's grant of tax-exempt status to racially segregated private schools discouraged whites from attending public schools and therefore interfered with the efforts of the courts and local school boards to desegregate them.

SECOND-GENERATION VOTING RIGHTS LITIGATION: THE PROBLEM OF MINORITY VOTE DILUTION

As indicated in the previous chapters, first-generation voting rights litigation sought to remove direct impediments to racial and ethnic minorities' right to vote. The Warren Court's commitment to egalitarian principles in the area of voting rights led to the formulation of the one person, one vote principle enunciated in *Reynolds v. Sims,* 377 U.S. 533 (1964). And the passage of the Voting Rights Act of 1965 proved to be a powerful statutory weapon in eradicating voting discrimination. During the late 1960s, blacks faced fewer barriers in their struggle to exercise the franchise. However, attempts were made in some states to dilute the true potential of the black vote. After all, more blacks were registered to vote, and blacks running for office at the local level were winning significant victories for slots in state legislatures, especially at the house or assembly level. In addition, blacks were being elected to Congress from majority black congressional districts for the first time in more than a century.

The Burger Court was confronted with demands to expand the concept of political equality to include the right to have racial and ethnic minorities' votes count as much as that of whites. This political equality norm encompasses the right to obtain a meaningful vote, or what is commonly referred to as being protected from minority vote dilution. Chandler Davidson defined *minority vote dilution* as a "process whereby election laws or practices, either singly or in concert, combine with systematic bloc voting among an identifiable group to dominate or cancel the voting strength of at least one minority group."[7] Gerrymandering, annexations, at-large elections, multimember districts, anti-single-shot devices, decreasing the size of a governmental body, exclusive slating groups, and runoff primaries posed serious threats to the maximization of black political influence. In this section, we illustrate how the Burger Court grappled with the problem of fashioning evidentiary standards in minority vote dilution cases (see Table 4.2).

**From *Whitcomb* to *Bolden:*
The Evolution of Constitutional Standards**

In the mid-1960s and early 1970s, the use of multimember districts was scrutinized by the federal courts. The Warren Court initially addressed the constitutionality of multimember districts in *Fortson v. Dorsey,* 379 U.S. 433 (1965) and *Burns v. Richardson,* 384 U.S. 73 (1966) in vote dilution cases.

The Court established in these cases that a claim of vote dilution could rest on either discriminatory purpose or effect. In *Whitcomb v. Chavis,* 403 U.S. 124 (1971), the issue of racial vote dilution was directly before the Burger Court. In *Whitcomb* black voters residing in Marion County, Indiana, challenged the validity of the multimember district scheme for electing state senators and representatives. Justice White, writing for the plurality, struck down the district court's finding that multimember districts unconstitutionally operated to dilute blacks votes. The Court found that the plaintiffs failed to prove under the *Fortson/Burns* standard that the multimember districts were conceived or operated as purposeful devices to further racial discrimination. In writing for the dissenters, Justice Douglas argued that black plaintiffs had met the burden of proof as established in *Fortson* and *Burns.* For Justice Douglas, "It is asking the impossible for us to demand that blacks first show that the effect of the scheme was to discourage or prevent poor blacks from voting or joining such party as they choose. On this record, the voting rights of the blacks have been 'abridged,' as I read the Constitution."

Two years later, in *White v. Regester,* 412 U.S. 755 (1973), the Court held that multimember districts for Mexican Americans in Bexar County, Texas, and for blacks in Dallas County, Texas, invidiously discriminated against these groups, in violation of the equal protection clause. The evidence revealed that a history of official racial and ethnic discrimination in Texas hindered the ability of blacks and Mexican Americans to register and effectively participate in the nomination and election process. Justice White, writing for the majority, argued that multimember districts are not unconstitutional per se but are invalid if they have the adverse effect of giving an electoral minority fewer opportunities to participate in the political process, compared with other residents. On the basis of the totality of the circumstances, the Court affirmed the district court's ruling that the use of multimember districts excluded blacks and Mexican Americans from effective participation in the political process.

A ruling by the Court of Appeals for the Fifth Circuit was instrumental in elaborating on the standards established in *Whitcomb* and *White.* In *Zimmer v. McKeithen,* 485 F.2d 1297 (1973), the court struck down the use of an at-large electoral scheme for the election of police juries and school board members because it diluted the voting strength of blacks in East Carroll Parish, Louisiana. The court concluded that access to the political process, not population, was the barometer of vote dilution as established in *Whitcomb* and *White* and that the showing of past purposeful discrimination against black voters had met this standard of testing vote dilution. The *Zimmer* Court interpreted the ruling in *White v. Regester* as requiring two standards of proof in vote dilution cases: (a) Plaintiffs must maintain the burden of showing a racially motivated gerrymander or a plan drawn along racial lines and (b) plaintiffs must prove that, designedly or otherwise, an apportionment scheme under the circumstances of a particular case would operate to minimize or cancel out the voting strength of racial or political elements of the voting population. The appeals court did not, however, require plaintiffs challenging vote dilution schemes to meet both standards.

Table 4.2 Minority Vote Dilution and the Burger Court: Major Cases

Case	Vote	Ruling
Whitcomb v. Chavis, 403 U.S. 124 (1971)	5-4	Justice White struck down a lower court's finding that multimember districts unconstitutionally diluted blacks' votes because the black plaintiffs had failed to prove that the districts were conceived or operated as purposeful devices to further racial discrimination.
Perkins v. Matthews, 400 U.S. 379 (1971)	7-2	Justice Brennan found that changes in the location of polling places, annexation changes, and changes from ward to at-large elections fall under § 5 of the Voting Rights Act.
Connor v. Johnson, 402 U.S. 690 (1971)	per curiam	The Supreme Court invalidated a judicially devised reapportionment plan and declared that single-member districts were preferable to multimember districts.
City of Petersburg v. United States, 410 U.S. 962 (1973)	9-0	The Supreme Court held that an annexation of an area with a white majority and an at-large city council operated to deny or abridge the right to vote within the meaning of § 5 of the Voting Rights Act.
Georgia v. United States, 411 U.S. 526 (1973)	6-3	The Supreme Court found that Georgia's 1972 house reapportionment plan had the potential of diluting black voting strength.
White v. Regester, 412 U.S. 755 (1973)	6-3	Justice White held that multimember districts are not unconstitutional per se but that they are invalid if they have the adverse effect of giving an electoral minority fewer opportunities to participate in the political process, compared with other residents.
City of Richmond v. United States, 422 U.S. 358 (1975)	5-3	Justice White held that an annexation does not violate § 5 of the Voting Rights Act as long as the minority's political potential is recognized.
Beer v. United States, 425 U.S. 130 (1976)	5-3	Justice Stewart established that the purpose of § 5 is to ensure that no voting procedure changes would be made that led to a retrogression of minorities' votes.
United Jewish Organizations, Inc. v. Carey, 430 U.S. 144 (1977)	7-1	Justice White upheld a 1974 reapportionment plan wherein the Hasidic Jewish community alleged that its voting strength had been diminished, in violation of the Fourteenth and Fifteenth Amendments.

Table 4.2 *continued*

Case	Vote	Ruling
Connor v. Finch, 431 U.S. 407 (1977)	7-1	The Supreme Court held that a court-devised reapportionment plan is held to stricter standards than a legislatively devised plan and that legislative districts should be drawn so as to avoid diluting black voting strength.
Briscoe v. Bell, 432 U.S. 404 (1977)	9-0	Justice Marshall held that a bailout suit under § 4(a) of the Voting Rights Act is Texas' sole remedy for getting out from under the 1975 Voting Rights Act Amendments.
United States v. Board of Commissioners of Sheffield, Alabama, 435 U.S. 110 (1978)	6-3	Justice Brennan held that a city is a subdivision as defined by § 5 of the Voting Rights Act and that voting changes must be precleared.
Doughtery County Board of Education v. White, 439 U.S. 32 (1978)	5-4	Justice Marshall held that a requirement that candidates take an unpaid leave of absence is subject to preclearance under § 5 of the Voting Rights Act.
City of Mobile v. Bolden, 446 U.S. 55 (1980)	6-3	Justice Stewart required that minority plaintiffs must show intent to discriminate in challenging the constitutionality of an at-large system.
City of Rome v. United States, 466 U.S. 156 (1980)	6-3	Justice Marshall held that a city may not use § 4(a)'s bailout procedure to escape § 5's preclearance requirement.
McDaniel v. Sanchez, 452 U.S. 130 (1981)	7-2	The Supreme Court held that a new reapportionment plan approved by a district court under objections by Mexican Americans must be precleared under § 5.
Rogers v. Lodge, 458 U.S. 613 (1982)	6-3	In distinguishing *Rogers* from *Bolden*, Justice White held that Burke County, Georgia's, at-large election of members to the Board of Commissioners violated the Fourteenth Amendment rights of black citizens.
City of Port Arthur v. United States, 459 U.S. 159 (1982)	6-3	Justice White upheld a lower court's finding that an annexation plan could not be approved under § 5 because the annexations had substantially reduced the relative political strength of the black population.
City of Lockhart v. United States, 460 U.S. 125 (1983)	6-3	Justice Powell applied the nonretrogression principle and rejected Mexican Americans' argument that the use of the numbered post system and staggered terms had a retrogressive effect on minority voting strength.
Thornburg v. Gingles, 478 U.S. 30 (1986)	5-4	Justice Brennan established a three-part test that made it easier to prove minority vote dilution.

By 1980 the Burger Court had become increasingly conservative because of changes in its personnel. By this time, there was enough support on the Court to apply the Washington v. Davis 426 U.S. 229 (1976) intent standard in the context of minority vote dilution under the Fourteenth and Fifteenth Amendments. In CITY OF MOBILE V. BOLDEN, 446 U.S. 55 (1980), the at-large system of electing Mobile, Alabama's three commissioners was challenged by black residents who claimed that the voting strength of blacks was diluted, in violation of the Fourteenth and Fifteenth Amendments and § 2 of the Voting Rights Act of 1965.[8] The district court applied the *Zimmer* criteria and found that no black had ever been elected to the city commission in a city that was 40% black, that racially polarized voting existed, and that the city officials had not been responsive to the interests of blacks. In a 6-3 plurality opinion, Justice Stewart reversed the lower court's decision and declared that disproportionate effects standing alone are insufficient to establish racially based vote dilution. Moreover, the Fifteenth Amendment does not ensure the right to have blacks elected but does require that the plaintiff show evidence of purposeful discrimination. Rather than elaborate on how the intent standard should be applied in future vote dilution cases, Justice Stewart chose instead to attack Justice Marshall's dissent in what the plurality saw as his advocacy of proportional representation. In his dissent, Justice Marshall explicitly rejected the notion that the Constitution contains any such requirement. For Justice Marshall, the "group is also required to carry the far more onerous burden of demonstrating that it has been effectively fenced out of the political process" and that the vote dilution doctrines can "logically apply only to groups whose electoral discreetness and insularity allow dominating political factions to ignore them."

The *Bolden* decision was heavily criticized on a number of grounds. First, the Court, in *Bolden,* failed to distinguish between cases prohibiting discrimination in the governmental distribution of constitutionally gratuitous benefits (e.g., government employment in *Washington v. Davis*) and cases involving the denials of fundamental rights (e.g., the right to vote). The result was to deny to minority voters the special protection accorded to fundamental constitutional rights. Second, the intent requirement was overly burdensome because (a) proving discriminatory purpose required evidence of legislative intent found in legislative history, which frequently does not exist on the state level; (b) courts have adopted rules that bar direct evidence of discriminatory intent, such as testimony from authors or supporters of discriminatory legislation, (c) the Court failed to elaborate on how intent may be inferred in future vote dilution cases, and (d) the intent standard encourages the search for discriminatory motivation, which results in undue intrusion into the local legislative process.[9]

Only two years after the *Bolden* decision and two days after President Reagan signed into law the Voting Rights Act Amendments of 1982, the Burger Court appeared to retreat from the intent requirement. In *Rogers v. Lodge,* 458 U.S. 613 (1982), officials in Burke County, Georgia, used an at-large system for electing commission members. Although blacks comprised a majority of the population, no black had ever been elected to the commission. Distinguishing *Rogers* from *Bolden,* the Court approved of the district court judge's application of the *Zimmer* criteria in determining discriminatory intent. Justice White observed that the unmistakable fact that no black had ever been elected to the commission is important evidence of purposeful exclusion. He also concluded that persistent bloc voting bears heavily on the issue of intentional discrimination in at-large electoral systems. Justice Stevens, in his dissent, elaborated on his disapproval of the majority's reliance on the subjective intent standard for minority vote dilution cases.

Congressional Response to *Bolden:* Amending § 2 of the Voting Rights Act of 1965

A galvanized voting rights triangle consisting of various civil rights groups, administrative agencies, and congressional committees was forceful in marshalling support for "overturning" *Bolden* when the Voting Rights Act was scheduled for renewal in 1982.[10] This could be accomplished statutorily because, in *Bolden,* the Court concluded that the language of § 2 was a restatement of the Fifteenth Amendment and therefore added nothing to the Fifteenth Amendment claim. Extensive congressional hearings revealed that racial and ethnic discrimination in voting was still pervasive throughout the United States. Congress subsequently rejected the intent standard required in *Bolden* in favor of a results test when it amended § 2 of the Voting Rights Act. The 1982 Amendments restored the previous standard enunciated in *White v. Regester* and *Zimmer* (see Box 4.1). Thus, discriminatory intent is not required to prove a violation of § 2. Minority plaintiffs can prevail under § 2 by demonstrating that a challenged election practice has resulted in the denial or abridgement of the right to vote based on race or color. Prior to the 1982 Amendments, § 2 was generally considered a restatement of the Fifteenth Amendment with little operative effect. Because § 2 is a permanent feature of the Voting Rights Act and applies nationwide, the amended § 2 has become a formidable weapon in striking down electoral schemes that dilute minorities' votes.

Black plaintiffs won a significant victory during the last term of the Burger Court when the Court for the first time construed the amended § 2. In THORNBURG V. GINGLES, 478 U.S. 30 (1986), black citizens in North Carolina claimed that the one single-member district and six multimember districts impaired their ability to elect state legislators of their choice, in violation of § 2 of the Voting Rights Act as amended. Writing for the 5-4 plurality, Justice Brennan invalidated the multimember districting scheme because a close examination of the totality of the circumstances revealed with clarity that the political process was not open equally to minority voters to elect legislators of their choice when multimember electoral structures were employed. In *Thornburg* the Court formulated a three-part test that made it easier for minorities to challenge electoral schemes that diluted their votes. In vote dilution cases, (a) it must be shown that the minority group is significantly large and geographically compact to constitute a majority in a single-member

BOX 4.1

**§ 2 of the 1965 Voting Rights Act of 1965:
1982 Amendments**

§2(a) [§1973]. No voting qualification or prerequisite to voting or standard, practice, or procedure shall be imposed or applied by any State or political subdivision in a manner which results in a denial or abridgment of the right to any citizen of the United States to vote on account of race or color, or in contravention of the guarantees set forth in § 4(f)(2), as provided in subsection (b).

(b) A violation of subsection (a) is established if, based on the totality of the circumstances, it is shown that the political processes leading to nomination or election in the State or political subdivision are not equally open to participation by members of a class of citizens protected by subsection (a) in that its members have less opportunity than other members of the electorate to participate in the political process and to elect representatives of their choice. The extent to which members of a protected class has been elected to office in the State or political subdivision is one circumstance which may be considered: *Provided,* That nothing in this section establishes a right to have members of a protected class elected in numbers equal to their proportion in the population.

district, (b) the group must show that it is politically cohesive, and (c) the minority group must be able to demonstrate that the white majority was sufficient as a bloc to enable it—in the absence of special circumstances such as the minority candidate running unopposed—to defeat the minority's preferred candidate. Additional factors may also be relevant to a finding of voting rights violations according to *Thornburg.* Justice O'Connor, concurring in the judgment, argued that the three-part test moved the Court closer to mandatory proportional representation. Because *Thornburg* "creates what amounts to a right to *usual, roughly* proportional representation on the part of sizable, compact cohesive minority groups," according to Justice O'Connor, it constitutes a ruling that significantly undergirds the contention that the absence of proportional representation evidences unconstitutional vote dilution.

The Significance of § 5 of the Voting Rights Act

Section 5 of the Voting Rights Act of 1965 prohibits any state or subdivision from implementing any voting changes unless they have been approved by the Attorney General of the Department of Justice or by a declaratory judgment issued by a three-judge district court in the District of Columbia. To receive administrative or judicial preclearance, covered jurisdictions must establish that the proposed changes do not have the purpose or effect of denying or abridging the right to vote on account of race or color. Most jurisdictions seek administrative preclearance from the attorney general, rather than file a lawsuit. Between 1965 and April 1, 1991, the Department of Justice reviewed 188,048 voting changes from covered jurisdictions. Between 1965 and December 1989, fewer than 20 jurisdictions sought judicial preclearance.[11] Voting rights litigation under § 5 proved to be a powerful statutory weapon in eradicating discriminatory practices and procedures that affect racial and ethnic minorities' right to vote. Congress also responded favorably to § 5 when it extended the provision in 1970 and 1975, and in 1982 § 5 was extended for 25 years.[12]

The Warren Court's ruling in *Allen v. State Board of Elections,* 393 U.S. 544 (1969) established that § 5 should be given the broadest scope possible to reach any state enactment that altered the election law of a covered jurisdiction in even a minor way. The Burger Court expanded this principle in *Perkins v. Matthews,* 400 U.S. 379 (1971). In *Perkins* black voters sought to enjoin the 1969 election for mayor and aldermen when the city of Canton, Mississippi, sought to enforce voting changes pertaining to (a) changes in the locations of polling places, (b) annexation changes, and (c) change from ward to at-large election of aldermen, without first seeking administrative or judicial preclearance. Justice Brennan, writing for the majority, relied on *Allen* and found that changes in polling places, changing boundary lines through annexations, and changes from ward to at-large elections fall within the scope of § 5 as a standard, practice or procedure with respect to voting different from that in force or effect on November 1, 1964, and required preclearance. In his dissenting opinion, Justice Black restated his position that § 5 violated the U.S. Constitution because it usurps the functions of local governments to make their own laws without advance federal approval.

Allen and *Perkins* remained significant constructions of § 5 for determining whether voting changes enacted by a city within a covered state under § 5 must be precleared. In *United States v. Board of Commissioners of Sheffield, Alabama,* 435 U.S. 110 (1978), the city of Sheffield scheduled at-large council elections in 1976 without obtaining preclearance when it adopted a mayor-council form of government. A three-judge district court held that the city was not covered by § 5 because it was not a political subdivision as defined by the Voting Rights Act. In writing for the 6-3 majority, Justice Brennan rejected the absurd result reached by the district court, arguing that its interpretation of the Act was contrary to congressional intent. The Burger Court also ruled that a requirement in which candidates for elective office take an unpaid leave of absence is subject to § 5 preclearance. In *Dougherty County Board of Education v. White,* 439 U.S. 32 (1978), a black employee of the Dougherty County Board of Education ran for the Georgia House of Representatives but was forced to take three unpaid leaves of absence while campaigning for office. Less than one month after White announced his candidacy, the school board adopted Rule 58, which required that any employee of the school system who becomes a candidate for any elective office must take an unpaid leave of absence for the duration of the political activity and during the period of service in the office. Rejecting the school board's characterization that Rule 58 is "a neutral personnel practice governing all forms of absenteeism," Justice Marshall, writing for the Court, viewed it as a policy that imposes "substantial economic disincentives on employees who wish to seek elective office" [and] "the Rule burdens entry into elective campaigns and . . . limits the choices available to Dougherty County voters." Also important for the majority, "the circumstances surrounding its adoption and its effect on the political process are sufficiently suggestive of the potential for discrimination to demonstrate the need for preclearance." Justice Powell, writing for the dissenters, expressed the view that the Court's ruling was contrary to the language and legislative history of the Voting Rights Act.

The Burger Court also addressed the issue of how annexations should be dealt with under § 5. In *City of Petersburg v. United States,* 410 U.S. 962 (1973), the Supreme Court affirmed on appeal without opinion a three-judge district court's ruling that an annexation of an area with a white majority in concert with at-large city council elections operated to deny or abridge the right to vote within the meaning of § 5. A setback occurred in 1975, however, involving the applicability of § 5 to annexations that would guarantee no change in racial minorities' preannexation voting strength. The city of Richmond, Virginia, sought approval of an annexation plan that had the effect of reducing the black population from 52% to 42%. The city and the attorney general approved a plan for nine wards in Richmond where four had substantial black majorities, four had substantial white majorities, and the ninth had a 59%-41% white-black division. The district court declared that the proportion of blacks was reduced substantially by the annexation and that black political power had been diluted. Justice White, writing for the 5-3 majority in *City of Richmond v. United States,* 422 U.S. 358 (1975), vacated the district court's judgment and held that the annexation is not violative of § 5 as long as the minority's political potential is recognized. Furthermore, if the ward system affords black representation equivalent to their political strength in the postannexation system, it would be unreasonable to conclude that black voting strength is undervalued. Writing for the dissenters, Justice Brennan argued that the Richmond annexation plan was motivated by discrimination in an effort to avert political control to an eventual black population majority. It was also clear to the dissenters that significant dilution of black voting strength occurred as a result of postannexation.

In a case decided on the same day as *Bolden,* Justice Marshall, writing for a 6-3 majority in *City of Rome v. United States,* 466 U.S. 156 (1980), agreed with the district court's finding that electoral changes and annexations made by the city of Rome, Georgia, diluted black voting strength. More important, the Court ruled in *Rome* that a city may not use § 4(a)'s bailout procedure to escape § 5's preclearance requirement. Justice Marshall also emphasized that Congress plainly intended that a voting practice not be precleared unless both discriminatory purpose and effect are absent. In his dissenting opinion, Justice

Powell argued that the Court's ends could not justify the means of continued federal rule of local governments in a state, especially when local governments act diligently to meet the Voting Rights Act's requirements.

The Burger Court addressed the validity of reapportionment plans under § 5 of the Voting Rights Act. For example, in *Connor v. Johnson,* 402 U.S. 690 (1971), the Court had to decide the constitutionality of a judicially devised plan that called for some multimember districts in Mississippi's upper and lower houses. In a per curiam opinion, the Court invalidated the plan, declaring that single-member districts were preferable to multimember districts in court-devised apportionment plans unless there are insurmountable barriers. In *Georgia v. United States,* 411 U.S. 526 (1973), the Court found that Georgia's 1972 House reapportionment changes had the potential for diluting black voting strength and that the burden was placed on Georgia as the submitting party to prove that the reapportionment plan did not have a racially discriminatory purpose or effect on voting. In *Connor v. Finch,* 431 U.S. 407 (1977), the Court held that a court-devised reapportionment plan is held to stricter standards than a legislatively devised plan and that the court plan should draw legislative districts that are reasonably contiguous and compact so as to avoid dilution of black voting strength.

In *Beer v. United States,* 425 U.S. 130 (1976), the city of New Orleans proposed two reapportionment plans for the city council, based on the 1970 census figures. The attorney general objected to the first reapportionment plan, arguing that it diluted black voting strength. The attorney general also objected to the second plan on the same grounds that the plan that used north-to-south districts would divide the predominantly black city neighborhoods located in an east-west progression. The district court refused to allow the second plan to go into effect. In a 5-3 majority opinion written by Justice Stewart, the Court established that "the purpose of § 5 has always been to insure that no voting-procedure changes would be made that would lead to a retrogression in the position of racial minorities with respect to their effective exercise of the electoral franchise." Justice Stewart reasoned that under the 1961 apportionment plan, no blacks were elected to the city council but that under the second plan adapted after the 1970 census, blacks would have a majority of the population in two of the five districts and a voting majority in one of the districts. Therefore, the Court concluded that, under § 5, the second reapportionment plan did not have the effect of diluting the right to vote on account of race. In his dissenting opinion, Justice Marshall argued that because blacks were underrepresented by the second reapportionment plan, they were denied equal access to the political processes in New Orleans.

The Court approved of the use of numerical targets in the reapportionment of legislative districts and, in the process, interpreted § 5 of the Voting Rights Act literally in UNITED JEWISH ORGANIZATIONS INC. V. CAREY, 430 U.S. 144 (1977). New York State devised a reapportionment plan in 1974 that reassigned a portion of the Hasidic Jewish community to an adjoining district for the purpose of affording fair representation to racial groups numerous enough to comprise majority voting strength in some districts. The reassignment meant that the Hasidic community would be split into two senatorial districts under the 1972 plan. The United Jewish Organizations sued on behalf of the Hasidic community, alleging that its voting strength had been diminished, in violation of the Fourteenth and Fifteenth Amendments. Writing for the plurality, Justice White held that the reapportionment plan was valid and complied with § 5 because it was sometimes necessary to use racial considerations in drawing district lines so as to preserve black majorities in some districts. He also argued that the 1974 revisions to the reapportionment plan simply restored the voting strength of nonwhites to 1966 levels and did not fence "out the white population from participation in the political processes of the county and the plan did not minimize or unfairly cancel out white voting strength." In his dissent, Chief Justice Burger argued that the reapportionment plan was a strict quota and that the Court should have relied on *Gomillion v. Lightfoot,* 364 U.S. 339 (1960). He also felt strongly that the marshaling of racial or religious groups into enclaves decreases the possibility of the nation becoming a genuinely homogeneous society.

When Congress extended the Voting Rights Act in 1975, it broadened the Act's coverage to include language minorities—that is, citizens living in environments where the dominant language is not English (Asian Americans, American Indians, Alaskan natives, and persons of Spanish heritage). Because Mexican Americans have historically experienced political subjugation, especially in Southwestern states, extending § 5 coverage to language minorities proved to be a potent weapon aimed at eradicating Chicano underrepresentation in the electoral process. In an effort to prevent application of the 1975 Amendments of the Voting Rights Act, Texas officials brought suit in district court. In an opinion by Justice Marshall, the Court held, in *Briscoe v. Bell,* 432 U.S. 404 (1977), that the lower courts erred in holding that they had jurisdiction to review Texas officials' claims. The Court found that a bailout suit under § 4(a) of the Voting Rights Act was Texas' sole remedy and that this interpretation was supported by the language and legislative history of the Act.

FAIR EMPLOYMENT AND THE EMERGENCE OF AFFIRMATIVE ACTION

During the 1960s, blacks made real strides in gaining equal access to hotels, restaurants, parks, public beaches, interstate carriers, and recreational facilities. Despite these gains, many blacks lacked sufficient economic resources because of racial discrimination in the labor market to pay for hotel rooms, interstate bus rides, and dinners in upscale restaurants. William Darity and Samuel Myers found that discrimination is the fundamental problem facing black males who are excluded from participating in the labor market on an equal basis with white males with similar qualifications.[13] A gap also exists in the wages that males and females make. Charles Dale found in his

BOX 4.2

Title VII of the Civil Rights Act of 1964:
Main Provisions

§ 703 [2000e-2]. *Unlawful employment practices.*
(a) Employer practices. It shall be an unlawful employment practice for an employer—
    (1) to fail or refuse to hire or to discharge any individual, or otherwise to discriminate against any individual with respect to his compensation, terms, conditions of employment, because of such individual's race, color, religion, sex, or national origin; or
    (2) to limit, segregate, or classify his employees or applicants for employment in any way which would deprive or tend to deprive any individual of employment opportunities or otherwise adversely affect his status as an employee, because of such individual's race, color, religion, sex, or national origin.

study that, in 1991, "women earned about 70 cents for every $1.00 earned by men."[14] The logical course of action was to focus the struggle for racial equality on eradicating job bias and receiving a fair share of the economic pie. The Philadelphia Plan, which came into existence in 1967, was viewed as a solution to the lack of black employees in the building trades. The idea behind the plan was to persuade white contractors to affirmatively guard against discriminatory practices or lose federal contracts. The Office of Federal Contract Compliance was responsible for evaluating the level of progress being made by contractors.

The Civil Rights Act of 1964 had become one of the most important pieces of legislation enacted by Congress in the 20th century. Title VII prohibits discriminatory employment practices against any person on account of race, color, religion, gender, or national origin (see Box 4.2). It applies to employment agencies; labor unions; public employers at the federal, state, and local levels; and to employers with 15 or more employees. The Equal Employment Opportunity Commission (EEOC) was created by Congress to enforce Title VII's provisions. In addition to Title VII, President Lyndon Johnson issued Executive Order 11246, which prohibited federal contractors from practicing employment discrimination on account of race. Minority groups and women challenged discriminatory employment practices in the courts and used Title VII of the Civil Rights Act of 1964 as their chief statutory weapon. The Burger Court was activist in its attempt to delineate the legality of employment practices that promote or restrict equal employment opportunities of minorities and women.

Title VII and the Elimination
of Racial Bias in the Labor Market

Title VII withstood statutory challenge for the first time in GRIGGS V. DUKE POWER CO., 401 U.S. 424 (1971). Black employees challenged Duke Power Company's educational requirements of a high school diploma and aptitude tests as prerequisites for employment and transfer under Title VII of the Civil Rights Act of 1964. Writing for a unanimous Court, Chief Justice Burger found that education and aptitude test requirements were unrelated to job performance and that "Congress has commanded . . . that any tests used must measure the person for the job and not the person in the abstract." Thus, *Griggs* established the principle of adverse impact; that is, Title VII is violated when employer practices have a discriminatory impact on minorities regardless of the employer's intent unless business necessity justifies such practices.

The Burger Court elaborated further on the standards of proof under Title VII (see Table 4.3). For example, in *McDonnell Douglas Corp. v. Green*, 411 U.S. 792 (1973), a civil rights activist who participated in a protest demonstration against the company's hiring practices alleged that his discharge violated § 703(a)(1) of Title VII, which prohibits discriminatory employment decisions. Justice Powell, writing for a unanimous Court, held that the complainant in Title VII suits has the burden of establishing a prima facie case of racial discrimination. The Court, in *McDonnell Douglas,* established the following three-part test for employment discrimination cases: (a) a job applicant must show that he or she applied and was qualified for an available job and that a white person was hired instead; (b) the company must show that it had a legitimate, nondiscriminatory reason for not hiring the minority job applicant; and (c) the job applicant must show that the reason cited by the company was a pretext or cover-up. The Supreme Court refined the *McDonnell Douglas* framework in *Texas Department of Community Affairs v. Burdine*, 450 U.S. 248 (1981) and *United States Postal Service Board of Governors v. Aikens*, 460 U.S. 711 (1983). *McDonnell Douglas* became a cornerstone of employment discrimination law because alleged victims of job bias could win suits by establishing such a pretext; there was no need to prove intentional discrimination.

In WASHINGTON V. DAVIS, 426 U.S. 229 (1976), the Court had to decide whether a written personnel test (Test 21) for Washington, D.C., police applicants was racially discriminatory in violation of the due process clause of the Fifth Amendment. In a decision viewed as a setback for black Americans in their quest for economic justice, the Burger Court declared that the test was not unconstitutional simply because it resulted in a racially disproportionate impact. According to the Court's reasoning in *Davis,* because Test 21 was neutral on its face, disproportionate impact alone was not enough to prove a violation of equal protection. In rejecting that Title VII standards should control in *Davis,* the Court established that discriminatory purpose or intent must be shown when race-neutral governmental action is challenged under the equal protection clauses of the Fifth and Fourteenth Amendments. As illustrated in this chapter, the impact of the *Davis* intent standard was felt in other areas, such as school desegregation, housing, and voting rights cases. Interestingly, the impact of the *Davis* ruling in the employment context was lessened significantly when Title VII was amended in 1972 to cover governmental employees; thus, there was no need to bring these suits under the equal protection clause.

Just 18 days after the *Davis* decision, the Burger Court was confronted with the question of whether Title VII applies to whites. In *McDonald v. Santa Fe Trail Transportation Co.,* 427 U.S. 273 (1976), two white employees discharged by the company for misappropriating property and a black worker similarly charged but not dismissed alleged a Title VII and § 1981 violation. In writing for the majority, Justice Marshall found that the language and legislative history of Title VII apply to both whites and nonwhites. Similarly, the Court held that § 1981 is applicable to racial discrimination in private employment against white persons. In *Johnson v. Railway Express Agency,* 421 U.S. 454 (1975), the Burger Court held that § 1981 affords a federal remedy against racial discrimination in private employment separate from Title VII. Thus, 1981 overlaps with Title VII and also has broader coverage, such as allowing monetary damages. Justices White and Rehnquist dissented in *McDonald* because they disagreed that § 1981 applied in the case.

The Supreme Court has established that one of the purposes behind Title VII is to make persons whole for injuries suffered because of unlawful employment discrimination. As indicated in § 706(g) of Title VII, Congress has provided for a back-pay provision if a court finds that an employer has intentionally engaged in unlawful employment practices. In *Albemarle Paper Co. v. Moody,* 422 U.S. 405 (1975), the Burger Court elaborated on the standards governing the award of back pay for losses sustained by minority plaintiffs under a discriminatory system under Title VII. The Court established in *Moody* that back pay should be denied only for reasons that would not frustrate the central purpose of Title VII—that is, eradicating discrimination in the labor force and making persons whole for injuries suffered through past discrimination.

In *Hazelwood School District v. United States,* 433 U.S. 299 (1977), the Burger Court considered the role of statistics in pattern or practice suits under Title VII. In *Hazelwood* the federal government brought a pattern or practice suit of teacher employment discrimination against the Hazelwood, Missouri, school district. The government's evidence was based on (a) a history of alleged racial discriminatory practices, (b) statistical disparities in hiring, (c) standardless and subjective hiring procedures, and (d) specific instances of discrimination against 55 black applicants for teaching jobs. The school district offered virtually no additional evidence in response, relying instead on perceived deficiencies in the government's case. The issue before the Burger Court in *Hazelwood* was whether the appellate court's finding of a pattern or practice of discrimination based on the small percentage of black teachers in the school district was adequate. In an 8-1 opinion written by Justice Stewart, the Court found that the court of appeals was correct when it based its findings on the relevant comparisons of black teachers in the school

Table 4.3 Employment and Affirmative Action: Major Cases

Case	Vote	Ruling
Griggs v. Duke Power Co., 401 U.S. 424 (1971)	9-0	Chief Justice Burger established that Title VII is violated when employer practices have a disproportionate impact on minorities unless business necessity justifies such practices.
McDonnell Douglas Corp. v. Green, 411 U.S. 792 (1973)	9-0	Justice Powell devised a three-part test for establishing a prima facie case of racial discrimination under Title VII.
Alexander v. Gardner-Denver Co., 415 U.S. 36 (1974)	9-0	Justice Powell held that the legislative history of Title VII allows an individual to pursue independently his or her rights under Title VII and other applicable federal statutes.
DeFunis v. Odegaard, 416 U.S. 312 (1974)	per curiam	The Supreme Court held moot a case in which a white male who had been denied admission to the University of Washington School of Law claimed that he was denied the equal protection of the laws.
Emporium Capwell Co. v. Western Addition Community Organization, 420 U.S. 50 (1975)	8-1	Justice Marshall held that the discharge of black workers for failure to discontinue picketing, thereby bypassing the union representatives, did not violate the National Labor Relations Act.
Albemarle Paper Co. v. Moody, 422 U.S. 405 (1975)	7-1	Justice Stewart held that back pay should be denied only for reasons that do not frustrate the central purpose of Title VII.
Johnson v. Railway Express Agency, 421 U.S. 454 (1975)	6-3	Justice Blackmun established that Title VII and § 1981 are distinct and are separate statutes of relief for victims of employment discrimination.
McDonald v. Santa Fe Trail Transportation Co., 427 U.S. 273 (1976)	7-2	Justice Marshall declared that the language and legislative history of Title VII apply to whites and nonwhites alike.
Franks v. Bowman Transportation Co. Inc., 424 U.S. 747 (1976)	5-3	Justice Brennan ruled that an award of seniority that was retroactive to a class of black truck drivers under § 706(g) of Title VII was appropriate because they had been the victims of discrimination by the company.
Teamsters v. United States, 431 U.S. 324 (1977)	7-2	Justice Stewart held that victims of discrimination could not be granted retroactive seniority.
Hazelwood School District v. United States, 433 U.S. 299 (1977)	8-1	Justice Stewart held that once a prima facie case has been established by statistical workforce disparities, the employer must be given an opportunity to attack the validity of the statistical evidence.

Table 4.3 *continued*

Case	Vote	Ruling
Furnco Construction Corp. v. Waters, 438 U.S. 567 (1978)	7-2	Justice Rehnquist relaxed the *Green* prima facie showing to the extent that employers must be given latitude to introduce statistics on the question of whether the workforce was racially balanced.
Regents of the University of California v. Bakke, 438 U.S. 265 (1978)	5-4	Justice Powell ordered Allan Bakke, a white male, admitted to the University of California at Davis Medical School but also ruled that race may be a factor in the admissions process in the first affirmative action case considered by the Court.
United Steelworkers of America v. Weber, 443 U.S. 193 (1979)	5-2	Justice Brennan upheld a voluntary affirmative action plan in the private sector under Title VII.
Fullilove v. Klutznick, 448 U.S. 448 (1980)	6-3	Chief Justice Burger upheld Congress' 10% set-aside against a challenge by white construction contractors as an exercise of Congress' Spending Power authority under Article I, § 8, Clause 1.
Texas Department of Community Affairs v. Burdine, 450 U.S. 248 (1981)	9-0	The Supreme Court ruled that when the plaintiff in a Title VII case has proven a prima facie case of employment discrimination, the defendant bears only the burden of explaining clearly the nondiscriminatory reason for its action.
American Tobacco Company v. Patterson, 456 U.S. 63 (1982)	5-4	Justice White held that seniority plans adopted after Title VII became effective are not subject to challenge under the disparate impact standard.
Pullman-Standard v. Swint, 456 U.S. 273 (1982)	7-2	Justice White struck down black employees' challenge to an alleged discriminatory seniority system on the ground that absent a discriminatory purpose, the operation of a seniority system cannot be an unlawful unemployment practice even if the system has discriminatory consequences.
United States Postal Service Board of Governors v. Aikens, 460 U.S. 711 (1983)	9-0	Justice Rehnquist ruled that a district court erred when it required a black plaintiff to submit direct evidence of discriminatory intent and in its focusing on the question of a prima facie case rather than directly on the question of discrimination.

continued

Table 4.3 *continued*

Case	Vote	Ruling
Firefighters v. Stotts, 467 U.S. 561 (1984)	6-3	Justice White invalidated a modified layoff plan aimed at protecting black employees under Title VII because there was no finding that any of the blacks protected from layoffs had been victims of identified discrimination.
Sheet Metal Workers v. EEOC, 478 U.S. 421 (1986)	5-4	Justice Brennan held that, under Title VII, a district court may order race-conscious relief that may benefit individuals who were not victims of identified discrimination.
Firefighters v. Cleveland, 478 U.S. 501 (1986)	6-3	Justice Brennan held that § 706(g) of Title VII does not preclude the adoption of a consent decree that may benefit individuals who were not the actual victims of the city's discriminatory practices.
Wygant v. Jackson Board of Education, 476 U.S. 267 (1986)	5-4	Justice Powell, in employing strict scrutiny, invalidated an affirmative action plan whereby white teachers with more seniority were laid off and black teachers with less seniority retained their jobs.

district and in the labor market area. However, the Court found that this prima facie statistical proof might, at the trial court level, be rebutted by statistics offered by the school district after it became subject to Title VII in 1972 (when Title VII was extended to public employers). The Court noted that "once a prima facie case has been established by statistical workforce disparities, the employer must be given an opportunity to show that 'the claimed discriminatory pattern is a product of pre-Act hiring rather than unlawful post-Act discrimination.'" The Court vacated the court of appeals ruling and held that the trial court must evaluate what figures provide the ultimate determination of whether the school district engaged in a pattern or practice of racial discrimination.

The extent to which a court could award retroactive seniority to victims of discrimination under Title VII was addressed in *Teamsters v. United States,* 431 U.S. 324 (1977). Section 703(h) of Title VII provides, in part, that

> It shall not be an unlawful employment practice for an employer to apply different standards of compensation, or different terms, conditions, or privileges of employment pursuant to a bona fide seniority . . . system, . . . provided that such differences are not the result of an intention to discriminate because of race . . . or national origin.

Teamsters involved a suit instituted by the United States government against a nationwide motor freight carrier for engaging in a pattern of discrimination against blacks and individuals with Spanish surnames, in violation of Title VII. The court of appeals held that the discriminatees could bid for higher paying jobs and use all of their seniority even if it antedated Title VII's effective date. Writing for the majority, Justice Stewart vacated the judgment of the appeals court and declared that "the unmistakable purpose of § 703(h) was to make clear that the routine application of a bona fide seniority system would not be unlawful under Title VII." Consequently, seniority rights were not outlawed because employers had engaged in discriminatory practices before the 1964 Act was passed. The scarcity of jobs intensified the debate concerning "who gets what, when, and how" and the federal courts were caught in the middle of this explosive controversy.

Trying to achieve more equity in the marketplace for blacks without adversely affecting many whites who had more seniority because of discriminatory hiring practices was a formidable task for the Burger Court. In *Franks v. Bowman Transportation Co., Inc.,* 424 U.S. 747 (1976), the Court ruled that an award of seniority that was retroactive to a class of black truck drivers was appropriate under § 706(g) of Title VII because they had been the victims of discrimination by the company. In the majority opinion, Justice Brennan pointed out that although an award of seniority status is not requisite in all circumstances, in this case it is consistent with one of the central purposes of Title VII:—to make persons whole for injuries suffered on account of unlawful employment discrimination. Justice Powell, dissenting in part, argued that the Court's ruling denies district courts the power to "investigate and weigh competing equities with respect to individual claimants."

Six years later, in *American Tobacco Company v. Patterson,* 456 U.S. 63 (1982) and *Pullman-Standard v. Swint,* 456 U.S. 273 (1982), the seniority system was before the Supreme Court once again. In *Patterson* the Court, in a 5-4 decision, ruled that § 703(h) is applicable to a seniority system that was established after the passage of Title VII. Relying on *Teamsters,* Justice White concluded that "a construction of § 703(h) limiting its application to seniority systems in place prior to the effective date of the statute would be contrary to its plain language, [would be] inconsistent with prior cases, and would run counter to the national labor policy." Justice Brennan, joined by Justices Marshall and Blackmun, contended in his dissenting opinion that seniority plans adopted after the passage of § 703(h) are subject to challenge under the disparate impact standard established in *Griggs.* In *Swint,* which was decided 22 days after *Patterson,* the Court declared that, under § 703(h), a showing of disparate impact alone cannot invalidate a seniority system even though pre-Act discrimination is perpetuated. Justice White argued that a seniority system that has discriminatory consequences will not be considered unlawful unless there is proof of a discriminatory purpose.

The Emergence of Affirmative Action

By the end of the 1960s, it had become abundantly clear that the mere prohibition of discriminatory practices against black Americans was only part of the solution to the inequities in the labor market. The enactment of Title

VII was an important legal weapon that blacks and women could use because it forbade discrimination in employment. The belief emerged that affirmative action was necessary to compensate for the detrimental effects of past discrimination and that Title VII would assist blacks and women in their quest for fair play in the job market. Affirmative action has become one of the most controversial issues of public discussion involving race. President Franklin Roosevelt mandated an end to discrimination in federal construction projects when he issued Executive Order 8802 in 1941, but he never used the phrase "affirmative action." President John Kennedy first used the term in Executive Order 10925 in 1961. Four years later, President Lyndon Johnson launched federal affirmative action by signing Executive Order 11246. At the commencement exercises at Howard University on June 4, 1965, he stated, "You do not take a person who, for years, has been hobbled by chains and liberate him, bring him up to the starting line of a race and then say, 'You are free to compete with all others,' and still justly believe you have been completely fair."[15]

Support or opposition to affirmative action is manifested in the different terminology used to describe the policy. For example, the federal government defines it as those "actions appropriate to overcome the effects of past or present practices, policies or . . . barriers to equal employment opportunity."[16] For others it means eliminating barriers to job opportunities, especially in a wide range of policy contexts. For still others, it means "preferential treatment," "quotas" for black Americans, or "reverse discrimination." The latter interpretation has caused a great deal of controversy, divisiveness, hostility, and antiblack attitudes because of the widespread belief that many unqualified blacks are receiving various positions over more qualified whites. Thus, many whites believe they are being penalized for the sins of their forefathers. Whatever the philosophic or group self-interest differences inherent in the affirmative action debate, the problem of how to best rectify past and present discriminatory practices still remains.

The Legality of Preferential
Admissions in Higher Education

In *DeFunis v. Odegaard*, 416 U.S. 312 (1974), affirmative action appeared destined to receive its first test of constitutionality. Marco DeFunis, a white male, had been denied admission to the University of Washington School of Law even though minority students with lower grades and lower Law School Admissions Test (LSAT) scores were admitted. He sued, claiming that he was denied equal protection of the laws. The lower court ordered him admitted to the law school while his case was in the courts. DeFunis was in the final term of his final year when the case reached the Supreme Court. In a per curiam decision, the Burger Court held the case moot because DeFunis was about to graduate. According to the Court's rationale in *DeFunis,* the limitations of Article III's case or controversy requirements prohibit the Court from considering the substantive constitutional issues of the case. The only Justice to reach the merits in this case was Justice Douglas. In a sharply worded dissent, he emphasized, on the one hand, that the LSAT exam discriminates against minorities and that it would make more sense to place minorities in a separate class in order to obtain a fairer assessment of their true potential. On the other hand, he argued that the "Equal Protection Clause commands the elimination of racial barriers, not their creation in order to satisfy our theory as to how society ought to be organized."

Four years later, the Court reached the merits of this controversial issue and was sharply divided. In REGENTS OF THE UNIVERSITY OF CALI-FORNIA V. BAKKE, 438 U.S. 265 (1978), the medical school at the University of California at Davis had a minority admissions program in which 16 of the 100 slots for the entering class were allotted to members of minority groups. Allan Bakke, a white male, was denied admission for one of the 84 slots in 1973 and 1974 and charged that students with lower grade point averages, Medical College Admission Test (MCAT) scores, and total benchmark scores were admitted under the special admissions program. He therefore alleged that he was the victim of reverse discrimination, in violation of Title VI of the Civil Rights Act of 1964 and the equal protection clause of the Fourteenth Amendment. The California Supreme Court ruled that the special admissions program violated the equal protection clause and ordered Bakke admitted because the university had not satisfied the burden of demonstrating that he would not have been admitted even if the special admissions program did not exist. The university appealed to the Supreme Court. Justice Powell announced the judgment for the 5-4 plurality in a 157-page opinion, holding that Bakke must be admitted to the medical school and also holding that race could be considered a factor in the admissions process. The *Bakke* ruling generated two opposing viewpoints on the legality of affirmative action in the higher education context. The first bloc, consisting of Justices Brennan, White, Marshall, and Blackmun, agreed with part of Justice Powell's opinion, holding that race could be considered a factor in the admissions process, but disagreed with Justice Powell on the question of whether past racial discrimination justified affirmative action. They also argued that the intermediate level of scrutiny was the appropriate standard of review in affirmative action cases. The second bloc, consisting of Justices Stevens, Stewart, Rehnquist, and Chief Justice Burger, argued that the special admissions program violated Title VI of the Civil Rights Act of 1964 and that Bakke should be admitted. This bloc would not have reached the constitutional issues presented in the case. Justice Marshall's concurring opinion in *Bakke* is considered to be one of the most eloquent justifications for affirmative action programs.

The landmark *Bakke* ruling increased uncertainty and apprehension in the black community about voluntary affirmative action efforts.[17] At the same time, many whites increasingly viewed affirmative action programs as a threat to their chances of gaining admission to the nation's law and medical schools. Rather than provide clear-cut answers to the permissibility of race-conscious remedies in the higher education context, the *Bakke* decision simply raised more questions about their applicability in other contexts.

Race-Conscious Remedies in the Labor Market

In UNITED STEELWORKERS OF AMERICA V. WEBER, 443 U.S. 193 (1979), the Kaiser Aluminum Company had instituted a voluntary affirmative action plan that reserved for black employees 50% of the openings in an in-plant training program designed to eradicate racial imbalances in Kaiser's workforce. Brian Weber, a white male, applied for the training program but was denied admission although he had more seniority than black coworkers. He filed a suit charging that he was the victim of racial bias and reverse discrimination under Title VII. In a 5-2 decision, the Court held that the training program was consistent with the spirit of Title VII because its purpose was to remedy the effects of racial discrimination in skilled craft positions that were the result of past patterns of racial segregation. In writing for the majority, Justice Brennan established the following criteria in determining whether affirmative action plans violate Title VII: (a) whether the plan unnecessarily trammels the interest of white employees, (b) whether the plan requires the discharge of white workers and their replacement with new black hires, (c) whether the plan creates an absolute bar to the advancement of white employees, (d) whether the plan is a temporary measure, and (e) whether the plan is intended to maintain a racial balance or to eliminate a manifest racial imbalance. Thus, the majority concluded that a private, voluntary, race-conscious affirmative action plan does not violate §§ 703(a) and (d) of Title VII. In his dissenting opinion, Justice Rehnquist relied extensively on legislative history and the language of Title VII and concluded that Title VII outlaws all racial discrimination, especially in the context of Kaiser's racially discriminatory admissions quota.

In 1977 Congress passed a law requiring that 10% of public works funds be set aside for minority business enterprises. White construction contractors challenged the law, which they characterized as an impermissible quota under the equal protection clause of the Fourteenth Amendment, the equal protection component of the due process clause of the Fifth Amendment, and various statutory provisions. Writing for the majority in FULLILOVE V. KLUTZNICK, 448 U.S. 448 (1980), Chief Justice Burger, in upholding the law, observed that the Spending Power (Art. 1, § 8, cl. 1) gave Congress the power to prohibit federal funds from being used in a discriminatory manner and that deference should be given to Congress when it acts as a co-equal branch of government. He also noted that although racial classifications require strict judicial scrutiny, Congress is authorized with broad powers to remedy the present effects of past discrimination. In concurring in the judgment, Justices Marshall, Brennan, and Blackmun restated their *Bakke* position that the minority set-aside program should be evaluated under the intermediate level of scrutiny. Justices Stewart and Rehnquist, in their dissent, argued that the minority set-aside was unconstitutional "for the same reason that *Plessy* was wrong." They argued that the Constitution is colorblind and prohibits invidious discrimination by government.

The intense pressure for equal job opportunities persuaded many municipalities to develop affirmative action programs. Whites objected because scarce economic resources limited the number of jobs that were available, and such programs were viewed by many whites as a threat to their job seniority. Conflict was inevitable, and the Court, which was sharply divided, had to decide between affirmative action programs and seniority. In *Firefighters v. Stotts,* 467 U.S. 561 (1984), a district court entered a preliminary injunction against the Memphis fire department that prohibited it from following its seniority system in determining who would be laid off because of budgetary cutbacks. A modified layoff plan aimed at protecting black employees was approved. The plan was upheld by the court of appeals, and the fire department and the union appealed to the Supreme Court. In a 6-3 ruling, the Court struck down the modified layoff plan on the grounds that there was no evidence that the black firefighters were victims of identified discrimination and that it was a violation of Title VII to lay off white employees with more senority under a bona fide seniority system.

During its final term, the Burger Court decided three important affirmative action cases. In two of the cases, the Court broadened its interpretation of Title VII, and blacks and Hispanics were on the winning side in *Sheet Metal Workers v. EEOC,* 478 U.S. 421 (1986) and *Firefighters v. Cleveland,* 478 U.S. 501 (1986). In *Sheet Metal Workers,* a sheet metal workers' union was found guilty of engaging in a pattern or practice of discrimination against blacks and Hispanics, in violation of Title VII. The union was ordered to cease its discriminatory practices and to admit minorities to the union; however, it disobeyed the court's orders and was found guilty of civil contempt. The issue presented in *Sheet Metal Workers* was whether Title VII empowers a district court to order race-conscious relief that may benefit individuals who were not identified victims of unlawful discrimination. In a 5-4 plurality opinion written by Justice Brennan, the Court ruled that the sanctions imposed by the district court were proper and were designed to coerce compliance. In addition, the language and legislative history of § 706(g) of Title VII do not prohibit a court from ordering race-conscious relief as a remedy for past discrimination.

In *Firefighters v. Cleveland,* decided on the same day as *Sheet Metal Workers,* an organization of black and Hispanic firefighters alleged that the city discriminated against them in hiring and promotion practices, in violation of Title VII. The district court adopted a consent decree that provided for the use of race-conscious relief in promoting firefighters. The union objected to the decree, and on appeal the sixth circuit affirmed the judgment of the lower court. In a 6-3 opinion written by Justice Brennan, the Court ruled that § 706(g) of Title VII does not preclude the adoption of a consent decree that may benefit individuals who were not the actual victims of the city's discriminatory practices. In addition, Justice Brennan found that Congress intended voluntary compliance to be the preferred means of achieving Title VII's objectives and that § 706(g) by itself does not restrict the ability of employers or unions to enter into voluntary agreements providing race-conscious relief. Justices White and Rehnquist and Chief Justice Burger dissented in both cases. Their principal argument was that *Stotts* controlled both cases and that the language and legislative history of § 706(g) "prevent courts from unduly interfering with the managerial discretion of employers or unions."

In one of the most important affirmative action cases decided by the Burger Court, an affirmative action plan found itself on a collision course with the seniority system, and white teachers who had the most to lose challenged it. In WYGANT V. JACKSON BOARD OF EDUCATION, 476 U.S. 267 (1986), the school board and teachers' union agreed to a collective bargaining agreement whereby white teachers with more seniority were laid off when layoffs became necessary, whereas black teachers with less seniority retained their jobs. Some laid-off white teachers brought an action alleging that their rights to equal protection had been violated. A sharply divided Court agreed with the white teachers. Applying strict scrutiny, Justice Powell's plurality opinion stressed that societal discrimination is too amorphous to impose a race-conscious remedy. Moreover, the layoff plan was not narrowly tailored, and less intrusive means to achieve the desired objectives were available. Justice White, in a concurring opinion, argued that discharging white teachers while retaining other teachers solely on the basis of race is not permissible under the equal protection clause. Justice Marshall, joined by Justices Brennan and Blackmun, dissented. He emphasized that the evidence presented by the union and school officials made it abundantly clear that the goal of integrating the faculty could not be achieved by eliminating those last hired when layoffs become necessary.

The Burger Court's affirmative action jurisprudence can be understood by its approach to Title VII and equal protection cases. The *Weber* criteria suggest that voluntary efforts in the private sphere designed to alleviate discriminatory practices do not run counter to Title VII and are consistent with its broad purposes in promoting equal employment opportunities. With respect to affirmative action plans adopted by governments, strict scrutiny is imposed; that is, a racial classification must be justified by a compelling governmental interest, and the means chosen to carry out the state's purpose must be narrowly tailored to the achievement of that goal (see *Wygant* case excerpt). The common thread underlying both approaches is that the Burger Court was more likely to strike down affirmative action plans that adversely affected the interests of white workers—that is, innocent parties. Critics charge, however, that the Burger Court's affirmative action jurisprudence did not take into account the fact that innocent white workers who obtain jobs because of a biased job market clearly benefit from such a system even though they are not responsible for it.

HOUSING DISCRIMINATION: THE INCREASING SIGNIFICANCE OF RACE AND CLASS

Pervasive segregated housing patterns in the United States are no coincidence. The housing industry worked in concert with the federal government to create this problem. Dennis Judd described the nature of the partnership in these words: "The FHA suburban preference went . . . beyond a simple matter of geography. FHA administrators actively promoted the idea that housing, and therefore neighborhoods, should be racially segregated. They shared the real estate industry's view that racial segregation was closely linked to neighborhood stability and housing values."[18]

Blacks were prevented from moving into integrated neighborhoods for several other reasons. First, there is institutional racism within the real estate profession. Studies show that real estate agents use racial steering, a practice whereby real estate agents show blacks only those properties in which they are already domiciled extensively.[19] Furthermore, blacks are more likely to experience blatant discrimination in trying to rent an apartment or purchase a home from real estate agents. Second, blacks and Hispanics are more likely than whites or Asian Americans to be denied credit. Third, private homeowners simply refuse to sell houses to blacks and never openly espouse their racist beliefs. However, when white and black testers are sent out to purchase homes, the evidence shows that the whites are told that homes are available but the blacks are informed that all of the homes have been sold or are under contract. Fourth, segregated housing reflects income disparities between blacks and whites. Because blacks as a group make less money than whites, they simply cannot afford to live in many suburban white neighborhoods. In 1993, for example, the median income for a white family was $39,308, compared with $21,548 for a black family.[20] It is important to emphasize, however, that income disparities do not fully account for segregated housing. Reynolds Farley found in his study that high-income blacks were as segregated as low-income blacks and that upper-class blacks and whites were segregated from their lower-class counterparts.[21] Fifth, local governmental units use their exclusionary zoning authority to exclude blacks, especially those with low incomes. Sixth, redlining—the practice of lending institutions refusing to lend money to or insuring any individuals residing in a particular neighborhood—places blacks at a tremendous disadvantage. Thus, poor people with excellent credit who happen to live in a deteriorating neighborhood are perpetually trapped in a no-win situation. Federal district courts have held that Title VIII prohibits redlining. For example, in *Laufmann v. Oakley Building and Loan Company,* 408 F. Supp. 489 (1976), a white couple claimed they had been refused a mortgage loan because of their plans to move into a racially integrated neighborhood. District Judge David Porter found that Congress intended to prohibit such practices when it enacted Title VIII and that the Act should be construed liberally. Individuals can rely on *Laufmann* to fight redlining, but lending institutions continue to use this form of housing discrimination. Seventh, real estate agents engage in the practice of blockbusting, whereby an agent (a) sells a home to a black in a targeted neighborhood, (b) then spreads the word around to whites in the neighborhood that it is "changing," and (c) finally encourages the whites to sell their properties before their values decrease. Agents reap the profits from such tactics. Finally, public opinion polls have indicated that blacks express a preference for residential integration.

Public Housing Referendums
as a Barrier to Fair Housing

The Burger Court addressed the issue of site selection and voter approval for building low-income housing in *James v. Valtierra,* 402 U.S. 137 (1971). Article XXXIV of the California Constitution was challenged by plaintiffs who qualified for low-cost public housing. This article provided that no low-rent housing project could be constructed or developed without approval by a majority of those voting in a referendum. The district court, relying on *Hunter v. Erickson,* 393 U.S. 385 (1969), enjoined enforcement of the referendum as a denial of equal protection. The Supreme Court reversed the lower court's decision by distinguishing *Hunter* and *James.* Justice Black, writing for the majority, declared that mandatory referendums are not limited to those proposals involving low-cost public housing and that they guarantee democratic decision making. He also reasoned that, unlike the *Hunter* case, Article XXXIV is not a racial classification because "California's entire history demonstrates the repeated use of referendums to give citizens a voice on questions of public policy." In his dissenting opinion, Justice Marshall argued that Article XXXIV was an "explicit classification on the basis of poverty—a suspect classification which demands exacting judicial scrutiny." In *City of Eastlake v. Forest City Enterprises, Inc.,* 426 U.S. 668 (1976), the Burger Court relied on *James v. Valtierra* in upholding a challenge to a city charter provision requiring that proposed land use changes be ratified by 55% of the voters.

Access to the Courts:
Fair Housing and Standing to Sue

The issue of whether a person who has directly or indirectly been a victim of housing discrimination has standing to sue in court shaped fair housing jurisprudence of the Burger Court. The jurisdictional concept of standing stems from Article III's case or controversy requirement in that a plaintiff must show that he or she is the proper party to a lawsuit. Standing rules, many of which are judge-made, can be liberally construed, which means greater access to the courts in challenging discriminatory fair housing practices. Restrictive standing rules mean, of course, that persons or groups may have to look elsewhere in resolving discriminatory housing problems.

Section 810(a) of the Fair Housing Act of 1968 provides, in part: "Any person who claims to have been injured by a discriminatory housing practice or who believes that he will be irrevocably injured by a discriminatory housing practice that is about to occur (hereafter 'person aggrieved') may file a complaint with the Secretary." In *Trafficante Metropolitan Life Insurance Company,* 409 U.S. 205 (1972), a black tenant and a white tenant of an apartment complex filed a complaint under § 810(a) of the Fair Housing Act, alleging that the owner had discriminated against nonwhites on the basis of race in the rental of apartments. The tenants claimed they had been injured in that they lost the social, business, and professional advantages of living in an integrated community. The lower court ruled that the tenants did not have standing to sue under § 810(a) because the Act permits only persons who are the objects of discriminatory housing practices to sue. In a unanimous opinion written by Justice Douglas, the Court interpreted the words "person aggrieved" in § 810(a) broadly, "which gives standing to sue to all in the same housing unit who are injured by racial discrimination in the management of those facilities within the coverage of the statute." Justice Douglas also noted the benefits that white residents would be deprived of by not being afforded the right to live in an integrated community.

Three years later, the Burger Court was confronted with another standing issue in WARTH V. SELDIN, 422 U.S. 490 (1975). In *Warth*, black low- and moderate-income and Puerto Rican plaintiffs brought an action against the town of Penfield (a suburb of Rochester, New York), claiming that the town's zoning ordinance had the effect of excluding moderate- and low-income persons from living in the town, in violation of §§ 1981, 1982, and 1983. The appeals court affirmed the district court's decision to dismiss the complaint on the ground that petitioners lacked standing. The Court, in a 5-4 decision, affirmed the decision of the appeals court. In writing for the majority, Justice Powell held that petitioners had not been personally injured and that "a plaintiff who seeks to challenge exclusionary zoning practices must allege specific, concrete facts demonstrating that the challenged practices harm *him*, and that he personally would benefit in a tangible way from the court's intervention." Justice Douglas, in a sharply worded dissent, argued that "standing has become a basic barrier to access to the federal courts, just as 'the political question' was in earlier decades." Justice Brennan argued in his dissent that Penfield purposely excluded low- and moderate-income persons from residing within Penfield and that the Court would not allow them to prove what they had alleged.

In *Gladstone, Realtors v. Village of Bellwood*, 441 U.S. 91 (1979), the Burger Court had another opportunity to elaborate on the doctrine of standing in the federal courts. In *Gladstone* one black and four white residents of Bellwood (a suburb of Chicago) brought suit against two real estate brokerage firms, alleging that the firms had violated § 804 of the Fair Housing Act by racial steering—that is, directing prospective home buyers interested in equivalent properties to different areas according to their race. The individual respondents were not seeking to buy homes but were acting as testers in an attempt to determine whether the real estate firms were engaging in racial steering. An appeals court reversed a lower court's finding that the respondents lacked standing to sue. In a 7-2 opinion written by Justice Powell, the Court agreed with the appeals court's broad interpretation of §§ 810 and 812 as being available to the same class of plaintiffs. In addition, the Court found that the respondents as residents of Bellwood had standing on the basis of their claim that the transformation of their neighborhood deprived them of "the social and professional benefits of living in an integrated society." In his dissenting opinion, Justice Rehnquist argued that, under § 812, only direct victims of housing discrimination had standing to sue. He also adhered to a narrower reading of § 810 and rejected the Court's construction of that section in *Trafficante.*

It is important to note that, in *Gladstone,* the residents of Bellwood did not press their claim that they had standing to sue because of their tester status; therefore, the Court did not reach that question. The Burger Court directly confronted the question of whether testers had standing to sue for alleged racial steering practices in the landmark case of HAVENS REALTY CORP. V. COLEMAN, 455 U.S. 363 (1982). In *Havens,* Housing Opportunities Made Equal (HOME), a nonprofit corporation, hired a white and a black tester to find out whether the Havens Realty Corporation was engaged in racial steering. The white tester was informed that vacancies were available, whereas the black tester was told that no apartments were available. Justice Brennan, writing for a unanimous Court, held that the black tester had standing to sue under § 804(d) of Title VIII because she had been the victim of a misrepresentation. The fact that the black tester had no intention of renting an apartment and expected to receive false information "does not negate the simple fact of injury within the meaning of Section 804(d)." He also noted that HOME had standing to sue because its ability to provide referral services and counseling to low-income persons seeking homes who had been seriously impaired by the steering practices.

Site Selection and Rezoning

Critics have always questioned the procedures for selecting sites for public housing. The Supreme Court has made it clear that it will fashion judicial policies for the site selection problem when local governments fail to develop clear-cut policy directives or behave in a discriminatory manner (see Table 4.4). For example, in *Hills v. Gautreaux,* 425 U.S. 284 (1976), black tenants brought suit against the Chicago Housing Authority (CHA) and the Department of Housing and Urban Development (HUD), alleging that they intentionally selected sites for public housing in Chicago on a racially discriminatory basis, in violation of the Fourteenth Amendment. Justice Stewart, writing for a unanimous Court, held that a metropolitan area remedy to correct segregated housing was permissible because the actions of the two agencies had violated federal statutes and the Fourteenth Amendment. He also argued that HUD's conduct in the area beyond the geographical boundaries of Chicago would not interfere with the authority of local governments or suburban housing authorities. The Court distinguished this case from *Milliken v. Bradley (Milliken I)* (1974) because remedial relief was ordered beyond the city's boundaries as a direct consequence of a constitutional violation.

Approximately one year after the *Gautreaux* decision, the *Davis* intent standard was applied in the context of housing. In *Arlington Heights v. Metropolitan Housing Development Corp.,* 429 U.S. 252 (1977), a nonprofit developer planned to build federally subsidized, racially integrated, low-income housing contingent on securing rezoning from a single-family to a multiple-family classification. The rezoning application was denied, and the court of appeals ruled that the denial was racially discriminatory and would affect blacks disproportionately. In reversing the appeals court's decision, Justice Powell declared, in a 5-4 ruling, that the action of officials that results in a racially disproportionate impact is not unconstitutional unless there is proof that a racially discriminatory purpose or intent led to the rezoning decision. Relying on *Washington v. Davis,* he concluded his opinion with these words: "If the property involved here always had been zoned R-5 but suddenly changed to R-3 when the town learned of MHDC's plans to erect integrated housing, we would have a far different case." The dissenters argued that the proper result in the case would be to remand the case to the lower court in light of *Davis* because *Arlington Heights* was tried in the lower courts before the Court reached its decision in *Davis.*

Providing adequate housing for the poor remains a critical nationwide problem. In many instances, deteriorated housing for them is torn down and the new housing is out of their price range. This situation forces the poor to move into already overcrowded enclaves where crime, unemployment, and a multiplicity of other problems increase in magnitude. It is worth emphasizing that the Fair Housing Act of 1968 has been a major disappointment because of ineffective enforcement efforts.[22]

Fair Housing Issues in the Contexts of Exclusionary Zoning and Street Closings

According to Professor Charles Lamb's analysis of equal housing opportunity, one common discriminatory method used to keep blacks out of white neighborhoods is exclusionary zoning laws.[23] Exclusionary zoning practices "require minimum lot sizes, maximum square footage in the size of houses, and high-quality building materials that could make such property too expensive for minorities."[24] Such laws may also prohibit federally subsidized housing or multifamily units. Lamb pointed out that zoning laws are used to control urban and suburban growth but that "exclusionary zoning is negative, however, when deliberately used to keep out those who could otherwise move into a community and wish to do so but are denied that right because of their race or ethnicity."[25]

The Burger Court was confronted with the impact of a municipal zoning ordinance on the definition of the family in MOORE V. CITY OF EAST CLEVELAND, 431 U.S. 494 (1977). In *Moore,* Inez Moore, a black grandmother, lived in her East Cleveland home with her son and her two grandsons who were first cousins. An East Cleveland housing ordinance defined *family* in such a way that one of her grandsons was an illegal occupant. When Moore failed to remove him from her home, the city filed criminal charges against her. The legal issue before the Court in *Moore* was whether the East Cleveland ordinance violated the due process clause of the Fourteenth Amendment. In a 6-3 plurality opinion written by Justice Powell, the Court found the ordinance unconstitutional on the rationale that the government intruded on the choice of family living arrangements, in violation of substantive due process. Justices Brennan and Marshall's concurring opinion emphasized the prominent role

Table 4.4 Fair Housing and the Burger Court: Major Cases

Case	Vote	Ruling
James v. Valtierra, 402 U.S. 137 (1971)	5-3	Justice Black declared that a public housing referendum was not an impermissible racial classification under the equal protection clause.
Lindsey v. Normet, 405 U.S. 56 (1972)	5-2	Justice White rejected the argument that the right to housing is fundamental under strict scrutiny.
Trafficante Metropolitan Life Insurance Company, 409 U.S. 205 (1972)	9-0	Justice Douglas interpreted § 801(a) of Title VIII broadly in allowing persons to have standing to sue when they alleged that the owner had discriminated against nonwhites on the basis of race in the rental of apartments.
Warth v. Seldin, 422 U.S. 490 (1975)	5-4	Justice Powell held that minority plaintiffs lacked standing to bring a challenge to a town's exclusionary zoning practices.
Hills v. Gautreaux, 425 U.S. 284 (1976)	9-0	Justice Stewart held that a metropolitan remedy was appropriate to correct segregated housing because the Chicago Housing Authority and HUD had intentionally selected sites for public housing in Chicago, in violation of the Fourteenth Amendment.
City of Eastlake v. Forest City Enterprises, Inc., 426 U.S. 668 (1976)	6-3	The Supreme Court upheld a challenge to a city charter provision requiring proposed land use changes to be ratified by 55% of the voters.
Arlington Heights v. Metropolitan Housing Development Corp., 429 U.S. 252 (1977)	5-4	Justice Powell declared that racially discriminatory intent was required in challenging the denial of a rezoning application to build federally subsidized, racially integrated, low-income housing.
Moore v. City of East Cleveland, 431 U.S. 494 (1977)	6-3	Justice Powell struck down a municipal zoning ordinance that defined *family* in such a way that a grandmother's grandson was an illegal occupant on the ground that it violated substantive due process under the Fourteenth Amendment.

the extended family plays in the black community. In contrast, Justices Stewart and Rehnquist rejected the Court's expansion of due process to the extended family. They found East Cleveland's definition of family constitutional under the equal protection clause.

Table 4.4 *continued*

Case	Vote	Ruling
Gladstone, Realtors v. Village of Bellwood, 441 U.S. 91 (1979)	7-2	Justice Powell held that black plaintiffs and white plaintiffs had standing to sue under §§ 810 and 812 of Title VIII even though they were acting as testers to buy homes in an attempt to determine whether real estate firms were engaging in racial steering.
Memphis v. Greene, 451 U.S. 100 (1981)	6-3	Justice Stevens held that a street closing that adjoined a black neighborhood at the request of an all-white neighborhood did not violate § 1982 or the Thirteenth Amendment.
Havens Realty Corp. v. Coleman, 455 U.S. 363 (1982)	9-0	Justice Brennan held that testers had standing to sue for alleged racial steering practices under § 804(d) of Title VIII.

Do street closings reflect racial discrimination? The Burger Court grappled with this problem in MEMPHIS V. GREENE, 451 U.S. 100 (1981). In *Greene* the city, at the request of residents of an affluent, all-white neighborhood, closed off a street at the point where it adjoined a black neighborhood. Black residents sued the city, alleging that the street closing violated § 1982 and the Thirteenth Amendment. In a 6-3 opinion, the Court rejected both contentions raised by the black residents. In the majority opinion, Justice Stevens found that the street closing did not impair the kind of property interests within the scope of § 1982. In reference to the Thirteenth Amendment argument, Justice Stevens found that the city's interest in safety and tranquility was sufficient to justify the adverse impact on black motorists who were inconvenienced by the street closing. For Justice Stevens, "That inconvenience cannot be equated to an actual restraint on the liberty of black citizens that is in any sense comparable to the odious practice the Thirteenth Amendment was designed to eradicate." Justice Marshall, in his dissenting opinion, argued that ample evidence existed in the record to indicate that the city's actions were racially motivated. Moreover, he suggested that blacks' property values would deteriorate because of the street closing and that the street closing would foster racial hostility.

THE DEATH PENALTY AND THE PERVASIVE INFLUENCE OF RACE

In 1972 the Burger Court addressed for the first time the issue whether the Eighth Amendment's ban on cruel and unusual punishments prohibited the

Table 4.5 Major Capital Punishment Cases During the Burger Court Era

Case	Vote	Ruling
McGautha v. California, 402 U.S. 183 (1971)	6-3	Justice Harlan ruled that permitting juries to impose the death penalty without any governing standards does not violate the Constitution.
Furman v. Georgia, 408 U.S. 238 (1972)	5-4	The Supreme Court ruled that the death penalty as presently administered in the states violated the cruel and unusual punishments provisions of the Eighth and Fourteenth Amendments.
Gregg v. Georgia, 428 U.S. 153 (1976)	7-2	Justice Stewart upheld Georgia's death penalty statutes under the Eighth Amendment.
Proffitt v. Florida, 428 U.S. 242 (1976)	7-2	The Supreme Court upheld the revised death penalty statutes in Florida.
Jurek v. Texas, 428 U.S. 262 (1976)	7-2	The Supreme Court upheld Texas' revised death penalty statutes.
Woodson v. North Carolina, 428 U.S. 280 (1976)	5-4	Justice Stewart held that a North Carolina statute that imposed the mandatory death penalty in all cases involving first-degree murder violated the Eighth and Fourteenth Amendments.
Stanislaus Roberts v. Louisiana, 428 U.S. 325 (1976)	5-4	The Supreme Court overturned Louisiana's mandatory death sentence for five categories of homicide.
Harry Roberts v. Louisiana, 431 U.S. 633 (1977)	per curiam	The Supreme Court held that the mandatory death sentence imposed on the defendant for first-degree murder of a police officer violated the Eighth and Fourteenth Amendments.
Coker v. Georgia, 433 U.S. 584 (1977)	6-3	Justice White declared that the punishment of death was an excessive penalty for the crime of rape.
Lockett v. Ohio, 438 U.S. 586 (1978)	6-2	Chief Justice Burger held that the Ohio death penalty statute did not permit the type of individualized consideration of mitigating factors required by the Eighth Amendment.

imposition of the death penalty (see Table 4.5). Opponents of the death penalty argued that its imposition was disproportionately given to black males, especially for the crime of rape. In the 1960s, groups such as the ACLU and the NAACP Legal Defense Fund began a litigation strategy of attacking the

Table 4.5 *continued*

Case	Vote	Ruling
Barefoot v. Estelle, 463 U.S. 880 (1983)	6-3	Justice White upheld procedures adopted to facilitate the speedy disposition of fedeal habeas corpus petitions by inmates on death row.
Beck v. Alabama, 447 U.S. 625 (1980)	7-2	The Supreme Court invalidated an Alabama death penalty statute that required the jury to convict and impose the death penalty or acquit the defendant of the capital offense but prohibited it from convicting for the lesser included offense.
Enmund v. Florida, 458 U.S. 782 (1982)	5-4	Justice White invalidated a Florida death penalty statute that allowed the death penalty to be imposed for someone who participated in a murder but did not take a life.
Pulley v. Harris, 465 U.S. 37 (1984)	7-2	The Supreme Court declared that the lack of proportionality review does not violate the Eighth Amendment.
Ford v. Wainwright, 477 U.S. 399 (1986)	5-4	Justice Marshall held that the Eighth Amendment prohibited states from inflicting the death penalty on a prisoner who is insane.

constitutionality of the death penalty. In 1971 the Burger Court ruled, in *McGautha v. California,* 402 U.S. 183 (1971), that permitting juries to impose the death penalty without any governing standards does not violate the Constitution.

In FURMAN V. GEORGIA, 408 U.S. 238 (1972), the Burger Court was directly confronted with the question of whether the imposition of the death penalty violated the Eighth and Fourteenth Amendments. In *Furman* and two companion cases, two black men were sentenced to death for raping two white women, and a black man was sentenced to death for murder. In a 233-page plurality opinion, five Justices agreed that the imposition of the death sentences in these cases violated the cruel and unusual punishments provision, but they could not agree on the rationale for their holding. Justice Douglas argued that the death penalty was applied discriminatorily against minorities and the poor under the equal protection clause. Justice Brennan argued that the death penalty served no penal purpose that was more effective than imprisonment and does not comport with human dignity under the Eighth Amendment. Justice Stewart argued that the death penalty was cruel and unusual because it was so wantonly and freakishly imposed. Justice White argued that the death penalty violated the cruel and unusual punishments provision because of its infrequent imposition and did not justify the social ends it was deemed to serve. And Justice Marshall argued that the death penalty was cruel and unusual punishment because it (a) served no valid legislative purpose; (b) was morally unacceptable, cruel, and unusual because of its infliction of physical pain, excessiveness, arbitrariness; and (c) was discriminatory. The Burger Court did not rule in *Furman* that the death penalty was unconstitutional in all circumstances. The impact of *Furman* was that 35 states with death penalty statutes on their books revised them in the light of concerns expressed by the Justices in *Furman.*

The Court's ruling in *Furman* in many ways intensified the debate concerning the death penalty. For example, Norman Dorsen and others found that of the 3,859 individuals executed in the United States between 1930 and 1967, over 50% were nonwhite. Over 90% of the individuals executed for rape for the same period were nonwhite.[26] Professor Welsh White also found that a disproportionate number of blacks received the death penalty and that the greatest disparity was in rape cases.[27] He also reported that during the 1930-1967 period, "approximately 49 percent (1,630 out of 3,334) of those executed for murder were black."[28] White concluded in his study that an individual who kills a white person, regardless of race, is more likely to receive the death penalty than an individual who kills a black person. Consequently, race lies at the heart of the death penalty controversy.

In many instances, the revised death penalty statutes required a bifurcated trial that separated the determination of guilt or innocence from the sentencing proceeding, and required that juries examine specific aggravating and mitigating circumstances before imposing a capital sentence. The rationale given for this approach was to reduce the significance of race when juries considered the death penalty. White found, however, that the revised statutes did not achieve the desired result because of the intensity and pervasiveness of race prejudice in the United States.[29]

On July 2, 1976, approximately four years after *Furman* was decided, opponents of the death penalty received a major setback from the Burger Court when it rendered three decisions concerning revised death penalty statutes in Georgia, Florida, and Texas. In *Gregg v. Georgia,* 428 U.S. 153 (1976), the Court ruled, in a 7-2 plurality opinion, that the punishment of death for murder is not disproportionate to the crime and therefore does not violate the Eighth Amendment under all circumstances. In writing for the plurality, Justice Stewart pointed out that Georgia's carefully drafted statutory system had dealt effectively with the element of arbitrariness, which was of great concern to the Court in *Furman.* In their separate dissenting opinions and in all subsequent death penalty cases, Justices Brennan and Marshall restated their objections to the imposition of the death penalty. In *Proffitt v. Florida,* 428 U.S. 242 (1976) and *Jurek v. Texas,* 428 U.S. 262 (1976), the Burger Court upheld the revised death penalty statutes in Florida and Texas as it had done in *Gregg.* The Texas and Florida statutes permitted juries to consider aggravating and mitigating circumstances before the death penalty may be imposed.

In *Woodson v. North Carolina,* 428 U.S. 280 (1976), also decided on the same day as *Gregg,* the Court, in a 5-4 plurality opinion written by Justice Stewart, held that a North Carolina statute that imposed a mandatory death penalty in all cases involving first-degree murder violated the Eighth and Fourteenth Amendments. For Justice Stewart, individualized sentencing was illustrative of enlightened policy and takes into consideration the "relevant aspects of the character and record of each convicted defendant." Relying on *Woodson,* the Court reached a similar conclusion in *Stanislaus Roberts v. Louisiana,* 428 U.S. 325 (1976) when it overturned Louisiana's mandatory death sentence for five categories of homicide. The Court also ruled, in *Harry Roberts v. Louisiana,* 431 U.S. 633 (1977), that the mandatory death sentence imposed on the defendant for the first-degree murder of a police officer violated the Eighth and Fourteenth Amendments because the statute did not allow for consideration of particularized mitigating factors.

In *Coker v. Georgia,* 433 U.S. 584 (1977), Justice White, writing for a 6-3 plurality, declared that the punishment of death is a disproportionate penalty for the crime of raping an adult woman. Chief Justice Burger and Justice Rehnquist, in their dissenting opinion, expressed the view that the Georgia death penalty statute was constitutional and that the "Cruel and Unusual Punishments Clause does not give the Members of this Court license to engraft their conception of proper public policy onto the considered legislative judgments of the States."

By 1983 the Burger Court signaled its dissatisfaction toward the lengthy appeals process in capital cases. *Barefoot v. Estelle,* 463 U.S. 880 (1983) is illustrative of this attitudinal transformation. In 1978 Thomas Barefoot was convicted of the capital murder of a police officer in Texas and was sentenced to death. Barefoot objected to the state's use of psychiatric testimony at his sentencing hearing, in which psychiatrists stated there was a probability he would commit further criminal acts of violence. After the Texas Court of Criminal Appeals rejected Barefoot's contention, the Supreme Court denied certiorari in the case. When the Texas Court of Criminal Appeals denied Barefoot's habeas corpus application, his execution date was scheduled. He then filed a petition for habeas corpus in federal district court, raising the same claims with respect to the use of psychiatric testimony. The district court rejected his contentions, and the court of appeals refused to stay Barefoot's execution pending appeal of the district court's ruling. In a 6-3 ruling, the Court held that the court of appeals was not in error for refusing to stay Barefoot's death sentence. Justice White, writing for the majority, expressed the following concerns:

> The role of federal habeas proceedings, while important in assuring that constitutional rights are observed, is secondary and limited. Federal courts are not forums on which to relitigate state trials. Even less is federal habeas a means by which a defendant is entitled to delay an execution indefinitely. The procedures adopted to facilitate the orderly consideration and disposition of habeas petitions are not legal entitlements that a defendant has a right to pursue irrespective of the contribution these procedures make toward uncovering constitutional error. . . . Furthermore, unlike a term of years, a death sentence cannot begin to be carried out by the State while substantial legal issues remain outstanding.

Justice Marshall, joined by Justice Brennan, stated in his dissenting opinion, "In view of the irreversible nature of the death penalty and the extraordinary number of death sentences that have been found to suffer from some constitutional infirmity, it would be grossly improper for a court of appeals to establish special summary procedures for capital cases."

One year after the *Barefoot* decision, black criminal defendants suffered another setback. In *Pulley v. Harris,* 465 U.S. 37 (1984), the Burger Court rejected the claim of Robert Harris, a black male, that failure to compare his sentence with sentences imposed in similar capital cases was a violation of the Eighth Amendment. Justice Brennan, joined by Justice Marshall, wrote a sharply worded dissent expressing the need for proportionality review to ensure that the death penalty will not be imposed in a wanton and freakish manner. As he put it, "Comparative proportionality review serves to eliminate some, if only a small part, of the irrationality that currently infects imposition of the death penalty by the various states."

During the last term of the Burger Court, the Court, in a 5-4 plurality opinion, held in *Ford v. Wainwright,* 477 U.S. 399 (1986) that the Eighth Amendment prohibits states from inflicting the death penalty on a prisoner who is insane. In writing for the plurality, Justice Marshall reasoned that inflicting the death penalty on a prisoner who is insane has questionable retributive and deterrence value and simply offends humanity. For the dissenters, the Court ignored "the fact that the Florida scheme it finds unconstitutional, in which the Governor is assigned the ultimate responsibility of deciding whether a condemned prisoner is currently insane, is fully consistent with the 'common-law heritage' and current practice on which the Court purports to rely."

JURY DISCRIMINATION: NEW ERA, OLD PRACTICES

Racial, Ethnic, and Gender Bias in Jury Selection

During the Burger Court era, blacks, Mexican Americans, and women were experiencing discrimination in the selection of juries similar to what they had experienced 100 years earlier. Prior to 1970, only criminal defendants could challenge their convictions on the grounds of systematic exclusion of blacks from grand or petit juries. In *Carter v. Jury Commission of Greene County,* 396 U.S. 320 (1970), the Court considered for the first time whether black plaintiffs have standing to sue for declaratory and injunctive relief in attacking racial discrimination in the selection of juries. In an 8-1 opinion, Justice Stewart ruled that black citizens of Greene County, Alabama, who brought a class action suit against Alabama officials, alleging discriminatory exclusion of blacks from grand and petit juries, had standing to bring a civil suit to attack systematic jury discrimination. Justice Stewart held that:

Once the State chooses to provide grand and petit jurors, whether or not constitutionally required to do so, it must hew to federal constitutional criteria in ensuring that the selection of membership is free of racial bias. . . . That kind of discrimination contravenes the very idea of a jury—"a body truly representative of the community," composed of "the peers or equals of the person whose rights it is selected or summoned to determine; that is, of his neighbors, fellows, associates, persons having the same legal status in society as that which he holds."

On the merits of the case, the Court refused to overturn the ruling of the three-judge district court that refused to invalidate the Alabama statute. Dissenting in part, Justice Douglas argued that systematic exclusion of blacks was amply demonstrated in the record and that the only way to correct the problem of all-white jury commissions is proportional representation.

In *Peters v. Kiff,* 407 U.S. 493 (1972), the Court considered for the first time whether a white defendant could challenge the exclusion of blacks from jury service. Dean Peters claimed that Georgia's systematic exclusion of blacks from the grand jury that indicted him and from the petit jury that convicted him of burglary denied him due process and equal protection of the laws. In a 6-3 plurality opinion written by Justice Marshall, the Court held that the systematic exclusion of blacks from juries violated his due process rights. For Justice Marshall, "unconstitutional jury selection procedures cast doubts on the integrity of the whole judicial process. They create the appearance of bias in the decision of individual cases; and they increase the risk of actual bias as well." Chief Justice Burger, joined by Justices Blackmun and Rehnquist, argued in the dissent that the alleged exclusion in the case was extraneous to the due process question.

In *Alexander v. Louisiana,* 405 U.S. 625 (1972), Russell Alexander, a black defendant who was convicted and sentenced to life imprisonment for rape, challenged his conviction on the ground that the grand jury selection procedures discriminated against blacks and women. In Lafayette Parish, Louisiana, all-white jury commissioners sent out questionnaires that included a space for racial designation to those on a list compiled from nonracial sources. Of the 7,000 returns, only 14% were from blacks although they constituted 21% of the parish population eligible for grand jury service. The jury pool was reduced to 400, of whom 27 (7%) were black, from which the 20-person grand jury venires were drawn. Alexander's venire included one black, and the grand jury that indicted him had none. In a unanimous opinion, the Court held that the defendant made out a prima facie case of racial discrimination in the selection of the grand jury by showing that the selection procedures were not racially neutral.

In *Castaneda v. Partida,* 430 U.S. 482 (1977), Rodrigo Castaneda, a Mexican American who had been convicted of burglary with intent to rape, filed a habeas corpus petition in federal court, alleging a denial of due process and equal protection because Mexican Americans had been systematically excluded from the state grand jury selection process under Texas' key man system. The evidence indicated that Mexican Americans made up 79% of the

Table 4.6 Jury Discrimination and the Burger Court: Major Cases

Case	Vote	Ruling
Carter v. Jury Commission of Greene County, 396 U.S. 320 (1970)	8-1	Justice Stewart ruled that black plaintiffs have standing to sue for declaratory and injunctive relief in attacking racial discrimination in the selection of juries.
Turner v. Fouche, 396 U.S. 346 (1970)	9-0	The Supreme Court held that black residents made out a prima facie case of jury discrimination in attacking the constitutionality of the statutory system used to select juries and school boards.
Peters v. Kiff, 407 U.S. 493 (1972)	6-3	Justice Marshall held that a white defendant could challenge the exclusion of blacks from jury service.
Alexander v. Louisiana, 405 U.S. 625 (1972)	9-0	The Supreme Court held that a black defendant had made out a prima facie case of racial discrimination in the selection of the grand jury by showing that the selection procedures were not racially neutral.
Taylor v. Louisiana, 419 U.S. 522 (1975)	8-1	Justice White held that the Sixth Amendment guarantee that a petit jury be selected from a representative cross section of the community is violated when women are systematically excluded from jury panels.
Daniel v. Louisiana, 420 U.S. 1 (1975)	per curiam	The Supreme Court refused to apply *Taylor v. Louisiana* retroactively to convictions obtained by juries empaneled prior to the date of the decision.
Castaneda v. Partida, 430 U.S. 482 (1977)	5-4	Justice Blackmun held that substantial statistical disparities where Mexican Americans had been systematically excluded from the state grand jury selection process validated the existence of intentional discrimination in grand jury selection and that the state had failed to rebut the presumption by competent evidence.

population in Hidalgo County, Texas, but that only 39% were summoned for grand jury service over an 11-year period. Justice Blackmun, writing for the 5-4 majority, held that the substantial statistical disparities validated the existence of intentional discrimination in grand jury selection and that the state had failed to rebut the presumption by competent evidence. Justice Powell indicated in his dissenting opinion that the statistical disparity pre-

Table 4.6 *continued*

Case	Vote	Ruling
Ham v. South Carolina, 409 U.S. 524 (1973)	7-2	Justice Rehnquist held that the trial court's refusal to make any inquiry of the jurors as to racial bias violated Ham's due process rights under the Fourteenth Amendment.
Ristaino v. Ross, 424 U.S. 589 (1976)	6-2	Justice Powell held that black defendants' due process rights were not violated when the judge refused the request to ask the jury specifically about racial prejudice because the circumstances in the case did not rise to constitutional dimensions.
Rosales-Lopez v. United States, 451 U.S. 182 (1981)	6-3	The Supreme Court, relying on *Ristaino v. Ross,* held that the due process rights of a person of Mexican descent were not violated when the trial judge refused to ask questions concerning possible prejudice against Mexicans during the voir dire.
Turner v. Murray, 476 U.S. 28 (1986)	5-4	Justice White held that a black man indicted on charges of capital murder for fatally shooting a white man in the course of a robbery is entitled to have prospective jurors informed of the victim's race and questioned on the issue of racial bias.
Batson v. Kentucky, 476 U.S. 79 (1986)	7-2	Justice Powell declared that the equal protection clause prohibits a prosecutor from challenging black jurors on the assumption that they will be unable to consider the case against a black man impartially.

sented in the case stemmed from neutral causes, rather than from any intention to discriminate against Mexican Americans.

In one of the best-known studies concerning the influence of racial prejudice on jury decisions (see Table 4.6), Kalven and Zeisel found that racial considerations did influence the decisions that juries made in the same cases.[30] Many defense attorneys have attempted to weed out prospective jurors who bring their racist beliefs into the courtroom. For example, in *Ham v. South Carolina,* 409 U.S. 524 (1973), Gene Ham, a well-known black civil rights worker in South Carolina, was convicted of possession of marijuana. Prior to the trial judge's voir dire examination of prospective jurors, Ham's counsel requested the judge to ask jurors four questions relating to possible prejudice against him. The first two questions sought to elicit racial prejudice against blacks, the third question related to possible prejudice against beards, and the fourth dealt with pretrial publicity relating to the drug problem. The trial judge declined to ask any of the four questions, but instead asked three general questions as to bias, prejudice, and partiality as required by South Carolina law. Ham alleged that the trial court's refusal to examine jurors on voir dire as to possible prejudice against him violated his constitutional rights. In a 7-2 opinion, Justice Rehnquist held that the trial court's refusal to make any inquiry of the jurors as to racial bias violated Ham's due process rights under the Fourteenth Amendment. The majority emphasized, however, that it was not constitutional error for the trial judge to refuse to inquire as to juror prejudice against beards because bias against beards does not reach the same level of constitutional violation as that of racial prejudice. Justice Douglas, concurring in part and dissenting in part, thought the trial judge abused his discretion on the question of bias against beards. Justice Marshall also emphasized that the trial judge acted improperly in totally foreclosing other reasonable and relevant avenues of inquiry as to possible prejudice.

In *Ristaino v. Ross,* 424 U.S. 589 (1976), three blacks were tried for armed robbery and assault with intent to murder a white security guard. Counsel for the defendants requested the trial judge to ask the jury specifically about racial prejudices; however, the judge denied the request. The defendants, relying on *Ham,* argued that due process required the need for specific questioning about racial prejudice. In a 6-2 ruling delivered by Justice Powell, the Court found that the "circumstances in *Ham* strongly suggested the need for *voir dire* to include specific questioning about racial prejudice." The majority found, however, that the circumstances in *Ristaino* did not rise to constitutional dimensions, observing that the "mere fact that the victim of the crimes alleged was a white man and the defendants were Negroes was less likely to distort the trial than were the specific factors involved in *Ham.*" In *Rosales-Lopez v. United States,* 451 U.S. 182 (1981), a man of Mexican descent was convicted for his participation in a plan by which Mexicans were smuggled into the country. Defendant Humberto Rosales-Lopez requested that during the voir dire examination of prospective jurors the judge ask a question concerning possible prejudice against Mexicans. The trial judge refused to ask such a question, but he did ask questions concerning the possible bias against aliens. In a 6-3 plurality opinion, the Court relied on *Ristaino* and found that the case presented no special circumstances of constitutional dimension requiring an inquiry as to racial or ethnic bias because the issues in the trial did not involve allegations of racial or ethnic prejudice. The Court also noted that the case did not involve a violent criminal act with a victim of a different racial or ethnic group from that of the defendant; nor did the circumstances of the case indicate a reasonable possibility that racial or ethnic prejudice would influence the jury's evaluation of the evidence. In his dissenting opinion, Justice Stevens expressed the view that the voir dire "was inadequate as a matter of law because it wholly ignored the risk that potential jurors in the Southern District of California might be prejudiced against the defendant simply because he is a person of Mexican descent."

Prosecutorial Peremptory
Challenges and Juror Bias: *Swain* **Revisited**

During its final term, the Burger Court revisited the issue of whether prosecutors may use their peremptory challenges to strike blacks from the venire to secure an all-white jury. The Warren Court, in *Swain v. Alabama,* 380 U.S. 202 (1965), upheld the use of peremptories as not violative of the equal protection clause. In BATSON V. KENTUCKY, 476 U.S. 79 (1986), the Court held that a prosecutor could not remove all black jurors in a trial of a black defendant without violating the equal protection clause. Justice Powell argued that a defendant can prove purposeful discrimination by relying on the facts in his or her particular case concerning jury selection and that the burden then shifts to the prosecutor to show that the black jurors were not excluded for racial reasons. He also argued that the equal protection clause prohibits the prosecutor from challenging black jurors on the assumption that they will be unable to consider impartially the case against a black man. Justice Marshall, in a concurring opinion, argued that racial discrimination resulting from peremptories will not end until peremptory challenges are abolished. Chief Justice Burger, who would retire within five months of this decision, joined Justice Rehnquist, his successor, dissenting. They expressed the view that they could not "subscribe to the Court's unprecedented use of the Equal Protection clause to restrict the historic scope of the peremptory challenge, which has been described as 'a necessary part of trial by jury.' "

PRIVATE DISCRIMINATION:
SOPHISTICATED SEGREGATION

White men with wealth, power, and status have consistently fraternized in private settings to engage in business activities to the exclusion of blacks and women. After the passage of the Civil Rights Act of 1964, an attack on private discriminatory practices emerged. Private clubs presented a difficult and unique problem because they were viewed as being outside the purview of the equal protection clause and were exempted from civil rights legislation by Congress. Despite these difficulties, blacks and women have won a series of victories in the midst of an occasional setback.

The Burger Court made it more difficult for blacks to challenge private discrimination because of its constriction of the state action requirement. In *Moose Lodge No. 107 v. Irvis,* 407 U.S. 163 (1972), a black male who had been invited as a guest to a private club in Harrisburg, Pennsylvania, was refused service in the dining room and bar solely on account of his race. The Court ruled that granting a liquor license to the club did not sufficently implicate the state in Moose Lodge's discriminatory guest practices so as to make those practices state action within the ambit of the Fourteenth Amendment's equal protection clause. Justice Rehnquist, writing for the majority, argued that the regulatory scheme cannot be viewed as an approval of Moose Lodge's discriminatory acts. Justice Brennan, joined by Justice Marshall, dissented. He emphasized that the state's regulations were so closely interconnected with the club's bar that state involvement in racial discrimination was undoubtedly present. After the decision in this case, Irvis's claim prevailed because of Pennsylvania's public accommodations law.

One year later, in *Tillman v. Wheaton-Haven Recreation Assn., Inc.,* 410 U.S. 431 (1973), the Court, relying on *Sullivan v. Little Hunting Park, Inc.,* 396 U.S. 229 (1969), invalidated a whites-only association policy for use of a community swimming pool, a policy that had existed even though a black couple lived within the geographical preference area that automatically qualified them for membership. Writing for a unanimous Court, Justice Blackmun contended that § 1982 was violated because membership was open to every white person within the geographical area but was not available to the black couple. The crux of his opinion was stated succinctly: "When an organization links membership benefits to residency in a narrow geographical area, that decision infuses those benefits into the bundle of rights for which an individual pays when buying or leasing within the area."

Is there an affirmative duty to desegregate voluntary associations, such as 4-H clubs? The Burger Court addressed this question during its last term in *Bazemore v. Friday,* 478 U.S. 385 (1986). In *Bazemore* the North Carolina Extension Service, which operated in four areas (home economics, agriculture, 4-H, and youth and community resource development), was divided into two branches, a white branch and a black branch, prior to August 1, 1965. After the Civil Rights Act of 1964 was passed, the state merged the two branches into a single organization. In 1971 black employees of the Extension Service, recipients of its services, members of the homemaker clubs, and parents of 4-H club youths brought suit, alleging racial discrimination in employment and in provision of services, in violation of the First, Fifth, and Fourteenth Amendments. In 1972 the United States intervened in the case and amended its complaint to include the claim that the Extension Service violated Titles VI and VII of the Civil Rights Act of 1964. The district court found that the black plaintiffs had not proven that the Extension Service had discriminated against black employees in violation of Title VII by paying them less than whites employed in the same position. The court of appeals upheld this finding. In a 5-4 per curiam opinion, the Court held, in a concurring opinion written by Justice Brennan, that the court of appeals erred when it held that the Extension Service had no duty to eradicate salary disparities between white and black workers that originated prior to the date that Title VII was made applicable to public employers. However, the Court, in a concurring opinion by Justice White, affirmed that portion of the court of appeals' ruling that found no discrimination in the operation of the 4-H and homemaker clubs. Justice White found no violation of the Fourteenth Amendment because the Extension Service had discontinued its prior discriminatory practices and adopted a neutral admissions policy. For Justice White, the "mere continued existence of single-race clubs does not make out a constitutional violation."

Unlike *Green v. County School Board of New Kent County,* 391 U.S. 430 (1968), in which voluntary choice programs were inadequate and the schools had to take affirmative action to integrate their student bodies, *Green* does not apply because one's choice of a club is voluntary. Justice Brennan, joined by Justices Marshall, Blackmun, and Stevens, dissented from this portion of Justice White's concurrence. In a sharply worded dissent, Justice Brennan wrote:

> It is absurd to contend that the requirement that States take "affirmative action" is satisfied when the Extension Service simply declares a neutral admissions policy and refrains from illegal segregative activities. Moreover, the Court simply ignores the portion of the regulation that plainly requires that affirmative action be taken to *"overcome the effects of prior discrimination."* There is no room to doubt, and the Court does not even bother to argue otherwise, that one of the *effects* of prior discrimination is the legacy of single-race Clubs that still exist in North Carolina.

Justice Brennan rejected Justice White's assertion that *Bazemore* was distinguishable from *Green.* For Justice Brennan, "the State's obligation to desegregate formerly segregated entities extends beyond those programs where participation is compulsory to voluntary public amenities such as parks and recreational facilities."

Private Discrimination Versus Right of Association

One commonly held view of the First Amendment's right of freedom of association is the right of individuals to choose without state interference those persons with whom they will associate for whatever purpose. But does the freedom of association permit groups to exclude blacks and women in certain social and business activities? And are the associational rights of the excluded groups violated as well? The Burger Court confronted this dual nature of associational rights in a series of cases involving whether private clubs, under the First Amendment, can discriminate against blacks and women by refusing to extend them memberships.

In *Hishon v. King & Spalding,* 467 U.S. 69 (1984), the Court rejected a law firm's argument that Title VII infringed on its associational rights. This case involved a female lawyer who was employed as an associate with an Atlanta law firm and who, on being informed that she would not be invited to become a partner, was notified to seek employment elsewhere. Elizabeth Hishon claimed that the firm discriminated against her on the basis of sex, in violation of Title VII. In a unanimous opinion written by Chief Justice Burger, the Court held that Hishon could sue under Title VII because a benefit that is part of an employment relationship cannot be meted out discriminatorily. The Court explicitly rejected the law firm's claim that applying Title VII in this case would infringe on the rights of expression or association because the law firm did not show how its associational rights would be infringed. Moreover, the Court concluded that although private discrimination may be characterized as a form of freedom of association, it has never been accorded affirmative constitutional protection.

Fewer than two months later, the Court, in a unanimous decision, ruled in *Roberts v. United States Jaycees,* 468 U.S. 609 (1984), that a Minnesota law that made it "an unfair discriminatory practice . . . [t]o deny any person the full and equal enjoyment of the goods, services, facilities, . . . and accommodations of a place of public accommodations because of race, color, creed, religion, disability, national origin or sex," was constitutional. Women and older men were eligible for associate membership in the Jaycees, but the bylaws limited membership to men between the ages of 18 and 35. After the national organization threatened to revoke the charters of two local chapters that admitted women in order to conform to state law, the local chapters filed discrimination charges. In a 7-0 decision, the Court held that the law did not abridge the male members' right of association because that right is not absolute. Justice Brennan, writing for the Court, pointed out that the law was not overbroad because the state's compelling interest is to eradicate discrimination against females in order for them to have equal access to the goods and advantages offered to Jaycees, including full voting privileges.

The Rehnquist Court applied the principle of *Roberts* in two cases decided in 1987 and 1988. In *Board of Directors of Rotary International v. Rotary Club of Duarte,* 481 U.S. 537 (1987), the Court, in a unanimous decision, relied on *Roberts* and upheld the Unruh Act, a California statute that provides that all persons are entitled to equal accommodations, facilities, and privileges in all business establishments regardless of gender. In the majority opinion, Justice Powell argued that the Act did not interfere with members' freedom of private association or expressive association and that admitting women would not affect the ability of existing members to carry out any of their activities. One year later, in *New York State Club Association, Inc. v. City of New York,* 487 U.S. 1 (1988), the Court upheld a New York City law that prohibited discrimination on the basis of race, religion, or gender in any place of public accommodation in private clubs that have more than 400 members and that receive dues and serve meals "for the furtherance of trade or business." Writing for the majority, Justice White concluded that the law is not overbroad and does not infringe on members' right of expressive association because it "does not affect 'in any significant way' the ability of individuals to form associations that will advocate public or private viewpoints." Finally, the Court emphasized that religious and benevolent organizations were exempted from the law because business activity for women and minorities is not prevalent among them.

PROTEST RIGHTS AND ACTIVITY

The Constitutional Status of Economic Boycotts

Blacks have used a number of strategies to protest legal and political subjugation in the United States. The previous chapter examined how the Warren Court grappled with the legal status of the sit-in cases under the First

Amendment. Another weapon used by blacks during the civil rights era was the economic boycott. Historically, the economic boycott has been an effective way to bring about political and social change. One prime example was the Montgomery bus boycott led by Dr. Martin Luther King, Jr. The constitutional status of organized boycotts was uncertain, however, until the Burger Court in 1982 resolved a 16-year battle involving the Port Gibson, Mississippi, boycott. In NAACP V. CLAIBORNE HARDWARE CO., 458 U.S. 886 (1982), white business owners in Claiborne County sued the NAACP for approximately $1.5 million in economic losses. In 1982 Justice Stevens delivered an 8-0 opinion (Justice Marshall did not participate) upholding the constitutionality of the boycott activities under the First Amendment. In recognizing that "concerted action is a powerful weapon," Justice Stevens concluded that "one of the foundations of our society is the right of individuals to combine with other persons in pursuit of a common goal by lawful means." Coincidentally, the opinion in the case was announced during the NAACP's 73rd annual convention.

Vagrancy Laws and Minorities:
Police Harassment or Protecting Society?

In general, vagrancy laws allow police officers to arrest anyone loitering or wandering without any apparent reason, particularly if that person refuses to produce identification. The laws are often used by police officers to stop people who appear suspicious. A major problem with vagrancy laws is that they are often vague. How does one define "loitering" or "wandering"? Could a walk in a park be considered loitering? Vagueness is only one aspect of the problem of how vagrancy laws have been applied in the United States. Racial and ethnic minorities complain bitterly that police use vagrancy laws to single them out and harass them because they look different. In particular, blacks and Latinos assert that police officers often detain them for no reason, especially if they are spotted in a white, upper-class neighborhood.

In *Papachristou v. City of Jacksonville,* 405 U.S. 156 (1972), a unanimous Burger Court struck down a Jacksonville, Florida, vagrancy ordinance as void for vagueness. In *Papachristou* eight defendants were convicted in a Florida municipal court for violating Jacksonville Ordinance Code 26-57, which provided at the time of arrest:

> Rogues and vagabonds, or dissolute persons who go about begging, common gamblers, persons who use juggling or unlawful games or plays, common drunkards, common night walkers, thieves, pilferers or pickpockets, traders in stolen property, lewd, wanton and lascivious persons, keepers of gambling places, common railers and brawlers, persons wandering or strolling around from place to place without any lawful purpose or object, habitual loafers, disorderly persons neglecting all lawful business and habitually spending their time frequenting houses of ill fame, gaming houses, or places where alcoholic beverages are sold or served, persons able to work but habitually living upon the earnings of their wives or minor children shall be deemed vagrants and, upon conviction in the Municipal Court shall be punished as provided for Class D offenses.

Justice Douglas, writing for the Court, held that the ordinance violated the due process clause on vagueness grounds because "those convicted may be punished for no more than vindicating affronts to police authority." For Justice Douglas, the ordinance "results in a regime in which the poor and the unpopular are permitted to 'stand on a public sidewalk . . . only at the whim of any police officer.' "

The Burger Court confronted a facial challenge to California's vagrancy law in *Kolender v. Lawson,* 461 U.S. 352 (1983). Edward Lawson, a tall black man who wore shoulder-length dreadlocks, often took long walks in predominantly white neighborhoods in San Diego. He was arrested 15 times but was convicted only once under California's vagrancy law, which required a person to identify him- or herself and to account for his or her presence. Lawson challenged the constitutionality of the statute in federal district court. In a 7-2 decision, Justice O'Connor ruled that the law was vague and must be struck down because it gives police virtually complete discretion to determine whether the suspect has satisfied the statute. In a concurring opinion, Justice Brennan argued that the vagrancy statute violated the Fourth Amendment. The dissenters, Justices White and Rehnquist, argued that the law should not be held unconstitutionally vague unless it is vague in all of its possible applications.

CONCLUSION

Our analysis of Burger Court jurisprudence in civil rights is consistent with previous assessments of the Burger Court. The Burger Court was not antagonistic to the Warren Court's egalitarian principles expressed in *Brown* and its progeny. Its legacy was quite mixed and does not form a coherent pattern. The Burger Court's rulings appeared to be sensitive to the policy context of the case. The Court's response to employment discrimination, affirmative action, and minority voting rights was often supportive but at times was fraught with major stumbling blocks to the realization of full equality, such as the intent test and the application of strict scrutiny in affirmative action cases. With respect to death penalty jurisprudence, the Court, in the subsequent round of capital punishment cases, removed some of the discretionary aspects of its application.

NOTES

1. See Blasi, V. (Ed.). (1983). *The Burger Court: Counter-revolution that wasn't.* New Haven, CT: Yale University Press, Chapter 4. Also see the preface to the paperbound edition of *The Burger Court,* pp. xi-xviii.

2. Kahn, R. (1994). *The Supreme Court and constitutional theory, 1953-1993.* Lawrence: University Press of Kansas, p. 168.

3. Support for this perspective is found in Lamb, C. M., & Halpern, S. C. (Eds.). (1991). *The Burger Court: Political and judicial profiles.* Urbana: University of Illinois Press, Chapter 15.

4. Burns, H. (Ed.). (1988). The activism is not affirmative. In H. Schwartz (Ed.), *The Burger years.* New York: Penguin, p. 107.

5. O'Brien, D. (1993). *Storm center: The Supreme Court in American politics* (3rd ed.). New York: Norton, pp. 120-121.

6. State-Justice appropriation veto text. (1980, December 13). *Congressional Quarterly Weekly Report, 38,* 3633.

7. Davidson, C. (1992). The Voting Rights Act: A brief history. In B. Grofman & C. Davidson (Eds.), *Controversies in minority vote dilution: The Voting Rights Act in perspective.* Washington, DC: Brookings Institution, p. 24.

8. See Parker, F. (1983). The "results" test of Section 2 of the Voting Rights Act: Abandoning the intent standard. *Virginia Law Review, 69,* 737-746.

9. See Senate Report No. 417, 97th Congress, 2d sess., p. 3, reprinted in 1982 *U.S. Code Congressional and Administrative News,* pp. 177, 214 for additional criticisms of the *Bolden* standard.

10. For a discussion of these efforts, see Defner, A. (1982). Vote dilution and the Voting Rights Act Amendments of 1982. In C. Davidson (Ed.), *Minority vote dilution.* Washington, DC: Howard University Press, pp. 145-163; Pinderhughes, D. M. (1985). Interest groups and the passage of the Voting Rights Act in 1982. Cited in L. S. Foster (Ed.), *The Voting Rights Act: Consequences and implications.* New York: Praeger, p. 94. Also see Caldeira, G. A. (1992). Litigation, lobbying, and the Voting Rights bar. In B. Grofman & C. Davidson (Eds.), *Controversies in minority vote dilution: The Voting Rights Act in perspective.* Washington, DC: Brookings Institution, pp. 230-257.

11. Department of Justice. (1992). Number of changes submitted under Section 5 and reviewed by the Department of Justice, by state and year, 1965, April 1, 1991. Cited in B. Grofman & C. Davidson (Eds.), *Controversies in minority vote dilution: The Voting Rights Act in perspective.* Washington, DC: Brookings Institution, p. 53, footnote 2.

12. For a discussion of § 5's implementation, see Days, D. S. (1992). Section 5 and the role of the Justice Department. In B. Grofman & C. Davidson (Eds.), *Controversies in minority vote dilution: The Voting Rights Act in perspective.* Washington, DC: Brookings Institution, pp. 52-65.

13. Darity, W., Jr., & Myers, S., Jr., (1991, March). *Sex ratios, marriageability, and the marginalization of black males.* Paper presented at the Third National Meeting of the Status of Black Men in America, Morehouse College, Atlanta, GA, pp. 8, 10.

14. Dale, C. (1991, August 6). *Civil rights.* (Library of Congress, Congressional Research Service), p. 5.

15. Commencement Address delivered by President Lyndon Johnson at Howard University on June 4, 1965.

16. 29 C.F.R. 1608.1 (c) (1985).

17. John Gruhl and Susan Welch, in their 1990 study, examined the impact of *Bakke* on black and Hispanic enrollments in first-year classes of medical and law schools. Despite concerns by blacks that the *Bakke* ruling would adversely affect the chances of blacks gaining entry into the nation's professional schools, Gruhl and Welch concluded in their study that *Bakke* had a limited impact on minority enrollment. They found that the ruling "may have slightly slowed the trend toward increasing numbers of black and Hispanics in medical schools and Hispanics in law schools. However, what modest effect it may have had has been overshadowed by other factors." See Gruhl, J., & Welch, S. (1990, September). The impact of the *Bakke* decision on black and Hispanic enrollment in medical and law schools. *Social Science Quarterly, 71*(3), 458-473.

18. Judd, D. (1991, December 9). Segregation forever? *The Nation,* p. 740.

19. For an article concerning schemes to discriminate against black Americans in the housing market, see Dale, C. (1983). *Discrimination in housing: A legal perspective,* prepared by the Congressional Research Service for the Committee on Banking, Finance and Urban Affairs, 98th Cong. 1st sess., Washington, DC: Library of Congress, p. 147. Also see Lamb, C. M. (1984). Equal housing opportunity. In C. S. Bullock & C. M. Lamb (Eds.), *Implementation of civil rights policy.* Belmont, CA: Brooks/Cole, pp. 148-183.

20. U.S. Department of Commerce, Bureau of the Census, *The black population in the United States.* (Washington, DC, March 1994 and 1993 editions), p. 21.

21. See Farley, R. (1977). Residential segregation in urbanized areas of the United States in 1970: An analysis of social class and racial differences. *Demography, 14,* 510, 514.

22. Lamb, C. M. (1982). Congress, the courts, and civil rights: The Fair Housing Act of 1968 revisited. *Villanova Law Review, 28,* 1115-1162.

23. Lamb, C. M. (1984). Equal housing opportunity. In C. S. Bullock & C. M. Lamb (Eds.), *Implementation of civil rights policy.* Belmont, CA. Brooks/Cole, pp. 148-183.

24. Lamb, C. M. (1984). Equal housing opportunity. In C. S. Bullock & C. M. Lamb (Eds.), *Implementation of civil rights policy.* Belmont, CA: Brooks/Cole, p. 150.

25. Lamb, C. M. (1984). Equal housing opportunity. In C. S. Bullock & C. M. Lamb (Eds.), *Implementation of civil rights policy.* Belmont, CA: Brooks/Cole, p. 150.

26. Dorsen, N., Bender, P., Neuborne, B., & Law, S. (1979). *Political and civil rights in the United States.* Boston: Little, Brown, p. 1445.

27. White, W. (1991). *The death penalty in the nineties.* Ann Arbor: University of Michigan Press, p. 136.

28. White, W. (1991). *The death penalty in the nineties.* Ann Arbor: University of Michigan Press, p. 136.

29. White, W. (1991). *The death penalty in the nineties*. Ann Arbor: University of Michigan Press, p. 137.

30. Kalven, H., Jr., & Zeisel, H. (1966). *The American jury*. Chicago: University of Chicago Press, pp. 210-211.

CASES

SWANN V. CHARLOTTE-MECKLENBURG BOARD OF EDUCATION
402 U.S. 1 (1971)

The scope of permissible remedies in eliminating state-mandated school segregation was addressed in *Swann* and four companion cases: *McDaniel v. Barresi,* 402 U.S. 39 (1971); *Davis v. Board of School Commissioners of Mobile County,* 402 U.S. 33 (1971); *Moore v. Charlotte-Mecklenburg Board of Education,* 402 U.S. 47 (1971); and *North Carolina State Board of Education v. Swann,* 402 U.S. 43 (1971). During the 1968-69 school year, the Charlotte-Mecklenburg, North Carolina, school system had more than 84,000 students in 107 schools. Approximately 29% of the students were black, and 14,000 of those attended schools that were at least 99% black. This racial balance resulted from a desegregation plan approved by a district court in 1965. In 1968 James Swann challenged the desegregation plan, alleging that it failed to achieve a unitary school system under *Green v. County School Board* (1968). After numerous hearings and the admission of voluminous evidence, the district court found that the school board's action was discriminatory and that residential segregation contributed to segregated education in Charlotte and the surrounding area. The district court then appointed Dr. James Finger to prepare a desegregation plan. In 1970 the court was presented with two plans: the school board's plan and the Finger plan. The school board's plan placed heavy emphasis primarily on rezoning school attendance lines for the high schools, junior high schools, and elementary schools. The Finger plan was similar except in two respects: It required that 300 black students be bused to a nearly all-white high school and that zoning, pairing, grouping, and busing techniques be used for the elementary schools. On February 5, 1970, the district court adopted the board plan, as modified by Dr. Finger, for the junior and senior high schools, but the court adopted the Finger plan for the elementary schools. In *Swann* the Supreme Court addressed the validity of the student assignment remedies. *Vote: 9-0.*

* * *

MR. CHIEF JUSTICE BURGER delivered the opinion of the Court.

We granted certiorari in this case to review important issues as to the duties of school authorities and the scope of powers of federal courts under this Court's mandates to eliminate racially separate public schools established and maintained by state action. *Brown v. Board of Education,* 347 U.S. 483 (1954) (*Brown I*).

This case and those argued with it arose in States having a long history of maintaining two sets of schools in a single school system deliberately operated to carry out a governmental policy to separate pupils in schools solely on the basis of race. That was what *Brown v. Board of Education* was all about. These cases present us with the problem of defining in more precise terms than heretofore the scope of the duty of school authorities and district courts in implementing *Brown I* and the mandate to eliminate dual systems and establish unitary systems at once....

... The problems encountered by the district courts and courts of appeals make plain that we should now try to amplify guidelines, however incomplete and imperfect, for the assistance of school authorities and courts. The failure of local authorities to meet their constitutional obligations aggravated the massive problem of converting from the state-enforced discrimination of racially separate school systems. This process has been rendered more difficult by changes since 1954 in the structure and patterns of communities, the growth of student population, movement of families, and other changes, some of which have had marked impact on school planning, sometimes neutralizing or negating remedial action before it was fully implemented. Rural areas accustomed for half a century to the consolidated school systems implemented by bus transportation could make adjustments more readily than metropolitan areas with dense and shifting population, numerous schools, congested and complex traffic patterns.

The objective today remains to eliminate from the public schools all vestiges of state-imposed segregation. Segregation was the evil struck down by *Brown I* as contrary to the equal protection guarantees of the Constitution. That was the violation sought to be corrected by the remedial measures of *Brown II*

[*Brown v. Board of Education,* 349 U.S. 294 (1955)]. That was the basis for the holding in *Green* that school authorities are "clearly charged with the affirmative duty to take whatever steps might be necessary to convert to a unitary system in which racial discrimination would be eliminated root and branch" [*Green v. County School Board of New Kent County,* 391 U.S. 430 (1969)]. . . .

If school authorities fail in their affirmative obligations under these holdings, judicial authority may be invoked. Once a right and a violation have been shown, the scope of a district court's equitable powers to remedy past wrongs is broad, for breadth and flexibility are inherent in equitable remedies.

. . . This allocation of responsibility once made, the Court attempted from time to time to provide some guidelines for the exercise of the district judge's discretion and for the reviewing function of the courts of appeals. However, a school desegregation case does not differ fundamentally from other cases involving the framing of equitable remedies to repair the denial of a constitutional right. The task is to correct, by a balancing of the individual and collective interests, the condition that offends the Constitution.

. . . The school authorities argue that the equity powers of federal district courts have been limited by Title IV of the Civil Rights Act of 1964. . . . The language and the history of Title IV show that it was enacted not to limit but to define the role of the Federal Government in the implementation of the *Brown I* decision. . . .

. . . The central issue in this case is that of student assignment, and there are essentially four problem areas:

(1) to what extent racial balance or racial quotas may be used as an implement in a remedial order to correct a previously segregated system;

(2) whether every all-Negro and all-white school must be eliminated as an indispensable part of a remedial process of desegregation;

(3) what the limits are, if any, on the rearrangement of school districts and attendance zones, as a remedial measure; and

(4) what the limits are, if any, on the use of transportation facilities to correct state-enforced racial school segregation.

(1) Racial Balances or Racial Quotas

. . . In this case it is urged that the District Court has imposed a racial balance requirement of 71%-29% on individual schools. The fact that no such objective was actually achieved—and would appear to be impossible—tends to blunt that claim, yet in the opinion and order of the District Court of December 1, 1969, we find that court directing "that efforts be made to reach a 71-29 ratio in the various schools so that there will be no basis for contending that one school is racially different from the others . . . [t]hat no school [should] be operated with an all-black or predominantly black student body, [and] [t]hat pupils of all grades [should] be assigned in such a way that as nearly as practicable the various schools at various grade levels have about the same proportion of black and white students."

The District Judge went on to acknowledge that variation "from that norm may be unavoidable." This contains intimations that the "norm" is a fixed mathematical racial balance reflecting the pupil constituency of the system. If we were to read the holding of the District Court to require, as a matter of substantive constitutional right, any particular degree of racial balance or mixing, that approach would be disapproved and we would be obliged to reverse. The constitutional command to desegregate schools does not mean that every school in every community must always reflect the racial composition of the school system as a whole.

As the voluminous record in this case shows, the predicate for the District Court's use of the 71%-29% ratio was twofold: first, its express finding, approved by the Court of Appeals and not challenged here, that a dual school system had been maintained by the school authorities at least until 1969; second, its finding, also approved by the Court of Appeals, that the school board had totally defaulted in its acknowledged duty to come forward with an acceptable plan of its own, notwithstanding the patient efforts of the District Judge who, on at least three occasions, urged the board to submit plans. As the statement of facts shows, these findings are abundantly supported by the record. It was because of this total failure of the school board that the District Court was obliged to turn to other qualified sources, and Dr. Finger was designated to assist the District Court to do what the board should have done.

We see therefore that the use made of mathematical ratios was no more than a starting point in the process of shaping a remedy, rather than an inflexible requirement. From that starting point the District Court proceeded to frame a decree that was within its discretionary powers, as an equitable remedy for the particular circumstances. As we said in *Green,* a school authority's remedial plan or a district court's remedial decree is to be judged by its effectiveness. Awareness of the racial composition of the whole school system is likely to be a useful starting point in shaping a remedy to correct past constitutional violations. In sum, the very limited use made of mathematical ratios was within the equitable remedial discretion of the District Court.

(2) One-Race Schools

The record in this case reveals the familiar phenomenon that in metropolitan areas minority groups are often found concentrated in one part of the city. In some circumstances certain schools may remain all or largely of one race until new schools can be provided or neighborhood patterns change. Schools all or predominantly of one race in a district of mixed population will require close scrutiny to determine that school assignments are not part of state-enforced segregation.

In light of the above, it should be clear that the existence of some small number of one-race, or virtually one-race, schools within a district is not in and of itself the mark of a system that still practices segregation by law. The district judge or school authorities should make every effort to achieve the greatest possible degree of actual desegregation and will thus necessarily be concerned with the elimination of one-race schools. No *per se* rule can adequately embrace all the difficulties of reconciling the competing interests involved; but in a system with a history of segregation the need for remedial criteria of sufficient specificity to assure a school authority's compliance with its constitutional duty warrants a presumption against schools that are substantially disproportionate in their racial composition. Where the school authority's proposed plan for conversion from a dual to a unitary system contemplates the continued existence of some schools that are all or predominantly of one race, they have the burden of showing that such school assignments are genuinely nondiscriminatory. The court should scrutinize such schools, and the burden upon the school authorities will be to satisfy the court that their racial composition is not the result of present or past discriminatory action on their part.

An optional majority-to-minority transfer provision has long been recognized as a useful part of every desegregation plan. Provision for optional transfer of those in the majority racial group of a particular school to other schools where they will be in the minority is an indispensable remedy for those students willing to transfer to other schools in order to lessen the impact on them of the state-imposed stigma of segregation. In order to be effective, such a transfer arrangement must grant the transferring student free transportation and space must be made available in the school to which he desires to move. . . . The court orders in this and the companion *Davis* case now provide such an option.

(3) Remedial Altering of Attendance Zones

The maps submitted in these cases graphically demonstrate that one of the principal tools employed by school planners and by courts to break up the dual school system has been a frank—and sometimes drastic—gerrymandering of school districts and attendance zones. An additional step was pairing, "clustering," or "grouping," of schools with attendance assignments made deliberately to accomplish the transfer of Negro students out of formerly segregated Negro schools and transfer of white students to formerly all-Negro schools. More often than not, these zones are neither compact nor contiguous; indeed they may be on opposite ends of the city. As an interim corrective measure, this cannot be said to be beyond the broad remedial powers of a court.

Absent a constitutional violation there would be no basis for judicially ordering assignment of students on a racial basis. All things being equal, with no history of discrimination, it might well be desirable to assign pupils to schools nearest their homes. But all things are not equal in a system that has been deliberately constructed and maintained to enforce racial segregation. The remedy for such segregation may be administratively awkward, inconvenient, and even bizarre in some situations and may impose burdens on some; but all awkwardness and inconvenience cannot be avoided in the interim period when remedial adjustments are being made to eliminate the dual school systems.

No fixed or even substantially fixed guidelines can be established as to how far a court can go, but it must be recognized that there are limits. The objective is to dismantle the dual school system. "Racially neutral" assignment plans proposed by school authorities to a district court may be inadequate; such plans may fail to counteract the continuing effects of past school segregation resulting from discriminatory location of school sites or distortion of school size in order to achieve or maintain an artificial racial separation. When school authorities present a district court with a "loaded game board," affirmative action in the form of remedial altering of attendance zones is proper to achieve truly nondiscriminatory assignments. In short, an assignment plan is not acceptable simply because it appears to be neutral.

. . . We hold that the pairing and grouping of noncontiguous school zones is a permissible tool and such action is to be considered in light of the objectives sought. Judicial steps in shaping such zones going beyond combinations of contiguous areas should be examined in light of what is said in subdivisions (1), (2), and (3) of this opinion concerning the objectives to be sought. Maps do not tell the whole story since noncontiguous school zones may be more accessible to each other in terms of the critical travel time, because of traffic patterns and good highways, than schools geographically closer together. Conditions in different localities will vary so widely that no rigid rules can be laid down to govern all situations.

(4) Transportation of Students

The scope of permissible transportation of students as an implement of a remedial decree has never been defined by this Court and by the very nature of the problem it cannot be defined with precision. No rigid guidelines as to student transportation can be given for application to the infinite variety of problems presented in thousands of situations. Bus transportation has been an integral part of the public education system for years, and was perhaps the single most important factor in the transition from the one-room schoolhouse to the consolidated school. Eighteen million of the Nation's public school children, approximately 39%, were transported to their schools by bus in 1969-1970 in all parts of the country.

The importance of bus transportation as a normal and accepted tool of educational policy is readily discernible in this and the companion case, *Davis*. . . . The Charlotte school authorities did not purport to assign students on the basis of geographically drawn zones until 1965 and then they allowed almost unlimited transfer privileges. The District Court's conclusion that assignment of children to the school nearest their home serving their grade would not produce an effective dismantling of the dual system is supported by the record.

Thus the remedial techniques used in the District Court's order were within that court's power to provide equitable relief; implementation of the decree is well within the capacity of the school authority.

The decree provided that the buses used to implement the plan would operate on direct routes. Students would be picked up at schools near their homes and transported to the schools they were to attend. The trips for elementary school pupils average about seven miles and the District Court found that they would take "not over 35 minutes at the most." This system compares favorably with the transportation plan previously operated in Charlotte under which each day 23,600 students on all grade levels were transported an average of 15 miles one way for an average trip requiring over an hour. In these circumstances, we find no basis for holding that the local school authorities may not be required to employ bus transportation as one tool of school desegregation. Desegregation plans cannot be limited to the walk-in school.

An objection to transportation of students may have validity when the time or distance of travel is so great as to either risk the health of the children or significantly impinge on the educational process. District courts must weigh the soundness of any transportation plan in light of what is said in subdivisions (1), (2), and (3) above. It hardly needs stating that the limits on time of travel will vary with many factors, but probably with none more than the age of the students. The reconciliation of competing values in a desegregation case is, of course, a difficult task with many sensitive facets but fundamentally no more so than remedial measures courts of equity have traditionally employed.

. . . At some point, these school authorities and others like them should have achieved full compliance with this Court's decision in *Brown I*. The systems would then be "unitary" in the sense required by our decisions in *Green* and *Alexander* [v. *Holmes County Board of Education*, 396 U.S. 19 (1969)].

It does not follow that the communities served by such systems will remain demographically stable, for in a growing, mobile society, few will do so. Neither school authorities nor district courts are constitutionally required to make year-by-year adjustments of the racial composition of student bodies once the affirmative duty to desegregate has been accomplished and racial discrimination through official action is eliminated from the system. This does not mean that federal courts are without power to deal with future problems; but in the absence of a showing that either the school authorities or some other agency of the State has deliberately attempted to fix or alter demographic patterns to affect the racial composition of the schools, further intervention by a district court should not be necessary.

For the reasons herein set forth, the judgment of the Court of Appeals is affirmed as to those parts in which it affirmed the judgment of the District Court. The order of the District Court, dated August 7, 1970, is also affirmed.

It is so ordered.

MILLIKEN V. BRADLEY (MILLIKEN I)
418 U.S. 717 (1974)

In 1970 the NAACP brought a class action suit on behalf of Ronald Bradley and other black school children in Detroit against the governor of Michigan, William Milliken, and other state officials, alleging that the Detroit public school system was racially segregated as a result of official action. The district court concluded that state officials had created and perpetuated school segregation in Detroit and ordered them to submit desegregation plans encompassing the three-county metropolitan area despite the fact that the 85 outlying school districts in these three counties were not parties to the lawsuit, nor had claims been made against them. The district court ruled that the Detroit-only plans submitted by the school board were inadequate to accomplish desegregation. The Court then appointed a panel to devise a plan for the 1972-73 school year that required interdistrict busing in an area consisting of 53 of the 85 school districts plus Detroit. The court of appeals affirmed the part of the district court's ruling that found unconstitutional violations committed by state officials and that the metropolitan area plan embracing the 53 outlying districts was the only feasible solution. The appeals court remanded so that all suburban districts could be made parties to the litigation and thus have an opportunity to be heard as to the scope and implementation of the remedy. *Vote: 5-4.*

* * *

MR. CHIEF JUSTICE BURGER delivered the opinion of the Court.

We granted certiorari in these consolidated cases to determine whether a federal court may impose a multidistrict, areawide remedy to a single-district *de jure* segregation problem absent any finding that the other included school districts have failed to operate unitary school systems within their districts, absent any claim or finding that the boundary lines of any affected school district were established with the purpose of fostering racial segregation in public schools, absent any finding that the included districts committed acts which effected segregation within the other districts, and absent a meaningful opportunity for the included neighboring school districts to present evidence or be heard on the propriety of a multidistrict remedy or on the question of constitutional violations by those neighboring districts.

. . . Viewing the record as a whole, it seems clear that the District Court and the Court of Appeals shifted the primary focus from a Detroit remedy to the metropolitan area only because of their conclusion that total desegregation of Detroit would not produce the racial balance which they perceived as desirable. Both courts proceeded on an assumption that the Detroit schools could not be truly desegregated—in their view of what constituted desegregation—unless the racial composition of the student body of each school substantially reflected the racial composition of the population of the metropolitan area as whole. The metropolitan area was then defined as Detroit plus 53 of the outlying school districts. . . .

In *Swann,* which arose in the context of a single independent school district, the Court held:

"If we were to read the holding of the District Court to require, as a matter of substantive constitutional right, any particular degree of racial balance or mixing, that approach would be disapproved and we would be obliged to reverse." . . .

The clear import of this language from *Swann* [*v. Charlotte-Mecklenburg Board of Education,* 402 U.S. 1 (1971)] is that desegregation, in the sense of dismantling a dual school system, does not require any particular racial balance in each "school, grade or classroom." . . .

Here the District Court's approach to what constituted "actual desegregation" raises the fundamental question, not presented in *Swann,* as to the circumstances in which a federal court may order desegregation relief that embraces more than a single school district. The court's analytical starting point was its conclusion that school district lines are no more than arbitrary lines on a map drawn "for political convenience." Boundary lines may be bridged where there has been a constitutional violation calling for interdistrict relief, but the notion that school district lines may be casually ignored or treated as a mere administrative convenience is contrary to the history of public education in our country. No single tradition in public education is more deeply rooted than local control over the operation of schools; local autonomy has long been thought essential both to the maintenance of community concern and support for public schools and to quality of the educational process. . . .

The Michigan educational structure involved in this case, in common with most States, provides for a large measure of local control, and a review of the scope and character of these local powers indicates the extent to which the interdistrict remedy approved by the two courts could disrupt and alter the structure of public education in Michigan. The metropolitan remedy would require, in effect, consolidation of 54 independent school districts historically administered as separate units into a vast new super school district. . . . Entirely apart from the logistical and other serious problems attending large-scale transportation of students, the consolidation would give rise to an array of other problems in financing and operating this new school system. Some of the more obvious questions would be: What would be the status and authority of the present popularly elected school boards? Would the children of Detroit be within the jurisdiction and operating control of a school board elected by the parents and residents of other districts? What board or boards would levy taxes for school operations in these 54 districts constituting the consolidated metropolitan area? What provisions could be made for assuring substantial equality in tax levies among the 54 districts, if this were deemed requisite? What provisions would be made for financing? Would the validity of long-term bonds be jeopardized unless approved by all of the component districts as well as the State? What body would determine that portion of the curricula now left to the discretion of local school boards? Who would establish attendance zones, purchase school equipment, locate and construct new schools, and indeed attend to all the myriad day-to-day decisions that are necessary to school operations affecting potentially more than three-quarters of a million pupils? . . .

It may be suggested that all of these vital operational problems are yet to be resolved by the District Court, and that this is the purpose of the Court of Appeals' proposed remand. But it is obvious from the scope of the interdistrict remedy itself that absent a complete restructuring of the laws of Michigan relating to school districts the District Court will become first, a *de facto* "legislative authority" to resolve these complex questions, and then the "school superintendent" for the entire area. This is a task which few, if any, judges are qualified to perform and one which would deprive the people of control of schools through their elected representatives.

Of course, no state law is above the Constitution. School district lines and the present laws with respect to local control, are not sacrosanct and if they conflict with the Fourteenth Amendment federal courts have a duty to prescribe appropriate remedies. . . . But our prior holdings have been confined to violations and remedies within a single school district. We therefore turn to address, for the first time, the validity of a remedy mandating cross-district or interdistrict consolidation to remedy a condition of segregation found to exist in only one district.

The controlling principle consistently expounded in our holdings is that the scope of the remedy is determined by the nature and extent of the constitutional violation. . . . Before the boundaries of separate and autonomous school districts may be set aside by consolidating the separate units for remedial purposes or by imposing a cross-district remedy, it must be first shown that there has been a constitutional violation within one district that produces a significant segregative effect in another district. Specifically, it must be shown that racially discriminatory acts of the state or local school districts, or of a single school district have been a substantial cause of interdistrict segregation. Thus an interdistrict remedy might be in order where the racially discriminatory acts of one or more school districts caused racial segregation in an adjacent district, or where district lines have been deliberately drawn on the basis of race. In such circumstances an interdistrict remedy would be appropriate to eliminate the interdistrict segregation directly caused by the constitutional violation. Conversely, without an interdistrict violation and interdistrict effect, there is no constitutional wrong calling for an interdistrict remedy.

The record before us, voluminous as it is, contains evidence of *de jure* segregated conditions only in the Detroit schools; indeed, that was the theory on which the litigation was initially based and on which the District Court took evidence. . . . With no showing of significant violation by the 53 outlying school districts and no evidence of any interdistrict violation or effect, the court went beyond the original theory of the case as framed by the pleadings and mandated a metropolitan area remedy. To approve the remedy ordered by the court would impose on the outlying districts, not shown to have committed any constitutional violation, a wholly impermissible remedy based on a standard not hinted at in *Brown I* and *II* or any holding of this Court.

. . . We recognize that the six-volume record presently under consideration contains language and some specific incidental findings thought by the District Court to afford a basis for interdistrict relief. However, these comparatively isolated findings and brief comments concern only one possible interdistrict violation and are found in the context of a proceeding that, as the District Court conceded, included no proof of segregation practiced by any of the 85 suburban school districts surrounding Detroit. . . .

. . . Petitioners have urged that they were denied due process by the manner in which the District Court limited their participation after intervention was allowed, thus precluding adequate opportunity to present evidence that they had committed no acts having a segregative effect in Detroit. In light of our holding that, absent an interdistrict violation, there is no basis for an interdistrict remedy, we need not reach these claims. It is clear, however, that the District Court, with the approval of the Court of Appeals, has provided an interdistrict remedy in the face of a record which shows no constitutional violations that would call for equitable relief except within the city of Detroit. In these circumstances there was no occasion for the parties to address, or for the District Court to consider whether there were racially discriminatory acts for which any of the 53 outlying districts were responsible and which had direct and significant segregative effect on schools of more than one district.

We conclude that the relief ordered by the District Court and affirmed by the Court of Appeals was based upon an erroneous standard and was unsupported by record evidence that acts of the outlying districts effected the discrimination found to exist in the schools of Detroit. Accordingly, the judgment of the Court of Appeals is reversed and the case is remanded for further proceedings consistent with this opinion leading to prompt formulation of a decree directed to eliminating the segregation found to exist in Detroit city schools, a remedy which has been delayed since 1970.

Reversed and remanded.

[The concurring opinion of MR. JUSTICE STEWART is omitted.]

* * *

MR. JUSTICE WHITE, with whom MR. JUSTICE DOUGLAS, MR. JUSTICE BRENNAN, and MR. JUSTICE MARSHALL join, dissenting.

. . . Regretfully, and for several reasons, I can join neither the Court's judgment nor its opinion. The core of my disagreement is that deliberate acts of segregation and their consequences will go unremedied, not because a remedy would be infeasible or unreasonable in terms of the usual criteria governing school desegregation cases, but because an effective remedy would cause what the Court considers to be undue administrative inconvenience to the State. The result is that the State of Michigan, the entity at which the Fourteenth Amendment is directed, has successfully insulated itself from its duty to provide effective desegregation remedies by vesting sufficient power over its public schools in its local school districts. If this is the case in Michigan, it will be the case in most States.

. . . I am surprised that the Court, sitting at this distance from the State of Michigan, claims better insight than the Court of Appeals and the District Court as to whether an interdistrict remedy for equal protection violations practiced by the State of Michigan would involve undue difficulties for the State in the management of its public schools. . . . Obviously, whatever difficulties there might be, they are surmountable; for the Court itself concedes that, had there been sufficient evidence of an interdistrict violation, the District Court could have fashioned a single remedy for the districts implicated rather than a different remedy for each district in which the violation had occurred or had an impact.

I am even more mystified as to how the Court can ignore the legal reality that the constitutional violations, even if occurring locally, were committed by governmental entities for which the State is responsible and that it is the State that must respond to the command of the Fourteenth Amendment. An interdistrict remedy for the infringements that occurred in this case is well within the confines and powers of the State, which is the governmental entity ultimately responsible for desegregating its schools. . . .

. . . Finally, I remain wholly unpersuaded by the Court's assertion that "the remedy is necessarily designed, as all remedies are, to restore the victims of discriminatory conduct to the position they would have occupied in the absence of such conduct." . . . In the first place, under this premise the Court's judgment is itself infirm; for had the Detroit school system not followed an official policy of segregation throughout the 1950's and 1960's, Negroes and whites would have been going to school together. There would have been no, or at least not as many, recognizable Negro schools and no, or at least not as many, white schools, but "just schools," and neither Negroes nor whites would have suffered from the effects of segregated education, with all its shortcomings. Surely the Court's remedy will not restore to the Negro community, stigmatized as it was by the dual school system, what it would have enjoyed over all or most of this period if the remedy is confined to present Detroit; for the maximum remedy available within that area will leave many of the schools almost totally black, and the system itself will be predominantly black and will become increasingly so. Moreover, when a State has engaged in acts of official segregation over a lengthy period of time, as in the case before us, it is unrealistic to suppose that the children who were victims of the State's unconstitutional conduct could now be provided the benefits of which they were wrongfully deprived. Nor can the benefits which accrue to school systems in which schoolchildren have not been officially segregated, and to the communities supporting such school systems, be fully and immediately restored after a substantial period of unlawful segregation. The education of children of different races in a desegregated environment has unhappily been lost, along with the social, economic, and political advantages which accompany a desegregated school system as compared with an unconstitutionally segregated system. It is for these reasons that the Court has consistently followed the course of requiring the effects of past official segregation to be eliminated "root and branch" by imposing, in the present, the duty to provide a remedy which will achieve "the greatest possible degree of actual desegregation, taking into account the practicalities of the situation." It is also for these reasons that once a constitutional violation has been found, the district judge obligated to provide such a remedy "will thus necessarily be concerned with the elimination of one-race schools." These concerns were properly taken into account by the District Judge in this case. Confining the remedy to the boundaries of the Detroit district is quite unrelated either to the goal of achieving maximum desegregation or to those intensely practical considerations, such as the extent and expense of transportation, that have imposed limits on remedies in cases such as this. The Court's remedy, in the end, is essentially arbitrary and will leave serious violations of the Constitution substantially unremedied.

[The dissenting opinion of MR. JUSTICE MARSHALL, with whom MR. JUSTICE BRENNAN and MR. JUSTICE WHITE join, is omitted.]

[The dissenting opinion of MR. JUSTICE DOUGLAS is omitted.]

KEYES V. SCHOOL DISTRICT NO. 1, DENVER, COLORADO
413 U.S. 189 (1973)

Keyes was the first school desegregation case outside the South considered by the Supreme Court. The case involved segregation in the Denver, Colorado, public schools, especially in the Park Hill area in the northeast portion of the city. The parents of Denver school children sought to desegregate the schools in the Park Hill area, and the district court ordered the school board to desegregate. Not satisfied with their success in obtaining relief for Park Hill, the plaintiffs expanded their suit to secure desegregation of the remaining schools of the Denver school district, particularly those in the core city area. The district court denied further relief, finding that deliberate racial segregation of the Park Hill schools did not impose on the school board an affirmative duty to eliminate segregation throughout the entire district. Instead, the court found that the core city schools were inferior to the white schools and ordered the school board to provide substantially equal facilities for those schools. The court of appeals reversed the latter order, however, and accepted the district court's finding that plaintiffs had not proven that the school board had a like policy addressed specifically to the core city schools. *Vote: 7-1.*

* * *

MR. JUSTICE BRENNAN delivered the opinion of the Court.

This school desegregation case concerns the Denver, Colorado, school system. That system has never been operated under a constitutional or statutory provision that mandated or permitted racial segregation in public education. Rather, the gravamen of this action, . . . is that respondent School Board alone, by use of various techniques such as the manipulation of student attendance zones, schoolsite selection and a neighborhood school policy, created or maintained racially or ethnically (or both racially and ethnically) segregated schools throughout the school district, entitling petitioners to a decree directing desegregation of the entire school district.

. . . In our view, the only other question that requires our decision at this time is . . . whether the District Court and the Court of Appeals applied an incorrect legal standard in addressing petitioners' contention that respondent School Board engaged in an unconstitutional policy of deliberate segregation in the core city schools. Our conclusion is that those courts did not apply the correct standard in addressing that contention.

Petitioners apparently conceded for the purposes of this case that in the case of a school system like Denver's, where no statutory dual system has ever existed, plaintiffs must prove not only that segregated schooling exists but also that it was brought about or maintained by intentional state action. Petitioners proved that for almost a decade after 1960 respondent School Board had engaged in an unconstitutional policy of deliberate racial segregation in the Park Hill Schools. Indeed, the District Court found that "[b]etween 1960 and 1969 the Board's policies with respect to these northeast Denver schools show an undeviating purpose to isolate Negro students" in segregated schools "while preserving the Anglo character of [other] schools." . . . This finding did not relate to an insubstantial or trivial fragment of the school system. On the contrary, respondent School Board was found guilty of following a deliberate segregation policy at schools attended, in 1969, by 37.69% of Denver's total Negro school population, including one-fourth of the Negro elementary pupils, over two-thirds of the Negro junior high pupils, and over two-fifths of the Negro high school pupils. In addition, there was uncontroverted evidence that teachers and staff had for years been assigned on the basis of a minority teacher to a minority school system throughout the school. Respondent argues, however, that a finding of state-imposed segregation as to a substantial portion of the school system can be viewed in isolation from the rest of the district, and that even if state-imposed segregation does exist in a substantial part of the Denver school system, it does not follow that the District Court could predicate on that fact a finding that the entire school system is a dual system. We do not agree. We have never suggested that plaintiffs in school desegregation cases must bear the burden of proving the elements of *de jure* segregation as to each and every school or each and every student within the school system. Rather, we have held that where plaintiffs prove that a current condition of segregated schooling exists within a school district where a dual system was compelled or authorized by statute at the time of our decision in *Brown v. Board of Education*, 347 U.S. 483 (1954) (*Brown I*), the State automatically assumes an affirmative duty "to effectuate a transition to a racially nondiscriminatory school system," . . . that is, to eliminate from the public schools within their system "all vestiges of state-imposed segregation." . . .

This is not a case, however, where a statutory dual system has never existed. Nevertheless, where plaintiffs prove that the school authorities have car-

Issue of legal standard

de jure

ried out a systematic program of segregation affecting a substantial portion of the students, schools, teachers, and facilities within the school system, it is only common sense to conclude that there exists a predicate for a finding of the existence of a dual school system. Several considerations support this conclusion. First, it is obvious that a practice of concentrating Negroes in certain schools by structuring attendance zones or designating "feeder" schools on the basis of race has the reciprocal effect of keeping other nearby schools predominantly white. Similarly, the practice of building a school—such as the Barrett Elementary School in this case—to a certain size and in a certain location, "with conscious knowledge that it would be a segregated school," . . . has a substantial reciprocal effect on the racial composition of other nearby schools. So also, the use of mobile classrooms, the drafting of student transfer policies, the transportation of students, and the assignment of faculty and staff, on racially identifiable bases, have the clear effect of earmarking schools according to their racial composition, and this, in turn, together with the elements of student assignment and school construction, may have a profound reciprocal effect on the racial composition of residential neighborhoods within a metropolitan area, thereby causing further racial concentration within the schools. . . .

In short, common sense dictates the conclusion that racially inspired school board actions have an impact beyond the particular schools that are the subjects of those actions. This is not to say, of course, that there can never be a case in which the geographical structure of, or the natural boundaries within, a school district may have the effect of dividing the district into separate, identifiable and unrelated units. Such a determination is essentially a question of fact to be resolved by the trial court in the first instance, but such cases must be rare. In the absence of such a determination, proof of state-imposed segregation in a substantial portion of the district will suffice to support a finding by the trial court of the existence of a dual system. Of course, where that finding is made, as in cases involving statutory dual systems, the school authorities have an affirmative duty "to effectuate a transition to a racially nondiscriminatory school system." . . .

On remand, therefore, the District Court should decide in the first instance whether respondent School Board's deliberate racial segregation policy with respect to the Park Hill schools constitutes the entire Denver school system a dual school system. . . .

. . . On the question of segregative intent, petitioners presented evidence tending to show that the Board, through its actions over a period of years, intentionally created and maintained the segregated character of the core city schools. Respondents countered this evidence by arguing that the segregation in these schools is the result of a racially neutral "neighborhood school policy" and that the acts of which petitioners complain are explicable within the bounds of that policy. Accepting the School Board's explanation, the District Court and the Court of Appeals agreed that a finding of de jure segregation as to the core city schools was not permissible since petitioners had failed to prove "(1) a racially discriminatory purpose and (2) a causal relationship between the acts complained of and the racial imbalance admittedly existing in those schools." . . . This assessment of petitioners' proof was clearly incorrect.

Although petitioners had already proved the existence of intentional school segregation in the Park Hill schools, this crucial finding was totally ignored when attention turned to the core city schools. Plainly, a finding of intentional segregation as to a portion of a school system is not devoid of probative value in assessing the school authorities' intent with respect to other parts of the same school system. On the contrary, where, as here, the case involves one school board; a finding of intentional segregation on its part in one portion of a school system is highly relevant to the issue of the board's intent with respect to other segregated schools in the system. This is merely an application of the well-settled evidentiary principle that "the prior doing of other similar acts, whether clearly a part of a scheme or not, is useful as reducing the possibility that the act in question was done with innocent intent." . . .

Applying these principles in the special context of school desegregation cases, we hold that a finding of intentionally segregative school board actions in a meaningful portion of a school system, as in this case, creates a presumption that other segregated schooling within the system is not adventitious. It establishes, in other words, a prima facie case of unlawful segregative design on the part of school authorities, and shifts to those authorities the burden of proving that other segregated schools within the system are not also the result of intentionally segregative actions. This is true even if it is determined that different areas of the school district should be viewed independently of each other because, even in that situation, there is high probability that where school authorities have effectuated an intentionally segregative policy in a meaningful portion of the school system, similar impermissible considerations have motivated their actions in other areas of the system. We emphasize that the differentiating factor between de jure segregation and so-called de facto segregation to which we referred to in Swann is purpose or intent to segregate. [Swann v. Charlotte-Mecklenburg Board of Education, 402 U.S. 1 (1971)] Where school authorities have been found to have practiced purposeful segregation in part of a school system, they may be expected to oppose system-wide desegregation, as did the respondents in this case, on the ground that their purposefully segregative actions were isolated and individual events, thus leaving plaintiffs with the burden of proving otherwise. But at that point where an intentionally segregative policy is practiced in a meaningful or significant segment of a school system, as in this case, the school authorities cannot be heard to argue that plaintiffs have proved only "isolated and individual" unlawfully segregative actions. In that circumstance, it is both fair and reasonable to require that the school authorities bear the burden of showing that their actions as to other segregated schools within the system were not also motivated by segregative intent.

. . . The respondent School Board invoked at trial its "neighborhood school policy" as explaining racial and ethnic concentrations within the core city schools, arguing that since the core city area population had long been Negro and Hispano, the concentrations were necessarily the result of residential patterns and not of purposefully segregative policies. We have no occasion to consider in this case whether a "neighborhood school policy" of itself will justify racial or ethnic concentrations in the absence of a finding that school authorities have committed acts constituting *de jure* segregation. It is enough that we hold that the mere assertion of such a policy is not dispositive where, as in this case, the school authorities have been found to have practiced *de jure* segregation in a meaningful portion of the school system by techniques that indicate that the "neighborhood school" concept has not been maintained free of manipulation. . .

. . . The judgment of the Court of Appeals is modified to vacate instead of reverse the parts of the Final Decree that concern the core city schools, and the case is remanded to the District Court for further proceedings consistent with this opinion.

It is so ordered.

MR. CHIEF JUSTICE BURGER concurs in the result.

MR. JUSTICE WHITE took no part in the decision of this case.

[The concurring opinion of MR. JUSTICE DOUGLAS is omitted.]

* * *

MR. JUSTICE POWELL concurring in part and dissenting in part.

. . . The situation in Denver is generally comparable to that in other large cities across the country in which there is a substantial minority population and where desegregation has not been ordered by the federal courts. There is segregation in the schools of many of these cities fully as pervasive as that in southern cities prior to the desegregation decrees of the past decade and a half. The focus of the school desegregation problem has now shifted from the South to the country as a whole. Unwilling and footdragging as the process was in most places, substantial progress toward achieving integration has been made in Southern States. No comparable progress has been made in many nonsouthern cities with large minority populations primarily because of the *de facto/de jure* distinction nurtured by the courts and accepted complacently by many of the same voices which denounced the evils of segregated schools in the South. But if our national concern is for those who attend such schools, rather than for perpetuating a legalism rooted in history rather than present reality, we must recognize that the evil of operating separate schools is no less in Denver than in Atlanta.

In my view we should abandon a distinction which long since has outlived its time, and formulate constitutional principles of national rather than merely regional application. When [*Brown I*] was decided, the distinction between *de jure* and *de facto* segregation was consistent with the limited constitutional rationale of that case. The situation confronting the Court, largely confined to the Southern States, was officially imposed racial segregation in the schools extending back for many years and usually embodied in constitutional and statutory provisions.

. . . The Court's decision today, while adhering to the *de jure/de facto* distinction, will require the application of the *Green/Swann* doctrine of "affirmative duty" to the Denver School Board despite the absence of any history of state-mandated school segregation. The only evidence of a constitutional violation was found in various decisions of the School Board. I concur in the Court's position that the public school authorities are the responsible agency of the State, and that if the affirmative-duty doctrine is sound constitutional law for Charlotte, it is equally so for Denver. I would not, however, perpetuate the *de jure/de facto* distinction nor would I leave to petitioners the initial tortuous effort of identifying "segregative acts" and deducing "segregative intent." I would hold, quite simply, that where segregated public schools exist within a school district to a substantial degree, there is a prima facie case that the duly constituted public authorities (I will usually refer to them collectively as the "school board") are sufficiently responsible to warrant imposing upon them a nationally applicable burden to demonstrate they nevertheless are operating a genuinely integrated school system.

The principal reason for abandonment of the *de jure/de facto* distinction is that, in view of the evolution of the holding in *Brown I* into the affirmative-duty doctrine, the distinction no longer can be justified on a principled basis. In decreeing remedial requirements for the Charlotte-Mecklenburg school district, *Swann* dealt with a metropolitan, urbanized area in which the basic causes of segregation were generally similar to those in all sections of the country, and also largely irrelevant to the existence of historic, state-imposed segregation at the time of the *Brown* decision. Further, the extension of the affirmative duty concept to include compulsory student transportation went well beyond the mere remedying of that portion of school segregation for which former state segregation laws were ever responsible. Moreover, as the Court's opinion today abundantly demonstrates, the facts deemed necessary to establish *de jure* discrimination present problems of subjective intent which the courts cannot fairly resolve.

* * *

MR. JUSTICE REHNQUIST dissenting.

. . . It is quite possible, of course, that a school district purporting to adopt racially neutral boundary zones might, with respect to every such zone, invidiously discriminate against minorities, so as to produce substantially the same result as was produced by the statutorily decreed segregation involved in *Brown*. If that were the case, the consequences would necessarily have to be the same as were the consequences in *Brown*. But, in the absence of a statute requiring segregation, there must necessarily be the sort of factual inquiry which was unnecessary in those jurisdictions where racial mixing in the schools was forbidden by law.

Underlying the Court's entire opinion is its apparent thesis that a district judge is at least permitted to find that if a single attendance zone between two individual schools in the large metropolitan district is found by him to have been "gerrymandered," the school district is guilty of operating a "dual" school system, and is apparently a candidate for what is in practice a federal receivership. Not only the language of the Court in the opinion, but its reliance on the case of *Green* . . . indicates that such would be the case. It would therefore presumably be open to the District Court to require, *inter alia,* that pupils be transported great distances throughout the district to and from schools whose attendance zones have not been gerrymandered. Yet, unless the Equal Protection Clause of the Fourteenth Amendment now be held to embody a principle of "taint," found in some primitive legal systems but discarded centuries ago in ours, such a result can only be described as the product of judicial fiat.

. . . The drastic extension of *Brown* which *Green* represented was barely, if at all, explicated in the latter opinion. To require that a genuinely "dual" system be disestablished, in the sense that the assignment of a child to a particular school is not made to depend on his race, is one thing. To require that school boards affirmatively undertake to achieve racial mixing in schools where such mixing is not achieved in sufficient degree by neutrally drawn boundary lines is quite obviously something else.

The Court's own language in *Green* makes it unmistakably clear that this significant extension of *Brown*'s prohibition against discrimination, and the conversion of that prohibition into an affirmative duty to integrate, was made in the context of a school system which had for a number of years rigidly excluded Negroes from attending the same schools as were attended by whites. Whatever may be the soundness of that decision in the context of a genuinely "dual" school system, where segregation of the races had once been mandated by law, I can see no constitutional justification for it in a situation such as that which the record shows to have obtained in Denver.

. . . The Court's opinion totally confuses the concept of a permissible inference in such a situation, of which the District Court indicated it was well aware, with what the Court calls a "presumption," which apparently "shifts . . . the burden of proving" to the defendant school authority. No case from this Court has ever gone further in this area than to suggest that a finding of intent in one factual situation may support a finding of fact in another related factual situation involving the same factor, a principle with which, as indicated above, the District Court was thoroughly familiar.

RUNYON V. McCRARY
427 U.S. 160 (1976)

Raymond and Margaret Gonzales responded to a mailed brochure and a yellow pages advertisement for the Fairfax-Brewster School in May 1969. After visiting the school, they submitted an application for their son Colin to attend the day camp. The school responded with a form letter stating that the school was unable to accommodate Colin's application, and the chairman of the board of the Fairfax-Brewster School explained the reason for Colin's rejection as the school not being integrated. In August 1972, Mrs. McCrary telephoned Bobbe's School in response to an advertisement in the telephone book. When she inquired about nursery school facilities for her son Michael and asked whether the school was integrated, the answer was no. The parents of Michael McCrary and Colin Gonzales filed a class action suit against Russell and Katheryne Runyon, owners of Bobbe's School in

Arlington, Virginia, and the Fairfax-Brewster School, Inc., which had prevented their children from attending school on account of race, in violation of § 1981. Both suits were consolidated for trial. The district court found that the Fairfax-Brewster School and Bobbe's School had denied both children admission on racial grounds, in violation of § 1981. The court of appeals, sitting en banc, affirmed the district court's grant of equitable and compensatory relief but reversed on its award of attorneys' fees. *Vote: 7-2.*

* * *

MR. JUSTICE STEWART delivered the opinion of the Court.

. . . It is now well established that § 1 of the Civil Rights Act of 1866, . . . § 1981, prohibits racial discrimination in the making and enforcement of private contracts. See *Johnson v. Railway Express Agency,* 421 U.S. 454, 459-460 [1975]; *Tillman v. Wheaton-Haven Recreation Assn.,* 410 U.S. 431, 439-440 [1973]. Cf. *Jones v. Alfred H. Mayer Co.,* 392 U.S. 409, 441-443, n. 78 [1968].

In *Jones* the Court held that the portion of § 1 of the Civil Rights Act of 1866 presently codified as . . . 42 U.S.C. § 1982 prohibits private racial discrimination in the sale or rental of real or personal property. . . .

As the Court indicated in *Jones,* . . . that holding necessarily implied that the portion of § 1 of the 1866 Act presently codified as 42 U.S.C. § 1981 likewise reaches purely private acts of racial discrimination. . . . Just as in *Jones* a Negro's § 1 right to purchase property on equal terms with whites was violated when a private person refused to sell the prospective purchaser solely because he was a Negro, so also a Negro's § 1 right to "make and enforce contracts" is violated if a private offeror refuses to extend to a Negro, solely because he is a Negro, the same opportunity to enter into contracts as he extends to white offerees.

. . . It is apparent that the racial exclusion practiced by the Fairfax-Brewster School and Bobbe's Private School amounts to a classic violation of § 1981. The parents of Colin Gonzales and Michael McCrary sought to enter into contractual relationships with Bobbe's School for educational services. Colin Gonzales' parents sought to enter into a similar relationship with the Fairfax-Brewster School. Under those contractual relationships, the schools would have received payments for services rendered, and the prospective students would have received instruction in return for those payments. The educational services of Bobbe's School and the Fairfax-Brewster School were advertised and offered to members of the general public. But neither school offered services on an equal basis to white

and nonwhite students. . . . The Court of Appeals' conclusion that § 1981 was thereby violated follows inexorably from the language of that statute, as constructed in *Jones, Tillman,* and *Johnson.*

The petitioning schools and school association argue principally that § 1981 does not reach private acts of racial discrimination. That view is wholly inconsistent with *Jones'* interpretation of the legislative history of 1 of the Civil Rights Act of 1866, an interpretation that was reaffirmed in *Sullivan v. Little Hunting Park, Inc.,* 396 U.S. 229 [1969], and again in *Tillman.* . . . And this consistent interpretation of the law necessarily requires the conclusion that § 1981, like § 1982, reaches private conduct. . . .

. . . The question remains whether § 1981, as applied, violates constitutionally protected rights of free association and privacy, or a parent's right to direct the education of his children.

. . . In *NAACP v. Alabama,* 357 U.S. 449 [1958], and similar decisions, the Court has recognized a First Amendment right "to engage in association for the advancement of beliefs and ideas." . . . That right is protected because it promotes and may well be essential to the "[e]ffective advocacy of both public and private points of view, particularly controversial ones" that the First Amendment is designed to foster. . . .

From this principle it may be assumed that parents have a First Amendment right to send their children to educational institutions that promote the belief that racial segregation is desirable, and that the children have an equal right to attend such institutions. But it does not follow that the *practice* of excluding racial minorities from such institutions is also protected by the same principle. As the Court stated in *Norwood v. Harrison,* 413 U.S. 455 [1973], "the Constitution . . . places no value on discrimination," . . . and while "[i]nvidious private discrimination may be characterized as a form of exercising freedom of association protected by the First Amendment . . . it has never been accorded affirmative constitutional protections. And even some private discrimination is subject to special remedial legislation in certain circumstances under § 2 of the Thirteenth Amendment; Congress has made such discrimination unlawful in other significant contexts." . . . In any event, as the Court of Appeals noted, "there is no showing that discontinuance of [the] discriminatory admission practices would inhibit in any way the teaching in these schools of any ideas or dogma." . . .

. . . In *Meyer v. Nebraska,* 262 U.S. 390 [1923], the Court held that the liberty protected by the Due Process Clause of the Fourteenth Amendment includes the right "to acquire useful knowledge, to marry, establish a home and bring up children," . . . and, concomitantly, the right to send one's children to a private school that offers specialized training—in that case, instruction in the German language. In

Pierce v. Society of Sisters, 268 U.S. 510 [1925], the Court applied "the doctrine of *Meyer v. Nebraska,*" . . . to hold unconstitutional an Oregon law requiring the parent, guardian, or other person having custody of a child between 8 and 16 years of age to send that child to public school on pain of criminal liability. The Court thought it "entirely plain that the [statute] unreasonably interferes with the liberty of parents and guardians to direct the upbringing and education of children under their control." . . . In *Wisconsin v. Yoder,* 406 U.S. 205 [1972], the Court stressed the limited scope of *Pierce,* pointing out that it lent "no support to the contention that parents may replace state educational requirements with their own idiosyncratic views of what knowledge a child needs to be a productive and happy member of society" but rather "held simply that while a State may posit [educational] standards, it may not pre-empt the educational process by requiring children to attend public schools." . . . And in *Norwood v. Harrison,* . . . the Court once again stressed the "limited scope of *Pierce,*" . . . which simply "affirmed the right of private schools to exist and to operate." . . .

It is clear that the present application of § 1981 infringes no parental right recognized in *Meyer, Pierce, Yoder,* or *Norwood.* No challenge is made to the petitioner schools' right to operate or the right of parents to send their children to a particular private school rather than a public school. Nor do these cases involve a challenge to the subject matter which is taught at any private school. Thus, the Fairfax-Brewster School and Bobbe's School and members of the intervenor association remain presumptively free to inculcate whatever values and standards they deem desirable. *Meyer* and its progeny entitle them to no more.

. . . The Court has held that in some situations the Constitution confers a right of privacy. See *Roe v. Wade,* 410 U.S. 113, 152-153 [1973]; *Eisenstadt v. Baird,* 405 U.S. 438, 453 [1972]; *Stanley v. Georgia,* 394 U.S. 557, 564-565 [1969]; *Griswold v. Connecticut,* 381 U.S. 479, 484-485 [1965]. See also *Loving v. Virginia,* 388 U.S. 1, 12 [1967]; *Skinner v. Oklahoma ex rel. Williamson,* 316 U.S. 535, 541 [1942].

While the application of § 1981 to the conduct at issue here—a private school's adherence to a racially discriminatory admissions policy—does not represent governmental intrusion into the privacy of the home or a similarly intimate setting, it does implicate parental interests. These interests are related to the procreative rights protected in *Roe v. Wade* . . . and *Griswold v. Connecticut.* . . . A person's decision whether to bear a child and a parent's decision concerning the manner in which his child is to be educated may fairly be characterized as exercises of familial rights and responsibilities. But it does not follow that because government is largely or even entirely precluded from regulating the child-bearing decision, it is similarly restricted

by the Constitution from regulating the implementation of parental decisions concerning a child's education.

. . . Section 1981, as applied to the conduct at issue here, constitutes an exercise of federal legislative power under § 2 of the Thirteenth Amendment fully consistent with *Meyer, Pierce,* and the cases that followed in their wake. . . . The prohibition of racial discrimination that interferes with the making and enforcement of contracts for private educational services furthers goals closely analogous to those served by § 1981's elimination of racial discrimination in the making of private employment contracts and, more generally, by § 1982's guarantee that "a dollar in the hands of a Negro will purchase the same thing as a dollar in the hands of a white man." . . .

. . . For the reasons stated in this opinion, the judgment of the Court of Appeals is in all respects affirmed.

It is so ordered.

[The concurring opinions of MR. JUSTICE POWELL and MR. JUSTICE STEVENS are omitted.]

* * *

MR. JUSTICE WHITE, with whom MR. JUSTICE REHNQUIST joins, dissenting.

. . . Section 1981 has been on the books since 1870 and to so hold for the first time would be contrary to the language of the section, to its legislative history, and to the clear dictum of this Court in the *Civil Rights Cases,* 109 U.S. 3, 16-17 (1883), almost contemporaneously with the passage of the statute, that the section reaches only discriminations imposed by state law. The majority's belated discovery of a congressional purpose which escaped this Court only a decade after the statute was passed and which escaped all other federal courts for almost 100 years is singularly unpersuasive. I therefore respectfully dissent.

. . . The right to make contracts, enjoyed by white citizens, was therefore always a right to enter into binding agreements only with willing second parties. Since the statute only gives Negroes the "same rights" to contract as is enjoyed by whites, the language of the statute confers no right on Negroes to enter into a contract with an unwilling person no matter what that person's motivation for refusing to contract. What is conferred by . . . § 1981 is the *right*—which was enjoyed by whites—"to make contracts" with other willing parties and to "enforce" those contracts in court. Section 1981 would thus invalidate any state statute or court-made rule of law which would have the effect of disabling Negroes or any other class of persons from making contracts or enforcing contractual obligations or otherwise giving less weight to their obligations than is given to contractual obligations running to whites. The statute by its terms does not require any private individual or institution to enter into a contract or perform any other act under any circumstances; and it consequently fails to supply a cause of action by respondent students against petitioner schools based on the latter's racially motivated decision not to contract with them.

. . . The majority's holding that . . . § 1981 prohibits all racially motivated contractual decisions—particularly coupled with the Court's decision in *McDonald* [v. *Santa Fe Trail Transportation Co.,* 427 U.S. 273 (1976)] . . . that whites have a cause of action against others including blacks for racially motivated refusals to contract—threatens to embark the Judiciary on a treacherous course. Whether such conduct should be condoned or not, whites and blacks will undoubtedly choose to form a variety of associational relationships pursuant to contracts which exclude members of the other race. Social

clubs, black and white, and associations designed to further the interests of blacks or whites are but two examples. Lawsuits by members of the other race attempting to gain admittance to such an association are not pleasant to contemplate. As the associational or contractual relationships become more private, the pressures to hold § 1981 inapplicable to them will increase. Imaginative judicial construction of the word "contract" is foreseeable; Thirteenth Amendment limitations on Congress' power to ban "badges and incidents of slavery" may be discovered; the doctrine of the right to association may be bent to cover a given situation. In any event, courts will be called upon to balance sensitive policy considerations against each other—considerations which have never been addressed by any Congress—all under the guise of "construing" a statute. This is a task appropriate for the Legislature, not for the Judiciary.

BOB JONES UNIVERSITY
V. UNITED STATES
461 U.S. 574 (1983)

In *Bob Jones University v. United States,* together with *Goldsboro Christian Schools, Inc. v. United States,* the Burger Court was confronted with the question whether the Internal Revenue Service's (IRS) regulations prohibit tax-exempt status to private schools that discriminate on the basis of race. Bob Jones University, a religious and educational institution in Greenville, South Carolina, is not affiliated with any religious denomination but is dedicated to the teaching and propagation of its fundamentalist religious beliefs. The university administration believes that the Bible forbids interracial dating and marriage. To effectuate these views, blacks were completely excluded from the university until 1971. From 1971 to May 1975, it only accepted applications from blacks married within their race. Since May 29, 1975, the university has permitted unmarried blacks to enroll but continues its rule prohibiting interracial dating and marriage. Goldsboro Christian Schools, in Goldsboro, North Carolina, was established to conduct an institution of learning, giving special emphasis to the Christian religion and the ethics revealed in the Holy Scriptures. Since its incorporation in 1963, Goldsboro Christian Schools has maintained a racially discriminatory admissions policy based on its interpretation of the Bible. On occasion, the schools have accepted children from racially mixed marriages in which one of the parents is white. Until 1970 the IRS extended tax-exempt status to Bob Jones University under § 501(c)(3), but it formally notified the university of the change in IRS policy and announced its intention to chal-

lenge the tax-exempt status of private schools practicing racial discrimination in their admission policies after an injunction issued by a district court in *Green v. Kennedy,* 309 F. Supp. 1127 (1970). On January 19, 1976, the IRS officially revoked Bob Jones's tax-exempt status, effective as of December 1, 1970. The university subsequently filed a tax return and paid a total of $21 for one employee for the calendar year of 1975. After the university's request for a refund was denied, it sued in district court. The district court held that the revocation of the university's tax-exempt status exceeded the delegated powers of the IRS and ordered the refund. The court of appeals reversed. Goldsboro Christian Schools never received a determination by the IRS that it was entitled to a tax exemption. An IRS audit for the years 1969-1972 revealed that it was not entitled to a tax exemption and therefore was required to pay $3,459.93 in taxes. The district court rejected Goldsboro's claim to tax-exempt status, and the court of appeals affirmed for the reasons set forth in *Bob Jones University.* The Reagan administration attempted to terminate the IRS policy of denying tax-exempt status to schools that practiced racial discrimination, thus abandoning its support for the position argued in the lower courts. The Supreme Court appointed black attorney William T. Coleman, Jr., as amicus curiae to argue the position of the IRS. *Vote: 8-1.*

* * *

CHIEF JUSTICE BURGER delivered the opinion of the Court.

We granted certiorari to decide whether petitioners, nonprofit schools that prescribe and enforce racially discriminatory admissions standards on the basis of religious doctrine, qualify as tax-exempt organizations under § 501(c)(3) of the Internal Revenue Code of 1954.

. . . In Revenue Ruling 71-447, the IRS formalized the policy, first announced in 1970, that § 170 and § 501(c)(3) embrace the common-law "charity" concept. Under that view, to qualify for a tax exemption pursuant to § 501(c)(3), an institution must show, first, that it falls within one of the eight categories expressly set forth in that section, and second, that its activity is not contrary to settled public policy.

Section 501(c)(3) provides that "[c]orporations . . . organized and operated exclusively for religious, charitable . . . or educational purposes" are entitled to tax exemption. Petitioners argue that the plain language of the statute guarantees them tax-exempt status. They emphasize the absence of any language in the statute expressly requiring all exempt organizations to be "charitable" in the common-law sense, and they contend that the disjunctive "or" separating the categories in § 501(c)(3) precludes such a reading. Instead, they argue that if an institution falls within one or more of the specified categories it is automatically entitled to exemption, without regard to whether it also qualifies as "charitable." The Court of Appeals rejected that contention and concluded that petitioners' interpretation of the statute "tears section 501(c)(3) from its roots." . . .

. . . Section 501(c)(3) therefore must be analyzed and construed within the framework of the Internal Revenue Code and against the background of the congressional purposes. Such an examination reveals unmistakable evidence that, underlying all relevant parts of the Code, is the intent that entitlement to tax exemption depends on meeting certain common-law standards of charity—namely, that an institution seeking tax-exempt status must serve a public purpose and not be contrary to established public policy.

. . . When the Government grants exemptions or allows deductions all taxpayers are affected; the very fact of the exemption or deduction for the donor means that other taxpayers can be said to be indirect and vicarious "donors." Charitable exemptions are justified on the basis that the exempt entity confers a public benefit—a benefit which the society or the community may not itself choose or be able to provide, or which supplements and advances the work of public institutions already supported by tax revenues. History buttresses logic to make clear that, to warrant exemption under § 501(c)(3), an institution must fall within a category specified in that section and must demonstrably serve and be in

harmony with the public interest. The institution's purpose must not be so at odds with the common community conscience as to undermine any public benefit that might otherwise be conferred.

We are bound to approach these questions with full awareness that determinations of public benefit and public policy are sensitive matters with serious implications for the institutions affected; a declaration that a given institution is not "charitable" should be made only where there can be no doubt that the activity involved is contrary to a fundamental public policy. But there can no longer be any doubt that racial discrimination in education violates deeply and widely accepted views of elementary justice. Prior to 1954, public education in many places still was conducted under the pall of *Plessy v. Ferguson,* 163 U.S. 537 (1896); racial segregation in primary and secondary education prevailed in many parts of the country. . . . This Court's decision in *Brown v. Board of Education* [*Brown I*], 347 U.S. 483 (1954), signalled an end to that era. Over the past quarter of a century, every pronouncement of this Court and myriad Acts of Congress and Executive Orders attest a firm national policy to prohibit racial segregation and discrimination in public education.

An unbroken line of cases following *Brown v. Board of Education* establishes beyond doubt this Court's view that racial discrimination in education violates a most fundamental national public policy, as well as rights of individuals.

. . . In *Norwood v. Harrison,* 413 U.S. 455, 468-469 (1973), we dealt with a nonpublic institution:

"[A] private school—even one that discriminates—fulfills an important educational function; *however,* . . . [*that*] *legitimate educational function cannot be isolated from discriminatory practices.* . . . [*D*]*iscriminatory treatment exerts a pervasive influence on the entire educational process.*" (Emphasis added.) . . .

Congress, in Titles IV and VI of the Civil Rights Act of 1964, . . . clearly expressed its agreement that racial discrimination in education violates a fundamental public policy. Other sections of that Act, and numerous enactments since then, testify to the public policy against racial discrimination. . . .

. . . There can thus be no question that the interpretation of § 170 and § 501(c)(3) announced by the IRS in 1970 was correct. That it may be seen as belated does not undermine its soundness. It would be wholly incompatible with the concepts underlying tax exemption to grant the benefit of tax-exempt status to racially discriminatory educational entities, which "exer[t] a pervasive influence on the entire educational process." . . . Whatever may be the rationale for such private schools' policies, and however sincere the rationale may be, racial discrimination in education is contrary to public policy. Racially discriminatory educational institutions cannot be viewed as conferring a public benefit within the "charitable" concept discussed earlier, or within the congressional intent underlying § 170 and § 501(c)(3).

Petitioners contend that, regardless of whether the IRS properly concluded that racially discriminatory private schools violate public policy, only Congress can alter the scope of § 170 and § 501(c)(3). Petitioners accordingly argue that the IRS overstepped its lawful bounds in issuing its 1970 and 1971 rulings.

Yet ever since the inception of the Tax Code, Congress has seen fit to vest in those administering the tax laws very broad authority to interpret those laws. In an area as complex as the tax system, the agency Congress vests with administrative responsibility must be able to exercise its authority to meet changing conditions and new problems. Indeed as early as 1918, Congress expressly authorized the Commissioner "to make all needful rules and regulations for the enforcement" of the tax laws. . . . The same provision, so essential to efficient and fair administration of the tax laws, has appeared in Tax Codes ever since, . . . and this Court has long recognized the primary authority of the IRS and its predecessors in construing the Internal Revenue Code. . . .

Congress, the source of IRS authority, can modify IRS rulings it considers improper; and courts exercise review over IRS actions. In the first instance, however, the responsibility for construing the Code falls to the IRS. Since Congress cannot be expected to anticipate every conceivable problem that can arise or to carry out day-to-day oversight, it relies on the administrators and on the courts to implement the legislative will. Administrators, like judges, are under oath to do so.

In § 170 and § 501(c)(3), Congress has identified categories of traditionally exempt institutions and has specified certain additional requirements for tax exemption. Yet the need for continuing interpretation of those statutes is unavoidable. For more than 60 years, the IRS and its predecessors have constantly been called upon to interpret these and comparable provisions, and in doing so have referred consistently to principles of charitable trust law. . . .

. . . On the record before us, there can be no doubt as to the national policy. In 1970, when the IRS first issued the ruling challenged here, the position of all three branches of the Federal Government was unmistakably clear. The correctness of the Commissioner's conclusion that a racially discriminatory private school "is not 'charitable' within the common law concepts reflected in . . . the Code," . . . is wholly consistent with what Congress, the Executive, and the courts had repeatedly declared before 1970. Indeed, it would be anomalous for the Executive, Legislative, and Judicial Branches to reach conclusions that add up to a firm public policy on

racial discrimination, and at the same time have the IRS blissfully ignore what all three branches of the Federal Government had declared. Clearly an educational institution engaging in practices affirmatively at odds with this declared position of the whole Government cannot be seen as exercising a "beneficial and stabilizing influenc[e] in community life," . . . and is not "charitable," within the meaning of § 170 and § 501(c)(3). We therefore hold that the IRS did not exceed its authority when it announced its interpretation of § 170 and § 501(c)(3) in 1970 and 1971.

The actions of Congress since 1970 leave no doubt that the IRS reached the correct conclusion in exercising its authority. It is, of course, not unknown for independent agencies or the Executive Branch to misconstrue the intent of a statute; Congress can and often does correct such misconceptions, if the courts have not done so. Yet for a dozen years Congress has been made aware—acutely aware—of the IRS rulings of 1970 and 1971. As we noted earlier, few issues have been the subject of more rigorous and widespread debate and discussion in and out of Congress than those related to racial segregation in education. Sincere adherents advocating contrary views have ventilated the subject for well over three decades. Failure of Congress to modify the IRS rulings of 1970 and 1971, of which Congress was, by its own studies and by public discourse, constantly reminded, and Congress' awareness of the denial of tax-exempt status for racially discriminatory schools when enacting other related legislation make out an unusually strong case of legislative acquiescence in and ratification by implication of the 1970 and 1971 rulings.

. . . Nonaction by Congress is not often a useful guide, but the nonaction here is significant. During the past 12 years there have been no fewer than 13 bills introduced to overturn the IRS interpretation of § 501(c)(3). Not one of these bills has emerged from any committee, although Congress has enacted numerous amendments to § 501 during this same period, including an amendment to § 501(c)(3) itself. . . . It is hardly conceivable that Congress—and in this setting, any Member of Congress—was not abundantly aware of what was going on. In view of its prolonged and acute awareness of so important an issue, Congress' failure to act on the bills proposed on this subject provides added support for concluding that Congress acquiesced in the IRS rulings of 1970 and 1971. . . .

. . . Even more significant is the fact that both [House and Senate Committee] Reports focus on this Court's affirmance of *Green v. Connally,* 330 F. Supp. 1150 (1971), as having established that "discrimination on account of race is inconsistent with an *educational institution's* tax-exempt status." . . . These references in congressional Committee Reports on an enactment denying tax exemptions to racially discriminatory private social clubs cannot be read other than as indicating approval of the standards applied to racially discriminatory private schools by the IRS subsequent to 1970, and specifically of Revenue Ruling 71-447.

Petitioners contend that, even if the Commissioner's policy is valid as to nonreligious private schools, that policy cannot constitutionally be applied to schools that engage in racial discrimination on the basis of sincerely held religious beliefs. As to such schools, it is argued that the IRS construction of § 170 and § 501(c)(3) violates their free exercise rights under the Religion Clauses of the First Amendment. This contention presents claims not heretofore considered by this Court in precisely this context.

. . . The governmental interest at stake here is compelling. [T]he Government has a fundamental, overriding interest in eradicating racial discrimination in education—discrimination that prevailed, with official approval, for the first 165 years of this Nation's constitutional history. That governmental interest substantially outweighs whatever burden denial of tax benefits places on petitioners' exercise of their religious beliefs. The interests asserted by petitioners cannot be accommodated with that compelling governmental interest, . . . and no "less restrictive means," . . . are available to achieve the governmental interest.

The remaining issue is whether the IRS properly applied its policy to these petitioners. Petitioner Goldsboro Christian Schools admits that it "maintain[s] racially discriminatory policies," . . . but seeks to justify those policies on grounds we have fully discussed. The IRS properly denied tax-exempt status to Goldsboro Christian Schools.

Petitioner Bob Jones University, however, contends that it is not racially discriminatory. It emphasizes that it now allows all races to enroll, subject only to its restrictions on the conduct of all students, including its prohibitions of association between men and women of different races, and of interracial marriage. Although a ban on interracial marriage or interracial dating applies to all races, decisions of this Court firmly establish that discrimination on the basis of racial affiliation and association is a form of racial discrimination. . . . We therefore find that the IRS properly applied Revenue Ruling 71-447 to Bob Jones University.

The judgments of the Court of Appeals are, accordingly,

Affirmed.

[The opinion of JUSTICE POWELL, concurring in part and concurring in the judgment, is omitted.]

* * *

JUSTICE REHNQUIST dissenting.

The Court points out that there is a strong national policy in this country against racial discrimination. To the extent that the Court states that Congress in furtherance of this policy could deny tax-exempt status to educational institutions that promote racial discrimination, I readily agree. But, unlike the Court, I am convinced that Congress simply has failed to take this action and, as this Court has said over and over again, regardless of our view on the propriety of Congress' failure to legislate we are not constitutionally empowered to act for it.

In approaching this statutory construction question the Court quite adeptly avoids the statute it is construing. This I am sure is no accident, for there is nothing in the language of § 501(c)(3) that supports the result obtained by the Court. . . . With undeniable clarity, Congress has explicitly defined the requirements for § 501(c)(3) status. An entity must be (1) a corporation, or community chest, fund, or foundation, (2) organized for one of the eight enumerated purposes, (3) operated on a nonprofit basis, and (4) free from involvement in lobbing activities and political campaigns. Nowhere is there to be found some additional, undefined public policy requirement.

The Court first seeks refuge from the obvious reading of § 501(c)(3) by turning to § 170 of the Internal Revenue Code, which provides a tax deduction for contributions made to § 501(3)(c) organizations. . . . The Court seizes the words "charitable contribution" and with little discussion concludes that "[o]n its face, therefore, § 170 reveals that Congress' intention was to provide tax benefits to organizations serving charitable purposes," intimating that this implies some unspecified common-law charitable trust requirement. . . .

. . . The Court would have been well advised to look to subsection (c) where, as § 170(a)(1) indicates, Congress has defined a "charitable contribution." . . . Plainly, § 170(c) simply tracks the requirements set forth in § 501(c)(3). Since § 170 is no more than a mirror of § 501(c)(3) and, as the Court points out, § 170 followed § 501(c)(3) by more than two decades, . . . it is at best of little usefulness in finding the meaning of § 501(c)(3).

Making a more fruitful inquiry, the Court next turns to the legislative history of § 501(c)(3) and finds that Congress intended in that statute to offer a tax benefit to organizations that Congress believed were providing a public benefit. I certainly agree. But then the Court leaps to the conclusion that this history is proof Congress intended that an organization seeking § 501(c)(3) status "must fall within a category specified in that section *and must demonstrably serve and be in harmony with the public interest.*" . . . To the contrary, I think that the legislative history of § 501(c)(3) unmistakably makes clear that *Congress has decided* what organizations are serving a public purpose and providing a public benefit within the meaning of § 501(c)(3) and has clearly set forth in § 501(c)(3) the characteristics of such organizations. . . .

. . . But simply because I reject the Court's heavy handed creation of the requirement that an organization seeking § 501(c)(3) status must "serve and be in harmony with the public interest," . . . does not mean that I would deny to the IRS the usual authority to adopt regulations further explaining what Congress meant by the term "education." . . . I have little doubt that neither the "Fagin School for Pickpockets" nor a school training students for guerilla warfare and terrorism in other countries would meet the definitions contained in the regulations.

Prior to 1970, when the charted course was abruptly changed, the IRS had continuously interpreted § 501(c)(3) and its predecessors in accordance with the view I have expressed above. This, of course, is of considerable significance in determining the intended meaning of the statute. . . .

. . . Few cases would call for more caution in finding ratification by acquiescence than the present ones. The new IRS interpretation is not only far less than a long-standing administrative policy, it is at odds with a position maintained by the IRS, and unquestioned by Congress, for several decades prior to 1970. The interpretation is unsupported by the statutory language, it is unsupported by legislative history, the interpretation has led to considerable controversy in and out of Congress, and the interpretation gives to the IRS a broad power which until now Congress had kept for itself. Where in addition to these circumstances Congress has shown time and time again that it is ready to enact positive legislation to change the Tax Code when it desires, this Court has no business finding that Congress has adopted the new IRS position by failing to enact legislation to reverse it.

CITY OF MOBILE V. BOLDEN
446 U.S. 55 (1980)

Since 1911 the city of Mobile, Alabama, had been governed by a city commission consisting of three members elected at-large by the voters of the city. Black citizens brought a class action suit against city officials, alleging that the practice of electing city commissioners at-large unfairly diluted the voting strength of blacks, in violation of § 2 of the Voting Rights Act and the Fourteenth and Fifteenth Amendments. The district court held that the at-large electoral system violated the Fourteenth and Fifteenth Amendments and ordered that the city commission be disestablished and replaced by a mayor-city council form of government with members elected from single-member districts. The court of appeals affirmed the judgment in its entirety. *Vote: 6-3.*

* * *

MR. JUSTICE STEWART announced the judgment of the Court and delivered an opinion in which THE CHIEF JUSTICE [BURGER], MR. JUSTICE POWELL, and MR. JUSTICE REHNQUIST joined.

. . . Although required by general principles of judicial administration to do so, . . . neither the District Court nor the Court of Appeals addressed the complaint's statutory claim—that the Mobile electoral system violates § 2 of the Voting Rights Act of 1965. Even a cursory examination of that claim, however, clearly discloses that it address nothing to the appellee's complaint.

Section 2 of the Voting Rights Act provides:

"No voting qualification or prerequisite to voting, or standard, practice, or procedure shall be imposed or applied by any State or political subdivision to deny or abridge the right of any citizen of the United States to vote on account of race or color."

Assuming, for present purposes, that there exists a private right of action to enforce this statutory provision, it is apparent that the language of § 2 no more than elaborates upon that of the Fifteenth Amendment, and the sparse legislative history of § 2 makes clear that it was intended to have an effect no different from that of the Fifteenth Amendment itself.

. . . The Court's early decisions under the Fifteenth Amendment established that it imposes but one limitation on the powers of the States. It forbids them to discriminate against Negroes in matters having to do with voting. . . . The Amendment's command and effect are wholly negative. "The Fifteenth Amendment does not confer the right of suffrage upon any one," but has "invested the citizens of the United States with a new constitutional right which is within the protecting power of Congress. That right is exemption from discrimination in the exercise of the elective franchise on account of race, color, or previous condition of servitude." . . .

Our decisions, moreover, have made clear that action by a State that is racially neutral on its face violates the Fifteenth Amendment only if motivated by a discriminatory purpose. . . .

. . . In *Gomillion v. Lightfoot,* 364 U.S. 339 [1960], the Court held that allegations of a racially motivated gerrymander of municipal boundaries stated a claim under the Fifteenth Amendment. The constitutional infirmity of the state law in that case, . . . was that in drawing the municipal boundaries the legislature was "solely concerned with segregating white and colored voters by fencing Negro citizens out of town so as to deprive them of their pre-existing municipal vote." . . . The Court made clear that in the absence of such an invidious purpose, a State is constitutionally free to redraw political boundaries in any manner it chooses. . . .

In *Wright v. Rockefeller,* 376 U.S. 52 [1964], the Court upheld by like reasoning a state congressional reapportionment statute against claims that district lines had been racially gerrymandered, because the plaintiffs failed to prove that the legislature "was either motivated by racial considerations or in fact drew the districts on racial lines"; or that the statute "was a product of a state contrivance to segregate on the basis of race or place of origin." . . .

While other of the Court's Fifteenth Amendment decisions have dealt with different issues, none has questioned the necessity of showing purposeful discrimination in order to show a Fifteenth Amendment violation. The cases of *Smith v. Allwright,* 321 U.S. 649 [1944], and *Terry v. Adams,* 345 U.S. 461 [1953], for example, dealt with the question whether a State was so involved with racially discriminatory voting practices as to invoke the Amendment's protection. . . .

. . . The appellees have argued in this Court that *Smith v. Allwright* and *Terry v. Adams* support the conclusion that the at-large system of elections in Mobile is unconstitutional, reasoning that the effect of racially polarized voting in Mobile is the same as that of a racially exclusionary primary. The only characteristic, however, of the exclusionary primaries that offended the Fifteenth Amendment was that Negroes were not permitted to vote in them. . . .

The answer to appellees' argument is that, as the District Court expressly found, their freedom to vote has not been denied or abridged by anyone. The Fifteenth Amendment does not entail the right to have Negro candidates elected, and neither *Smith v. Allwright* nor *Terry v. Adams* contains any implication to the contrary. That Amendment prohibits only purposely discriminatory denial or abridgment by government of the freedom to vote "on account of race, color, or previous condition of servitude." Having found that Negroes in Mobile "register and vote without hindrance," the District Court and Court of Appeals were in error in believing that the appellants invaded the protection of that Amendment in the present case.

The Court of Appeals also agreed with the District Court that Mobile's at-large electoral system violates the Equal Protection Clause of the Fourteenth Amendment. There remains for consideration, therefore, the validity of its judgment on that score.

The claim that at-large electoral schemes unconstitutionally deny to some persons the equal protection of the laws has been advanced in numerous cases before this Court. That contention has been raised most often with regard to multimember constituencies within a state legislative apportionment system. The constitutional objection to multimember districts is not and cannot be that, as such, they depart from apportionment on a population basis in violation of *Reynolds v. Sims,* 377 U.S. 533 [1964], and its progeny. Rather the focus in such cases has been on the lack of representation multimember districts afford various elements of the voting population in a system of representative legislative democracy. . . .

Despite repeated constitutional attacks upon multimember legislative districts, the Court has consistently held that they are not unconstitutional *per se.* . . . We have recognized, however, that such legislative apportionments could violate the Fourteenth Amendment if their purpose were invidiously to minimize or cancel out the voting potential of racial or ethnic minorities. . . . To prove such a purpose it is not enough to show that the group allegedly discriminated against has not elected representatives in proportion to its numbers. . . . A plaintiff must prove that the disputed plan was "conceived or operated as [a] purposeful devic[e] to further racial . . . discrimination." . . .

This burden of proof is simply one aspect of the basic principle that only if there is purposeful discrimination can there be a violation of the Equal Protection Clause of the Fourteenth Amendment. See *Washington v. Davis,* 426 U.S. 229 [1976]; *Arlington Heights v. Metropolitan Housing Dev. Corp.,* 429 U.S. 252 [1977]; *Personnel Administrator of Mass. v. Feeney,* 442 U.S. 256 [1979]. The Court explicitly indicated in *Washington v. Davis* that this principle applies to claims of racial discrimination affecting voting just as it does to other claims of racial discrimination. Indeed, the Court's opinion in that case viewed *Wright v. Rockefeller* . . . as an apt illustration of the principle that an illicit purpose must be proved before a constitutional violation can be found. . . . More recently, in *Arlington Heights* . . . the Court again relied on *Wright v. Rockefeller* to illustrate the principle that "[p]roof of racially discriminatory intent or purpose is required to show a violation of the Equal Protection Clause." . . . Although dicta may be drawn from a few of the Court's earlier opinions suggesting that disproportionate effects alone may establish a claim of unconstitutional racial vote dilution, the fact is that such a view is not supported by any decision of this Court. More importantly, such a view is not consistent with the meaning of the Equal Protection Clause as it has been understood in a variety of other contexts involving alleged racial discrimination. *Washington v. Davis* . . . (employment); *Arlington Heights* . . . (zoning); *Keyes v. School District No. 1, Denver,*

Colo., 413 U.S. 189, 208 (1973) (public schools); *Akins v. Texas,* 325 U.S. 398, 403-404 [1945] (jury selection).

In only one case has the Court sustained a claim that multimember legislative districts unconstitutionally diluted the voting strength of a discrete group. That case was *White v. Regester* [412 U.S. 755 (1973)]. . . .

White v. Regester is thus consistent with "the basic equal protection principle that the invidious quality of a law claimed to be racially discriminatory must ultimately be traced to a racially discriminatory purpose," *Washington v. Davis* . . . The Court stated the constitutional question in *White* to be whether the "multimember districts [were] *being used invidiously* to cancel out or minimize the voting strength of racial groups," . . . strongly indicating that only a purposeful dilution of the plaintiffs' vote would offend the Equal Protection Clause. Moreover, much of the evidence on which the Court relied in that case was relevant only for the reason that "official action will not be held unconstitutional solely because it results in a racially disproportionate impact." . . . But where the character of a law is readily explainable on grounds apart from race, as would nearly always be true where, as here, an entire system of local governance is brought into question, disproportionate impact alone cannot be decisive, and courts must look to other evidence to support a finding of discriminatory purpose. . . .

We may assume, for present purposes, that an at-large election of city officials with all the legislative, executive, and administrative power of the municipal government is constitutionally indistinguishable from the election of a few members of a state legislative body in multimember districts—although this may be a rash assumption. But even making this assumption, it is clear that the evidence in the present case fell far short of showing that the appellants "conceived or operated [a] purposeful devic[e] to further racial . . . discrimination." . . .

The District Court assessed the appellees' claims in light of the standard that had been articulated by the Court of Appeals for the Fifth Circuit in *Zimmer v. McKeithen,* 485 F. 2d 1297 [1973]. That case, coming before *Washington v. Davis,* . . . was quite evidently decided upon the misunderstanding that it is not necessary to show a discriminatory purpose in order to prove a violation of the Equal Protection Clause—that proof of a discriminatory effect is sufficient. . . .

. . . In affirming the District Court, the Court of Appeals acknowledged that the Equal Protection Clause of the Fourteenth Amendment reaches only purposeful discrimination, but held that one way a plaintiff may establish this illicit purpose is by adducing evidence that satisfies the criteria of its decision in *Zimmer v. McKeithen.* . . . Thus, because the appellees had proved an "aggregate" of the *Zimmer* factors, the Court of Appeals concluded that a

discriminatory purpose had been proved. That approach, however, is inconsistent with our decisions in *Washington v. Davis* . . . and *Arlington Heights.* . . . Although the presence of the indicia relied on in *Zimmer* may afford some evidence of a discriminatory purpose, satisfaction of those criteria is not of itself sufficient proof of such a purpose. The so-called *Zimmer* criteria upon which the District Court and the Court of Appeals relied were most assuredly insufficient to prove an unconstitutionally discriminatory purpose in the present case.

. . . We turn finally to the arguments advanced in . . . MR. JUSTICE MARSHALL's dissenting opinion. The theory of this dissenting opinion—a theory much more extreme than that espoused by the District Court or the Court of Appeals—appears to be that every "political group," or at least every such group that is in the minority, has a federal constitutional right to elect candidates in proportion to its numbers. Moreover, a political group's "right" to have its candidates elected is said to be a "fundamental interest," the infringement of which may be established without proof that a State has acted with the purpose of impairing anybody's access to the political process. This dissenting opinion finds the "right" infringed in the present case because no Negro has been elected to the Mobile County Commission.

Whatever appeal the dissenting opinion's view may have as a matter of political theory, it is not the law. The Equal Protection Clause of the Fourteenth Amendment does not require proportional representation as an imperative of political organization. The entitlement that the dissenting opinion assumes to exist simply is not to be found in the Constitution of the United States.

. . . The judgment is reversed, and the case is remanded to the Court of Appeals for further proceedings.

It is so ordered.

[The opinion of MR. JUSTICE BLACKMUN, concurring in the result, is omitted.]

[The opinion of MR. JUSTICE STEVENS, concurring in the judgment, is omitted.]

* * *

MR. JUSTICE WHITE dissenting.

. . . Without questioning the vitality of *White v. Regester* and our other decisions dealing with challenges to multimember districts by racial or ethnic groups, the Court today inexplicably rejects a similar holding based on meticulous factual findings and scrupulous application of the principles of these cases by both the District Court and the Court of Appeals. The Court's decision is flatly inconsistent with *White v. Regester* and it cannot be understood to flow from our recognition in *Washington v. Davis* . . . that the Equal Protection Clause forbids only purposeful discrimination. Both the District Court and the Court of Appeals properly found that an invidious discriminatory purpose could be inferred from the totality of the facts in this case. The Court's cryptic rejection of their conclusions ignores the principles that an invidious discriminatory purpose can be inferred from objective factors of the kind relied on in *White v. Regester* and that the trial courts are in a special position to make such intensely local appraisals.

. . . In conducting "an intensely local appraisal of the design and impact" of the at-large election scheme, . . . the District Court's decision was fully consistent with our recognition in *Washington v. Davis* . . . that "an invidious discriminatory purpose may often be inferred from the totality of the relevant facts, including the fact, if it is true, that the law bears more heavily on one race than another." Although the totality of the facts relied upon by the District Court to support its inference of purposeful discrimination is even more compelling than that present in *White v. Regester*, the plurality today rejects the inference of purposeful discrimination apparently because each of the factors relied upon by the courts below is alone insufficient to support the inference. . . . By viewing each of the factors relied upon below in isolation, and ignoring the fact that racial bloc voting at the polls makes it impossible to elect a black commissioner under the at-large system, the plurality rejects the "totality of the circumstances" approach we endorsed in *White v. Regester*, . . . *Washington v. Davis*, . . . and *Arlington Heights v. Metropolitan Housing Dev. Corp.* . . . and leaves the courts below adrift on uncharted seas with respect to how to proceed on remand.

* * *

MR. JUSTICE MARSHALL dissenting.

. . . The District Court in both of these cases found that the challenged multimember districting schemes unconstitutionally diluted the Negro vote. These factual findings were upheld by the Court of Appeals, and the plurality does not question them. Instead, the plurality concludes that districting schemes do not violate the Equal Protection Clause unless it is proved that they were enacted or maintained for the purpose of minimizing or canceling out the voting potential of a racial minority. The plurality would require plaintiffs in vote-dilution cases to meet the stringent burden of establishing discriminatory intent within the meaning of *Washington v. Davis*, . . . *Arlington Heights v. Metropolitan Housing Dev. Corp.*, . . . and *Personnel Administrator of Mass. v. Feeney*. . . . In my view, our vote-dilution decisions require only a showing of discriminatory impact to justify the invalidation of a multimember districting scheme, and, because

they are premised on the fundamental interest in voting protected by the Fourteenth Amendment, the discriminatory-impact standard adopted by them is unaffected by *Washington v. Davis* . . . and its progeny. Furthermore, an intent requirement is inconsistent with the protection against denial or abridgment of the vote on account of race embodied in the Fifteenth Amendment and in § 2 of the Voting Rights Act of 1965. . . . Even if, however, proof of discriminatory intent were necessary to support a vote-dilution claim, I would impose upon the plaintiffs a standard of proof less rigid than that provided by *Personnel Administrator of Mass. v. Feeney*. . . .

. . . The plurality's response is that my approach amounts to nothing less than a constitutional requirement of proportional representation for groups. . . . That assertion amounts to nothing more than a red herring: I explicitly reject the notion that the Constitution contains any such requirement. . . . The constitutional protection against vote dilution found in our prior cases does not extend to those situations in which a group has merely failed to elect representatives in proportion to its share of the population. To prove unconstitutional vote dilution, the group is also required to carry the far more onerous burden of demonstrating that it has been effectively fenced out of the political process. . . . Typical of the plurality's mischaracterization of my position is its assertion that I would provide protection against vote dilution for "every 'political group,' or at least every such group that is in the minority." . . . The vote-dilution doctrine can logically apply only to groups whose electoral discreteness and insularity allow dominant political factions to ignore them. . . . In short, the distinction between a requirement of proportional representation and the discriminatory-effect test I espouse is by no means a difficult one, and it is hard for me to understand why the plurality insists on ignoring it.

Such judicial deference to official decisionmaking has no place under the Fifteenth Amendment. Section 1 of that Amendment differs from the Fourteenth Amendment's prohibition on racial discrimination in two crucial respects: it explicitly recognizes the right to vote free of hindrances related to race, and it sweeps no further. In my view, these distinctions justify the conclusion that proof of racially discriminatory impact should be sufficient to support a claim under the Fifteenth Amendment. The right to vote is of such fundamental importance in the constitutional scheme that the Fifteenth Amendment's command that it shall not be "abridged" on account of race must be interpreted as providing that the votes of citizens of all races shall be of substantially equal weight. Furthermore, a disproportionate-impact test under the Fifteenth Amendment would not lead to constant judicial intrusion into the process of official decisionmaking.

Rather, the standard would reach only those decisions having a discriminatory effect upon the minority's vote. The Fifteenth Amendment cannot tolerate that kind of decision, even if made in good faith, because the Amendment grants racial minorities the full enjoyment of the right to vote, not simply protection against the unfairness of intentional vote dilution along racial lines.

[The dissenting opinion of MR. JUSTICE BRENNAN is omitted.]

THORNBURG V. GINGLES
478 U.S. 30 (1986)

In 1982 the North Carolina General Assembly enacted a legislative redistricting plan for the state's senate and house of representatives. Ralph Gingles and other black citizens of North Carolina challenged seven districts—one single-member and six multimember districts—alleging that the redistricting scheme impaired black citizens' ability to elect representatives of their choice, in violation of the Fourteenth and Fifteenth Amendments and § 2 of the Voting Rights Act. After the lawsuit was filed but before trial, Congress amended § 2 of the Voting Rights Act, which statutorily overturned *City of Mobile v. Bolden*'s (1980) requirement of showing discriminatory intent in order to establish a violation of either § 2 or the Fifteenth Amendment. The district court applied the totality of the circumstances test of § 2 and, relying on the factors outlined in the Senate Report, held that the redistricting scheme violated § 2 because it diluted black citizens' votes in all seven disputed districts. The court did not reach the constitutional claims raised in the case. Lacy Thornburg, the Attorney General of North Carolina, appealed the case to the Supreme Court with respect to five of the multimember districts— House Districts 21, 23, 36, and 39 and Senate District 22. *Vote: 5-4.*

* * *

JUSTICE BRENNAN announced the judgment of the Court and delivered the opinion of the Court with respect to Parts I, II, III-A, III-B, IV-A, and V; an opinion with respect to Part III-C, in which JUSTICE MARSHALL, JUSTICE BLACKMUN, and JUSTICE STEVENS join; and an opinion with respect to Part IV-B, in which JUSTICE WHITE joins.

This case requires that we construe for the first time § 2 of the Voting Rights Act of 1965, as amended June 29, 1982. . . . The specific question to be decided is whether the three-judge District Court . . . correctly held that the use in a legislative redistricting plan of multimember districts in five North Carolina legislative districts violated § 2 by impairing the opportunity of black voters "to participate in the political process and to elect representatives of their choice." . . .

[Part II-B: Vote Dilution Through the Use of Multimember Districts]

Appellees contend that the legislative decision to employ multimember, rather than single-member, districts in the contested jurisdictions dilutes their votes by submerging them in a white majority, thus impairing their ability to elect representatives of their choice.

The essence of a § 2 claim is that a certain electoral law, practice, or structure interacts with social and historical conditions to cause an inequality in the opportunities enjoyed by black and white voters to elect their preferred representatives. This Court has long recognized that multimember districts and at-large voting schemes may " 'operate to minimize or cancel out the voting strength of racial [minorities in] the voting population.' " . . . The theoretical basis for this type of impairment is that where minority and majority voters consistently prefer different candidates, the majority, by virtue of its numerical superiority, will regularly defeat the choices of the minority voters. . . . Minority voters who contend that the multimember form of districting violates § 2 must prove that the use of a multimember electoral structure operates to minimize or cancel out their ability to elect their preferred candidates. . . .

While many or all of the factors listed in the Senate Report may be relevant to a claim of vote dilution through submergence in multimember districts, unless there is a conjunction of the following circumstances, the use of multimember districts generally will not impede the ability of minority voters to elect representatives of their choice. Stated succinctly, a bloc voting majority must *usually* be able to defeat candidates supported by a politically cohesive, geographically insular minority group. . . . These circumstances are necessary preconditions for multimember districts to operate to impair minority voters' ability to elect representatives of their choice for the following reasons. First, the minority group must be able to demonstrate that it is sufficiently large and geographically compact to constitute a majority in a single-member district. If it is not, as would be the case in a substantially integrated district, the *multimember form* of the district cannot be responsible for minority voters' inability to elect candidates. . . . Second, the minority group must be able to show that it is politically cohesive. If the minority group is not politically cohesive, it cannot be said that the selection of a multimember electoral structure thwarts distinctive minority group interests. . . . Third, the minority must be able to demonstrate that the white majority votes sufficiently as a bloc to enable it—in the absence of special circumstances, such as the minority candidate running unopposed . . .—usually to defeat the minority's preferred candidate. . . . In establishing this last circumstance, the minority group demonstrates that submergence in a white multimember district impedes its ability to elect its chosen representatives.

Finally, we observe that the usual predictability of the majority's success distinguishes structural dilution from the mere loss of an occasional election. . . .

[Part III-A: The District Court's Treatment of Racially Polarized Voting]

The investigation conducted by the District Court into questions of racial bloc voting credited some testimony of lay witnesses, but relied principally on statistical evidence presented by appellees' expert witnesses, in particular that offered by Dr. Bernard Grofman. . . . The court accepted Dr. Grofman's expert opinion that the correlation between race of the voter and the voter's choice of certain candidates was statistically significant. Finally, adopting Dr. Grofman's terminology, . . . the court found that in all but 2 of the 53 elections the degree of racial bloc voting was "so marked as to be substantively significant, in the sense that the results of the individual election would have been different depending upon whether it had been held among only the white voters or only the black voters.". . .

The court also reported its findings . . . that a high percentage of black voters regularly supported black candidates and that most white voters were extremely reluctant to vote for black candidates. The court then considered the relevance to the existence of legally significant white bloc voting of the fact that black candidates have won some elections. It determined that in most instances, special circumstances, such as incumbency and lack of opposition, rather than a diminution in usually severe white bloc voting, accounted for these candidates' success. The court also suggested that black voters' reliance on bullet voting was a significant factor in their successful efforts to elect candidates of their choice. Based on all of the evidence before it, the trial court concluded that each of the districts experienced racially polarized voting "in a persistent and severe degree." . . .

[Part III-B: The Degree of Bloc Voting That Is Legally Significant Under § 2]

[1. Appellants' Arguments.] North Carolina and the United States argue that the test used by the District Court to determine whether voting patterns in the disputed districts are racially polarized to an extent cognizable under § 2 will lead to results that are inconsistent with congressional intent. North Carolina maintains that the court considered legally significant racially polarized voting to occur whenever "less than 50% of the white voters cast a ballot for the black candidate." . . . Appellants also argue that racially polarized voting is legally significant only when it always results in the defeat of black candidates. . . .

The United States, on the other hand, isolates a single line in the court's opinion and identifies it as the court's complete test. According to the United States, the District Court adopted a standard under which legally significant racial bloc voting is deemed to exist whenever " 'the results of the individual election would have been different depending upon whether it had been held among only the white voters or only the black voters in the election.' " . . . We read the District Court opinion differently.

[2. The Standard for Legally Significant Racial Bloc Voting.] The Senate Report states that the "extent to which voting in the elections of the state or political subdivision is racially polarized" . . . is relevant to a vote dilution claim. Further, courts and commentators agree that racial bloc voting is a key element of a vote dilution claim. . . .

The purpose of inquiring into the existence of racially polarized voting is twofold: to ascertain whether minority group members constitute a politically cohesive unit and to determine whether whites vote sufficiently as a bloc usually to defeat the minority's preferred candidates. . . . Thus, the question whether a given district experiences legally significant racially polarized voting requires discrete inquiries into minority and white voting practices. A showing that a significant number of minority group members usually vote for the same candidates is one way of proving the political cohesiveness necessary to a vote dilution claim . . . and, consequently, establishes minority bloc voting within the context of § 2. And, in general, a white bloc vote that normally will defeat the combined strength of minority support plus white "crossover" votes rises to the level of legally significant white bloc voting. . . . The amount of white bloc voting that can generally "minimize or cancel" . . . black voters' ability to elect representatives of their choice, however, will vary from district to district according to a number of factors, including the nature of the allegedly dilutive electoral mechanism; the presence or absence of other potentially dilutive electoral devices, such as majority vote requirements, designated posts, and prohibitions against bullet voting; the percentage of registered voters in the district who are members of the minority group; the size of the district; and, in multimember districts, the number of seats open and the number of candidates in the field. . . .

Because loss of political power through vote dilution is distinct from the mere inability to win a particular election, . . . a pattern of racial bloc voting that extends over a period of time is more probative of a claim that a district experiences legally significant polarization than are the results of a single election. . . . Also for this reason, in a district where elections are shown usually to be polarized, the fact that racially polarized voting is not present in one or a few individual elections does not necessarily negate the conclusion that the district experiences legally significant bloc voting. Furthermore, the success of a minority candidate in a particular election does not necessarily prove that the district did not experience polarized voting in that election; special circumstances, such as the absence of an opponent, incumbency, or the utilization of bullet voting, may explain minority electoral success in a polarized contest.

[*3. Standard Used by the District Court.*] The District Court clearly did not employ the simplistic standard identified by North Carolina—legally significant bloc voting occurs whenever less than 50% of the white voters cast a ballot for the black candidate. . . . And, although the District Court did utilize the measure of "substantive significance" that the United States ascribes to it—" 'the result of the individual election would have been different depending on whether it had been held among only the white voters or only the black voters,' " . . .—the court did not reach its ultimate conclusion that the degree of racial bloc voting present in each district is *legally* significant through mechanical reliance on this standard. While the court did not phrase the standard for legally significant racial bloc voting exactly as we do, a fair reading of the court's opinion reveals that the court's analysis conforms to our view of the proper legal standard.

[Part III-C: Evidence of Racially Polarized Voting]

North Carolina and the United States also contest the evidence upon which the District Court relied in finding that voting patterns in the challenged districts were racially polarized. They argue that the term "racially polarized voting" must, as a matter of law, refer to voting patterns for which the *principal cause* is race. They contend that the District Court utilized a legally incorrect definition of racially polarized voting by relying on bivariate statistical analyses which merely demonstrated a *correlation* between the race of the voter and the level of voter support for certain candidates, but which did not prove that race was the primary determinant of voters' choices. According to appellants and the United States, only multiple regression analysis, which can take into account other variables which might also explain voters' choices, such as

"party affiliation, age, religion, income[,] incumbency, education, campaign expenditures," . . . "media use measured by cost, . . . name, identification, or distance that a candidate lived from a particular precinct," . . . can prove that race was the primary determinant of voter behavior.

Whether appellants and the United States believe that it is the voter's race or the candidate's race that must be the primary determinant of the voter's choice is unclear; indeed, their catalogs of relevant variables suggest both. Age, religion, income, and education seem most relevant to the voter; incumbency, campaign expenditures, name identification, and media use are pertinent to the candidate; and party affiliation could refer both to the voter and the candidate. In either case, we disagree: For purposes of § 2, the legal concept of racially polarized voting incorporates neither causation nor intent. It means simply that the race of the voters correlates with the selection of a certain candidate or candidates; that is, it refers to the situation where different races (or minority language groups) vote in blocs for different candidates. . . .

[*2. Causation Irrelevant to Section 2 Inquiry.*] The first reason we reject appellant's argument that racially polarized voting refers to voting patterns that are in some way *caused by race,* rather than to voting patterns that are merely *correlated with the race of the voter,* is that the reasons black and white voters vote differently have no relevance to the central inquiry of § 2. By contrast, the correlation between race of voter and the selection of certain candidates is crucial to that inquiry.

Both § 2 itself and the Senate Report make clear that the critical question in a § 2 claim is whether the use of a contested electoral practice or structure results in members of a protected group having less opportunity than other members of the electorate to participate in the political process and to elect representatives of their choice. . . . As we explained, . . . multimember districts may impair the ability of blacks to elect representatives of their choice where blacks vote sufficiently as a bloc to be able to elect their preferred candidates in a black majority, single-member district and where a white majority votes sufficiently as a bloc usually to defeat the candidates chosen by blacks. It is the *difference* between the choices made by blacks and whites— not the reasons for that difference—that results in blacks having less opportunity than whites to elect their preferred representatives. Consequently, we conclude that under the "results test" of § 2, only the correlation between race of the voter and selection of certain candidates, not the causes of the correlation, matters.

[*3. Race of the Voter as Primary Determinant of Voter Behavior.*] Appellants and the United States contend that the legal concept of "racially polarized voting" refers not to voting patterns that are merely *correlated with the voter's race,* but to voting patterns that are *determined primarily by the voter's race,* rather than by the voter's other socioeconomic characteristics.

The first problem with this argument is that it ignores the fact that members of geographically insular racial and ethnic groups frequently share socioeconomic characteristics, such as income level, employment status, amount of education, housing and other living conditions, religion, language, and so forth. . . . Where such characteristics are shared, race or ethnic group not only denotes color or place of origin, it also functions as a shorthand notation for common social and economic characteristics. Appellants' definition of racially polarized voting is even more pernicious where shared characteristics are causally related to race or ethnicity. The opportunity to achieve high employment status and income, for example, is often influenced by the presence or absence of racial or ethnic discrimination. A definition of racially polarized voting which holds that black bloc voting does not exist when black voters' choice of certain candidates is most strongly influenced by the fact that the voters have low incomes and menial jobs—when the reason most of those voters have menial jobs and low incomes is attributable to past or present racial discrimination—runs counter to the Senate Report's instruction to conduct a searching and practical evaluation of past and present reality . . . and interferes with the purpose of the Voting Rights Act to eliminate the negative effects of past discrimination on the electoral opportunities of minorities. . . .

Furthermore, under appellants' theory of racially polarized voting, even uncontrovertible evidence that candidates strongly preferred by black voters are *always* defeated by a bloc voting white majority would be dismissed for failure to prove racial polarization whenever the black and white population could be described in terms of other socioeconomic characteristics.

. . . Congress could not have intended that courts employ this definition of racial bloc voting. First, this definition leads to results that are inconsistent with the effects test adopted by Congress when it amended § 2 and with the Senate Report's admonition that courts take a "functional" view of the political process . . . and conduct a searching and practical evaluation of reality. . . . A test for racially polarized voting that denies the fact that race and socioeconomic characteristics are often closely correlated permits neither a practical evaluation of reality nor a functional analysis of vote dilution. . . .

Second, appellants' interpretation of "racially polarized voting" creates an irreconcilable tension between their proposed treatment of socioeconomic characteristics in the bloc voting context and the Senate Report's statement that "the extent to which members of the minority group . . . bear the effects of discrimination in such areas as education, employment and health" may be relevant to a § 2 claim.

. . . We can find no support in either logic or the legislative history for the anomalous conclusion to which appellants' position leads—that Congress intended, on the one hand, that proof that a minority group is predominantly poor, uneducated, and unhealthy should be considered a factor tending to prove a violation; but that Congress intended, on the other hand, that proof that the same socioeconomic characteristics greatly influence black voters' choice of candidates should destroy these voters' ability to establish one of the most important elements of a vote dilution claim.

[*4. Race of Candidate as Primary Determinant of Voter Behavior.*] North Carolina's and the United States' suggestion that racially polarized voting means that voters select or reject candidates *principally* on the basis of the *candidate's race* is also misplaced.

First, both the language of § 2 and a functional understanding of the phenomenon of vote dilution mandate the conclusion that the race of the candidate *per se* is irrelevant to racial bloc voting analysis. Section 2(b) states that a violation is established if it can be shown that members of a protected minority group "have less opportunity than other members of the electorate to . . . electing representatives *of their choice.*" . . . Because both minority and majority voters often select members of their own race as their preferred representatives, it will frequently be the case that a black candidate is the choice of blacks, while a white candidate is the choice of whites. . . . Indeed, the facts of this case illustrate that tendency— blacks preferred black candidates, whites preferred white candidates. . . . Nonetheless, the fact that race of voter and race of candidate is often correlated is not directly pertinent to a § 2 inquiry. Under § 2, it is the *status* of the candidate as the *chosen representative of a particular racial group,* not the race of the candidate, that is important.

. . . Second, appellants' suggestion that racially polarized voting refers to voting patterns where whites vote for white candidates because they prefer members of their own race or are hostile to blacks, as opposed to voting patterns where whites vote for white candidates because the white candidates spent more on their campaigns, utilized more media coverage, and thus enjoyed greater name recognition than the black candidates, fails for another, independent reason. This argument, like the argument that the race of the voter must be the primary determinant of the voter's ballot, is inconsistent with the purposes of § 2 and would render meaningless the Senate Report factor that addresses the impact of low socioeconomic status on a minority group's level of political participation.

[*5. Racial Animosity as Primary Determinant of Voter Behavior.*] Finally, we reject the suggestion that racially polarized voting refers only to white bloc voting which is caused by white voters' *racial hostility* toward black candidates. To accept this theory would frustrate the goals Congress sought to achieve by repudiating the intent test of *Mobile v. Bolden,* 446 U.S. 55 (1980), and would prevent minority voters who have clearly been denied an opportunity to elect representatives of their choice from establishing a critical element of a vote dilution claim.

In amending § 2, Congress rejected the requirement announced by this Court in *Bolden* . . . that § 2 plaintiffs must prove the discriminatory intent of state or local governments in adopting or maintaining the challenged electoral mechanism. Appellants' suggestion that the discriminatory intent of individual white voters must be proved in order to make out a § 2 claim must fail for the very reasons Congress rejected the intent test with respect to governmental bodies. . . .

The Senate Report states that one reason the Senate Committee abandoned the intent test was that "the Committee . . . heard persuasive testimony that the intent test is unnecessarily divisive because it involves charges of racism on the part of individual officials or entire communities." . . .

The grave threat to racial progress and harmony which Congress perceived from requiring proof that racism caused the adoption or maintenance of a challenged electoral mechanism is present to a much greater degree in the proposed requirement that plaintiffs demonstrate that racial animosity determined white voting patterns. Under the old intent test, plaintiffs might succeed by proving only that a limited number of elected officials were racist; under the new intent test plaintiffs would be required to prove that most of the white community is racist in order to obtain judicial relief. It is difficult to imagine a more racially divisive requirement.

A second reason Congress rejected the old intent test was that in most cases it placed an "inordinately difficult burden" on § 2 plaintiffs. . . . The new intent test would be equally, if not more, burdensome. In order to prove that a *specific factor*—racial hostility—*determined* white voters' ballots, it would be necessary to demonstrate that other potentially relevant *causal factors*, such as socioeconomic characteristics and candidate expenditures, do not correlate better than racial animosity with white voting behavior. . . .

The final and most dispositive reason the Senate Report repudiated the old intent test was that it "asks the wrong question." . . . Amended § 2 asks instead "whether minorities have equal access to the process of electing their representatives." . . .

Focusing on the discriminatory intent of the voters, rather than the behavior of the voters, also asks the wrong question. All that matters under § 2 and under a functional theory of vote dilution is voter behavior, not its explanations. Moreover, as we have explained in detail, . . . requiring proof that racial considerations actually *caused* voter behavior will result—contrary to congressional intent—in situations where a black minority that functionally has been totally excluded from the political process will be unable to establish a § 2 violation. . . .

[Part IV-A: The Legal Significance of Some Black Candidates' Success]

North Carolina and the United States maintain that the District Court failed to accord the proper weight to the success of some black candidates in the challenged districts. Black residents of these districts, they point out, achieved improved representation in the 1982 General Assembly election. They also note that blacks in House District 23 have enjoyed proportional representation consistently since 1973 and that blacks in the other districts have occasionally enjoyed nearly proportional representation. This electoral success demonstrates conclusively, appellants and the United States argue, that blacks in those districts do not have "less opportunity than other members of the electorate to participate in the political process and to elect representatives of their choice." . . .

. . . Nothing in the statute or its legislative history prohibited the court from viewing with some caution black candidates' success in the 1982 election, and from deciding on the basis of all the relevant circumstances to accord greater weight to blacks' relative lack of success over the course of several recent elections. Consequently, we hold that the District Court did not err, as a matter of law, in refusing to treat the fact that some black candidates have succeeded as dispositive of appellees' § 2 claim. Where multimember districting generally works to dilute the minority vote, it cannot be defended on the ground that it sporadically and serendipitously benefits minority voters.

The District Court did err, however, in ignoring the significance of the *sustained* success black voters have experienced in House District 23. In that district, the last six elections have resulted in proportional representation for black residents. This persistent proportional representation is inconsistent with appellees' allegation that the ability of black voters in District 23 to elect representatives of their choice is not equal to that enjoyed by the white majority.

[Part V: Ultimate Determination of Vote Dilution]

Finally, appellants and the United States dispute the District Court's ultimate conclusion that the multimember districting scheme at issue in this case deprived black voters of an equal opportunity to participate in the political process and to elect representatives of their choice.

. . . We reaffirm our view that the clearly-erroneous test of Rule 52(a) is the appropriate standard for appellate review of a finding of vote dilution. As both amended § 2 and its legislative history make clear, in evaluating a statutory claim of vote dilution through districting, the trial court is to consider the "totality of the circumstances" and to determine, based "upon a searching practical evaluation of the 'past and present reality,' " . . . whether the political process is equally open to minority voters. "This determination is peculiarly dependent upon the facts of each case" . . . and requires an "intensely local appraisal of the design and impact" of the contested electoral mechanisms. . . . The fact that amended § 2 and its legislative history provide legal standards which a court must apply to the facts in order to determine whether § 2 has been violated does not alter the standard of review. . . . Thus, the application of the clearly-erroneous standard to ultimate findings of vote dilution preserves the benefit of the trial court's particular familiarity with the indigenous political reality without endangering the rule of law.

. . . Excepting House District 23, with respect to which the District Court committed legal error, . . . we affirm the District Court's judgment. We cannot say that the District Court, composed of local judges who are well acquainted with the political realities of the State, clearly erred in concluding that use of a multimember electoral structure has caused black voters in the districts other than House District 23 to have less opportunity than white voters to elect representatives of their choice.

The judgment of the District Court is
Affirmed in part and reversed in part.

[The concurring opinion of JUSTICE WHITE is omitted.]

* * *

JUSTICE O'CONNOR, with whom THE CHIEF JUSTICE, JUSTICE POWELL, and JUSTICE REHNQUIST join, concurring in the judgment.

. . . The Court's definition of the elements of a vote dilution claim is simple and invariable: a court should calculate minority voting strength by assuming that the minority group is concentrated in a single-member district in which it constitutes a voting majority. Where the minority group is not large enough, geographically concentrated enough, or politically cohesive enough for this to be possible, the minority group's claim fails. Where the minority group meets these requirements, the representatives that it could elect in the hypothetical district or districts in which it constitutes a majority will serve as the measure of its undiluted voting strength. Whatever plan the State actually adopts must be assessed in terms of the effect it has on this undiluted voting strength. If this is indeed the single, universal standard for evaluating undiluted minority voting strength for vote dilution purposes, the standard is applicable whether what is challenged is a mul-

timember district or a particular single-member districting scheme.

The Court's statement of the elements of a vote dilution claim also supplies an answer to another question posed above: *how much* of an impairment of undiluted minority voting strength is necessary to prove vote dilution. The Court requires the minority group that satisfies the threshold requirements of size and cohesiveness to prove that it will *usually* be unable to elect as many representatives of its choice under the challenged districting scheme as its undiluted voting strength would permit. This requirement, then, constitutes the true test of vote dilution. Again, no reason appears why this test would not be applicable to a vote dilution claim challenging single-member as well as multimember districts.

This measure of vote dilution, taken in conjunction with the Court's standard for measuring undiluted minority voting strength, creates what amounts to a right to *usual, roughly* proportional representation on the part of sizable, compact, cohesive minority groups. If, under a particular multimember or single-member district plan, qualified minority groups usually cannot elect the representatives they would be likely to elect under the most favorable single-member districting plan, then § 2 is violated. Unless minority success under the challenged electoral system regularly approximates this rough version of proportional representation, that system dilutes minority voting strength and violates § 2.

. . . If a minority group is politically and geographically cohesive and large enough to constitute a voting majority in one or more single-member districts, then unless white voters usually support the minority's preferred candidates in sufficient numbers to enable the minority group to elect as many of those candidates as it could elect in such hypothetical districts, it will routinely follow that a vote dilution claim can be made out, and the multimember district will be invalidated. . . . But the fact remains that electoral success has now emerged, under the Court's standard, as the linchpin of vote dilution claims, and that the elements of a vote dilution claim create an entitlement to roughly proportional representation within the framework of single-member districts.

In my view, the Court's test for measuring minority voting strength and its test for vote dilution, operating in tandem, come closer to an absolute requirement of proportional representation than Congress intended when it codified the results test in § 2. It is not necessary or appropriate to decide in this case whether § 2 requires uniform measure of undiluted minority voting strength in every case, nor have appellants challenged the standard employed by the District Court for assessing undiluted minority voting strength.

UNITED JEWISH ORGANIZATIONS, INC. V. CAREY
430 U.S. 144 (1977)

Kings (Manhattan) and Bronx Counties in New York were subject to §§ 4 and 5 of the Voting Rights Act because they used a literacy test as of November 1, 1968, and thus had to obtain administrative or judicial approval for the 1972 reapportionment plan that concerned these counties. In January 1974, a reapportionment plan was submitted to the attorney general for his review. He also considered submissions from interested parties criticizing or defending the plan. In April the attorney general concluded that the state had not met its burden under § 5 demonstrating that certain districts in Kings County covering the Bedford-Stuyvesant area of Brooklyn had neither the purpose nor effect of abridging the right to vote on account of color. The state responded by submitting a revised plan in May 1974; this plan did not change the number of districts with nonwhite majorities but did change the size of the nonwhite majorities in most of those districts. One of the communities affected by these revisions in the Kings County reapportionment plan was the Williamsburgh area, where about 30,000 Hasidic Jews lived. The 1974 revisions split the Hasidic community between two senate and two assembly districts. State officials thought that Justice Department officials would approve the figure of 65% for the nonwhite population in the assembly district in which the Hasidic community was located. To attain the 65% figure, a portion of the white community, including part of the Hasidic community, was reassigned to an adjoining district. In 1974 the United Jewish Organizations sued Governor Carey on behalf of the Hasidic Jewish community, alleging that the 1974 plan would dilute the value of their vote by halving its effectiveness solely for the purpose of achieving a racial quota and that they were assigned to electoral districts on the basis of race. The district court dismissed the complaint, holding that (a) United Jewish Organizations had no constitutional right in reapportionment to separate community recognition as Hasidic Jews, (b) the redistricting did not disfranchise them, and (c) racial considerations were permissible to correct past discrimination. The court of appeals affirmed. *Vote: 7-1.*

* * *

MR. JUSTICE WHITE announced the judgment of the Court and filed an opinion in which MR. JUSTICE STEVENS joined; Parts I, II, and III of which are joined by MR. JUSTICE BRENNAN and MR. JUSTICE BLACKMUN; and Parts I and IV of which are joined by MR. JUSTICE REHNQUIST.

. . . The question presented is whether . . . the use of racial criteria by the State of New York in its attempt to comply with § 5 of the Voting Rights Act and to secure the approval of the Attorney General violated the Fourteenth Amendment.

. . . Petitioners argue that the New York Legislature, although seeking to comply with the Voting Rights Act as construed by the Attorney General, has violated the Fourteenth and Fifteenth Amendments by deliberately revising its reapportionment plan along racial lines. In rejecting petitioners' claims, we address four propositions: First, that whatever might be true in other contexts, the use of racial criteria in districting and apportionment is never permissible; second, that even if racial considerations may be used to redraw district lines in order to remedy the residual effects of past unconstitutional reapportionments, there are no findings here of prior discriminations that would require or justify as a remedy that white voters be reassigned in order to increase the size of black majorities in certain districts; third, that the use of a "racial quota" in redistricting is never acceptable; and fourth, that even if the foregoing general propositions are infirm, what New York actually did in this case was unconstitutional, particularly its use of a 65% nonwhite racial quota for certain districts. The first three arguments, as we now explain, are foreclosed by our cases construing and sustaining the constitutionality of the Voting Rights Act; the fourth we address in Parts III and IV.

. . . Implicit in [*Beer v. United States,* 425 U.S. 130 (1976)] and [*City of Richmond v. United States,* 422 U.S. 358 (1975)], then, is the proposition that the Constitution does not prevent a State subject to the Voting Rights Act from deliberately creating or preserving black majorities in particular districts in order to ensure that its reapportionment plan complies with § 5. That proposition must be rejected and § 5 held unconstitutional to that extent if we are to accept petitioners' view that racial criteria may never be used in redistricting or that they may be used, if at all, only as a specific remedy for past unconstitutional reapportionments. We are unwilling to overturn our prior cases, however. Section 5 and its authorization for racial redistricting where appropriate to avoid abridging the right to vote on account of race or color are constitutional. Contrary to petitioners' first argument, neither the Fourteenth nor the Fifteenth Amendment mandates any *per se* rule against using racial factors in districting and apportionment. Nor is petitioners' second argument valid. The permissible use of racial criteria is not confined to eliminating the effects of past discriminatory districting or apportionment.

Moreover, in the process of drawing black majority districts in order to comply with § 5, the State must decide how substantial those majorities must be in order to satisfy the Voting Rights Act. The figure used in drawing the *Beer* plan, for example, was 54% of registered voters. At a minimum and by definition, a "black majority district" must be more than 50% black. But whatever the specific percentage, the State will inevitably arrive at it as a necessary means to ensure the opportunity for the election of a black representative and to obtain approval of its reapportionment plan. Unless we adopted an unconstitutional construction of § 5 in *Beer* and *City of Richmond,* a reapportionment cannot violate the Fourteenth or Fifteenth Amendment merely because a State uses specific numerical quotas in establishing a certain number of black majority districts. Our cases under § 5 stand for at least this much.

[*Part III*] Having rejected these three broad objections to the use of racial criteria in redistricting under the Voting Rights Act, we turn to the fourth question, which is whether the racial criteria New York used in this case—the revision of the 1972 plan to create 65% nonwhite majorities in two additional senate and two additional assembly districts—were constitutionally infirm. We hold they are not, on two separate grounds. The first is addressed in this Part III, the second in Part IV.

The first ground is that petitioners have not shown, or offered to prove, that New York did more than the Attorney General was authorized to require it to do under the nonretrogression principle of *Beer,* a principle that . . . this Court has accepted as constitutionally valid. Under *Beer,* the acceptability of New York's 1972 reapportionment for purposes of § 5 depends on the change in nonwhite voting strength in comparison with the previous apportionment, which occurred in 1966. Yet there is no evidence in the record to show whether the 1972 plan increased or decreased the number of senate or assembly districts with substantial nonwhite majorities of 65%. For all that petitioners have alleged or proved, the 1974 revisions may have accomplished nothing more than the restoration of nonwhite voting strength to 1966 levels. To be successful in their constitutional challenge to the racial criteria used in New York's revised plan, petitioners must show at a minimum that minority voting strength was increased under the 1974 plan in comparison with the 1966 apportionment; otherwise the challenge amounts to a constitutional attack on compliance with the statutory rule of nonretrogression.

In the absence of any evidence regarding nonwhite voting strength under the 1966 apportionment, the creation of substantial nonwhite majorities in approximately 30% of the senate and assembly districts in Kings County was reasonably related to the constitutionally valid statutory mandate of maintaining nonwhite voting strength. The percentage of districts with nonwhite majorities was less than the percentage of nonwhites in the county as a whole (35%). The size of the nonwhites in those districts reflected the need to take account of the substantial difference between the nonwhite percentage of the total population in a district and the nonwhite percentage of the voting-age population. Because, as the Court said in *Beer,* the inquiry under § 5 focuses ultimately on "the position of racial minorities with respect to their effective exercise of the electoral franchise," . . . the percentage of eligible voters by district is of great importance to that inquiry. In the redistricting plan approved in *Beer,* for example, only one of the two districts with a black population majority also had a black majority of registered voters. . . . We think it was reasonable for the Attorney General to conclude in this case that a *substantial* nonwhite population majority—in the vicinity of 65%—would be required to achieve a nonwhite majority of eligible voters.

Petitioners have not shown that New York did more than accede to a position taken by the Attorney General that was authorized by our constitutionally permissible construction of § 5. New York adopted the 1974 plan because it sought to comply with the Voting Rights Act. This has been its primary defense of the plan, which was sustained on that basis by the Court of Appeals. Because the Court of Appeals was essentially correct, its judgment may be affirmed without addressing the additional argument by New York and by the United States that, wholly aside from New York's obligation under the Voting Rights Act to preserve minority voting strength in Kings County, the Constitution permits it to draw district lines deliberately in such a way that the percentage of districts with a nonwhite majority roughly approximates the percentage of nonwhites in the county.

[*Part IV*] This additional argument, however, affords a second, and independent, ground for sustaining the particulars of the 1974 plan for Kings County. Whether or not the plan was authorized by or was in compliance with § 5 of the Voting Rights Act, New York was free to do what it did as long as it did not violate the Constitution, particularly the Fourteenth and Fifteenth Amendments; and we are convinced that neither Amendment was infringed.

There is no doubt that in preparing the 1974 legislation, the State deliberately used race in a purposeful manner. But its plan represented no racial slur or stigma with respect to whites or any other race, and we discern no discrimination violative of the Fourteenth Amendment nor any abridgment of the right to vote on account of race within the meaning of the Fifteenth Amendment.

It is true that New York deliberately increased the nonwhite majorities in certain districts in order to enhance the opportunity for election of nonwhite representatives from those districts. Nevertheless, there was no fencing out of the white population from participation in the political processes of the county, and the plan did not minimize or unfairly cancel out white voting strength. . . . Petitioners have not objected to the impact of the 1974 plan on the representation of white voters in the county or in the State as a whole. As the Court of Appeals observed, the plan left white majorities in approximately 70% of the assembly and senate districts in Kings County, which had a countywide population that was 65% white. Thus, even if voting in the county occurred strictly according to race, whites would not be underrepresented relative to their share of the population.

In individual districts where nonwhite majorities were increased to approximately 65%, it became more likely, given racial bloc voting, that black candidates would be elected instead of their white opponents, and it became less likely that white voters would be represented by a member of their own race; but as long as whites in Kings County, as a group, were provided with fair representation, we cannot conclude that there was a cognizable discrimination against whites or an abridgment of their right to vote on the grounds of race. Furthermore, the individual voter in the district with a nonwhite majority has no constitutional complaint merely because his candidate has lost out at the polls and his district is represented by a person for whom he did not vote. Some candidate, along with his supporters, always loses. . . .

Where it occurs, voting for or against a candidate because of his race is an unfortunate practice. But it is not rare; and in any district where it regularly happens, it is unlikely that any candidate will be elected who is a member of the race that is in the minority in that district. However disagreeable this result may be, there is no authority for the proposition that the candidates who are found racially unacceptable by the majority, and the minority voters supporting those candidates, have had their Fourteenth or Fifteenth Amendment rights infringed by this process. Their position is similar to that of the Democratic or Republican minority that is submerged year after year by the adherents to the majority party who tend to vote a straight party line.

. . . In this respect New York's revision of certain district lines is little different in kind from the decision by a State in which a racial minority is unable to elect representatives from multimember districts to change to single-member districting for the purpose of increasing minority representation. This change might substantially increase minority representation at the expense of white voters, who previously elected all of the legislators but who with single-member districts could elect no more than their proportional share. If this intentional reduction of white voting power would be constitutionally permissible, as we think it would be, we think it also permissible for a State, employing sound districting principles such as compactness and population equality, to attempt to prevent racial minorities from being repeatedly outvoted by creating districts that will afford fair representation to the members of those racial groups who are sufficiently numerous and whose residential patterns afford the opportunity of creating districts in which they will be in the majority. . . .

The judgment is

Affirmed.

[The opinion of MR. JUSTICE BRENNAN, concurring in part, is omitted.]

[The opinion of MR. JUSTICE STEWART, with whom MR. JUSTICE POWELL joins, concurring in the judgment, is omitted.]

MR. JUSTICE MARSHALL took no part in the consideration or decision of this case.

* * *

MR. CHIEF JUSTICE BURGER dissenting.

. . . I begin with this Court's holding in *Gomillion v. Lightfoot,* 364 U.S. 339 (1960), the first case to strike down a state attempt at racial gerrymandering. If *Gomillion* teaches anything, I had thought that it was that drawing of political boundary lines with the sole, explicit objective of reaching a predetermined racial result cannot ordinarily be squared with the Constitution. The record before us reveals— and it is not disputed—that this is precisely what took place here. In drawing up the 1974 reapportionment scheme, the New York Legislature did not consider racial composition as merely *one* of several political characteristics; on the contrary, race appears to have been the one and only criterion applied.

. . . The words "racial quota" are emotionally loaded and must be used with caution. Yet this undisputed testimony shows that the 65% figure was viewed by the legislative reapportionment committee as so firm a criterion that even a fractional deviation was deemed impermissible. I cannot see how this can be characterized otherwise than a strict quota approach and I must therefore view today's holding as casting doubt on the clear-cut principles established in *Gomillion.*

My second inquiry is whether the action of the State of New York becomes constitutionally permissible because it was taken to comply with the remedial provisions of the federal Voting Rights Act. . . .

. . . Faced with the straightforward obligation to redistrict so as to avoid "a retrogression in the position of racial minorities with respect to their effective exercise of the electoral franchise," *Beer v. United States* . . . the state legislature mechanically adhered to a plan designed to maintain—without tolerance for even a 1.6% deviation—a "nonwhite" population of 65% within several of the new districts. There is no indication whatever that use of this rigid figure was in any way related—much less necessary—to fulfilling the State's obligation under the Voting Rights Act as defined in *Beer.*

... Although reference to racial composition of a political unit may, under certain circumstances, serve as "a starting point in the process of shaping a remedy," ... rigid adherence to quotas, especially in a case like this, deprives citizens such as petitioners of the opportunity to have the legislature make a determination free from unnecessary bias for or against any racial, ethnic, or religious group. I do not quarrel with the proposition that the New York Legislature may choose to take ethnic or community union into consideration in drawing its district lines. Indeed, petitioners are members of an ethnic community which, without deliberate purpose so far as shown on this record, has long been within a single assembly and senate district. While petitioners certainly have no constitutional right to remain unified within a single political district, they do have, in my view, the constitutional right not to be carved up so as to create a voting bloc composed of some other ethnic or racial group through the kind of racial gerrymandering the Court condemned in *Gomillion v. Lightfoot.*

GRIGGS V. DUKE POWER CO.
401 U.S. 424 (1971)

In 1955 Duke Power Company instituted a policy of requiring a high school education for initial assignment to any department except labor and for transfer from the Coal-Handling Department to any inside department. When in 1965 the company abandoned its policy of restricting blacks to the Labor Department, completion of high school was also made a prerequisite to transfer from labor to any other department. The company added a further requirement for new employees on July 2, 1965, the date on which Title VII became effective. To qualify for placement in any department except labor, an employee had to obtain satisfactory scores on two professionally prepared aptitude tests: the Wonderlic Personnel Test, which purported to measure general intelligence, and the Bennett Mechanical Comprehension Test. The employee also had to have a high school education. Neither test was directed or intended to measure the ability to learn to perform a particular job. Black employees brought a class action suit against Duke Power Company's Dan River Steam Station, a power-generating facility located at Draper, North Carolina, alleging that the company's requirement of a high school diploma or passing of intelligence tests as a condition of employment in or transfer to jobs at the plant was in violation of Title VII of the Civil Rights Act of 1964. The district court found that the company's former policy of racial discrimination had ended and that Title VII, being prospective only, did not reach prior inequities. The court of appeals reversed in part, rejecting the holding that residual discrimination arising from prior employment practices was insulated from remedial action but agreed with the district court that, in the absence of a discriminatory purpose, the use of such requirements was permitted by Title VII. *Vote: 8-0.*

* * *

MR. CHIEF JUSTICE BURGER delivered the opinion of the Court.

We granted the writ in this case to resolve the question of whether an employer is prohibited by the Civil Rights Act of 1964, Title VII, from requiring a high school education or passing of a standardized general intelligence test as a condition of employment in or transfer to jobs when (a) neither standard is shown to be significantly related to successful job performance, (b) both requirements operate to disqualify Negroes at a substantially higher rate than white applicants, and (c) the jobs in question formerly had been filled only by white employees as part of a longstanding practice of giving preference to whites.

... The objective of Congress in the enactment of Title VII is plain from the language of the statute. It was to achieve equality of employment opportunities and remove barriers that have operated in the past to favor an identifiable group of white employees over other employees. Under the Act, practices, procedures, or tests neutral on their face, and even neutral in terms of intent, cannot be maintained if they operate to "freeze" the status quo of prior discriminatory employment practices.

The Court of Appeals' opinion, and the partial dissent, agreed that, on the record in the present case, "whites register far better on the Company's alternative requirements" than Negroes. . . . This consequence would appear to be directly traceable to race. Basic intelligence must have the means of articulation to manifest itself in a testing process. Because they are Negroes, petitioners have long received inferior education in segregated schools and this Court expressly recognized these differences in *Gaston County [North Carolina] v. United States,* 395 U.S. 285 (1969). There, because of the inferior education received by Negroes in North Carolina, this Court barred the institution of a literacy test for voter registration on the ground that the test would abridge the right to vote indirectly on account of race. Congress did not intend by Title VII, however, to guarantee a job to every person regardless of qualifications. In short, the Act does not command that any person be hired because he was formerly the subject of discrimination, or because he is a member of a minority group. Discriminatory preference for any group, minority or majority, is precisely and only what Congress has proscribed. What is required by Congress is the removal of artificial, arbitrary, and unnecessary barriers to employment when the barriers operate invidiously to discriminate on the basis of racial or other impermissible classification.

Congress has now provided that tests or criteria for employment or promotion may not provide equality of opportunity merely in the sense of the fabled offer of milk to the stork and the fox. On the contrary, Congress has now required that the posture and condition of the jobseeker be taken into account. It has—to resort again to the fable—provided that the vessel in which the milk is proffered be one all seekers can use. The Act proscribes not only overt discrimination but also practices that are fair in form, but discriminatory in operation. The touchstone is business necessity. If an employment practice which operates to exclude Negroes cannot be shown to be related to job performance, the practice is prohibited.

On the record before us, neither the high school completion requirement nor the general intelligence test is shown to bear a demonstrable relationship to successful performance of the jobs for which it was used. Both were adopted, as the Court of Appeals noted, without meaningful study of their relationship to job-performance ability. Rather, a vice president of the Company testified, the requirements were instituted on the Company's judgment that they generally would improve the overall quality of the work force.

The evidence, however, shows that employees who have not completed high school or taken the tests have continued to perform satisfactorily and make progress in departments for which the high school and test criteria are now used. The promotion record of present employees who would not be able to meet the new criteria thus suggests the possibility that the requirements may not be needed even for the limited purpose of preserving the avowed policy of advancement within the Company. In the context of this case, it is unnecessary to reach the question whether testing requirements that take into account capability for the next succeeding position or related future promotion might be utilized upon a showing that such long-range requirements fulfill a genuine business need. In the present case the Company has made no such showing.

The Court of Appeals held that the Company had adopted the diploma and test requirements without any "intention to discriminate against Negro employees." . . . We do not suggest that either the District Court or the Court of Appeals erred in examining the employer's intent; but good intent or absence of discriminatory intent does not redeem employment procedures or testing mechanisms that operate as "built-in headwinds" for minority groups and are unrelated to measuring job capability.

The Company's lack of discriminatory intent is suggested by special efforts to help the undereducated employees through Company financing of two-thirds the cost of tuition for high school training. But Congress directed the thrust of the Act to the *consequences* of employment practices, not simply the motivation. More than that, Congress has placed on the employer the burden of showing that any given requirement must have a manifest relationship to the employment in question.

The facts of this case demonstrate the inadequacy of broad and general testing devices as well as the infirmity of using diplomas or degrees as fixed measures of capability. History is filled with examples of men and women who rendered highly effective performance without the conventional badges of accomplishment in terms of certificates, diplomas, or degrees. Diplomas and tests are useful servants, but Congress has mandated the commonsense proposition that they are not to become masters of reality.

The Company contends that its general intelligence tests are specifically permitted by § 703(h) of the Act. That section authorizes the use of any "professionally developed ability test" that is not "designed, intended *or used* to discriminate because of race." . . .

The Equal Employment Opportunity Commission, having enforcement responsibility, has issued guidelines interpreting § 703(h) to permit only the use of job-related tests. The administrative interpretation of the Act by the enforcing agency is entitled to great deference. . . . Since the Act and its legislative history support the Commission's construction, this affords good reason to treat the guidelines as expressing the will of Congress.

. . . Nothing in the Act precludes the use of testing or measuring procedures; obviously they are useful. What Congress has forbidden is giving these devices and mechanisms controlling force unless they are demonstrably a reasonable measure of job performance. Congress has not commanded that the less qualified be preferred over the better qualified simply because of minority origins. Far from disparaging job qualifications as such, Congress has made such qualifications the controlling factor, so that race, religion, nationality, and sex become irrelevant. What Congress has commanded is that any test used must measure the person for the job and not the person in the abstract.

The judgment of the Court of Appeals is, as to that portion of the judgment appealed from, reversed.

* * *

MR. JUSTICE BRENNAN took no part in the consideration or decision of this case.

WASHINGTON V. DAVIS
426 U.S. 229 (1976)

On April 10, 1970, Alfred E. Davis brought a class action suit against District of Columbia officials, including Mayor Washington, alleging that the promotion policies of the police department were racially discriminatory and violated the due process clause of the Fifth Amendment, § 1981, and the D.C. Code § 1-320, and sought a declaratory judgment and an injunction. George Harley and John Sellers were permitted to intervene, asserting that their applications to become officers in the department had been rejected and that the department's recruiting procedures discriminated on the basis of race against black applicants by a series of practices including, but not limited to, a written personnel test, Test 21. Test 21 was administered to determine whether applicants had acquired a particular level of verbal skill. The black respondents contended that the test bore no relationship to job performance and that it excluded a disproportionately high number of black applicants. The district court, noting the absence of any claim of intentional discrimination, found that the black respondents' evidence supporting their motion warranted the conclusions that (a) the number of black police officers was not proportionate to the city's population mix, (b) a higher percentage of blacks failed the test than whites, and (c) the test had not been validated to establish its reliability for measuring subsequent job performance. The court concluded, however, that the test was a useful indicator of training school performance and was not designed to discriminate against blacks. The court of appeals reversed, holding that the lack of discriminatory intent in the enactment and administering of Test 21 was irrelevant; that the critical fact was that four times as many blacks as whites failed the test; and that such disproportionate impact sufficed to establish a constitutional violation absent any proof by petitioners that the test adequately measured job performance. *Vote: 7-2.*

* * *

MR. JUSTICE WHITE delivered the opinion of the Court.

This case involves the validity of a qualifying test administered to applicants for positions as police officers in the District of Columbia Metropolitan Police Department. The test was sustained by the District Court but invalidated by the Court of Appeals. We are in agreement with the District Court and hence reverse the judgment of the Court of Appeals.

. . . Because the Court of Appeals erroneously applied the legal standards applicable to Title VII cases in resolving the constitutional issue before it, we reverse its judgment in respondents' favor. Although the petition for certiorari did not present this ground for reversal, our Rule 40(1)(d)(2) provides that we "may notice a plain error not presented"; and this is an appropriate occasion to invoke the Rule.

As the Court of Appeals understood Title VII, employees or applicants proceeding under it need not concern themselves with the employer's possibly discriminatory purpose but instead may focus solely on the racially differential impact of the challenged hiring or promotion practices. This is not the constitutional rule. We have never held that the constitutional standard for adjudicating claims of invidious racial discrimination is identical to the standards applicable under Title VII, and we decline to do so today.

The central purpose of the Equal Protection Clause of the Fourteenth Amendment is the prevention of official conduct discriminating on the basis of race. It is also true that the Due Process Clause of the Fifth Amendment contains an equal protection component prohibiting the United States from invidiously discriminating between individuals or groups. . . . But our cases have not embraced the proposition that a law or other official act, without regard to whether it reflects a racially discriminatory purpose, is unconstitutional *solely* because it has a racially disproportionate impact.

. . . A statute, otherwise neutral on its face, must not be applied so as invidiously to discriminate on the basis of race. . . . It is also clear from the cases dealing with racial discrimination in the selection of juries that the systematic exclusion of Negroes is itself such an "unequal application of the law . . . as to show intentional discrimination." . . . A prima facie case of discriminatory purpose may be proved as well by the absence of Negroes on a particular jury combined with the failure of the jury commissioners to be informed of eligible Negro jurors in a community . . . or with racially nonneutral selection procedures. . . . With a prima facie case made out, "the burden of proof shifts to the State to rebut the presumption of unconstitutional action by showing that permissible racially neutral selection criteria and procedures have produced the monochromatic result." . . .

Necessarily, an invidious discriminatory purpose may often be inferred from the totality of the relevant facts, including the fact, if it is true, that the law bears more heavily on one race than another. It is also not infrequently true that the discriminatory impact—in the jury cases for example, the total or seriously disproportionate exclusion of Negroes from jury venires—may for all practical purposes demonstrate unconstitutionality because in various circumstances the discrimination is very difficult to explain on nonracial grounds. Nevertheless, we have not held that a law, neutral on its face and serving ends otherwise within the power of government to pursue, is invalid under the Equal Protection Clause simply because it may affect a greater proportion of one race than of another. Disproportionate impact is not irrelevant, but it is not the sole touchstone of an invidious racial discrimination forbidden by the Constitution. Standing alone, it does not trigger the rule, *McLaughlin v. Florida,* 379 U.S. 184 (1964), that racial classifications are to be subjected to the strictest scrutiny and are justifiable only by the weightiest of considerations.

. . . As an initial matter, we have difficulty understanding how a law establishing a racially neutral qualification for employment is nevertheless racially discriminatory and denies "any person . . . equal protection of the laws" simply because a greater proportion of Negroes fail to qualify than members of other racial or ethnic groups. Had respondents, along with all others who had failed Test 21, whether white or black, brought an action claiming that the test denied each of them equal protection of the laws as compared with those who had passed with high enough scores to qualify them as police recruits, it is most unlikely that their challenge would have been sustained. Test 21, which is administered generally to prospective Government employees, concededly seeks to ascertain whether those who take it have acquired a particular level of verbal skill; and it is untenable that the Constitution prevents the Government from seeking modestly to upgrade the communicative abilities of its employees rather than to be satisfied with some lower level of competence, particularly where the job requires special ability to communicate orally and in writing. Respondents, as Negroes, could no more successfully claim that the test denied them equal protection than could white applicants who also failed. The conclusion would not be different in the face of proof that more Negroes than whites had been disqualified by Test 21. That other Negroes also failed to score well would, alone, not demonstrate that respondents individually were being denied equal protection of the laws by the application of an otherwise valid qualifying test being administered to prospective police recruits.

Nor on the facts of the case before us would the disproportionate impact of Test 21 warrant the conclusion that it is a purposeful device to discriminate against Negroes and hence an infringement of the constitutional rights of respondents as well as other black applicants. As we have said, the test is neutral on its face and rationally may be said to serve a purpose the Government is constitutionally empowered to pursue. Even agreeing with the District Court that the differential racial effect of Test 21 called for further inquiry, we think the District Court correctly held that the affirmative efforts of the Metropolitan Police Department to recruit black officers, the changing racial composition of the recruit classes and of the force in general, and the relationship of the test to the training program negated any inference that the Department discriminated on the basis of race or that "a police officer qualifies on the color of his skin rather than ability." . . .

Under Title VII, Congress provided that when hiring and promotion practices disqualifying substantially disproportionate numbers of blacks are challenged, discriminatory purpose need not be proved, and that it is an insufficient response to demonstrate some rational basis for the challenged practices. It is necessary, in addition, that they be "validated" in terms of job performance in any one of several ways, perhaps by ascertaining the minimum skill, ability, or potential necessary for the position at issue and determining whether the qualifying tests are appropriate for the selection of qualified applicants for the job in question. However this process proceeds, it involves a more probing judicial review of, and less deference to, the seemingly reasonable acts of administrators and executives than is appropriate under the Constitution where special racial impact, without discriminatory purpose, is claimed. We are not disposed to adopt this more rigorous standard for the purposes of applying the Fifth and the Fourteenth Amendments in cases such as this.

A rule that a statute designed to serve neutral ends is nevertheless invalid, absent compelling justification, if in practice it benefits or burdens one race more than another would be far reaching and would raise serious questions about, and perhaps invalidate, a whole range of tax, welfare, public service, regulatory, and licensing statutes that may be more burdensome to the poor and to the average black than to the more affluent white.

Given that rule, such consequences would perhaps be likely to follow. However, in our view, extension of the rule beyond those areas where it is already applicable by reason of statute, such as in the field of public employment, should await legislative prescription.

As we have indicated, it was error to direct summary judgment for respondents based on the Fifth Amendment.

We also hold that the Court of Appeals should have affirmed the judgment of the District Court granting the motions for summary judgment filed by petitioners and the federal parties. Respondents were entitled to relief on neither constitutional nor statutory grounds.

The submission of the defendants in the District Court was that Test 21 complied with all applicable statutory as well as constitutional requirements; and they appear not to have disputed that under the statutes and regulations governing their conduct standards similar to those obtaining under Title VII had to be satisfied. The District Court also assumed that Title VII standards were to control the case, identified the determinative issues as whether Test 21 was sufficiently job related and proceeded to uphold use of the test because it was "directly related to a determination of whether the applicant possesses sufficient skills requisite to the demands of the curriculum a recruit must master at the police academy." . . . The Court of Appeals reversed because the relationship between Test 21 and training school success, if demonstrated at all, did not satisfy what it deemed to be the crucial requirement of a direct relationship between performance on Test 21 and performance on the policeman's job.

We agree with petitioners and the federal parties that this was error. The advisability of the police recruit training course informing the recruit about his upcoming job, acquainting him with its demands, and attempting to impart a modicum of required skills seems conceded. It is also apparent to us, as it was to the District Judge, that some minimum verbal and communicative skill would be very useful, if not essential, to satisfactory progress in the training regimen. Based on the evidence before him, the District Judge concluded that Test 21 was directly related to the requirements of the police training program and that a positive relationship between the test and training-course performance was sufficient to validate the former, wholly aside from its possible relationship to actual performance as a police officer. This conclusion of the District Judge that training-program validation may itself be sufficient is supported by regulations of the Civil Service Commission, by the opinion evidence placed before the District Judge, and by the current views of the Civil Service Commissioners who were parties to the case. Nor is the conclusion foreclosed by either *Griggs* [*v. Duke Power Co.*] or *Albemarle Paper Co. v. Moody*, 422 U.S. 405 (1975); and it seems to us the much more sensible construction of the job-relatedness requirement.

The District Court's accompanying conclusion that Test 21 was in fact directly related to the requirements of the police training program was supported by a validation study, as well as by other evidence of record; and we are not convinced that this conclusion was erroneous.

The federal parties, whose views have somewhat changed since the decision of the Court of Appeals and who still insist that training-program validation is sufficient, now urge a remand to the District Court for the purpose of further inquiry into whether the training-program test scores, which were found to correlate with Test 21 scores, are themselves an appropriate measure of the trainee's mastership of the material taught in the course and whether the training program itself is sufficiently related to actual performance of the police officer's task. We think a remand is inappropriate. The District Court's judgment was warranted by the record before it, and we perceive no good reason to reopen it, particularly since we were informed at oral argument that although Test 21 is still being administered, the training program itself has undergone substantial modification in the course of this litigation. If there are now deficiencies in the recruiting practices under prevailing Title VII standards, those deficiencies are to be directly addressed in accordance with appropriate procedures mandated under that Title.

The judgment of the Court of Appeals accordingly is reversed.

So ordered.

MR. JUSTICE STEWART joins Parts I and II of the Court's opinion.

[The concurring opinion of MR. JUSTICE STEVENS is omitted.]

* * *

MR. JUSTICE BRENNAN, with whom MR. JUSTICE MARSHALL joins, dissenting.

. . . Nevertheless, although it appears unnecessary to reach the statutory questions, I will accept the Court's conclusion that respondents were entitled to summary judgment if they were correct in their statutory arguments, and I would affirm the Court of Appeals because petitioners have failed to prove that Test 21 satisfies the applicable statutory standards. All parties' arguments and both lower court decisions were based on Title VII standards. In this context, I think it wrong to focus on § 3304 to the exclusion of the Title VII standards, particularly because the Civil Service Commission views the job-relatedness standards of Title VII and § 3304 as identical. . . .

. . . It is hornbook law that the Court accord deference to the construction of an administrative regulation when that construction is made by the administrative authority responsible for the regulation. . . . It is worthy of note, therefore, that the brief filed by the CSC in this case interprets the instructions in a manner directly contrary to the Court, despite the Court's claim that its result is supported by the Commissioners' "current views."

. . . Today's decision is also at odds with EEOC regulations issued pursuant to explicit authorization in Title VII. . . . Although the dispute in this case is not within the EEOC's jurisdiction, . . . the proper construction of Title VII nevertheless is relevant. Moreover, the 1972 extension of Title VII to public employees gave the same substantive protection to those employees as had previously been accorded in the private sector, . . . and it is therefore improper to maintain different standards in the public and private sectors. . . .

. . . *Albemarle* read *Griggs* to require that a discriminatory test be validated through proof "by professionally acceptable methods" that it is "predictive of or significantly correlated with *important* elements of work behavior *which comprise or are relevant to the job or jobs for which candidates are being evaluated.*" . . . To me, therefore, these cases read Title VII as requiring proof of a significant relationship to job performance to establish the validity of a discriminatory test. . . . Petitioners do not maintain that there is a demonstrated correlation between Test 21 scores and job performance. Moreover, their validity study was unable to discern a significant positive relationship between training averages and job performance. Thus, there is no proof of a correlation—either direct or indirect—between Test 21 and performance of the job of being a police officer.

. . . Today's reduced emphasis on a relationship to job performance is also inconsistent with clearly expressed congressional intent. . . . The pre-1972 judicial decisions dealing with standardized tests used as job qualification requirements uniformly

follow the EEOC regulations discussed above and insist upon proof of a relationship to job performance to prove that a test is job related. Furthermore, the Court ignores Congress' explicit hostility toward the use of written tests as job-qualification requirements; Congress disapproved the CSC's "use of general ability tests which are not aimed at any direct relationship to specific jobs." . . . Petitioners concede that Test 21 was devised by the CSC for general use and was not designed to be used by police departments.

Finally, it should be observed that every federal court, except the District Court in this case, presented with proof identical to that offered to validate Test 21 has reached a conclusion directly opposite to that of the Court today. Sound policy considerations support the view that, at a minimum, petitioners should have been required to prove that the police training examinations either measure job-related skills or predict job performance. Where employers try to validate written qualification tests by proving a correlation with written examinations in a training course, there is a substantial danger that people who have good verbal skills will achieve high scores on both tests due to verbal activity, rather than "job-specific ability." As a result, employers could validate any entrance examination that measures only verbal ability by giving another written test that measures verbal ability at the end of a training course. Any contention that the resulting correlation between examination scores would be evidence that the initial test is "job-related" is plainly erroneous. It seems to me, however, that the Court's holding in this case can be read as endorsing this dubious proposition. Today's result will prove particularly unfortunate if it is extended to govern Title VII cases.

REGENTS OF THE UNIVERSITY
OF CALIFORNIA V. BAKKE
438 U.S. 265 (1978)

The medical school at the University of California at Davis opened in 1968 with an entering class of 50 students. In 1971 the size was increased to 100 students. The faculty devised a special admissions program to increase the representation of disadvantaged students in each medical school class; it consisted of a separate admission system operating in coordination with the regular admission process. Under the regular admissions procedure, candidates whose overall undergraduate grade point averages fell below 2.5 on a scale of 4.0 were summarily rejected. After personal interviews, candidates were rated on a scale of 1 to 100 by their interviewers and four other members of the admissions committee.

The ratings consisted of the interviewers' summaries, the candidates' overall grade point averages, grade point average in science courses, scores on the Medical College Admissions Test (MCAT), letters of recommendation, extracurricular activities, and other biographical data. The ratings were added together to arrive at each candidate's benchmark score. Depending on the numerical composition of the committee (e.g., five), a perfect score in 1973 was 500.

The special admissions committee operated with a separate committee, a majority of whom were members of minority groups. Sixteen of the 100 seats were set aside for minority group members. On the 1973 application form, candidates were asked to indicate whether they wished to be considered as economically disadvantaged and/or disadvantaged members of a minority group, which the medical school viewed as blacks, Chicanos, Asians, and American Indians. If an applicant was found to be disadvantaged, he or she would then be rated by the special committee in a fashion similar to that used by the general admissions committee, except these candidates did not have to meet the 2.5 grade point average cutoff. After personal interviews, the special committee assigned each special applicant a benchmark score, after which the committee presented its top choices to the general admissions committee. The special committee did not compare the candidates against the general applicants, but it could reject recommended special candidates for failure to meet course requirements or other specific deficiencies.

At the age of 32, Allan Bakke, a white male of Norwegian ancestry, decided that he wanted to change careers from engineering to medicine and applied for admission to medical schools, including the Davis Medical School. Bakke applied to two medical schools in 1972 and 11 more in 1973; all 13 turned him down, including his alma mater, the University of Minnesota. Bakke applied late to the Davis Medical School in 1973, and despite a favorable interview, a 3.46 grade point average, an 89th percentile MCAT score, and a strong benchmark score of 468 out of 500, he was rejected (no applicant with a score of 470 was accepted after Bakke's application). Fifteen students with a benchmark score one point higher than Bakke's were not selected for admission to the medical school at Davis in 1973. An additional 20 with a score identical to that of Bakke were placed on the alternative list. A total of 35 students would therefore have been considered ahead of Bakke in the absence of 16 slots that had been set aside for minority students. In 1973 eight whites who were admitted to the medical school at Davis and had lower benchmark scores than Bakke, and 36 applicants with lower undergraduate grades than Bakke, were admitted.

In his lawsuit, Bakke only objected to the minority students who were admitted with lower ratings. After the 1973 rejection, he wrote to the medical school, protesting that the special admissions program operated as a racial and ethnic quota. He applied early in 1974 but received a total benchmark score of 549 out of 600 and was again rejected. In neither year was Bakke placed on a waiting list, and applicants admitted under the special program had grade point averages, MCAT scores, and benchmark scores lower than Bakke's for both years. After the second rejection, Bakke filed suit in the superior (trial) court of California, alleging that the special admissions program at the medical school excluded him on the basis of race, in violation of the equal protection clause of the Fourteenth Amendment, § 601 of Title VI of the Civil Rights Act of 1964,

and the state Constitution. He sought a mandatory injunction and declaratory relief compelling his admission to medical school. The trial court found that the special admissions program was unconstitutional, but it refused to order his admission on the ground that Bakke had not proven that he would have been admitted but for the existence of the special program. The California Supreme Court held that (a) the special program was unconstitutional under strict scrutiny analysis, (b) the medical school could not take race into account in the admissions process, and (3) Bakke was entitled to admission to the medical school. *Vote: 5-4.*

* * *

MR. JUSTICE POWELL announced the judgment of the Court.

. . . For the reasons stated in the following opinion, I believe that so much of the judgment of the California court as holds petitioner's special admissions program unlawful and directs that respondent to be admitted to the Medical School must be affirmed. For the reasons expressed in a separate opinion, my Brothers THE CHIEF JUSTICE, MR. JUSTICE STEWART, MR. JUSTICE REHNQUIST, and MR. JUSTICE STEVENS concur in this judgment.

I also conclude for the reasons stated in the following opinion that the portion of the court's judgment enjoining petitioner from according any consideration to race in its admission process must be reversed. For reasons expressed in separate opinions, my Brothers MR. JUSTICE BRENNAN, MR. JUSTICE WHITE, MR. JUSTICE MARSHALL, and MR. JUSTICE BLACKMUN concur in this judgment.

Affirmed in part and reversed in part.

[*Part II-B*] The language of § 601 [of Title VI], like that of the Equal Protection Clause, is majestic in its sweep:

"No person in the United States shall, on the ground of race, color, or national origin, be excluded from participation in, be denied the benefits of, or be subjected to discrimination under any program or activity receiving Federal financial assistance."

. . . Examination of the voluminous legislative history of Title VI reveals a congressional intent to halt federal funding of entities that violate a prohibition of racial discrimination similar to that of the Constitution. Although isolated statements of various legislators, taken out of context, can be marshaled in support of the proposition that § 601 enacted a purely colorblind scheme, without regard to the reach of the Equal Protection Clause, these comments must be read against the background of both the problem that Congress was addressing and the broader view of the statute that emerges from a full examination of the legislative debates.

. . . In view of the clear legislative intent, Title VI must be held to proscribe only those racial classifications that would violate the Equal Protection Clause or the Fifth Amendment.

[*Part III-A*] Petitioner does not deny that decisions based on race or ethnic origin by faculties and administrations of state universities are reviewable under the Fourteenth Amendment. . . . For his part, respondent does not argue that all racial or ethnic classifications are *per se* invalid. . . . The parties do disagree as to the level of judicial scrutiny to be applied to the special admissions program. Petitioner argues that the court below erred in applying strict scrutiny, as this inexact term has been applied in our cases. That level of review, petitioner asserts, should be reserved for classifications that disadvantage "discrete and insular minorities." See *United States v. Carolene Products Co.,* 304 U.S. 144, 152 n. 4 (1938). Respondent, on the other hand, contends that the California court correctly rejected the notion that the degree of judicial scrutiny accorded a particular racial or ethnic classification hinges upon membership in a discrete and insular minority and duly recognized that the "rights established [by the Fourteenth Amendment] are personal rights." *Shelley v. Kraemer,* 334 U.S. 1, 22 (1948).

En route to this crucial battle over the scope of judicial review, the parties fight a sharp preliminary action over the proper characterization of the special admissions program. Petitioner prefers to view it as establishing a "goal" of minority representation in the Medical School. Respondent, echoing the courts below, labels it a racial quota.

This semantic distinction is beside the point: The special admissions program is undeniably a classification based on race and ethnic background. To the extent that there existed a pool of at least minimally qualified minority applicants to fill the 16 special admissions seats, white applicants could compete only for 84 seats in the entering class, rather than the 100 open to minority applicants. Whether this limitation is described as a quota or goal, it is a line drawn on the basis of race and ethnic status.

The guarantees of the Fourteenth Amendment extend to all persons. Its language is explicit: "No State shall . . . deny to any person within its jurisdiction the equal protection of the laws." It is settled beyond question that the "rights created by the first section of the Fourteenth Amendment are, by its terms, guaranteed to the individual. The rights established are personal rights." . . . The guarantee of equal protection cannot mean one thing when applied to one individual and something else when applied to a person of another color. If both are not accorded the same protection, then it is not equal.

Nevertheless, petitioner argues that the court below erred in applying strict scrutiny to the special admissions program because white males, such as respondent, are not a "discrete and insular minority" requiring extraordinary protection from the majoritarian political process. . . . This rationale, however, has never been invoked in our decisions as a prerequisite to subjecting racial or ethnic distinctions to strict scrutiny. Nor has this Court held that discreteness and insularity constitute necessary preconditions to a holding that a particular classification is invidious. . . . These characteristics may be relevant in deciding whether or not to add new types of classifications to the list of "suspect" categories or whether a particular classification survives close examination. . . . Racial and ethnic classifications, however, are subject to stringent examination without regard to these additional characteristics. We declared as much in the first cases explicitly to recognize racial distinctions as suspect [*Hirabayashi v. United States,* 320 U.S. 81 (1943); *Korematsu v. United States,* 323 U.S. 214 (1944)]. The Court has never questioned the validity of those pronouncements. Racial and ethnic distinctions of any sort are inherently suspect and thus call for the most exacting judicial examination.

[*Part III-B*] . . . Petitioner urges us to adopt for the first time a more restrictive view of the Equal Protection Clause and hold that discrimination against members of the white "majority" cannot be suspect if its purpose can be characterized as "benign." The clock of our liberties, however, cannot be turned back to 1868. . . . It is far too late to argue that the guarantee of equal protection to *all* persons permits the recognition of special wards entitled to a degree of protection greater than that accorded others. "The Fourteenth Amendment is not directed solely against discrimination due to a 'two-class theory'—that is, based upon differences between 'white' and Negro."

Once the artificial line of a "two-class theory" of the Fourteenth Amendment is put aside, the difficulties entailed in varying the level of judicial review according to a perceived "preferred" status of a particular racial or ethnic minority are intractable. The concepts of "majority" and "minority" necessarily reflect temporary arrangements and political judgments. As observed above, the white "majority" itself is composed of various minority groups, most of which can lay claim to a history of prior discrimination at the hands of the State and private individuals. Not all of these groups can receive preferential treatment and corresponding judicial tolerance of distinctions drawn in terms of race and nationality, for then the only "majority" left would be a new minority of white Anglo-Saxon Protestants. There is no principled basis for deciding which groups would merit "heightened judicial solicitude" and which would not. Courts would be asked to evaluate the extent of the prejudice and consequent harm suffered by various minority groups. Those whose societal injury is thought to exceed some arbitrary level of tolerability then would be entitled to preferential classifications at the expense of individuals belonging to other groups. Those classifications would be free from exacting judicial scrutiny. As these preferences began to have their desired effect, and the consequences of past discrimination were undone, new judicial rankings would be necessary. The kind of variable sociological and political analysis necessary to produce such rankings simply does not lie within the judicial competence—even if they otherwise were politically feasible and socially desirable.

Moreover, there are serious problems of injustice connected with the idea of preference itself. First, it may not always be clear that a so-called preference is in fact benign. Courts may be asked to validate burdens imposed upon individual members of a particular group in order to advance the group's general interest. See *United Jewish Organizations v. Carey,* [430 U.S. 144 (1977)] Nothing in the Constitution supports the notion that individuals may be asked to suffer otherwise impermissible burdens in order to enhance the societal standing of their ethnic groups. Second, preferential programs may only reinforce common stereotypes holding that certain groups are unable to achieve success without special protection based on a factor having no relationship to individual worth. . . . Third, there is a measure of inequity in forcing innocent persons in respondent's position to bear the burdens of redressing grievances not of their making.

By hitching the meaning of the Equal Protection Clause to these transitory considerations, we would be holding, as a constitutional principle, that judicial scrutiny of classifications touching on racial and ethnic background may vary with the ebb and flow of political forces. Disparate constitutional tolerance of such classifications well may serve to exacerbate racial and ethnic antagonisms rather than alleviate them. . . . Also, the mutability of a constitutional principle, based upon shifting political and social judgments, undermines the chances for consistent application of the Constitution from one generation to the next, a critical feature of its coherent interpretation. . . .

[*Part IV*] We have held that in "order to justify the use of a suspect classification, a State must show that its purpose or interest is both constitutionally permissible and substantial, and that its use of the classification is 'necessary . . . to the accomplishment' of its purpose or the safeguarding of its interest." . . . The special admissions program purports to serve the purposes of: (i) "reducing the historic deficit of traditionally disfavored minorities in medical schools and in the medical profession" . . .; (ii) countering the effects of societal discrimination; (iii) increasing the number of physicians who will practice in communities currently underserved; and (iv) obtaining the educational benefits that flow from an ethnically diverse student body. It is necessary to decide which, if any, of these purposes is substantial enough to support the use of a suspect classification.

If petitioner's purpose is to assure within its student body some specified percentage of a particular group merely because of its race or ethnic origin, such a preferential purpose must be rejected not as insubstantial but as facially invalid. Preferring members of any one group for no reason other than race or ethnic origin is discrimination for its own sake. This the Constitution forbids. . . .

The State certainly has a legitimate and substantial interest in ameliorating, or eliminating where feasible, the disabling effects of identified discrimination. The line of school desegregation cases, commencing with *Brown,* attests to the importance of this state goal and the commitment of the judiciary to affirm all lawful means toward its attainment. In the school cases, the States were required by court order to redress the wrongs worked by specific instances of racial discrimination. That goal was far more focused than the remedying of the effects of "societal discrimination," an amorphous concept of injury that may be ageless in its reach into the past.

We have never approved a classification that aids persons perceived as members of relatively victimized groups at the expense of other innocent individuals in the absence of judicial, legislative, or administrative findings of constitutional or statutory violations. . . .

. . . Hence, the purpose of helping certain groups whom the faculty of the Davis Medical School perceived as victims of "societal discrimination" does not justify a classification that imposes disadvantages upon persons like respondent, who bear no responsibility for whatever harm the beneficiaries of the special admissions program are thought to have suffered. To hold otherwise would be to convert a remedy heretofore reserved for violations of legal rights into a privilege that all institutions throughout the Nation could grant at their pleasure to whatever groups are perceived as victims of societal discrimination. That is a step we have never approved. . . .

Petitioner identifies, as another purpose of its program, improving the delivery of health-care services to communities currently underserved. It may be assumed that in some situations a State's interest in facilitating the health care of its citizens is sufficiently compelling to support the use of a suspect classification. But there is virtually no evidence in the record indicating that petitioner's special admissions program is either needed or geared to promote that goal. . . .

. . . The fourth goal asserted by petitioner is the attainment of a diverse student body. This clearly is a constitutionally permissible goal for an institution of higher education. Academic freedom, though not a specifically enumerated constitutional right, long has been viewed as a special concern of the First Amendment. The freedom of a university to make its own judgments as to education includes the selection of its student body. . . .

. . . The atmosphere of "speculation, experiment and creation"—so essential to the quality of higher education—is widely believed to be promoted by a diverse student body. . . .

Thus, in arguing that its universities must be accorded the right to select those students who will contribute the most to the "robust exchange of ideas," petitioner invokes a countervailing constitutional interest, that of the First Amendment. In this light, petitioner must be viewed as seeking to achieve a goal that is of paramount importance in the fulfillment of its mission.

It may be argued that there is greater force to these views at the undergraduate level than in a medical school where the training is centered primarily on professional competency. But even at the graduate level, our tradition and experience lend support to the view that the contribution of diversity is substantial. . . . Physicians serve a heterogeneous population. An otherwise qualified medical student with a particular background—whether it be ethnic, geographic, culturally advantaged or disadvantaged— may bring to a professional school of medicine experiences, outlooks, and ideas that enrich the training of its student body and better equip its graduates to render with understanding their vital service to humanity.

Ethnic diversity, however, is only one element in a range of factors a university properly may consider in attaining the goal of a heterogeneous student body. Although a university must have wide discretion in making the sensitive judgments as to who should be admitted, constitutional limitations protecting individual rights may not be disregarded. Respondent urges—and the courts below have held— that petitioner's dual admissions program is a racial classification that impermissibly infringes his rights under the Fourteenth Amendment. As the interest of diversity is compelling in the context of a university's admissions program, the question remains whether the program's racial classification is necessary to promote this interest. . . .

[*Part V*] It may be assumed that the reservation of a specified number of seats in each class for individuals from the preferred ethnic groups would contribute to the attainment of considerable ethnic diversity in the student body. But petitioner's argument that this is the only effective means of serving the interest of diversity is seriously flawed. In a most fundamental sense the argument misconceives the nature of the state interest that would justify consideration of race or ethnic background. It is not an interest in simple ethnic diversity, in which a specified percentage of the student body is in effect guaranteed to be members of selected ethnic groups, with the remaining percentage an undifferentiated aggregation of students. The diversity that furthers a compelling state interest encompasses a far broader array of qualifications and characteristics of which racial or ethnic origin is but a single though important element. Petitioner's special admissions program, focused *solely* on ethnic diversity, would hinder rather than further attainment of genuine diversity.

Nor would the state interest in genuine diversity be served by expanding petitioner's two-track system into a multitrack program with a prescribed number of seats set aside for each identifiable category of applicants. Indeed, it is inconceivable that a university would thus pursue the logic of petitioner's two-track program to the illogical end of insulating each category of applicants with certain desired qualifications from competition with all other applicants.

The experience of other university admissions programs, which take race into account in achieving the educational diversity valued by the First Amendment, demonstrates that the assignment of a fixed number of places to a minority group is not a necessary means toward that end. An illuminating example is found in the Harvard College program. . . .

In such an admissions program, race or ethnic background may be deemed a "plus" in a particular applicant's file, yet it does not insulate the individual from comparison with all other candidates for the available seats. The file of a particular black applicant may be examined for his potential contribution to diversity without the factor of race being decisive when compared, for example, with that of an applicant identified as an Italian-American if the latter is thought to exhibit qualities more likely to promote beneficial educational pluralism. Such qualities could include exceptional personal talents, unique work or service experience, leadership potential, maturity, demonstrated compassion, a history of overcoming disadvantage, ability to communicate with the poor, or other qualifications deemed important. In short, an admissions program operated in this way is flexible enough to consider all pertinent elements of diversity in light of the particular qualifications of each applicant, and to place them on the same footing for consideration, although not necessarily according them the same weight. Indeed, the weight attributed to a particular quality may vary from year to year depending upon the "mix" both of the student body and the applicants for the incoming class.

This kind of program treats each applicant as an individual in the admissions process. The applicant who loses out on the last available seat to another candidate receiving a "plus" on the basis of ethnic background will not have been foreclosed from all consideration for that seat simply because he was not the right color or had the wrong surname. It would mean only that his combined qualifications, which may have included similar nonobjective factors, did not outweigh those of the other applicant. His qualifications would have been weighed fairly and competitively, and he would have no basis to complain of unequal treatment under the Fourteenth Amendment.

It has been suggested that an admissions program which considers race only as one factor is simply a subtle and more sophisticated—but no less effective—means of according racial preference than the Davis program. A facial intent to discriminate, however, is evident in petitioner's preference program and not denied in this case. No such facial infirmity exists in an admissions program where race or ethnic background is simply one element— to be weighed fairly against other elements—in the selection process. . . . And a court would not assume that a university, professing to employ a facially nondiscriminatory admissions policy, would operate it as a cover for the functional equivalent of a quota system. In short, good faith would be presumed in the absence of a showing to the contrary in the manner permitted by our cases. . . .

In summary, it is evident that the Davis special admissions program involves the use of an explicit racial classification never before countenanced by this Court. It tells applicants who are not Negro, Asian, or Chicano that they are totally excluded from a specific percentage of the seats in an entering class. No matter how strong their qualifications, quantitative and extracurricular, including their own potential for contribution to educational diversity, they are never afforded the chance to compete with applicants from the preferred groups for the special admissions seats. At the same time, the preferred applicants have the opportunity to compete for every seat in the class.

The fatal flaw in petitioner's preferential program is its disregard of individual rights as guaranteed by the Fourteenth Amendment. . . . Such rights are not absolute. But when a State's distribution of benefits or imposition of burdens hinges on ancestry or the color of a person's skin, that individual is entitled to a demonstration that the challenged classification is necessary to promote a substantial state interest. Petitioner has failed to carry this burden. For this reason, that portion of the California court's judgment holding petitioner's special admissions program invalid under the Fourteenth Amendment must be affirmed.

In enjoining petitioner from ever considering the race of any applicant, however, the courts below failed to recognize that the State has a substantial interest that legitimately may be served by a properly devised admissions program involving the competitive consideration of race and ethnic origin. For this reason, so much of the California court's judgment as enjoins petitioner from any consideration of the race of any applicant must be reversed.

[*Part VI*] With respect to respondent's entitlement to an injunction directing his admission to the Medical School, petitioner has conceded that it could not carry its burden of proving that, but for the existence of its unlawful special admissions program, respondent still would not have been admitted. Hence, respondent is entitled to the injunction, and that portion of the judgment must be affirmed.

* * *

MR. JUSTICE BRENNAN, MR. JUSTICE WHITE, MR. JUSTICE MARSHALL, and MR. JUSTICE BLACKMUN, concurring in the judgment in part and dissenting in part.

. . . We agree with MR. JUSTICE POWELL that, as applied to the case before us, Title VI goes no further in prohibiting the use of race than the Equal Protection Clause of the Fourteenth Amendment itself. We also agree that the effect of the California Supreme Court's affirmance of the judgment of the Superior Court of California would be to prohibit the University from establishing in the future affirmative-action programs that take race into account. . . . Since we conclude that the affirmative admissions program at the Davis Medical School is constitutional, we would reverse the judgment below in all respects. MR. JUSTICE POWELL agrees that some uses of race in university admissions are permissible and, therefore, he joins with us to make five votes reversing the judgment below insofar as it prohibits the University from establishing race-conscious programs in the future.

. . . On the other hand, the fact that this case does not fit neatly into our prior analytic framework for race cases does not mean that it should be analyzed by applying the very loose rational-basis standard of review that is the very least that is always applied in equal protection cases. . . . Instead, a number of considerations—developed in gender-discrimination cases but which carry even more force when applied to racial classifications—lead us to conclude that racial classifications designed to further remedial purposes "must serve important governmental objectives and must be substantially related to achievement of those objectives." . . . *Craig v. Boren,* 429 U.S. 190, 197 (1976).

First, race, like, "gender-based classifications too often [has] been inexcusably utilized to stereotype and stigmatize politically powerless segments of society." . . . While a carefully tailored statute designed to remedy past discrimination could avoid these vices, . . . we nonetheless have recognized that the line between honest and thoughtful appraisal of the effects of past discrimination and paternalistic stereotyping is not so clear and that a statute based on the latter is patently capable of stigmatizing all women with a badge of inferiority. . . . State programs designed ostensibly to ameliorate the effects of past racial discrimination obviously create the same hazard of stigma, since they may promote racial separatism and reinforce the views of those who believe that members of racial minorities are inherently incapable of succeeding on their own. . . .

Second, race, like gender and illegitimacy, . . . is an immutable characteristic which its possessors are powerless to escape or set aside. While a classification is not *per se* invalid because it divides classes on the basis of an immutable characteristic, . . . it is nevertheless true that such divisions are contrary to our deep belief that "legal burdens should bear some relationship to individual responsibility or wrongdoing" . . . and that advancement sanctioned, sponsored, or approved by the State should ideally be based on individual merit or achievement, or at the least on factors within the control of an individual. . . .

. . . In sum, because of the significant risk that racial classifications established for ostensibly benign purposes can be misused, causing effects not unlike those created by invidious classifications, it is inappropriate to inquire only whether there is any conceivable basis that might sustain such a classification. Instead, to justify such a classification an important and articulated purpose for its use must be shown. In addition, any statute must be stricken that stigmatizes any group or that singles out those least well represented in the political processes to bear the brunt of a benign program. Thus, our review under the Fourteenth Amendment should be strict—not " 'strict' in theory and fatal in fact," because it is stigma that causes fatality—but strict and searching nonetheless.

Davis' articulated purpose of remedying the effects of past societal discrimination is, under our cases, sufficiently important to justify the use of race-conscious admissions programs where there is a sound basis for concluding that minority underrepresentation is substantial and chronic, and that the handicap of past discrimination is impeding access of minorities to the Medical School.

. . . Properly construed, therefore, our prior cases unequivocally show that a state government may adopt race-conscious programs if the purpose of such programs is to remove the disparate racial impact its actions might otherwise have and if there is reason to believe that the disparate impact is itself the product of past discrimination, whether its own or that of society at large. There is no question that Davis' program is valid under this test.

. . . The second prong of our test—whether the Davis program stigmatizes any discrete group or individual and whether race is reasonably used in light of the program's objectives—is clearly satisfied by the Davis program.

. . . Unlike discrimination against racial minorities, the use of racial preferences for remedial purposes does not inflict a pervasive injury upon individual whites in the sense that wherever they go or whatever they do there is a significant likelihood that they will be treated as second-class citizens because of their color. This distinction does not mean that the exclusion of a white resulting from the

preferential use of race is not sufficiently serious to require justification; but it does mean that the injury inflicted by such a policy is not distinguishable from disadvantages caused by a wide range of government actions, none of which has ever been thought impermissible for that reason alone.

* * *

The opinion of MR. JUSTICE MARSHALL.

I agree with the judgment of the Court only insofar as it permits a university to consider the race of an applicant in making admissions decisions. I do not agree that petitioner's admissions program violates the Constitution. For it must be remembered that, during most of the past 200 years, the Constitution as interpreted by this Court did not prohibit the most ingenious and pervasive forms of discrimination against the Negro. Now, when a State acts to remedy the effects of that legacy of discrimination, I cannot believe that this same Constitution stands as a barrier.

Three hundred and fifty years ago, the Negro was dragged to this country in chains to be sold into slavery. Uprooted from his homeland and thrust into bondage for forced labor, the slave was deprived of all legal rights. It was unlawful to teach him to read; he could be sold away from his family and friends at the whim of his master; and killing or maiming him was not a crime. The system of slavery brutalized and dehumanized both master and slave.

The denial of human rights was etched into the American Colonies' first attempts at establishing self-government. When the colonists determined to seek their independence from England, they drafted a unique document cataloguing their grievances against the King and proclaiming as "self-evident" that "all men are created equal" and are endowed "with certain unalienable Rights," including those to "Life, Liberty and the pursuit of Happiness." . . .

The implicit protection of slavery embodied in the Declaration of Independence was made explicit in the Constitution, which treated a slave as being equivalent to three-fifths of a person for purposes of apportioning representatives and taxes among the States. Art. I, § 2. The Constitution also contained a clause ensuring that the "Migration or Importation" of slaves into the existing States would be legal until at least 1808, Art. I § 9, and a fugitive slave clause requiring that when a slave escaped to another State, he must be returned on the claim of the master, Art. IV, § 2. In their declaration of the principles that were to provide the cornerstone of the new Nation, therefore, the Framers made it plain that "we the people," for whose protection the Constitution was designed, did not include those whose skins were the wrong color. . . .

The individual States likewise established the machinery to protect the system of slavery through the promulgation of the Slave Codes, which were designed primarily to defend the property interest of the owner in his slave. The position of the Negro slave as mere property was confirmed by this Court in *Dred Scott v. Sandford*, [60 U.S.] 19 How. 393 (1857), holding that the Missouri Compromise—which prohibited slavery in the portion of the Louisiana Purchase Territory north of Missouri—was unconstitutional because it deprived slave owners of their property without due process. . . . The Court further concluded that Negroes were not intended to be included as citizens under the Constitution but were "regarded as beings of an inferior order . . . altogether unfit to associate with the white race, either in social or political relations; and so far inferior, that they had no rights which the white man was bound to respect." . . .

The status of the Negro as property was officially erased by his emancipation at the end of the Civil War. But the long-awaited emancipation, while freeing the Negro from slavery, did not bring him citizenship or equality in any meaningful way. Slavery was replaced by a system of "laws which imposed upon the colored race onerous disabilities and burdens, and curtailed their rights in the pursuit of life, liberty, and property to such an extent that their freedom was of little value." *Slaughter-House Cases,* [83 U.S.] 16 Wall. 36, 70 (1873). Despite the passage of the Thirteenth, Fourteenth, and Fifteenth Amendments, the Negro was systematically denied the rights those Amendments were supposed to secure. The combined actions and inactions of the State and Federal Governments maintained Negroes in a position of legal inferiority for another century after the Civil War.

The Southern States took the first steps to re-enslave the Negroes. Immediately following the end of the Civil War, many of the provisional legislatures passed Black Codes, similar to the Slave Codes, which, among other things, limited the rights of the Negroes to own or rent property and permitted imprisonment for breach of employment contracts. Over the next several decades, the South managed to disenfranchise the Negroes in spite of the Fifteenth Amendment by various techniques, including poll taxes, deliberately complicated balloting processes, property and literacy qualifications, and finally the white primary.

Congress responded to the legal disabilities being imposed in the Southern States by passing the Reconstruction Acts of the Civil Rights Acts. Congress also responded to the needs of the Negroes at the end of the Civil War by establishing the Bureau of Refugees, Freedmen, and Abandoned Lands, better known as the Freedmen's Bureau, to supply food, hospitals, land, and education to the newly freed slaves. Thus, for a time it seemed as if the Negro might be protected from the continued denial of his civil rights and might be relieved of the disabilities

that prevented him from taking his place as a free and equal citizen.

That time, however, was short-lived. Reconstruction came to a close, and, with the assistance of this Court, the Negro was rapidly stripped of his new civil rights. In the words of C. Van Woodward: "By narrow and ingenious interpretation [the Supreme Court's] decisions over a period of years had whittled away a great part of the authority presumably given the government for protection of civil rights." . . .

. . . The position of the Negro today in America is the tragic but inevitable consequence of centuries of unequal treatment. Measured by any benchmark of comfort or achievement, meaningful equality remains a distant dream for the Negro.

A Negro child today has a life expectancy which is shorter by more than five years than that of a white child. The Negro child's mother is over three times more likely to die of complications in childbirth, and the infant mortality rate for Negroes is nearly twice that for whites. The median income of the Negro family is only 60% that of the median of a white family, and the percentage of Negroes who live in families with incomes below the poverty line is nearly four times greater than that of whites.

When the Negro child reaches working age, he finds that America offers him significantly less than it offers his white counterpart. For Negro adults, the unemployment rate is twice that of whites, and the unemployment rate for Negro teenagers is nearly three times that of white teenagers. A Negro male who completes four years of college can expect a median income of merely $110 more than a white male who has only a high school diploma. Although Negroes represent 11.5% of the population, they are only 1.2% of the lawyers and judges, 2% of the physicians, 2.3% of the dentists, 1.1% of the engineers and 2.6% of the college and university professors.

The relationship between those figures and the history of unequal treatment afforded to the Negro cannot be denied. At every point from birth to death the impact of the past is reflected in the still disfavored position of the Negro.

In light of the sorry history of discrimination and its devastating impact on the lives of Negroes, bringing the Negroes into the mainstream of American life should be a state interest of the highest order. To fail to do so is to ensure that America will forever remain a divided society.

I do not believe that the Fourteenth Amendment requires us to accept that fate. Neither its history nor our past cases lend any support to the conclusion that a university may not remedy the cumulative effects of society's discrimination by giving consideration to race in an effort to increase the number and percentage of Negro doctors.

. . . While I applaud the judgment of the Court that a university may consider race in its admissions process, it is more than a little ironic that, after several hundred years of class-based discrimination against Negroes, the Court is unwilling to hold that a class-based remedy for that discrimination is permissible. In declining to so hold, today's judgment ignores the fact that for several hundred years Negroes have been discriminated against, not as individuals, but rather solely because of the color of their skins. It is unnecessary in 20th-century America to have individual Negroes demonstrate that they have been victims of racial discrimination; the racism of our society has been so pervasive that none, regardless of wealth or position, has managed to escape its impact. The experience of Negroes in America has been different in kind, not just in degree, from that of other ethnic groups. It is not merely the history of slavery alone but also that a whole people were marked as inferior by the law. And that mark has endured. The dream of America as the great melting pot has not been realized for the Negro; because of his skin color he never even made it into the pot.

[The opinion of MR. JUSTICE WHITE is omitted.]

[The separate opinion of MR. JUSTICE BLACKMUN is omitted.]

* * *

MR. JUSTICE STEVENS, with whom THE CHIEF JUSTICE [BURGER], MR. JUSTICE STEWART, and MR. JUSTICE REHNQUIST join, concurring in the judgment in part and dissenting in part.

. . . The University, through its special admissions policy, excluded Bakke from participation in its program of medical education because of his race. The University also acknowledges that it was, and still is, receiving federal financial assistance. The plain language of the statute therefore requires affirmance of the judgment below. A different result cannot be justified unless that language misstates the actual intent of the Congress that enacted the statute or the statute is not enforceable in a private action. Neither conclusion is warranted.

. . . Petitioner contends, however, that exclusion of applicants on the basis of race does not violate Title

VI if the exclusion carries with it no racial stigma. No such qualification or limitation of § 601's categorical prohibition of "exclusion" is justified by the statute or its history. The language of the entire section is perfectly clear; the words that follow "excluded from" do not modify or qualify the explicit outlawing of any exclusion on the stated grounds.

The legislative history reinforces this reading. The only suggestion that § 601 would allow exclusion of nonminority applicants came from opponents of the legislation and then only by way of a discussion of the meaning of the word "discrimination." The opponents feared that the term "discrimination" would be read as mandating racial quotas and "racially balanced" colleges and universities, and they pressed for a specific definition of the term in order to avoid this possibility. In response, the proponents of the legislation gave repeated assurances that the Act would be "colorblind" in its application. . . .

In giving answers such as these, it seems clear that the proponents of Title VI assumed that the Constitution itself required a colorblind standard on the part of government, but that does not mean that the legislation only codifies an existing constitutional prohibition. The statutory prohibition against discrimination in federally funded projects contained in § 601 is more than a simple paraphrasing of what the Fifth or Fourteenth Amendment would require. The Act's proponents plainly considered Title VI consistent with their view of the Constitution and they sought to provide an effective weapon to implement that view. As a distillation of what the supporters of the Act believed the Constitution demanded of State and Federal Governments, § 601 has independent force, with language and emphasis in addition to that found in the Constitution.

As with other provisions of the Civil Rights Act, Congress' expression of its policy to end racial discrimination may independently proscribe conduct that the Constitution does not. However, we need not decide the congruence—or lack of congruence—of the controlling statute and the Constitution since the meaning of the Title VI ban on exclusion is crystal clear: Race cannot be the basis of excluding anyone from participation in a federally funded program.

UNITED STEELWORKERS OF AMERICA V. WEBER
443 U.S. 193 (1979)

In 1974 the United Steelworkers of America (USWA) and the Kaiser Aluminum & Chemical Corporation entered into a collective bargaining agreement covering terms and conditions of employment at 15 Kaiser plants. The agreement contained an affirmative action plan designed to eliminate racial imbalances in Kaiser's almost exclusively white craft workforces. The plan reserved for black employees 50% of the openings in in-plant craft-training programs until the percentage of black craftworkers in a plant was commensurate with the percentage of blacks in the local labor force. This case arose from the operation of the Kaiser plant in Gramercy, Louisiana, where, until 1974, Kaiser hired as craftworkers only persons who had prior craft experience. Prior to 1974, only 1.83% (5 out of 273) of the skilled craftworkers at the Gramercy plant were black, even though the local workforce was approximately 39% black. Pursuant to the national agreement, Kaiser, rather than continue its practice of hiring trained outsiders, established a program to train its own production workers to fill craft openings. Trainees were selected on the basis of seniority, with the proviso that at least 50% of the trainees were to be black until the percentage of black skilled craftworkers in the plant approximated the percentage of blacks in the local labor force. During 1974, the first year of the operation of the affirmative action plan, 13 craft trainees were selected; 7 were black, and 6 were white. The most senior black selected into the program had less seniority than several white production workers whose bids for admission were rejected. Brian Weber, one of those white production workers, brought a class action suit in district court, alleging that the affirmative action program discriminated against white employees, in violation of §§ 703(a) and (d) of Title VII. The district court held that the affirmative action plan violated Title VII. The court of appeals affirmed, holding that all employment preferences based on race, including those preferences incidental to bona fide affirmative action plans, violated Title VII. *Vote: 5-2.*

* * *

MR. JUSTICE BRENNAN delivered the opinion of the Court.

Challenged here is the legality of an affirmative action plan—collectively bargained by an employer and a union—that reserves for black employees 50% of the openings in an in-plant craft-training program until the percentage of black craftworkers in the plan is commensurate with the percentage of blacks in the local labor force. The question for decision is whether Congress, in Title VII of the Civil Rights Act of 1964, . . . left employers and unions in the private sector free to take such race-conscious steps to eliminate manifest racial imbalances in traditionally segregated job categories. We hold that Title VII does not prohibit such race-conscious affirmative action plans.

. . . We emphasize at the outset the narrowness of our inquiry. Since the Kaiser-USWA plan does not involve state action, this case does not present an alleged violation of the Equal Protection Clause of the Fourteenth Amendment. Further, since the Kaiser-USWA plan was adopted voluntarily, we are not concerned with what Title VII requires or with what a court might order to remedy a past proved violation of the Act. The only question before us is the narrow statutory issue of whether Title VII *forbids* private employers and unions from voluntarily agreeing upon bona fide affirmative action plans that accord racial preferences in the manner and for the purpose provided in the Kaiser-USWA plan. That question was expressly left open in *McDonald v. Santa Fe Trail Transp. Co.,* 427 U.S. 273, 281 n. 8 (1976) which held, in a case not involving affirmative action, that Title VII protects whites as well as blacks from certain forms of racial discrimination.

Respondent argues that Congress intended in Title VII to prohibit all race-conscious affirmative action plans. Respondent's argument rests upon a literal interpretation of §§ 703(a) and (d) of the Act. Those sections make it unlawful to "discriminate . . . because of . . . race" in hiring and in the selection of apprentices for training programs. Since, the argument runs, *McDonald v. Santa Fe Trail Transp. Co.,* . . . settled that Title VII forbids discrimination against whites as well as blacks, and since the Kaiser-USWA affirmative action plan operates to discriminate against white employees solely because they are white, it follows that the Kaiser-USWA plan violates Title VII.

Respondent's argument is not without force. But it overlooks the significance of the fact that the Kaiser-USWA plan is an affirmative action plan voluntarily adopted by the private parties to eliminate traditional patterns of racial segregation. In this context respondent's reliance upon a literal construction of §§ 703(a) and (d) and upon *McDonald* is misplaced. . . . The prohibition against racial discrimination in §§ 703(a) and (d) of Title VII must therefore be read against the background of the legislative history of Title VII and the historical context from which the Act arose. . . . Examination of those sources makes clear that an interpretation of the sections that forbade all race-conscious affirmative action would "bring about an end completely at variance with the purpose of the statute" and must be rejected.

Congress' primary concern in enacting the prohibition against racial discrimination in Title VII of the Civil Rights Act of 1964 was with "the plight of the Negro in our economy." . . . Before 1964, blacks were largely relegated to "unskilled and semi-skilled jobs." . . . Because of automation the number of such jobs was rapidly decreasing. . . . As a consequence, "the relative position of the Negro worker [was] steadily worsening. In 1947 the nonwhite unemployment rate was only 64 percent higher than the white rate; in 1962 it was 124 percent higher." . . . Congress considered this a serious social problem. . . .

Congress feared that the goals of the Civil Rights Act—the integration of blacks into the mainstream of American society—could not be achieved unless this trend were reversed. And Congress recognized that that would not be possible unless blacks were able to secure jobs "which have a future." . . . Accordingly, it was clear to Congress that "[t]he crux of the problem [was] to open employment opportunities for Negroes in occupations which have been traditionally closed to them," . . . and it was to this problem that Title VII's prohibition against racial discrimination in employment was primarily addressed.

It plainly appears from the House Report accompanying the Civil Rights Act that Congress did not intend wholly to prohibit private and voluntary affirmative action efforts as one method of solving this problem. The Report provides:

"No bill can or should lay claim to eliminating all of the causes and consequences of racial and other types of discrimination against minorities. There is reason to believe, however, that national leadership provided by the enactment of Federal legislation dealing with the most troublesome problems *will create an atmosphere conducive to voluntary or local resolution of other forms of discrimination.*"

Given this legislative history, we cannot agree with respondent that Congress intended to prohibit the private sector from taking effective steps to accomplish the goal that Congress designed Title VII to achieve. The very statutory words intended as a spur or catalyst to cause "employers and unions to self-examine and to self-evaluate their employment practices and to endeavor to eliminate, so far as possible, the last vestiges of an unfortunate and ignominious page in this country's history" . . . cannot be interpreted as an absolute prohibition against all private, voluntary, race-conscious affirmative action efforts to hasten the elimination of such vestiges. It would be ironic indeed if a law triggered by a Nation's concern over centuries of racial injustice and intended to improve the lot of those who had "been excluded from the American dream for so long" . . . constituted the first legislative prohibition of all voluntary, private, race-conscious efforts to abolish traditional patterns of racial segregation and hierarchy.

Our conclusion is further reinforced by examination of the language and legislative history of § 703(j) of Title VII. Opponents of Title VII raised two related arguments against the bill. First, they argued that the Act would be interpreted to *require* employers with racially imbalanced work forces to grant preferential treatment to racial minorities in order to integrate. Second, they argued that employers with racially imbalanced work forces would grant preferential treatment to racial minorities, even if not required to do so by the Act. . . . Had Congress meant to prohibit all race-conscious affirmative action, as respondent urges, it easily could have answered both objections by providing that Title VII would not require or *permit* racially preferential integration efforts. But Congress did not choose such a course. Rather, Congress added § 703(j)

which addresses only the first objection. The section provides that nothing contained in Title VII "shall be interpreted to *require* any employer . . . to grant preferential treatment . . . to any group because of the race . . . of such . . . group on account of" a *de facto* racial imbalance in the employer's work force. The section does *not* state that "nothing in Title VII shall be interpreted to *permit*" voluntary affirmative efforts to correct racial imbalances. The natural inference is that Congress chose not to forbid all voluntary race-conscious affirmative action.

The reasons for this choice are evident from the legislative record. Title VII could not have been enacted into law without substantial support from legislators in both Houses who traditionally resisted federal regulation of private business. Those legislators demanded as a price for their support that "management prerogatives, and union freedoms . . . be left undisturbed to the greatest extent possible." . . . Section 703(j) was proposed by Senator Dirksen to allay any fears that the Act might be interpreted in such a way as to upset this compromise. The section was designed to prevent § 703 of Title VII from being interpreted in such a way as to lead to undue "Federal Government interference with private businesses because of some Federal employee's ideas about racial balance or racial imbalance." . . . Clearly, a prohibition against all voluntary, race-conscious, affirmative action efforts would deserve these ends. Such a prohibition would augment the powers of the Federal Government and diminish traditional management prerogatives while at the same time impeding attainment of the ultimate statutory goals. In view of this legislative history and in view of Congress' desire to avoid undue federal regulation of private businesses, use of the word "require" rather than the phrase "require or permit" in § 703(j) fortifies the conclusion that Congress did not intend to limit traditional business freedom to such a degree as to prohibit all voluntary race-conscious affirmative action.

We therefore hold that Title VII's prohibition in §§ 703(a) and (d) against racial discrimination does not condemn all private, voluntary, race-conscious affirmative action plans.

We need not today define in detail the line of demarcation between permissible and impermissible affirmative action plans. It suffices to hold that the challenged Kaiser-USWA affirmative action plan falls on the permissible side of the line. The purposes of the plan mirror those of the statute. Both were designed to break down old patterns of racial segregation and hierarchy. Both were structured to "open employment opportunities for Negroes in occupations which have been traditionally closed to them." . . .

At the same time, the plan does not unnecessarily trammel the interests of the white employees. The plan does not require the discharge of white workers and their replacement with new black hires. . . . Nor does the plan create an absolute bar to the advancement of white employees; half of those trained in the program will be white. Moreover, the plan is a temporary measure; it is not intended to maintain racial balance, but simply to eliminate a manifest racial imbalance. Preferential selection of craft trainees at the Gramercy plant will end as soon as the percentage of black skilled craftworkers in the Gramercy plant approximates the percentage of blacks in the local labor force. . . .

We conclude, therefore, that the adoption of the Kaiser-USWA plan for the Gramercy plant falls within the area of discretion left by Title VII to the private sector voluntarily to adopt affirmative action plans designed to eliminate conspicuous racial imbalance in traditionally segregated job categories. Accordingly, the judgment of the Court of Appeals for the Fifth Circuit is

Reversed.

[The concurring opinion of MR. JUSTICE BLACKMUN is omitted.]

MR. JUSTICE POWELL and MR. JUSTICE STEVENS took no part in the consideration or decision of this case.

* * *

MR. JUSTICE REHNQUIST, with whom THE CHIEF JUSTICE joins, dissenting.

. . . Thus, by a *tour de force* reminiscent not of jurists such as Hale, Holmes, and Hughes, but of escape artists such as Houdini, the Court eludes clear statutory language, "uncontradicted" legislative history, and uniform precedent in concluding that employers are, after all, permitted to consider race in making employment decisions. It may be that one or more of the principal sponsors of Title VII would have preferred to see a provision allowing preferential treatment of minorities written into the bill. Such a provision, however, would have to have been expressly or impliedly excepted from Title VII's explicit prohibition on all racial discrimination in employment. There is no such exception on the Act. And a reading of the legislative debates concerning Title VII, in which proponents and opponents alike uniformly denounced discrimination

in favor of, as well as discrimination against, Negroes, demonstrates clearly that any legislator harboring an unspoken desire for such a provision could not possibly have succeeded in enacting it into law.

. . . Quite simply, Kaiser's racially discriminatory admission quota is flatly prohibited by the plain language of Title VII. This normally dispositive fact, however, gives the Court only momentary pause. An "interpretation" of the statute upholding Weber's claim would, according to the Court, "bring about an end completely at variance with the purpose of the statute." . . . To support this conclusion, the Court calls upon the "spirit" of the Act, which it divines from passages in Title VII's legislative history indicating that enactment of the statute was prompted by Congress' desire "to open employment opportunities for Negroes in occupations which [had] been traditionally closed to them." . . . But the legislative history invoked by the Court to avoid the plain language of §§ 703(a) and (d) simply misses the point. To be sure, the reality of employment discrimination against Negroes provided the primary impetus for passage of Title VII. But this fact by no means supports the proposition that Congress intended to leave employers free to discriminate against white persons. In most cases, "[l]egislative history . . . is more vague than the statute we are called upon to interpret." . . . Here, however, the legislative history of Title VII is as clear as the language of §§ 703(a) and (d), and it irrefutably demonstrates that Congress meant precisely what it said in §§ 703 (a) and (d)—that *no* racial discrimination in employment is permissible under Title VII, not even preferential treatment of minorities to correct racial imbalance.

. . . There is perhaps no device more destructive to the notion of equality than the *numerous clausus*— the quota. Whether described as "benign discrimination" or "affirmative action," the racial quota is nonetheless a creator of castes, a two-edged sword that must demean one in order to prefer another. In passing Title VII, Congress outlawed *all* racial discrimination, recognizing that no discrimination based on race is benign, that no action disadvantaging a person because of his color is affirmative.

[The dissenting opinion of MR. CHIEF JUSTICE BURGER is omitted.]

FULLILOVE V. KLUTZNICK
448 U.S. 448 (1980)

In May 1977, Congress passed the Public Works Employment Act, which authorized an additional $4 billion appropriation for federal grants to be made by the Secretary of Commerce, acting through the Economic Development Administration (EDA), to state and local governmental entities for use in local public works projects. Section 103(f)(2) of the Act, the minority business enterprise (MBE) provision, required that at least 10% of the federal funds granted for local public works projects must be used by the state or local grantee to procure services or supplies from businesses owned by minority group members, defined as blacks, Spanish-speaking, Orientals, Eskimos, and Aleuts, unless they obtain an administrative waiver. In November 1977, several associations of construction contractors and subcontractors and a firm engaged in heating, ventilation, and air conditioning work brought suit against Secretary of Commerce Klutznick in district court, alleging that the 10% MBE requirement violated the equal protection clause of the Fourteenth Amendment and the equal protection component of the due process clause of the Fifth Amendment and various statutory and anti-discrimination provisions. The district court upheld the validity of the MBE program, and the court of appeals affirmed. *Vote: 6-3.*

* * *

MR. CHIEF JUSTICE BURGER announced the judgment of the Court and delivered an opinion in which MR. JUSTICE WHITE and MR. JUSTICE POWELL joined.

. . . The clear objective of the MBE provision is disclosed by our necessarily extended review of its legislative and administrative background. The program was designed to ensure that to the extent federal funds were granted under the Public Works Employment Act of 1977, grantees who elect to participate would not employ procurement practices that Congress had decided might result in perpetuation of the effects of prior discrimination which had impaired or foreclosed access by minority businesses to public contracting opportunities. The MBE program does not mandate the allocation of federal funds according to inflexible percentages solely based on race or ethnicity.

Our analysis proceeds in two steps. At the outset, we must inquire whether the *objectives* of this legislation are within the power of Congress. If so, we must go on to decide whether the limited use of racial and ethnic criteria, in the context presented, is a constitutionally permissible *means* for achieving the congressional objectives and does not violate the equal protection component of the Due Process Clause of the Fifth Amendment.

In enacting the MBE provision, it is clear that Congress employed an amalgam of its specifically delegated powers. The Public Works Employment Act of 1977, by its very nature, is primarily an exercise of the Spending Power. U.S. Const. Art. I, § 8, cl. 1. This Court has recognized that the power to "provide for the . . . general Welfare" is an independent grant of legislative authority, distinct from other broad congressional powers. . . . Congress has frequently employed the Spending Power to further

broad policy objectives by conditioning receipt of federal moneys upon compliance by the recipient with federal statutory and administrative directives. This Court has repeatedly upheld against constitutional challenge the use of this technique to induce governments and private parties to cooperate voluntarily with federal policy. . . .

The MBE program is structured within this familiar legislative pattern. The program conditions receipt of public works grants upon agreement by the state or local governmental grantee that at least 10% of the federal funds will be devoted to contracts with minority businesses, to the extent this can be accomplished by overcoming barriers to access and by awarding contracts to bona fide MBE's. It is further conditioned to require that MBE bids on these contracts are competitively priced, or might have been competitively priced but for the present effects of prior discrimination. Admittedly, the problems of administering this program with respect to these conditions may be formidable. Although the primary responsibility for ensuring minority participation falls upon the grantee, when the procurement practices of the grantee involve the award of a prime contract to a general or prime contractor, the obligations to assure minority participation devolve upon the private contracting party; this is a contractual condition of eligibility for award of the prime contract.

Here we need not explore the outermost limitations on the objectives attainable through such an application of the Spending Power. The reach of the Spending Power within its sphere, is at least as broad as the regulatory powers of Congress. If, pursuant to its regulatory powers, Congress could have achieved the objectives of the MBE program, then it may do so under the Spending Power. And we have no difficulty perceiving a basis for accomplishing the objectives of the MBE program though the Commerce Power insofar as the program objectives pertain to the action of private contracting parties, and through the power to enforce the equal protection guarantees of the Fourteenth Amendment insofar as the program objectives pertain to the action of state and local grantees.

. . . Although the Act recites no preambulary "findings" on the subject, we are satisfied that Congress had abundant historical basis from which it could conclude that traditional procurement practices, when applied to minority businesses, could perpetuate the effects of prior discrimination. Accordingly, Congress reasonably determined that the prospective elimination of these barriers to minority firm access to public contracting opportunities generated by the 1977 Act was appropriate to ensure that those businesses were not denied equal opportunity to participate in federal grants to state and local governments, which is one aspect of the equal protection of the laws. Insofar as the MBE program pertains to the actions of state and local grantees, Congress could have achieved its objectives by use of its power under § 5 of the Fourteenth Amendment. We conclude that in this respect the objectives of the MBE provision are within the scope of the Spending Power.

. . . We now turn to the question whether, as a *means* to accomplish these plainly constitutional objectives, Congress may use racial and ethnic criteria, in this limited way, as a condition attached to a federal grant. . . . However, Congress may employ racial or ethnic classifications in exercising its Spending or other legislative powers only if those classifications do not violate the equal protection component of the Due Process Clause of the Fifth Amendment. We recognize the need for careful judicial evaluation to assure that any congressional program that employs racial or ethnic criteria to accomplish the objective of remedying the present effects of past discrimination is narrowly tailored to the achievement of that goal.

. . . Our review of the regulations and guidelines governing administration of the MBE provision reveals that Congress enacted the program as a strictly remedial measure; moreover, it is a remedy that functions prospectively, in the manner of an injunctive decree. Pursuant to the administrative program, grantees and their prime contractors are required to seek out all available, qualified, bona fide MBE's; they are required to provide technical assistance as needed, to lower or waive bonding requirements where feasible, to solicit the aid of the Office of Minority Business Enterprise, the SBA, or other sources for assisting MBE's to obtain required working capital, and to give guidance through the intricacies of the bidding process. . . . The program assumes that grantees who undertake these efforts in good faith will obtain at least 10% participation by minority business enterprises. It is recognized that, to achieve this target, contracts will be awarded to available, qualified, bona fide MBE's even though they are not the lowest competitive bidders, so long as their higher bids, when challenged, are found to reflect merely attempts to cover costs inflated by the present effects of prior disadvantage and discrimination. . . . There is available to the grantee a provision authorized by Congress for administrative waiver on a case-by-case basis should there be a demonstration that, despite affirmative efforts, this level of participation cannot be achieved without departing from the objectives of the program. . . . There is also an administrative mechanism, including a complaint procedure, to ensure that only bona fide MBE's are encompassed by the remedial program, and to prevent unjust participation in the program by those minority firms whose access to public contracting opportunities is not impaired by the effects of prior discrimination. . . .

As a threshold matter, we reject the contention that in the remedial context the Congress must act in a wholly "color-blind" fashion. . . .

. . . A more specific challenge to the MBE program is the charge that it impermissibly deprives nonminority businesses of access to at least some portion of the government contracting opportunities generated by the Act. It must be conceded that by its objective of remedying the historical impairment of access, the MBE provision can have the effect of awarding some contracts to MBE's which otherwise might be awarded to other businesses, who may themselves be innocent of any prior discriminatory actions. Failure of nonminority firms to receive certain contracts is, of course, an incidental consequence of the program, not part of its objective; similarly, past impairment of minority-firm access to public contracting opportunities may have been an incidental consequence of "business as usual" by public contracting agencies and among prime contractors.

It is not a constitutional defect in this program that it may disappoint the expectations of nonminority firms. When effectuating a limited and properly tailored remedy to cure the effects of prior discrimination, such "a sharing of the burden" by innocent parties is not impermissible. . . . The actual "burden" shouldered by nonminority firms is relatively light in this connection when we consider the scope of this public works program as compared with overall construction contracting opportunities. Moreover, although we may assume that the complaining parties are innocent of any discriminatory conduct, it was within congressional power to act on the assumption that in the past some nonminority businesses may have reaped competitive benefit over the years from the virtual exclusion of minority firms from these contracting opportunities.

Another challenge to the validity of the MBE program is the assertion that it is underinclusive—that it limits its benefit to specified minority groups rather than extending its remedial objectives to all businesses whose access to government contracting is impaired by the effects of disadvantage or discrimination. Such an extension would, of course, be appropriate for Congress to provide; it is not a function for the courts.

Even in this context, the well-established concept that a legislature may take one step at a time to remedy only part of a broader problem is not without relevance. . . . We are not reviewing a federal program that seeks to confer a preferred status upon a nondisadvantaged minority or give special assistance to only one of several groups established to be similarly disadvantaged minorities. Even in such a setting, the Congress is not without a certain authority. . . .

The Congress has not sought to give select minority groups a preferred standing in the construction industry, but has embarked on a remedial program to place them on a more equitable footing with respect to public contracting opportunities. There has been no showing in this case that Congress has inadvertently effected an invidious discrimination by excluding from coverage an identifiable minority group that has been the victim of a degree of disadvantage and discrimination equal to or greater than that suffered by the groups encompassed by the MBE program. It is not inconceivable that on very special facts a case might be made to challenge the congressional decision to limit MBE eligibility to the particular minority groups identified in the Act. . . . But on this record we find no basis to hold that Congress is without authority to undertake the kind of limited remedial effort represented by the MBE program. Congress, not the courts, has the heavy burden of dealing with a host of intractable economic and social problems.

It is also contended that the MBE program is overinclusive—that it bestows a benefit on businesses identified by racial or ethnic criteria which cannot be justified on the basis of competitive criteria or as a remedy for the present effects of identified prior discrimination. It is conceivable that a particular application of the program may have this effect; however, the peculiarities of specific applications are not before us in this case. We are not presented here with a challenge involving a specific award of a construction contract or the denial of a waiver request; such questions of specific application must await future cases.

. . . The administrative program contains measures to effectuate the congressional objective of assuring legitimate participation by disadvantaged MBE's. Administrative definition has tightened some less definite aspects of the statutory identification of the minority groups encompassed by the program. There is administrative scrutiny to identify and eliminate from participation in the program MBE's who are not "bona fide" within the regulations and guidelines; for example, spurious minority-front entities can be exposed. A significant aspect of this surveillance is the complaint procedure available for reporting "unjust participation by an enterprise or individuals in the MBE program." . . . And even as to specific contract awards, waiver is available to avoid dealing with an MBE who is attempting to exploit the remedial aspects of the program by charging an unreasonable price, *i.e.,* a price not attributable to the present effects of past discrimination. . . . We must assume that Congress intended close scrutiny of false claims and prompt action on them.

Grantees are given the opportunity to demonstrate that their best efforts will not succeed or have not succeeded in achieving the statutory 10% target for minority firm participation within the limitations of the program's remedial objectives. In these cir-

cumstances a waiver or partial waiver is available once compliance has been demonstrated. A waiver may be sought and granted at any time during the contracting process, or even prior to letting contracts if the facts warrant.

Nor is the program defective because a waiver may be sought by the grantee and not by prime contractors who may experience difficulty in fulfilling contract obligations to assure minority participation. It may be administratively cumbersome, but the wisdom of concentrating responsibility at the grantee level is not for us to evaluate; the purpose is to allow the EDA to maintain close supervision of the operation of the MBE program. The administrative complaint mechanism allows for grievances of prime contractors who assert that a grantee has failed to seek a waiver in an appropriate case. Finally, we note that where private parties, as opposed to governmental entities, transgress the limitations inherent in the MBE program, the possibility of constitutional violation is more removed. . . .

That the use of racial and ethnic criteria is premised on assumptions rebuttable in the administrative process gives reasonable assurance that application of the MBE program will be limited to accomplishing the remedial objectives contemplated by Congress and that misapplications of the racial and ethnic criteria can be remedied. In dealing with this facial challenge to the statute, doubts must be resolved in support of the congressional judgment that this limited program is a necessary step to effectuate the constitutional mandate for equality of economic opportunity. The MBE provision may be viewed as a pilot project, appropriately limited in extent and duration, and subject to reassessment and re-evaluation by the Congress prior to any extension or re-enactment. Miscarriages of administration could have only a transitory economic impact on businesses not encompassed by the program, and would not be irremedial.

. . . Any preference based on racial or ethnic criteria must necessarily receive a most searching examination to make sure that it does not conflict with constitutional guarantees. This case is one which requires, and which has received, that kind of examination. This opinion does not adopt, either expressly or implicitly, the formulas of analysis articulated in such cases as *University of California Regents v. Bakke,* 438 U.S. 265 (1978). However, our analysis demonstrates that the MBE provision would survive judicial review under either "test" articulated in the several *Bakke* opinions. The MBE provision of the Public Works Employment Act of 1977 does not violate the Constitution.

Affirmed.

[The concurring opinion of MR. JUSTICE POWELL is omitted.]

* * *

MR. JUSTICE MARSHALL, with whom MR. JUSTICE BRENNAN and MR. JUSTICE BLACKMUN join, concurring in the judgment.

My resolution of the constitutional issue in this case is governed by the separate opinion I coauthored in *University of California Regents v. Bakke.* . . . In my view, the 10% minority set-aside provision of the Public Works Employment Act of 1977 passes constitutional muster under the standard announced in that opinion.

. . . In our view, then, the proper inquiry is whether racial classifications designed to further remedial purposes serve important governmental objectives and are substantially related to achievement of those objectives. . . .

Judged under this standard, the 10% minority set-aside provision at issue in this case is plainly constitutional. Indeed, the question is not even a close one.

* * *

MR. JUSTICE STEWART, with whom MR. JUSTICE REHNQUIST joins, dissenting.

. . . The equal protection standard of the Constitution has one clear and central meaning—it absolutely prohibits invidious discrimination by government. That standard must be met by every State under the Equal Protection Clause of the Fourteenth Amendment. . . . And that standard must be met by the United States under the Due Process Clause of the Fifth Amendment. Under our Constitution, any official action that treats a person differently on account of his race or ethnic origin is inherently suspect and presumptively invalid. . . .

. . . On its face, the minority business enterprise (MBE) provision at issue in this case denies the equal protection of the laws. The Public Works Employment Act of 1977 directs that all project construction shall be performed by those private contractors who submit the lowest competitive bids and who meet established criteria of responsibility. . . . One class of contracting firms—defined solely according to the racial and ethnic attributes of their owners—is, however, excepted from the full rigor of these requirements with respect to a percentage of each federal grant. The statute, on its face and in effect, thus bars a class to which the petitioners belong from having the opportunity to receive a government benefit, and bars the members of that class solely on the basis of their race or ethnic background. This is precisely the kind of law that the guarantee of equal protection forbids.

[The dissenting opinion of MR. JUSTICE STEVENS is omitted.]

WYGANT V. JACKSON BOARD OF EDUCATION
476 U.S. 267 (1986)

In 1972 the Jackson, Michigan, Board of Education, because of racial tensions in the community that extended to its schools, considered adding a layoff provision to the collective bargaining agreement (CBA) between the board and the Jackson Education Association (union) that would protect employee members of certain minority groups against layoffs. The agreement (Article XII of the CBA) reached between the board and the union provided that if it became necessary to lay off teachers, those with the most seniority would be retained, except that at no time would there be a greater percentage · of minority personnel laid off than the current percentage of minority personnel employed at the time of the layoff. When layoffs became necessary in 1974, it was evident that adherence to the CBA would result in the layoff of tenured white teachers while minority teachers on probationary status were retained. Rather than comply with Article XII, the board retained the tenured teachers and laid off probationary minority teachers, thus failing to maintain the percentage of minority personnel that existed at the time of the layoff. The union, together with two minority teachers who had been laid off, brought suit in federal court, claiming that the board's failure to adhere to the layoff provision violated the equal protection clause of the Fourteenth Amendment and Title VII. The district court upheld the constitutionality of the layoff provision, holding that racial preferences granted by the board need not be grounded on a finding of prior discrimination but were permissible under the equal protection clause as an attempt to remedy societal discrimination by providing role models for minority school children. The court of appeals affirmed. *Vote: 5-4.*

* * *

JUSTICE POWELL announced the judgment of the Court and delivered an opinion in which CHIEF JUSTICE [BURGER] and JUSTICE REHNQUIST joined and in all but Part IV of which JUSTICE O'CONNOR joined.

This case presents the question whether a school board, consistent with the Equal Protection Clause, may extend preferential protection against layoffs to some of its employees because of their race or national origin.

. . . The Court has recognized that the level of scrutiny does not change merely because the challenged classification operates against a group that historically has not been subject to governmental discrimination. *Mississippi University for Women v. Hogan,* 458 U.S. 718, 724, n. 9 (1982) . . . In this case, Article XII of the CBA operates against whites and in favor of certain minorities, and therefore constitutes a classification based on race. . . . There are two prongs to this examination. First, any racial classification "must be justified by a compelling governmental interest." . . . Second, the means chosen by the State to effectuate its purpose must be "narrowly tailored to the achievement of that goal." . . . We must decide whether the layoff provision is supported by a compelling state purpose and whether the means chosen to accomplish that purpose are narrowly tailored.

The Court of Appeals, relying on the reasoning and language of the District Court's opinion, held that the Board's interest in providing minority role models for its minority students, as an attempt to alleviate the effects of societal discrimination, was sufficiently important to justify the racial classification embodied in the layoff provision. . . . The court discerned a need for more minority faculty role models by finding that the percentage of minority teachers was less than the percentage of minority students. . . .

This Court never has held that societal discrimination alone is sufficient to justify a racial classification. Rather, the Court has insisted upon some showing of prior discrimination by the governmental unit involved before allowing limited use of racial classifications in order to remedy such discrimination. This Court's reasoning in *Hazelwood School District v. United States,* 433 U.S. 299 (1977), illustrates that the relevant analysis in cases involving proof of discrimination by statistical disparity focuses on those disparities that demonstrate such prior governmental discrimination. . . .

Unlike the analysis in *Hazelwood,* the role model theory employed by the District Court has no logical stopping point. The role model theory allows the Board to engage in discriminatory hiring and layoff practices long past the point required by any legitimate remedial purpose. Indeed, by tying the required percentage of minority teachers to the percentage of minority students, it requires just the sort of year-to-year calibration the Court stated was unnecessary in *Swann* [*v. Charlotte-Mecklenburg Board of Education,* 402 U.S. 1 (1971)]. . . .

Moreover, because the role model theory does not necessarily bear a relationship to the harm caused by prior discriminatory hiring practices, it actually could be used to escape the obligation to remedy such practices by justifying the small percentage of black teachers by reference to the small percentage of black students. . . . Carried to its logical extreme, the idea that black students are better off with black teachers could lead to the very system the Court rejected in *Brown v. Board of Education,* 347 U.S. 483 (1954) (*Brown I*).

Societal discrimination, without more, is too amorphous a basis for imposing a racially classified remedy. The role model theory announced by the District Court and the resultant holding typify this indefiniteness. There are numerous explanations for a disparity between the percentage of minority students and the percentage of minority faculty, many of them completely unrelated to discrimination of any kind. In fact, there is no apparent connection between the two groups. Nevertheless, the District Court combined irrelevant comparisons between these two groups with an indisputable statement that there has been societal discrimination, and upheld state action predicated upon racial classifications. No one doubts that there has been serious racial discrimination in this country. But as the basis for imposing discriminatory *legal* remedies that work against innocent people, societal discrimination is insufficient and overexpansive. In the absence of particularized findings, a court could uphold remedies that are ageless in their reach into the past, and timeless in their ability to affect the future.

Respondents also now argue that their purpose in adopting the layoff provision was to remedy prior discrimination against minorities by the Jackson School District in hiring teachers. Public schools, like other public employers, operate under two interrelated constitutional duties. They are under a clear command from this Court, starting with *Brown v. Board of Education* [*Brown II*], 349 U.S. 294 (1955), to eliminate every vestige of racial segregation and discrimination in the schools. Pursuant to that goal, race-conscious remedial action may be necessary. . . . On the other hand, public employers, including public schools, also must act in accordance with a "core purpose of the Fourteenth Amendment" which is to "do away with all governmentally imposed discriminations based on race." *Palmore v. Sidote,* [466 U.S. 429, 432 (1984)]. These related constitutional duties are not always harmonious; reconciling them requires public employers to act with extraordinary care. In particular, a public employer like the Board must ensure that, before it embarks on an affirmative-action program, it has convincing evidence that remedial action is warranted. That is, it must have sufficient evidence to justify the conclusion that there has been prior discrimination.

Evidentiary support for the conclusion that remedial action is warranted becomes crucial when the remedial program is challenged in court by nonminority employees. In this case, for example, petitioners contended at trial that the remedial program—Article XII—had the purpose and effect of instituting a racial classification that was not justified by a remedial purpose. . . . In such a case, the trial court must make a factual determination that the employer had a strong basis in evidence for its conclusion that remedial action was necessary. The ultimate burden remains with the employees to demonstrate the unconstitutionality of an affirmative-action program. But unless such a determination is made, an appellate court reviewing a challenge by nonminority employees to remedial action cannot determine whether the race-based action is justified as a remedy for prior discrimination.

Despite the fact that Article XII has spawned years of litigation and three separate lawsuits, no such determination ever has been made. Although its litigation position was different, the Board [in two trial court cases at the federal and state levels] denied the existence of prior discriminatory hiring practices. . . . This precise issue was litigated in both those suits. Both courts concluded that any statistical disparities were the result of general societal discrimination, not of prior discrimination by the Board. The Board now contends that, given another opportunity, it could establish the existence of prior discrimination. Although this argument seems belated at this point in the proceedings, we need not consider the question since we conclude below that the layoff provision was not a legally appropriate means of achieving even a compelling purpose.

[*Part IV*] The Court of Appeals examined the means chosen to accomplish the Board's race-conscious purposes under a test of "reasonableness." That standard has no support in the decisions of this Court. As demonstrated . . . our decisions always have employed a more stringent standard—however articulated—to test the validity of the means chosen by a State to accomplish its race-conscious purposes. . . . Under strict scrutiny the means chosen to accomplish the State's asserted purpose must be specifically and narrowly framed to accomplish that purpose. . . .

We have recognized, however, that in order to remedy the effects of prior discrimination, it may be necessary to take race into account. As part of this Nation's dedication to eradicating discrimination, innocent persons may be called upon to bear some of the burden of the remedy. . . .

. . . Many of our cases involve union seniority plans with employees who are typically heavily dependent on wages for their day-to-day living. Even a temporary layoff may have adverse financial as well as psychological effects. A worker may invest many productive years in one job and one city with the expectation of earning the stability and security of seniority. "At that point, the rights and expectations surrounding seniority make up what is probably the most valuable capital asset that the worker

'owns,' worth even more than the current equity in his home." . . . Layoffs disrupt these settled expectations in a way that general hiring goals do not.

While hiring goals impose a diffuse burden, often foreclosing only one of several opportunities, layoffs impose the entire burden of achieving racial equality on particular individuals, often resulting in serious disruption of their lives. That burden is too intrusive. We therefore hold that, as a means of accomplishing purposes that otherwise may be legitimate, the Board's layoff plan is not sufficiently narrowly tailored. Other, less intrusive means of accomplishing similar purposes—such as the adoption of hiring goals—are available. For these reasons, the Board's selection of layoffs as the means to accomplish even a valid purpose cannot satisfy the demands of the Equal Protection Clause.

We accordingly reverse the judgment of the Court of Appeals for the Sixth Circuit.

It is so ordered.

[The opinion of JUSTICE O'CONNOR, concurring in part and concurring in the judgment, is omitted.]

[The opinion of JUSTICE WHITE, concurring in the judgment, is omitted.]

* * *

JUSTICE MARSHALL, with whom JUSTICE BRENNAN and JUSTICE BLACKMUN join, dissenting.

. . . The sole question posed by this case is whether the Constitution prohibits a union and a local school board from developing a collective-bargaining agreement that apportions layoffs between two racially determined groups as a means of preserving the effects of an affirmative hiring policy, the constitutionality of which is unchallenged.

Agreement upon a means for applying the Equal Protection Clause to an affirmative-action program has eluded this Court every time the issue has come before us. . . .

. . . Despite the Court's inability to agree on a route, we have reached a common destination in sustaining affirmative action against constitutional attack. In *Bakke,* we determined that a state institution may take race into account as a factor in its decisions, . . . and in *Fullilove,* the Court upheld a congressional preference for minority contractors because the measure was legitimately designed to ameliorate the present effects of past discrimination. . . .

In this case, it should not matter which test the Court applies. What is most important, under any approach to the constitutional analysis, is that a reviewing court genuinely consider the circumstances of the provision at issue. The history and application of Article XII, assuming verification upon a proper record, demonstrate that this provision would pass constitutional muster, no matter which standard the Court should adopt.

The principal state purpose supporting Article XII is the need to preserve the levels of faculty integration achieved through the affirmative hiring policy adopted in the early 1970's. . . . Justification for the hiring policy itself is found in the turbulent history of the effort to integrate the Jackson public schools—not even mentioned in the plurality opinion—which attests to the bona fides of the Board's current employment practices.

. . . Were I satisfied with the record before us, I would hold that the state purpose of preserving the integrity of a valid hiring policy—which in turn sought to achieve diversity and stability for the benefit of *all* students—was sufficient, in this case, to satisfy the demands of the Constitution.

The second part of any constitutional assessment of this disputed plan requires us to examine the means chosen to achieve the state purpose. Again, the history of Article XII, insofar as we can determine it, is the best source of assistance.

. . . Under JUSTICE POWELL's approach, the community of Jackson, having painfully watched the hard-won benefits of its integration efforts vanish as a result of massive layoffs, would be informed today, simply, that preferential layoff protection is never permissible because hiring policies serve the same purpose at a lesser cost. . . . As a matter of logic as well as fact, a hiring policy achieves no purpose at all if it is eviscerated by layoffs. JUSTICE POWELL's position is untenable.

JUSTICE POWELL has concluded, by focusing exclusively on the undisputed hardship of losing a job, that the Equal Protection Clause always bars race-conscious layoff plans. This analysis overlooks, however, the important fact that Article XII does not cause the loss of jobs; someone will lose a job under any layoff plan and, whoever it is, that person will not deserve it. Any *per se* prohibition against layoff protection, therefore, must rest upon a premise that the tradition of basing layoff decisions on seniority is so fundamental that its modification can never be permitted. Our cases belie that premise.

The general practice of basing employment decisions on relative seniority may be upset for the sake of other public policies. For example, a court may displace innocent workers by granting retroactive seniority to victims of employment discrimination. *Franks v. Bowman Transportation Co.,* 424 U.S. 747, 775 (1976). Further, this Court has long held that "employee expectations arising from a seniority system agreement may be modified by statutes furthering a strong public policy interest." . . . And we have recognized that collective-bargaining agreements may go further than statutes in enhancing the seniority of certain employees for the purpose of fostering legitimate interests. . . . Ac-cordingly, we have upheld one collectively bargained provision that bestowed enhanced seniority on those who had served in the military before employment . . . and another that gave preferred seniority status to union chairmen, to the detriment of veterans. . . .

. . . These cases establish that protection from layoff is not altogether unavailable as a tool for achieving legitimate societal goals. It remains to be determined whether the particular form of layoff protection embodied in Article XII falls among the permissible means for preserving minority proportions on the teaching staff.

Article XII is a narrow provision because it allocates the impact of an unavoidable burden proportionately between two racial groups. It places no absolute burden or benefit on one race, and, within the confines of constant minority proportions, it preserves the hierarchy of seniority in the selection of individuals for layoff. Race is a factor, along with seniority, in determining which individuals the school system will lose; it is not alone dispositive of any individual's fate. . . . Moreover, Article XII does not use layoff protection as a tool for *increasing* minority representation; achievement of that goal is entrusted to the less severe hiring policies. And Article XII is narrow in the temporal sense as well. The very bilateral process that gave rise to Article XII when its adoption was necessary will also occasion its demise when remedial measures are no longer required. Finally, Article XII modifies contractual expectations that do not themselves carry any connotation of merit or achievement; it does not interfere with the "cherished American ethos" of "[f]airness in individual competition," . . . depriving individuals of an opportunity that they could be said to deserve. In all of these important ways, Article XII metes out the hardship of layoffs in a manner that achieves its purpose with the smallest possible deviation from established norms.

The Board's goal of preserving minority proportions could have been achieved, perhaps, in a different way. For example, if layoffs had been determined by lottery, the ultimate effect would have been retention of current racial percentages. A random system, however, would place every teacher in equal jeopardy, working a much greater upheaval of the seniority hierarchy than that occasioned by Article XII; it is not at all a less restrictive means of achieving the Board's goal. Another possible approach would have been a freeze on layoffs of minority teachers. This measure, too, would have been substantially more burdensome than Article XII, not only by necessitating the layoff of a greater number of white teachers, but also by erecting an absolute distinction between the races, one to be benefited and one to be burdened, in a way that Article XII avoids. Indeed, neither petitioners nor any Justice of this Court has suggested an alternative to

Article XII that would have attained the stated goal in any narrower or more equitable a fashion. Nor can I conceive of one.

It is no accident that this least burdensome of all conceivable options is the very provision that the parties adopted. For Article XII was forged in the crucible of clashing interests. All of the economic powers of the predominantly white teachers' union were brought to bear against those of the elected Board, and the process yielded consensus.

[The dissenting opinion of JUSTICE STEVENS is omitted.]

WARTH V. SELDIN
422 U.S. 490 (1975)

Metro-Act of Rochester, Inc., a not-for-profit corporation that fostered action to alleviate the housing shortage for low- and moderate-income persons in the Rochester, New York, area, and eight individual plaintiffs filed a class action suit in 1974 against Penfield, a suburb of Rochester. They claimed that the town's zoning ordinance excluded persons of low and moderate income from living in the town, in violation of their constitutional rights and §§ 1981, 1982, and 1983. Plaintiffs Victor Vinkey, Lynn Reichert, Robert Warth, and Katherine Harris were residents of Rochester, all of whom owned real property in and paid property taxes to that city. Plaintiff Andelino Ortiz, of Spanish/Puerto Rican ancestry, owned property in and paid taxes to Rochester but resided in Wayland, some 42 miles from Penfield, where he was employed. Plaintiffs Clara Broadnax and Rosa Sinkler were black, and Angelea Reyes was Puerto Rican. The plaintiffs specifically alleged that Penfield's zoning ordinance allocated 98% of the town's vacant land to single-family detached housing and imposed unreasonable requirements relating to lot size, setback, floor area, and habitable space, which increased the cost of single-family detached housing beyond the means of persons of low and moderate income. They also alleged that only 0.3% of the land available for residential construction was allotted to multifamily structures and that members of Penfield's Town, Zoning, and Planning Boards had acted in an arbitrary and discriminatory manner by (a) delaying action on proposals for low- and moderate-cost housing, (b) refusing to grant necessary variances and permits, (c) failing to provide necessary support services for low- and moderate-cost housing projects, and (d) amending the ordinance to make approval of such projects virtually impossible. The Rochester Home Builders Association, an association of firms engaged in residential construction in the Rochester area, and the Housing Council in the Monroe County Area, Inc., a not-for-profit New York corporation comprising some 71 public and private organizations interested in housing problems, sought to intervene in the case as party-plaintiff. The district court held that (a) Home Builders and Housing Council lacked standing in the case, (b) the complaint failed to state a claim on which relief could be granted, (c) the suit should not proceed as a class action, and (d) Home Builders should not be permitted to intervene. The court of appeals affirmed, reaching only the standing questions. *Vote: 5-4.*

* * *

MR. JUSTICE POWELL delivered the opinion of the Court.

. . . [W]e turn first to the claims of petitioners Ortiz, Reyes, Sinkler and Broadnax, each of whom asserts standing as a person of low or moderate income and, coincidentally, as a member of a minority racial or ethnic group. We must assume, taking the allegation of the complaint as true, that Penfield's zoning ordinance and the pattern of enforcement by respondent officials have had the purpose and effect of excluding persons of low and moderate income, many of whom are members of racial or ethnic minority groups. We also assume, for purposes here, that such intentional exclusionary practices, if proved in a proper case, would be adjudged violative of the constitutional and statutory rights of the persons excluded.

But the fact that these petitioners share attributes common to persons who may have been excluded from residence in the town is an insufficient predicate for the conclusion that petitioners themselves have been excluded, or that the respondents' assertedly illegal actions have violated their rights. Petitioners must allege and show that they personally have been injured, not that injury has been suffered by other, unidentified members of the class to which they belong and which they purport to represent. Unless these petitioners can thus demonstrate the requisite case or controversy between themselves personally and respondents, "none may seek relief on behalf of himself or any other member of the class." *O'Shea v. Littleton*, 414 U.S. 488, 494 (1974) . . .

In their complaint, petitioners Ortiz, Reyes, Sinkler, and Broadnax alleged in conclusory terms that they are among the persons excluded by respondents' actions. None of them has ever resided in Penfield; each claims at least implicitly that he desires, or has desired, to do so. Each asserts, moreover, that he made some effort at some time, to locate housing in Penfield that was at once within his means and adequate for his family's needs. Each claims that his efforts proved fruitless. We may assume, as petitioners allege, that respondents' actions have contributed, perhaps substantially, to the cost of housing in Penfield. But there remains the question of whether petitioners' inability to locate suitable housing in Penfield reasonably can be said to have resulted, in any concretely demonstrable way, from respondents' alleged constitutional and statutory infractions. Petitioners must allege facts from which it reasonably could be inferred that, absent the respondents' restrictive zoning practices, there is a substantial probability that they would have been able to purchase or lease in Penfield and that, if the court affords the relief requested, the asserted inability of petitioners will be removed. . . .

We find the record devoid of the necessary allegations. As the Court of Appeals noted, none of the petitioners has a present interest in any Penfield property; none is himself subject to the ordinance's strictures; and none has ever been denied a variance or permit by respondent officials. . . . Instead, petitioners claim that respondents' enforcement of the ordinance against third parties—developers, builders, and the like—has had the consequence of precluding the construction of housing suitable to their needs at prices they might be able to afford. The fact that the harm to petitioners may have resulted indirectly does not in itself preclude standing. When a governmental prohibition or restriction imposed on one party causes specific harm to a third party, harm that a constitutional provision or statute was intended to prevent, the indirectness of the injury does not necessarily deprive the person harmed of standing to vindicate his rights. . . . But it may make it substantially more difficult to meet the minimum requirement of Art. III: to establish that, in fact, the asserted injury was the consequence of the defendants' actions, or that prospective relief will remove the harm.

Here, by their own admission, realization of petitioners' desire to live in Penfield always has depended on the efforts and willingness of third parties to build low- and moderate-cost housing. The record specifically refers to only two such efforts: that of Penfield Better Homes Corp., in late 1969, to obtain the rezoning of certain land in Penfield to allow the construction of subsidized cooperative townhouses that could be purchased by persons of moderate income; and a similar effort by O'Brien Homes, Inc., in late 1971. But the record is devoid of any indication that these projects, or other like projects, would have satisfied petitioners' needs at prices they could afford, or that, were the court to remove the obstructions attributable to respondents, such relief would benefit petitioners. Indeed, petitioners' descriptions of their individual financial situations and housing needs suggest precisely the

contrary—that their inability to reside in Penfield is the consequence of the economics of the area housing market, rather than of respondents' assertedly illegal acts. In short, the facts alleged fail to support an actionable causal relationship between Penfield's zoning practices and petitioners' asserted injury.

In support of their position, petitioners refer to several decisions in the District Courts and Courts of Appeals, acknowledging standing in low-income, minority-group plaintiffs to challenge exclusionary zoning practices. In those cases, however, the plaintiffs challenged zoning restrictions as applied to particular projects that would supply housing within their means, and of which they were intended residents. The plaintiffs thus were able to demonstrate that unless relief from assertedly illegal actions was forthcoming, their immediate and personal interests would be harmed. Petitioners here assert no like circumstances. Instead, they rely on little more than the remote possibility, unsubstantiated by allegations of fact, that their situation might have been better had respondents acted otherwise, and might improve were the court to afford relief.

We hold only that a plaintiff who seeks to challenge exclusionary zoning practices must allege specific, concrete facts demonstrating that the challenged practices harm *him,* and that he personally would benefit in a tangible way from the court's intervention. Absent the necessary allegations of demonstrable, particularized injury, there can be no confidence of "a real need to exercise the power of judicial review" or that relief can be framed "no broader than required by the precise facts to which the court's ruling would be applied." *Schlesinger v. Reservists to Stop the War,* 418 U.S., at 221-222 [1974].

The petitioners who assert standing on the basis of their status as taxpayers of the city of Rochester present a different set of problems. These "taxpayer-petitioners" claim that they are suffering economic injury consequent to Penfield's allegedly discriminatory and exclusionary zoning practices. Their argument, in brief, is that Penfield's persistent refusal to allow or to facilitate construction of low- and moderate-cost housing forces the city of Rochester to provide more such housing than it otherwise would do; that to provide such housing, Rochester must allow certain tax abatements; and that as the amount of tax-abated property increases, Rochester taxpayers are forced to assume an increased tax burden in order to finance essential public services.

"Of course, pleadings must be something more than an ingenious academic exercise in the conceivable." *United States v. SCRAP,* 412 U.S., at 688 [1973]. We think the complaint of the taxpayer-petitioners is little more than such an exercise. Apart from the conjectural nature of the asserted injury, the line of causation between Penfield's actions and such injury is not apparent from the complaint. Whatever may occur in Penfield, the injury complained of—increases in taxation—results only from decisions made by the appropriate Rochester authorities, who are not parties to this case.

... We turn next to the standing problems presented by the petitioner associations—Metro-Act of Rochester, Inc., one of the original plaintiffs; Housing Council in the Monroe County Area, Inc., which the original plaintiffs sought to join as a party-plaintiff; and Rochester Home Builders Association, Inc., which moved in the District Court for leave to intervene as plaintiff. There is no question that an association may have standing in its own right to seek judicial relief from injury to itself and to vindicate whatever rights and immunities the association itself may enjoy. Moreover, in attempting to secure relief from injury to itself the association may assert the rights of its members, at least so long as the challenged infractions adversely affect its members' associational ties. . . . With limited exception of Metro-Act, however, none of the associational petitioners here has asserted injury to itself.

... We do not understand Metro-Act to argue that Penfield residents themselves have been denied any constitutional rights, affording them a cause of action under . . . § 1983. Instead, their complaint is that they have been harmed directly by the exclusion of others. This is an attempt to raise putative rights of third parties, and none of the exceptions that allow such claims is present here. In these circumstances, we conclude that it is inappropriate to allow Metro-Act to invoke the judicial process.

... The rules of standing, whether as aspects of the Art. III case-or-controversy requirement or as reflections of prudential considerations defining and limiting the role of the courts, are threshold determinants of the propriety of judicial intervention. It is the responsibility of the complainant clearly to allege facts demonstrating that he is a proper party to invoke judicial resolution of the dispute and the exercise of the court's remedial powers. We agree with the District Court and Court of Appeals that none of the petitioners here has met this threshold requirement. Accordingly, the judgment of the Court of Appeals is

Affirmed.

* * *

MR. JUSTICE BRENNAN, with whom MR. JUSTICE WHITE and MR. JUSTICE MARSHALL join, dissenting.

... Here, the very fact that, as the Court stresses, these petitioners' claim rests in part upon proving the intentions and capabilities of third parties to build in Penfield suitable housing which they can afford, coupled with the exclusionary character of the claim on the merits, makes it particularly inappropriate to assume that these petitioners' lack of specificity reflects a fatal weakness in their theory of causation. Obviously they cannot be expected, prior to discovery and trial, to know the future plans of building companies, the precise details of the housing market in Penfield, or everything which has transpired in 15 years of application of the Penfield zoning ordinance, including every housing plan suggested and refused. To require them to allege such facts is to require them to prove their case on paper in order to get into court at all, reverting to the form of fact pleading long abjured in the federal courts. This Court has not required such unachievable specificity in standing cases in the past, . . . and the fact that it does so now can only be explained by an indefensible determination by the Court to close the doors of the federal courts to claims of this kind. Understandably, today's decision will be read as revealing hostility to breaking down even unconstitutional zoning barriers that frustrate the deep human yearning of low-income and minority groups for decent housing they can afford in decent surroundings.

[The dissenting opinion of MR. JUSTICE DOUGLAS is omitted.]

HAVENS REALTY CORP. V. COLEMAN
455 U.S. 363 (1982)

A class action suit was brought against Havens Realty Corporation, which owned and operated two apartment complexes in Henrico County, Virginia, a suburb of Richmond, and one of its employees, Rose Jones. The complaint was filed in district court by Paul Coles, Sylvia Coleman, R. Kent Willis, and Housing Opportunities Made Equal (HOME), a nonprofit corporation whose purpose was to make equal employment in housing a reality in the Richmond metropolitan area. They alleged that the de-fendants engaged in racial steering practices, in violation of § 804 of the Fair Housing Act. Paul Coles, who was black, attempted to rent an apartment from Havens but was told that no apartments were available. Coleman and Willis were testers employed by HOME to determine whether Havens practiced racial steering. Coleman, the black tester, was told that no apartments were available, whereas Willis, the white tester, was told that there were vacancies. Later, Coleman made another inquiry and was told that there were no vacancies, and a white tester for HOME, who was not a party to the complaint, was given contrary information that same day. The complaint alleged that Havens's practices had deprived the plaintiffs the important social, professional, business and economic, and political and aesthetic benefits of interracial association that arise from living in integrated communities. They also alleged that Havens's steering practices had frustrated HOME's housing counseling and referral services.

The district court held that the plaintiffs lacked standing and that their claims were barred by the Act's 180-day statute of limitations. The court of appeals reversed and remanded, holding that the allegations of injury to the respondents were sufficient to withstand a motion to dismiss and that their claims were not time-barred because Havens's conduct constituted a continuing violation lasting through the time of the alleged Coles incident, which was within the 180-day period. The Supreme Court agreed with the court of appeals on the statute of limitations issue. *Vote: 9-0.*

* * *

JUSTICE BRENNAN delivered the opinion of the Court.

. . . Our inquiry with respect to the standing issues raised in this case is guided by our decision in *Gladstone, Realtors v. Village of Bellwood,* 441 U.S. 91 (1979). There we considered whether six individuals and the village of Bellwood had standing to sue under § 812 of the Fair Housing Act . . . to redress injuries allegedly caused by the racial steering practices of two real estate brokerage firms. Based on the complaints, "as illuminated by subsequent discovery," . . . we concluded that the village and four of the individual plaintiffs did have standing to sue under the Fair Housing Act. . . . In reaching that conclusion, we held that "Congress intended standing under § 812 to extend to the full limits of Art. III" and that the courts accordingly lack the authority to create prudential barriers to standing in suits brought under that section. . . . Thus the sole requirement for standing to sue under § 812 is the Art. III minima of injury in fact: that the plaintiff alleges that as a result of the defendant's actions he has suffered "a distinct and palpable injury." . . . With this understanding, we proceed to determine whether each of the respondents in the present case has the requisite standing.

The Court of Appeals held that Coleman and Willis have standing to sue in two capacities: as "testers" and as individuals deprived of the benefits of interracial association. We first address the question of "tester" standing.

In the present context, "testers" are individuals who, without an intent to rent or purchase a home or apartment, pose as renters or purchasers for the purpose of collecting evidence of unlawful steering practices. Section 804(d) states that it is unlawful for an individual or firm covered by the Act "[t]o represent to *any person* because of race, color, religion, sex, or national origin that any dwelling is not available for inspection, sale, or rental when such dwelling is in fact so available," . . . a prohibition made enforceable through the creation of an explicit cause of action in § 812(a) of the Act. . . . Congress has thus conferred on all "persons" a legal right to truthful information about available housing.

This congressional intention cannot be overlooked in determining whether testers have standing to sue. As we have previously recognized, "[t]he actual or threatened injury required by Art. III may exist solely by virtue of 'statutes creating legal rights, the invasion of which creates standing. . . .' " *Warth v. Seldin,* [422 U.S. 490, 500 (1975)] . . . Section 804(d), which, in terms, establishes an enforceable right to truthful information concerning the availability of housing, is such an enactment. A tester who has been the object of a misrepresentation made unlawful under § 804(d) has suffered injury in precisely the form the statute was intended to guard against, and therefore has standing to maintain a claim for damages under the Act's provisions. That the tester may have approached the real estate agent fully expecting that he would receive false information, and without any intention of buying or renting a home, does not negate the simple fact of injury within the meaning of § 804(d). . . . Whereas Congress, in prohibiting discriminatory refusals to sell or rent in § 804(a) of the Act, . . . required that there be a "bona fide offer" to rent or purchase, Congress plainly omitted any such requirement insofar as it banned discriminatory representations in § 804(d).

In the instant case, respondent Coleman—the black tester—alleged injury to her statutorily created right to truthful housing information. As part of the complaint, she averred that petitioners told her on four different occasions that apartments were not available in the Henrico Country complexes while informing white testers that apartments were available. If the facts are as alleged, then respondent has suffered "specific injury" from the challenged acts of petitioners, . . . and the Art. III requirement of injury in fact is satisfied.

Respondent Willis' situation is different. He made no allegation that petitioners misrepresented to him that apartments were unavailable in two apartment complexes. To the contrary, Willis alleged that on each occasion that he inquired he was informed that apartments *were* available. As such,

Willis has alleged no injury to his statutory right to accurate information concerning the availability of housing. We thus discern no support for the Court of Appeals' holding that Willis has standing to sue in his capacity as a tester. More to the point, because Willis does not allege that he was a victim of discriminatory misrepresentation, he has not pleaded a cause of action under § 804(d). We must therefore reverse the Court of Appeals' judgment insofar as it reversed the District Court's dismissal of Willis' "tester" claims.

Coleman and Willis argue in this Court, and the Court of Appeals held, that irrespective of their status as testers, they should have been allowed to proceed beyond the pleading stage inasmuch as they have alleged that petitioners' steering practices deprived them of the benefits that result from living in an integrated community. This concept of "neighborhood" standing differs from that of "tester" standing in that the injury asserted is an indirect one: an adverse impact on the neighborhood in which the plaintiff resides resulting from the steering of persons other than the plaintiff. By contrast, the injury underlying tester standing—the denial of the tester's own statutory right to truthful housing information caused by misrepresentations to the tester—is a direct one. . . . The distinction is between "third-party" and "first-party" standing.

This distinction is, however, of little significance in deciding whether a plaintiff has standing to sue under § 812 of the Fair Housing Act. . . . *Bellwood* . . . held that the only requirement for standing to sue under § 812 is the Art. III requirement of injury in fact. As long as respondents have alleged distinct and palpable injuries that are "fairly traceable" to petitioners' actions, the Art. III requirement of injury in fact is satisfied. . . . The question before us, then, is whether injury in fact has been sufficiently alleged.

The two individual respondents, who according to the complaint were "residents of the City of Richmond or Henrico County," alleged that the racial steering practices of petitioners have deprived them of "the right to the important social, professional, business, economic, political and aesthetic benefits of interracial associations that arise from living in integrated communities free from discriminatory housing practices." . . . The type of injury alleged thus clearly resembles that which we found palpable in *Bellwood*. . . .

Petitioners do not dispute that the loss of social, professional, and economic benefits resulting from steering practices constitutes palpable injury. Instead, they contend that Coleman and Willis, by pleading simply that they were residents of the Richmond metropolitan area, have failed to demonstrate how the asserted steering practices of petitioners in Henrico County may have affected the *particular*

neighborhoods in which the individual respondents resided.

It is indeed implausible to argue that petitioners' alleged acts of discrimination could have palpable effects throughout the *entire* Richmond metropolitan area. . . . We have not suggested that discrimination within a single housing complex might give rise to "distinct and palpable injury" . . . throughout a metropolitan area.

Nonetheless, in the absence of further factual development, we cannot say as a matter of law that no injury could be proved. . . . Under the liberal federal pleading standards, we therefore agree with the Court of Appeals that dismissal on the pleadings is inappropriate at this stage of the litigation. At the same time, we note that the extreme generality of the complaint makes it impossible to say that respondents have made factual averments sufficient if true to demonstrate injury in fact. . . .

HOME brought suit against petitioners both as a representative of its members and on its own behalf. In its representative capacity, HOME sought only injunctive relief. . . .

In determining whether HOME has standing under the Fair Housing Act, we conduct the same inquiry as in the case of an individual: Has the plaintiff "alleged such a personal stake in the outcome of the controversy, as to warrant his invocation of federal court jurisdiction"? . . .

If, as broadly alleged, petitioners' steering practices have perceptibly impaired HOME's ability to provide counseling and referral services for low- and moderate-income homeseekers, there can be no question that the organization has suffered injury in fact. Such concrete and demonstrable injury to the organization's activities—with the consequent drain on the organization's resources—constitutes far more than simply a setback to the organization's abstract social interests. See *Sierra Club v. Morton*, 405 U.S., at 739 [1972]. We therefore conclude, as did the Court of Appeals, that in view of HOME's allegation of injury it was improper for the District Court to dismiss for lack of standing the claims of the organization in its own right.

. . . In sum, we affirm the judgment of the Court of Appeals insofar as the judgment reversed the District Court's dismissal of the claims of Coleman and Willis as individuals allegedly deprived of the benefits of interracial association, and the claims of HOME as an organization allegedly injured by the racial steering practices of petitioners; we reverse the judgment insofar as it directed that Coleman and Willis may proceed to trial on their tester claims. Further proceedings on the remand directed by the Court of Appeals shall be consistent with this opinion.

It is so ordered.

[The concurring opinion of JUSTICE POWELL is omitted.]

MOORE V. CITY OF EAST CLEVELAND
431 U.S. 494 (1977)

The City of East Cleveland, a predominantly black community with a black city manager and a city commission, is a suburb of the Cleveland metropolitan area with a population of 40,000. East Cleveland's housing ordinance, § 1351.02 defined *family* in such a way that only a few categories of related individuals could live together. For example, the ordinance defined a family to include, in addition to the spouse of the head of household, the couple's childless unmarried children, but only one dependent child (married or unmarried) having dependent children, and one parent of the head of the household or of his or her spouse. Mrs. Inez Moore, a black grandmother, resided in her home in East Cleveland together with her son, Dale Moore, Jr., and her two grandsons, Dale Jr. and John Moore Jr. The two boys were first cousins, rather than brothers. John came to live with his grandmother after his mother's death. In early 1973, Mrs. Moore received a notice of violation from the city, stating that the presence of her grandson John Jr. violated the ordinance and directed her to remove him from her home. After she failed to do this, the city filed a criminal charge against her. Mrs. Moore moved to dismiss the charge, claiming that the ordinance was unconstitutional. Her motion was overruled, and she was sentenced to five days in jail and a $25 fine. The Ohio Court of Appeals affirmed, and the Ohio Supreme Court denied review of the case. *Vote: 5-4.*

* * *

MR. JUSTICE POWELL announced the judgment of the Court and delivered an opinion in which MR. JUSTICE BRENNAN, MR. JUSTICE MARSHALL, and MR. JUSTICE BLACKMUN joined.
. . . The city argues that our decision in *Village of Belle Terre v. Boraas,* 416 U.S. 1 (1974), requires us to sustain the ordinance attacked here. Belle Terre, like East Cleveland, imposed limits on the types of groups that could occupy a single dwelling unit. Applying the constitutional standard announced in this Court's leading land-use case, *Euclid v. Ambler Realty Co.,* 272 U.S. 365 (1926), we sustained the Belle Terre ordinance on the ground that it bore a rational relationship to permissible state objectives.
But one overriding factor sets this case apart from *Belle Terre.* The ordinance there affected only *unrelated* individuals. It expressly allowed all who were related by "blood, adoption, or marriage" to live together, and in sustaining the ordinance we were careful to note that it promoted "family needs" and "family values." . . . East Cleveland, in contrast, has chosen to regulate the occupancy of its housing by slicing deeply into the family itself. This is no mere incidental result of the ordinance. On its face it selects certain categories of relatives who may live together and declares that others may not. In particular, it makes a crime of a grandmother's choice to live with her grandson in circumstances like those presented here.
When a city undertakes such intrusive regulation of the family, neither *Belle Terre* nor *Euclid* governs; the usual judicial deference to the legislature is inappropriate. "This Court has long recognized that freedom of personal choice in matters of marriage and family life is one of the liberties protected by the Due Process Clause of the Fourteenth Amendment." *Cleveland v. Board of Education v. LaFleur,* 414 U.S. 632, 639-640 (1974). A host of cases, tracing their lineage to *Meyer v. Nebraska,* 262 U.S. 390, 399-401 (1923), and *Pierce v. Society of Sisters,* 268 U.S. 510, 534-535 (1925), have consistently acknowledged a "private realm of family life which the state cannot enter." *Prince v. Massachusetts,* 321 U.S. 158, 166 (1944). See, *e.g., Roe v. Wade,* 410 U.S. 113, 152-153 (1973); *Wisconsin v. Yoder,* 406 U.S. 205, 231-233 (1972); *Stanley v. Illinois,* 405 U.S. 645, 651 (1972); *Ginsberg v. New York,* 390 U.S. 629, 639 (1968); *Griswold v. Connecticut,* 381 U.S. 479 (1965); *id.* at 495-496 . . . *Poe v. Ullman,* 367 U.S. 497, 542-544, 549-553 (1961) . . . Of course, the family is not beyond regulation. . . . But when the government intrudes on choices concerning family living arrangements, this Court must examine carefully the importance of the governmental interests advanced and the extent to which they are served by the challenged regulation. . . .
When thus examined, this ordinance cannot survive. The city seeks to justify it as a means of preventing overcrowding, minimizing traffic and parking congestion, and avoiding an undue financial burden on East Cleveland's school system. Although these are legitimate goals, the ordinance before us serves them marginally, at best. For example, the ordinance permits any family consisting only of husband, wife, and unmarried children to live together, even if the family contains a half dozen licensed drivers, each with his or her own car. At the same time it forbids an adult brother or sister to share a household, even if both faithfully use public transportation. The ordinance would permit a grandmother to live with a single dependent son and children, even if his school-age children number a dozen, yet it forces Mrs. Moore to find another dwelling for her grandson John, simply because of the presence of his uncle and cousin in the same household. We need not labor the point. Section

1341.08 has but a tenuous relation to alleviation of the conditions mentioned by the city.

The city would distinguish the cases based on *Meyer* and *Pierce*. It points out that none of them "gives grandmothers any fundamental rights with respect to grandsons" . . . and suggests that any constitutional right to live together as a family extends only to the nuclear family—essentially a couple and their dependent children.

To be sure, these cases did not expressly consider the family relationship presented here. They were immediately concerned with freedom of choice with respect to childbearing, *e.g., LaFleur, Roe v. Wade, Griswold,* . . . or with the rights of parents to the custody and companionship for their own children, *Stanley v. Illinois,* . . . or with traditional parental authority in matters of childrearing and education. *Yoder, Ginsberg, Pierce, Meyer.* . . . But unless we close our eyes to the basic reasons why certain rights associated with the family have been accorded shelter under the Fourteenth Amendment's Due Process Clause, we cannot avoid applying the force and rationale of these precedents to the family choice involved in this case.

Understanding those reasons requires careful attention to this Court's function under the Due Process Clause. . ..

Substantive due process has at times been a treacherous field for this Court. There *are* risks when the judicial branch gives enhanced protection to certain substantive liberties without the guidance of the more specific provisions of the Bill of Rights. As the history of the *Lochner* [*v. New York,* 198 U.S. 45 (1905)] era demonstrates, there is reason for concern lest the only limits to such judicial intervention become the predilections of those who happen at the time to be Members of this Court. That history counsels caution and restraint. But it does not counsel abandonment, nor does it require what the city urges here: cutting off any protection of family rights at the first convenient, if arbitrary boundary— the boundary of the nuclear family.

Appropriate limits on substantive due process come not from drawing arbitrary lines but rather from careful "respect for the teachings of history [and] solid recognition of the basic values that underlie our society." . . . Our decisions establish that the Constitution protects the sanctity of the family precisely because the institution of the family is deeply rooted in this Nation's history and tradition. It is through the family that we inculcate and pass down many of our most cherished values, moral and cultural.

Ours is by no means a tradition limited to respect for the bonds uniting the members of the nuclear family. The tradition of uncles, aunts, cousins, and especially grandparents sharing a household along with parents and children has roots equally venerable and equally deserving of constitutional recognition. Over the years millions of our citizens have grown up in just such an environment, and most have profited from it. Even if conditions of modern society have brought about a decline in extended family households, they have not erased the accumulated wisdom of civilization, gained over the centuries and honored throughout our history, that supports a larger conception of the family. Out of choice, necessity, or a sense of family responsibility, it has been common for close relatives to draw together and participate in the duties and the satisfactions of a common home. Decisions concerning child rearing, which *Yoder, Meyer,* and *Pierce* and other cases have recognized as entitled to constitutional protection, long have been shared with grandparents or other relatives who occupy the same household—indeed who may take on major responsibility for the rearing of children. Especially in times of adversity, such as the death of a spouse or economic need, the broader family has tended to come together for mutual sustenance and to maintain or rebuild a secure home life. This is apparently what happened here.

Whether or not a household is established because of personal tragedy, the choice of relatives in this degree of kinship to live together may not lightly be denied by the State. *Pierce* struck down an Oregon law requiring all children to attend the State's public schools, holding that the Constitution "excludes any general power of the State to standardize its children by forcing them to accept instruction from public teachers only." . . . By the same token the Constitution prevents East Cleveland from standardizing its children—and its adults—by forcing all to live in certain narrowly defined family patterns.

Reversed.

* * *

MR. JUSTICE BRENNAN, with whom MR. JUSTICE MARSHALL joins, concurring.

. . . I write only to underscore the cultural myopia of the arbitrary boundary drawn by the East Cleveland ordinance in the light of the tradition of the American home that has been a feature of our society since our beginning as a Nation—the "tradition" in the plurality's words, "of uncles, aunts, cousins, and especially grandparents sharing a household along with parents and children." . . . The line drawn by this ordinance displays a depressing insensitivity toward the economic and emotional needs of a very large part of our society.

In today's America, the "nuclear family" is the pattern so often found in much of white suburbia. . . . The Constitution cannot be interpreted, however, to tolerate the imposition by government upon the rest of us white suburbia's preference in patterns of family living. The "extended family" that provided generations of early Americans with social services and economic and emotional support in times of hardship, and was the beachhead for successive waves of immigrants who populated our cities, remains not merely still a pervasive living pattern, but under the goad of brutal economic necessity, a prominent pattern—virtually a means of survival—for large numbers of the poor and deprived minorities of our society. For them compelled pooling of scant resources requires compelled sharing of a household.

The "extended" form is especially familiar among black families. We may suppose that this reflects the truism that black citizens, like generations of white immigrants before them, have been victims of economic and other disadvantages that would worsen if they were compelled to abandon extended, for nuclear, living patterns. Even in husband and wife households, 13% of black families compared to 3% of white families include relatives under 18 years old, in addition to the couple's own children. In black households whose head is an elderly woman, as in this case, the contrast is even more striking: 48% of such black households, compared with 10% of counterpart white households, include related minor children not offspring of the head of household.

I do not wish to be understood as implying that East Cleveland's enforcement of its ordinance is motivated by a racially discriminatory purpose: The record of this case would not support that implication. But the prominence of other than nuclear families among ethnic and racial minority groups, including our black citizens, surely demonstrates that the "extended family" pattern remains a vital tenet of our society. It suffices that in prohibiting this pattern of family living as a means of achieving its objectives, appellee city has chosen a device that deeply intrudes into family associational rights that historically have been central, and today remain central to a large proportion of our population.

[The opinion of MR. JUSTICE STEVENS, concurring in the judgment, is omitted.]

* * *

MR. JUSTICE STEWART, with whom, MR. JUSTICE REHNQUIST joins, dissenting.

. . . Viewed in the light of these principles, I do not think East Cleveland's definition of "family" offends the Constitution. The city has undisputed power to ordain single-family residential occupancy. . . . And that power plainly carries with it the power to say what a "family" is. Here the city has defined "family" to include not only father, mother, and dependent children, but several other close relatives as well. The definition is rationally designed to carry out the legitimate governmental purposes identified in the *Belle Terre* opinion: "The police power is not confined to elimination of filth, stench, and unhealthy places. It is ample to lay out zones where family values, youth values, and the blessings of quiet seclusion and clean air make the area a sanctuary for people."

[The dissenting opinions of MR. JUSTICE WHITE and MR. CHIEF JUSTICE BURGER are omitted.]

MEMPHIS V. GREENE
451 U.S. 100 (1981)

Hein Park, a small, predominantly white community in Memphis, Tennessee, is bounded on three sides by thoroughfares and on the west by the campus of Southwestern University. West Drive, one of three streets that enter Hein Park from the north, is a two-lane street about half a mile long passing through the center of Hein Park. The two other streets, Jackson Avenue and Springdale Street, are two heavily traveled four-lane avenues that enter Hein Park from the east. In 1970 the residents of Hein Park requested the city to close four streets leading into the subdivision. After receiving objections from the Police, Fire, and Sanitation Departments, the city denied the request. The city's Traffic Engineering Department noted that much of the traffic through the subdivision could be eliminated by closing West Drive at Jackson Avenue. In July 1973, members of the Hein Park Civic Association sought to close West Drive for the stated reasons to reduce the flow of traffic using Hein Park streets, to increase safety to children who live in Hein Park, and to reduce traffic pollution in the residential area In November the city approved the street closing.

Residents of the predominantly black area north of Jackson Avenue and west of Springdale Street, and two civic associations brought a class action suit alleging that the street closing violated § 1982, which entitles all citizens to have the same right as is enjoyed by white persons to inherit, purchase, lease, sell, hold, and convey real property, and the Thirteenth Amendment as constituting a badge of slavery. They sought an injunction requiring the city to keep West Drive open for through traffic. The district court held that (a) the street closing did not create a benefit for white citizens that was denied to black citizens, (b) racially discriminatory intent or purpose had not been proven, and (c) the city had not departed significantly from normal procedures in authorizing the closing. The court of appeals reversed and remanded, holding that the street closing was invalid because it adversely affected the black residents' ability to hold and enjoy their property. *Vote: 6-3.*

* * *

JUSTICE STEVENS delivered the opinion of the Court.

The question presented is whether a decision by the city of Memphis to close the north end of West Drive, a street that traverses a white residential community, violated § 1 of the Civil Rights Act of 1866, . . . 42 U.S.C. § 1982, or the Thirteenth Amendment to the United States Constitution. The city's action was challenged by respondents who resided in a predominantly black area to the north. The Court of Appeals ultimately held the street closing invalid because it adversely affected respondents' ability to hold and enjoy their property. . . . We reverse because the record does not support that holding.

Most of the relevant facts concerning geography, the decision to close the street, and the course of the litigation are not in dispute. The inferences to be drawn from the evidence, however, are subject to some disagreement.

. . . In summary, then, the critical facts established by the record are these: The city's decision to close West Drive was motivated by its interest in protecting the safety and tranquility of a residential neighborhood. The procedures followed in making the decision were fair and were not affected by any racial or other impermissible factors. The city has conferred a benefit on certain white property owners but there is no reason to believe that it would refuse to confer a comparable benefit on black property owners. The closing has not affected the value of the property owned by black citizens, but it has caused some slight inconvenience to black motorists.

Under the Court's recent decisions in *Washington v. Davis,* 426 U.S. 229 [1976], and *Arlington Heights v. Metropolitan Housing Dev. Corp.,* 429 U.S. 252 [1977], the absence of proof of discriminatory intent forecloses any claim that the official action challenged in this case violates the Equal Protection Clause of the Fourteenth Amendment. Petitioners ask us to hold that respondents' claims under § 1982 and the Thirteenth Amendment are likewise barred by the absence of proof of discriminatory purpose. We note initially that the coverage of both § 1982 and the Thirteenth Amendment is significantly different from the coverage of the Fourteenth Amendment. The prohibitions of the latter apply only to official action, or, as implemented by . . . § 1983 . . . to action taken under color of state law. We have squarely decided, however, that § 1982 is directly applicable to private parties, *Jones v. Alfred H. Mayer Co.,* 392 U.S. 409 [1968]; . . . and it has long been settled that the Thirteenth Amend-

ment "is not a mere prohibition of State laws establishing or upholding slavery, but an absolute declaration that slavery or involuntary servitude shall not exist in any part of the United States." *Civil Rights Cases,* 109 U.S. 3, 20 [1883]. Thus, although respondents challenge official action in this case, the provisions of the law on which the challenge is based cover certain private action as well. Rather than confront prematurely the rather general question whether either § 1982 or the Thirteenth Amendment requires proof of a specific unlawful purpose, we first consider the extent to which either provision applies at all to this street closing case. We of course deal first with the statutory question.

Section 1982 provides:

"All citizens of the United States shall have the same right, in every State and Territory, as is enjoyed by white citizens thereof to inherit, purchase, lease, sell, hold, and convey real and personal property."

To effectuate the remedial purposes of the statute, the Court has broadly construed this language to protect not merely the enforceability of property interests acquired by black citizens but also their right to acquire and use property on an equal basis with white citizens. . . .

Therefore, as applied to this case, the threshold inquiry under § 1982 must focus on the relationship between the street closing and the property interests of the respondents. As the Court of Appeals correctly noted in its first opinion, the statute would support a challenge to municipal action benefiting white property owners that would be refused to similarly situated black property owners. For official action of that kind would prevent blacks from exercising the same property rights as whites. But respondents' evidence failed to support this legal theory. Alternatively, as the Court of Appeals held in its second opinion, the statute might be violated by official action that depreciated the value of property owned by black citizens. But this record discloses no effect on the value of property owned by any member of the respondent class. Finally, the statute might be violated if the street closing severely restricted access to black homes, because blacks would then be hampered in the use of their property. Again, the record discloses no such restriction.

The injury to respondents established by the record is the requirement that one public street rather than another must be used for certain trips within the city. We need not assess the magnitude of that injury to conclude that it does not involve any impairment to the kind of property interests that we have identified as being within the reach of § 1982. We therefore must consider whether the street closing violated respondents' constitutional rights.

In relevant part, the Thirteenth Amendment provides:

"Neither slavery nor involuntary servitude, except as a punishment for crime whereof the party shall have been duly convicted, shall exist within the United States, or any place subject to the their jurisdiction."

In this case respondents challenge the conferring of a benefit upon white citizens by a measure that places a burden on black citizens as an unconstitutional "badge of slavery." Relying on JUSTICE BLACK's opinion for the Court in *Palmer v. Thompson*, 403 U.S. 217 [1971], the city argues that in the absence of a violation of a specific enabling legislation enacted pursuant to § 2 of the Thirteenth Amendment, any judicial characterization of an isolated street closing as a badge of slavery would constitute the usurpation of "a law-making power far beyond the imagination of the amendment's authors." . . .

Pursuant to the authority created by § 2 of the Thirteenth Amendment, Congress has enacted legislation to abolish both the conditions of involuntary servitude and the "badges and incidents of slavery." The exercise of that authority is not inconsistent with the view that the Amendment has self-executing force. . . . In *Jones,* the Court left open the question whether § 1 of the Amendment by its own terms did anything more than abolish slavery. It is also appropriate today to leave that question open because a review of the justification for the official action challenged in this case demonstrates that its disparate impact on black citizens could not, in any event, be fairly characterized as a badge or incident of slavery.

We begin our examination of the respondents' Thirteenth Amendment argument by reiterating the conclusion that the record discloses no racially discriminatory motive on the part of the City Council. Instead, the record demonstrates that the interests that did motivate the Council are legitimate. Proper management of the flow of vehicular traffic within a city requires the accommodation of a variety of conflicting interests: the motorist's interest in unhindered access to his destination, the city's interest in the efficient provision of municipal services, the commercial interest in adequate parking, the residents' interest in relative quiet, and the pedestrians' interest in safety. Local governments necessarily exercise wide discretion in making the policy decisions that accommodate these interests.

. . . Whether the individual privacy interests of the residents of Hein Park, coupled with the interest in safety, should be considered strong enough to overcome the more general interest in the use of West Drive as a thoroughfare is the type of question that a multitude of local governments must resolve every day. Because there is no basis for concluding that the interests favored by the city in its decision were contrived or pretextual, the District Court correctly concluded that it had no authority to review the wisdom of the city's policy decision. . . .

The interests motivating the city's action are thus sufficient to justify an adverse impact on motorists who are somewhat inconvenienced by the street closing. That inconvenience cannot be equated to an actual restraint on the liberty of black citizens that is in any sense comparable to the odious practice the Thirteenth Amendment was designed to eradicate. The argument that the closing violates the Amendment must therefore rest, not on the actual consequences of the closing, but rather on the symbolic significance of the fact that most of the drivers who will be inconvenienced by the action are black.

But the inconvenience of the drivers is a function of where they live and where they regularly drive—not a function of their race; the hazards and the inconvenience that the closing is intended to minimize are a function of the number of vehicles involved, not the race of their drivers or of the local residents. Almost any traffic regulation—whether it be a temporary detour during construction, a speed limit, a one-way street, or a no-parking sign—may have a differential impact on residents of adjacent or nearby neighborhoods. Because urban neighborhoods are so frequently characterized by a common ethnic or racial heritage, a regulation's adverse impact on a particular neighborhood will often have a disparate effect on an identifiable ethnic or racial group. To regard an inevitable consequence of that kind as a form of stigma so severe as to violate the Thirteenth Amendment would trivialize the great purpose of that charter of freedom. Proper respect for the dignity of the residents of any neighborhood requires that they accept the same burdens as well as the same benefits of citizenship regardless of their racial or ethnic origin.

This case does not disclose a violation of any of the enabling legislation enacted by Congress pursuant to § 2 of the Thirteenth Amendment. To decide the narrow constitutional question presented by this record we need not speculate about the sort of impact on a racial group that might be prohibited by the Amendment itself. We merely hold that the impact of the closing of West Drive on nonresidents of Hein Park is a routine burden of citizenship; it does not reflect a violation of the Thirteenth Amendment.

The judgment of the Court of Appeals is *Reversed.*

[The opinion of JUSTICE WHITE, concurring in the judgment, is omitted.]

* * *

JUSTICE MARSHALL, with whom JUSTICE BRENNAN and JUSTICE BLACKMUN join, dissenting.

. . . Indeed, until today I would have thought that a city's erection of a barrier, at the behest of a historically all-white community, to keep out predominantly Negro traffic, would have been among the least of the statute's prohibitions. Certainly I suspect that the Congress that enacted § 1982 would be surprised to learn that it has no application to such a case. Even the few portions of the debate that I have cited make clear that a major concern of the statute's supporters was the elimination of the effects of local prejudice on Negro residents. In my view, the evidence before us supports a strong inference that the operation of such prejudice is precisely what has led to the closing of West Drive. And against this record, the government should be required to do far more than it has here to justify an action that so obviously damages and stigmatizes a racially identifiable group of its citizens.

FURMAN V. GEORGIA
408 U.S. 238 (1972)

Beginning in the 1960s, the NAACP Legal Defense and Education Fund implemented a legal strategy to abolish capital punishment. The Fund's litigation campaign reached a climax in 1972 in *Furman v. Georgia. Furman* and two other cases involved the constitutionality of the death penalty for murder and rape by three black men. In the lead case, *Furman v. Georgia,* William Furman was convicted of murdering a white man and was sentenced to death. In *Jackson v. Georgia,* Lucious Jackson was convicted of the rape of a 21-year-old white woman and was sentenced to death. And in *Branch v. Texas,* Elmer Branch was convicted of raping a 65-year-old widow and was sentenced to death. Each of the Justices wrote a separate opinion in the case. *Vote: 5-4.*

* * *

Per Curiam
    . . . Certiorari was granted limited to the following question: "Does the imposition and carrying out of the death penalty in [these cases] constitute cruel and unusual punishment in violation of the Eighth and Fourteenth Amendments?" . . . The Court holds that the imposition and carrying out of the death penalty in these cases constitute cruel and unusual punishment in violation of the Eighth and Fourteenth Amendments. The judgment in each case is therefore reversed insofar as it leaves undisturbed the death sentence imposed, and the cases are remanded for further proceedings.
    So ordered.
    MR. JUSTICE DOUGLAS, MR. JUSTICE BRENNAN, MR. JUSTICE STEWART, MR. JUSTICE WHITE, and MR. JUSTICE MARSHALL filed separate opinions in support of the judgments. THE CHIEF JUSTICE [BURGER], MR. JUSTICE BLACKMUN, MR. JUSTICE POWELL, and MR. JUSTICE REHNQUIST filed separate dissenting opinions.

* * *

MR. JUSTICE DOUGLAS concurring.

    . . . There is increasing recognition of the fact that the basic theme of equal protection is implicit in "cruel and unusual" punishments. "A penalty . . . should be considered 'unusually' imposed if it is administered arbitrarily or discriminatorily." The same authors add that "[t]he extreme rarity with which applicable death penalty provisions are put to use raises a strong inference of arbitrariness." . . .
    . . . We cannot say from facts disclosed in these records that these defendants were sentenced to death because they were black. Yet our task is not restricted to an effort to divine what motives impelled these death penalties. Rather, we deal with a system of law and of justice that leaves to the uncontrolled discretion of judges or juries the determination whether defendants committing these crimes should die or be imprisoned. Under these laws no standards govern the selection of the penalty. People live or die, dependent on the whim of one man or of 12.
    . . . Those who wrote the Eighth Amendment knew what price their forbears had paid for a system based, not on equal justice, but on discrimination. In those days the target was not the blacks or the poor, but the dissenters, those who opposed absolutism in government, who struggled for a parliamentary regime, and who opposed governments' recurring efforts to foist a particular religion on the people. . . . But the tool of capital punishment was used with vengeance against the opposition and those unpopular with the regime. One cannot read this history without realizing that the desire for equality was reflected in the ban against "cruel and unusual punishments" contained in the Eighth Amendment.
    In a Nation committed to equal protection of the laws there is no permissible "caste" aspect of law enforcement. Yet we know that the discretion of judges and juries in imposing the death penalty enables the penalty to be selectively applied, feeding prejudices against the accused if he is poor and despised, and lacking political clout, or if he is a member of a suspect or unpopular minority, and saving those who by social position may be in a more protected position. In ancient Hindu law a Brahman was exempt from capital punishment, and under that law, "[g]enerally, in the law books, pun-

ishment increased in severity as social status diminished." We have, I fear, taken in practice the same position, partially as a result of making the death penalty discretionary and partially as a result of the ability of the rich to purchase the services of the most respected and most resourceful legal talent in the Nation.

. . . Any law which is nondiscriminatory on its face may be applied in such a way as to violate the Equal Protection Clause of the Fourteenth Amendment. . . . Such conceivably might be the fate of a mandatory death penalty, where equal or lesser sentences were imposed on the elite, a harsher one on the minorities or members of the lower castes. Whether a mandatory death penalty would otherwise be constitutional is a question I do not reach.

* * *

MR. JUSTICE BRENNAN concurring.

. . . Judicial enforcement of the Clause, then, cannot be evaded by invoking the obvious truth that legislatures have the power to prescribe punishments for crimes. That is precisely the reason the Clause appears in the Bill of Rights. The difficulty arises, rather, in formulating the "legal principles to be applied by the courts" when a legislatively prescribed punishment is challenged as "cruel and unusual." . . .

. . . At bottom, then, the Cruel and Unusual Punishments Clause prohibits the infliction of uncivilized and inhuman punishments. The State, even as it punishes, must treat its members with respect for their intrinsic worth as human beings. A punishment is "cruel and unusual," therefore, if it does not comport with human dignity.

This formulation, of course, does not of itself yield principles for assessing the constitutional validity of particular punishments. Nevertheless . . . there are principles recognized in our cases inherent in the Clause sufficient to permit a judicial determination whether a challenged punishment comports with human dignity.

. . . There are, then, four principles by which we may determine whether a particular punishment is "cruel and unusual." The primary principle, which I believe supplies the essential predicate for the application of the others, is that a punishment must not by its severity be degrading to human dignity. The paradigm violation of this principle would be the infliction of a torturous punishment of the type that the Clause has always prohibited. Yet "[i]t is unlikely that any State at this moment in history" . . . would pass a law providing for the infliction of such a punishment. Indeed, no such punishment has ever been before this Court. The same may be said of the other principles. It is unlikely that this Court will confront a severe punishment that is obviously inflicted in wholly arbitrary fashion; no State would

engage in a reign of blind terror. Nor is it likely that this Court will be called upon to review a severe punishment that is clearly and totally rejected throughout society; no legislature would be able even to authorize the infliction of such a punishment. Nor, finally, is it likely that this Court will have to consider a severe punishment that is patently unnecessary; no State today would inflict a severe punishment knowing that there was no reason whatever for doing so. In short, we are unlikely to have occasion to determine that a punishment is fatally offensive under any one principle.

Since the Bill of Rights was adopted, this Court has adjudged only three punishments to be within the prohibition of the Clause. See *Weems v. United States* [217 U.S. 349 (1910)] (12 years in chains at hard and painful labor); *Trop v. Dulles* [356 U.S. 86 (1958)] (expatriation); *Robinson v. California* [370 U.S. 660 (1962)] . . . (imprisonment for narcotics addiction). Each punishment, of course, was degrading to human dignity, but of none could it be said conclusively that it was fatally offensive under one or the other of the principles. Rather, these "cruel and unusual punishments" seriously implicated several of the principles, and it was the application of the principles in combination that supported the judgment. That, indeed, is not surprising. The function of these principles, after all, is simply to provide means by which a court can determine whether a challenged punishment comports with human dignity. They are, therefore, interrelated, and in most cases it will be their convergence that will justify the conclusion that a punishment is "cruel and unusual." The test, then, will ordinarily be a cumulative one: If a punishment is unusually severe, if there is a strong probability that it is inflicted arbitrarily, if it is substantially rejected by contemporary society, and if there is no reason to believe that it serves any penal purpose more effectively than some less severe punishment, then the continued infliction of that punishment violates the command of the Clause and the State may not inflict inhuman and uncivilized punishments upon those convicted of crimes.

. . . The question, then, is whether the deliberate infliction of death is today consistent with the command of the Clause that the State may not inflict punishments that do not comport with human dignity. I will analyze the punishment of death in terms of the principles set out above and the cumulative test to which they lead: It is a denial of human dignity for the State arbitrarily to subject a person to an unusually severe punishment that society has indicated it does not regard as acceptable, and that cannot be shown to serve any penal purpose more effectively than a significantly less drastic punishment. Under these principles and this test, death is today a "cruel and unusual" punishment.

. . . The only explanation for the uniqueness of death is its extreme severity. Death is today an unusually severe punishment, unusual in its pain, in its finality, and in its enormity. No other existing punishment is comparable to death in terms of physical and mental suffering. Although our information is not conclusive, it appears that there is no method available that guarantees an immediate and painless death. Since the discontinuance of flogging as a constitutionally permissible punishment, . . . death remains as the only punishment that may involve the conscious infliction of physical pain. In addition, we know that mental pain is an inseparable part of our practice of punishing criminals by death, for the prospect of pending execution exacts a frightful toll during the inevitable long wait between the imposition of sentence and the actual infliction of death. . . .

The unusual severity of death is manifested most clearly in its finality and enormity. Death, in these respects, is in a class by itself. . . .

. . . In comparison to all other punishments today, then, the deliberate extinguishment of human life by the State is uniquely degrading to human dignity. I would not hesitate to hold, on that ground alone, that death is today a "cruel and unusual" punishment, were it not that death is a punishment of longstanding usage and acceptance in this country. I therefore turn to the second principle—that the State may not arbitrarily inflict an unusually severe punishment.

The outstanding characteristic of our present practice of punishing criminals by death is the infrequency with which we resort to it. The evidence is conclusive that death is not the ordinary punishment for any crime.

There has been a steady decline in the infliction of this punishment in every decade since the 1930's, the earliest period for which accurate statistics are available. . . .

. . . When a country of over 200 million people inflicts an unusually severe punishment no more than 50 times a year, the inference is strong that the punishment is not being regularly and fairly applied. To dispel it would indeed require a clear showing of nonarbitrary infliction.

. . . When the punishment of death is inflicted in a trivial number of the cases in which it is legally available, the conclusion is virtually inescapable that it is being inflicted arbitrarily. Indeed, it smacks of little more than a lottery system. The States claim, however, that this rarity is evidence not of arbitrariness, but of informed selectivity: Death is inflicted, they say, only in "extreme" cases.

. . . When there is a strong probability that an unusually severe and degrading punishment is being inflicted arbitrarily, we may well expect that society will disapprove of its infliction. I turn, therefore, to the third principle. An examination of the history and present operation of the American practice of punishing criminals by death reveals that this punishment has been almost totally rejected by contemporary society.

. . . The progressive decline in, and the current rarity of, the infliction of death demonstrate that our society seriously questions the appropriateness of this punishment today. The States point out that many legislatures authorize death as the punishment for certain crimes and that substantial segments of the public, as reflected in opinion polls and referendum votes, continue to support it. Yet the availability of this punishment through statutory authorization, as well as the polls and referenda, which amount simply to approval of that authorization, simply underscores the extent to which our society has in fact rejected this punishment. When an unusually severe punishment is authorized for widescale application but not, because of society's refusal, inflicted save in a few instances, the inference is compelling that there is a deep-seated reluctance to inflict it. Indeed, the likelihood is great that the punishment is tolerated only because of its disuse. The objective indicator of society's view of an unusually severe punishment is what society does with it, and today society will inflict death upon only a small sample of the eligible criminals. Rejection could hardly be more complete without becoming absolute. At the very least, I must conclude that contemporary society views this punishment with substantial doubt.

The final principle to be considered is that an unusually severe and degrading punishment may not be excessive in view of the purposes for which it is inflicted. This principle, too, is related to the others. When there is a strong probability that the State is arbitrarily inflicting an unusually severe punishment that is subject to grave societal doubts, it is likely also that the punishment cannot be shown to be serving any penal purpose that could not be served equally well by some less severe punishment.

The State's primary claim is that death is a necessary punishment because it prevents the commission of capital crimes more effectively than any less severe punishment. The first part of this claim is that the infliction of death is necessary to stop the individuals executed from committing further crimes. The sufficient answer to this is that if a criminal convicted of a capital crime poses a danger to society, effective administration of the State's pardon and parole laws can delay or deny his release from prison, and techniques of isolation can eliminate or minimize the danger while he remains confined.

The more significant argument is that the threat of death prevents the commission of capital crimes because it deters potential criminals who would not be deterred by the threat of imprisonment. The argument is not based upon evidence that the threat of death is a superior deterrent. Indeed, as my Brother MARSHALL establishes, the available evidence uniformly indicates, although it does not conclusively prove, that the threat of death has no greater deterrent effect than the threat of imprisonment. The

States argue, however, that they are entitled to rely upon common human experience, and that experience, they say, supports the conclusion that death must be a more effective deterrent than any less severe punishment. Because people fear death the most, the argument runs, the threat of death must be the greatest deterrent.

It is important to focus upon the precise import of this argument. It is not denied that many, and probably most, capital crimes cannot be deterred by the threat of punishment. Thus the argument can apply only to those who think rationally about the commission of capital crimes. Particularly is that true when the potential criminal, under this argument, must not only consider the risk of punishment, but also distinguish between two possible punishments. The concern, then, is with a particular type of potential criminal, the rational person who will commit a capital crime knowing that the punishment is long-term imprisonment, which may well be for the rest of his life, but will not commit the crime knowing that the punishment is death. On the face of it, the assumption that such persons exist is implausible.

. . . A rational person contemplating a murder or rape is confronted, not with the certainty of a speedy death, but with the slightest possibility that he will be executed in the distant future. The risk of death is remote and improbable; in contrast, the risk of long-term imprisonment is near and great. In short, whatever the speculative validity of the assumption that the threat of death is a superior deterrent, there is no reason to believe that as currently administered the punishment of death is necessary to deter the commission of capital crimes. Whatever might be the case were all or substantially all eligible criminals quickly put to death, unverifiable possibilities are an insufficient basis upon which to conclude that the threat of death today has any greater deterrent efficacy than the threat of imprisonment.

There is, however, another aspect to the argument that the punishment of death is necessary for the protection of society. The infliction of death, the States urge, serves to manifest the community's outrage at the commission of the crime. It is, they say, a concrete public expression of moral indignation that inculcates respect for the law and helps assure a more peaceful community. Moreover, we are told, not only does the punishment of death exert this widespread moralizing influence upon community values, it also satisfies the popular demand for grievous condemnation of abhorrent crimes and thus prevents disorder, lynching, and attempts by private citizens to take the law into their own hands.

The question, however, is not whether death serves these supposed purposes of punishment, but whether death serves them more effectively than imprisonment. There is no evidence whatever that utilization of imprisonment rather than death encourages private blood feuds and other disorders.

Surely if there were such a danger, the execution of a handful of criminals each year would not prevent it. The assertion that death alone is a sufficiently emphatic denunciation for capital crimes suffers from the same defect. If capital crimes require the punishment of death in order to provide moral reinforcement for the basic values of the community, those values can only be undermined when death is so rarely inflicted upon the criminals who commit the crimes. Furthermore, it is certainly doubtful that the infliction of death by the State does in fact strengthen the community's moral code; if the deliberate extinguishment of human life has any effect at all, it more likely tends to lower our respect for life and brutalize our values. That, after all, is why we no longer carry out public executions. In any event, this claim simply means that one purpose of punishment is to indicate social disapproval of crime. To serve that purpose our laws distribute punishments according to the gravity of crimes and punish more severely the crimes society regards as more serious. That purpose cannot justify any particular punishment as the upper limit of severity. ͜

* * *

MR. JUSTICE STEWART concurring.

. . . Instead, the death sentences now before us are the product of a legal system that brings them, I believe, within the very core of the Eighth Amendment's guarantee against cruel and unusual punishments, a guarantee applicable against the States through the Fourteenth Amendment. . . . In the first place, it is clear that these sentences are "cruel" in the sense that they excessively go beyond, not in degree but in kind, the punishments that the state legislatures have determined to be necessary. . . . In the second place, it is equally clear that these sentences are "unusual" in the sense that the penalty of death is infrequently imposed for murder, and that its imposition for rape is extraordinarily rare. But I do not rest my conclusion upon these propositions alone.

These death sentences are cruel and unusual in the same way that being struck by lightning is cruel and unusual. For, of all of the people convicted of rapes and murders in 1967 and 1968, many just as reprehensible as these, the petitioners are among a capriciously selected random handful upon whom the sentence of death has in fact been imposed. My concurring Brothers have demonstrated that, if any basis can be discerned for the selection of these few to be sentenced to die, it is the constitutionally impermissible basis of race. . . . But racial discrimination has not been proved, and I put it to one side. I simply conclude that the Eighth and Fourteenth Amendments cannot tolerate the infliction of a sentence of death under legal systems that permit this unique penalty to be so wantonly and so freakishly imposed.

* * *

MR. JUSTICE WHITE concurring.

... The narrower question to which I address myself concerns the constitutionality of capital punishment statutes under which (1) the legislature authorizes the imposition of the death penalty for murder or rape; (2) the legislature does not itself mandate the penalty in any particular class or kind of case (that is, legislative will is not frustrated if the penalty is never imposed), but delegates to judges or juries the decisions as to those cases, if any, in which the penalty will be utilized; and (3) judges and juries have ordered the death penalty with such infrequency that the odds are now very much against imposition and execution of the penalty with respect to any convicted murderer or rapist. It is in this context that we must consider whether the execution of these petitioners would violate the Eighth Amendment.

I begin with what I consider a near truism: that the death penalty could so seldom be imposed that it would cease to be a credible deterrent or measurably to contribute to any other end of punishment in the criminal justice system. It is perhaps true that no matter how infrequently those convicted of rape or murder are executed, the penalty so imposed is not disproportionate to the crime and those executed may deserve exactly what they received. It would also be clear that executed defendants are finally and completely incapacitated from again committing rape or murder or any other crime. But when imposition of the penalty reaches a certain degree of infrequency, it would be very doubtful that any existing general need for retribution would be measurably satisfied. Nor could it be said with confidence that society's need for specific deterrence justifies death for so few when for so many in like circumstances life imprisonment or shorter prison terms are judged insufficient, or that community values are measurably reinforced by authorizing a penalty so rarely invoked.

Most important, a major goal of the criminal law—to deter others by punishing the convicted criminal—would not be substantially served where the penalty is so seldom invoked that it ceases to be the credible threat essential to influence the conduct of others. For present purposes I accept the morality and utility of punishing one person to influence another. I accept also the effectiveness of punishment generally and need not reject the death penalty as a more effective deterrent than a lesser punishment. But common sense and experience tell us that seldom-enforced laws become ineffective measures for controlling human conduct and that the death penalty, unless imposed with sufficient frequency, will make little contribution to deterring those crimes for which it may be exacted.

The imposition and execution of the death penalty are obviously cruel in the dictionary sense. But the penalty has not been considered cruel and unusual punishment in the constitutional sense because it was thought justified by the social ends it was deemed to serve. At the moment that it ceases realistically to further these purposes, however, the emerging question is whether its imposition in such circumstances would violate the Eighth Amendment. It is my view that it would, for its imposition would then be the pointless and needless extinction of life with only marginal contributions to any discernable social or public purposes. A penalty with such negligible returns to the State would be patently excessive and cruel and unusual punishment violative of the Eighth Amendment.

It is also my judgment that this point has been reached with respect to capital punishment as it is presently administered under the statutes involved in these cases. Concededly, it is difficult to prove as a general proposition that capital punishment, however administered, more effectively serves the ends of the criminal law than does imprisonment. But however that may be, I cannot avoid the conclusion that as the statutes before us now administered, the penalty is so infrequently imposed that the threat of execution is too attenuated to be of substantial service to criminal justice.

* * *

MR. JUSTICE MARSHALL concurring.

... In order to assess whether or not death is an excessive or unnecessary penalty, it is necessary to consider the reasons why a legislature might select it as punishment for one or more offenses, and examine whether less severe penalties would satisfy the legitimate legislative wants as well as capital punishment. If they would, then the death penalty is unnecessary cruelty, and, therefore, unconstitutional.

There are six purposes conceivably served by capital punishment: retribution, deterrence, prevention of repetitive criminal acts, encouragement of guilty pleas and confessions, eugenics, and economy. These are considered *seriatim* below.

A. The concept of retribution is one of the most misunderstood in all of our criminal jurisprudence. The principal source of confusion derives from the fact that, in dealing with the concept, most people confuse the question "why do men in fact punish?" with the question "what justifies men in punishing?" Men may punish for any number of reasons, but the one reason that punishment is morally good or morally justifiable is that someone has broken the law. Thus, it can correctly be said that breaking the law is the *sine qua non* of punishment, or, in other words, that we only tolerate punishment as it is imposed on one who deviates from the norm established by the criminal law.

. . . It is plain that the view under the *Weems* Court was that punishment for the sake of retribution was not permissible under the Eighth Amendment. This is the only view the Court could have taken if the "cruel and unusual" language were to be given any meaning. . . . If retribution alone could serve as a justification for any particular penalty, then all penalties selected by the legislature would by definition be acceptable means for designating society's moral approbation of a particular act. The "cruel and unusual" language would thus be read out of the Constitution and the fears of Patrick Henry and the other Founding Fathers would become realities.

B. The most hotly contested issue regarding capital punishment is whether it is better than life imprisonment as a deterrent to crime.

. . . There is no more complex problem than determining the deterrent efficacy of the death penalty. "Capital punishment has obviously failed as a deterrent when a murder is committed. We can number its failures. But we cannot number its successes. No one can ever know how many people have refrained from murder because of the fear of being hanged." This is the nub of the problem and it is exacerbated by the paucity of useful data. The United States is more fortunate than most countries, however, in that it has what are generally considered to be the world's most reliable statistics.

. . . In sum, the only support for the theory that capital punishment is an effective deterrent is found in the hypotheses with which we began and the occasional stories about a specific individual being deterred from doing a contemplated criminal act. These claims of specific deterrence are often spurious, however, and may be more than counterbalanced by the tendency of capital punishment to incite certain crimes.

C. Much of what must be said about the death penalty as a device to prevent recidivism is obvious—if a murderer is executed, he cannot possibly commit another offense. The fact is, however, that murderers are extremely unlikely to commit other crimes either in prison or upon their release. For the most part, they are first offenders, and when released from prison they are known to become model citizens. Furthermore, most persons who commit capital crimes are not executed. With respect to those who are sentenced to die, it is critical to note that the jury is never asked to determine whether they are likely to be recidivists. In light of these facts, if capital punishment were justified purely on the basis of preventing recidivism, it would have to be considered to be excessive; no general need to obliterate all capital offenders could have been demonstrated, nor any specific need in individual cases.

D. The three final purposes which may underlie utilization of a capital sanction—encouraging guilty pleas and confessions, eugenics, and reducing state expenditures—may be dealt with quickly. If the death penalty is used to encourage guilty pleas and thus to deter suspects from exercising their rights under the Sixth Amendment to jury trials, it is unconstitutional. . . . Its elimination would do little to impair the State's bargaining position in criminal cases, since life imprisonment remains a severe sanction which can be used as leverage for bargaining for pleas or confessions in exchange either for charges of lesser offenses or recommendations of leniency.

. . . In light of the previous discussion on deterrence, any suggestions concerning the eugenic benefits of capital punishment are obviously meritless. As I pointed out above, there is not even any attempt made to discover which capital offenders are likely to be recidivists, let alone which are positively incurable. No test or procedure presently exists by which incurables can be screened from those who would benefit from treatment. One the one hand, due process would seem to require that we have some procedure to demonstrate incurability before execution; and, on the other hand, equal protection would then seemingly require that all incurables be executed. . . . In addition, the "cruel and unusual" punishment language would require that life imprisonment, treatment, and sterilization be inadequate for eugenic purposes. More importantly, this Nation has never formally professed eugenic goals, and the history of the world does not look kindly on them. If eugenics is one of our purposes, then the legislatures should say so forthrightly and design procedures to serve this goal. Until such time, I can only conclude, as has virtually everyone else who has looked at the problem, that capital punishment cannot be defended on the basis of any eugenic purposes.

As for the argument that it is cheaper to execute a capital offender than to imprison him for life, even assuming that such an argument, if true, would support a capital sanction, it is simply incorrect. A disproportionate amount of money spent on prisons is attributable to death row. Condemned men are not productive members of the prison community, although they could be, and executions are expensive. Appeals are often automatic, and courts admittedly spend more time with death cases.

E. There is but one conclusion that can be drawn from all of this—*i.e.,* the death penalty is an excessive and unnecessary punishment that violates the Eighth Amendment. The statistical evidence is not convincing beyond all doubt, but it is persuasive. . . .

In addition, even if capital punishment is not excessive, it nonetheless violates the Eighth Amendment because it is morally unacceptable to the people of the United States at this time in their history.

In judging whether or not a given penalty is morally acceptable, most courts have said that the punishment is valid unless "it shocks the conscience and sense of justice of the people."

. . . While a public opinion poll obviously is of some assistance in indicating public acceptance or rejection of a specific penalty, its utility cannot be very great. This is because whether or not a punishment is cruel and unusual depends, not on whether its mere mention "shocks the conscience and sense of justice of the people," but on whether people who were fully informed as to the purposes of the penalty and its liabilities would find the penalty shocking, unjust, and unacceptable.

In other words, the question with which we must deal is not whether a substantial proportion of American citizens would today, if polled, opine that capital punishment is barbarously cruel, but whether they would find it to be so in the light of all information presently available.

. . . I believe that the following facts would serve to convince even the most hesitant of citizens to condemn death as a sanction: capital punishment is imposed discriminatorily against certain identifiable classes of people; there is evidence that innocent people have been executed before their innocence can be proved; and the death penalty wreaks havoc with our entire criminal justice system. . . .

. . . Indeed, a look at the bare statistics regarding executions is enough to betray much of the discrimination. A total of 3,859 persons have been executed since 1930, of whom 1,751 were white and 2,066 were Negro. Of the executions, 3,334 were for murder; 1,664 of the executed murderers were white and 1,630 were Negro; 455 persons, including 48 whites and 405 Negroes, were executed for rape. It is immediately apparent that Negroes were executed far more often than whites in proportion to their percentage of the population. Studies indicate that while the higher rate of execution among Negroes is partially due to a higher rate of crime, there is evidence of racial discrimination. . . .

There is also evidence that the death penalty is employed against men and not women. Only 32 women have been executed since 1930, while 3,827 men have met a similar fate. It is difficult to understand why women have received such favored treatment since the purposes allegedly served by capital punishment seemingly are equally applicable to both sexes.

It also is evident that the burden of capital punishment falls upon the poor, the ignorant, and the underprivileged members of society. It is the poor, and the members of minority groups who are least able to voice their complaints against capital punishment. Their impotence leaves them victims of a sanction that the wealthier, better-represented, just-as-guilty person can escape. So long as the capital sanction is used only against the forlorn, easily forgotten members of society, legislators are content to maintain the status quo, because change would draw attention to the problem and concern might develop. Ignorance is perpetuated and apathy soon becomes its mate, and we have today's situation.

Just as Americans know little about who is executed and why, they are unaware of the potential dangers of executing an innocent man. Our "beyond a reasonable doubt" burden of proof in criminal cases is intended to protect the innocent, but we know it is not foolproof. Various studies have shown that people whose innocence is later convincingly established are convicted and sentenced to death.

Proving one's innocence after a jury finding of guilt is almost impossible. While reviewing courts are willing to entertain all kinds of collateral attacks where a sentence of death is involved, they very rarely dispute the jury's interpretation of the evidence. This is, perhaps, as it should be. But, if an innocent man has been found guilty, he must then depend on the good faith of the prosecutor's office to help him establish his innocence. There is evidence, however, that prosecutors do not welcome the idea of having convictions, which they labored hard to secure, overturned, and that their cooperation is highly unlikely.

No matter how careful courts are, the possibility of perjured testimony, mistaken honest testimony, and human error remain all too real. We have no way of judging how many innocent persons have been executed but we can be certain that there were some. Whether there were many is an open question made difficult by the loss of those who were most knowledgeable about the crime for which they were convicted. Surely there will be more as long as capital punishment remains part of our penal law.

. . . Assuming knowledge of all the facts presently available regarding capital punishment, the average citizen would, in my opinion, find it shocking to his conscience and sense of justice. For this reason alone capital punishment cannot stand.

* * *

MR. CHIEF JUSTICE BURGER, with whom MR. JUSTICE BLACKMUN, MR. JUSTICE POWELL, and MR. JUSTICE REHNQUIST join, dissenting.

... In the 181 years since the enactment of the Eighth Amendment, not a single decision of this Court has cast the slightest shadow of a doubt on the constitutionality of capital punishment. ... In these cases the Court confined its attention to the procedural aspects of capital trials, it being implicit that the punishment itself could be constitutionally imposed. Nonetheless, the Court has now been asked to hold that a punishment clearly permissible under the Constitution at the time of its adoption and accepted as such by every member of the Court until today, is suddenly so cruel as to be incompatible with the Eighth Amendment.

Before recognizing such an instant evolution in the law, it seems fair to ask what factors have changed that capital punishment should now be "cruel" in the constitutional sense as it has not been in the past. It is apparent that there has been no change of constitutional significance in the nature of the punishment itself. Twentieth century modes of execution surely involve no greater physical suffering than the means employed at the time of the Eighth Amendment's adoption. And although a man awaiting execution must inevitably experience extraordinary mental anguish, no one suggests that this anguish is materially different from that experienced by condemned men in 1791, even though protracted appellate review processes have greatly increased the waiting time on "death row." To be sure, the ordeal of the condemned man may be thought cruel in the sense that all suffering is thought cruel. But if the Constitution proscribed every punishment producing severe emotional distress, then capital punishment would clearly have been impermissible in 1791.

However, the inquiry cannot end here. For reasons unrelated to any change in intrinsic cruelty, the Eighth Amendment prohibition cannot fairly be limited to those punishments thought excessively cruel and barbarous at the time of the adoption of the Eighth Amendment. ... Nevertheless, the Court up to now has never actually held that a punishment has become impermissibly cruel due to a shift in the weight of accepted social values; nor has the Court suggested judicially manageable criteria for measuring such a shift in moral consensus.

The Court's quiescence in this area can be attributed to the fact that in a democratic society legislatures, not courts, are constituted to respond to the will and consequently the moral values of the people. ... Accordingly, punishments such as branding and the cutting off of ears, which were commonplace at the time of the adoption of the Constitution, passed the penal scene without judicial intervention because they became basically offensive to the people and the legislatures responded to this sentiment.

... The critical fact is that this Court has never had to hold that a mode of punishment authorized by a domestic legislature was so cruel as to be fundamentally at odds with our basic notions of decency. ... Judicial findings of impermissible cruelty have been limited, for the most part, to offensive punishments devised without specific authority by prison officials, not by legislatures. ... The paucity of judicial decisions invalidating legislatively prescribed punishments is powerful evidence that in this country legislatures have in fact been responsive—albeit belatedly at times—to changes in social attitudes and moral values.

I do not suggest that the validity of legislatively authorized punishments presents no justiciable issue under the Eighth Amendment, but, rather, that the primacy of the legislative role narrowly confines the scope of judicial inquiry. Whether or not provable, and whether or not true at all times, in a democracy the legislative judgment is presumed to embody the basic standards of decency prevailing in the society. This presumption can only be negated by unambiguous and compelling evidence of legislative default.

There are no obvious indications that capital punishment offends the conscience of society to such a degree that our traditional deference to the legislative judgment must be abandoned. ... Capital punishment is authorized by statute in 40 States, the District of Columbia, and in the federal courts for the commission of certain crimes. On four occasions in the last 11 years Congress has added to the list of federal crimes punishable by death. In looking for reliable indicia of contemporary attitude, none more trustworthy has been advanced.

... The rate of imposition of death sentences falls far short of providing the requisite unambiguous evidence that the legislatures of 40 States and the Congress have turned their backs on current or evolving standards of decency in continuing to make the death penalty available. For, if selective imposition evidences a rejection of capital punishment in those cases where it is not imposed, it surely evidences a correlative affirmation of the penalty in those cases where it is imposed. Absent some clear indication that the continued imposition of the death penalty on a selective basis is violative of prevailing standards of civilized conduct, the Eighth Amendment cannot be said to interdict its use.

In two of these cases we have been asked to rule on the narrower question whether capital punishment offends the Eighth Amendment when imposed as the punishment for the crime of forcible rape. It is true that the death penalty is authorized for rape in fewer States than it is for murder, and that even in those States it is applied more sparingly for rape than for murder. But for the reason aptly brought out in the opinion of MR. JUSTICE POWELL, ... I do not believe these differences can be elevated to the level of an Eighth Amendment distinction. This blunt constitutional command cannot be sharpened to carve neat distinctions corresponding to the categories of crimes defined by the legislatures.

Capital punishment has also been attacked as violative of the Eighth Amendment on the ground that it is not needed to achieve legitimate penal aims and is thus "unnecessarily cruel." As a pure policy matter, this approach has much to recommend it, but it seeks to give a dimension to the Eighth Amendment that it was never intended to have and promotes a line of inquiry that this Court has never before pursued.

. . . Thus, apart from the fact that the Court in *Weems* concerned itself with the crime committed as well as the punishment imposed, the case marks no departure from the largely unarticulable standard of extreme cruelty. However intractable that standard may be, that is what the Eighth Amendment is all about. The constitutional provision is not addressed to social utility and does not command that enlightened principles of penology always be followed.

By pursuing the necessity approach, it becomes even more apparent that it involves matters outside the purview of the Eighth Amendment. Two of the several aims of punishment are generally associated with capital punishment—retribution and deterrence. It is argued that retribution can be discounted because that, after all, is what the Eighth Amendment seeks to eliminate. There is no authority suggesting that the Eighth Amendment was intended to purge the law of its retributive elements, and the Court has consistently assumed that retribution is a legitimate dimension of the punishment of crimes. . . . Furthermore, responsible legal thinkers of widely varying persuasions have debated the sociological and philosophical aspects of the retribution question for generations, neither side being able to convince the other. It would be reading a great deal into the Eighth Amendment to hold that the punishments authorized by legislatures cannot constitutionally reflect a retributive purpose.

. . . Today the Court has not ruled that capital punishment is *per se* violative of the Eighth Amendment; nor has it ruled that the punishment is barred for any particular class or classes of crimes. . . . The actual scope of the Court's ruling, which I take to be embodied in these concurring opinions, is not entirely clear. This much, however, seems apparent: if the legislatures are to continue to authorize capital punishment for some crimes, juries and judges can no longer be permitted to make the sentencing determination in the same manner they have in the past. This approach—not urged in oral arguments or briefs—misconceives the nature of the constitutional command against "cruel and unusual punishments," disregards controlling case law, and demands a rigidity in capital cases which, if possible of achievement, cannot be regarded as a welcome change. Indeed the contrary seems to be the case.

. . . While I would not undertake to make a definitive statement as to the parameters of the Court's ruling, it is clear that if state legislatures and the Congress wish to maintain the availability of capital punishment, significant statutory changes will have to be made. Since the two pivotal concurring opinions turn on the assumption that the punishment of death is now meted out in a random and unpredictable manner, legislative bodies may seek to bring their laws into compliance with the Court's ruling by providing standards for juries and judges to follow in determining the sentence in capital cases or by more narrowly defining the crimes for which the penalty is to be imposed. If such standards can be devised or the crimes more meticulously defined, the result cannot be detrimental.

[The dissenting opinion of MR. JUSTICE BLACKMUN is omitted.]

[The dissenting opinion of MR. JUSTICE POWELL, with whom MR. CHIEF JUSTICE, MR. JUSTICE BLACKMUN, and MR. JUSTICE REHNQUIST join, is omitted.]

[The dissenting opinion of MR. JUSTICE REHNQUIST, with whom MR. CHIEF JUSTICE, MR. JUSTICE BLACKMUN, and MR. JUSTICE POWELL join, is omitted.]

BATSON V. KENTUCKY
476 U.S. 79 (1986)

James Batson, a black male, was indicted in Kentucky on charges of second-degree burglary and receipt of stolen goods. During the trial, the judge conducted the voir dire examination of the jury venire, excused certain jurors for cause, and permitted the parties to exercise peremptory challenges. The prosecutor used his peremptory challenges to strike all four black persons on the venire, and a jury composed of only white persons was selected. Defense counsel moved to discharge the jury on the ground that the prosecutor's removal of the black members of the venire violated Batson's rights under the Sixth and Fourteenth Amendments to a jury drawn from a cross section of the community and under the Fourteenth Amendment's equal protection of the laws. Without expressly ruling on Batson's request for a hearing, the trial judge denied the motion; the jury ultimately convicted Batson. The Kentucky Supreme Court, relying on *Swain v. Alabama* (1965), affirmed the conviction and held that a defendant alleging lack of a fair cross section must demonstrate systematic exclusion of a group of jurors from the venire. *Vote: 7-2.*

* * *

JUSTICE POWELL delivered the opinion of the Court.

This case requires us to reexamine that portion of *Swain v. Alabama,* 380 U.S. 202 (1965), concerning the evidentiary burden placed on a criminal defendant who claims that he has been denied equal protection through the State's use of peremptory challenges to exclude members of his race from the petit jury.

. . . In *Swain v. Alabama,* this Court recognized that a "State's purposeful or deliberate denial to Negroes on account of race of participation as jurors in the administration of justice violates the Equal Protection Clause." . . . This principle has been "consistently and repeatedly" reaffirmed . . . in numerous decisions of this Court both preceding and following *Swain.* We reaffirm the principle today.

More than a century ago, the Court decided that the State denies a black defendant equal protection of the laws when it puts him on trial before a jury from which members of his race have been purposefully excluded. *Strauder v. West Virginia,* 100 U.S. 303 (1880). That decision laid the foundation for the Court's unceasing efforts to eradicate racial discrimination in the procedures used to select the venire from which individual jurors are drawn. In *Strauder,* the Court explained that the central concern of the recently ratified Fourteenth Amendment was to put an end to governmental discrimination on account of race. . . . Exclusion of black citizens from service as jurors constitutes a primary example of the evil the Fourteenth Amendment was designed to cure.

In holding that racial discrimination in jury selection offends the Equal Protection Clause, the Court in *Strauder* recognized, however, that a defendant has no right to a "petit jury composed in whole or in part of persons of his own race." . . . But the defendant does have the right to be tried by a jury whose members are selected pursuant to nondiscriminatory criteria. . . . *Martin v. Texas,* 200 U.S. 316, 321 (1906); *Ex parte Virginia,* 100 U.S. [10 Otto] 339, 345 (1880). The Equal Protection Clause guarantees the defendant that the State will not exclude members of his race from the jury venire on account of race . . . or on the false assumption that members of his race as a group are not qualified to serve as jurors. See *Norris v. Alabama,* 294 U.S. 587, 599 (1935); *Neal v. Delaware,* 103 U.S. [13 Otto] 370, 397 (1880).

Purposeful racial discrimination in selection of the venire violates a defendant's right to equal protection because it denies him the protection that a trial by jury is intended to secure. . . . "The very idea of a jury is a body . . . composed of the peers or equals of the person whose rights it is selected or summoned to determine; that is, of his neighbors, fellows, associates, persons having the same legal status in society as that which he holds." . . . The petit jury has occupied a central position in our system of justice by safeguarding a person accused of crime against the arbitrary exercise of power by prosecutor or judge. *Duncan v. Louisiana,* 391 U.S. 145, 156 (1968). Those on the venire must be "indifferently chosen," to secure the defendant's right under the Fourteenth Amendment to "protection of life and liberty against race or color prejudice." . . .

. . . A number of lower courts following the teaching of *Swain* reasoned that proof of repeated striking of blacks over a number of cases was necessary to establish a violation of the Equal Protection Clause. Since this interpretation of *Swain* has placed on defendants a crippling burden of proof, prosecutors' peremptory challenges are now largely immune from constitutional scrutiny. For reasons that follow, we reject this evidentiary formulation as inconsistent with standards that have been developed since *Swain* for assessing a prima facie case under the Equal Protection Clause.

Since the decision in *Swain,* we have explained that our cases concerning selection of the venire reflect the general equal protection principle that the "invidious quality" of governmental action claimed to be racially discriminatory "must ultimately be traced to a racially discriminatory purpose." *Washington v. Davis,* 426 U.S. 229, 240 (1976). As in any equal protection case, the "burden is, of course," on the defendant who alleges discriminatory selection of the venire "to prove the existence of purposeful discrimination." . . . In deciding if the defendant has carried his burden of persuasion, a court must undertake "a sensitive inquiry into such circumstantial and direct evidence of intent as may be available." . . . Circumstantial evidence of invidious intent may include proof of disproportionate impact. . . . We have observed that under some circumstances proof of discriminatory impact "may for all practical purposes demonstrate unconstitutionality because in various circumstances the discrimination is very difficult to explain on nonracial grounds." . . . For example, "total or seriously disproportionate exclusion of Negroes from jury venires" . . . "is itself such an 'unequal application of the law . . . as to show intentional discrimination.' " . . .

Moreover, since *Swain,* we have recognized that a black defendant alleging that members of his race have been impermissibly excluded from the venire may make out a prima facie case of purposeful discrimination by showing that the totality of the relevant facts gives rise to an inference of discriminatory purpose. . . . Once the defendant makes the requisite showing, the burden shifts to the State to explain adequately the racial exclusion. . . . The State cannot meet this burden on mere general assertions that its officials did not discriminate or that they properly performed their official duties. . . . Rather, the State must demonstrate that "permissible racially neutral selection criteria and procedures have produced the monochromatic result." . . .

. . . The standards for assessing a prima facie case in the context of discriminatory selection of the venire have been fully articulated since *Swain.* See *Castaneda v. Partida,* [430 U.S. 482 (1977)], . . . *Washington v. Davis,* [426 U.S. 229 (1976)], . . . *Alexander v. Louisiana,* [405 U.S. 625 (1972)]. . . . These principles support our conclusion that a defendant may establish a prima facie case of purposeful discrimination in selection of the petit jury solely on evidence concerning the prosecutor's exercise of peremptory challenges at the defendant's trial. To establish such a case, the defendant first must show that he is a member of a cognizable racial group . . . and that the prosecutor has exercised peremptory challenges to remove from the venire members of the defendant's race. Second, the defendant is entitled to rely on the fact, as to which there can be no dispute, that peremptory challenges constitute a jury selection practice that permits "those to discriminate who are of a mind to discriminate." . . . Finally, the defendant must show that these facts and any other relevant circumstances raise an inference that the prosecutor used that practice to exclude the veniremen from the petit jury on account of their race. This combination of factors in the empaneling of the petit jury, as in the selection of the venire, raises the necessary inference of purposeful discrimination.

In deciding whether the defendant has made the requisite showing, the trial court should consider all relevant circumstances. For example, a "pattern" of strikes against black jurors included in the particular venire might give rise to an inference of discrimination. Similarly, the prosecutor's questions and statements during *voir dire* examination and in exercising his challenges may support or refute an inference of discriminatory purpose. These examples are merely illustrative. We have confidence that trial judges, experienced in supervising *voir dire,* will be able to decide if the circumstances concerning the prosecutor's use of peremptory challenges creates a prima facie case of discrimination against black jurors.

Once the defendant makes a prima facie showing, the burden shifts to the State to come forward with a neutral explanation for challenging black jurors. Though this requirement imposes a limitation in some cases on the full peremptory character of the historic challenge, we emphasize that the prosecutor's explanation need not rise to the level justifying exercise of a challenge for cause. . . . But the prosecutor may not rebut the defendant's prima facie case of discrimination by stating merely that he challenged jurors of the defendant's race on

the assumption—or his intuitive judgment—that they would be partial to the defendant because of their shared race. . . . Just as the Equal Protection Clause forbids the States to exclude black persons from the venire on the assumption that blacks as a group are unqualified to serve as jurors, so it forbids the States to strike black veniremen on the assumption that they will be biased in a particular case simply because the defendant is black. The core guarantee of equal protection, ensuring citizens that their State will not discriminate on account of race, would be meaningless were we to approve the exclusion of jurors on the basis of such assumptions, which arise solely from the jurors' race. Nor may the prosecutor rebut the defendant's case merely by denying that he had a discriminatory motive or "affirm[ing] [his] good faith in making individual selections." . . . If these general assertions were accepted as rebutting a defendant's prima facie case, the Equal Protection Clause "would be but a vain and illusory requirement." . . . The prosecutor therefore must articulate a neutral explanation related to the particular case to be tried. The trial court then will have the duty to determine if the defendant has established purposeful discrimination.

The State contends that our holding will eviscerate the fair trial values served by the peremptory challenge. Conceding that the Constitution does not guarantee a right to peremptory challenges and that *Swain* did state that their use ultimately is subject to the strictures of equal protection, the State argues that the privilege of unfettered exercise of the challenge is of vital importance to the criminal justice system.

While we recognize, of course, that the peremptory challenge occupies an important position in our trial procedures, we do not agree that our decision today will undermine the contribution the challenge generally makes to the administration of justice. The reality of practice, amply reflected in many state- and federal-court opinions, shows that the challenge may be, and unfortunately at times has been, used to discriminate against black jurors. By requiring trial courts to be sensitive to the racially discriminatory use of peremptory challenges, our decision enforces the mandate of equal protection and furthers the ends of justice. In view of the heterogeneous population of our Nation, public respect for our criminal justice system and the rule of law will be strengthened if we ensure that no citizen is disqualified from jury service because of his race.

Nor are we persuaded by the State's suggestion that our holding will create serious administrative difficulties. In those States applying a version of the evidentiary standard we recognized today, courts have not experienced serious administrative burdens, and the peremptory challenge system has survived. We decline, however, to formulate particular procedures to be followed upon a defendant's timely objection to a prosecutor's challenges.

In this case, petitioner made a timely objection to the prosecutor's removal of all black persons on the venire. Because the trial court flatly rejected the objection without requiring the prosecutor to give an explanation for his action, we remand this case for further proceedings. If the trial court decides that the facts establish, prima facie, purposeful discrimination and the prosecutor does not come forward with a neutral explanation for his action, our precedents require that petitioner's conviction be reversed. . . .

It is so ordered.

* * *

JUSTICE WHITE concurring.

The Court overturns the principal holding in *Swain v. Alabama,* . . . that the Constitution does not require in any given case an inquiry into the prosecutor's reasons for using his peremptory challenges to strike blacks from the petit jury panel in the criminal trial of a black defendant and that in such a case it will be presumed that the prosecutor is acting for legitimate trial-related reasons. The Court now rules that such use of peremptory challenges in a given case may, but does not necessarily, raise an inference, which the prosecutor carries the burden of refuting, that his strikes were based on the belief that no black citizen could be a satisfactory juror or fairly try a black defendant.

I agree that, to this extent, *Swain* should be overruled. I do so because *Swain* itself indicated that the presumption of legitimacy with respect to the striking of black venire persons could be overcome by evidence that over a period of time the prosecution had consistently excluded blacks from petit juries. This should have warned prosecutors that using peremptories to exclude blacks on the assumption that no black juror could fairly judge a black defendant would violate the Equal Protection Clause.

* * *

JUSTICE MARSHALL concurring.

. . . I wholeheartedly concur in the Court's conclusion that use of the peremptory challenge to remove blacks from juries, on the basis of their race, violates the Equal Protection Clause. I would go further, however, in fashioning a remedy adequate to eliminate that discrimination. Merely allowing defendants the opportunity to challenge the racially discriminatory use of peremptory challenges in individual cases will not end the illegitimate use of the peremptory challenge.

. . . The inherent potential of peremptory challenges to distort the jury process by permitting the exclusion of jurors on racial grounds should ideally lead the Court to ban them entirely from the criminal

justice system. . . . JUSTICE GOLDBERG, dissenting in *Swain,* emphasized that "[w]ere it necessary to make an absolute choice between the right of a defendant to have a jury chosen in conformity with the requirements of the Fourteenth Amendment and the right to challenge peremptorily, the Constitution compels a choice of the former." . . . I believe that this case presents just such a choice, and I would resolve that choice by eliminating peremptory challenges entirely in criminal cases.

[The concurring opinion of JUSTICE STEVENS, with whom JUSTICE BRENNAN joins, is omitted.]

[The concurring opinion of JUSTICE O'CONNOR is omitted.]

* * *

CHIEF JUSTICE BURGER, with whom JUSTICE REHNQUIST joins, dissenting.

. . . Today the Court sets aside the peremptory challenge, a procedure which has been part of the common law for many centuries and part of our jury system for nearly 200 years. It does so on the basis of a constitutional argument that was rejected, without a single dissent, in *Swain v. Alabama.* . . . Reversal of such settled principles would be unusual enough on its own terms, for only three years ago we said that "*stare decisis,* while perhaps never entirely persuasive on a constitutional question, is a doctrine that demands respect in a society governed by the rule of law." . . . What makes today's holding truly extraordinary is that it is based on a constitutional argument that the petitioner has *expressly* declined to raise, both in this Court and in the Supreme Court of Kentucky.

. . . Instead of even considering the history or function of the peremptory challenge, the bulk of the Court's opinion is spent recounting the well-established principle that intentional exclusion of racial groups from jury venires is a violation of the Equal Protection Clause. I too reaffirm that principle, which has been a part of our constitutional tradition since at least *Strauder v. West Virginia.* . . . But if today's decision is nothing more than mere "application" of the "principles announced in *Strauder,*" as the Court maintains, . . . some will consider it curious that the application went unrecognized for over a century. The Court in *Swain* had no difficulty in unanimously concluding that cases such as *Strauder* did not require inquiry into the basis for a peremptory challenge. . . . More recently, we held that "[d]efendants are not entitled to a jury of any particular composition." . .

. . . Today we mark the return of racial differentiation as the Court accepts a positive evil for a perceived one. Prosecutors and defense attorneys alike will build records in support of their claims that peremptory challenges have been exercised in a racially discriminatory fashion by asking jurors to state their racial background and national origin for the record, despite the fact that "such questions may be offensive to some jurors and thus are not ordinarily asked on voir dire." . . . This process is sure to tax even the most capable counsel and judges since determining whether a prima facie case has been established will "require a continued monitoring and recording of the 'group' composition of the panel present and prospective."

[The dissenting opinion of JUSTICE REHNQUIST, with whom THE CHIEF JUSTICE joins, is omitted.]

NAACP V. CLAIBORNE HARDWARE CO.
458 U.S. 886 (1982)

In late 1965 or early 1966, Charles Evers, the Field Secretary of the NAACP, helped organized the Claiborne County, Mississippi, branch of the NAACP. Black residents of Port Gibson and areas of Claiborne County formed a Human Relations Committee and presented white civic and business leaders a petition for redress of grievances. After a series of unproductive meetings, the committee then prepared a petition entitled "Demands for Racial Justice." It was approved at a local NAACP meeting in March 1966 by approximately 500 black persons. The petition called for the desegregation of public schools and public facilities, the hiring of black police officers, public improvements in black residential areas, the selection of blacks for jury duty, the integration of bus stations, and an end to verbal abuse by police. It also stated that blacks are not to be addressed by terms such as *boy, girl, shine, uncle,* or any other offensive term, but as *Mr., Mrs.,* or *Miss,* as is the case with other citizens. When a favorable response was not received, the Claiborne County NAACP conducted another meeting at the First Baptist Church, and the several hundred attending the meeting voted unanimously to boycott white merchants of Port Gibson and Claiborne County. In February 1967, Mississippi Action for Progress, Inc. (MAP), which was organized to develop community action programs, authorized its Claiborne County representatives to purchase food for the Head Start program from only black-owned stores.

On February 1, 1967, Port Gibson employed its first black police officer, and during that month the boycott was lifted on a number of merchants. After Dr. Martin Luther King, Jr. was assassinated in 1968, a young black man, Roosevelt Jackson, was shot and killed by two Port Gibson police officers, and tensions heightened in the black community. On April 19, Charles Evers spoke to black citizens at the First Baptist Church and led a march to the courthouse. After his demand that the entire Port Gibson police force be discharged was not met, the boycott was reimposed on all merchants. During his speech, Evers stated that the boycott violators would be disciplined and warned that the sheriff could not sleep with boycott violators at night. In another speech on April 21, Evers stated, "If we catch any of you going in any of these racist stores, we're going to break your damn neck." During the boycott, some individuals, known as the "Black Hats" or "Deacons," stood outside the stores and identified those blacks who traded with the white merchants. Their names were read at NAACP meetings and published in a black newspaper. Blacks also held marches and pickets that were used to advertise the boycott without incident. In about 10 instances, however, blacks who violated the boycott experienced instances of violence such as shots fired in homes, bricks thrown in windshields, and slashed tires.

In October 1969, 17 white merchants filed a lawsuit in Mississippi Chancery Court against two corporations (NAACP and MAP), two NAACP officials (Aaron Henry and Charles Evers), and 144 other individuals who had participated in the boycott. The trial began in 1973, and in August 1976 the chancellor found that the black defendants were liable for the tort of malicious interference with the plaintiffs' businesses—a violation of state statutory prohibition against secondary boycotts and a violation of a Mississippi restraint of trade statute. The chancellor rejected the black defendants' claim that their conduct was protected by the First Amendment. The chancellor found that, during an 11-year period (1966-1977), the black defendants were liable for $1,250,699 plus interest for the business losses of 12 white merchants. In addition to imposing damages liability, the chancellor entered a permanent injunction enjoining black citizens from "store watching," picketing, or patrolling white merchants and from persuading or using violence against any person to withhold patronage from white merchants. In December 1980, the Mississippi Supreme Court reversed portions of the trial court's judgment on secondary boycott and restraint of trade violations but upheld the imposition of liability on the basis that the entire boycott was unlawful. *Vote: 8-0.*

* * *

JUSTICE STEVENS delivered the opinion of the Court.

The term "concerted action" encompasses unlawful conspiracies and constitutionally protected assemblies. The "looseness and pliability" of legal doctrine applicable to concerted action led Justice Jackson to note that certain joint activities have a "chameleon-like" character. The boycott of white merchants in Claiborne County, Miss., that gave rise to this litigation had such a character; it included elements of criminality and elements of majesty. Evidence that fear of reprisals caused some black citizens to withhold their patronage from respondents' businesses convinced the Supreme Court of Mississippi that the entire boycott was unlawful and that each of the 92 petitioners was liable for all of its economic consequences. Evidence that persuasive rhetoric, determination to remedy past injustices, and a host of voluntary decisions by free citizens were the critical factors in the boycott's success presents us with the question whether the state court's judgment is consistent with the Constitution of the United States.

. . . This Court's jurisdiction to review the judgment of the Mississippi Supreme Court is, of course, limited to the federal questions necessarily decided by that court. We consider first whether petitioners' activities are protected in any respect by the Federal Constitution and, if they are, what effect such protection has on a lawsuit of this nature.

The boycott of white merchants at issue in this case took many forms. The boycott was launched at a meeting of a local branch of the NAACP attended by several hundred persons. Its acknowledged purpose was to secure compliance by both civic and business leaders with a lengthy list of demands for equality and racial justice. The boycott was supported by speeches and nonviolent picketing. Participants repeatedly encouraged others to join in its cause.

Each of these elements of the boycott is a form of speech or conduct that is ordinarily entitled to protection under the First and Fourteenth Amendments. The black citizens named as defendants in this action banded together and collectively expressed their dissatisfaction with a social structure that had denied them rights to equal treatment and respect. . . .

. . . The right to associate does not lose all constitutional protection merely because some members of the group may have participated in conduct or advocated doctrine that itself is not protected. In *De Jonge v. Oregon,* 299 U.S. 353 [1937], the Court unanimously held that an individual could not be penalized simply for assisting in the conduct of an otherwise lawful meeting held under the auspices of the Communist Party, an organization that advocated "criminal syndicalism." . . .

Of course, the petitioners in this case did more than assemble peaceably and discuss among themselves their grievances against governmental and business policy. Other elements of the boycott, however, also involved activities ordinarily safeguarded by the First Amendment. In *Thornhill v. Alabama,*

310 U.S. 88 [1940], the Court held that peaceful picketing was entitled to constitutional protection, even though, in that case, the purpose of the picketing "was concededly to advise customers and prospective customers of the relationship existing between the employer and its employees and thereby to induce such customers not to patronize the employer." . . . In *Edwards v. South Carolina,* 372 U.S. 229 [1963], we held that a peaceful march and demonstration was protected by the rights of free speech, free assembly, and freedom to petition for a redress of grievances.

Speech itself also was used to further the aims of the boycott. Nonparticipants repeatedly were urged to join the common cause, both through public address and through personal solicitation. These elements of the boycott involve speech in its most direct form. In addition, names of boycott violators were read aloud at meetings at the First Baptist Church and published in a local black newspaper. Petitioners admittedly sought to persuade others to join the boycott through social pressure and the "threat" of social ostracism. Speech does not lose its protected character, however, simply because it may embarrass others or coerce them into action. . . .

. . . In sum, the boycott clearly involved constitutionally protected activity. The established elements of speech, assembly, association, and petition, "though not identical, are inseparable." . . . Through exercise of these First Amendment rights, petitioners sought to bring about political, social, and economic change. Through speech, assembly, and petition—rather than through riot or revolution—petitioners sought to change a social order that had consistently treated them as second-class citizens.

The presence of protected activity, however, does not end the relevant constitutional inquiry. Governmental regulation that has an incidental effect on First Amendment freedoms may be justified in certain narrowly defined instances. See *United States v. O'Brien,* 391 U.S. 367 [1968]. A nonviolent and totally voluntary boycott may have a disruptive effect on local economic conditions. This Court has recognized the strong governmental interest in certain forms of economic regulation, even though such regulation may have an incidental effect on rights of speech and association. . . . The right of business entities to "associate" to suppress competition may be curtailed. . . . Unfair trade practices may be restricted. Secondary boycotts and picketing by labor unions may be prohibited, as part of "Congress' striking of the delicate balance between union freedom of expression and the ability of neutral employers, employees, and consumers to remain free from coerced participation in industrial strife." . . .

While States have broad power to regulate economic activity, we do not find a comparable right to prohibit peaceful political activity such as that found in the boycott in this case. This Court has recognized that expression on public issues "has always rested on the highest rung of the hierarchy of First Amendment values." . . .

. . . We hold that the nonviolent elements of petitioners' activities are entitled to the protection of the First Amendment.

The Mississippi Supreme Court did not sustain the chancellor's imposition of liability on a theory that state law prohibited a nonviolent, politically motivated boycott. The fact that such activity is constitutionally protected, however, imposes a special obligation on this Court to examine critically the basis on which liability was imposed. In particular, we consider here the effect of our holding that much of petitioners' conduct was constitutionally protected on the ability of the State to impose liability for elements of the boycott that were not so protected.

The First Amendment does not protect violence. . . . Although the extent and significance of the violence in this case are vigorously disputed by the parties, there is no question that acts of violence occurred. No federal rule of law restricts a State from imposing tort liability for business losses that are caused by violence and by threats of violence. When such conduct occurs in the context of constitutionally protected activity, however, "precision of regulation" is demanded. . . . Specially, the presence of activity protected by the First Amendment imposes restraints on the grounds that may give rise to damages liability and on the person who may be held accountable for those damages.

. . . The principles announced in *Scales* [*v. United States,* 367 U.S. 203 (1961)], *Noto* [*v. United States,* 367 U.S. 290 (1961)], and *Healy* [*v. James,* 408 U.S. 169 (1972)] are relevant to this case. Civil liability may not be imposed merely because an individual belonged to a group, some members of which committed acts of violence. For liability to be imposed by reason of association alone, it is necessary to establish that the group itself possessed unlawful goals and that the individual held a specific intent to further those illegal aims. . . .

The chancellor awarded respondents damages for all business losses that were sustained during a 7-year period beginning in 1966 and ending in December 31, 1972. With the exception of Aaron Henry, all defendants were held jointly and severally liable for these losses. The chancellor's findings were consistent with his view that voluntary participation in the boycott was a sufficient basis on which to impose liability. The Mississippi Supreme Court properly rejected that theory; it nevertheless held that petitioners were liable for all damages "resulting from the boycott." In light of the principles set forth above, it is evident that such a damages award may not be sustained in this case.

. . . It is indeed inconceivable that a boycott launched by the unanimous vote of several hundred persons succeeded solely through fear and intimidation. Moreover, the fact that the boycott "intensified" following the shootings of Martin Luther King, Jr., and Roosevelt Jackson demonstrates that factors other than force and violence (by the petitioners) figured prominently in the boycott's success. The chancellor made no finding that any act of violence occurred after 1966. While the timing of the acts of violence was not important to the chancellor's imposition of liability, it is a critical factor under the narrower rationale of the Mississippi Supreme Court. The court has completely failed to demonstrate that business losses suffered in 1972—three years after this lawsuit was filed—were proximately caused by the isolated acts of violence found in 1966. It is impossible to conclude that state power has not been exerted to compensate respondents for the direct consequences of nonviolent, constitutionally protected activity.

. . . Respondents' supplemental brief also demonstrates that on the present record no judgment may be sustained against most of the petitioners. Regular attendance and participation at the Tuesday meetings of the Claiborne County Branch of the NAACP is an insufficient predicate on which to impose liability. The chancellor's findings do not suggest that any illegal conduct was authorized, ratified, or even discussed at any of the meetings. The Sheriff testified that he was kept informed of what transpired at the meetings; he made no reference to any discussion of unlawful activity. To impose liability for presence at weekly meetings of the NAACP would—ironically—not even constitute "guilt by association," since there is no evidence that the association possessed unlawful aims. Rather, liability could only be imposed on a "guilt *for* association" theory. Neither is permissible under the First Amendment.

Respondents also argue that liability may be imposed on individuals who were either "store watchers" or members of the "Black Hats." There is nothing unlawful in standing outside a store and recording names. Similarly, there is nothing unlawful in wearing black hats, although such apparel may cause apprehension in others. As established above, mere association with either group—absent a specific intent to further an unlawful aim embraced by that group—is an insufficient predicate for liability. At the same time, the evidence does support the conclusion that some members of each of these groups engaged in violence or threats of violence. Unquestionably, these individuals may be held responsible for the injuries that they caused; a judgment tailored to the consequence of their unlawful conduct may be sustained.

. . . For the reasons set forth above, liability may not be imposed on Evers for his presence at NAACP meetings or his active participation in the boycott itself. To the extent that Evers caused respondents to suffer business losses through his organization of the boycott, his emotional and persuasive appeals for unity in the joint effort, or his "threats" of vilification or social ostracism, Evers' conduct is constitutionally protected and beyond the reach of a damages award. Respondents point to Evers' speeches, however, as a justification for the chancellor's damages award. Since respondents would impose liability on the basis of a public address—which predominantly contained highly charged political rhetoric lying at the core of the First Amendment—we approach this suggested basis of liability with extreme care.

. . . The emotionally charged rhetoric of Charles Evers' speeches did not transcend the bounds of protected speech set forth in *Brandenburg* [*v. Ohio,* 395 U.S. 444 (1969)]. The lengthy addresses generally contained an impassioned plea for black citizens to unify, to support and respect each other, and to realize the political and economic power available to them. In the course of those pleas, strong language was used. If that language had been followed by acts of violence, a substantial question would be presented whether Evers could be held liable for the consequences of that unlawful conduct. In this case, however—with the possible exception of the Cox incident—the acts of violence identified in 1966 occurred weeks or months after the April 1, 1966, speech; the chancellor made no finding of any violence after the challenged 1969 speech. Strong and effective extemporaneous rhetoric cannot be nicely channeled in purely dulcet phrases. An advocate must be free to stimulate his audience with spontaneous and emotional appeals for unity and action in a common cause. When such appeals do not incite lawless action, they must be regarded as protected speech. To rule otherwise would ignore the "profound national commitment" that "debate on public issues should be uninhibited, robust, and wide-open." . . .

For these reasons, we conclude that Evers' addresses did not exceed the bounds of protected speech. . . .

. . . The associational rights of the NAACP and its members have been recognized repeatedly by this Court. The NAACP—like any other organization—of course may be held responsible for the acts of its agents throughout the country that are undertaken within the scope of their actual or apparent authority. . . . Moreover, the NAACP may be found liable for other conduct of which it had knowledge and specifically ratified.

The chancellor made no finding that Charles Evers or any other NAACP member had either actual or apparent authority to commit acts of violence or to threaten violent conduct. The evidence in the record suggests the contrary. . . .

To impose liability without a finding that the NAACP authorized—either actually or apparently—or ratified unlawful conduct would impermissibly burden the rights of political association that are protected by the First Amendment. . . . The chancellor's findings are not adequate to support the judgment against the NAACP.

In litigation of this kind the stakes are high. Concerted action is a powerful weapon. History teaches that special dangers are associated with conspiratorial activity. And yet one of the foundations of our society is the right of individuals to combine with other persons in pursuit of a common goal by lawful means.

. . . The judgment is reversed. The case is remanded for further proceedings not inconsistent with this opinion.

It is so ordered.

JUSTICE REHNQUIST concurs in the result.

JUSTICE MARSHALL took no part in the consideration or decision of this case.

5

The Rehnquist Court

THE ERA OF RETRENCHMENT
AND UNPREDICTABILITY, 1986-1995

The result of a Rehnquist-led majority would be an equal protection clause that offers little protection to racial minorities; virtually no protection to women, aliens and illegitimates; and no "special" preferential treatment to members of traditionally disadvantaged groups.

Sue Davis*

A MORE CONSERVATIVE
POLICY DIRECTION FOR CIVIL RIGHTS

The Reagan administration (1980-1988) took a restrictive approach to federal civil rights enforcement.[1] For example, when the authorization of the U.S. Commission on Civil Rights was about to expire in 1983, President Ronald Reagan, disturbed by the activist agenda of the commission, fired the three Democratic Commissioners—Mary Frances Berry, Blandina Cardenas Ramirez, and Murray Saltzman. His nominees, Morris Abram, John Bunzel, and Robert Destro, along with Linda Chavez, who was recommended to fill the position of staff director, shared President Reagan's views on civil rights. President Reagan had earlier appointed Clarence Pendleton, an outspoken black conservative, to head the commission. The dismissals of the commission

---

*Sue Davis (1984). Justice Rehnquist's Equal Protection Clause: An Interim Analysis. *Nebraska Law Review, 63,* 313.

members outraged the civil rights community because the commission was generally regarded as genuinely committed to equal opportunity for all citizens, and it acted independently of the White House. Congress responded to the president's action by enacting compromise legislation that included an eight-member, bipartisan commission with four members appointed by the president and four members appointed by Congress for staggered terms.[2]

The Reagan administration also attempted to use the federal judiciary to implement its conservative social agenda. The Reagan jurisprudence became more forcefully articulated when Edwin Meese was appointed to the position of attorney general in 1985. Attorney General Meese argued that the only legitimate way to interpret the Constitution was to adhere to the intent of the framers.[3] He also criticized the Supreme Court's selective incorporation of the Bill of Rights as resting on an "intellectually shaky foundation" and as contrary to original intent theory.[4] The Reagan jurisprudence was aggressively pursued by the solicitor general in arguing cases before the Supreme Court and in filing amicus curiae briefs. Lincoln Caplan traced the transformation of the solicitor general's office from one of having "the independence to exercise his craft as a lawyer on behalf of the institution of government without being a mouthpiece for the President" to one of becoming "a partisan advocate for the Administration" who viewed the law "as no more than the instrument of politics" because so much of the Court's docket deals with the legal aspects of social policy.[5] The federal government's position before the Court as a party and as amicus curiae reflected a more restrictive interpretation of individual and civil rights.

As part of the 1980 campaign, President Reagan promised that he would place on the federal courts conservatives who adhered to a philosophy of judicial self-restraint and to counteract the activist federal judges appointed by President Jimmy Carter.[6] Ideology clearly emerged as the most important factor in selecting federal judges, especially Supreme Court nominees, during the Reagan administration. The first vacancy was filled by Sandra Day O'Connor, a conservative judge on the Arizona Court of Appeals, whose notoriety as the first female Justice overshadowed her conservative judicial philosophy in favor of "state-prerogatives, judicial restraint and deference to the political branches of government."[7]

On September 26, 1986, after 17 years as Chief Justice of the United States, Warren E. Burger resigned to work full time as Chairman of the Commission on the Bicentennial, which had the responsibility of planning the Constitution's 200th-year celebration. On June 20, 1986, President Reagan nominated William H. Rehnquist, an Associate Justice, to replace Burger. Rehnquist had graduated first in his class from the Stanford Law School. O'Connor had been one of his classmates. He became one of only three sitting Associate Justices to be elevated to the position of Chief Justice. During the confirmation hearings, he was sharply confronted with questions concerning his views on civil rights. Fifteen years earlier, when he was nominated to serve as an Associate Justice on the high court by President Richard Nixon, questions were raised concerning a memorandum he allegedly wrote as a law clerk for Justice Robert Jackson that favored "separate but equal" schools for whites and blacks. He responded to the allegations by pointing out that the views in the memorandum were not his but those of Justice Jackson.[8]

After his clerkship with Justice Jackson, Rehnquist became associated with the most conservative wing of the Republican Party. Robert Riggs and Thomas Proffitt, in their study of Rehnquist following his 11th year as an Associate Justice, pinpointed the core of his philosophy: "His support for state sovereignty and autonomy, his manifest reluctance to reverse criminal convictions, his narrow reading of first amendment rights, and his general willingness to subordinate civil liberty claims to governmental authority are readily identifiable as conservative positions as the term is currently understood."[9] Approximately 10 years before being confirmed as Chief Justice, Rehnquist revealed the quintessence of his judicial philosophy in a lecture at the University of Texas School of Law on March 12, 1976. He emphasized that the federal judiciary should not fashion solutions to problems simply because the legislative and executive branches have failed to act within a given time period. For him, such an approach would be "genuinely corrosive of the fundamental values of our democratic society."[10] Deference to positive law and state authority is the sine qua non for Chief Justice Rehnquist. He stated:

> Representative government is predicated upon the idea that one who feels deeply upon a question as a matter of conscience will seek out others of like view or will attempt to persuade others who do not initially share that view. When adherents to the belief become sufficiently numerous, he will have the necessary armaments required in a democratic society to press his views upon the elected representatives of the people, and to have them embodied into positive law.[11]

On September 17, 1986, Rehnquist was confirmed by the Senate by a vote of 65-33. It is important to note that, with the exception of Justice Clarence Thomas, Justice Rehnquist received more negative votes than any other nominee to the Supreme Court during this century. President Reagan nominated Antonin Scalia to fill the Rehnquist vacancy. Scalia, one of the Court's most conservative members, received a 98-0 vote. Because Scalia filled the seat previously occupied by Rehnquist, major ideological shifts on the Court were not expected to occur. When Justice Lewis F. Powell resigned in June, 1987, however, President Reagan attempted to upset the delicate ideological balance on the Supreme Court by appointing the intellectually powerful conservative judge Robert Bork, of the Court of Appeals for the District of Columbia. The widespread perception of Judge Bork's insensitivity to individual and civil rights and his seeming disavowal of earlier controversial stances he had taken in extensive writings and speeches over two decades facilitated interest group mobilization against his confirmation that was unprecedented in the history of Supreme Court nominations. Judge Bork's views on civil rights issues also contributed to the lack of support by key Southern senators who were elected by a large percentage of the black vote. The Senate rejected the Bork nomination by a 58-42 vote in October 1987. In February

1988, the Senate unanimously approved, by a vote of 97-0, the less controversial appointment of conservative Anthony M. Kennedy of the Court of Appeals for the Ninth Circuit to fill Powell's vacancy.

In 1990 and 1991, the nation witnessed the departure of the two leading proponents of liberty and equality on the Supreme Court. Justice William J. Brennan, Jr., retired in July 1990, after serving 33 years on the high court. President George Bush nominated David H. Souter, a justice on the Supreme Court of New Hampshire, to replace him. Approximately one year later, President Bush nominated Clarence Thomas, a black conservative, to succeed the Court's only remaining liberal and black Justice, Thurgood Marshall, who retired in June 1991 (the Thomas nomination is discussed later in this chapter). The replacement of the two most liberal Justices with conservatives and the elevation of Rehnquist to the position of Chief Justice solidified and accelerated the Court's ideological shift to the right.

On March 19, 1993, Justice Byron R. White announced that he would retire in June at the end of his 31st year on the Supreme Court. Approximately three months later, President Bill Clinton nominated Ruth Bader Ginsburg, a 60-year-old jurist of the U.S. Court of Appeals for the District of Columbia and former litigator of women's rights cases, to fill White's vacancy. Her appointment came as a surprise to many Court observers because Clinton administration officials had claimed that Judge Stephen G. Breyer would receive the nomination. On July 29, 1993, the Senate Judiciary Committee unanimously approved Ginsburg's nomination to become the second woman Justice, the sixth Jewish Justice, and the first nominee to be appointed by a Democratic president since 1967. On August 3, 1993, Ginsburg was confirmed by a vote of 96-3. Judge Ginsburg's testimony during the Senate hearings and her brief tenure on the Court reveal that she is a moderate on the Court, with a propensity to practice judicial self-restraint.

In April 1994, Justice Harry A. Blackmun formally announced his retirement after serving 23 years on the Court. Despite several prospective nominees, Judge Stephen G. Breyer emerged as President Clinton's second nominee to the Supreme Court. Breyer, who was chief judge of the Court of Appeals for the First Circuit, was also former chief counsel of the Senate Judiciary Committee and was well known among members of the committee. The most controversial aspect of his confirmation hearing dealt with allegations that he acted improperly in pollution cases while holding investments in an insurance syndicate. No single approach to constitutional interpretation or clear judicial philosophy emerged during the Breyer hearings. Court observers have characterized Breyer as a judicial pragmatist or moderate whose appointment is not likely to alter the Court's ideological direction. Breyer was confirmed as the nation's 108th Supreme Court Justice by a vote of 87-9.

In this chapter, our analysis reveals that the Rehnquist Court narrowly interpreted constitutional provisions and federal statutes that provide protection for civil rights of racial and ethnic minorities. In particular, minorities experienced setbacks in affirmative action, employment discrimination, and voting rights. The Rehnquist Court's leading civil rights cases in many

Table 5.1 School Desegregation and the Rehnquist Court: Leading Cases

Case	Vote	Ruling
Missouri v. Jenkins, 495 U.S. 33 (1990)	5-4	Justice White held that a federal district court judge could not order a tax increase himself to finance a magnet school desegregation plan but that he should have ordered the school board to raise the taxes.
Board of Education of Oklahoma City Public Schools v. Dowell, 498 U.S. 237 (1991)	5-3	Chief Justice Rehnquist held that formerly segregated school districts must be released from a desegregation decree once they have taken steps to eliminate vestiges of past discrimination.
Freeman v. Pitts, 112 S.Ct. 1430 (1992)	8-0	Justice Kennedy held that a district court may relinquish supervisory authority of a school district in incremental stages before achieving full compliance in all aspects of school operations.
United States v. Fordice, 112 S.Ct. 2727 (1992)	8-1	Justice White held that merely adopting and implementing race-neutral policies to govern colleges and universities did not necessarily fulfill the state's affirmative obligation to disestablish a prior de jure segregated system.

instances eroded previously won victories. Its policy making in the area of civil rights has frustrated the quest for equality.

SCHOOL DESEGREGATION: A RELAXATION OF FEDERAL COURT SUPERVISION

The impetus that school desegregation received during the Warren and Burger Courts slowed dramatically during the Rehnquist Court. The *Brown,* 347 U.S. 483 (1954), era had come to an end, and truly desegregated schools were, at most, an ideal. Many schools resegregated because of demographic changes and the lack of genuine political support. School desegregation cases remained off the Supreme Court's agenda until the 1990s. The major cases before the Rehnquist Court (see Table 5.1) addressed the issue of whether there were limits to a federal court's supervision of school desegregation decrees. A divided Court defied expectations when it upheld the broad authority of federal courts to remedy constitutional violations in *Missouri v. Jenkins,* 495 U.S. 33 (1990). In *Jenkins* a federal district court judge—Judge Russell G. Clark—ordered a property tax increase to finance a magnet school desegregation plan in Kansas City, Missouri, when voters repeatedly rejected the tax increase to pay for the plan. The court of appeals modified Judge Clark's order when it held that the district court should not have imposed the tax increase itself but that it should have ordered the school board to raise the taxes. The Court was unanimous only on the question of whether Judge Clark abused his discretion by imposing the tax increase himself. In an opinion written by Justice White, the Court held that the district judge's order intruded on the authority of the local government when it assumed the important power of taxation. A five-member majority upheld the court of appeals' modification order, however, insisting that "authorizing and directing local government institutions to devise and implement remedies not only protects the function of those institutions but . . . also places the responsibility for solutions to the problem of segregation upon those who have themselves created the problems." In a lengthy concurring opinion, Justice Kennedy, joined by Chief Justice Rehnquist and Justices O'Connor and Scalia, was sharply critical of the expensive and far-reaching magnet school plan. Justice Kennedy argued that by allowing unelected, life-appointed judges to authorize a tax and to enjoin state law limitations was beyond the power of Article III courts and "disregards fundamental precepts for the democratic control of public institutions." He also pointed out that the principles established in this case were not necessarily limited to the school desegregation context and could realistically extend to "judicial taxation in cases involving prisons, hospitals, or other public institutions."

A number of school boards sought an end to federal court supervision because they believed they were in compliance. Fifteen years after *Pasadena City Board of Education v. Spangler,* 427 U.S. 424 (1976) was decided, the Rehnquist Court revisited the question whether there were time limits to a federal court's supervision of a desegregation decree. In BOARD OF EDUCATION OF OKLAHOMA CITY PUBLIC SCHOOLS V. DOWELL, 498 U.S. 237 (1991), Chief Justice Rehnquist, writing for the 5-3 majority, declared that desegregation decrees were intended to operate temporarily to remedy past discrimination. Otherwise, a school district could be condemned "to judicial tutelage for the indefinite future" or in perpetuity. He also asserted that after local authorities have complied with a decree for a reasonable time period and the evidence indicates they are not likely to return to their former ways, dissolution of a decree is appropriate. The majority developed the following standard to apply in desegregation decree cases: Formerly segregated school districts must be released from a desegregation decree once they have taken steps to eliminate vestiges of past discrimination. Justice Marshall, joined in his dissent by Justices Blackmun and Stevens, argued forcefully that the decree had not been achieved because one-race schools could have been avoided. For Marshall, the majority opinion had failed to adequately examine Oklahoma's history of vigorously resisting desegregation.

The *Dowell* decision was ambiguous in providing guidance for lower courts and those school districts that were once segregated and that now wanted to escape judicial supervision. The Rehnquist Court agreed to hear another school desegregation case, involving the DeKalb County, Georgia, school system, in which many Court observers thought the Rehnquist Court would clarify the questions left open in *Dowell*. In FREEMAN V. PITTS, 112 S.Ct. 1430 (1992), the DeKalb County school system had been under federal court supervision since 1969, and it filed a motion for final dismissal in 1986. The district court, in its order, relinquished remedial control in four categories in which unitary status had been achieved but retained judicial control over two other categories (faculty assignments and resource allocations) because the school district was not in full compliance. Relying on the *Pasadena* case, the Rehnquist Court held in *Pitts* that a district court may relinquish supervisory authority of a school district in incremental stages before achieving full compliance in all aspects of school operations. Justice Kennedy, writing for the unanimous Court, believed that this approach would allow a district court and the school district involved to concentrate their resources those areas in which full compliance had not been achieved. For him, the return of local autonomy to school authorities where justified is an integral part of our national tradition.

During the 1994-1995 term, the Rehnquist Court accepted yet another challenge to the Kansas City school desegregation plan. In *Missouri v. Jenkins*, No. 93-1823, the state of Missouri argued that it had spent $1.3 billion to help Kansas City desegregate its public schools and requested that the Court declare the schools partially unitary. Missouri also argued that the lower federal court exceeded its authority when it declared that overall academic performance of the students must improve as part of the plan. How the Rehnquist Court rules in this case may affect approximately 200 other school systems under federal court supervision.

Dismantling De Jure
Segregation in Higher Education

Public colleges and universities, like elementary and secondary schools, desegregated very slowly before 1964. After the enactment of the Civil Rights Act of 1964, an increase occurred in the number of black students attending predominantly white Southern universities, but genuine progress was still slow despite the ruling in *Adams v. Richardson,* 356 F. Supp. 1159 (1972); *affirmed per curiam,* 480 F.2d 1159 (1973). In *Adams,* several civil rights organizations complained to the Department of Health, Education and Welfare (HEW) that the public colleges and universities in 10 states had failed to desegregate. The Legal Defense Fund of the NAACP initiated a suit against HEW, alleging that it had not acted to enforce Title VI of the Civil Rights Act of 1964. The district court held that HEW must commence enforcement proceedings against all institutions that had not complied with Title VI.

The concerted efforts of Congress, the executive branch, and the courts resulted in only token progress in desegregating public colleges and universities in the South.[12] The Rehnquist Court for the first time addressed the issue of de jure segregation at the university level in the case of UNITED STATES

V. FORDICE, 112 S.Ct. 2727 (1992). Thirty years after *Brown I,* Mississippi maintained five all-white universities and three universities that were almost 100% black. Initially, the parties agreed to solve the problem voluntarily, but the case proceeded to trial when it became clear that the student bodies at Mississippi's public universities were still segregated. The district court declared that the defendants had taken steps to dismantle their de jure segregated system, and the court of appeals, on rehearing en banc, agreed and held that the defendants had implemented race-neutral policies that afforded students the freedom to attend the college or university of their choice. The Rehnquist Court reversed the holding of the appeals court and contended that a seemingly race-neutral policy does not necessarily cure a constitutional violation. Writing for the 8-1 majority, Justice White examined four policies (admission standards, duplication of programs, institutional mission assignments, and the continued operation of all-white universities) and concluded that they were the relics of the state's prior de jure system of higher education. He also emphasized the Court's rejection of the plaintiffs' request to upgrade the three predominantly black institutions on the ground that they are for all of the state's citizens and cannot remain exclusively black enclaves by private choice. Justice Scalia dissented to the part of the judgment that required previously segregated universities to demonstrate that they were complying with the *Brown* mandate because he thought this requirement had no prior application to institutions of higher learning and provided inadequate guidance to the states. Some civil rights advocates view *Fordice* as an important ruling that will result in changes at predominantly white institutions. Other observers contend, however, that *Fordice* could actually threaten the existence of historically black colleges and universities.

VOTING RIGHTS
AND RACE IN THE 1990s

When Congress amended the Voting Rights Act in 1982 and when the Supreme Court first construed the 1982 Amendments in *Thornburg v. Gingles,* 478 U.S. 30 (1986), the stage was set for the attainment of meaningful progress in minority political representation at the state and national levels of government. Redistricting after the 1990 census led to record numbers of blacks and Latinos elected to office in 1992 throughout the South. For example, the Southern Regional Council found that the 1992 election produced 16 new black state senators, for a total of 64 (a 33% increase); 42 new black state representatives were elected, for a total of 199 (a 26.8% increase).[13] Florida and Texas experienced the greatest increase in Latino representatives at the state level, and one new Latino senator was elected in Florida (for a total of 9). Thirty-six new Latino representatives were elected in Florida and Texas, a 24.1% increase.[14] Impressive gains were made at the national level as well. In 1992, 16 African Americans were newly elected to the U.S. House of Representatives, with 13 of them coming from Southern states.[15] For the first time in this century, Virginia, Alabama, Florida, North Carolina, and South Carolina sent African American representatives to the U.S. House of Representatives. A record number of black women—six—were elected to Congress, including Carol Moseley Braun of Illinois to the U.S. Senate. In 1992 eight new Latino representatives were elected, with three of them coming from Florida and Texas. In addition, Ben Nighthorse Campbell, a Native American from Colorado, was elected to the Senate, and California elected its first Korean American representative to Congress, Jay C. Kim.

The political landscape changed dramatically in Congress in November 1994. Republicans gained control of both houses in Congress for the first time in 40 years. In contrast to the 103rd Congress, fewer minorities won seats in the House of Representatives for the 104th Congress. J.C. Watts (Republican, Oklahoma), Sheila Jackson Lee (Democrat, Texas), and Chaka Fattah (Democrat, Pennsylvania) joined the 36 black incumbents. Hispanics and Asians, however, made no electoral gains to the 104th Congress.

Thus, despite these impressive gains and milestones in American electoral politics, a major gap still exists between the percentage of the minority voting-age population and representation at the state and national levels. The important question to consider in this section is whether and to what extent Rehnquist Court rulings in the area of voting rights will advance minority electoral gains.

The Continuing Significance of §§ 2 and 5 of the Voting Rights Act

Sections 2 and 5 of the Voting Rights Act continued to be important statutory weapons in protecting minority voting rights during the Rehnquist Court era (see Table 5.2). For example, during the Rehnquist Court's first term, the Court barred an all-white city from annexing an all-white area while refusing to annex adjacent black areas under § 5. In *City of Pleasant Grove v. United States,* 479 U.S. 462 (1987), Justice White, writing for the 6-3 majority, found that the city's failure to annex black areas while simultaneously annexing nonblack areas was highly sufficient in demonstrating that the annexations were racially motivated. The Court also rejected Pleasant Grove's contention that because the city had no black voters at the time of the annexations, there was no impermissible effect on black voting and thus no discriminatory purpose. Justice White stated that it is incorrect to assume that § 5 relates only to present circumstances; that is, it looks also to their future effects, and an impermissible purpose under § 5 may relate to anticipated as well as present circumstances. Writing for the dissenters, Justice Powell argued that because "the actions challenged in this case would not have had *any* effect on minority voting rights, much less a retrogressive effect, it is clear that the city of Pleasant Grove could not have acted with such an intent respecting either of the annexations at issue in this case."

Black and Latino voters won a significant victory in a series of cases that affect the racial and ethnic composition of the elected state judiciary (see Table

Table 5.2 Minority Voting Rights Cases and the Rehnquist Court

Case	Vote	Ruling
City of Pleasant Grove v. United States, 479 U.S. 462 (1987)	6-3	Justice White held that the refusal of an all-white city to annex black areas while simultaneously annexing nonblack areas violated § 5 of the Voting Rights Act.
Chisom v. Roemer, 501 U.S. 380 (1991)	6-3	Justice Stevens held for the first time that § 2 of the Voting Rights Act applies to judicial elections of state supreme court justices.
Houston Lawyers' Association v. Attorney General of Texas, and League of United Latin American Citizens v. Attorney General of Texas, 501 U.S. 419 (1991)	6-3	Relying on *Chisom v. Roemer*, the Court held that the election of trial judges is covered under § 2 of the Voting Rights Act.
Clark v. Roemer, 500 U.S. 646 (1991)	9-0	The Court held that a district court was in error for not enjoining elections for certain state court judgeships for which the attorney general had raised valid objections under the Voting Rights Act.
Presley v. Etowah County Commission, 112 S. Ct. 820 (1992)	6-3	Justice Kennedy held that charges in the way county boards reallocated decisionmaking authority did not have a direct relation to voting or the election process and therefore did not require preclearance under § 5.
Growe v. Emison, 113 S.Ct. 1075 (1993)	9-0	Justice Scalia held that a district court erred in its conclusion that the state court's redistricting plan violated § 2 of the Voting Rights Act and that the district court ignored the *Thornburg v. Gingles* prerequisites.
Voinovich v. Quilter, 113 S.Ct. 1149 (1993)	9-0	The Supreme Court refused to decide whether influence districts claims are viable under § 2.
Shaw v. Reno, 113 S.Ct. 2816 (1993)	5-4	Justice O'Connor established that white voters can challenge the creation of majority black congressional districts under the equal protection clause and that strict scrutiny is required in the reapportionment context.

5.2). In the landmark case of *Chisom v. Roemer*, 501 U.S. 380 (1991), the Court held for the first time that § 2 of the Voting Rights Act applies to state judicial elections. This case involved a class action suit that challenged the way Louisiana selected its state supreme court justices from the New Orleans area. Two of the seven members of the court were elected at-large from one

Table 5.2 *continued*

Case	Vote	Ruling
Holder v. Hall, 114 S.Ct. 2581 (1994)	5-4	Justice Kennedy held that the size of a governing authority is not subject to a vote dilution challenge under § 2. Justices Thomas and Scalia asserted that minority vote dilution claims do not fall under § 2 and that *Thornburg v. Gingles* should be overruled.
Johnson v. DeGrandy, 114 S.Ct. 2647 (1994)	7-2	Justice Souter rejected black and Hispanic voters' claims that Florida's reapportionment plan unlawfully diluted their voting strength in Dade County because the Voting Rights Act does not necessarily require creating the maximum number of legislative districts in which minority voters make up a majority.

multimember district (Orleans Parish), whereas the remainder were elected from single-member districts. No black had ever been elected to the Louisiana Supreme Court from any of the districts. Black voters alleged that the electoral scheme impermissibly diluted minority voting strength, in violation of § 2 of the Voting Rights Act. Justice Stevens, writing for the 6-3 majority, rejected the state's contention that Congress intended to exclude judicial elections from the Voting Rights Act's coverage. For the Court, when Congress used the word *representative* in the language of § 2, it indicated at the very least that Congress intended to cover more than legislative elections. In his dissenting opinion, Justice Scalia, relying heavily on rules of statutory interpretation and linguistic analysis, argued that an ordinary reading of § 2 leads to the conclusion that the word *representative* does not include judges.

The refusal of the Supreme Court to consider a case dealing with remedies under a biased judicial election system may actually threaten opportunities for minority voters to elect judges of their choice. On April 23, 1995, the Supreme Court denied certiorari in *Nipper v. Smith,* No. 94-1463, an important judicial election case. The Court of Appeals for the Eleventh Circuit sitting en banc struck down a ruling by an Eleventh Circuit panel that found that at-large judicial districts impermissibly diluted black voting power. The en banc panel in *Nipper v. Smith,* 39 F.3d. 1494 (1994) found that vote dilution occurred but denied the black appellants' remedies on the ground that the state's interest in linking the jurisdictional and electoral bases of its judges precludes the fashioning of any remedy the appellants suggest or a court could devise. The court stated that, "By altering the current electoral schemes for the express purpose of electing more black judges, the federal court in fashioning the alteration, and the state courts in implementing it, would be proclaiming that race matters in the administration of justice. . . . Like other race-conscious remedies, this tends to entrench the very practices and stereotypes the Equal Protection Clause is set against."

A leading voting rights scholar, Lani Guinier, has criticized second-generation voting rights lawsuits that focus too much on simple representation and not enough on minority legislative influence.[16] For Guinier, "Political equality requires both a standard for evaluating legislative influence and explicit mechanisms for overcoming inequality within the governing policy-making body."[17] Once second-generation lawsuits have succeeded in getting blacks elected to various positions in government, third-generation voting rights lawsuits focus on the ability of blacks to govern effectively. During the 1990 term, the Rehnquist Court signaled that it would be unsympathetic to third-generation voting rights lawsuits when it decided PRESLEY V. ETOWAH COUNTY COMMISSION, 502 U.S. 491 (1992). In the first major civil rights case since he joined the Court, Justice Clarence Thomas voted with the 6-3 majority, in which the Court narrowed the scope of § 5 of the Voting Rights Act.

In *Presley,* blacks won elections in 1986 to previously all-white Etowah and Russell County commissions in Alabama. The county commissions subsequently adopted changes that, in effect, took budgetary powers away from the newly elected black commissioners' offices. The black commissioners brought suit, alleging that the commission's failure to preclear the changes in decision-making authority violated § 5 of the Voting Rights Act. Justice Kennedy, writing for the 6-3 majority, held that the common fund resolution in Etowah County and the adoption of the unit system in Russell County did not involve changes covered by the Voting Rights Act. Justice Kennedy reasoned that *Allen v. State Board of Elections,* 393 U.S. 544 (1969) and its progeny established that changes subject to § 5 preclearance pertain only to voting. The majority then formulated a new standard: Under § 5, substantive or procedural changes must have a direct relation to voting and the election process. In the dissenting opinion, Justice Stevens, joined by Justices White and Blackmun, argued that the changes in the reallocation of decision-making authority in an elective office, such as the Etowah and Russell Counties commission changes, were "at least in its most blatant form, indistinguishable from, and just as unacceptable as, gerrymandering boundary lines or switching elections from a district to an at-large basis."

Race-Conscious Remedies and Legislative Redistricting

In 1993 the Rehnquist Court was confronted with a question not addressed in *Thornburg v. Gingles*—that is, whether § 2 of the Voting Rights Act permits minority groups to bring vote dilution claims on the ground that a districting scheme hinders their ability to influence elections. In *Voinovich v. Quilter,* 113 S.Ct. 1149 (1993), the Rehnquist Court had to consider whether Ohio's creation of seven legislative districts under a state reapportionment plan dominated by minority voters violated § 2. Ohio Democrats challenged the Republican plan, arguing that the plan should have created a large number of influence districts—districts in which black voters would not constitute a majority but in which they could, with a number of crossover voters from whites, elect candidates of their choice. The Republican-sponsored plan argued that it enhanced the strength of black voters by providing safe minority districts by "packing" or overconcentrating them into districts. Writing for the Court, Justice O'Connor held that the Court has not yet decided whether influence district claims are viable under § 2. The Court refused to resolve the question, but it did disagree with the lower court that § 2 prohibits the creation of majority-minority districts unless such districts are necessary to remedy a statutory violation.

In one of the most controversial rulings of the 1992 term, the Rehnquist Court ruled that creating a majority black congressional district may violate the constitutional rights of white voters under the equal protection clause. In SHAW V. RENO, 113 S.Ct. 2816 (1993), a 5-4 majority demonstrated its willingness to employ affirmative action jurisprudence in the context of redistricting. In *Shaw* the North Carolina legislature created a second majority-minority congressional district in response to the Justice Department's objection to its first reapportionment plan, which included one majority-black congressional district. The second district's boundary lines were of dramatically irregular shape: The lines were described as winding in a snakelike fashion along Interstate 85. White voters challenged the district on the ground that it constituted a racial gerrymander, in violation of the Fourteenth Amendment. A three-judge district court dismissed the complaint. In a sharply divided opinion, Justice O'Connor, writing for the majority, rejected the district court's conclusion that the white voters did not state a claim under the equal protection clause. Justice O'Connor reasoned from her examination of past precedents that the North Carolina plan closely resembled that of the "uncouth twenty-eight-sided" municipal boundary line in *Gomillion v. Lightfoot,* 364 U.S. 339 (1960). For the majority, "reapportionment is one area in which appearances do matter," and a "reapportionment plan that includes in one district individuals who belong to the same race, but who are otherwise widely separated by geographical and political boundaries, and who may have little in common with one another but for the color of their skin, bears an uncomfortable resemblance to political apartheid." Justice O'Connor then established that strict scrutiny is required in the reapportionment context; but at the same time, she maintained that creating majority-minority districts in order to comply with the Voting Rights Act does not by itself meet the compelling interest requirement under strict scrutiny. Relying on *City of Richmond v. J. A. Croson Co.*, 488 U.S. 469 (1989) (discussed in the next section), Justice O'Connor argued that a state must have a strong basis in evidence for concluding that remedial action was warranted.

On his final day on the Supreme Court (June 28, 1993), Justice White, a conservative though key supporter of minority voting rights, contended in his lengthy dissenting opinion that the lower court properly relied on *United Jewish Organizations, Inc. v. Carey,* 430 U.S. 144 (1977), which mirrors the facts in the *Shaw* case. Justice White argued that he could not understand how the white voters presented a cognizable claim in the case, especially because "whites constituted roughly 76 percent of the total population and 79 percent of the voting age population in North Carolina. Yet, under the State's plan, they still constitute a voting majority in 10 (or 83 percent) of the 12 Congressional districts." Criticizing the majority for being fascinated with irregularly shaped districts as an indicator of some form of gerrymandering, Justice White argued that the Constitution does not require compactness and that a "regularly shaped district can just as effectively effectuate racially discriminatory gerrymandering as an odd-shaped one." Justice White concluded his dissent by stating that "state efforts to remedy minority vote dilution are wholly unlike what typically has been labeled 'affirmative action' "; instead, it involves "an attempt to *equalize* treatment, and to provide minority voters with an effective voice in the political process."

On the last day of the Court's 1993-94 term, Justice Thomas articulated his voting rights philosophy in *Holder v. Hall,* 114 S.Ct. 2581 (1994) in a lengthy concurring opinion. He described the Court's voting rights rulings as a disastrous misadventure of 30 years of judicial interpretation of the Voting Rights Act. In 1985, black voters challenged Bleckley County's sole commissioner form of government under § 2 of the Voting Rights Act. They claimed that Bleckley County must have a county commission of sufficient size and that, with single-member districts, the county's black citizens would constitute a majority in one of the single-member districts. In a sharply divided Court, Justice Kennedy, joined by Chief Justice Rehnquist and Justice O'Connor, held that the size of a governing authority is not subject to a vote dilution challenge under § 2. According to Justice Kennedy, "There is no principled reason why one size should be picked over another as the benchmark for comparison." Justice Thomas, joined by Justice Scalia, concurring in the judgment, expressed the view that the size of a governing body cannot be attacked under § 2 because it is not a "standard, practice or procedure" within the terms of § 2. For Justice Thomas, § 2's text refers only to those practices that affect minority citizens' access to the ballot. Going further, he argued that minority vote dilution claims are simply beyond the purview of the Voting Rights Act and that *Thornburg v. Gingles*—which interpreted § 2 to reach claims of vote dilution—should be overruled. Justice Thomas then stated that *Gingles* was based on a flawed method of statutory interpretation, that it is at odds with the text of the Voting Rights Act, and that it has proven unworkable in practice. Justice Blackmun, joined by Justices Stevens, Souter, and Ginsburg, dissented. Justice Blackmun argued that subtler, more complex means of infringing minority voting strength, including submergence or dispersion of minority voters, are still prevalent. He stated, "It is clear that the practice of electing a single-member county commission can be one such dilutive practice. It is equally clear that a five-member commission is an appropriate benchmark against which to measure the alleged dilutive effect of Bleckley County's practice of electing a sole commissioner." In a separate opinion, Justice Stevens criticized Justice Thomas's views as a "radical reinterpretation of the Voting Rights Act" that would require the Court to overrule or reconsider a large number of decisions and congressional reenactments.

The Supreme Court is expected to clarify its ruling in *Shaw* in two cases accepted by the Court during its 1994-1995 term. *United States v. Hays,* No. 94-558, and *Miller v. Johnson,* No. 94-631, involve challenges to congressional redistricting plans that created majority black districts with the objective of increasing black representation in Congress. Relying on *Shaw v. Reno,* the lower courts found both plans lacking under strict scrutiny. A number of important legal issues have been raised in these cases: Can congressional districts be drawn according to race? Does any person have standing to challenge these plans, even if he or she does not live in the district? To what extent is a district's "bizarre shape" constitutionally suspect? The broader question raised by these cases is whether the Court will resolve the tension between the Voting Rights Act and the Constitution. How the Rehnquist Court decides these cases may have serious consequences for black and Hispanic representation in Congress and other legislative bodies.

THE REHNQUIST COURT'S ASSAULT ON AFFIRMATIVE ACTION AND EMPLOYMENT DISCRIMINATION JURISPRUDENCE

The Continuing Confusion
Over Affirmative Action Jurisprudence

Mention of the terms *quota, affirmative action,* and *reverse discrimination* automatically evokes instant controversy. The landmark affirmative action decisions of the Rehnquist Court (see Table 5.3) intensified the debate and opposition by the Reagan administration to affirmative action policies and simply added fuel to this explosive issue. The Reagan administration's position was rejected, however, in *United States v. Paradise,* 480 U.S. 149 (1987). Because of the systematic exclusion of blacks from employment as state troopers, the district court ordered that one black trooper be promoted for each white trooper who was elevated in rank, until an acceptable promotion procedure was implemented by the Department of Public Safety. The constitutionality of this order was challenged by the U.S. Department of Justice and a group of white troopers. In a 5-4 decision, the Rehnquist Court declared that the race-conscious relief was justified by a compelling governmental interest in eliminating the systematic and discriminatory exclusion of blacks. Writing for the plurality, Justice Brennan concluded that the race-conscious relief was narrowly tailored to serve the district court's praiseworthy purposes. Justice O'Connor, writing for the dissenters, argued that the one-for-one quota was not justified in the case and did not survive strict scrutiny because the district court failed to consider other alternatives in achieving the consent decrees.

Table 5.3 Employment Discrimination, Affirmative Action, and the Rehnquist Court: Cases

Case	Vote	Ruling
United States v. Paradise, 480 U.S. 149 (1987)	5-4	Justice Brennan upheld a district court's order requiring one black state trooper to be promoted for each white trooper elevated in rank under strict scrutiny.
St. Francis College v. Al-Khazraji, 481 U.S. 604 (1987)	9-0	The Supreme Court held that U.S. citizens of Arab descent can sue under § 1981.
Shaare Tefila Congregation v. Cobb, 481 U.S. 615 (1987)	9-0	The Supreme Court held that Jews can bring a § 1982 claim against white defendants.
Watson v. Fort Worth Bank and Trust, 487 U.S. 977 (1988)	8-0	Justice O'Connor, writing for the plurality, established that employees are responsible for isolating and identifying the specific employment practices that are allegedly responsible for any observed statistical disparity.
City of Richmond v. J. A. Croson Co., 488 U.S. 469 (1989)	6-3	Justice O'Connor struck down a city's affirmative action plan that required city contractors to subcontract 30% of the dollar amount to minority business enterprises under strict scrutiny.
Wards Cove Packing Co., Inc. v. Atonio, 490 U.S. 642 (1989)	5-4	The Court shifted the burden of proof from the employer to the employee in Title VII lawsuits, and minority plaintiffs must prove that a specific employment practice was responsible for the disparate impact.
Price Waterhouse v. Hopkins, 490 U.S. 228 (1989)	6-3	Justice Brennan held that an employer who had been motivated by discriminatory reasons could avoid liability under Title VII if it could be shown by a preponderance of the evidence that the same decision would have been made concerning the plaintiff even in the absence of a discriminatory motive or if gender had not been taken into account.
Martin v. Wilks, 490 U.S. 755 (1989)	5-4	Chief Justice Rehnquist held that white firefighters who failed to intervene in a lawsuit involving an affirmative action consent decree could later challenge the provisions as constituting reverse discrimination even though the firefighters had not been parties to the proceedings in which the decrees were entered.
Lorance v. AT&T Technologies, Inc. 490 U.S. 900 (1989)	5-3	Justice Scalia placed strict time limits on female employees who received demotions that they should not have received had a former seniority system remained in place and who wanted to file a complaint challenging the revised seniority system.

Table 5.3 *continued*

Case	Vote	Ruling
Independent Federation of Flight Attendants v. Zipes, 491 U.S. 754 (1989)	6-2	Justice Scalia, in upholding the lower court's awarding of attorneys' fees against a union that intervened in a sex discrimination suit on behalf of female flight attendants, held that district courts may award Title VII attorneys' fees against those who intervene to protect their own rights only where the intervention is frivolous, unreasonable, or without foundation.
Patterson v. McLean Credit Union, 491 U.S. 164 (1989)	5-4	Justice Kennedy held that racial harassment does not extend to the job under § 1981.
University of Pennsylvania v. EEOC, 493 U.S. 182 (1990)	9-0	Justice Blackmun held that the government's compelling interest in eradicating sexual and racial discrimination in universities outweighs the need for confidentiality of the peer review process when a university refused to produce tenure review files requested by the EEOC for a Title VII lawsuit.
Metro Broadcasting Inc., v. FCC and *Astroline Communications Company Limited Partnership v. Shurberg Broadcasting of Hartford, Inc.*, 497 U.S. 547 (1990)	5-4	Justice Brennan upheld the FCC's affirmative action policies under the intermediate standard of review.
EEOC v. Arabian American Oil Co., 499 U.S. 244 (1991)	6-3	The Supreme Court held that Title VII does not cover American citizens employed by an American company in a foreign country.
West Virginia University Hospitals v. Casey, 499 U.S. 83 (1991)	6-3	The Court held that expert witnesses' fees in civil rights litigation may not be shifted to the losing party as part of the attorneys' fees under § 1988.
Northeastern Florida Contractors v. Jacksonville, 113 S.Ct. 2297 (1993)	7-2	Justice Thomas held that a construction contractor's association had standing to challenge a minority set-aside plan.
St. Mary's Honor Center v. Hicks, 113 S.Ct. 2742 (1993)	5-4	Justice Scalia required that Title VII plaintiffs must prove evidence of intentional discrimination beyond showing that the employer's explanation was pretextual.
Landgraf v. USI Film Products, 114 S.Ct. 1483 (1994)	8-1	Justice Stevens ruled that § 102 of the Civil Rights Act of 1991 does not apply retroactively.
Rivers v. Roadway Express, Inc., 114 S.Ct. 1510 (1994)	8-1	Justice Stevens ruled that § 101 of the Civil Rights Act of 1991 does not apply retroactively.

A number of state and local governmental units implemented policies that set aside a portion of their contracts for minority businesses after the Court's opinion in *Fullilove v. Klutznick,* 448 U.S. 448 (1980). The city of Atlanta had such a program, and a few black contractors received a fair share of the funds for the first time. Opposition to these programs intensified. The critics asserted that the most qualified individuals should be rewarded with employment opportunities. In CITY OF RICHMOND v. J. A. CROSON CO., 488 U.S. 469 (1989), blacks seeking contracts received a serious setback when a white contractor challenged the set-aside provision adopted by the Richmond, Virginia, City Council, on the ground that it constituted reverse discrimination. Richmond adopted a Minority Business Utilization Plan that required prime contractors with city contracts to subcontract 30% of the dollar amount of each contract to one or more minority business enterprises. The plan was challenged as a violation of the equal protection clause. The city argued that the plan was constitutional under the *Fullilove* rationale. Justice O'Connor, writing for the 6-3 majority, declared that the Constitution requires all governmental racial classifications to be subject to strict judicial scrutiny. She also argued that the record did not pinpoint any instances of past discrimination in city contracting and that the city of Richmond had failed to narrowly tailor the remedy to some compelling state interest. Emphasizing that the city did not consider alternatives to a racial quota as a means to eradicate barriers facing minorities interested in receiving city contracts, she concluded that the plan was overinclusive because it applied to Asians, Indians, Eskimos, and Aleuts, against whom there was absolutely no evidence of past discrimination. Justice Marshall, joined by Justices Brennan and Blackmun, dissented. He emphasized that the Court should not second-guess the judgment of the Richmond City Council that past discrimination prevented minorities from fully participating in the city's construction industry. Justice Marshall also forcefully restated his view that affirmative action jurisprudence should be evaluated under the intermediate standard of scrutiny.

Within approximately one year of the *Croson* decision, blacks won a victory in METRO BROADCASTING, INC. V. FCC, 497 U.S. 547 (1990) and its companion case, *Astroline Communications Company Limited Partnership v. Shurberg Broadcasting of Hartford, Inc.,* 497 U.S. 547 (1990). The issue in *Metro Broadcasting* was whether two minority-preference policies of the Federal Communications Commission (FCC) were violative of the equal protection component of the Fifth Amendment. The policies included a program that awarded an enhancement for minority ownership in comparative proceedings for licenses that were new, and the minority distress sale program, which allowed a limited category of existing television and radio broadcast stations to be transferred only to firms that are minority controlled. A nonminority applicant challenged these policies. The divisiveness over affirmative action was exemplified in this case during the Bush administration, when the Justice Department filed an amicus curiae brief claiming that the policies were unconstitutional, whereas the FCC defended the policies. A sharply divided Court declared that the policies did not violate the equal protection clause because they were mandated by Congress and are substantially related to achieving the important governmental objective of broadcast diversity. Relying on *Fullilove,* Justice Brennan, writing for the five-member majority, held that the intermediate standard of review would be applied to benign, race-conscious, congressionally mandated policies. He also asserted that the distress sale policy does not constitute a quota and cannot be viewed as imposing an undue burden on nonminorities because only a small number of broadcast licenses are involved in the policies. In a sharply worded dissent, Justice O'Connor argued that strict scrutiny was appropriate for evaluating the challenged racial classification under the *Croson* rationale. For her, such classifications intensify racial hostility by reinforcing the view of a country that is divided into racial blocs.

During the 1994-1995 term, the Rehnquist Court heard arguments in *Adarand Constructors v. Pena,* No. 93-1841, where the Court may impose limits on Congress' ability to establish a disadvantaged business enterprise program. In *Pena,* a white-owned construction company is seeking to overturn a federal program that provides incentives for prime contractors to award subcontracts to minority-owned firms. This case may provide the Court the opportunity to revisit its rulings in *Fullilove v. Klutznick* and *Metro Broadcasting, Inc. v. FCC.*

Employment Discrimination and the Rehnquist Court: A Cramped View of Title VII

The 1988-89 Supreme Court term was a watershed year for employment discrimination jurisprudence. The Rehnquist Court rendered several important decisions that represented an emerging consensus in its approach to employment discrimination cases (see Table 5.3). Its jurisprudence was taking shape in ways not done in the past. Racial and ethnic minorities witnessed the Rehnquist Court working out the contours of policy change, resulting in a cramped view on rights.

In WARDS COVE PACKING, CO., INC. V. ATONIO, 490 U.S. 642 (1989), the Rehnquist Court reversed *Griggs v. Duke Power Co.,* 401 U.S. 424 (1971). In *Wards Cove,* a class of Filipino and Alaska Native cannery workers brought suit under Title VII, claiming the company that operated salmon canneries in Alaska maintained discriminatory hiring and promotion practices that were responsible for the workforce's racial stratification and denied them employment on account of race. In a 5-4 opinion written by Justice White, the Rehnquist Court shifted the burden of proving liability from the employer to the employee in Title VII lawsuits. This shift was a severe blow to minority plaintiffs, who were now required to prove that a specific employment practice was responsible for the disparate impact. In addition, the business justification standard was relaxed. Justice Stevens, writing for the dissenters, regarded the majority's abandonment of the *Griggs* rationale as "a sojourn into judicial activism" and argued that *Griggs* "correctly reflected the intent of Congress that enacted Title VII."

The Rehnquist Court shifted the burden of proof in *Price Waterhouse v. Hopkins,* 490 U.S. 228 (1989). In *Price* a female senior manager in an accounting firm was denied a partnership. She sued under Title VII, charging discrimination on the basis of sex. The lower courts ruled that an employer who has allowed a discriminatory motive to play a part in an employment decision must prove by clear and convincing evidence that it would have made the same decision in the absence of discrimination. In a 6-3 plurality opinion written by Justice Brennan, the Court reversed the lower courts and held that an employer motivated by discriminatory reasons could avoid liability under Title VII if it could be shown by a preponderance of the evidence that the same decision would have been made concerning the plaintiff even in the absence of a discriminatory motive or even if gender had not been taken into account.

In *Martin v. Wilks,* 490 U.S. 755 (1989), the Rehnquist Court struck a blow to court decrees that provided for affirmative action. In *Martin,* the Court, in a 5-4 decision written by Chief Justice Rehnquist, held that white firefighters who failed to intervene in a lawsuit involving an affirmative action consent decree could later challenge the provisions as constituting reverse discrimination even though the firefighters had not been parties to the proceedings in which the decrees were entered. According to the Court, an individual who is a nonparty cannot be deprived of his or her right to reject the doctrine of impermissible collateral attack and challenge actions pursuant to a consent decree. Justice Stevens, writing for the dissenters, argued, "The fact that one of the effects of a decree is to curtail the job opportunities of nonparties does not mean that the nonparties have been deprived of legal rights or that they have standing to appeal from that decree without becoming parties."

When the case was sent back to the lower courts, the white firefighters lost their reverse discrimination claim at the district court level but won on appeal. In 1994, the Court of Appeals for the Eleventh Circuit ruled that a 1981 consent decree that reserved to blacks 50% of all lieutenant promotions in the city fire department violated both Title VII and the equal protection clause. During the 1994-1995 term, the Rehnquist Court denied certiorari to black firefighters' appeal of the ruling in *Arrington v. Wilks,* No. 94-1397, and *Martin v. Wilks,* No. 94-1422.

On the same day that *Martin* was decided, the Rehnquist Court, in *Lorance v. AT&T Technologies, Inc.,* 490 U.S. 900 (1989), held that seniority plans cannot be challenged as discriminatory under Title VII in complaints filed soon after the plans were adopted. In the 5-3 opinion written by Justice Scalia (Justice O'Connor did not participate), the Court placed strict time limits on female employees who received demotions that they would not have received had the former seniority system remained in place and who wanted to file a complaint challenging the revised seniority system. Justice Marshall, writing for the dissenters, argued, "This severe interpretation of § 706(e) will come as a surprise to Congress, whose goals in enacting Title VII surely never included conferring absolute immunity on discriminatorily adopted seniority systems that survive their first 300 days."

BOX 5.1

The Civil Rights Act of 1991: Main Provisions

§ 101. Reversed *Patterson v. McLean Credit Union* (1989). This section provides that the phrase *make and enforce contracts* includes "the making, performance, modification and termination of contracts, and the enjoyment of all benefits, privileges, terms and conditions of the contractual relationship."

§ 102. Created a new section, § 1981a (1977A), which provides that a person complaining of unlawful intentional discrimination may recover compensatory and punitive damages under Title VII. This section also permits jury trials.

§ 105. Reversed *Wards Cove Packing, Co., Inc. v. Atonio* (1989). This section shifts the burden of proof back to the employer, who is required to show "that the challenged practice is job related for the position in question and consistent with business necessity."

§ 106. Prohibits the discriminatory use of test scores when considering applicants for employment.

§ 107. Reversed *Price Waterhouse v. Hopkins* (1989). This section provides that "an unlawful employment practice is established when the complaining party demonstrates that race, color, religion, sex or national origin was a motivating factor for any employment practice, even though other factors also motivated the practices."

§ 108. Reversed *Martin v. Wilks* (1989). This section provides that individuals who have had "actual notice of proposed judgment or order" are barred from challenging a consent judgment unless an individual can establish that the judgment was obtained through collusion or fraud.

§ 109. Reversed *EEOC v. Arabian American Oil Company* (1991). This section provides that American citizens employed by an American company in a foreign country are covered by Title VII.

§ 112. Reversed *Lorance v. AT&T Technologies, Inc.* (1989). This section provides that "an unlawful employment practice occurs, with respect to a seniority system that has been adopted for an intentionally discriminatory purpose . . . when the seniority system is adopted, when an individual becomes subject to the seniority system or when a person aggrieved is injured by the application of the seniority system."

§ 113. Reversed *West Virginia University Hospitals v. Casey* (1991). This section provides that civil rights litigants who won their cases could recover expert fees as part of the attorneys' fees.

SOURCE: Pub. L. No. 102-166, 105 Stat. 1071 (codified as amended in several sections of 42 U.S.C.A., 2 U.S.C.A, 16 U.S.C.A. and 29 U.S.C.A.).

In *Independent Federation of Flight Attendants v. Zipes,* 491 U.S. 754 (1989), a class of female flight attendants alleged that Trans World Airlines' policy of dismissing flight attendants who became mothers constituted sex discrimination, in violation of Title VII. They entered into an agreement with airline management in which it agreed to credit the class with full company and competitive seniority. The collective bargaining agent for the flight attendants intervened in the suit on behalf of those flight attendants who would be adversely affected by the agreement. After this challenge was rejected, the lower court awarded attorneys' fees against the union. In a 6-2 opinion written by Justice Scalia, the Court held that district courts may award Title VII attorneys' fees against those who are not charged with Title VII violations but intervene to protect their own rights only where the intervention is frivolous, unreasonable, or without foundation.

Narrowing the Scope of § 1981
of the Civil Rights Act of 1866

Three days after the *Martin v. Wilks* decision, the Rehnquist Court, in PATTERSON V. McLEAN CREDIT UNION, 491 U.S. 164 (1989), refused to overturn *Runyon v. McCrary,* 427 U.S. 160 (1976) but instead restricted § 1981 to cases involving the making and enforcement of employment contracts alone. In *Patterson* a black woman brought a § 1981 suit against her employers at a credit union, alleging that they harassed her, failed to promote her, and then discharged her on account of race. In a 5-4 opinion written by Justice Kennedy, the Court held that § 1981 did not extend to racial harassment on the job. For Justice Kennedy, § 1981 "covers conduct at the initial formation of the contract and conduct which impairs the right to enforce obligations through the legal process." The Court suggested that whereas Title VII might cover racial harassment on the job, interpreting § 1981 to do so would be inconsistent with the statute's limitation to the making and enforcement of contracts and would undermine the procedures for resolving Title VII claims. In a strongly worded dissent, Justice Brennan criticized the majority's "formalistic method of interpretation antithetical to Congress' vision of a society in which contractual opportunities are equal."

Congress Reacts:
The Civil Rights Acts of 1990 and 1991

Congress immediately responded to the series of Supreme Court decisions rendered in 1989 that seriously eroded equal employment opportunities for minorities and women. Legislation was introduced to reverse these decisions and restore previously won protections. Initially, President Bush and Congress could not agree on key aspects of the legislation, and the two political branches found themselves on a collision course. In early February 1990, bills were introduced in both Houses of Congress that would have overturned the rulings in the five cases decided in 1989. On October 22, 1990, however, President

Bush vetoed the Civil Rights Act of 1990 because he thought it would literally force employers to resort to "the destructive force of quotas" in the employment arena.[18] In his veto message, the president noted that employers would resort to the adoption of quotas to avoid liability because of their inability to defend legitimate practices in court. The Senate failed by one vote to override the veto (66-34). The 1990 Act, in § 13, clearly stated, "Nothing in the amendments made by this Act shall be construed to require or encourage an employer to adopt hiring or promotion quotas on the basis of race, color, religion, sex, or national origin."

The Civil Rights Act of 1991 was the major civil rights measure awaiting approval of both Houses during the 102nd Congress. Like the 1990 Act, it reversed parts of the five 1989 Supreme Court decisions. In addition, the 1991 Act reversed parts of two 1991 Rehnquist Court decisions (see Box 5.1). Congress was, in effect, reminding the conservative Rehnquist Court that its interpretation of a series of federal laws concerning employment discrimination was at odds with Congressional intentions. After an intense struggle that lasted more than a year, Congress finally approved the Act on November 7, 1992. One of the purposes of the Act was "to respond to recent decisions of the Supreme Court by expanding the scope of relevant civil rights statutes in order to provide adequate protection to victims of discrimination." Because this Act explicitly addressed race and ethnicity in the employment context, controversy could not be averted. Eighteen hours before the president was expected to sign this piece of legislation, White House Counsel C. Boyden Gray circulated a policy statement that stated racial preferences and quotas in hiring at the federal level would end. Expecting protests from civil rights organizations and lawmakers alike, President Bush ordered his press secretary, Marlin Fitzwater, to inform the American people that Gray had acted without the president's knowledge and that regulations concerning affirmative action would not be eliminated. On November 21, 1991, President Bush signed the Act and stated, "Nothing in this bill overturns the Government's affirmative action programs."[19]

Immediately after the Civil Rights Act of 1991 was enacted, legal challenges raised the question whether the Act applied retroactively to cases that were pending when the Act was signed into law. In *Landgraf v. USI Film Products,* 114 S.Ct. 1483 (1994) and *Rivers v. Roadway Express, Inc.,* 114 S.Ct. 1510 (1994), the Court ruled that §§ 101 and 102 of the Civil Rights Act do not apply retroactively.

Despite Congress' efforts at restoring Title VII precedents when it passed the Civil Rights Act of 1991, the Rehnquist Court continued its course of making it difficult for minorities and women to prove discrimination in the workplace. In *St. Mary's Honor Center v. Hicks,* 113 S.Ct. 2742 (1993), the Court revisited the three-step process established in *McDonnell Douglas Corp. v. Green* 411 U.S. 792 (1973) in disparate treatment cases. In *Hicks* a black correctional officer was dismissed from his job, and he brought a Title VII disparate treatment claim. Melvin Hicks met the first two requirements of the *McDonnell Douglas* framework: He was qualified for his job as supervisor,

---

BOX 5.2

The 1988 Fair Housing Amendments

Under the Fair Housing Act of 1968, only the Department of Housing and Urban Development (HUD) could mediate disputes and the Justice Department could bring lawsuits for a pattern or practice of housing discrimination, and private individuals could bring their own lawsuits. Under the 1988 Amendments, a two-track enforcement scheme was set into place. The enforcement process begins when HUD issues a charge of discrimination based on its own investigation. The aggrieved party, the violator, or HUD has 20 days to choose one of two forums for resolution of the discrimination complaint: an administrative law judge or a federal district court. Decisions of the administrative law judge could be reviewed by the Secretary of HUD. If any party chooses the federal district court, then that choice prevails. HUD represents the aggrieved party in court, and the party is subject to all remedies available in federal court. The Act gave judges the authority to impose fines as high as $50,000 against violators, and it removed the $1,000 cap on punitive damages. The Act extended coverage to residential real estate transactions, which were defined to include "the making or purchasing of loans, or providing other financial assistance for purchasing, constructing, improving, repairing or maintaining a dwelling; or . . . the selling, brokering or appraising of residential real property." The 1988 Amendments are also significant because they prohibited housing discrimination on the basis of physical or mental disability and against families with children under the age of 18.

---

and he eventually was replaced by a white man. At issue in *Hicks* was whether the third step requires the Title VII plaintiff to prove evidence of intentional discrimination beyond showing that the employer's explanation was pretextual. In a 5-4 opinion written by Justice Scalia, the Court held that it was not enough for Hicks to show that St. Mary's Honor Center gave a dishonest reason for dismissing him. Justice Scalia then established that Hicks must prove that the employer intentionally discriminated against him because of race. In his dissenting opinion, Justice Souter, joined by Justices White, Blackmun, and Stevens, argued that the majority abandoned the framework for settling disparate treatment cases and found that its scheme "will be unfair to plaintiffs, unworkable in practice, and inexplicable in forgiving employers who present false evidence in court." Justice Souter went on to explain how difficult it will be for Title VII plaintiffs to show intentional discrimination because they often will lack direct evidence of an employer's intent to discriminate. It appears that, with the passage of the Civil Rights Act of 1991, civil rights advocates won the battle but not the war. The Rehnquist Court has yet to indicate any signs of altering its cramped view of Title VII jurisprudence.

The Definition of Race and §§ 1981 and 1982

It is important to note that Arabs and Jews have successfully sued under §§ 1981 and 1982 of the Civil Rights Act of 1866, rather than Title VII, concerning claims of discrimination on the basis of race. For example, in *St. Francis College v. Al-Khazraji,* 481 U.S. 604 (1987), a college professor and U.S. citizen born in Iraq filed a suit alleging that he was denied tenure three years earlier on the basis of his Arabian race, in violation of § 1981. Writing for a unanimous Court, Justice White stated that when § 1981 became law in the 19th century, "all those who might be deemed Caucasian today were not thought to be of the same race at the time § 1981 became law." Therefore, on remand, the respondent can sue under § 1981 if he can prove he was a victim of discrimination solely because he was born an Arab. In *Shaare Tefila Congregation v. Cobb,* 481 U.S. 615 (1987), the Court relied on the *St. Francis* case and held that Jews could state a § 1982 claim against white defendants who had sprayed anti-Semitic slogans on the outside walls of a synagogue in Silver Spring, Maryland. Justice White, writing for a unanimous Court, reasoned that when § 1982 was adopted, "Jews and Arabs were among the peoples then considered to be distinct races and hence within the protection of the statute."

HOUSING DISCRIMINATION:
A PROBLEM FOR THE 21st CENTURY

Charles Dale captured the gravity of housing discrimination in the United States for the 1980s and 1990s in these words: "[W]e live in a divided nation in which residential housing segregation is a pervasive fact of life and . . . rather than declining, the degree of separation is actually on the increase."[20] Housing discrimination will undoubtedly be a serious problem facing the nation in the 21st century. Laws and favorable Supreme Court decisions have had limited success in solving this seemingly intractable problem. Many real estate agents operate as if the Congress and the courts have not addressed this issue. In September 1988, President Bush signed the Fair Housing Amendments Act; the amendments were designed to address the inadequate enforcement mechanism of Title VIII of the Fair Housing Act of 1968 (see Box 5.2). Among the important provisions, the 1988 Amendments extended coverage to residential real estate transactions and prohibited housing discrimination on the grounds of physical or mental disability and against families with children under the age of 18.

In December 1991, a lower federal court awarded one of the largest settlements ever obtained from a private landlord to a group of minority housing applicants who alleged that Investment Concepts Incorporated in

Southern California had refused to rent apartments to them solely on the basis of race, in violation of the Fair Housing Act.[21] They were awarded $1.1 million. In another case that received public attention in 1991, the mayor of Covington, Georgia, was sued for refusing to rent one of his apartments to a black and agreed to pay $27,500.[22] In this case, the mayor vehemently denied that he discriminated against blacks, but the American Civil Liberties Union used four sets of black and white testers who attempted to rent some of the mayor's apartments. In every instance, the whites were given information about vacancies, but the blacks were told no apartments were available. Two black couples and a nonprofit fair housing group in New York obtained one of the largest awards ever in a real estate advertising case. They will share $450,000 from the owners of an apartment complex in New York who were accused of using only white models in their property advertisements.[23]

Whites and blacks alike have supported the dispersal of public housing units, but only if they are not dispersed in their backyards. The tenants of public housing received a setback from the Rehnquist Court in 1990 in SPALLONE V. UNITED STATES, 493 U.S. 265 (1990). In 1980 the Department of Justice brought a suit against the city of Yonkers, New York, and its community development agency for perpetuating segregated housing, in violation of the equal protection clause and Title VIII of the Fair Housing Act of 1968. In 1985 the district court ordered the city to take steps to disperse public housing in all sections of Yonkers. Delaying its actions persistently, the city council defeated by a 4-3 vote an ordinance the district court required that it enact to carry out the consent decree it had signed. The district court order also provided for contempt citations, escalating daily fines for the city, and fines and imprisonment for disobedient council members for failure to enact the ordinance. Writing for a sharply divided Court, Chief Justice Rehnquist held that the district court had abused its discretion in imposing contempt sanctions against members of the city council because sanctions against the city alone would have produced the desired outcome. According to the majority, council members would be more likely to vote in favor of the ordinance because of the threat of bankruptcy to the city for whose welfare they are in part responsible, whereas monetary sanctions against legislators would motivate them to vote for the ordinance to avoid personal bankruptcy. The majority judged the personal fines as being more intrusive in the normal legislative process. Justice Brennan, joined by Justices Marshall, Stevens, and Blackmun, dissented. He argued that the Court had not taken the council members' stubborn defiance seriously and that its judgment could very well encourage them to respond only to intense public opinion, rather than to do what is just.

Despite the fact that the 5-4 majority held that the individual contempt fines were an abuse of judicial discretion, the Court, in *Spallone,* left undisturbed Judge Sand's original ruling that the city of Yonkers had engaged in intentional housing discrimination. The ruling in *Spallone* turned on the traditional limits of the use of the contempt power to force compliance with a judicial order—that a judge should use the least possible power adequate to

Table 5.4 The Rehnquist Court and Capital Punishment

Case	Vote	Ruling
McCleskey v. Kemp, 481 U.S. 279 (1987)	5-4	Justice Powell held that a black defendant must provide evidence that decision makers acted discriminatorily in his case in receiving the death penalty. The Court rejected the Baldus study, which indicated that black defendants were more likely than white defendants to receive the death penalty when the victim was white.
McCleskey v. Zant, 499 U.S. 467 (1991)	6-3	The Supreme Court made it more difficult for state prisoners to file subsequent habeas corpus petitions under the abuse of the writ doctrine.
Payne v. Tennessee, 501 U.S. 808 (1991)	6-3	Chief Justice Rehnquist permitted the use of victim impact statements during capital sentencing.
Keeney v. Tamayo-Reyes, 504 U.S. 1 (1992)	5-4	The Court held that federal judges can reject a habeas corpus petition if evidence vital to a case had not been properly presented in state courts even if the cause was due to a negligent attorney's failure to present the critical facts.
Wright v. West, 112 S.Ct. 2482 (1992)	9-0	In a unanimous but highly fragmented ruling, the Court would have required a federal judge to accept the findings of state court judges without additional evaluations in habeas corpus proceedings.
Dawson v. Delaware, 503 U.S. 159 (1992)	8-1	The Court rejected, on First Amendment grounds, attempts by a prosecutor who introduced evidence at the sentencing phase of a death penalty hearing that a defendant was a member of a white supremacist prison gang.
Herrera v. Collins, 113 S.Ct. 853 (1993)	6-3	Chief Justice Rehnquist refused to consider claims of innocence raised in habeas corpus petitions years later unless the evidence was truly persuasive.

the end proposed. The dissenters suggested, however, that the ruling in *Spallone* sends the message that trial court judges' remedial decrees will be second-guessed by the Supreme Court and that recalcitrant state and local officials will view the Yonkers case as giving them the green light to test the ultimate reach of judicial authority in remedial decree litigation by the use of blatant acts of noncompliance.

Another critical problem facing blacks in their quest to obtain equal housing opportunities in the 1990s is invidious discrimination by lending institutions. In a study done by *The Atlanta Journal/Constitution,* it was reported that black families with incomes comparable to those of white families in metropolitan Atlanta were two and one half times more likely to be denied a loan for buying a home in 1990.[24] The study also revealed that 1 in 4 black applicants was denied a mortgage, compared with 1 in 10 white applicants. The most interesting finding was that as income increased, the disparity between loan approvals for blacks and whites increased.[25] Moreover, whites who applied for loans in middle-class black neighborhoods were twice as likely to be turned down for a mortgage loan than whites who applied for loans in predominantly white middle-class neighborhoods.

In 1993 the Rehnquist Court refused to grant certiorari in a seventh circuit case, *American Family Mutual Insurance Co. v. N.A.A.C.P.,* 978 F.2d 287; *cert. denied,* 111 S.Ct. 2335 (1993), which addressed the question of whether redlining violates the Fair Housing Act. The Fair Housing Act Amendments of 1988 do not specifically mention discrimination in housing insurance. In *American Family Mutual,* the Milwaukee branch of the NAACP brought a class action suit alleging that the American Family Mutual Insurance Company engaged in redlining—charging higher rates or declining to write insurance for people who live in particular areas—in and near Milwaukee. The district court judge dismissed the Title VIII claims. Judge Frank H. Easterbrook, writing for the seventh circuit panel, ruled that although Congress was ambiguous in the 1988 amendments, deference should be given to HUD regulations that prohibit insurance redlining. After the appeals court's ruling, American Family Mutual Insurance Company agreed to a consent decree to expand its business in the African American community.

THE DEATH PENALTY: REMOVING BARRIERS TO EXPEDITIOUS EXECUTIONS

After the Burger Court's decision in *Gregg v. Georgia,* 428 U.S. 153 (1976), the controversy concerning the role of racial discrimination in death penalty cases continued. The controversy intensified during the Rehnquist Court (see Table 5.4), and black criminal defendants were dealt a serious setback after the landmark decision in McCLESKEY V. KEMP, 481 U.S. 279 (1987). Warren McCleskey, a black man, was convicted and sentenced to death for murdering a white police officer during the robbery of a furniture store in Fulton County, Georgia. McCleskey's attorney presented the results of the Baldus study, which was the most definitive analysis concerning the relationship between race and capital sentencing ever undertaken. Professors David Baldus, Charles Pulaski, and George Woodworth examined more than 2,000 murder cases that occurred in the state during the 1970s. The data revealed

Table 5.5 Peremptory Challenges, Jury Discrimination, and the Rehnquist Court

Case	Vote	Ruling
Holland v. Illinois, 493 U.S. 474 (1990)	5-4	Justice Scalia held that *Batson v. Kentucky* (1986) could not be incorporated into the Sixth Amendment and that the Sixth Amendment guarantees an impartial jury, not one that is representative.
Ford v. Georgia, 498 U.S. 411 (1991)	9-0	Justice Souter held that a defendant could make out a prima facie equal protection violation by examining prosecutorial use of peremptory challenges because *Batson* had dropped the *Swain* requirement of proving prior discrimination.
Powers v. Ohio, 499 U.S. 400 (1991)	7-2	Justice Kennedy declared that *Batson* applied to cases in which the excluded jurors and the defendants were not from the same race.
Edmonson v. Leesville Concrete Company, Inc., 500 U.S. 614 (1991)	6-3	Justice Kennedy applied the *Batson* principle to civil cases in which peremptory challenges were used to exclude jurors on the basis of race.
Hernandez v. New York, 500 U.S. 352 (1991)	6-3	Justice Kennedy argued that race-based discrimination was not present in a case in which a prosecutor had stricken several Latino jurors who were bilingual because he was uncertain whether they would be able to listen and follow the interpreter.
Georgia v. McCollum, 112 S.Ct. 2348 (1992)	7-2	Justice Blackmun held that a criminal defendant is prohibited by the Constitution from practicing racial discrimination in using his or her peremptory challenges.
J.E.B. v. Alabama ex rel. T.B., 114 S.Ct. 1419 (1994)	6-3	Justice Blackmun held that the equal protection clause prohibits discrimination in jury selection on the basis of gender or on the assumption that an individual will be biased in a particular case solely because that person happens to be a woman or a man.

that black defendants received the death penalty in 11% of the cases when their victims were white, but in 1% of the cases when their victims were black. The Baldus study also revealed that the killer of a white person was 4.3 times more likely to receive the death sentence than the killer of a black person. In a 5-4 decision, Justice Powell, writing for the Court, held that the defendant provided no evidence showing that racial considerations were crucial in his case or that the judges acted in a discriminatory manner. He argued, "Apparent disparities in sentencing are an inevitable part of our criminal justice system." For McCleskey to prevail, he would have to prove that the "decisionmakers in *his* case acted with discriminatory purposes." Justice Brennan, joined by Justices Marshall, Blackmun, and Stevens, dissented. He asserted that "McCleskey's claim is not a fanciful product of mere statistical artifice" and that ignoring it leaves all of us "imprisoned by the past as long as we deny its influence in the present."

On receiving the death sentence, McCleskey appealed the sentence and also filed petitions for habeas corpus relief in state and federal courts over a 10-year period. McCleskey's case reached the Supreme Court again in 1991 on the question of whether his successive habeas corpus petitions constituted an abuse of the writ of habeas corpus. In *McCleskey v. Zant,* 499 U.S. 467 (1991), the Court held that McCleskey's failure to raise a claim in the first habeas corpus petition that incriminating statements were made without the assistance of counsel constituted abuse of the writ when he raised the claim in the second federal habeas petition. The Court then established a new standard that will make it more difficult for valid constitutional claims to be heard in habeas corpus petitions. In a sharply worded dissent, Justice Marshall, joined by Justices Blackmun and Stevens, referred to the majority as a "backup legislature for the reconsideration of failed attempts to amend existing statutes" when it established a new standard contrary to Congress' intent. After the ruling in *Zant,* McCleskey was executed on September 25, 1991.

In another federal habeas corpus case, *Herrera v. Collins,* 113 S.Ct. 853 (1993), the Rehnquist Court signaled that it would be unsympathetic to claims of innocence raised in habeas petitions years later unless the evidence is truly persuasive. In this case, Herrera was convicted of murder and sentenced to death in 1982. After unsuccessful appeals in the Texas state court system, he raised a claim, in a federal habeas proceeding 10 years after his conviction, that newly discovered evidence in the form of affidavits demonstrated he was innocent of the crime. He alleged that the Eighth Amendment's ban on cruel and unusual punishments prohibited his execution and that he was therefore entitled to a new hearing. In a 6-3 opinion written by Chief Justice Rehnquist, the Court held, "Once a defendant has been afforded a fair trial and convicted of the offense for which he was charged, the presumption of innocence disappears." Chief Justice Rehnquist found the newly discovered evidence unconvincing and suggested that Herrera could petition the governor of Texas for clemency as a "remedy for preventing miscarriages of justice where the judicial process has been exhausted." In his dissenting opinion, Justice Blackmun argued, "The execution of an innocent person is at odds with any standard of decency that I can imagine" and that the "execution of a person who can show that he is innocent comes perilously close to simple murder." Herrera was executed in May 1993, after the governor refused to stay the appeal and the Texas court did not waive the 30-day limit on new claims.

REMOVING THE REMAINING
VESTIGES OF THE DISCRIMINATORY
USE OF PEREMPTORY CHALLENGES

One vexing problem the Supreme Court had in the area of discrimination in the selection of jurors was the prosecutorial use of peremptories to exclude all blacks from juries in criminal cases. The Rehnquist Court supported a line of opinions, spanning more than 100 years, that culminated in the eradication of the practice of selecting jurors on the basis of race incrementally (see Table 5.5). However, a setback occurred before the final assault on the discriminatory use of peremptories began. In 1990 a white man charged with rape, kidnapping, and armed robbery objected to the state's peremptory challenges that struck two blacks from the petit jury. He claimed that excluding them deprived him of the right to be tried by a representative cross section of the community, in violation of the Sixth Amendment. His objection was overruled by the trial judge, and the man was convicted. Justice Scalia, writing for the majority in *Holland v. Illinois,* 493 U.S. 474 (1990), declared that *Batson v. Kentucky,* 476 U.S. 79 (1986) could not be incorporated into the Sixth Amendment because the prohibition of excluding racial groups from the venire was set forth under the equal protection clause. He also contended that the Sixth Amendment guarantees an impartial jury, rather than a representative one. Justice Marshall dissented and argued that the assumption that an impartial jury is the primary goal of the representative cross-section requirement is a false one and that the exclusion of blacks from a petit jury contravenes the Sixth Amendment. Justice Stevens also dissented and pointed out that a jury chosen by such a racially discriminatory process cannot be an impartial one within the meaning of the Sixth Amendment.

The final assault on the discriminatory use of peremptory challenges began in 1991. In POWERS V. OHIO, 499 U.S. 400 (1991), the Court ruled that *Batson* applied not only to those cases in which the defendant and the jurors are of the same race but also to those cases in which the excluded jurors and the defendant are of different races. In this case, a white man convicted of murder had objected when the prosecutor used his first peremptory challenge to exclude a black venireperson for racial reasons. Writing for the Court, Justice Kennedy reasoned that a white defendant could object to the discriminatory exclusion of black jurors because such discrimination reflects negatively on the integrity and fairness of the judicial process. Justice Scalia, joined by Justice Rehnquist, dissented. He stated, "Today's supposed blow against racism, while enormously self-satisfying, is unmeasured and misdirected. If for any reason the state is unable to reconvict Powers for double murder at issue here, later victims may pay the price for our extravagance."

In *Edmonson v. Leesville Concrete Company, Inc.,* 500 U.S. 614 (1991), the Rehnquist Court ruled that *Batson* applied not only to criminal cases but also to civil cases in which peremptory challenges are used to exclude jurors on the basis of race. This case involved a black construction worker who sued a concrete company for an on-the-job-site injury. Two of the defendant's three peremptory challenges were used to remove prospective black jurors. Justice Kennedy, writing for the 6-3 majority, declared that a private litigant in a civil case violates the equal protection clause when peremptory challenges are used to exclude jurors on a racial basis. He also emphasized that the injury caused by a discriminatory peremptory challenge becomes even more serious because it is allowed to happen with governmental permission. Summing up, he observed, "The selection of jurors represents a unique governmental function delegated to private litigants by the government and attributable to the government for purposes of invoking constitutional protections against discrimination by reason of race."

In 1992 the Rehnquist Court had to determine whether a criminal defendant is prohibited by the Constitution from practicing racial discrimination in using his or her peremptory challenges. In *Georgia v. McCollum,* 112 S.Ct. 2348 (1992), the Court answered in the affirmative in a 7-2 decision. Justice Blackmun reasoned that the state's contention that 18 of 42 jurors would be black if a statistically representative panel was assembled and that respondents could therefore eliminate all potential black jurors with 20 peremptory challenges must be taken seriously. He also argued that the court's exclusion of jurors on a racial basis, be it at the hands of the state or the defense, would undoubtedly undermine the core of the criminal justice system and that this evil would be imputed to the state. Justices O'Connor and Scalia dissented in *McCollum.* Justice Scalia contended that the *Edmonson* case had been wrongly decided. He also argued that the majority had simply used the Constitution to destroy criminal defendants' age-old right to resort to peremptory challenges to impanel a jury that they believed would be fair for the primary purpose of advancing race relations in the nation.

HATE SPEECH AND HATE CRIMES: THE CLASH BETWEEN FREE SPEECH AND EQUALITY

Hate Crimes

During the late 1980s and early 1990s, the United States experienced an alarming increase in the number of hate crime incidents. *Hate crimes* are defined as crimes that manifest prejudice based on certain group characteristics. For example, in June 1989, a white federal judge and a black civil rights lawyer were killed by pipe bombs that were sent through the U.S. mail to two Southern cities.[26] John Castillo, director of Michigan's Department of Civil Rights, reported that "the number of hate-related crimes rose from virtually none reported before 1988 to 59 in 1990."[27] The state of Oregon reported an increase in such crimes in 1991. The FBI reported that, in 1991, 60% of the hate crimes in the United States were committed against blacks. Racial bias accounted for 2,963 of the 4,558 hate crimes reported.[28] The report also pointed out that intimidation was the most common hate crime, followed by vandalism and assault.[29] Jews were the second most likely targets of hate crimes.[30] It is worth noting that FBI officials concluded that many local governmental units failed to report statistical information on hate crimes because of their "lack of sensitivity to the problem."[31]

Dubuque, Iowa, a city with only 331 blacks in a population of 57,546, embarked on a social experiment during the spring of 1991 to recruit 100 black families to the city. The city council adopted the plan by a 6-1 vote in May 1991. During a three-month period, the city experienced 12 cross burnings, fights between blacks and whites in one of the high schools, and racist graffiti scrawled throughout the city. The governor announced at a news conference that he would consider strengthening laws that pertain to hate crimes as a result of the unfortunate incidents that had occurred in the state.[32]

In January 1992, two separate racial attacks that were categorized as hate crimes took place in New York City. In the first incident, a 14-year-old black youth and his 12-year-old sister were reproached with sarcastic words, robbed, and sprayed with white polish by three white youngsters. In the second incident, a 12-year-old Hispanic male was punched and smeared with white paint by three white youths who also shouted several ethnic slurs.[33] Klanwatch, an arm of the Southern Poverty Law Center in Montgomery, Alabama, reported that 1992 was the deadliest and most violent year for hate crimes since it began collecting data in 1979.[34] The organization reported that, in 1992, 31 people were killed in hate crimes (3 of them in the Los Angeles riots). A rise also occurred in other forms of hate-inspired violence: a 49% increase in vandalism and 16% more cross burnings. Klanwatch also reported a significant increase in hate crimes against gays and violence in the public schools through college level. A number of explanations have been presented for the increase in hate crimes. They include shrinking job opportunities, benign societal support for racist actions, a recessionary economy, and family and peer group beliefs and attitudes.

The increase in hate crimes and racially divisive campaign tactics by the major political parties prompted the U.S. Commission on Civil Rights to send identical letters to President Bush and congressional leaders in both houses of Congress. The letters stressed that the reduction of hate crimes and racial tensions in educational institutions should be a top priority.[35] The federal government and some states have responded to hate crimes. Although some states have compiled data on hate crimes, no national statistics were collected before 1990. To combat hate crimes by improving the reporting of it, the Hate Crimes Statistics Act, Pub. L. 101-275, 104 Stat. 140, was signed into law by President Bush on April 23, 1990. Section (b)(1) of the Act provides that the attorney general shall acquire data

> . . . about crimes that manifest evidence of prejudice based on race, religion, sexual orientation, or ethnicity, including where appropriate the crimes of murder, non-negligent manslaughter, forcible rape, aggravated assault, simple assault, intimidation, arson, and destruction, damage or vandalism of property.

Under this law, the attorney general is required to collect hate crimes data for five years to be used for research and statistical purposes. The Act makes it very clear, however, that an individual is not permitted to file a complaint of discrimination on the basis of sexual orientation. Many lawmakers were concerned that without this explicit language, the Act could be interpreted to grant homosexuals class status. Historically, homosexuals have been victims of verbal assaults and physical violence in a number of states, and a few have been killed.

Many states have responded to the rise in hate crimes by enacting legislation designed to curtail violence against racial minorities, Jews, and homosexuals. The Supreme Court ruled for the first time on the constitutionality of a hate crime law in R.A.V. v. CITY OF ST. PAUL, MINNESOTA, 112 S.Ct. 2538 (1992). In 1990 St. Paul enacted an ordinance known as the St. Paul Bias-Motivated Crime Ordinance, which provide that

> [w]hoever places on public or private property a symbol, object appellation, characterization or graffiti, including, but not limited to, a burning cross or Nazi swastika, which one knows or has reasonable grounds to know arouses anger, alarm or resentment in others on the basis of race, color, creed, religion or gender commits disorderly conduct and shall be guilty of a misdemeanor.

This case involved a white teenager, Robert A. Viktora, who burned a cross in the yard of a black family on June 21, 1990. Although this conduct could have been punished under several laws, St. Paul officials decided to charge him under the Bias-Motivated Crime Ordinance. Viktora argued that the ordinance was overbroad and impermissibly content-based and therefore on its face unconstitutional under the First Amendment. The Minnesota Supreme Court held that the ordinance was valid on the ground that it reaches only conduct that constitutes fighting words. Writing for a unanimous but philosophically divided Court, Justice Scalia, joined by Chief Justice Rehnquist and Justices Kennedy, Souter, and Thomas, declared the ordinance unconstitutional because of its content-based discrimination. He contended that the ordinance prohibited only those fighting words that arouse anger on the basis of race, creed, color, religion, or gender. Such selectivity, for Justice Scalia, enhanced the possibility that St. Paul sought to prohibit the expression of particular ideas. The remaining four Justices argued that the ordinance was overbroad because it criminalized speech that is protected by the First Amendment and could easily be decided under established First Amendment law.

Many states have adopted penalty-enhancement legislation, similar to the model statute developed by the Anti-Defamation League of B'nai B'rith, which provides for increased sentences if the crime is motivated by bias.[36] In WISCONSIN V. MITCHELL, 113 S.Ct. 2194 (1993), Wisconsin's law, unlike the St. Paul ordinance, imposed a harsher sentence on defendants if the crime was motivated "because of the race, religion, color, disability, sexual orientation, national origin or ancestry of that person." After viewing the movie *Mississippi Burning,* which portrayed a white man beating a black boy while he was praying, black youths gathered on a street in Kenosha, Wisconsin, and attacked a 14-year-old white boy who was walking on the opposite side of the street. He was beaten severely and remained in the hospital for four days in a coma. Todd Mitchell, a 19-year-old black youth in the group, made the following statement before attacking the white youth: "Do you all feel hyped up to move on some white people?" Shortly thereafter, he said, "There goes a white boy; go get him." Mitchell was sentenced to two years in prison for aggravated battery, but the judge added two additional years to his sentence under Wisconsin's hate crime law because the victim was selected on the basis of his race. The Wisconsin Supreme Court, relying on *R.A.V. v. City of St. Paul,* rejected the lower court's extra two-year sentence because it believed that the Wisconsin hate crime law had a chilling effect on the First Amendment. Writing for a unanimous Court, Chief Justice Rehnquist reversed the decision of the Wisconsin Supreme Court by distinguishing the St. Paul ordinance from the Wisconsin law in *Mitchell* and, in the process, granted its approval of this innovative approach to punishing hate crimes. Chief Justice Rehnquist held that the St. Paul ordinance was directed at protected expression, whereas the Wisconsin law was aimed at conduct that is not protected by the First Amendment. For him, "the Wisconsin statute singles out for enhancement bias-inspired conduct because this conduct is thought to inflict greater individual and societal harm."

Hate Speech in the University Setting

Racial slurs and hate crime incidents are not limited to poor, uneducated whites and members of the Ku Klux Klan. Many of the nation's leading colleges and universities have experienced an increase in racial incidents, especially hate speech. According to a *Newsweek* article, "The list of name schools that have been rocked by race-related controversies in recent years include Yale, Brown, Penn State, Georgetown, the University of Texas, the University of Michigan and many others.[37] On April 2, 1992, at Olivet College in rural Michigan, racial tensions came to a head when white members of a fraternity confronted two black students who had been accused of harassing a white female student. A fight broke out between black and white students in the lobby of a dormitory; one black student was injured and had to be taken to a hospital. The racial hostility that permeated the campus resulted in the vast majority of the college's 55 black students leaving the campus out of fear.[38] A number of black students commented that the racist comments made by some of the white students were more alarming than the fight. Henry Henderson, a black student, made the following comment: "Everybody dropped their mask and showed themselves. People who nudged you for answers on a test were calling you coon and spear-chucker."[39]

On October 7, 1992, officials at the University of Georgia filed charges against the Pi Kappa Phi fraternity for using a highly offensive racial slur against blacks in a pamphlet that was given to pledges. The NAACP chapter at Georgia requested a meeting with University President Charles Knapp. The chapter also requested that the fraternity be suspended from the university for three years.[40] Nineteen days later, the fraternity was suspended from all activities sponsored by the university (with the exception of service and educational programs) for one year.[41]

Perhaps the most problematic aspect of the hate speech controversy is the conceptual difficulties underlying "hate speech." It is also referred to as "racist speech" and "racial insults speech." Little consensus exists on the definition of hate speech. One of the leading scholars on hate speech, Mari Matsuda, professor at the School of Law and at the Center for Asian American Studies at UCLA, narrowly defines racist speech in order to respect First Amendment values. She offers three identifying characteristics of racist hate messages that distinguish them from other forms of nonracist speech:

1. The message is of racial inferiority.
2. The message is directed against a historically oppressed group.
3. The message is persecutory, hateful, and degrading.[42]

Matsuda argues that "making each element a prerequisite to prosecution prevents opening of the dreaded floodgates of censorship."[43] Central to understanding Matsuda's analysis is that hate speech must be understood from the victims' perspective because it causes real harm to them.

Serious questions about hate speech policy on college campuses have arisen. They concern the contours of permissible and impermissible hate speech. Underlying hate speech policies is the assumption that hate speech stigmatizes minority students in an insulting manner and in the process impairs their educational experience. Calling a black student a "dumb nigger" would be an obvious violation of the policy. But what about a sincere but naive white student asking a black person with a Ph.D., "Are you a coach?" or "Did you attend college?" Some blacks may find the latter questions as insulting, threatening, and denigrating as the former comment. Others may be insulted by the questions but would argue that they are constitutionally protected under the First Amendment.

Because the nation's colleges and universities have been confronted with numerous racial incidents,[44] those institutions that have sought to address the problem have adopted hate speech codes. In UWM POST, INC. V. BOARD OF REGENTS OF THE UNIVERSITY OF WISCONSIN SYSTEM, 774 F. Supp. 1163 (1991), a federal district judge had to determine the constitutional validity of a hate speech code. The Board of Regents for the University of Wisconsin System responded to an increase in incidents of discriminatory harassment by adopting a rule prohibiting speech intended to demean an individual's race, gender, religion, sexual orientation, or disability, thereby increasing the potential of creating a hostile learning environment. The university contended that the rule was permissible under the fighting words doctrine. However, District Judge Robert Warren declared in October 1991 that the UW rule was overbroad because it reached beyond the confines of fighting words and therefore violated the First Amendment. A new code was adopted in February 1992 that is more explicit than the original code and is expected to satisfy some of the reservations that Judge Warren expressed.

The University of Michigan adopted a racist speech policy because of an increase in racial incidents during the late 1980s. The policy at Michigan, like the original policy at Wisconsin, was invalidated by District Court Judge Avern Cohn in *Doe v. University of Michigan,* 721 F. Supp. 852 (1989). He argued that the policy was unconstitutionally vague and overbroad, in violation of the First Amendment. Within two weeks, the University of California at Davis adopted a hate speech policy that was similar to the revised policy approved by the Faculty Senate at the University of Wisconsin-Madison. The chancellor may impose discipline on students for using fighting words that are abusive epithets and that could provoke a violent response when addressed to an ordinary individual. Although the exact number of institutions with such policies is unknown, considerable evidence suggests that the number has increased since 1989.[45]

The increase in racist speech policies at many of the nation's universities has not deterred racist and/or sexist behavior. On April 4, 1991, the Iota Xi Chapter of the Sigma Chi fraternity at George Mason University held an "ugly woman contest" to raise funds for charity. Fraternity members dressed as women; one participant dressed as a black woman with stringy hair lined with curlers. His outfit was stuffed with pillows to exaggerate a woman's breasts and buttocks. Moreover, he spoke in slang to imitate the speech pattern of many African Americans. A number of students protested to university officials that the contest was offensive, sexist, and racist. After a meeting with the Dean of Student Services, a number of sanctions were imposed against the fraternity, including a suspension from all activities for the remainder of the spring semester. On June 5, 1991, the fraternity brought an action in federal district court against the university to nullify the sanctions as a violation of the First and Fourteenth Amendments. The district court ruled that even though the skit was nothing short of "low-grade entertainment," it is expressive entertainment entitled to protection by the First Amendment. The court of appeals affirmed the district court's ruling in *Iota Xi Chapter of Sigma Chi Fraternity v. George Mason University,* 993 F.2d 386 (1993). The court of appeals held that the Sigma Chi skit was expressive in the same fashion as nude dancing, as low-grade entertainment, and is entitled to First Amendment protection. Moreover, the court of appeals relied on the *R.A.V. v. City of St. Paul* rationale and concluded that the university sanctioned the fraternity because "the message conveyed by the 'ugly woman contest' ran counter to the views the University sought to communicate to its students and the community."

Charles R. Lawrence III, professor of law at Stanford University, has forcefully argued that opponents of regulating racist hate speech often ignore the constitutional rights of the victims. He suggests that *Brown I* articulated the principle that the practice of segregation that the Court held unconstitutional was "speech" because of the message conveyed by separation of the races—it "stamps a badge of inferiority upon Blacks, and this badge communicates a message to others in the community."[46] According to Lawrence,

racial insults, like fighting words, are undeserving of First Amendment protection because

> the experience of being called "nigger," "spic," "Jap," or "kike" is like receiving
> a slap in the face. The injury is instantaneous. . . . The second reason that racial
> insults should not fall under protected speech relates to the purpose underlying
> the first amendment. The purpose of the first amendment is to foster the greatest
> amount of speech. Racial insults disserve that purpose. Assaultive racist speech
> functions as a preemptive strike. The racial invective is experienced as a blow,
> not a proffered idea, and once the blow is struck, it is unlikely that dialogue will
> follow. Racial insults are undeserving of first amendment protection because
> the perpetrator's intention is not to discover truth or initiate dialogue, but to
> inure the victim.[47]

Lawrence goes on to argue, "Words like 'nigger,' 'kike,' and 'faggot' produce
physical symptoms that temporarily disable the victim," and "Many victims do
not find words of response until well after the assault, when the cowardly
assaulter has departed."[48]

In contrast, critics of hate speech policies, such as Nadine Strossen and
Gerald Gunther, have argued that hate speech policies violate the First Amendment because they seek to regulate the marketplace of ideas.[49] They contend
that constitutionally permissible speech could be discouraged if individuals
have doubts that what they say might possibly violate the policy. The language
used in these policies is ambiguous and overbroad and could easily have a
chilling effect on the First Amendment. In sum, they argue that hate speech
codes amount to censorship, result in reverse discrimination, are thought to
enforce "politically correct" attitudes, and act as the "thought police" and that
no workable solution to the problem exists.

The goals of hate speech policies are admirable. Tolerance, diversity, a
nonhostile educational environment, and genuine respect for the human dignity of all racial groups are time-tested values. Hate crimes and hate speech
cases are illustrative of the tension between the core constitutional principles
of free speech and equality. As Lawrence states, "We must weigh carefully
and critically the competing constitutional values expressed in the first and
fourteenth amendments."[50]

THE SECOND AFRICAN AMERICAN
SUPREME COURT JUSTICE:
THE POLITICS OF RACE AND
THE ROLE OF IDEOLOGY

On June 27, 1991, Thurgood Marshall delivered a letter to President Bush,
stating that he had decided to retire but would stay on until "my successor is
qualified." He also stated, "The strenuous demands of court work and its
related duties required or expected of a Justice appear at this time to be incompatible with my advancing age and medical condition."[51] Justice Marshall had

had a heart attack in 1976 and had also suffered from pneumonia, bronchitis, and glaucoma.[52] At the time of his retirement, he was 83 years old. Long before Marshall made his decision to retire, among the rumors about President Bush's choice to succeed him the name of Clarence Thomas kept coming up. Thomas, a judge on the U.S. Court of Appeals for the District of Columbia (a 1990 Bush appointment), was nominated to replace Justice Marshall on July 1, 1991. At the early age of 43, Judge Thomas was confronted with the formidable task of following in the steps of a highly respected jurist and one of the greatest contributors to legal thought in this century. After all, Justice Marshall had graduated first in his class from the Howard University School of Law in 1933.[53] His classmates at Lincoln University, in Pennsylvania, an undergraduate school for black males, included Langston Hughes and Nnamdi Azikiwe, who later became the President of Nigeria. After law school, Marshall worked at the local and national levels of the NAACP before being appointed Solicitor General and judge for the U.S. Court of Appeals for the Second Circuit. In 1967 he was appointed to the Supreme Court by President Lyndon Johnson.

In comparison with other Supreme Court Justices, Justice Marshall contributed immensely to the development of constitutional law. The May 17, 1954, landmark *Brown* decision turned out to be his most important legal victory. Winning 29 of 32 cases he argued before the U.S. Supreme Court still stands out as a remarkable accomplishment.[54] Marshall not only was a spokesman for black Americans but also was concerned about fairness and equality for all Americans.

On Sunday, January 24, 1993, Thurgood Marshall died of heart failure at the Bethesda Naval Medical Center at 2:00 p.m. at the age of 84.[55] Failing health had prevented him from administering the oath of office five days earlier to Al Gore, Vice President of the United States. On January 27, 1993, people from all walks of life came to the Great Hall of the Supreme Court at the rate of 1,000 each hour to pay their respects.[56] The tributes reflected the accomplishments of one of America's legal giants. At Marshall's funeral in the National Cathedral on January 28, 1993, Chief Justice William Rehnquist, who disagreed with Marshall on a number of important constitutional issues, eulogized his colleague in these words: "Under his leadership, the American Constitutional landscape in the area of equal protection of the laws was literally rewritten."[57] Justice Thomas, who replaced Marshall, said, "He was a great lawyer, a great jurist, and a great man, and the country is better for his having lived."[58] James O. Freeman, President of Dartmouth College and a former clerk for Justice Marshall when he was an appeals court judge, remarked, "He is probably the only person ever to have been appointed to the Supreme Court who would have had a place in American history before his appointment."[59] Finally, Medell Ford, a black, 68-year-old retired postal worker, emphasized that because of Marshall's work in the civil rights arena, he was afforded the opportunity to support his family. Five of his six children attended colleges that were previously closed to black Americans.[60]

Marshall's successor, Clarence Thomas, was born in Pin Point, Georgia, and moved to Savannah when he was very young. Having received a Catholic education, he had considered becoming a priest. He graduated from Holy Cross College with an English honors degree in 1970 and received his law degree from the Yale Law School in 1974. He worked for Attorney General John Danforth of Missouri (who later became a U.S. senator) as an assistant attorney general until 1977, when he joined the Monsanto Company's law department. In 1979 Thomas became a legislative assistant for Senator Danforth, and in 1981 President Reagan appointed him Assistant Secretary for Civil Rights in the Department of Education. From 1982 to 1990, Thomas served as Chairman of the Equal Employment Opportunity Commission. President Bush, who appointed Thomas to the Court of Appeals for the District of Columbia, stated that Thomas was "the best person for the position" to fill Marshall's vacancy.[61]

The Thomas nomination caused deep divisions in the black community. Justices Marshall and Brennan, the Court's two most liberal voices, had left the Court. President Reagan's appointment of William Rehnquist to the position of Chief Justice and his subsequent appointments of Sandra Day O'Connor, Anthony Kennedy, and Antonin Scalia solidified the Court's conservative majority. The split in the black community over Thomas's nomination was reflected in the support or lack thereof that he received from a number of civil rights organizations. For example, the NAACP opposed Judge Thomas, and the Southern Christian Leadership Conference (SCLC) was the only major civil rights organization that supported him. Benjamin Hooks, Executive Director of the NAACP, disagreed with Thomas's opposition to affirmative action, especially quotas, and with his antipathy toward the welfare state. He remarked that it was ironic that Judge Thomas opposed affirmative action despite the fact that it had afforded him the opportunity to attend Holy Cross and the Yale Law School.

As expected, questions from Senate Democrats focused on Judge Thomas's conservative judicial philosophy on a wide range of issues. In one of his most controversial positions, Judge Thomas indicated to the senators that he never debated *Roe v. Wade,* 410 U.S. 113 (1973) even while he was in law school and that he had abandoned his previously articulated natural rights approach to constitutional adjudication. Within minutes of the Committee's 7-7 vote on October 27, 1991, Judge Thomas's nomination was sent to the full Senate without a recommendation. Even those committee members who opposed the nomination believed he would be confirmed as the 106th Supreme Court Justice. However, no one anticipated the pending controversy over the sexual harassment charges brought against Judge Thomas by University of Oklahoma law professor and former EEOC attorney Anita Hill and made public on Sunday, October 6, 1991. The Senate postponed its vote, scheduled for October 8, 1991, to hear both sides. Professor Hill's electrifying testimony was presented during the morning of October 11, 1991. She accused Judge Thomas of using work situations to discuss sex with her and of boasting of his own sexual prowess. She also testified that she declined several invitations to go out with him. Some of her allegations against him were shocking to many people. At one point in her testimony, she stated:

My working relationship became even more strained when Judge Thomas began to use work situations to discuss sex. . . . He spoke about acts that he had seen in pornographic films involving such matters as women having sex with animals, and films showing group sex or rape scenes. He talked about pornographic materials depicting individuals with large penises or large breasts involved in various sex acts.

. . . One of the oddest episodes I remember was an occasion in which Thomas was drinking a Coke in his office, he got up from the table, at which we were working, went over to his desk to get the Coke, looked at the can and asked, "Who put pubic hair on my Coke?"[62]

On the evening of October 11, 1991, Judge Thomas testified and categorically denied all of Professor Hill's accusations. He stated that he and his family had been deeply hurt by the false allegations and expressed doubts whether the job he was pursuing was worth the humiliation and pain he was experiencing. Thomas expressed the crux of his feelings in these words: "No job is worth what I have been through, no job. No horror in my life has been so debilitating. Confirm me if you want, don't confirm me if you are so led, but let this process end. Let me and my family regain our lives."[63] Thomas also invoked race into the nomination process in the following manner:

This is a circus. It is a national disgrace. And from my standpoint, as a black American, as far as I am concerned, it is a high-tech lynching for uppity-blacks who in any way deign to think for themselves, to have different ideas, and it is a message that, unless you kow-tow to an old order, this is what will happen to you, you will be lynched, destroyed, caricatured by a committee of the U.S. Senate, rather than hung from a tree.[64]

In answering a question posed by Republican Senator Orrin Hatch of Utah concerning stereotypes, Judge Thomas remarked:

Senator, language throughout the history of this country, and certainly throughout my life, language about the sexual prowess of black men, language about the sex organs of black men and the sizes, etc., that kind of language has been used about black men as long as I have been on the face of this Earth. These charges that play into racist, bigoted stereotypes and these are the kind of charges that are impossible to wash off . . . And this plays into the most bigoted, racist stereotypes that any black man will face.[65]

Describing his ordeal as "Kafka-esque," Judge Thomas commented, "I think that this day is a travesty. I think that it is disgusting. I think that this hearing should never occur in America."[66] Having invoked the significance of race to defend himself caused Democratic Senators Robert Byrd of West Virginia and Barbara Mikulski of Maryland to invoke race to justify why they could not vote to confirm him. During the Senate debate that preceded the vote, Senator Byrd expressed his position in these words:

I believe Anita Hill. I believe what she said. . . . I frankly was offended by his injection of racism into these hearings. This was a diversionary tactic intended to divert both the committee's and the American public's attention away from the issue at hand, the issue being, which one is telling the truth? I was offended. I thought we were past that stage in this country.[67]

Senator Mikulski remarked, "The same people who gave us the worst of racial stereotypes in political campaigns, the Willie Horton ad, have now smeared Anita Hill. Much is said about the ruined reputation of Clarence Thomas, but what about Anita Hill?"[68]

At approximately 6:20 p.m. on October 15, 1991, Judge Thomas was confirmed to the Supreme Court by the narrowest margin in the history of Supreme Court appointments. The Senate vote was 52-48 (41 Republicans and 11 Democrats voted for him). He became the second black to serve on the highest court in the land. Louis Brandeis, Hugo Black, Abe Fortas, Homer Thornberry, Clement Haynesworth, William Rehnquist, Robert Bork, and others had to answer their critics' embarrassing allegations before the Senate Judiciary Committee, but none of them were subjected to what Judge Thomas described as a "circus" and "national disgrace" that the American people witnessed during prime time television.

On October 18, 1991, Judge Thomas took the Oath of Government Service, which was administered by Associate Justice Byron White. Mr. M. C. Thomas, Judge Thomas's father, left home when his son was only two years old. Judge Thomas learned of his whereabouts shortly before President Bush nominated Thomas and requested that he be invited to the ceremony. At the 15-minute ceremony, Justice Thomas stated, "Today, now, is a time to move forward, a time to look for what is good in others, what is good in our country. It's a time to see what we have in common, what we share as human beings and citizens."[69] The judicial oath is usually a public ceremony attended by other Justices and by members of Congress. Judge Thomas requested a short, private ceremony, which was held on October 31, 1991, and attended only by his wife, Virginia; Senator John Danforth; and Chief Justice Rehnquist's top aid, Robb Jones. It is important to note that the event was not announced by the Public Information Officer of the Supreme Court, Toni House, until after it had occurred. The judicial swearing-in ceremony had been planned for November 1, 1991. However, Judge Thomas requested that the ceremony take place earlier to allow him the opportunity to begin carrying out his awesome responsibilities.

Prior to his appointment to the Supreme Court, Thomas was highly critical of civil rights organizations and of the Supreme Court's role in civil rights cases, especially *Brown I*. Yet under intense questioning by Democrats during his confirmation hearings, Thomas seemed to suggest that, if confirmed, he would be compassionate toward underprivileged groups. Such concern prompted A. Leon Higginbotham, Jr., Chief Judge Emeritus of the U.S. Court of Appeals for the Third Circuit and Senior Fellow of the University of Pennsylvania School of Law, to write an open letter to Justice Thomas, dated November 29, 1991, and reprinted verbatim in the *University of Pennsylvania Law Review*.[70] The purpose of the letter was to remind Justice Thomas of the history of racial discrimination in the United States and to point out that if it were not for those civil rights organizations and leaders criticized by Thomas, he would probably still be in Pin Point or Savannah, Georgia, working as a laborer and not as a member of the Supreme Court. Judge Higginbotham recounted how conservatives at every turn tried to derail the struggle for equal rights in this country. He emphasized how the eradication of barriers to voting, housing, and privacy have personally affected Justice Thomas's life and career. Despite Judge Higginbotham's concerns, Justice Thomas's brief tenure on the Court clearly indicates that he is a staunch conservative who votes often with Justice Scalia, the Court's most conservative member, on a wide range of issues.

THE RODNEY KING TAPE:
RACE AND THE CRIMINAL JUSTICE SYSTEM

Since our analysis thus far clearly illustrates how the issue of race reemerged during each historical period that we have examined, we decided to include an examination of the highly publicized Rodney King incident in our book. Although this case never reached the Supreme Court and did not raise any major constitutional issues, it persuasively demonstrates how the nation's legal agenda has been dominated by the racial issue even in many lower level courts.

The prevalent view in the black community has always been that blacks are treated more harshly than their white counterparts in the American criminal justice system. However, the critics of this view have contended that the evidence is lacking. Black Americans pointed to the early morning hours of March 3, 1991, to validate what they have always suspected and alleged. Unlike incidents in prior allegations, the brutal beating of Rodney King, a black man, was captured on video. King was stopped in Los Angeles after a 15-minute high-speed chase and brutally beaten by four white police officers who were among approximately two dozen officers who showed up at the scene. The 81-second amateur videotape of the beating was shown repeatedly on national and international television, and many Americans, regardless of color, concluded that what they had seen was undoubtedly police brutality. Many Americans watched in disbelief and were shocked that such behavior by police officers could have happened in an American city. President Bush commented that the videotape literally sickened him.[71] Ross Perot, the 1992 independent candidate for president, on first viewing the videotape, commented, "The thing that just leaped at me was the shock that a group of men could do that. Second, I couldn't believe that the other guys didn't stop it."[72] In addition, similar feelings were expressed about the brutal assault against Reginald Denny, the white truck driver who was pulled from his truck and beaten by three blacks—Antoine Miller, Henry Watson, and Damian Williams— during the first hour of the rioting in Los Angeles that erupted after the police officers were found not guilty of beating King. The beating of Denny was equally repulsive to blacks and whites.

On April 1, 1991, Mayor Tom Bradley appointed a commission headed by Warren Christopher, former deputy secretary of state under the Carter administration, to investigate the Los Angeles Police Department (LAPD). On July 9, 1991, the commission released its report and concluded that the LAPD tolerated excessive force and overt racism among a significant number of officers; it called for the ouster of police chief Daryl Gates.[73] Gates, the controversial Los Angeles police chief, contended that the commission's recommendations, which included greater civilian control of the LAPD, were either already policy in the department or were unnecessary and that the problem had been traced to a few officers.

Without the videotape, Rodney King would have become another statistic in the criminal justice system in Los Angeles. The police officers would have denied having used excessive force, as they did during the trial, and would have testified that this lawless man's injuries were due to his resisting arrest. On April 29, 1992, approximately 13 months after the incident, a jury of 10 whites, 1 Latino, and 1 Asian American returned a verdict of not guilty for the four officers on charges of assault with a deadly weapon and excessive use of force as police officers.[74] The jury had studied the videotape and had listened to approximately seven weeks of thorough testimony. Immediately after the verdict, outrage and charges of racism catapulted to center stage. After the verdict, President Bush stated, "We must respect the process of law, whether or not you agree with the outcome. In a civilized society there can be no excuse for the murder, arson and vandalism."[75] Mayor Tom Bradley of Los Angeles remarked, "The jury's verdict will never blind us to what we saw on that videotape. The men who beat Rodney King do not deserve to wear the uniform of the LAPD."[76] Outside the courthouse where the separate verdicts of not guilty were read, arguments erupted between blacks and whites. A black man yelled, "What race are you?" Shouting back, a white man said, "I'm an American!" In reply, the black man commented, "We're not judged as Americans!"[77]

The outrage that many blacks felt was intensified because the venue for the trial had been changed from the city of Los Angeles to Simi Valley, California, a predominantly white conservative community that houses the Ronald Reagan Presidential Library. In addition to the change of venue issue, blacks were still seething with anger because Soon Ja Du, a Korean American shopkeeper, had been sentenced to five years probation rather than prison time for killing an unarmed black girl, 15-year-old Latasha Harlins, after a dispute over a bottle of orange juice at Ja Du's store.[78] A videotape had also captured this brutal and senseless killing. Members of the victim's family insisted that the sentence was not severe enough because the defendant could have been sentenced to as much as 16 years in prison. The tape, like the one involving Rodney King, was highlighted again and again on television. The videotape removed any reasonable doubt as to what really happened. On many occasions in the past, conflicting testimony clouded the issue of who was telling the truth, and the testimony of police officers was more often than not accepted as the most credible by judges and juries alike. Blacks contended that what they saw on the videotape was not that shocking. They pointed out that it simply reflected what had happened to blacks on many occasions in the past.

Shortly after the verdict was rendered, anger and rage turned into rioting and deadly violence that was worse than the rioting in the Watts section of Los Angeles in August 1965 and the violence that occurred in more than 120 cities after the assassination of Martin Luther King Jr. in April 1968. The Watts riots left 34 people dead and more than 1,000 people injured. Damages were estimated at $40 million.[79] Forty-six people were killed and damages were estimated at $67 million were reported after Dr. King's death.[80] During five days of rioting following the Rodney King beating trial in Los Angeles, 60 people were killed, more than 2,000 people were injured, and property damage estimated at $1 billion occurred.[81] Everado Garcia, a 20-year-old unemployed immigrant from El Salvador, believed that the United States was a place of peace but remarked that what had happened in Los Angeles was similar to a war.[82] Rodney King, the recipient of the beating, was so upset with the violence destroying Los Angeles and with the unnecessary loss of life that he pleaded for peace. On May 1, 1992, he stated, "We've got to quit, we've got to quit. Please, can we get along here—we can all get along. We're all stuck here for a while. Let's try to work it out. . . . We'll get our justice. . . . We'll get our day in court."[83] The Los Angeles riots triggered the eruption of violence on a smaller scale in San Francisco, Seattle, Miami, Las Vegas, and Atlanta. Some patrol cars were damaged in Madison, Wisconsin.

Approximately three months after the not-guilty verdict in the Rodney King beating trial (August 5, 1992), a federal grand jury indicted the four white police officers who had beaten King on federal charges of violating his civil rights. The three officers who actually beat King were charged with violating his Fourth Amendment rights against unreasonable arrest. The sergeant was charged for failing to restrain the three officers. Unlike in the first trial, King indicated that he would testify.[84] On March 9, 1993, he testified that he was not sure whether the police officers chanted the word *killer* or *nigger* at him. He said at one point during his testimony, "Sometimes I forget what happened. But I never added anything to make the situation [sound] worse than what it was."[85] On March 10, 1993, King denied that the officers used racial slurs while he was being beaten. He attributed the denial to his mother telling it a bigger issue than it already is."[86]

Unlike in the first trial, which evoked much controversy because the jury was comprised of 10 whites, 1 Latino, and 1 Asian American, the jury in the federal trial consisted of 9 whites, 2 blacks, and 1 Hispanic. As the 7-week trial was about to end, heightened anxiety permeated Los Angeles because of the fear of civil unrest and violence similar to that which erupted after the acquittal of the four white police officers in the state trial. Dr. Daniela Alloro, a psychologist from Los Angeles, reported that she had seen a number of patients who were suffering from anxiety because of their fear of another riot.[87] On April 17, 1993, the jury announced its long-awaited verdict, having listened to the testimony of 61 witnesses and viewed more than 130 exhibits, including the 81-second videotape, which they had watched repeatedly at various speeds.[88] Sergeant Stacey Koon and Officer Laurence Powell were found guilty; Officer Theodore Briseno and former Officer Timothy Wind were found not guilty. Officer Powell, who delivered the most blows, was found guilty of using unreasonable force during the arrest of Rodney King while acting under color of law. Sergeant Koon was found guilty of violating King's constitutionally protected right to be kept from harm while acting under the color of law. The acquittal of officers Briseno and Wind can be explained in large measure by the evidence, which clearly showed they played lesser roles in the beating of King.

After the verdict, intense anxiety was replaced with tears of joy. A genuine feeling that justice had prevailed brought a sigh of relief and probably averted a repeat of the violence and unnecessary loss of life that Los Angeles had experienced approximately one year earlier. The corner of Florence and Normandie Avenues, the South Central Los Angeles location that ignited the April 1992 riots, was peaceful. Photographers captured drivers giving the peace sign. President Clinton, in a speech in Pittsburgh shortly after the verdict was handed down, commented that the outcome of this trial should inspire the American people with "a determination to reaffirm our common humanity and to make a strength of our diversity."[89] Mayor Tom Bradley expressed his feelings in these words: "Today a jury representing the diversity of our city found the truth. Today a measure of simple justice has been delivered to our community. Today, Los Angeles has turned the corner."[90] Deputy Police Chief Matthew Hunt expressed the feeling of the Los Angeles community when he said, "Hopefully, this long nightmare that has gone on for the last two years is finally behind us."[91]

On August 4, 1993, the long-awaited sentences for Officers Stacey Koon and Laurence Powell were announced by U.S. District Court Judge John G. Davies. He sentenced them to two and one-half years in prison for the beating of Rodney King. Under the federal sentencing guidelines, the officers could have faced up to 10 years in prison. The judge waived the fines, which could have reached $250,000. In arriving at what many legal experts called a lenient sentence, Judge Davies concluded, "The victim's wrongful conduct contributed significantly to provoking the [officers'] behavior."[92] In explaining his decision, the judge emphasized that the violent blows that were played over and over again by television stations were justified by King's continuing movements.[93] He also pointed out that the six blows that made the officers culpable occurred during the last 20 seconds of the videotape, which for the most part the public had never seen.

After the sentencing, Richard Riordan, the newly elected mayor of Los Angeles, made a call for healing in a televised statement. The city was still tense from the riots that had occurred approximately 15 months earlier. Some black leaders voiced outrage at the lenient sentences. For example, Representative Maxine Waters, whose U.S. congressional district suffered immensely from the riots, called the sentences "a slap on the wrist."[94] Rodney King remarked, "I was glad that they did get some jail time. It's more time than I've ever spent in jail, that's for sure."[95] Laurie Levenson, a professor at the Loyola Law School who attended the trial as an observer, commented that Judge Davies's remarks made it appear that he was partial to the two officers.[96] Although the sentences were viewed by many persons as being too lenient, they did not provoke the outrage that followed the acquittals in the state trial and spared Los Angeles from a repeat of the violence and unnecessary loss of life that tore the city asunder in 1992. Federal prosecutors announced that they would appeal the lenient sentences.[97] On August 19, 1994, the Court of Appeals for the Ninth Circuit ruled, in *United States v. Koon,* 34 F.3d 1416 (1994), that the sentences imposed by the district court judge were inconsistent with federal sentencing guidelines. The ninth circuit vacated the sentences and remanded the case for resentencing. Under federal sentencing guidelines, Koon and Powell could receive a sentence of up to five years in prison.

Blacks had argued that they were the victims of unfair and often brutal treatment, but many whites refused to believe it because of their indifference and because such treatment was not happening to them. In fact, many whites who were extremely upset and vocal concerning the violence that had taken place in their city were not upset or at all vocal concerning the violence that King had endured. Indifference concerning injustices meted out to blacks was obvious, as it had been historically. Nevertheless, the videotape had convinced some whites that blacks had been painting an accurate picture all along.

The issue of race reemerged in a dramatic fashion in the trial of Damian Williams, 18, Henry Watson, 28, and Antoine Miller, 20, who were charged with beating white truck driver Reginald Denny during the initial stages of the Los Angeles riots. The beating in South Central Los Angeles was televised after having been captured by helicopter cameras. District Attorney Ira Reiner was accused of racism by a defense lawyer and by the mother of one of the defendants for removing Superior Court Judge Roosevelt Dorn, a black American, from the case to allow another black judge to preside. Reiner cited Judge Dorn's busy schedule for his actions. New charges of racism could not have been raised at a worse time. Between August 28 and August 30, 1992, Los Angeles witnessed one of the most violent weekends ever. A staggering 45 homicides occurred in this brief time span.[98] Judge Dorn accused Reiner of lying during a press conference, and shortly thereafter the district attorney's office was flooded with calls from angry citizens. After protracted jury deliberations, Williams was acquitted of attempted murder because the jury was unable to find the requisite intent to kill. However, he was convicted of simple mayhem, which is a felony. Watson was convicted of a charge of misdemeanor assault. Miller had pleaded guilty to grand theft from Reginald Denny, to receiving stolen property (a purse from a riot victim), and to felony assault on Marisa Bejar. People from all walks of life eagerly awaited the sentences for the three defendants. They wanted to find out whether the sentences would be similar to those meted out to the white police officers who had beaten Rodney King. On December 7, 1993, after the final showing of the beating that had been captured on videotape, Judge John Ouderkirk sentenced

Damian Williams to 10 years, which was the maximum punishment allowed.[99] Speaking to Williams, the judge said, "Mr. Williams, it is intolerable in this society to attack and maim people because of their race."[100] Williams could serve approximately three and one-half years in prison. The 17 months he spent in jail was subtracted from the sentence, and allowances could be made for good behavior. In an interview with the Wave Newspaper Group, Williams made the following comment concerning the riots: "People were just out of control like a pack of rats running after cheese. I was just caught up in the rapture. What we did was wrong."[101]

Henry Watson had already spent 17 months in jail, and Judge Ouderkirk ruled that he would not have to serve further time because of a plea bargain. However, the judge ordered him to perform 320 hours of community service and placed him on probation for three years.[102] On December 1, 1993, Antoine Miller was sentenced by a different judge (Cecil Miller) to 27 months of probation and 100 hours of community service.[103] After the sentence, Antoine Miller said, "It was pretty fair. I need to straighten out my life. I know I can't mess up anymore again."[104]

Supporters of Williams felt strongly that his sentence was too harsh compared with the 30-month prison sentence that the white officers received, and that racial prejudice still permeates the criminal justice system. Believing that the laws of Rome do not apply equally to all Romans, Reverend Cecil Murray, one of the most respected and influential clergyman in Los Angeles, observed, "Some say these cases are legally different, but contextually this says to blacks that the pattern of history continues."[105] Two of the most highly publicized and talked-about trials in recent American history had come to an end. However, the issues of race and racial divisions that have become a permanent component of the body politic remained.

On September 24, 1992, approximately five months after the verdict was rendered in the Rodney King beating case, Tom Bradley, the first black mayor of Los Angeles, announced that he would not seek a sixth term. After serving the city for 20 years, the 74-year-old mayor reminisced about his feelings concerning the violence that had further fragmented his city along racial lines. He said, "The April unrest tore at my heart, and I will not be at peace till we have healed our wounds and rebuilt our neighborhoods."[106]

On October, 21, 1992, 27 days after Mayor Bradley announced that he would not run for reelection, the 222-page report *The City in Crisis* was released.[107] This five-month study examined the performance of police officers before and during the rioting that tore at the heart of Los Angeles. William H. Webster, former CIA and FBI director, headed the panel, which volunteered its time and expertise to complete the reports that criticized Mayor Bradley, Police Chief Daryl Gates, the city council, and the Civilian Police Commission. It pointed the finger at Daryl Gates for misleading officials into believing that he had a plan for controlling the disorders when, in fact, there was no plan. Gates reacted angrily to the findings in the report and called the panel members "liars."[108] Gates was also criticized for the "department's warlike stance," which intensified tensions between community residents and police officers. The report also stated that Gates's decision to attend a fundraising event after the verdict was read was "mystifying." Mayor Bradley, who had not spoken to Gates for more than a year, was criticized for his failure to take control and for not having a riot plan. Inadequate planning for a crisis was brought to light, and the report recommended a reorganization of the police department. The new police chief, Willie Williams, promised that he would implement a number of the recommendations. The report emphasized that poverty, loss of hope, and racial intolerance were some of the causes for the riots in Los Angeles. Unfortunately, the causes have not been addressed, and the potential for future disturbances cannot be ruled out.

Police Officers and the Use of Excessive Force: A Nationwide Problem

Many whites have argued that what happened to Rodney King was an isolated occurrence and represented an exception to the rule. However, the perceptions by blacks that the use of excessive force against black Americans was not an isolated incident but has happened on a historically persistent basis was reinforced on April 30, 1992, one day after the verdict was rendered in the first Rodney King beating case. In Columbus, Ohio, Ronald Poole, the acting public safety director, concluded that excessive force had been used against Oleatha Waugh, a black American and former Ohio State University varsity wrestler, by police officer Michael Exline. Waugh testified that the officer struck him in the head twice with a flashlight and sprayed him with mace repeatedly for walking in the street to avoid a fight that was taking place on the sidewalk. The jury found the officer not guilty, as in the Rodney King beating case. Despite the acquittal, the officer was charged by the police department with using excessive force. Poole, however, stayed the decision, provided that the officer complete counseling and training within one year.[109] The officer was placed in another job, pending the successful completion of training and counseling. Many blacks contend that such verdicts and relaxed disciplinary action encourage police officers to use excessive force against minorities.

Fewer than 60 days after the Rodney King beating verdict, six police officers in New Jersey were suspended from the force without pay because they admitted to lying about a shooting in which a 17-year-old unarmed black youth suspected of car theft was seriously wounded.[110] Approximately four and one-half months after the Rodney King beating verdict, more than 2,000 police officers participated in an unruly demonstration at city hall in New York City to protest a proposal by Mayor David Dinkins to create an independent civilian agency to investigate misconduct by police officers. Many police officers who had taken an oath to enforce the law blocked the entrance to city hall and marched on the Brooklyn Bridge. Traffic was tied up for approximately one hour.[111] Some of the officers yelled, "The Mayor's on crack."[112] Some carried signs that read, "Dear Mayor, have you hugged a drug dealer today?"[113] Some of the shouts by the police officers were racially derogatory.

Such behavior reflects the real feelings of many white police officers toward black Americans and leads to the type of behavior that was captured on videotape in Los Angeles and to the excessive force that was used against Oleatha Waugh, the black wrestler from Ohio State University.

Fewer than seven months after the verdict in the Rodney King beating case, it became abundantly clear that some police officers were continuing to use excessive force. On November 5, 1992, 35-year-old Malice Green, an unemployed black steelworker, was beaten to death in Detroit by two white plainclothes police officers—Larry Nevers and Walter Bodzyn, nicknamed Starsky and Hutch within their precinct—who had a history of complaints against them for acts of brutality.[114] A spokesperson for the police department commented that at least two flashlights had been used in the beating. Numerous head wounds were cited by the medical examiner's office as the cause of death.[115] At a preliminary hearing in Detroit on December 14, 1992, a pathologist testified that a portion of Green's scalp had been torn off as a result of the blows he received. Stanley Knox, the black Detroit police chief, said he saw similarities between the beating of Rodney King and Malice Green and that what had happened in Detroit "was disgraceful and a total embarrassment."[116] On November 16, 1992, the two white officers were charged with second-degree murder. A third white officer, Robert Lessnau, was charged with aggravated assault, and Sergeant Freddie Douglas, a black 19-year veteran of the police force, was charged with involuntary manslaughter and willful neglect of duty.[117] It is worth noting that, according to a criminal justice expert, it is highly unusual for police officers to be charged with murder in cases involving beating deaths.[118] It is indeed ironic that Malice Green was the victim of brutality in Detroit. After all, Coleman Young became mayor in 1974 in large measure because he promised the voters he would work to eliminate the brutalization of blacks by white police officers.[119] On August 23, 1993, former police officers Bodzyn and Nevers were convicted of second-degree murder in the beating death of Malice Green. The third officer, Robert Lessnau, in a bench trial, was acquitted of assault with intent to do great bodily harm.[120] On October 12, 1993, Larry Nevers was sentenced to a term of 12 to 15 years and Walter Bodzyn received 8 to 18 years in prison.

Mayor Young has been less than successful at eliminating police brutality against blacks in Detroit. Southfield attorney Lauri Ellias filed approximately 100 police brutality lawsuits against the department within a 10-year period.[121] From 1987 to 1992, Detroit police officers were in more than 1,000 legal actions involving misconduct, and settlements estimated at $20 million were paid by the taxpayers in 1991.[122] This amount represents a 770% increase in cash settlements, when compared with the $2.59 million that was paid out in 1980. *The New York Times* reported in March 1993 that Detroit "has become one of the most violent and drug-ridden cities in America."[123]

Racial stereotyping also increases the likelihood that blacks will be the victims of police violence much more frequently than their white counterparts. On the evening of November 17, 1992, Derwin Pannell, a black plainclothes officer, was shot by two white transit authority officers in Brooklyn, New

York, when they observed him holding a gun on a woman while his partner, who was white, searched her pocketbook. The two officers fired 21 times before they realized that they had shot an undercover officer who had chased a woman because she had evaded paying the subway fare.[124] In an editorial in the *New York Times,* the issue of racial stereotyping was addressed in these words:

> When a group of Transit Police Officers opened fire on two of their fellow officers, they taught New Yorkers . . . that racial stereotyping can distort judgment. . . . The Transit Police acknowledge the possibility that the officers who fired did so because Officer Pannell is black. The disproportionate number of young black men committing crime feeds the belief that it is safe to assume the criminality of any black man behaving suspiciously—certainly one with a gun. That dangerously complicates life for black officers working under-cover.[125]

Transit police commanders moved quickly to assure the citizens that more sensitivity training would be instituted to address this serious problem. Studies have shown that blacks are shot more frequently than whites when police officers suspect that a crime is being committed. Twenty-eight days after the Pannell incident (December 15, 1992), Reginald Miller, a black under-cover police officer in Nashville, Tennessee, was stopped by five white police officers for a minor traffic violation. A gun was placed to his head. He was then kicked and beaten while being removed from the truck he was driving.[126] At the time of the incident, Miller was investigating prostitution on the same shift and in the same precinct as the officers who beat him. Robert Kirchner, the police chief, commented that the incident was not racially motivated. Miller informed the chief, however, that the beating was racially motivated. "If I were white, it never would have happened," he said.[127] Cindy Donnelly, a white woman who witnessed the incident, said the beating was much worse than the picture painted by the police. She also observed, "I wish I had a camera like they did for Rodney King, but I didn't. I'll never forget it as long as I live."[128] Two of the officers were fired for their role in the Miller beating.

Three years earlier, in 1989, Don Jackson, a former black detective, was treated like Officer Miller for a routine traffic violation. Two white officers in Long Beach, California, shoved him "face-first into a plate glass store window."[129] Racial stereotyping also adversely affects black defendants who are represented by some white lawyers. An example involves Dennis Palmeiri, the former attorney for Damian Williams, one of the four black men charged with beating Reginald Denny, the white truck driver, during the initial hours of the Los Angeles riots. Palmeiri testified at a superior court hearing that Frederick Celani, Deputy Director of the Center for Constitutional Law and Justice, which was defending Williams, ordered Palmeiri not to pursue the case aggressively and to withdraw a motion that was filed to suppress some damaging statements that Williams had made to police officers. He also testified that Celani referred to Williams as an "animal" and that Celani commented "Damian Williams was black, what does it matter?"[130]

Years before the Los Angeles riots, black Americans had pointed to similar racial disturbances as evidence that indifference to racial injustices would only delay future eruptions of violence. Their clarion call that something be done fell on deaf ears. For example, in May 1980, an all-white jury acquitted four Miami police officers of fatally beating a black insurance executive. Eighteen people were killed and approximately 400 people were injured in the following three days of rioting in Liberty City.[131] Approximately nine years later, violence was triggered in three sections of the same city after the killing of Clement Lloyd, a black motorcycle rider, by William Lozano, a Hispanic police officer.[132] On March 21, 1981, Henry Hays, a Ku Klux Klan leader, and his accomplice, Tiger Knowles, drove around the streets of Mobile, Alabama, literally "looking for a black man to hang."[133] Michael Donald became their victim simply because he was alone. Eight Los Angeles deputy sheriffs lost their jobs after the fatal shooting and beating of Arthur Jones, a black man, in 1990. During a 10-minute chase, he was shot in the neck and beaten with a flashlight on exiting the car. The beating could have killed him, according to the coroner's report.[134]

Other ethnic groups have also expressed outrage at how they have been unfairly treated by police officers. In May 1991, rioting broke out in the Mount Pleasant Latino community of Washington, D.C., after the shooting of a Hispanic man by a police officer.[135] After the rioting in the Mount Pleasant community, a number of witnesses at public hearings expressed their discontent with the treatment of Latinos by police officers. In July 1992, a Hispanic man was shot and killed in New York under questionable circumstances. The shooting touched off an ugly riot by angry residents in the Washington Heights section of the city. Charges of police wrongdoing were echoed throughout the community. Fermin Alameda, 63, died of wounds he suffered at the hands of a police officer in Miami on August, 9, 1992. In addition to internal bleeding, he had a dislocated shoulder, a ruptured liver, and five broken ribs.[136] A paramedic accused Officer Emilio Lopez of repeatedly striking Alameda.

The persistent pattern of brutality against blacks that has been examined in this chapter is illustrative of the significance of race in the administration of criminal justice. Police indifference to brutality and even to the deaths of blacks serves as a green light indicating that such behavior is acceptable. Historically, white politicians and law enforcement officials have opted not to be out front in discussions of explosive racial issues. They prefer that such discussions be left on the back burner. Failure to seriously address these problems openly and honestly has created a societal time bomb capable of a violent eruption at any moment.

CONCLUSION

Our analysis of the Rehnquist Court's decisions in the area of civil rights clearly suggests that the cyclical pattern of winning and losing cases is operative.

The decisional propensities of the Rehnquist Court in the areas of school desegregation, voting rights, employment discrimination, and affirmative action will make it very difficult for politically disadvantaged groups to realize the full promise of equality. As evidenced in some cases, most notably those involving jury discrimination and the use of the peremptory challenge, the Court still appears to be in transition, and the conservative bloc does not always vote together. What is clear from our discussion of the Rehnquist Court's interpretation of the Fourteenth Amendment and federal civil rights statutes is that its solidified conservative policy stance has seriously questioned the Supreme Court's contemporary role as protector and guardian of minority rights and interests. Only major shifts in the current composition of the Court, such as those that took place in previous eras, are likely to reverse this trend.

The Rehnquist Court will have ample opportunity to address potential landmark cases of sweeping significance and delineate the contours of policy change in the civil rights area. During the 1994-1995 term, the Court heard arguments in several high-profile cases in the areas of school desegregation, voting rights, affirmative action, and employment discrimination. Several important civil rights cases are now in the pipeline to the Court. Will the Rehnquist Court use these cases to limit or overturn precedents? Will civil rights interest groups be successful in pressuring a Republican-dominated, conservative Congress in overturning or limiting adverse rulings from the Court, as they did with the 1990 and 1991 Civil Rights Acts, or will the Court "follow the election returns"? Will the Clinton appointments to the Court result in a new consensus on civil rights issues, or will the Court continue its present path? Answers to these questions must await future consideration.

NOTES

1. Amaker, N. C. (1988). *Civil rights and the Reagan administration*. Washington, DC: Urban Institute Press, p. 157.

2. The Civil Rights Commission Act of 1983, Pub. L. 98-182, 197 Stat. 1301 (1983).

3. Witt, E. (1985). *A different justice: Reagan and the Supreme Court*. Washington, DC: Congressional Quarterly, p. 177.

4. Witt, E. (1985). *A different justice: Reagan and the Supreme Court*. Washington, DC: Congressional Quarterly, p. 176.

5. Caplan, L. (1987). *The tenth justice: The solicitor general and the rule of law*. New York: Vintage, pp. 18, 271.

6. Cohodas, N. (1981). How Reagan will pick judges is unclear, but philosophy will play an important role. *Congressional Quarterly Weekly Report, 39*, 299.

7. Witt, E. (1985). *A different justice: Reagan and the Supreme Court*. Washington, DC: Congressional Quarterly, p. 45.

8. Witt, E. (1991). *Congressional Quarterly's guide to the United States Supreme Court*. Washington, DC: Congressional Quarterly, p. 878.

9. Riggs, R. E., & Profitt, T. D. (1983, Spring). The judicial philosophy of Justice Rehnquist. *Akron Law Review, 16*, pp. 597-598. Also see Kleven, T. (1983, Spring). The constitutional philosophy of Justice William H. Rehnquist. *Vermont Law Review, 8*, p. 53; and Davis, S. (1989). *Justice Rehnquist and the Constitution*. Princeton, NJ: Princeton University Press.

10. Rehnquist, W. H. (1976, May). The notion of a living Constitution. *Texas Law Review, 54*, 706.

11. Rehnquist, W. H. (1976, May). The notion of a living Constitution. *Texas Law Review, 54*, 705.

12. Rosenburg, G. (1991). *The hollow hope: Can courts bring about social change?* Chicago: University of Chicago Press, pp. 104-105.

13. Southern Regional Council. (1993, Spring). Election analysis: Clear progress at the state level. *Voting Rights Review*, p. 3.

14. Southern Regional Council. (1993, Spring). Election analysis: Clear progress at the state level. *Voting Rights Review,* p. 3.

15. Southern Regional Council. (1993, Spring). 1992 election analysis: More clout in Congress for black and Latino legislators. *Voting Rights Review,* p. 1.

16. See Guinier, L. (1991). No two seats: The elusive quest for political equality. *Virginia Law Review, 77,* 1413-1514; Guinier, L. (1991). The triumph of tokenism: The Voting Rights Act and the theory of black electoral success. *Michigan Law Review, 89,* 1077-1154; and Guinier, L. (1992). Voting rights and democratic theory: Where do we go from here? In B. Grofman & C. Davidson (Eds.), *Controversies in minority voting: The Voting Rights Act in perspective.* Washington, DC: Brookings Institution. pp. 283-292.

17. Guinier, L. (1992). Voting rights and democratic theory: Where do we go from here? In B. Grofman & C. Davidson (Eds.), *Controversies in minority voting: The Voting Rights Act in perspective.* Washington, DC: Brookings Institution, p. 288.

18. "Message to the Senate returning without approval the Civil Rights Act of 1990." 26 Weekly Comp. Pres. Doc. 1632, October 22, 1990.

19. "Remarks on the Civil Rights Act of 1991," 27 Weekly Comp. Pres. Doc. 1699, November 20, 1991.

20. Dale, C. (1993, July). *Discrimination in housing: A legal perspective.* Congressional Research Service, Library of Congress, prepared for the Committee on Banking, Finance and Urban Affairs, 98th Congress, 1st Sess. Washington, DC: Government Printing Office.

21. 1.1 million awarded. (1991, December 25). *The Atlanta Journal/Constitution,* p. D2.

22. Corvette, D. (1991, December 6). Covington mayor will pay $27,000 in bias suit. *The Atlanta Journal/Constitution,* p. F2.

23. Bias suit settled. (1991, December 25). *The Atlanta Journal/Constitution,* p. D2.

24. King, J. (1992, March 15). Loan gap plagues Atlanta blacks. *The Atlanta Journal/Constitution,* pp. A1, G1.

25. King, J. (1992, March 15). Loan gap plagues Atlanta blacks. *The Atlanta Journal/Constitution,* p. A1.

26. Johnston, D. (1989, December 20). U.S. finds evidence linking bombings. *The New York Times,* p. A1, col. 1.

27. U.S. Commission on Civil Rights. (1991, September-October). *Civil Rights Update,* p. 4.

28. Race bias fuels most hate crimes. (1993, January 5). *The Atlanta Journal/Constitution,* p. A5.

29. Labaton, S. (1993, January 6). Poor cooperation deflates F.B.I. report on hate crimes. *The New York Times,* p. A8, col. 5.

30. Labaton, S. (1993, January 6). Poor cooperation deflates F.B.I. report on hate crimes. *The New York Times,* p. A8, col. 5.

31. Labaton, S. (1993, January 6). Poor cooperation deflates F.B.I. report on hate crimes. *The New York Times,* p. A8, col. 5.

32. See generally, Wilkerson, I. (1991, November 3). Seeking a racial mix, Dubuque finds tension. *The New York Times,* p. 1, sec. 1, pt. 1, col. 2.

33. Hispanic child victim of racial attack. (1992, January 14). *The Atlanta Journal/Constitution,* p. A4.

34. Walker, T. (1993, February 27). 31 died as crimes of bias rose in '92. *The Atlanta Journal/Constitution,* p. A3.

35. U.S. Commission on Civil Rights. (1991, September-October). *Civil Rights Update,* p. 1.

36. Greenhouse, L. (1993, June 12). Justices uphold stiffer sentences for hate crimes. *The New York Times,* p. A1.

37. Morganthau, T., et al. "Race on campus: Failing the test," p. 27. From Newsweek, May 6, 1991, ©1991, Newsweek, Inc. All rights reserved. Reprinted by permission.

38. Racial conflicts at Olivet College: Or, why desegregation is not enough. (1992, April 15). *The Daily Cardinal* (University of Wisconsin-Madison), p. 2.

39. Racial conflicts at Olivet College: Or, why desegregation is not enough. (1992, April 15). *The Daily Cardinal* (University of Wisconsin-Madison), p. 2.

40. UGA files charges against fraternity for racial slur. (1992, October 8). *The Atlanta Journal/Constitution,* p. D3.

41. McCarthy, R. (1992, October 27). UGA fraternity suspended for racial slur administrator rules after closed hearing. *The Atlanta Journal/Constitution,* p. C4.

42. Matsuda, M. J. (1993). Public response to racist speech: Considering the victim's story. In M. J. Matsuda, C. R. Lawrence, III., R. Delgado, & K. W. Crenshaw, *Words that wound: Critical race theory, assaultive speech, and the First Amendment.* Boulder, CO: Westview, p. 36.

43. Matsuda, M. J. (1993). Public response to racist speech: Considering the victim's story. In M. J. Matsuda, C. R. Lawrence, III., R. Delgado, & K. W. Crenshaw, *Words that wound: Critical race theory, assaultive speech, and the First Amendment.* Boulder, CO: Westview, p. 36.

44. See Wilkerson, I. (1989, April 17). Campus blacks feel racism's nuances. *The New York Times,* p. B1; Gibbs, N. (1990, May 7). Bigots in the

ivory tower: An alarming rise in hatred roils U.S. campus. *Time*, pp. 104-106; Brown, D. (1990). Racism and the university. *Virginia Law Review, 76*, 295.

45. For several articles on hate speech, see (1991). *Wayne Law Review, 37*, 1313-1468.

46. Lawrence, C. R. III. (1993). If he hollers let him go: Regulating racist speech on campus. In M. J. Matsuda, C. R. Lawrence, III., R. Delgado, & K. W. Crenshaw, *Words that wound: Critical race theory, assaultive speech, and the First Amendment*, p. 59.

47. Lawrence, C. R. III. (1993). If he hollers let him go: Regulating racist speech on campus. In M. J. Matsuda, C. R. Lawrence, III., R. Delgado, & K. W. Crenshaw, *Words that wound: Critical race theory, assaultive speech, and the First Amendment*, pp. 67-68.

48. Lawrence, C. R. III. (1993). If he hollers let him go: Regulating racist speech on campus. In M. J. Matsuda, C. R. Lawrence, III., R. Delgado, & K. W. Crenshaw, *Words that wound: Critical race theory, assaultive speech, and the First Amendment*, pp. 67-68.

49. See Strossen, N. (1990). Regulating racist speech on campus: A modest proposal? *Duke Law Journal, 1990*, 484-573; Gunther, G. (1990, Spring). Good speech, bad speech: A debate. *Stanford Lawyer, 24*, 4, 9, 41.

50. Lawrence, C. R. III. (1993). If he hollers let him go: Regulating racist speech on campus. In M. J. Matsuda, C. R. Lawrence, III., R. Delgado, & K. W. Crenshaw, *Words that wound: Critical race theory, assaultive speech, and the First Amendment*, p. 86.

51. President nominates Judge Clarence Thomas for the Supreme Court. (1991, July). *Third Branch: Newsletter of the Federal Courts, 23*(7), p. 1.

52. Davis, M. D., & Clark, H. R. (1992). *Thurgood Marshall: Warrior at the bar, rebel on the bench*. New York: Birch Lane, p. 5.

53. Williams, J. (1992). Marshall's law. In R. Goldman & D. Gallen, *Thurgood Marshall: Justice for all*. New York: Carroll & Graf, pp. 140-159.

54. Williams, J. (1992). Marshall's law. In R. Goldman & D. Gallen, *Thurgood Marshall: Justice for all*. New York: Carroll & Graf. p. 15.

55. Greenhouse, L. (1993, January 25). Ex-Justice Thurgood Marshall dies at 84. *The New York Times*, p. A1, col. 3.

56. Barringer, F. (1993, January 28). Thousands bid farewell to Marshall. *The New York Times*, p. A18, col. 4.

57. Labaton, S. (1993, January 25). Thousands fill cathedral to pay tribute to Marshall. *The New York Times*, p. C11, col. 1. Copyright ©1993 by The New York Times Company. Reprinted by permission.

58. Steinberg, J. (1993, January 25). Marshall is remembered as more than a Justice. *The New York Times*, p. C11, col. 1. Copyright ©1993 by The New York Times Company. Reprinted by permission.

59. Steinberg, J. (1993, January 25). Marshall is remembered as more than a Justice. *The New York Times*, p. C11, col. 1. Copyright ©1993 by The New York Times Company. Reprinted by permission.

60. Barringer, F. (1993, January 28). Thousands bid farewell to Marshall. *The New York Times*, p. A18, col. 4.

61. The Supreme Court: Excerpts from news conference announcing Court nominee. (1991, July 2). *The New York Times*, p. A14, col. 1. Copyright ©1991 by The New York Times Company. Reprinted by permission.

62. U.S. Congress, Senate Committee on the Judiciary, *Nomination of Judge Clarence Thomas to be Associate Justice of the Supreme Court of the United States*, 102nd Cong., 1st sess., Part 4, October 11, 1991, pp. 37-38.

63. U.S. Congress, Senate Committee on the Judiciary, *Nomination of Judge Clarence Thomas to be Associate Justice of the Supreme Court of the United States*, 102nd Cong., 1st sess., Part 4, October 11, 1991, p. 9.

64. U.S. Congress, Senate Committee on the Judiciary, *Nomination of Judge Clarence Thomas to be Associate Justice of the Supreme Court of the United States*, 102nd Cong., 1st sess., Part 4, October 11, 1991, pp. 157-158.

65. U.S. Congress, Senate Committee on the Judiciary, *Nomination of Judge Clarence Thomas to be Associate Justice of the Supreme Court of the United States*, 102nd Cong., 1st sess., Part 4, October 11, 1991, p. 202.

66. U.S. Congress, Senate Committee on the Judiciary, *Nomination of Judge Clarence Thomas to be Associate Justice of the Supreme Court of the United States*, 102nd Cong., 1st sess., Part 4, October 11, 1991, p. 157.

67. Congress, Senate, Senator Byrd of West Virginia, speaking against the nomination of Judge Clarence Thomas to the Supreme Court of the United States, 102nd Cong., 1st sess., (1991, October 15). *Congressional Record, 137*(147), pp. 14631, 14632.

68. Congress, Senate, Senator Mikulski of Maryland, speaking against the nomination of Judge Clarence Thomas to the Supreme Court of the United States, 102nd Cong., 1st sess., (1991, October 15). *Congressional Record, 137*(147), pp. 14651. Interestingly, after the confirmation hearings, public opinion polls indicated that most Americans believed Clarence Thomas. One year later, however, several opinion polls indicated a

shift in favor of Anita Hill. See Lewis, N. A. (1992, October 17). Anita Hill says she's skeptical about Specter. *The New York Times*, p. A14, col. 6.

69. Devroy, A. (1991, October 19). "There is joy," Thomas tells crowd. *The Washington Post*, p. A8.

70. Higginbotham, A. L. Jr. (1992, January). An open letter to Justice Clarence Thomas from a federal judicial colleague. *University of Pennsylvania Law Review, 140,* 1005-1028.

71. Mydans, S. (1992, April 30). Los Angeles policemen acquitted in taped beating. *The New York Times*, p. A1.

72. Hayes, T. (1992, May 4). The 1992 campaign: Undeclared candidate. *The New York Times*, p. A14. Copyright ©1992 by The New York Times Company. Reprinted by permission.

73. Reinhold, R. (1991, July 10). Violence and racism are routine in Los Angeles police, study says. *The New York Times*, p. A1.

74. Mydans, S. (1992, April 30). The police verdict. *The New York Times*, p. A1.

75. Please, we can get along here. (1992, May 2). *Milwaukee Sentinel*, p. 1.

76. Mydans, S. (1992, April 30). The police verdict. *The New York Times*, p. A1. Copyright ©1992 by The New York Times Company. Reprinted by permission.

77. Mydans, S. (1992, April 30). The police verdict. *The New York Times*, p. A1. Copyright ©1992 by The New York Times Company. Reprinted by permission.

78. Wilkinson, T., & Clifford, F. (1991, November 16). Korean grocer who killed black teen gets probation. *The Los Angeles Times*, p. A1, col. 5.

79. (1992, May 7). *Facts on File, 52*(2685), 328.

80. (1992, May 7). *Facts on File, 52*(2685), 328.

81. Reinhold, R. (1992, August 6). U.S. jury indicts 4 police officers in King beating. *The New York Times*, p. A1, col. 5.

82. Terry, D. (1992, May 4). Riots in Los Angeles: The overview. *The New York Times*, p. A1, col. 6.

83. An emotional plea to end the violence. (1992, May 2). *Milwaukee Sentinel*, p. 1.

84. Reinhold, R. (1992, August 6). U.S. jury indicts 4 police officers in King beating. *The New York Times*, p. A1.

85. King says mom stopped him from reporting racial taunts. (1993, March 11). *The Atlanta Journal/Constitution*, p. A4.

86. King says mom stopped him from reporting racial taunts. (1993, March 11). *The Atlanta Journal/Constitution*, p. A4.

87. Mydans, S. (1993, April 13). Trial-induced anxiety in Los Angeles. *The New York Times*, p. A14.

88. Mydans, S. (1993, April 17). Jury in beating trial sets announcement for today. *The New York Times*, p. Y6, col. 5.

89. Mydans, S. (1993, April 18). Verdict in Los Angeles: 2 of 4 officers found guilty in Los Angeles beating. *The New York Times*, p. A1, sec. 1, col. 6. Copyright ©1993 by The New York Times Company. Reprinted by permission.

90. Reinhold, R. (1993, April 18). Verdict in Los Angeles: Calm relief where rage once ruled. *The New York Times*, p. 1., col. 1. Copyright ©1993 by The New York Times Company. Reprinted by permission.

91. Reinhold, R. (1993, April 18). Verdict in Los Angeles: Calm relief where rage once ruled. *The New York Times*, p. 1., col. 1. Copyright ©1993 by The New York Times Company. Reprinted by permission.

92. Mydans, S. (1993, August 5). Sympathetic judge gives officers 2½ years in Rodney King beating. *The New York Times*, p. A1, col. 1. Copyright ©1993 by The New York Times Company. Reprinted by permission.

93. Mydans, S. (1993, August 5). Sympathetic judge gives officers 2½ years in Rodney King beating. *The New York Times*, p. A1, col. 1.

94. Mydans, S. (1993, August 6). Behind beating sentence: Guidelines and sympathy. *The New York Times*, p. B6, col. 3. Copyright ©1993 by The New York Times Company. Reprinted by permission.

95. Mydans, S. (1993, August 6). Behind beating sentence: Guidelines and sympathy. *The New York Times*, p. B6, col. 3. Copyright ©1993 by The New York Times Company. Reprinted by permission.

96. Mydans, S. (1993, August 6). Behind beating sentence: Guidelines and sympathy. *The New York Times*, p. B6, col. 3. A poll conducted by the Gallup Organization for the American Bar Association in June 1993 found that 27% of 401 state and federal judges believed that the federal trial following the acquittal of the officers in the state trial constituted double jeopardy; 62% of the judges believed that the federal trial did not constitute double jeopardy; 8% of the judges polled said they did not know; and 3% were not willing to answer the question. See (1993, August 6). 27% of judges call 2d trial unconstitutional. *The New York Times*, p. B6, col. 3.

97. U.S. is appealing sentences in Rodney King's beating. (1993, August 28). *The New York Times*, p. 6, col. 1.

98. El Nasser, H. (1992, August 28). Race looms over L.A. riot trial. *USA Today*, p. A6.

99. Mydans, S. (1993, December 8). Maximum sentence in riot beatings. *The New York Times*, p. A1.

100. Mydans, S. (1993, December 8). Maximum sentence in riot beatings. *The New York Times,* p. A1. Copyright ©1993 by The New York Times Company. Reprinted by permission.

101. Mydans, S. (1993, December 8). Maximum sentence in riot beatings. *The New York Times,* p. A13. Copyright ©1993 by The New York Times Company. Reprinted by permission.

102. Hamilton, W. (1993, December 8). Maximum 10-year sentence imposed in Denny beating case. *The Washington Post,* p. 2.

103. Anderson, J. (1993, December 2). Judge biased, says lawyer in LA riot case. *The Atlanta Journal/Constitution,* p. A16.

104. Anderson, J. (1993, December 2). Judge biased, says lawyer in LA riot case. *The Atlanta Journal/Constitution,* p. A16.

105. Mydans, S. (1993, December 8). Maximum sentence in riot beating. *The New York Times,* p. A13. Copyright ©1993 by The New York Times Company. Reprinted by permission.

106. Mydans, S. (1992, September 25). Los Angeles mayor won't run again. *The New York Times,* p. A12, col. 4. Copyright ©1992 by The New York Times Company. Reprinted by permission.

107. Yang, J. E. (1992, October 22). L.A. riot inquiry decries lack of planning by city, police officials. *The Washington Post,* p. A3.

108. Mydans, S. (1992, October 22). Failures of city blamed for riot in Los Angeles. *The New York Times,* p. A12, col. 6.

109. Cadwallader, B. (1992, April 30). Two officers disciplined. *The Columbus Dispatch,* p. A1.

110. Six policemen suspended in shooting probe. (1992, June 13). *The Atlanta Journal/Constitution,* p. A5.

111. McKinley, J. C. (1992, September 17). Officers rally and Dinkins is their target. *The New York Times,* p. B1, col. 5.

112. McKinley, J. C. (1992, September 17). Officers rally and Dinkins is their target. *The New York Times,* p. B1, col. 5. Copyright ©1992 by The New York Times Company. Reprinted by permission.

113. McKinley, J. C. (1992, September 17). Officers rally and Dinkins is their target. *The New York Times,* p. B1, col. 5. Copyright ©1992 by The New York Times Company. Reprinted by permission.

114. Levin, D. P. (1992, November 7). Detroit suspends policemen in fatal beating of motorist. *The New York Times,* p. Y7, col. 1.

115. Levin, D. P. (1992, November 7). Detroit suspends policemen in fatal beating of motorist. *The New York Times,* p. Y7, col. 1.

116. Levin, D. P. (1992, November 7). Detroit suspends policemen in fatal beating of motorist. *The New York Times,* p. Y7, col. 1. Copyright ©1992 by The New York Times Company. Reprinted by permission.

117. Levin, D. P. (1992, November 17). Four Detroit officers charged in death. *The New York Times,* p. A1, col. 5.

118. Levin, D. P. (1992, November 17). Four Detroit officers charged in death. *The New York Times,* p. A1, col. 5.

119. Levin, D. P. (1992, November 17). Four Detroit officers charged in death. *The New York Times,* p. A1, col. 5.

120. Terry, D. (1993, August 24). Ex-officers in Detroit guilty in beating death of motorist. *The New York Times,* p. A1, col. 1. The charge of involuntary manslaughter was dropped against the black supervisor, Freddie Douglas, although he faces a trial on a misdemeanor charge of neglect of duty.

121. Cannon, A., & Lengel, A. (1992, November 10). Who's policing the police? *The Detroit News,* p. A4.

122. Cannon, A., & Lengel, A. (1992, November 10). Who's policing the police? *The Detroit News,* p. A10.

123. Levin, D. P. (1993, March 23). For mayor of Detroit, this race is different. *The New York Times,* p. A14, col. 1. Copyright ©1993 by The New York Times Company. Reprinted by permission.

124. Mistaken for mugger, officer shot. (1992, November 20). *The Atlanta Journal/Constitution,* p. A10.

125. When police shoot police. (1992, November 21). *The New York Times,* p. 18, col. 1. Copyright ©1992 by The New York Times Company. Reprinted by permission.

126. Two Nashville officers dismissed in beating. (1992, December 19). *The New York Times,* p. 7, col. 4.

127. Fears, D. (1992, December 19). Policeman's beating exposes risks when blacks go undercover. *The Atlanta Journal/Constitution,* p. A3. Reprinted with permission from The Atlanta Journal and The Atlanta Constitution.

128. Fears, D. (1992, December 19). Policeman's beating exposes risks when blacks go undercover. *The Atlanta Journal/Constitution,* p. A3. Reprinted with permission from The Atlanta Journal and The Atlanta Constitution.

129. Fears, D. (1992, December 19). Policeman's beating exposes risks when blacks go undercover. *The Atlanta Journal/Constitution,* p. A3. Reprinted with permission from The Atlanta Journal and The Atlanta Constitution.

130. McMillan, P. (1992, November 20). Attorney tells of discord in Denny case defense. *The Los Angeles Times,* p. B2, col. 3.

131. (1992, May 7). *Facts on File, 52*(2685), 328.

132. (1992, May 7). *Facts on File, 52*(2685), 328.

133. Court lets employers cut insurance benefits for grave diseases: Other Court action. (1992, November 10). *The Atlanta Journal/Constitution,* p. A4.

134. Eight reported fired in death of black in '90. (1992, November 22). *The Orlando Sentinel,* p. A7.

135. (1992, May 7). *Facts on File, 52*(2685), p. 328. See also U.S. Commission on Civil Rights. (1992, May/June). L.A. riots underscore urgency of racial tensions project. *Civil Rights Update,* p. 1.

136. Epstein, G. (1992, November 21). Officer "was being rough" during arrest, paramedic says. *The Miami Herald,* p. B2.

CASES

BOARD OF EDUCATION OF OKLAHOMA CITY PUBLIC SCHOOLS V. DOWELL
498 U.S. 237 (1991)

In 1963, a federal district court found that Oklahoma City had intentionally segregated both schools and housing. In 1965 the district court found that the school board's attempt to desegregate by using neighborhood zoning failed to remedy past segregation because residential segregation resulted in one-race schools. After previous efforts had not been successful at eliminating de jure segregation in 1972, the district court ordered the school board to adopt the Finger Plan, under which (a) kindergartners would be assigned to neighborhood schools unless their parents opted otherwise, (b) black children in grades 1 through 4 would be bused to formerly all-white schools, (c) white children in grade 5 would be bused to formerly all-black schools, (d) students in the upper grades would be bused to various areas in order to maintain integrated schools, and (e) integrated neighborhoods would have stand-alone schools for all grades. In 1977, after complying with the desegregation decree for five years, the school board made a motion to close the case. The district court found that the school district had achieved unitary status, and the court issued an order terminating the case, which black parents and students did not appeal. In 1984, as more neighborhoods became integrated and more stand-alone schools were established, young black students had to be bused farther from their inner-city homes to outlying white areas. In an effort to alleviate this burden, the school board adopted the Student Reassignment Plan (SRP), which relied on neighborhood assignments for students in grades K through 4, beginning in the 1985-1986 school year. Busing continued for students in grades 5 through 12, and any student could transfer from a school where he or she was in the majority to a school where he or she would be in the minority. Faculty and staff integration was retained.

In 1985, black parents filed a motion to reopen the case, contending that the school district had not achieved unitary status and that the SRP was a return to segregation. Under the SRP, 11 of 64 elementary schools would be more than 90% black, 22 would be more than 90% white plus other minorities, and 31 would be racially mixed. The district court refused to reopen the case, holding that the district remained unitary and that court-ordered desegregation must end. The court of appeals reversed, holding that black parents could challenge the SRP because the school district was still subject to the desegregation decree and because nothing in the 1977 district court order terminated the 1972 injunction. On remand, the district court dissolved the injunction, finding that (a) the original plan was no longer workable, (b) the school board had complied in good faith for more than a decade with the court's orders, and (c) the SRP was not designed with discriminatory intent. The court of appeals reversed again, holding that a desegregation decree remains in effect until a school district can show "grievous wrong evoked by new and unforeseen conditions" and that the circumstances had not changed enough to justify modification of the 1972 decree. *Vote: 5-3.*

* * *

CHIEF JUSTICE REHNQUIST delivered the opinion of the Court.

. . . We must first consider whether respondents may contest the District Court's 1987 order dissolving the injunction which had imposed the desegregation decree. Respondents did not appeal from the District Court's 1977 order finding that the school system had achieved unitary status, and petitioners contend that the 1977 order bars respondents from contesting the 1987 order. We disagree, for the 1977 order did not dissolve the desegregation decree, and the District Court's unitariness finding was too ambiguous to bar respondents from challenging later action by the Board.

The lower courts have been inconsistent in their use of the term "unitary." Some have used it to identify a school district that has completely remedied all vestiges of past discrimination. . . . Under that interpretation of the word, a unitary school district is one that has met the mandate of *Brown v. Board of Education* [*Brown II*], 349 U.S. 294 (1955), and *Green v. New Kent County School Board,* 391 U.S. 430 (1968). Other courts, however, have used "unitary" to describe any school district that has currently desegregated student assignments, whether or not that status is solely the result of a court-imposed desegregation plan. . . . In other words, such a school district could be called unitary and nevertheless still contain vestiges of past discrimination. . . .

We think it is a mistake to treat words such as "dual" and "unitary" as if they were actually found in the Constitution. The constitutional command of the Fourteenth Amendment is that "[n]o State shall . . . deny to any person . . . the equal protection of the laws." Courts have used the terms "dual" to denote a school system which has engaged in intentional segregation of students by race, and "unitary" to describe a school system which has been brought into compliance with the command of the Constitution. We are not sure how useful it is to define these terms more precisely, or to create subclasses within them. But there is no doubt that the differences in usage described above do exist. The District Court's 1977 order is unclear with respect to what it meant by unitary and the necessary result of that finding. We therefore decline to overturn the conclusion of the Court of Appeals that while the 1977 order of the District Court did bind the parties as to the unitary character of the district, it did not finally terminate the Oklahoma City school litigation. In *Pasadena City Bd. of Education v. Spangler,* 427 U.S. 424 (1976), we held that the school board is entitled to a rather precise statement of its obligations under a desegregation decree. If such a decree is to be terminated or dissolved, respondents as well as the school board are entitled to a like statement from the court.

The Court of Appeals relied upon language from this Court's decision in *United States v. Swift and Co.,* [286 U.S. 106 (1932)] for the proposition that a desegregation decree could not be lifted or modified absent a showing of "grievous wrong evoked by new and unforeseen conditions." . . . It also held that "compliance alone cannot become the basis for modifying or dissolving an injunction." . . . We hold that its reliance was mistaken.

. . . In the present case, a finding by the District Court that the Oklahoma City School District was being operated in compliance with the commands of the Equal Protection Clause of the Fourteenth Amendment, and that it was unlikely that the school board would return to its former ways, would be a finding that the purposes of the desegregation litigation had been fully achieved. No additional showing of "grievous wrong evoked by new and unforeseen conditions" is required of the school board.

In *Milliken v. Bradley* (*Milliken II*), 433 U.S. 267 (1977), we said:

> "[F]ederal-court decrees must directly address and relate to the constitutional violation itself. Because of this inherent limitation upon federal judicial authority, federal-court decrees exceed appropriate limits if they are aimed at eliminating a condition that does not violate the Constitution or does not flow from such a violation." . . .

From the very first, federal supervision of local school systems was intended as a temporary measure to remedy past discrimination. *Brown* considered the "complexities arising from the *transition* to a system of public education freed of racial discrimination" in holding that the implementation of desegregation was to proceed "with all deliberate speed." . . . *Green* also spoke of the "*transition* to a unitary, nonracial system of public education." . . .

Considerations based on the allocation of powers within our federal system, we think, support our view that quoted language from *Swift* does not provide the proper standard to apply to injunctions entered in school desegregation cases. Such decrees, unlike the one in *Swift,* are not intended to operate in perpetuity. Local control over the education of children allows citizens to participate in decision-making, and allows innovation so that school programs can fit local needs. . . . The legal justification for displacement of local authority by an injunctive decree in a school desegregation case is a violation of the Constitution by the local authorities. Dissolving a desegregation decree after the local authorities have operated in compliance with it for a reasonable period of time properly recognizes that necessary concern for the important values of local control of public school systems dictates that a federal court's regulatory control of such systems not extend beyond the time required to remedy the effects of past intentional discrimination. . . .

. . . A district court need not accept at face value the profession of a school board which has intentionally discriminated that it will cease to do so in the future. But in deciding whether to modify or dissolve a desegregation degree, a school board's compliance with previous court orders is obviously relevant. In this case the original finding of *de jure* segregation was entered in 1961, the injunctive decree from which the Board seeks relief was entered in 1972, and the Board complied with the decree in good faith until 1985. Not only do the personnel of school boards change over time, but the same passage of time enables the District Court to observe the good faith of the school board in complying with the decree. The test espoused by the Court of Appeals would condemn a school district, once governed by a board which intentionally discriminated, to judicial tutelage for the indefinite future. Neither the principles governing the entry and dissolution of injunctive decrees, nor the commands of the Equal Protection Clause of the Fourteenth Amendment, require any such Draconian result.

Petitioners urge that we reinstate the decision of the District Court terminating the injunction, but we think that the preferable course is to remand the case to that court so that it may decide, in accordance with this opinion, whether the Board made a sufficient showing of constitutional compliance as of 1985, when the SRP was adopted, to allow the injunction to be dissolved. The District Court should address itself to whether the Board had complied in good faith with the desegregation decree since it was entered, and whether the vestiges of past discrimination had been eliminated to the extent practicable.

In considering whether the vestiges of *de jure* segregation had been eliminated as far as practicable, the District Court should look not only at student assignments, but "to every facet of school operations— faculty, staff, transportation, extra-curricular activities and facilities." . . .

After the District Court decides whether the Board was entitled to have the decree terminated, it should proceed to decide respondent's challenge to the SRP. A school district which has been released from an injunction imposing a desegregation plan no longer requires court authorization for the promulgation of policies and rules regulating matters such as assignment of students and the like, but it of course remains subject to the mandate of the Equal Protection Clause of the Fourteenth Amendment. If the Board was entitled to have the decree terminated as of 1985, the District Court should then evaluate the Board's decision to implement the SRP under appropriate equal protection principles. . . .

The judgment of the Court of Appeals is reversed, and the case is remanded to the District Court for further proceedings consistent with this opinion.

It is so ordered.

JUSTICE SOUTER took no part in the consideration or decision of this case.

* * *

JUSTICE MARSHALL, with whom JUSTICE BLACKMUN and JUSTICE STEVENS join, dissenting.

. . . In my view, the standard for dissolution of a school desegregation decree must reflect the central aim of our school desegregation precedents. In [*Brown I*], a unanimous Court declared that racially "[s]eparate educational facilities are inherently unequal." . . . This holding rested on the Court's recognition that state-sponsored segregation conveys a message of "inferiority as to th[e] status [of Afro-American school children] in the community that may affect their hearts and minds in a way unlikely ever to be undone." . . . Remedying this evil and preventing its recurrence were the motivations animating our requirement that formerly *de jure* segregated school districts take all feasible steps to *eliminate* racially identifiable schools. . . .

I believe a desegregation decree cannot be lifted so long as conditions likely to inflict the stigmatic injury condemned in *Brown I* persist and there remain feasible methods of eliminating such conditions. Because the record here shows, and the Court of Appeals found, that feasible steps could be taken to avoid one-race schools, it is clear that the purposes of the decree have not yet been achieved and the Court of Appeals' reinstatement of the decree should be affirmed. I therefore dissent.

. . . I agree with the majority that the proper standard for determining whether a school desegregation decree should be dissolved is whether the purposes of the desegregation litigation, as incorporated in the decree, have been fully achieved. . . . I strongly disagree with the majority, however, on what must be shown to demonstrate that a decree's purposes have been fully realized. In my view, a standard for dissolution of a desegregation decree must take into account the unique harm associated with a system of racially identifiable schools and must expressly demand the elimination of such schools.

FREEMAN V. PITTS
112 S.Ct. 1430 (1992)

This case involved a court-ordered desegregation decree for the DeKalb County School System (DCSS), located in a major suburban area of Atlanta, Georgia, which serves 73,000 students. In 1969 the DCSS was ordered to dismantle its dual school system. In 1986 the DCSS filed a motion to dismiss the litigation, seeking a declaration that the school system had achieved unitary status. The district court approached the question of whether the DCSS had achieved unitary status by asking whether it was unitary with respect to the factors identified in *Green v. New Kent County School Board* (1968).

The district court also considered another factor not identified in *Green:* the quality of education being offered to the white and black student population. The district court found that the school system was a unitary system with regard to student assignment, transportation, physical facilities, and extracurricular activities and ruled that it would order no further relief in those areas. The court also found that subsequent and continuing racial imbalance with respect to student assignment was a product of independent demographic changes unrelated to the school system's actions and not a vestige of the prior de jure system and that actions taken by the school system had achieved maximum practical desegregation from 1969 to 1986. However, the district court did not dismiss the case because it found that the DCSS was not unitary in every respect. The court stated that the vestiges of the dual system remained in the areas of teacher and principal assignments, resource allocation, and quality of education.

The court of appeals affirmed the district court's ultimate conclusion that the school system had not yet achieved unitary status but reversed the district court's conclusion that the DCSS has no further duties in the area of student assignment. Furthermore, the court held that a district court should retain full remedial authority over a school system until it achieves unitary status in all *Green* categories at the same time for several years. According to the court of appeals, because the school system had never achieved unitary status, it could not shirk its constitutional duties by pointing to demographic shifts occurring prior to unitary status, and the DCSS would have to take further actions to correct the racial imbalance even though such actions might be administratively awkward, inconvenient, and even bizarre in some situations. *Vote: 8-0.*

* * *

JUSTICE KENNEDY delivered the opinion of the Court.

. . . Two principal questions are presented. The first is whether a district court may relinquish its supervision and control over those aspects of a school system in which there has been compliance with a desegregation decree if other aspects of the system remain in noncompliance. As we answer this question in the affirmative, the second question is whether the Court of Appeals erred in reversing the District Court's order providing for incremental withdrawal of supervision in all the circumstances of this case.

The duty and responsibility of a school district once segregated by law is to take all steps necessary to eliminate the vestiges of the unconstitutional *de jure* system. This is required in order to insure that the principal wrong of the *de jure* system, the injuries and stigma inflicted upon the race disfavored by the

violation, is no longer present. This was the rationale and the objective in *Brown I* and *Brown II*. . . .

The objective of *Brown I* was made more specific by our holding in *Green [v. New Kent County School Bd.,* 391 U.S. 430 (1968)] that the duty of a former *de jure* district is to "take whatever steps might be necessary to convert to a unitary system in which racial discrimination would be eliminated root and branch." . . . We also identified various parts of the school system which, in addition to student attendance patterns, must be free from racial discrimination before the mandate of *Brown* is met: faculty, staff, transportation, extracurricular activities and facilities. . . . The *Green* factors are a measure of the racial identifiability of schools in a system that is not in compliance with *Brown,* and we instructed the District Courts to fashion remedies that address all these components of elementary and secondary school systems.

. . . Today, we make explicit the rationale that was central in [*Pasadena City Board of Education v. Spangler,* 427 U.S. 424 (1976)]. A federal court in a school desegregation case has the discretion to order an incremental or partial withdrawal of its supervision and control. This discretion derives both from the constitutional authority which justified its intervention in the first instance and its ultimate objectives in formulating the decree. The authority of the court is invoked at the outset to remedy particular constitutional violations. In construing the remedial authority of the district courts, we have been guided by the principles that "judicial powers may be exercised only on the basis of a constitutional violation," and that "the nature of the violation determines the scope of the remedy." . . . A remedy is justifiable only insofar as it advances the ultimate objective of alleviating the initial constitutional violation.

We have said that the court's end purpose must be to remedy the violation and in addition to restore state and local authorities to the control of a school system that is operating in compliance with the Constitution. *Milliken v. Bradley [Milliken II]*, 433 U.S. 267, 280-281 (1977) . . . Partial relinquishment of judicial control, where justified by the facts of the case, can be an important and significant step in fulfilling the district court's duty to return the operations and control of schools to local authorities. In *Dowell [v. Board of Education of Oklahoma City Public Schools,* 396 U.S. 269 (1969)], we emphasized that federal judicial supervision of local school systems was intended as a "temporary measure." . . . Although this temporary measure has lasted decades, the ultimate objective has not changed—to return school districts to the control of local authorities. Just as a court has the obligation at the outset of a desegregation decree to structure a plan so that all available resources of the court are directed to comprehensive supervision of its decree, so too must a court provide an orderly means for withdrawing from control when it is shown that the school district has attained the requisite degree of compliance. A transition phase in which control is relinquished in a gradual way is an appropriate means to this end.

. . . As we discuss below, one of the prerequisites to relinquishment of control in whole or in part is that a school district has demonstrated its commitment to a course of action that gives full respect to the equal protection guarantees of the Constitution. Yet it must be acknowledged that the potential for discrimination and racial hostility is still present in our country, and its manifestations may emerge in new and subtle forms after the effects of *de jure* desegregation have been eliminated. It is the duty of the State and its subdivisions to ensure that such forces do not shape or control the policies of its school systems. Where control lies, so too does responsibility.

We hold that, in the course of supervising desegregation plans, federal courts have the authority to relinquish supervision and control of school districts in incremental stages, before full compliance has been achieved in every area of school operations. While retaining jurisdiction over the case, the court may determine that it will not order further remedies in areas where the school district is in compliance with the decree. That is to say, upon a finding that a school system subject to a court-supervised desegregation plan is in compliance in some but not all areas, the court in appropriate cases may return control to the school system in those areas where compliance has been achieved, limiting further judicial supervision to operations that are not yet in full compliance with the court decree. In particular, the district court may determine that it will not order further remedies in the area of student assignments where racial imbalance is not traceable, in a proximate way, to constitutional violations.

A court's discretion to order the incremental withdrawal of its supervision in a school desegregation case must be exercised in a manner consistent with the purposes and objectives of its equitable power. Among the factors which must inform the sound discretion of the court in ordering partial withdrawal are the following: whether there has been full and satisfactory compliance with the decree in those aspects of the system where supervision is to be withdrawn; whether retention of judicial control is necessary or practicable to achieve compliance with the decree in other facets of the school system; and whether the school district has demonstrated, to the public and to the parents and students of the once disfavored race, its good faith commitment to the whole of the court's decree and to those provisions of the law and the constitution that were the predicate for judicial intervention in the first instance.

In considering these factors a court should give particular attention to the school system's record of compliance. A school system is better positioned to demonstrate its good-faith commitment to a constitutional course of action when its policies form a consistent pattern of lawful conduct directed to eliminating earlier violations. And with the passage of time the degree to which racial imbalances continue to represent vestiges of a constitutional violation may diminish, and the practicability and efficacy of various remedies can be evaluated with more precision.

These are the premises that guided our formulation in *Dowell* of the duties of a district court during the final phases of a desegregation case: "The District Court should address itself to whether the Board had complied in good faith with the desegregation decree since it was entered, and whether the vestiges of past discrimination had been eliminated to the extent practicable." . . .

We reach now the question whether the Court of Appeals erred in prohibiting the District Court from returning to DCSS partial control over some of its affairs. We decide that the Court of Appeals did err in holding that, as a matter of law, the District Court had no discretion to permit DCSS to regain control over student assignment, transportation, physical facilities, and extracurricular activities, while retaining court supervision over the areas of faculty and administrative assignments and the quality of education, where full compliance had not been demonstrated.

It was an appropriate exercise of its discretion for the District Court to address the elements of a unitary system discussed in *Green,* to inquire whether other elements ought to be identified, and to determine whether minority students were being disadvantaged in ways that required the formulation of new and further remedies to insure full compliance with the court's decree. Both parties agreed that quality of education was a legitimate inquiry in determining DCSS' compliance with the desegregation decree, and the trial court found it workable to consider the point in connection with its findings on resource allocation. Its order retaining supervision over this aspect of the case has not been challenged by the parties and we need not examine it except as it underscores the school district's record of compliance in some areas but not others. The District Court's approach illustrates that the *Green* factors need not be a rigid framework. It illustrates also the uses of equitable discretion. By withdrawing control over areas where judicial supervision is no longer needed, a district court can concentrate both its own resources and those of the school district on the areas where the effects of *de jure* discrimination have not been eliminated and further action is necessary in order to provide real and tangible relief to minority students.

The Court of Appeals' rejection of the District Court's order rests on related premises: first, that given noncompliance in some discrete categories, there can be no partial withdrawal of judicial control; and second, until there is full compliance, heroic measures must be taken to ensure racial balance in student assignments systemwide. Under our analysis and our precedents, neither premise is correct.

The Court of Appeals was mistaken in ruling that our opinion in *Swann* [v. *Charlotte-Mecklenburg Board of Education,* 402 U.S. 1 (1971)] requires "awkward," "inconvenient" and "even bizarre" measures to achieve racial balance in student assignments in the late phases of carrying out a decree, when the imbalance is attributable neither to the prior *de jure* system nor to a later violation by the school district but rather to independent demographic forces. . . .

That there was racial imbalance in student attendance zones was not tantamount to a showing that the school district was in noncompliance with the decree or with its duties under the law. Racial balance is not to be achieved for its own sake. It is to be pursued when racial imbalance has been caused by a constitutional violation. Once the racial imbalance due to the *de jure* violation has been remedied, the school district is under no duty to remedy imbalance that is caused by demographic factors. . . .

The findings of the District Court that the population changes which occurred in DeKalb County were not caused by the policies of the school district, but rather by independent factors, are consistent with the mobility that is a distinct characteristic of our society. . . . In such a society it is inevitable that the demographic makeup of school districts, based as they are on political subdivisions such as counties and municipalities, may undergo rapid change.

. . . Where resegregation is a product not of state action but of private choices, it does not have constitutional implications. It is beyond the authority and beyond the practical ability of the federal courts to try to counteract these kinds of continuous and massive demographic shifts. To attempt such results would require ongoing and never-ending supervision by the courts of school districts simply because they were once *de jure* segregated. Residential housing choices, and their attendant effects on the racial composition of schools, present an ever-changing pattern, one difficult to address through judicial remedies.

. . . As the *de jure* violation becomes more remote in time and these demographic changes intervene, it becomes less likely that a current racial imbalance in a school district is a vestige of the prior *de jure* system. The causal link between current conditions and the prior violation is even more attenuated if the school district has demonstrated its good faith. In light of its finding that the demographic changes in DeKalb County are unrelated to the prior violation, the District Court was correct to entertain the suggestion that DCSS had no duty to achieve systemwide racial balance in the student population. It was appropriate for the District Court to examine the reasons for the racial imbalance before ordering an impractical, and no doubt massive, expenditure of funds to achieve racial balance after 17 years of efforts to implement the comprehensive plan in a district where there were fundamental changes in demographics, changes not attributable to the former *de jure* regime or any later actions by school officials. The District Court's determination to order instead the expenditure of scarce resources in areas such as the quality of education, where full compliance had not yet been achieved, underscores the uses of discretion in framing equitable remedies.

To say, as did the Court of Appeals, that a school district must meet all six *Green* factors before the trial court can declare the system unitary and relinquish its control over school attendance zones, and to hold further that racial balancing by all necessary means is required in the interim, is simply to vindicate a legal phase. The law is not so formalistic. A proper rule must be based on the necessity to find a feasible remedy that insures systemwide compliance with the court decree and that is directed to curing the effects of the specific violation.

We next consider whether retention of judicial control over student attendance is necessary or practicable to achieve compliance in other facets of the school system. Racial balancing in elementary and secondary school student assignments may be a legitimate remedial device to correct other fundamental inequities that were themselves caused by the constitutional violation. We have long recognized that the *Green* factors may be related or interdependent. . . .

There was no showing that racial balancing was an appropriate mechanism to cure other deficiencies in this case. It is true that the school district was not in compliance with respect to faculty assignments, but the record does not show that student reassignments would be a feasible or practicable way to remedy this defect. To the contrary, the District Court suggests that DCSS could solve the faculty assignment problem by reassigning a few teachers per school. The District Court, not having our analysis before it, did not have the opportunity to make specific findings and conclusions on this aspect of the case, however. Further proceedings are appropriate for this purpose.

The requirement that the school district show its good faith commitment to the entirety of a desegregation plan so that parents, students and the public have assurance against further inquiries or stigma also should be a subject for more specific findings. . . .

. . . The judgment is reversed and the case is remanded to the Court of Appeals. It should determine what issues are open for its further consideration in light of the previous briefs and arguments of the parties and in light of the principles set forth in this opinion. Thereupon it should order further proceedings as necessary or order an appropriate remand to the District Court.

It is so ordered.

JUSTICE THOMAS took no part in the consideration or decision of this case.

[The concurring opinions of JUSTICE SCALIA and JUSTICE SOUTER are omitted.]

[The opinion of JUSTICE BLACKMUN, with whom JUSTICE STEVENS and JUSTICE O'CONNOR join, concurring in the judgment, is omitted.]

UNITED STATES V. FORDICE
112 S.Ct. 2727 (1992)

Mississippi launched its public university system in 1848 by establishing the University of Mississippi exclusively for white students. Subsequently, the state erected additional single-race universities: four white institutions (Mississippi State, Mississippi University for Women [MUW], University of Southern Mississippi, and Delta State) and three black institutions (Alcorn State, Jackson State, and Mississippi Valley State). The first black student, James Meredith, was not admitted to the University of Mississippi until 1962, and only then by court order. For the next 12 years, the segregated public university system in Mississippi remained largely intact. Mississippi State, MUW, University of Southern Mississippi, and Delta State each admitted at least one black student during these years, and Jackson State and Mississippi Valley State were exclusively black. Alcorn State had admitted five white students by 1968.

In 1969 the U.S. Department of Health, Education and Welfare (HEW) initiated efforts to enforce Title VI of the Civil Rights Act of 1964, which required that Mississippi devise a plan to disestablish the formerly de jure segregated system. In June 1973, the board of trustees submitted a plan, but HEW rejected it because it did not go far enough in the areas of student recruitment and enrollment, faculty hiring, elimination of unnecessary program duplication, and institutional funding practices. In 1975 black plaintiffs brought suit, alleging that Mississippi had maintained the racially segregative effects of this prior dual system in higher education, in violation of, among other things, the equal protection clause and Title VI. After the lawsuit was filed, the parties attempted for 12 years to achieve a consensual resolution of their differences through voluntary dismantlement of the segregated university system. In 1981 the board of trustees issued mission statements classifying the three flagship universities (University of Mississippi, Mississippi State, and Southern Mississippi) as comprehensive universities having the most varied programs and offering doctoral degrees and Jackson State as an urban university with more limited research and degree functions; and characterized the rest of the universities as regional institutions that functioned primarily in an undergraduate role. When the student bodies at the universities were predominantly

segregated by the mid-1980s, the lawsuit against the governor of Mississippi proceeded to trial. The district court concluded that, in the higher education context, the affirmative duty to desegregate does not contemplate either restricting choice or the achievement of any degree of racial balance. The district court found no violations of federal law and concluded that the state was fulfilling its affirmative duty to disestablish the former de jure segregated system of higher education. The court of appeals affirmed the decision of the lower court. *Vote: 8-1.*

* * *

JUSTICE WHITE delivered the opinion of the Court.

. . . The District Court, the Court of Appeals, and respondents recognize and acknowledge that the State of Mississippi had the constitutional duty to dismantle the dual school system that its laws once mandated. Nor is there any dispute that this obligation applied to its higher education system. If the State has not discharged this duty, it remains in violation of the Fourteenth Amendment. *Brown v. Board of Education* [*Brown I,* 347 U.S. 483 (1954)] and its progeny clearly mandate this observation. Thus, the primary issue in this case is whether the State has met its affirmative duty to dismantle its prior dual university system.

Our decisions establish that a State does not discharge its constitutional obligations until it eradicates policies and practices traceable to its prior *de jure* dual system that continue to foster segregation. Thus we have consistently asked whether existing racial identifiability is attributable to the State . . . and examined a wide range of factors to determine whether the State has perpetuated its formerly *de jure* segregation in any facet of its institutional system. . . .

The Court of Appeals concluded that the State had fulfilled its affirmative obligation to disestablish its prior *de jure* segregated system by adopting and implementing race-neutral policies governing its college and university system. Because students seeking higher education had "real freedom" to choose the institution of their choice, the State need do no more. . . .

Like the United States, we do not disagree with the Court of Appeals' observation that a state university system is quite different in very relevant respects from primary and secondary schools. Unlike attendance at the lower level schools, a student's decision to seek higher education has been a matter of choice. The State historically has not assigned university students to a particular institution. Moreover, like public universities throughout the country, Mississippi's institutions of higher learning are not fungible—they have been designated to perform certain missions. Students who qualify for admissions enjoy a range of choices of which institution to attend. . . .

We do not agree with the Court of Appeals or the District Court, however, that the adoption and implementation of race-neutral policies alone suffice to demonstrate that the State has completely abandoned its prior dual system. That college attendance is by choice and not by assignment does not mean that a race-neutral admissions policy cures the constitutional violation of a dual system. In a system based on choice, student attendance is determined not simply by admissions policies but also by many other factors. Although some of these factors clearly cannot be attributed to State policies, many can be. Thus, even after a State dismantles its segregative *admissions* policy, there may still be state action that is traceable to the State's prior *de jure* segregation and that continues to foster segregation. . . . We also disagree with respondents that the Court of Appeals and District Court properly relied on our decision in *Bazemore v. Friday* [478 U.S. 385 (1986)]. . . . *Bazemore* neither requires nor justifies the conclusions reached by the two courts below.

. . . *Bazemore* plainly does not excuse inquiry into whether Mississippi has left in place certain aspects of its prior dual system that perpetuate the racially segregated higher education system. If the State perpetuates policies and practices traceable to its prior system that continue to have segregative effects—whether by influencing student enrollment decisions or by fostering segregation in other facets of the university system—and such policies are without sound educational justification and can be practicably eliminated, the State has not satisfied its burden of proving that it has dismantled its prior system. Such policies run afoul of the Equal Protection Clause, even though the State has abolished the legal requirement that whites and blacks be educated separately and has established racially neutral policies not animated by a discriminatory purpose. Because the standard applied by the District Court did not make these inquiries, we hold that the Court of Appeals erred in affirming the District Court's ruling that the State had brought itself into compliance with the Equal Protection Clause in the operation of its higher education system.

Had the Court of Appeals applied the correct legal standard, it would have been apparent from the undisturbed factual findings of the District Court that there are several surviving aspects of Mississippi's prior dual system which are constitutionally suspect; for even though such policies may be race-neutral on their face, they substantially restrict a person's choice of which institution to enter and they contribute to the racial identifiability of the eight public universities. Mississippi must justify these policies or eliminate them.

. . . [W]e address four policies of the present system: admission standards, program duplication, institutional mission assignments, and continued operation of all eight public universities.

. . . The present admission standards are not only traceable to the *de jure* system and were originally adopted for a discriminatory purpose, but they also have present discriminatory effects. Every Mississippi resident under 21 seeking admission to the university system must take the ACT. Any applicant who scores at least 15 qualifies for automatic admission to any of the five historically white institutions except Mississippi University for Women, which requires a score of 18 for automatic admission unless the student has a 3.0 high school grade average. Those scoring less than 15 but at least 13 automatically qualify to enter Jackson State University, Alcorn State University, and Mississippi Valley State University. Without doubt, these requirements restrict the range of choices of entering students as to which institution they may attend in a way that perpetuates segregation. . . .

The segregative effect of this automatic entrance standard is especially striking in light of the differences in minimum automatic entrance scores among the regional universities in Mississippi's system. The minimum score for automatic admission to Mississippi University for Women (MUW) is 18; it is 13 for the historically black universities. Yet MUW is assigned the same institutional mission as two other regional universities, Alcorn State and Mississippi Valley—that of providing quality undergraduate education. The effects of the policy fall disproportionately on black students who might wish to attend MUW; and though the disparate impact is not as great, the same is true of the minimum standard ACT score of 15 at Delta State University—the other "regional" university—as compared to the historically black "regional" universities where a score of 13 suffices for automatic admission. The courts below made little if any effort to justify in educational terms those particular disparities in entrance requirements or to inquire whether it was practicable to eliminate them.

We also find inadequately justified by the court below or by the record before us the differential admissions requirements between universities with dissimilar programmatic missions. We do not suggest that absent a discriminatory purpose different programmatic missions accompanied by different admission standards would be constitutionally suspect simply because one or more schools are racially identifiable. But here the differential admission standards are remnants of the dual system with a continuing discriminatory effect, and the mission assignments "to some degree follow the historical racial assignments." . . . Moreover, the District Court did not justify the differing admission standards based on the different mission assignments. . . .

Another constitutionally problematic aspect of the State's use of the ACT test scores is its policy of denying automatic admission if an applicant fails to earn the minimum ACT score specified for the particular institution, without also resorting to the applicant's high school grades as an additional factor in predicting college performance. The United States produced evidence that the American College Testing Program (ACTP), the administering organization of the ACT, discourages use of ACT scores as the sole admissions criterion on the ground that it gives an incomplete "picture" of the student applicant's ability to perform adequately in college. . . . The record also indicated that the disparity between black and white students' high school grade averages was much narrower than the gap between their average ACT scores, thereby suggesting that an admissions formula which included grades would increase the number of black students eligible for automatic admission to all of Mississippi's public universities.

The United States insists that the State's refusal to consider information which would better predict college performance than ACT scores alone is irrational in light of most States' use of high school grades and other indicators along with standardized test scores. The District Court observed that the Board of Trustees was concerned with grade inflation and the lack of comparability in grading practices and course offerings among the State's diverse high schools. Both District Court and the Court of Appeals found this concern ample justification for the failure to consider high school grade performance along with ACT scores. In our view, such justification is inadequate because the ACT requirement was originally adopted for discriminatory purposes, the current requirement is traceable to that decision and seemingly continues to have segregative effects, and the State has so far failed to show that the "ACT-only" admissions standard is not susceptible to elimination without eroding sound educational policy.

A second aspect of the present system that necessitates further inquiry is the widespread duplication of programs. "Unnecessary" duplication refers, under the District Court's definition, "to those instances where two or more institutions offer the same nonessential or noncore program. Under this definition, all duplication at the bachelor's level of nonbasic liberal arts and sciences course work and all duplication at the master's level and above are considered to be unnecessary." . . . The District Court found that 34.6 percent of the 29 undergraduate programs at historically black institutions are "unnecessarily duplicated" by the historically white universities, and that 90 percent of the graduate programs at the historically black institutions are unnecessarily duplicated at the historically white institutions. . . . In its conclusions of law on this point, the District Court nevertheless determined that "there is no proof" that such duplication "is directly associated with the racial identifiability of institutions," and that "there is no proof that the elimination of unnecessary program duplication would be justifiable from an educational standpoint or that its elimination would have a substantial effect on student choice." . . .

The District Court's treatment of this issue is problematic from several different perspectives. First, the court appeared to impose the burden of proof on the plaintiffs to meet a legal standard the court itself acknowledged was not yet formulated. It can hardly be denied that such duplication was part and parcel of the prior dual system of higher education—the whole notion of "separate but equal" required duplicative programs in two sets of schools—and that the present unnecessary duplication is a continuation of that practice. *Brown* and its progeny, however, established that the burden of proof falls on the *State,* and not the aggrieved plaintiffs, to establish that it has dismantled its prior *de jure* segregated system. . . . Second, implicit in the District Court's finding of "unnecessary" duplication is the absence of any education justification and the fact that some if not all duplication may be practically eliminated. Indeed, the District Court observed that such duplication "cannot be justified economically or in terms of providing quality education." . . . Yet by stating that "there is no proof" that elimination of unnecessary duplication would decrease institutional racial identifiability, affect student choice, and promote educationally sound policies, the court did not make clear whether it had directed the parties to develop evidence on these points, and if so, what that evidence revealed. . . . Finally, by treating this issue in isolation, the court failed to consider the combined effects of unnecessary program duplication with other policies, such as differential admissions standards, in evaluating whether the State had met its duty to dismantle its prior *de jure* segregated system.

We next address Mississippi's scheme of institutional mission classification, and whether it perpetuates the State's formerly *de jure* dual system. The District Court found that, throughout the period of *de jure* segregation, University of Mississippi, Mississippi State University, and University of Southern Mississippi were the flagship institutions in the state system. They received the most funds, initiated the most advanced and specialized programs, and developed the widest range of curricular functions. At their inception, each was restricted for the education solely of white persons. . . . The missions of Mississippi University for Women and Delta State University (DSU), by contrast, were more limited than their other all-white counterparts during the period of legalized segregation. MUW and DSU were each established to provide undergraduate education solely for white students in the liberal arts and such other fields as music, art, education, and home economics. . . . When they were founded, the three exclusively black universities were more limited in their assigned academic missions than the five all-white institutions. Alcorn State, for example, was designated to serve as "an agricultural college for the education of Mississippi's black youth." . . . Jackson State and Mississippi Valley State were established to train black teachers. . . . Though the District Court's findings do not make this point explicit, it is reasonable to infer that state funding and curriculum decisions throughout the period of *de jure* segregation were based on the purposes for which these institutions were established.

In 1981, the State assigned certain missions to Mississippi's public universities as they then existed. It classified University of Mississippi, Mississippi State, and Southern Mississippi as "comprehensive" universities having the most varied programs and offering graduate degrees. Two of the historically white institutions, Delta State University and Mississippi University for Women, along with two of the historically black institutions, Alcorn State University and Mississippi Valley State University, were designated as "regional" universities with more limited programs and devoted primarily to undergraduate education. Jackson State University was classified as an "urban" university whose mission was defined by its urban location.

The institutional mission designations adopted in 1981 have as their antecedents the policies enacted to perpetuate racial separation during the *de jure* segregated regime. The Court of Appeals expressly disagreed with the District Court by recognizing that the "inequalities among the institutions largely follow the mission designations, and the mission designations to some degree follow the historical racial assignments." . . . It nevertheless upheld this facet of the system as constitutionally acceptable based on the existence of good-faith racially neutral policies and procedures. That different missions are assigned to the universities surely limits to some extent an entering student's choice as to which university to seek admittance. . . . We do not suggest that absent discriminatory purpose the assignment of different missions to various institutions in a State's higher education system would raise an equal protection issue where one or more of the institutions become or remain predominantly black or white. But here the issue is whether the State has sufficiently dismantled its prior dual system; and when combined with the differential admission practices and unnecessary program duplication, it is likely that the mission designations interfere with student choice and tend to perpetuate the segregated system. On remand, the court should inquire whether it would be practicable and consistent with sound educational practices to eliminate any such discriminatory effects of the State's present policy of mission assignments.

Fourth, the State attempted to bring itself into compliance with the Constitution by continuing to maintain and operate all eight higher educational institutions. The existence of eight instead of some lesser number was undoubtedly occasioned by State laws forbidding the mingling of the races. . . . It was evident to the District Court that "the defendants undertake to fund more institutions of higher learning than are justified by the amount of financial resources available to the state," . . . but the court concluded that such fiscal irresponsibility was a policy choice of the legislature rather than a feature of a system subject to constitutional scrutiny.

Unquestionably, a larger rather than a smaller number of institutions from which to choose in itself makes for different choices, particularly when examined in the light of other factors present in the operation of the system, such as admissions, program duplication, and institutional mission designation. Though certainly closure of one or more institutions would decrease the discriminatory effects of the present system, . . . based on the present record we are unable to say whether such action is constitutionally required. Elimination of program duplication and revision of admissions criteria may make institutional closure unnecessary. However, on remand this issue should be carefully explored by inquiring and determining whether retention of all eight institutions itself affects student choice and perpetuates the segregated higher education system, whether maintenance of each of the universities is educationally justifiable, and whether one or more of them can be practicably closed or merged with other existing institutions.

Because the former *de jure* segregated system of public universities in Mississippi impeded the free choice of prospective students, the State in dismantling that system must take the necessary steps to ensure that this choice now is truly free. The full range of policies and practices must be examined with this duty in mind. That an institution is predominantly white or black does not in itself make out a constitutional violation. But surely the State may not leave in place policies rooted in its prior officially-segregated system that serve to maintain the racial identifiability of its universities if those policies can practically be eliminated without eroding sound educational policies.

If we understand private petitioners to press us to order the upgrading of Jackson State, Alcorn State, and Mississippi Valley *solely* so that they may be publicly financed, exclusively black enclaves by private choice, we reject that request. The State provides these facilities for *all* its citizens and it has not met its burden under *Brown* to take affirmative steps to dismantle its prior *de jure* system when it perpetuates a separate, but "more equal" one. Whether such an increase in funding is necessary to achieve a full dismantlement under the standards we have outlined, however, is a different question, and one that must be addressed on remand.

Because the District Court and the Court of Appeals failed to consider the State's duties in their proper light, the cases must be remanded. To the extent that the State has not met its affirmative obligation to dismantle its prior dual system, it shall be adjudged in violation of the Constitution and Title VI and remedial proceedings shall be conducted. The decision of the Court of Appeals is vacated, and the cases are remanded for further proceedings consistent with this opinion.

It is so ordered.

[The concurring opinion of JUSTICE O'CONNOR is omitted.]

* * *

JUSTICE THOMAS concurring.

. . . I think it undisputable that these institutions have succeeded in part because of their distinctive histories and traditions; for many, historically black colleges have become "a symbol of the highest attainments of black culture." . . . Obviously, a State cannot maintain such traditions by closing particular institutions, historically white or historically black, to particular racial groups. Nonetheless, it hardly follows that a State cannot operate a diverse assortment of institutions—including historically black institutions—open to all on a race-neutral basis, but with established traditions and programs that might disproportionately appeal to one race or another. No one, I imagine, would argue that such institutional *diversity* is without "sound educational justification," or that it is even remotely akin to program *duplication,* which is designed to separate the races for the sake of separating the races. The Court at least hints at the importance of this value when it distinguishes *Green* in part on the ground that colleges and universities "are not fungible." . . . Although I agree that a State is not constitutionally *required* to maintain its historically black institutions as such, . . . I do not understand our opinion to

hold that a State is *forbidden* from doing so. It would be ironic, to say the least, if the institutions that sustained blacks during segregation were themselves destroyed in an effort to combat its vestiges.

* * *

JUSTICE SCALIA, concurring in the judgment in part and dissenting in part.

. . . It is my view that the requirement of compelled integration (whether by student assignment, as in *Green* itself, or by elimination of nonintegrated options, as the Court today effectively decrees) does not apply to higher education. Only one aspect of an historically segregated university system need be eliminated: discriminatory admissions standards. The burden is upon the formerly *de jure* system to show that that has been achieved. Once that has been done, however, it is not just unprecedented, but illogical as well, to establish that former *de jure* States continue to deny equal protection of the law to students whose choices among public university offerings are unimpeded by discriminatory barriers. Unless one takes the position that *Brown I* required States not only to provide equal access to their universities but also to correct lingering disparities between them, that is, to remedy institutional non-compliance with the "equal" requirement of *Plessy* [*v. Ferguson*], a State is in compliance with *Brown I* once it establishes that it has dismantled all discriminatory barriers to its public universities. Having done that, a State is free to govern its public institutions of higher learning as it will, unless it is convicted of discriminating anew—which requires both discriminatory intent and discriminatory causation. See *Washington v. Davis,* 426 U.S. 229 (1976).

That analysis brings me to agree with the judgment that the Court of Appeals must be reversed in part—for the reason (quite different from the Court's) that Mississippi has not borne the burden of demonstrating that intentionally discriminatory admissions standards have been eliminated. It has been established that Mississippi originally adopted ACT assessments as an admissions criterion because that was an effective means of excluding blacks from the HWIs. . . . Given that finding, the District Court should have required Mississippi to prove that its continued use of ACT requirements does not have a racially exclusionary purpose and effect—a not insubstantial task. . . .

PRESLEY V. ETOWAH COUNTY COMMISSION
502 U.S. 491 (1992)

Newly elected black commissioners in Alabama challenged how county boards reallocated decision-making authority under § 5 of the Voting Rights Act in *Presley v. Etowah County Commission* and its companion case *Mack v. Russell County Commission.* In *Presley* the county commission was restructured in 1986 under a consent decree that required each member of the six-member commission to be elected from a different district. Two members were elected to the commission, one of whom was black (Lawrence Presley). In 1987 the commission passed a road supervision resolution that stripped the new commissioners' authority over road districts. A common fund resolution was passed that stripped the commissioners' authority to determine how funds were to be allocated to their own districts. Prior to the 1986 consent decree, individual commissioners had control over spending priorities within the district. The Etowah commission did not seek preclearance of either resolution under § 5 of the Voting Rights Act. In the *Russell County* case, newly elected black commissioners Nathaniel Gosha and Ed Mack challenged the adoption of the unit system that abolished individual road districts and transferred responsibility for road operations to a county engineer appointed by the entire commission. They alleged that failure to preclear the unit system violated § 5. A three-judge district court held that the changes were not subject to § 5 preclearance. *Vote: 6-3.*

* * *

JUSTICE KENNEDY delivered the opinion of the Court.

. . . Our cases since *Allen* [*v. State Board of Elections,* 393 U.S. 544 (1969)] reveal a consistent requirement that changes subject to § 5 pertain only to voting. Without implying that the four typologies exhaust the statute's coverage, we can say these later cases fall within one of the four factual contexts presented in the *Allen* cases. First, we have held that § 5 applies to cases like *Allen v. State Board of Elections* itself, in which the changes involved the manner of voting. See *Perkins v. Matthews,* 400 U.S. 379 (1971) (location of polling places). Second, we have held that § 5 applies to cases like *Whitley v. Williams* [392 U.S. 902 (1968)], which involve candidacy requirements and qualifications. . . . Third, we have applied § 5 to cases like *Fairley v. Patterson* [393 U.S. 544 (1969)], which concerned changes in the composition of the electorate that may vote for candidates for a given office. . . . Fourth, we have made clear that § 5 applies to changes, like the one in *Bunton v. Patterson* [393 U.S. 544 (1969)], affecting the creation or abolition of an elective office. . . .

The first three categories involve changes in election procedures, while all the examples within the fourth category might be termed substantive changes as to which offices are elective. But whether the changes are of procedure or substance, each has a direct relation to voting and the election process.

A comparison of the changes at issue here with those in our prior decisions demonstrates that the present cases do not involve changes covered by the Act.

The Etowah County Commission's Common Fund Resolution is not a change within any of the categories recognized in *Allen* or our later cases. It has no connection to voting procedures: It does not affect the manner of holding elections, it alters or imposes no candidacy qualifications or requirements, and it leaves undisturbed the composition of the electorate. It also has no bearing on the substance of voting power, for it does not increase or diminish the number of officials for whom the electorate may vote. Rather, the Common Fund Resolution concerns the internal operations of an elected body.

The appellants argue that the Common Fund Resolution is a covered change because after its enactment each commissioner has less individual power than before the resolution. A citizen casting a ballot for a commissioner today votes for an individual with less authority than before the resolution, and so, it is said, the value of the vote has been diminished.

Were we to accept the appellants' proffered reading of § 5, we would work an unconstrained expansion of its coverage. Innumerable state and local enactments having nothing to do with voting affect the power of elected officials. When a state or local body adopts a new governmental program or modifies an existing one it will often be the case that it changes the powers of elected officials. So too, when a state or local body alters its internal operating procedures, for example by modifying its subcommittee assignment system, it "implicate[s] an elected official's *decision-making authority.*" . . .

Appellants and the United States fail to provide a workable standard for distinguishing between changes in rules governing voting and changes in the routine organization and functioning of government. Some standard is necessary, for in a real sense every decision taken by government implicates voting. This is but the felicitous consequence of democracy, in which power derives from the people. Yet no one would contend that when Congress enacted the Voting Rights Act it meant to subject all or even most decisions of government in covered jurisdictions to federal supervision. . . .

. . . Under the view advanced by appellants and the United States, every time a state legislature acts to diminish or increase the power of local officials, preclearance would be required. Governmental action decreasing the power of local officials could carry with it a potential for discrimination against those who represent racial minorities at the local level. At the same time, increasing the power of local officials will entail a relative decrease in the power of state officials, and that too could carry with it a potential for discrimination against state officials who represent racial minorities at the state level. The all but limitless minor changes in the allocation of power among officials and the constant adjustments required for the efficient governance of every covered State illustrate the necessity for us to formulate workable rules to confine the coverage of § 5 to its legitimate sphere: voting.

Changes which affect only the distribution of power among officials are not subject to § 5 because such changes have no direct relation to, or impact on, voting. The Etowah County Commission's Common Fund Resolution was not subject to the preclearance requirement.

We next consider Russell County's adoption of the Unit System and its concomitant transfer of operations to the county engineer. Of the four categories of changes in rules governing voting we have recognized to date, there is not even an arguable basis for saying that adoption of the Unit System fits within any of the first three. As to the fourth category, it might be argued that the delegation of authority to an appointed official is similar to the replacement of an elected official with an appointed one, the change we held subject to § 5 in *Bunton v. Patterson*. This approach, however, would ignore the rationale for our holding: "after the change, [the citizen] is prohibited from electing an officer formerly subject to the approval of the voters." . . . In short, the change in *Bunton v. Patterson* involved a rule governing voting not because it affected a change in the relative authority of various governmental officials, but because it changed an elective office to an appointive one.

The change in *Russell County* does not prohibit voters "from electing an officer formerly subject to the[ir] approval." . . . Both before and after the change the citizens of Russell County were able to vote for the members of the Russell County Commission. To be sure, after the 1979 resolution each commissioner exercised less direct authority over road operations, that authority having been delegated to an official answerable to the commission. But as we concluded with respect to Etowah County, the fact that an enactment alters an elected official's powers does not in itself render the enactment a rule governing voting.

It is a routine part of governmental administration for appointive positions to be created or eliminated, and for their powers to be altered. Each time this occurs the relative balance of authority is altered in some way. The making or unmaking of an appointive post often will result in the erosion or accretion of the powers of some official responsible to the electorate, but it does not follow that those changes are covered by § 5. By requiring preclearance of changes with respect to voting, Congress did not mean to subject such routine matters of governance to federal supervision. Were the rule otherwise, neither state nor local governments could exercise power in a responsible manner within a federal system.

The District Court, wrestling with the problem we now face and recognizing the need to draw principled lines, held that Russell County's adoption of the Unit System is not a covered change because it did not transfer power among officials answerable to different constituencies. Even upon the assumption (the assumption we reject in this case) that some transfers of power among government officials could be changes with respect to voting as that term is used in the Act, we disagree with the District Court's test. The question whether power is shifted among officials answerable to the same or different constituencies is quite distinct from the question whether the power voters exercise over elected officials is affected. Intraconstituency changes may have a large indirect effect on the voters while interconstituency changes may have a small indirect effect, but in neither case is the effect a change in voting for purposes of the Act. The test adopted by the District Court does not provide the workable rule we seek. In any event, because it proceeds from the faulty premise that reallocations of authority within government can constitute voting changes, we cannot accept its approach.

. . . The United States urges that despite our understanding of the language of § 5, we should defer to its administrative construction of the provision. . . .

We do not believe that in its use of the phrase "voting qualification or prerequisite to voting, or standard, practice, or procedure with respect to voting," . . . the statute is ambiguous as to the question whether § 5 extends beyond changes in rules governing voting. To be sure, reasonable minds may differ as to whether some particular changes in the law of a covered jurisdiction should be classified as changes in rules governing voting. In that sense § 5 leaves a gap for interpretation to fill. . . . When the Attorney General makes a reasonable argument that a contested change should be classified as a change in a rule governing voting, we can defer to that judgment. But § 5 is unambiguous with respect to the question whether it covers changes other than changes in rules governing voting: It does not. The administrative position in the present cases is not entitled to deference, for it suggests the contrary. The United States argues that the changes are covered by § 5 because they implicate the decisionmaking authority of elected officials, even though they are not changes in rules governing voting. This argument does not meet the express requirement of the statute.

Nothing we say implies that the conduct at issue in these cases is not actionable under a different remedial scheme. The Voting Rights Act is not an all-purpose antidiscrimination statute. The fact that the intrusive mechanisms of the Act do not apply to other forms of pernicious discrimination does not undermine its utility in combating the specific evils it was designed to address.

. . . If federalism is to operate as a practical system of governance and not a mere poetic ideal, the States must be allowed both predictability and efficiency in structuring their governments. Constant minor adjustments in the allocation of power among state and local officials serve this elemental purpose.

Covered changes must bear a direct relation to voting itself. That direct relation is absent in both cases now before us. The changes in Etowah and Russell Counties affected only the allocation of power among governmental officials. They had no impact on the substantive question whether a particular office would be elective or the procedural question how an election would be conducted. Neither change involves a new "voting qualification or prerequisite to voting, or standard, practice, or procedure with respect to voting." . . .

The judgment of the District Court is affirmed. *It is so ordered.*

* * *

JUSTICE STEVENS, with whom JUSTICE WHITE and JUSTICE BLACKMUN join, dissenting.

In 1986, an important event occurred in each of two Alabama counties with long histories of white-dominated political processes. In Etowah County, a black commissioner was elected to the county commission for the first time in recent history, and in Russell County, two black commissioners were elected to the county commission for the first time in "modern times." . . . Because of the three resolutions at issue in this case—two adopted in Etowah County after Commissioner Presley's election and one adopted in Russell County before the election of Commissioners Mack and Gosha—none of the three newly-elected black commissioners was able to exercise the decisionmaking authority that had been traditionally associated with his office.

. . . At the very least, I would hold that the reallocation of decisionmaking authority of an elective office that is taken (1) after the victory of a black candidate, and (2) after the entry of a consent decree designed to give black voters an opportunity to have representation on an elective body, is covered by § 5.

. . . Although the test I propose here may not adequately implement § 5, it would certainly provide a workable rule that would result in the correct disposition of this case without opening the Pandora's box that the Court seems to fear.

. . . Changes from district voting to at-large voting, the gerrymandering of district boundary lines, and the replacement of an elected official with an appointed official, all share the characteristic of enhancing the power of the majority over a segment of the political community that might otherwise be adequately represented. A resolution that reallocates decisionmaking power by transferring authority from an elected district representative to an official, or a group, controlled by the majority, has the same potential for discrimination against the constituents in the disadvantaged districts. The Russell County Resolution satisfies that test, and therefore, like both Etowah County Resolutions, should have been precleared. To hold otherwise, as the Court does today, leaves covered States free to evade the requirements of § 5, and to undermine the purpose of the Act, simply by transferring the authority of an elected official, who happens to be black, to another official or group controlled by the majority.

SHAW V. RENO
113 S.Ct. 2816 (1993)

As a result of the 1990 census, North Carolina gained a 12th seat in the U.S. House of Representatives. The North Carolina General Assembly enacted a reapportionment plan that included one majority-black congressional district. After the Justice Department objected to the plan under § 5 of the Voting Rights Act on the ground that the legislature could have created a second majority-minority district to give effect to black and Native American voting strength, the legislature revised the plan and created a second majority-black district. This district contained boundary lines of irregular shape. The district stretched approximately 160 miles along Interstate 85, and for much of its length it was no wider than the interstate's corridor. It was also described as winding "in a snake-like fashion through tobacco country, financial centers, and manufacturing areas until it gobbles in enough enclaves of black neighborhoods." The attorney general did not object to the revised plan. The North Carolina Republican Party and individual white voters brought suit in federal district court, alleging that the plan was an unconstitutional political gerrymander. That claim was dismissed, and the Supreme Court summarily affirmed. Ruth Shaw and four other white residents of Durham County, North Carolina, filed suit against Attorney General Janet Reno, alleging that the state had created an unconstitutional racial gerrymander. A three-judge district court dismissed the complaint on the ground that the white voters had failed to state an equal protection claim under *United Jewish Organizations, Inc. v. Carey* (1977) because favoring minority voters was not discriminatory in the constitutional sense. *Vote: 5-4.*

* * *

JUSTICE O'CONNOR delivered the opinion of the Court.

. . . In our view, the District Court properly dismissed appellants' claims against the federal appellees. Our focus is on appellants' claim that the State engaged in unconstitutional racial gerrymandering. That argument strikes a powerful historical chord: It is unsettling how closely the North Carolina plan resembles the most egregious racial gerrymanders of the past.

An understanding of the nature of appellants' claim is critical to our resolution of the case. In their complaint, appellants did not claim that the General Assembly's reapportionment plan unconstitutionally "diluted" white voting strength. They did not even claim to be white. Rather, appellants' complaint alleged that the deliberate segregation of voters into separate districts on the basis of race violated their constitutional right to participate in a "color-blind" electoral process. . . .

Despite their invocation of the ideal of a "color-blind" Constitution, . . . appellants appear to concede that race-conscious redistricting is not always unconstitutional. . . . That concession is wise: This Court never had held that race-conscious state decisionmaking is impermissible in *all* circumstances. What appellants object to is redistricting legislation that is so extremely irregular on its face that it rationally can be viewed only as an effort to segregate the races for purposes of voting, without regard for traditional districting principles and without sufficiently compelling justification. For the reasons that follow, we conclude that appellants have stated a claim upon which relief can be granted under the Equal Protection Clause. . . .

The Equal Protection Clause provides that "[n]o State shall . . . deny to any person within its jurisdiction the equal protection of the laws." . . . Its central purpose is to prevent the States from purposefully discriminating between individuals on the basis of race. *Washington v. Davis,* 426 U.S. 229, 239 (1976). Laws that explicitly distinguish between individuals on racial grounds fall within that core of that prohibition.

No inquiry into legislative purpose is necessary when the racial classification appears on the face of the statute. . . . Express racial classifications are immediately suspect because, "[a]bsent searching judicial inquiry . . ., there is simply no way of determining what classifications are 'benign' or 'remedial' and what classifications are in fact motivated by illegitimate notions of racial inferiority or simple racial politics." *Richmond v. J. A. Croson Co.,* 488 U.S. 469, 493 (1989). . . .

Classifications of citizens solely on the basis of race "are by their very nature odious to a free people whose institutions are founded upon the doctrine of equality." . . . They threaten to stigmatize individuals by reason of their membership in a racial group and to incite racial hostility. . . . Accordingly, we have held that the Fourteenth Amendment requires state legislation that expressly distinguishes among citizens because of their race to be narrowly tailored to further a compelling governmental interest. . . .

These principles apply not only to legislation that contains explicit racial distinctions, but also to those "rare" statutes that, although race-neutral, are, on their face, "unexplainable on grounds other than race." . . .

Appellants contend that redistricting legislation that is so bizarre on its face that it is "unexplainable on grounds other than race" . . . demands the same close scrutiny that we give other state laws that classify by race. Our voting rights precedents support that conclusion.

In *Guinn v. United States,* 238 U.S. 347 (1915), the Court invalidated under the Fifteenth Amendment a statute that imposed a literacy requirement on voters but contained a "grandfather clause" applicable to individuals and their lineal descendants entitled to vote "on [or prior to] January 1, 1866." . . . The determinative consideration for the Court was that the law, though ostensibly race-neutral, on its face "embod[ied] no exercise of judgment and rest[ed] upon no discernible reason" other than to circumvent the prohibitions of the Fifteenth Amendment. . . . In other words, the statute was invalid because, on its face, it could not be explained on grounds other than race.

The Court applied the same reasoning to the "uncouth twenty-eight-sided" municipal boundary line at issue in *Gomillion* [*v. Lightfoot,* 364 U.S. 339 (1960)]. Although the statute that redrew the city limits of Tuskegee was race-neutral on its face, plaintiffs alleged that its effect was impermissibly to remove from the city virtually all black voters and no white voters. The Court reasoned:

"If these allegations upon a trial remained uncontradicted or unqualified, the conclusion would be irresistible, tantamount for all practical purposes to a mathematical demonstration, that the legislation is solely concerned with segregating white and colored voters by fencing Negro citizens out of town so as to deprive them of their pre-existing municipal vote."

The majority resolved the case under the Fifteenth Amendment. . . . JUSTICE WHITTAKER, however, concluded that the "unlawful segregation of races of citizens" into different voting districts was cognizable under the Equal Protection Clause. . . . This Court's subsequent reliance on *Gomillion* in other Fourteenth Amendment cases suggests the correctness of JUSTICE WHITTAKER's view. . . . *Gomillion* thus supports appellants' contention that district lines obviously drawn for the purpose of separating voters by race require careful scrutiny under the Equal Protection Clause regardless of the motivations underlying their adoption.

The Court extended the reasoning of *Gomillion* to congressional districting in *Wright v. Rockefeller,* 376 U.S. 52 (1964). . . .

Wright illustrates the difficulty of determining from the face of a single-member districting plan that it purposefully distinguishes between voters on the basis of race. A reapportionment statute typically does not classify persons at all; it classifies tracts of land, or addresses. Moreover, redistricting differs from other kinds of state decisionmaking in that the legislature always is *aware* of race when it draws district lines, just as it is aware of age, economic status, religious and political persuasion, and a variety of other demographic factors. That sort of race consciousness does not lead inevitably to impermissible race discrimination. As *Wright* demonstrates, when members of a racial group live together in one community, a reapportionment plan that concentrates members of the group in one district and excludes them from others may reflect wholly legitimate purposes. The district lines may be drawn, for example, to provide for compact districts of contiguous territory, or to maintain the integrity of political subdivisions. . . .

The difficulty of proof, of course, does not mean that a racial gerrymander, once established, should receive less scrutiny under the Equal Protection Clause than other state legislation classifying citizens by race. Moreover, it seems clear to us that proof sometimes will not be difficult at all. In some exceptional cases, a reapportionment plan may be so highly irregular that, on its face, it rationally cannot be understood as anything other than an effort to "segregate . . . voters" on the basis of race. . . . *Gomillion,* in which a tortured municipal boundary line was drawn to exclude black voters, was such a case. So, too, would be a case in which a State concentrated a dispersed minority population in a single district by disregarding traditional districting principles such as compactness, contiguity, and respect for political subdivisions. We emphasize that these criteria are important not because they are constitutionally required—they are not, cf. *Gaffney v. Cummings,* 412 U.S. 735, 752 (1973)—but because they are objective factors that may serve to defeat a claim that a district has been gerrymandered on racial lines. . . .

Put differently, we believe that reapportionment is one area in which appearances do matter. A reapportionment plan that includes in one district individuals who belong to the same race, but who are otherwise widely separated by geographical and political boundaries, and who may have little in common with one another but the color of their skin, bears an uncomfortable resemblance to political apartheid. It reinforces the perception that members of the same racial group—regardless of their age, education, economic status, or the community in which they live—think alike, share the same political interests, and will prefer the same candidates at the pools. We have rejected such perceptions elsewhere as impermissible racial stereotypes. [*Holland v. Illinois,* 493 U.S. 474, 484 (1990); *Edmonson v. Leesville Concrete Co.,* 500 U.S. 614 (1991)] By perpetuating such notions, a racial gerrymander may exacerbate the very patterns of racial bloc voting that majority-minority districting is sometimes said to counteract.

The message that such districting sends to elected representatives is equally pernicious. When a district obviously is created solely to effectuate the perceived common interests of one racial group, elected officials are more likely to believe that their primary obligation is to represent only the members of that group, rather than their constituency as a whole. This is altogether antithetical to our system of representative democracy. . . .

For these reasons, we conclude that a plaintiff challenging a reapportionment statute under the Equal Protection Clause may state a claim by alleging that the legislation, though race-neutral on its face, rationally cannot be understood as anything other than an effort to separate voters into different districts on the basis of race, and that the separation lacks sufficient justification. It is unnecessary for us to decide whether or how a reapportionment plan that, on its face, can be explained in nonracial terms successfully could be challenged. Thus, we express no view as to whether "the intentional creation of majority-minority districts, without more" always gives rise to an equal protection claim. . . . We hold only that, on the facts of this case, plaintiffs have stated a claim sufficient to defeat the state appellees' motion to dismiss.

The dissenters consider the circumstances of this case "functionally indistinguishable" from multimember districting and at-large voting systems, which are loosely described as "other varieties of gerrymandering." . . . We have considered the constitutionality of these practices in other Fourteenth Amendment cases and have required plaintiffs to demonstrate that the challenged practice has the purpose and effect of diluting a racial group's voting strength. . . . At-large and multimember schemes, however, do not classify voters on the basis of race. Classifying citizens by race, as we have said, threatens special harms that are not present in our vote-dilution cases. It therefore warrants different analysis.

. . . Finally, nothing in the Court's highly fractured decision in *UJO* [*United Jewish Organizations, Inc. v. Carey,* 430 U.S. 144 (1971)]—on which the District Court almost exclusively relied, and which the dissenters evidently believe controls, . . . forecloses the claim we recognize today. *UJO* concerned New York's revision of a reapportionment plan to include additional majority-minority districts in response to the Attorney General's denial of administrative preclearance under § 5. In that regard, it closely resembles the present case. But the cases are critically different in another way. The plaintiffs in *UJO*—members of a Hasidic community split between two districts under New York's redistricting plan—did not allege that the plan, on its face, was so highly irregular that it rationally could be understood only as an effort to segregate voters by race. Indeed, the facts of the case would not have supported such a claim. Three Justices approved the New York statute, in part, precisely because it adhered to traditional districting principles. . . .

. . . The District Court below relied on these portions of *UJO* to reject appellants' claim. . . . In our view, the court used the wrong analysis. *UJO*'s framework simply does not apply where, as here, a reapportionment plan is alleged to be so irrational on its face that it immediately offends principles of racial equality. *UJO* set forth a standard under which white voters can establish unconstitutional vote dilution. But it did not purport to overrule *Gomillion* or *Wright*. Nothing in the decision precludes white voters (or voters of any other race) from bringing the analytically distinct claim that a reapportionment plan rationally cannot be understood as anything other than an effort to segregate citizens into separate voting districts on the basis of race without sufficient justification. Because appellants here stated such a claim, the District Court erred in dismissing their complaint.

Justice SOUTER contends that exacting scrutiny of racial gerrymanders under the Fourteenth Amendment is inappropriate because reapportionment "nearly always require[s] some consideration of race for legitimate reasons." . . . "As long as members of racial groups have [a] commonality of interest" and "racial bloc voting takes place," he argues, "legislators will have to take race into account" in order to comply with the Voting Rights Act. . . . Justice SOUTER's reasoning is flawed.

Earlier this Term, we unanimously reaffirmed that racial bloc voting and minority-group political cohesion never can be assumed, but specifically must be proved in each case in order to establish that a redistricting plan dilutes minority voting strength in violation of § 2. See *Growe v. Emison,* 113 S.Ct. 1075 (1993). . . . That racial bloc voting or minority political cohesion may be found to exist in *some* cases, of course, is no reason to treat *all* racial gerrymanders differently from other kinds of racial classification. Justice SOUTER apparently views racially gerrymandering of the type presented here as a special category of "benign" racial discrimination that should be subject to relaxed judicial review. . . . As we have said, however, the very reason that the Equal Protection Clause demands strict scrutiny of all racial classifications is because without it, a court cannot determine whether or not the discrimination truly is "benign." . . . Thus, if appellants'

allegations of a racial gerrymander are not contradicted on remand, the District Court must determine whether the General Assembly's reapportionment plan satisfies strict scrutiny. We therefore consider what that level of scrutiny requires in the reapportionment context.

The state appellees suggest that a covered jurisdiction may have a compelling interest in creating majority-minority districts in order to comply with the Voting Rights Act. The States certainly have a very strong interest in complying with federal antidiscrimination laws that are constitutionally valid as interpreted and as applied. But in the context of a Fourteenth Amendment challenge, courts must bear in mind the difference between what the law permits, and what it requires.

. . . Appellants maintain that the General Assembly's revised plan could not have been required by § 2. They contend that the State's black population is too dispersed to support two geographically compact majority-black districts, as the bizarre shape of District 12 demonstrates, and that there is no evidence of black political cohesion. They also contend that recent black electoral successes demonstrate the willingness of white voters in North Carolina to vote for black candidates. Appellants point out that blacks currently hold the positions of State Auditor, Speaker of the North Carolina House of Representatives, and chair of the North Carolina State Board of Elections. They also point out that in 1990 a black candidate defeated a white opponent in the Democratic Party run-off for a United States Senate seat before being defeated narrowly by the Republican incumbent in the general election. Appellants further argue that if § 2 did require adoption of North Carolina's revised plan, § 2 is to that extent unconstitutional. These arguments were not developed below, and the issues remain open for consideration on remand.

The state appellees alternatively argue that the General Assembly's plan advanced a compelling interest entirely distinct from the Voting Rights Act. We previously have recognized a significant state interest in eradicating the effects of past racial discrimination. . . . But the State must have a "strong basis in evidence for [concluding] that remedial action [is] necessary." . . .

The state appellees submit that two pieces of evidence gave the General Assembly a strong basis for believing that remedial action was warranted here: the Attorney General's imposition of the § 5 preclearance requirement on 40 North Carolina counties, and the [*Thornburg v. Gingles,* 478 U.S. 30 (1986)] District Court's findings of a long history of official racial discrimination in North Carolina's political system and of pervasive racial bloc voting. The state appellees assert that the deliberate creation of majority-minority districts is the most precise way—indeed the only effective way—to overcome the effects of racially polarized voting. This question also need not be decided at this stage of the litigation. . . .

. . . In this case, the Attorney General suggested that North Carolina could have created a reasonably compact second majority-minority district in the south-central to southeastern part of the State. We express no view as to whether appellants successfully could have challenged such a district under the Fourteenth Amendment. We also do not decide whether appellants' complaint stated a claim under constitutional provisions other than the Fourteenth Amendment. Today we hold only that appellants have stated a claim under the Equal Protection Clause by alleging that the North Carolina General Assembly adopted a reapportionment scheme so irrational on its face that it can be understood only as an effort to segregate voters into separate voting districts because of their race, and that the separation lacks sufficient justification. If the allegation of racial gerrymandering remains uncontradicted, the District Court further must determine whether the North Carolina plan is narrowly tailored to further a compelling governmental interest. Accordingly, we reverse the judgment of the District Court and remand the case for further proceedings consistent with this opinion.

It is so ordered.

* * *

JUSTICE WHITE, with whom JUSTICE BLACKMUN and JUSTICE STEVENS join, dissenting.

The facts of this case mirror those presented in *United Jewish Organizations of Williamsburgh, Inc. v. Carey* . . . where the Court rejected a claim that creation of a majority-minority district violated the Constitution, either as a *per se* matter or in light of the circumstances leading to the creation of such a district. Of particular relevance, five of the Justices reasoned that members of the white majority could not plausibly argue that their influence over the political process had been unfairly cancelled . . . or that such had been the State's intent. . . . Accordingly, they held that plaintiffs were not entitled to relief under the Constitution's Equal Protection Clause. On the same reasoning, I would affirm the district court's dismissal of appellants' claim in this instance.

The Court today chooses not to overrule, but rather to sidestep, *UJO*. It does so by glossing over the striking similarities, focusing on surface differences, most notably the (admittedly unusual) shape of the newly created district, and imagining an entirely new cause of action. Because the holding is limited to such anomalous circumstances, . . . it perhaps will not substantially hamper a State's legitimate efforts to redistrict in favor of racial minorities. Nonetheless, the notion that North Carolina's plan,

under which whites remain a voting majority in a disproportionate number of congressional districts, and pursuant to which the State has sent its *first* black representative since Reconstruction to the United States Congress, might have violated appellants' constitutional rights is both a fiction and departure from settled equal protection principles. Seeing no good reason to engage in either, I dissent.

The grounds for my disagreement with the majority are simply stated: Appellants have not presented a cognizable claim, because they have not alleged a cognizable injury. To date, we have held that only two types of state voting practices could give rise to a constitutional claim. The first involves direct and outright deprivation of the right to vote, for example by means of a poll tax or literacy test. See, *e.g., Guinn v. United States.* . . . Plainly, this variety is not implicated by appellants' allegations and need not detain us further. The second type of unconstitutional practice is that which "affects the political strength of various groups" [*City of*] *Mobile v. Bolden,* 446 U.S. 55, 83 (1980) . . . in violation of the Equal Protection Clause. As for this latter category, we have insisted that members of the political or racial group demonstrate that the challenged actions have the intent and effect of unduly diminishing their influence on the political process. Although this severe burden has limited the number of successful suits, it was adopted for sound reasons.

. . . With these considerations in mind, we have limited such claims by insisting upon a showing that "the political processes . . . were not equally open to participation by the group in question—that its members had less opportunity than did other residents in the district to participate in the political processes and to elect legislators of their choice." . . . Indeed, as a brief survey of decisions illustrates, the Court's gerrymandering cases all carry this theme—that it is not mere suffering at the polls but discrimination in the polity with which the Constitution is concerned.

. . . The other part of the majority's explanation of its holding is related to its simultaneous discomfort and fascination with irregularly shaped districts. Lack of compactness or contiguity, like uncouth district lines, certainly is a helpful indicator that some form of gerrymandering (racial or other) might have taken place and that "something may be amiss." . . . Disregard for geographic divisions and compactness often goes hand in hand with partisan gerrymandering. . . .

But while district irregularities may provide strong indicia of a potential gerrymander, they do no more than that. In particular, they have no bearing on whether the plan ultimately is found to violate the Constitution. Given two districts drawn on similar, race-based grounds, the one does not become more injurious than the other simply by virtue of being snake-like, at least so far as the Constitution is concerned and absent any evidence of differential racial impact. The majority's contrary view is perplexing in light of its concession that "compactness or attractiveness has never been held to constitute an independent federal constitutional requirement for state legislative districts." . . . It is shortsighted as well, for a regularly shaped district can just as effectively effectuate racially discriminatory gerrymandering as an odd-shaped one. By focusing on looks rather than impact, the majority "immediately casts attention in the wrong direction—toward superficialities of shape and size, rather than toward the political realities of district composition." . . .

Limited by its own terms to cases involving unusually-shaped districts, the Court's approach nonetheless will unnecessarily hinder to some extent a State's voluntary effort to ensure a modicum of minority representation. This will be true in areas where the minority population is geographically dispersed. It also will be true where the minority population is not scattered but, for reasons unrelated to race—for example incumbency protection—the State would rather not create the majority-minority district in its most "obvious" location. When, as is the case here, the creation of a majority-minority district does not unfairly minimize the voting power of any other group, the Constitution does not justify, much less mandate, such obstruction. . . .

[The dissenting opinions of JUSTICE BLACKMUN, JUSTICE STEVENS, and JUSTICE SOUTER are omitted.]

CITY OF RICHMOND v. J. A. CROSON CO.
488 U.S. 469 (1989)

In 1983 the Richmond, Virginia, City Council adopted the Minority Business Utilization Plan, which required prime contractors to whom the city awarded construction contracts to subcontract at least 30% of the dollar amount of the contract to one or more minority business enterprises (MBEs). The plan identified an MBE as a business that was at least 51% minority owned and controlled. Minorities were defined as blacks, Spanish-speaking, Orientals, Indians, Eskimos, or Aleuts, and a qualified MBE from anywhere in the United States could participate in the plan. The plan was declared remedial in nature and was enacted for the purpose of promoting wider participation by MBEs in public construction contracts. The plan also provided for a waiver if a qualified MBE was unable or unwilling to participate. After the J. A. Croson Construction Company, the sole bidder on a city contract, was denied a waiver and lost its contract, it brought suit under § 1983 in district court, arguing that the plan was unconstitutional on its face and as applied. The district court upheld the plan, and the court of appeals affirmed. The Supreme Court, in 1986, vacated the court of appeals' decision in the light of the *Wygant v. Jackson Board of Education* (1986) case; on remand, the court of appeals struck down the Richmond set-aside plan as violating both prongs of strict scrutiny. *Vote: 6-3.*

* * *

JUSTICE O'CONNOR announced the judgment of the Court and delivered the opinion of the Court with respect to Parts I, III-B, and IV, an opinion with respect to Part II, in which THE CHIEF JUSTICE [REHNQUIST] and JUSTICE WHITE join, and an opinion with respect to Parts III-A and V, in which THE CHIEF JUSTICE, JUSTICE WHITE, and JUSTICE KENNEDY join.

. . . [*Part II*] The parties and their supporting *amici* fight an initial battle over the scope of the city's power to adopt legislation designed to address the effects of past discrimination. Relying on our decision in *Wygant* [*v. Jackson Board of Education,* 476 U.S. 267 (1986)], appellee argues that the city must limit any race-based remedial efforts to eradicating the effects of its own prior discrimination. This is essentially the position taken by the Court of Appeals below. Appellant argues that our decision in *Fullilove* [*v. Klutznick,* 448 U.S. 448 (1980)] is controlling, and that as a result the city of Richmond enjoys sweeping legislative power to define and attack the effects of prior discrimination in its local construction industry. We find that neither of these two rather stark alternatives can withstand analysis.

. . . What appellant ignores is that Congress, unlike any State or political subdivision, has a specific constitutional mandate to enforce the dictates of the Fourteenth Amendment. The power to "enforce" may at times also include the power to define situations which *Congress* determines threaten principles of equality and to adopt prophylactic rules to deal with those situations. . . .

That Congress may identify and redress the effects of society-wide discrimination does not mean that, *a fortiori,* the States and their political subdivisions are free to decide that such remedies are appropriate. Section 1 of the Fourteenth Amendment is an explicit *constraint* on state power, and the States must undertake any remedial efforts in accordance with that provision. To hold otherwise would be to cede control over the content of the Equal Protection Clause to the 50 state legislatures and their myriad political subdivisions. . . .

. . . It would seem equally clear, however, that a state or local subdivision (if delegated the authority from the State) has the authority to eradicate the effects of the private discrimination within its own legislative jurisdiction. This authority must, of course, be exercised within the constraints of § 1 of the Fourteenth Amendment. Our decision in *Wygant* is not to the contrary. *Wygant* addressed the constitutionality of the use of racial quotas by local school authorities pursuant to an agreement reached with the local teachers' union. It was in the context of addressing the school board's power to adopt a race-based layoff program affecting its own work force that the *Wygant* plurality indicated that the Equal Protection Clause required "some showing or prior discrimination by the governmental unit involved." . . . As a matter of state law, the city of Richmond has legislative authority over its procurement policies, and can use its spending powers to remedy private discrimination, if it identifies that discrimination with the particularity required by the Fourteenth Amendment. To this extent, on the question of the city's competence, the Court of Appeals erred in following *Wygant* by rote in a case involving a state entity which has state-law authority to address discriminatory practices within local commerce under its jurisdiction.

Thus, if the city could show that it had essentially become a "passive participant" in a system of racial exclusion practiced by elements of the local construction industry, we think it clear that the city could take affirmative steps to dismantle such a system. It is beyond dispute that any public entity, state or federal, has a compelling interest in assuring that public dollars, drawn from the tax contributions of all citizens, do not serve to finance the evil of private prejudice. . . .

[*Part III-A*] The Equal Protection Clause of the Fourteenth Amendment provides that "[n]o State shall . . . deny to *any person* within its jurisdiction the equal protection of the laws." . . . As this Court has noted in the past, the "rights created by the first section of the Fourteenth Amendment are, by its terms, guaranteed to the individual. The rights established are personal rights." . . . The Richmond Plan denies certain citizens the opportunity to compete for a fixed percentage of public contracts based solely upon their race. To whatever racial group these citizens belong, their "personal rights" to be treated with equal dignity and respect are implicated by a rigid rule erecting race as the sole criterion in an aspect of public decisionmaking.

Absent searching judicial inquiry into the justification for such race-based measures, there is simply no way of determining what classifications are "benign" or "remedial" and what classifications are in fact motivated by illegitimate notions of racial inferiority or simple racial politics. Indeed, the purpose of strict scrutiny is to "smoke out" illegitimate uses of race by assuring that the legislative body is

pursuing a goal important enough to warrant use of a highly suspect tool. The test also ensures that the means chosen "fit" this compelling goal so closely that there is little or no possibility that the motive for the classification was illegitimate racial prejudice or stereotype.

Classifications based on race carry a danger of stigmatic harm. Unless they are strictly reserved for remedial settings, they may in fact promote notions of racial inferiority and lead to a politics of racial hostility. See *University of California Regents v. Bakke,* [438 U.S. 265 (1978)]. . . . We thus reaffirm the view expressed by the plurality in *Wygant* that the standard of review under the Equal Protection Clause is not dependent on the race of those burdened or benefited by a particular classification. . . .

. . . In this case, blacks constitute approximately 50% of the population of the city of Richmond. Five of the nine seats on the city council are held by blacks. The concern that a political majority will more easily act to the disadvantage of a minority based on unwarranted assumptions or incomplete facts would seem to militate for, not against, the application of heightened judicial scrutiny in this case. . . .

. . . [*Part III-B*] We think it clear that the factual predicate offered in support of the Richmond Plan suffers from the same defects identified as fatal in *Wygant.* The District Court found the city council's "findings sufficient to endure that, in adopting the Plan, it was remedying the present effects of past discrimination in the *construction industry.*" . . . Like the "role model" theory employed in *Wygant,* a generalized assertion that there has been past discrimination in an entire industry provides no guidance for a legislative body to determine the precise scope of the injury it seeks to remedy. It "has no logical stopping point." . . . "Relief" for such an ill-defined wrong could extend until the percentage of public contracts awarded to MBE's in Richmond mirrored the percentage of minorities in the population as a whole.

Appellant argues that it is attempting to remedy various forms of past discrimination that are alleged to be responsible for the small number of minority businesses in the local contracting industry. Among these the city cites the exclusion of blacks from skilled construction trade unions and training programs. This past discrimination has prevented them "from following the traditional path from laborer to entrepreneur." . . . The city also lists a host of non-racial factors which would seem to face a member of any racial group attempting to establish a new business enterprise, such as deficiencies in working capital, inability to meet bonding requirements, unfamiliarity with bidding procedures, and disability caused by an inadequate track record. . . .

While there is no doubt that the sorry history of both private and public discrimination in this country has contributed to a lack of opportunities for black entrepreneurs, this observation, standing alone, cannot justify a rigid racial quota in the awarding of public contracts in Richmond, Virginia. Like the claim that discrimination in primary and secondary schooling justifies a rigid racial preference in medical school admissions, an amorphous claim that there has been past discrimination in a particular industry cannot justify the use of an unyielding racial quota.

It is sheer speculation how many minority firms there would be in Richmond absent past societal discrimination, just as it was sheer speculation how many minority medical students would have been admitted to the medical school at Davis absent past discrimination in educational opportunities. Defining these sorts of injuries as "identified discrimination" would give local governments license to create a patchwork of racial preferences based on statistical generalizations about any particular field of endeavor.

These defects are readily apparent in this case. The 30% quota cannot in any realistic sense be tied to any injury suffered by anyone. The District Court relied upon five predicate "facts" in reaching its conclusion that there was an adequate basis for the 30% quota: (1) the ordinance declares itself to be remedial; (2) several proponents of the measure stated their views that there had been past discrimination in the construction industry; (3) minority businesses received 0.67% of prime contracts from the city while minorities constituted 50% of the city's population; (4) there were very few minority contractors in local and state contractors' associations; and (5) in 1977, Congress made a determination that the effects of past discrimination had stifled minority participation in the construction industry nationally. . . .

None of these "findings," singly or together, provide the city of Richmond with a "strong basis in evidence for its conclusion that remedial action was necessary." . . . There is nothing approaching a prima facie case of a constitutional or statutory violation by *anyone* in the Richmond construction industry. . . .

The District Court accorded great weight to the fact that the city council designated the Plan as "remedial." But the mere recitation of a "benign" or legitimate purpose for a racial classification is entitled to little or no weight. . . . Racial classifications are suspect, and that means that simple legislative assurances of good intention cannot suffice.

. . . In sum, none of the evidence presented by the city points to any identified discrimination in the Richmond construction industry. We, therefore, hold that the city has failed to demonstrate a compelling interest in apportioning public contracting opportunities on the basis of race. To accept Richmond's claim that past societal discrimination alone can serve as the basis for rigid racial preferences would be to open the door to competing claims for "remedial relief" for every disadvantaged group. The dream of a Nation of equal citizens in a society where race is irrelevant to personal opportunity and achievement would be lost in a mosaic of shifting preferences based on inherently unmeasurable claims of past wrongs. . . . We think such a result would be contrary to both the letter and spirit of a constitutional provision whose central command is equality.

The foregoing analysis applies only to the inclusion of blacks within the Richmond set-aside program. There is *absolutely no evidence* of past discrimination against Spanish-speaking, Oriental, Indian, Eskimo, or Aleut persons in any aspect of the Richmond construction industry. The District Court took judicial notice of the fact that the vast majority of "minority" person in Richmond were black. . . . It may well be that Richmond has never had an Aleut or Eskimo citizen. The random inclusion of racial groups that, as a practical matter, may never have suffered from discrimination in the construction industry in Richmond suggests that perhaps the city's purpose was not in fact to remedy past discrimination.

[*Part IV*] As noted by the court below, it is almost impossible to assess whether the Richmond Plan is narrowly tailored to remedy prior discrimination since it is not linked to identified discrimination in any way. We limit ourselves to two observations in this regard.

First, there does not appear to have been any consideration of the use of race-neutral means to increase minority business participation in city contracting. . . . Many of the barriers to minority participation in the construction industry relied upon by the city to justify a racial classification appear to be race neutral. If MBE's disproportionately lack capital or cannot meet bonding requirements, a race-neutral program of city financing for small firms would, *a fortiori*, lead to greater minority participation. The principal opinion in *Fullilove* found that Congress had carefully examined and rejected race-neutral alternatives before enacting the MBE set-aside. . . . There is no evidence in this record that the Richmond City Council has considered any alternatives to a race-based quota.

Second, the 30% quota cannot be said to be narrowly tailored to any goal, except perhaps outright racial balancing. It rests upon the "completely unrealistic" assumption that minorities will choose a particular trade in lockstep proportion to their representation in the local population. . . .

. . . [*Part V*] Nothing we say today precludes a state or local entity from taking action to rectify the effects of identified discrimination within its jurisdiction. If the city of Richmond had evidence before it that nonminority contractors were systematically excluding minority businesses from subcontracting opportunities, it could take action to end the discriminatory exclusion. Where there is a significant statistical disparity between the number of qualified contractors willing and able to perform a particular service and the number of such contractors actually engaged by the locality or the locality's prime contractors, an inference of discriminatory exclusion could arise. See *Bazemore v. Friday* [478 U.S. 385 (1986)]. . . . Under such circumstances, the city could act to dismantle the closed business system by taking appropriate measures against those who discriminate on the basis of race or other illegitimate criteria. . . . In the extreme case, some form of narrowly tailored racial preference might be necessary to break down patterns of deliberate exclusion.

Nor is local government powerless to deal with individual instances of racially motivated refusals to employ minority contractors. Where such discrimination occurs, a city would be justified in penalizing the discriminator and providing appropriate relief to the victim of such discrimination. . . . Moreover, evidence of a pattern of individual discriminatory acts can, if supported by appropriate statistical proof, lend support to a local government's determination that broader remedial relief is justified. . . .

Even in the absence of evidence of discrimination, the city has at its disposal a whole array of race-neutral devices to increase the accessibility of city contracting opportunities to small entrepreneurs of all races. Simplification of bidding procedures, relaxation of bonding requirements, and training and financial aid for disadvantaged entrepreneurs of all races would open the public contracting market to all those who have suffered the effects of past societal discrimination or neglect. Many of the formal barriers to new entrants may be the product of bureaucratic inertia more than actual necessity, and may have a disproportionate effect on the opportunities open to new minority firms. Their elimination or modification would have little detrimental effect on the city's interests and would serve to increase the opportunities available to minority business without classifying individuals on the basis of race. The city may also act to prohibit discrimination in the provision of credit or bonding by local suppliers and banks. Business as usual should not mean business pursuant to the unthinking exclusion of certain members of our society from its rewards.

. . . Proper findings in this regard are necessary to define both the scope of the injury and the extent of the remedy necessary to cure its effects. Such findings also serve to assure all citizens that the deviation from the norm of equal treatment of all racial and ethnic groups is a temporary matter, a measure taken in the service of the goal of equality itself. Absent such findings, there is a danger that a racial classification is merely the product of unthinking stereotypes or a form of racial politics. . . . Because the city of Richmond has failed to identify the need for remedial action in the awarding of its public construction contracts, its treatment of its citizens on a racial basis violates the dictates of the Equal Protection Clause. Accordingly, the judgment of the Court of Appeals for the Fourth Circuit is *Affirmed.*

[The opinions of JUSTICE STEVENS and JUSTICE KENNEDY, concurring in part and concurring in the judgment, are omitted.]

[The opinion of JUSTICE SCALIA, concurring in the judgment, is omitted.]

* * *

JUSTICE MARSHALL, with whom JUSTICE BRENNAN and JUSTICE BLACKMUN join, dissenting.

It is a welcome symbol of racial progress when the former capital of the Confederacy acts forthrightly to confront the effects of racial discrimination in its midst. In my view, nothing in the Constitution can be construed to prevent Richmond, Virginia, from allocating a portion of its contracting dollars for businesses owned or controlled by members of minority groups. Indeed, Richmond's set-aside program is indistinguishable in all meaningful respects from—and in fact was patterned upon—the federal set-aside plan which this Court upheld in *Fullilove v. Klutznick.* . . .

A majority of this Court hold today, however, that the Equal Protection Clause of the Fourteenth Amendment blocks Richmond's initiative. The essence of the majority's position is that Richmond has failed to catalog adequate findings to prove that past discrimination has impeded minorities from joining or participating fully in Richmond's construction contracting industry. I find deep irony in second-guessing Richmond's judgment on this point. As much as any municipality in the United States, Richmond knows what racial discrimination is; a century of decisions by this and other federal courts has richly documented the city's disgraceful history of public and private racial discrimination. In any event, the Richmond City Council *has* supported its determination that minorities have been wrongly excluded from local construction contracting. Its proof includes statistics showing that minority-owned businesses have received virtually no city contracting dollars and rarely if ever belonged to area trade associations; testimony by municipal officials that discrimination has been widespread in the local construction industry; and the same exhaustive and widely publicized federal studies relied on in *Fullilove,* studies which showed that pervasive discrimination in the nation's tight-knit construction industry had operated to exclude minorities from public contracting. These are precisely the types of statistical and testimonial evidence which, until today, this Court had credited in cases approving of race-conscious measures designed to remedy past discrimination.

More fundamentally, today's decision marks a deliberate and giant step backward in this Court's affirmative-action jurisprudence. Cynical of one municipality's attempt to redress the effects of past racial discrimination in a particular industry, the majority launches a grapeshot attack on race-conscious remedies in general. The majority's unnecessary pronouncements will inevitably discourage or prevent governmental entities, particularly States and localities, from acting to rectify the scourge of past discrimination. This is the harsh reality of the majority's decision, but it is not the Constitution's command.

. . . I would ordinarily end my analysis at this point and conclude that Richmond's ordinance satisfies both the governmental interest and substantial relationship prongs of our Equal Protection Clause analysis. However, I am compelled to add more, for the majority has gone beyond the facts of this case to announce a set of principles which unnecessarily restricts the power of governmental entities to take race-conscious measures to redress the effects of prior discrimination.

Today, for the first time, a majority of this Court has adopted strict scrutiny as its standard of Equal Protection Clause review of race-conscious remedial measures. . . . This is an unwelcome development. A profound difference separates governmental actions that themselves are racist, and governmental actions that seek to remedy the effects of prior racism or to prevent neutral governmental activity from perpetuating the effects of such racism. . . .

[The dissenting opinion of JUSTICE BLACK-MUN, with whom JUSTICE BRENNAN joins, is omitted.]

METRO BROADCASTING, INC. V. FCC
497 U.S. 547 (1990)

In an attempt to satisfy its obligation under the Communications Act of 1934 to promote diversification of programming, the Federal Communications Commission (FCC) adopted two minority ownership preference policies. Under the comparative proceedings policy, the FCC awarded an enhancement for minority ownership and participation in management, which it weighed together with all relevant factors in comparing mutually exclusive applications for licenses for new radio or broadcast stations. Under the distress sale policy, a radio or television broadcaster whose license is about to be revoked could assign that licensee to an FCC-approved minority enterprise. Metro Broadcasting sought review in the court of appeals of an FCC order awarding a new television license to Rainbow Broadcasting in a comparative proceeding when the Commission Review Board awarded Rainbow a substantial enhancement on the ground that it was 90% Hispanic owned. The court of appeals affirmed the commission's order awarding the license to Rainbow. In the companion case, *Astroline Communications Company Limited Partnership v. Shurberg Broadcasting of Hartford, Inc.,* the Faith Center sought the FCC's approval for a distress sale of its station to Astroline Communications Company, a minority applicant. Shurberg Broadcasting, which had applied to the FCC for a permit to build a television station in Hartford, opposed the distress sale of the station to Astroline on the ground that the FCC's distress sale policy violated Shurberg's right to equal protection. The FCC rejected Shurberg's equal protection challenge as without merit and approved the sale to Astroline. Shurberg appealed the order to the court of appeals, where it invalidated the FCC's minority distress sale policy. *Vote: 5-4.*

* * *

JUSTICE BRENNAN delivered the opinion of the Court.

The issue in these cases, consolidated for decision today, is whether certain minority preference policies of the Federal Communications Commission violate the equal protection component of the Fifth Amendment. The policies in question are (1) a program awarding an enhancement for minority ownership in comparative proceedings for new licenses, and (2) the minority "distress sale" program, which permits a limited category of existing radio and television broadcast stations to be transferred only to minority-controlled firms. We hold that these policies do not violate equal protection principles.

. . . A majority of the Court in *Fullilove* [*v. Klutznick,* 448 U.S. 448 (1980)] did not apply strict scrutiny to the race-based classification at issue. Three Members inquired "whether the *objectives* of th[e] legislation are within the power of Congress" and "whether the limited use of racial and ethnic criteria . . . is a constitutionally permissible *means* for achieving the congressional objectives." . . . Three other Members would have upheld benign racial classifications that "serve important governmental objectives and are substantially related to achievement of those objectives." . . . We apply that standard today. We hold that benign race-conscious measures mandated by Congress—even if those measures are not "remedial" in the sense of being designed to compensate victims of past governmental or societal discrimination—are constitutionally permissible to the extent that they serve important governmental objectives within the power of Congress and are substantially related to achievement of those objectives.

Our decision last Term in [*City of*] *Richmond v. J. A. Croson Co.,* 488 U.S. 469 (1989), concerning a minority set-aside program adopted by a municipality, does not prescribe the level of scrutiny to be applied to a benign racial classification employed by Congress. As JUSTICE KENNEDY noted, the question of congressional action was not before the Court . . . and so *Croson* cannot be read to undermine our decision in *Fullilove.* In fact, much of the language and reasoning in *Croson* reaffirmed the lesson of *Fullilove* that race-conscious classifications adopted by Congress to address racial and ethnic discrimination are subject to a different standard than such classifications prescribed by state and local governments. . . .

We hold that the FCC minority ownership policies pass muster under the test we announce today. First, we find that they serve the important governmental objective of broadcast diversity. Second, we conclude that they are substantially related to the achievement of that objective.

Congress found that "the effects of past inequities stemming from racial and ethnic discrimination have resulted in a severe underrepresentation of minorities in the media of mass communications." . . . Congress and the Commission do not justify the minority ownership policies strictly as remedies for victims of this discrimination, however. Rather, Congress and the FCC have selected the minority ownership policies primarily to promote programming diversity, and they urge that such diversity is an important governmental objective that can serve as a constitutional basis for the preference policies. We agree.

. . . Against this background, we conclude that the interest in enhancing broadcast diversity is, at the very least, an important governmental objective and is therefore a sufficient basis for the Commission's minority ownership policies. Just as a "diverse student body" contributing to a "robust exchange of ideas" is a "constitutionally permissible goal" on which a race-conscious university admissions program may be predicated, *Regents of University of California v. Bakke,* 438 U.S. 265, 311-313 (1978) . . . the diversity of views and information on the airways serves important First Amendment values. . . .

We also find that the minority ownership policies are substantially related to the achievement of the Government's interest. One component of this inquiry concerns the relationship between expanded minority ownership and greater broadcast diversity; both the FCC and Congress have determined that such a relationship exists. . . .

The FCC has determined that increased minority participation in broadcasting promotes programming diversity. . . . As the Commission observed in its 1978 Statement of Policy on Minority Ownership of Broadcasting Facilities, "ownership of broadcast facilities by minorities is [a] significant way of fostering the inclusion of minority views in the area of programming," and "[f]ull minority participation in the ownership and management of broadcast facilities results in a more diverse selection of programming." . . . Four years later, the FCC explained that it had taken "steps to enhance the ownership and participation of minorities in the media" in order to "increas[e] the diversity in the control of the media and thus diversity in the selection of available programming, benefitting the public and serving the principle of the First Amendment." . . . The FCC's conclusion that there is an empirical nexus between minority ownership and broadcasting diversity is a product of its expertise, and we accord its judgment deference.

. . . The judgment that there is a link between expanded minority ownership and broadcast diversity does not rest on impermissible stereotyping. Congressional policy does not assume that in every case minority ownership and management will lead to more minority-oriented programming or to the expression of a discrete "minority viewpoint" on the airwaves. Neither does it pretend that all programming that appeals to minority audiences can be labeled "minority programming" or that programming that might be described as "minority" does not appeal to nonminorities. Rather, both Congress and the FCC maintain simply that expanded minority ownership of broadcast outlets will, in the aggregate, result in greater broadcast diversity. A broadcasting industry with representative minority participation will produce more variation and diversity than will one whose ownership is drawn from a single racially and ethnically homogeneous group. . . .

. . . In short, the Commission established minority ownership preferences only after long experience demonstrated that race-neutral means could not produce adequate broadcasting diversity. The FCC did not act precipitately in devising the programs we uphold today; to the contrary, the Commission undertook thorough evaluations of its policies *three* times—in 1960, 1971, and 1978—before adopting the minority ownership programs. In endorsing the minority ownership preferences, Congress agreed with the Commission's assessment that race-neutral alternatives had failed to achieve the necessary programming diversity.

Moreover, the considered nature of the Commission's judgment in selecting the particular minority ownership policies at issue today is illustrated by the fact that the Commission has rejected other types of minority preferences. For example, the Commission has studied but refused to implement the more expansive alternative of setting aside certain frequencies for minority broadcasters. . . .

The minority ownership policies, furthermore, are aimed directly at the barriers that minorities face in entering the broadcasting industry. The Commission's task force identified as key factors hampering the growth of minority ownership a lack of adequate financing, paucity of information regarding license availability, and broadcast inexperience. . . . The Commission assigned a preference to minority status in the comparative licensing proceeding, reasoning that such an enhancement might help to compensate for a dearth of broadcasting experience. Most license acquisitions, however, are by necessity purchases of existing stations, because only a limited number of new stations are available, and those are often in less desirable markets or on less profitable portions of spectrum, such as the UHF band. Congress and the FCC therefore found a need for the minority distress sale policy, which helps to overcome the problem of inadequate access to capital by lowering the sale price and the problem of lack of information by providing existing licensees with an incentive to seek out minority buyers. The Commission's choice of minority ownership policies thus addressed the very factors it had isolated as being responsible for minority underrepresentation in the broadcast industry.

The minority ownership policies are "appropriately limited in extent and duration, and subject to reassessment and reevaluation by the Congress prior to any extension or reenactment." . . . Although it has underscored emphatically its support for the minority ownership policies, Congress has manifested that support through a series of appropriations acts of finite duration, thereby ensuring future reevaluations of the need for the minority ownership program as the number of minority broadcasters increases. In addition, Congress has continued to hold hearings on the subject of minority ownership. The FCC has noted with respect to the minority preferences contained in the lottery statute . . . that Congress instructed the Commission to "report annually on the effect of the preference system and whether it is serving the purposes intended. Congress will be able to further tailor the program based on that information, and may eliminate the preferences when appropriate." . . . Furthermore, there is provision for administrative and judicial review of all Commission decisions, which guarantees both that the minority ownership policies are applied correctly in individual cases, and that there will be frequent opportunities to revisit the merits of those policies. Congress and the Commission have adopted a policy of minority ownership not as an end to itself, but rather as a means of achieving

greater programming diversity. Such a goal carries its own natural limit, for there will be no need for further minority preferences once sufficient diversity has been achieved. The FCC's plan, like the Harvard admissions program discussed in *Bakke,* contains the seed of its own termination. . . .

Finally, we do not believe that the minority ownership policies at issue impose impermissible burdens on nonminorities. Although the nonminority challengers in these cases concede that they have not suffered the loss of an already-awarded broadcast license, they claim that they have been handicapped in their ability to obtain one in the first instance. But just as we have determined that "[a]s part of this Nation's dedication to eradicating racial discrimination, innocent persons may be called upon to bear some of the burden of the remedy," . . . we similarly find that a congressionally mandated, benign race-conscious program that is substantially related to the achievement of an important governmental interest is consistent with equal protection principles so long as it does not impose *undue* burdens on nonminorities. . . .

In the context of broadcasting licenses, the burden on nonminorities is slight. . . . Applicants have no settled expectation that their applications will be granted without consideration of public interest factors such as minority ownership. Award of a preference in a comparative hearing or transfer of a station in a distress sale thus contravenes "no legitimate firmly rooted expectation[s]" of competing applicants. . . .

Respondent Shurberg insists that because the minority distress sale policy operates to exclude nonminority firms completely from consideration in the transfer of certain stations, it is a greater burden than the comparative hearing preference for minorities, which is simply a "plus" factor considered together with other characteristics of the applicants. . . . We disagree that the distress sale policy imposes an undue burden on nonminorities. By its terms, the policy may be invoked at the Commission's discretion only with respect to a small fraction of broadcast licenses—those designated for revocation or renewal hearings to examine basic qualification issues—and only when the licensee chooses to sell out at a distress price rather than to go through with the hearing. The distress sale policy is not a quota or fixed quantity set-aside. Indeed, the nonminority firm exercises control over whether a distress sale will ever occur at all, because the policy operates only where the qualifications of an existing licensee to continue broadcasting have been designated for hearing and no other applications for the station in question have been filed with the Commission at the time of the designation. . . . Thus, a nonminority can prevent the distress sale procedures from ever being invoked by filing a competing application in a timely manner.

In practice, distress sales have represented a tiny fraction—less than 0.4 percent— of all broadcast sales since 1979. . . . There have been only 38 distress sales since the policy was commenced in 1978. . . . This means that, on average, only about 0.20 percent of renewal applications filed each year have resulted in distress sales since the policy was commenced in 1978. . . . Nonminority firms are free to compete for the vast remainder of license opportunities available in a market that contains over 11,000 broadcast properties. Nonminorities can apply for a new station, buy an existing station, file a competing application against a renewal application of an existing station, or seek financial participation in enterprises that qualify for distress sale treatment. . . . The burden on nonminority firms is at least as "relatively light" as that created by the program at issue in *Fullilove,* which set aside for minorities 10 percent of federal funds granted for local public works projects. . . .

The Commission's minority ownership policies bear the *imprimatur* of longstanding congressional support and direction and are substantially related to the achievement of the important governmental objective of broadcast diversity. The judgment in [*Metro Broadcasting*] is affirmed, the judgment in [*Astroline Communications Company*] is reversed, and the cases are remanded for proceedings consistent with this opinion.

It is so ordered.

[The concurring opinion of JUSTICE STEVENS is omitted.]

* * *

JUSTICE O'CONNOR, with whom THE CHIEF JUSTICE [REHNQUIST], JUSTICE SCALIA, and JUSTICE KENNEDY join, dissenting.

. . . As we recognized last Term, the Constitution requires that the Court apply a strict standard of scrutiny to evaluate racial classifications such as those contained in the challenged FCC distress sale and comparative licensing policies. See *Richmond v. J. A. Croson Co.,* . . . see also *Bolling v. Sharpe,* 347 U.S. 497 (1954). "Strict scrutiny" requires that, to be upheld, racial classifications must be determined to be necessary and narrowly tailored to achieve a compelling state interest. The Court abandons this traditional safeguard against discrimination for a lower standard of review, and in practice applies a standard like that applicable to routine legislation. Yet the Government's different treatment of citizens according to race is no routine concern. This Court's precedents in no way justify the Court's marked departure from our traditional treatment of race classifications and its conclusion that different equal protection principles apply to these federal actions.

In both the challenged policies, the Federal Communications Commission (FCC) provides benefits to some members of our society and denies benefits to others based on race or ethnicity. Except in the narrowest of circumstances, the Constitution bars such racial classifications as a denial to particular individuals, of any race or ethnicity, of "the equal protection of the laws." . . . The dangers of such classifications are clear. They endorse race-based reasoning and the conception of a Nation divided into racial blocs, thus contributing to an escalation of racial hostility and conflict. . . . Such policies may embody stereotypes that treat individuals as the product of their race, evaluating their thoughts and efforts—their very worth as citizens—according to a criterion barred to the Government by history and the Constitution. . . .

[The dissenting opinion of JUSTICE KENNEDY, with whom JUSTICE SCALIA joins, is omitted.]

WARDS COVE PACKING CO., INC. V. ATONIO
490 U.S. 642 (1989)

This case involved the employment practices of two salmon canneries in remote Alaska. The canneries operated only during the summer months and were inoperative for the rest of the year. Jobs at the canneries were of two types: cannery jobs, which were unskilled positions, and noncannery jobs, which were classified as skilled positions. The cannery jobs were filled predominantly by nonwhites—Filipinos and Alaska natives. The noncannery jobs were filled by predominately white workers. Virtually all of the noncannery jobs paid more than cannery positions, and the cannery and noncannery workers lived in separate dormitories and ate in separate dining areas.

In 1974 Frank Atonio, a U.S. citizen of Samoan descent, brought a Title VII class action suit on behalf of nonwhite cannery workers against the company, claiming that a variety of practices—nepotism, a rehire preference, a lack of objective hiring criteria, separate hiring channels, and a practice of not promoting from within—were responsible for the racial stratification of the workforce and had denied them and other nonwhites employment as noncannery workers on the basis of race. These claims were advanced under both the disparate-treatment and disparate-impact theories of Title VII liability. The district court rejected the claims, finding that nonwhite workers were overrepresented in cannery jobs because many of those jobs were filled under a hiring hall agreement with a predominantly nonwhite union. The court of appeals reversed, in part, holding that the cannery workers had made out a prima facie case of disparate impact in the hiring for both skilled and unskilled noncannery jobs by relying solely on their statistics showing a high percentage of nonwhite workers in cannery jobs and a low percentage of such workers in noncannery positions. The court of appeals also concluded that once a plaintiff class has shown disparate impact caused by specific, identifiable employment practices or criteria, the burden shifts to the employer to prove the challenged practice's business necessity. *Vote: 5-4.*

* * *

JUSTICE WHITE delivered the opinion of the Court.

Title VII of the Civil Rights Act of 1964 . . . makes it an unfair employment practice for an employer to discriminate against any individual with respect to hiring or the terms and conditions of employment because of such individual's race, color, religion, sex, or national origin; or to limit, segregate, or classify his employees in ways that would adversely affect any employee because of the employee's race, color, religion, sex or national origin. . . . *Griggs v. Duke Power Company,* 401 U.S. 424, 431 (1971), construed Title VII to proscribe "not only overt discrimination but also practices that are fair in form but discriminatory in practice." Under this basis for liability, which is known as the "disparate-impact" theory and which is involved in this case, a facially neutral employment practice may be deemed violative of Title VII without evidence of the employer's subjective intent to discriminate that is required in a "disparate-treatment" case.

. . . In holding that respondents had made out a prima facie case of disparate impact, the Court of Appeals relied solely on respondents' statistics showing a high percentage of nonwhite workers in the cannery jobs and a low percentage of such workers in the noncannery positions. Although statistical proof can alone make out a prima facie case, see *Teamsters v. United States,* 431 U.S. 324, 339 (1977); *Hazelwood School Dist. v. United States,* 433 U.S. 299, 307-308 (1977), the Court of Appeals' ruling here misapprehends our precedents and the purposes of Title VII, and we therefore reverse.

. . . It is such a comparison—between the racial composition of the qualified persons in the labor market and the persons holding at-issue jobs—that generally forms the proper basis for the initial inquiry in a disparate-impact case. Alternatively, in cases where such labor market statistics will be difficult if not impossible to ascertain, we have

recognized that certain other statistics—such as measures indicating the racial composition of "otherwise-qualified applicants" for at-issue jobs—are equally probative for this purpose. See, *e.g., New York City Transit Authority v. Beazer,* 440 U.S. 568, 585 (1979).

It is clear to us that the Court of Appeals' acceptance of the comparison between the racial composition of the cannery work force and that of the noncannery work force, as probative of a prima facie case of disparate impact in the selection of the latter group of workers, was flawed for several reasons. Most obviously, with respect to the skilled noncannery jobs at issue here, the cannery work force in no way reflected "the pool of *qualified* job applicants" or the "*qualified* population in the labor force." Measuring alleged discrimination in the selection of accountants, managers, boat captains, electricians, doctors, and engineers—and the long list of other "skilled" noncannery positions found to exist by the District Court . . .—by comparing the number of nonwhites occupying these jobs to the number of nonwhites filling cannery worker positions is nonsensical. If the absence of minorities holding such skilled positions is due to a dearth of qualified nonwhite applicants (for reasons that are not petitioners' fault), petitioners' selection methods or employment practices cannot be said to have had a "disparate impact" on nonwhites.

One example illustrates why this must be so. Respondents' own statistics concerning the noncannery work force at one of the canneries at issue here indicate that approximately 17% of the new hires for menial jobs, and 15% of the new hires for officer worker positions, were nonwhite. . . . If it were the case that less than 15 to 17% of the applicants for these jobs were nonwhite and that nonwhites made up a lower percentage of the relevant qualified labor market, it is hard to see how respondents, without more, . . . would have made out a prima facie case of disparate impact. Yet, under the Court of Appeals' theory, simply because nonwhites comprise 52% of the cannery workers at the cannery in question, . . . respondents would be successful in establishing a prima facie case of racial discrimination under Title VII.

Such a result cannot be squared with our cases or with the goals behind the statute. The Court of Appeals' theory, at the very least, would mean that any employer who had a segment of his work force that was—for some reason—racially imbalanced, could be haled into court and forced to engage in the expensive and time-consuming task of defending the "business necessity" of the methods used to select the other members of his work force. The only practicable option for many employers would be to adopt racial quotas, insuring that no portion of their work forces deviated in racial composition from the other portions thereof; this is a result that Congress expressly rejected in drafting Title VII. . . .

The Court of Appeals also erred with respect to the unskilled noncannery positions. Racial imbalance in one segment of an employer's work force does not, without more, establish a prima facie case of disparate impact with respect to the selection of workers for the employer's other positions, even where workers for the different positions may have somewhat fungible skills (as is arguably the case for cannery and unskilled noncannery workers). As long as there are no barriers or practices deterring qualified nonwhites from applying for noncannery positions, . . . if the percentage of selected applicants who are nonwhite is not significantly less than the percentage of qualified applicants who are nonwhite, the employer's selection mechanism probably does not operate with a disparate impact on minorities. Where this is the case, the percentage of nonwhite workers found in other positions in the employer's labor force is irrelevant to the question of a prima facie statistical case of disparate impact. As noted above, a contrary ruling on this point would almost inexorably lead to the use of numerical quotas in the workplace, a result that Congress and this Court has rejected repeatedly in the past.

Moreover, isolating the cannery workers as the potential "labor force" for unskilled noncannery positions is at once both too broad and too narrow in its focus. It is too broad because the vast majority of these cannery workers did not seek jobs in unskilled noncannery positions; there is no showing that many of them would have done so even if none of the arguably "deterring" practices existed. Thus, the pool of cannery workers cannot be used as a surrogate for the class of qualified job applicants because it contains many persons who have not (and would not) be noncannery job applicants. Conversely, if respondents propose to use the cannery workers for comparison purposes because they represent the "qualified labor population" generally, the group is too narrow because there are obviously many qualified persons in the labor market for noncannery jobs who are not cannery workers.

The peculiar facts of this case further illustrate why a comparison between the percentage of nonwhite cannery workers and nonwhite noncannery workers is an improper basis for making out a claim of disparate impact. Here, the District Court found that nonwhites were "overrepresent[ed] among cannery workers because petitioners had contracted with a predominantly nonwhite union (local 37) to fill these positions. . . . As a result, if petitioners (for some permissible reason) ceased using local 37 as its hiring channel for cannery positions, it appears (according to the District Court's findings) that the racial stratification between the cannery and noncannery workers might diminish to statistical insignificance. Under the Court of Appeals' approach, therefore, it is possible that *with no change whatso-*

ever in their hiring practices for noncannery workers—the jobs at issue in this lawsuit—petitioners could make respondents' prima facie case of disparate impact "disappear." But *if* there would be no prima facie case of disparate impact in the selection of noncannery workers absent petitioners' use of local 37 to hire cannery workers, surely petitioners' reliance on the union to fill the cannery jobs not at issue here (and its resulting "overrepresentation" of nonwhites in those positions) does not—standing alone—make out a prima facie case of disparate impact. Yet it is precisely such an ironic result that the Court of Appeals reached below.

Consequently, we reverse the Court of Appeals' ruling that a comparison between the percentage of cannery workers who are nonwhite and the percentage of noncannery workers who are nonwhite makes out a prima facie case of disparate impact. Of course, this leaves unresolved whether the record made in the District Court will support a conclusion that a prima facie case of disparate impact has been established on some basis other than the racial disparity between cannery and noncannery workers. This is an issue that the Court of Appeals or the District Court should address in the first instance.

. . . Our disparate-impact cases have always focused on the impact of *particular* hiring practices on employment opportunities for minorities. Just as an employer cannot escape liability under Title VII by demonstrating that, "at the bottom line" his work force is racially balanced (where particular hiring practices may operate to deprive minorities of employment opportunities), see *Connecticut v. Teal* [457 U.S. 440, 450 (1982)], a Title VII plaintiff does not make out a case of disparate impact simply by showing that, "at the bottom line," there is a racial *imbalance* in the work force. As a general matter, a plaintiff must demonstrate that it is the application of a specific or particular employment practice that has created the disparate impact under attack. Such a showing is an integral part of the plaintiff's prima facie case in a disparate impact suit under Title VII.

Here, respondents have alleged that several "objective" employment practices (*e.g.*, nepotism, separate hiring channels, rehire preferences), as well as the use of "subjective decision making" to select noncannery workers, have had a disparate impact on nonwhites. Respondents base this claim on statistics that allegedly show a disproportionately low percentage of nonwhites in the at-issue positions. However, even if on remand respondents can show that nonwhites are underrepresented in the at-issue jobs in a manner that is acceptable under the standards set forth in Part II, . . . this alone will *not* suffice to make out a prima facie case of disparate impact. Respondents will also have to demonstrate that the disparity they complain of is the result of one or more of the employment practices that they are attacking here, specifically showing that each challenged practice has a significantly disparate impact on employment opportunities for whites and nonwhites. To hold otherwise would result in employers being potentially liable for "the myriad of innocent causes that may lead to statistical imbalances in the composition of their work forces." . . .

Some will complain that this specific causation requirement is unduly burdensome on Title VII plaintiffs. But liberal civil discovery rules give plaintiffs broad access to employers' records in an effort to document their claims. Also, employers falling within the scope of the Uniform Guidelines on Employee Selection Procedures . . . are required to "maintain . . . records or other information which will disclose the impact which its tests and other selection procedures have upon employment opportunities of persons by identifiable race, sex, or ethnic group[s]." . . .

. . . Though we have phrased the query differently in different cases, it is generally well established that at the justification stage of such a disparate-impact case, the dispositive issue is whether a challenged practice serves, in a significant way, the legitimate employment goals of the employer. . . . The touchstone of this inquiry is a reasoned review of the employer's justification for his use of the challenged practice. A mere insubstantial justification in this regard will not suffice, because such a low standard of review would permit discrimination to be practiced through the use of spurious, seemingly neutral employment practices. At the same time, though, there is no requirement that the challenged practice be "essential" or "indispensable" to the employer's business for it to pass muster: this degree of scrutiny would be almost impossible for most employers to meet, and would result in a host of evils we have identified above. . . .

. . . For the reasons given above, the judgment of the Court of Appeals is reversed, and the case is remanded for further proceedings consistent with this opinion.

It is so ordered.

* * *

JUSTICE STEVENS, with whom JUSTICE BRENNAN, JUSTICE MARSHALL, and JUSTICE BLACKMUN join, dissenting.

. . . Our opinions always have emphasized that in a disparate-impact case the employer's burden is weighty. "The touchstone," the Court said in *Griggs*, "is business necessity." . . . I am thus astonished to read that the "touchstone of this inquiry is a reasoned review of the employer's justification for this use of the challenged practice. . . . [T]here is no requirement that the challenged practice be . . . 'essential.' " . . . This casual—almost summary—rejection of the statutory construction that developed in the wake of *Griggs* is most disturbing. I have always believed that the *Griggs* opinion correctly reflected the intent of the Congress that enacted Title VII. Even if I were not so persuaded, I could not join a rejection of a consistent interpretation of a federal statute. Congress frequently revisits this statutory scheme and can readily correct our mistakes if we misread its meaning. . . .

Also troubling is the Court's apparent redefinition of the employees' burden of proof in a disparate-impact case. No prima facie case will be made, it declares, unless the employees "isolat[e] and identif[y] the specific employment practices that are allegedly responsible for any observed statistical disparities." . . . This additional proof requirement is unwarranted. It is elementary that a plaintiff cannot recover upon proof of injury alone; rather, the plaintiff must connect the injury to an act of the defendant in order to establish prima facie that the defendant is liable. . . . Although the causal link must have substance, the act need not constitute the sole or primary cause of the harm. . . . Thus in a disparate-impact case, proof of numerous questionable employment practices ought to fortify an employee's assertion that the practices caused racial disparities. Ordinary principles of fairness require that Title VII actions be tried like "any lawsuit." . . . The changes the majority makes today, tipping the scales in favor of employers, are not faithful to those principles.

[The dissenting opinion of JUSTICE BLACKMUN, with whom JUSTICE BRENNAN and JUSTICE MARSHALL join, is omitted.]

PATTERSON V. McLEAN CREDIT UNION
491 U.S. 164 (1989)

In 1972 Brenda Patterson, a black woman, was employed by McLean Credit Union as a teller and a file coordinator. She was laid off in 1982. After the termination, she brought a § 1981 suit against the credit union, alleging that her bosses had harassed her, failed to promote her to an intermediate accounting clerk position, and then discharged her, all because of race. During the trial, Patterson testified how Robert Stevenson, the general manager and later president of the credit union, subjected her to racial harassment by making such statements as, "Blacks are known to work slower than whites by nature." She also testified that despite her stated desire to advance at McLean, she was not offered training but that white employees were offered training (including a less senior white employee). Patterson was also given more demeaning tasks to perform (dusting, sweeping) than white employees. She was heavily criticized during staff meetings, whereas white employees were criticized in private, and when she was given more work than white employees, she was told she always had the option of quitting. The district court determined that a claim of racial harassment is not actionable under § 1981, but the court upheld Patterson's claim based on alleged discrimination in her discharge and the failure to promote her. The court of appeals affirmed. When the Supreme Court granted certiorari to hear the case, it instructed both parties to brief and argue the question not raised by the parties, whether *Runyon v. McCrary* (1976) should be overruled. *Vote: 5-4.*

* * *

JUSTICE KENNEDY delivered the opinion of the Court.

. . . [*Part II*] In *Runyon* [*v. McCrary,* 427 U.S. 160 (1976)], the Court considered whether § 1981 prohibits private schools from excluding children who are qualified for admission, solely on the basis of race. We held that § 1981 did prohibit such conduct, noting that it was already well established in prior decisions that § 1981 "prohibits racial discrimination in the making and enforcement of private contracts." . . . The arguments about whether *Runyon* was decided correctly in light of the language and history of the statute were examined and discussed with great care in our decision. . . .

. . . We conclude, upon direct consideration of the issue, that no special justification has been shown for overruling *Runyon*. In cases where statutory precedents have been overruled, the primary reason for the Court's shift in position has been the intervening development of the law, through either the growth of judicial doctrine or further action taken by Congress. Where such changes have removed or weakened conceptual underpinnings from the prior decision . . . or where the later law has rendered the decision irreconcilable with competing legal doctrines or policies, . . . the Court has not hesitated to overrule an earlier decision. Our decision in *Runyon* has not been undermined by subsequent changes or development in the law.

. . . [*Part III*] Our conclusion that we should adhere to our decision in *Runyon* that § 1981 applies to private conduct is not enough to decide this case.

We must decide also whether the conduct of which petitioner complains falls within one of the enumerated rights protected by § 1981.

Section 1981 reads as follows:

"All persons within the jurisdiction of the United States shall have the same right in every State and Territory to make and enforce contracts, to sue, be parties, give evidence, and to the full and equal benefit of all laws and proceedings for the security of persons and property as is enjoyed by white citizens, and shall be subject to like punishment, pains, penalties, taxes, licenses, and exactions of every kind, and to no other." . . .

The most obvious feature of the provision is the restriction of its scope to forbidding discrimination in the "mak[ing] and enforce[ment]" of contracts alone. Where an alleged act of discrimination does not involve the impairment of one of these specific rights, § 1981 provides no relief. Section 1981 cannot be construed as a general proscription of racial discrimination in all aspects of contract relations, for it expressly prohibits discrimination only in the making and enforcement of contracts. See also *Jones v. Alfred H. Mayer Co.,* 392 U.S. 409, 436 (1968). . . .

By its plain terms, the relevant provision in § 1981 protects two rights: "the same right . . . to make . . . contracts" and "the same right . . . to . . . enforce contracts." The first of these protections extends only to the formation of a contract, but not to problems that may arise later from the conditions of continuing employment. . . . The statute prohibits, when based on race, the refusal to enter into a contract with someone, as well as the offer to make a contract only on discriminatory terms. But the right to make contracts does not extend, as a matter of either logic or semantics, to conduct by the employer after the contract relation has been established, including breach of the terms of the contract or imposition of discriminatory working conditions. Such postformation conduct does not involve the right to make a contract, but rather implicates the performance of established contract obligations and the conditions of continuing employment, matters more naturally governed by state contract law and Title VII. . . .

The second of these guarantees, "the same right . . . to . . . enforce contracts . . . as is enjoyed by white citizens," embraces protection of a legal process, and of a right of access to legal process, that will address and resolve contract-law claims without regard to race. In this respect, it prohibits discrimination that infects the legal process in ways that prevent one from enforcing contract rights, by reason of his or her race, and this is so whether this discrimination is attributed to a statute or simply to existing practices. It also covers wholly *private* efforts to impede access to the courts or obstruct nonjudicial methods of adjudicating disputes about the force of binding obligations, as well as discrimination by private entities, such as labor unions, in enforcing the terms of a contract. Following this principle and consistent with our holding in *Runyon* that § 1981 applies to private conduct, we have held that certain private entities such as labor unions, which bear explicit responsibilities to process grievances, press claims, and represent members in disputes over the terms of binding obligations that run from the employer to the employee, are subject to liability under § 1981 for racial discrimination in the enforcement of labor contracts. See *Goodman v. Lukens Steel Co.,* 482 U.S. 656 (1987). The right to enforce contracts does not, however, extend beyond conduct by an employer which impairs an employee's ability to enforce through legal process his or her established contract rights. . . .

Applying these principles to the case before us, we agree with the Court of Appeals that petitioner's racial harassment claim is not actionable under § 1981. Petitioner has alleged that during her employment with respondent, she was subjected to various forms of racial harassment from her supervisor. . . .

With the exception perhaps of her claim that respondent refused to promote her to a position as an accountant, . . . none of the conduct which petitioner alleges as part of the racial harassment against her involves either a refusal to make a contract with her or the impairment of her ability to enforce her established contract rights. Rather, the conduct which petitioner labels as actionable racial harassment is postformation conduct by the employer relating to the terms and conditions of continuing employment. . . .

This type of conduct, reprehensible though it be true, is not actionable under § 1981, which covers only conduct at the initial formation of the contract and conduct which impairs the right to enforce contract obligations through legal process. Rather, such conduct is actionable under the more expansive reach of Title VII of the Civil Rights Act of 1964. . . . While this Court has not yet had the opportunity to pass directly upon this interpretation of Title VII, the lower federal courts have uniformly upheld this view, and we implicitly have approved it in a recent decision concerning sexual harassment, *Meritor Savings Bank v. Vinson,* 477 U.S. 57, 65-66 (1986). As we stated in that case, "harassment [which is] sufficiently severe or pervasive 'to alter the conditions of [the victim's] employment and create an abusive working environment' " . . . is actionable under Title VII because it "affects a 'term, condition, or privilege' of employment." . . .

Interpreting § 1981 to cover postformation conduct unrelated to an employee's right to enforce her contract, such as incidents relating to the conditions of employment, is not only inconsistent with

that statute's limitation to the making and enforcement of contracts, but would also undermine the detailed and well-created procedures for conciliation and resolution of Title VII claims. In Title VII, Congress set up an elaborate administrative procedure, implemented through the EEOC, that is designed to assist in the investigation of claims of racial discrimination in the workplace and to work towards the resolution of these claims through conciliation rather than litigation. . . . Only after these procedures have been exhausted, and the plaintiff has obtained a "right to sue" letter from the EEOC, may she bring a Title VII action in court. . . . Section 1981, by contrast, provides no administrative review or opportunity for conciliation.

Where conduct is covered by both § 1981 and Title VII, the detailed procedures of Title VII are rendered a dead letter, as the plaintiff is free to pursue a claim by bringing suit under § 1981 without resort to those statutory prerequisites. We agree that, after *Runyon,* there is some necessary overlap between Title VII and § 1981, and that where the statutes do in fact overlap we are not at liberty "to infer any positive preference for one over the other." *Johnson v. Railway Express Agency, Inc.,* [421 U.S. 452, 461 (1975)]. We should be reluctant, however, to read an earlier statute broadly where the result is to circumvent the detailed remedial scheme constructed in a later statute. . . . That egregious racial harassment of employees is forbidden by a clearly applicable law (Title VII), moreover, should lessen the temptation for this Court to twist the interpretation of another statute (§ 1981) to cover the same conduct. In the particular case before us, we do not know for certain why petitioner chose to pursue only remedies under § 1981, and not under Title VII. . . . But in any event, the availability of the latter statute should deter us from a tortuous construction of the former statute to cover this type of claim.

. . . In sum, we affirm the Court of Appeals' dismissal of petitioner's racial harassment claim as not actionable under § 1981. The Court of Appeals erred, however, in holding that petitioner could succeed in her discriminatory promotion claim under § 1981 only by proving that she was better qualified for the position of intermediate accounting clerk than the white employee who in fact was promoted. The judgment of the Court of Appeals is therefore vacated insofar as it relates to petitioner's discriminatory promotion claim, and the case is remanded for further proceedings consistent with this opinion.

It is so ordered.

* * *

JUSTICE BRENNAN, with whom JUSTICE MARSHALL and JUSTICE BLACKMUN join, and with whom JUSTICE STEVENS joins as to Parts

II-B, II-C, and III, concurring in the judgment in part and dissenting in part.

. . . The Court holds that § 1981, insofar as it gives an equal right to make a contract, "covers only conduct at the initial formation of the contract." . . . This narrow interpretation is not, as the Court would have us believe, . . . the inevitable result of the statutory grant of an equal right "to make contracts." On the contrary, the language of § 1981 is quite naturally read as extending to cover postformation conduct that demonstrates that the contract was not really made on equal terms at all. It is indeed clear that the statutory language of § 1981 imposes some limit upon the type of harassment claims that are cognizable under § 1981, for the statute's prohibition is against discrimination in the making and enforcement of contracts; but the Court mistakes the nature of that limit. In my view, harassment is properly actionable under the language of § 1981 mandating that all persons "shall have the same right . . . to make . . . contracts . . . as is enjoyed by white citizens" if it demonstrates that the employer has in fact imposed discriminatory terms and hence has not allowed blacks to make a contract on an equal basis.

The question in a case in which an employee makes a § 1981 claim alleging racial harassment should be whether the acts constituting harassment were sufficiently severe or pervasive as effectively to belie any claim that the contract was entered into in a racially neutral manner. Where a black employee demonstrates that she has worked in conditions substantially different from those enjoyed by similarly situated white employees, and can show the necessary racial animus, a jury may infer that the black employee has not been afforded the same right to make an employment contract as white employees. . . .

Having reached its decision based upon a supposedly literal reading of § 1981, the Court goes on to suggest that its grudging interpretation of this civil rights statute has the benefit of not undermining Title VII. . . . It is unclear how the interpretation of § 1981 to reach pervasive postcontractual harassment could be thought in any way to undermine Congress' intentions as regards Title VII. . . .

The Court's use of Title VII is not only question-begging; it is also misleading. Section 1981 is a statute of general application, extending not just to employment contracts, but to *all* contracts. . . .

Even as regards their coverage of employment discrimination, § 1981 and Title VII are quite different. As we have previously noted, "the remedies available under Title VII and under § 1981, although related, and although directed to most of the same ends, are separate, distinct, and independent." . . . Perhaps most important, § 1981 is not limited in scope to employment discrimination by businesses with 15 or more employees . . . and hence may reach the nearly 15% of the workforce not covered by Title VII. . . . A § 1981 backpay award may also extend beyond the two-year limit of Title VII. . . . Moreover, a § 1981 plaintiff is not limited to recovering backpay: she may also obtain damages, including punitive damages in an appropriate case. . . . Other differences between the two statutes include the right to a jury trial under § 1981, but not Title VII; a different statute of limitations in § 1981 cases . . . and the availability under Title VII, but not § 1981, of administrative machinery designed to provide assistance in investigation and conciliation. . . . The fact that § 1981 provides a remedy for a type of racism that remains a serious social ill broader than that available under Title VII hardly provides a good reason to see it, as the Court seems to, as a disruptive blot on the legal landscape, a provision to be construed as narrowly as possible.

[The opinion of JUSTICE STEVENS, concurring in the judgment in part and dissenting in part, is omitted.]

SPALLONE V. UNITED STATES
493 U.S. 265 (1990)

In 1980 the Department of Justice brought suit against the city of Yonkers, New York, for intentionally engaging in housing discrimination, in violation of Title VIII of the Fair Housing Act of 1968 and the equal protection clause of the Fourteenth Amendment. The federal government and the NAACP (as plaintiff-intervenor) charged that the city had engaged in housing discrimination over 40 years by restricting new subsidized housing projects to southwest Yonkers, an area of the city already predominantly populated by minorities. In 1985 federal district court judge Leonard Sand issued a remedial decree enjoining the city from further discrimination and ordered that the city take affirmative steps to disperse public housing throughout Yonkers. The city failed to comply with the order and appealed to the second circuit in 1987. The appeals court affirmed Judge Sand's order, and the parties agreed to a consent decree to implement the remedial order, which required the construction of 200 public housing units, and set a goal of 800 units to be built over a period of 10 years. However, the city subsequently refused to abide by the plan and proceeded to invite public opposition against it and then refused to enact the legislation it had earlier approved. In July 1988, the district court required the city council members to enact the plan and provided that failure to do so would result in contempt citations for the city and for the council members. Judge Sand eventually imposed a fine of $100 a day on the city, to double every day, and a fine of $500 on Henry Spallone and the other three city council members who voted against the legislation. The appeals court upheld both the city and the individual council members' fines. The Supreme Court agreed to hear the city council members' appeal of the fines but refused to hear the city's appeal, thus making that part of the lower court's order final. *Vote: 5-4.*

* * *

CHIEF JUSTICE REHNQUIST delivered the opinion of the Court.

This case is the most recent episode of a lengthy lawsuit in which the city of Yonkers was held liable for intentionally enhancing racial segregation in housing in Yonkers. The issue here is whether it was a proper exercise of judicial power for the District Court to hold petitioners, four Yonkers city councilmembers, in contempt for refusing to vote in favor of legislation implementing a consent decree earlier approved by the city. We hold that in the circumstances of this case the District Court abused its discretion.

. . . Petitioners contend that the District Court's order violates their rights to freedom of speech under the First Amendment, and they also contend that they are entitled as legislators to absolute immunity for actions taken in discharge of their legislative responsibilities. We find it unnecessary to reach either of these questions, because we conclude that the portion of the District Court's order of July 26 imposing contempt sanctions against the petitioners if they failed to vote in favor of the court-proposed ordinance was an abuse of discretion under traditional equitable principles.

. . The nub of the matter, then, is whether in the light of the reasonable probability that sanctions against the city would accomplish the desired result, it was within the court's discretion to impose sanctions on the petitioners as well under the circumstances of this case.

In *Tenny v. Brandhove,* 341 U.S. 367 (1951), we held that state legislators were absolutely privileged in their legislative acts in an action against them for damages. We applied this same doctrine of legislative immunity to regional legislatures in *Lake Country Estates, Inc. v. Tahoe Regional Planning Agency,* 440 U.S. 391 (1979), and to actions for both damages and injunctive relief in *Supreme Court of Virginia v. Consumers Union of United States, Inc.,* 446 U.S. 719 (1980). The holdings in these cases do not control the question whether local legislators such as petitioners should be immune from contempt sanctions imposed for failure to vote in favor of a particular legislative bill. But some of the same considerations on which the immunity

doctrine is based must inform the District Court's exercise of its discretion in a case such as this. "Freedom of speech and action in the legislature," we observed, "was taken as a matter of course by those who served the Colonies from the Crown and founded our Nation." . . .

In perhaps the earliest American case to consider the import of the legislative privilege, the Supreme Judicial Court of Massachusetts, interpreting a provision of the Massachusetts Constitution granting the rights of freedom of speech and debate to state legislators, recognized that "the privilege secured by it is not so much the privilege of the house as an organized body, *as of each individual member composing it, who is entitled to this privilege, even against the declared will of the house.* For he does not hold this privilege at the pleasure of the house; but derives it from the will of the people . . ." *Coffin v. Coffin,* 4 Mass. 1, 27 (1808). This theme underlies our cases interpreting the Speech or Debate Clause and the federal common law of legislative immunity, where we have emphasized that any restriction on a legislator's freedom undermines the "public good" by interfering with the rights of the people to representation in the democratic process. . . .

Sanctions directed against the city for failure to take action such as required by the consent decree coerce the city legislators and, of course, restrict the freedom of those legislators to act in accordance with their current view of the city's best interests. But we believe there are significant differences between the two types of fines. The imposition of sanctions on individual legislators is designed to cause them to vote, not with a view to the interest of the constituents or of the city, but with a view solely to their own personal interests. Even though an individual legislator took the extreme position—or felt that his constituents took the extreme position—that even a huge fine against the city was preferable to enacting the Affordable Housing Ordinance, monetary sanctions against him individually would motivate him to vote to enact the ordinance simply because he did not want to be out of pocket financially. Such fines thus encourage legislators, in effect, to declare that they favor an ordinance not in order to avoid bankrupting the city for which they legislate, but in order to avoid bankrupting themselves.

This sort of individual sanction effects a much greater perversion of the normal legislative process than does the imposition of sanctions on the city for the failure of these same legislators to enact an ordinance. In that case, the legislator is only encouraged to vote in favor of an ordinance that he would not otherwise favor by reason of the adverse sanctions imposed on the city. A councilman who felt that his constituents would rather have the city enact the Affordable Housing Ordinance than pay a "bankrupting fine" would be motivated to vote in favor of such an ordinance because the sanctions were a threat to the fiscal solvency of the city for whose welfare he was in part responsible. This is the sort of calculus in which legislators engage regularly.

We hold that the District Court, in view of the "extraordinary" nature of the imposition of sanctions against the individual councilmembers, should have proceeded with such contempt sanctions first against the city alone in order to secure compliance with the remedial orders. Only if that approach failed to produce compliance within a reasonable time should the question of imposing contempt sanctions against petitioners even have been considered. "This limitation accords with the doctrine that a court must exercise '[t]he least possible power adequate to the end proposed.' "...

The judgment of the Court of Appeals is *Reversed.*

* * *

JUSTICE BRENNAN, with whom JUSTICE MARSHALL, JUSTICE BLACKMUN, and JUSTICE STEVENS join, dissenting.

. . . The Court today recognizes that it was appropriate for the District Court to hold in contempt and fine the city of Yonkers to encourage the city councilmembers to comply with their prior promise to redress the city's history of racial discrimination. Yet the Court also reprimands the District Court for simultaneously fining the individual councilmembers whose continuing defiance was the true source of the impasse, holding that personal sanctions should have been considered only after the city sanctions first proved fruitless.

I cannot accept this parsimonious view of the District Court's discretion to wield the power of contempt. Judge Sand's intimate contact for many years with the recalcitrant councilmembers and his familiarity with the city's political climate gave him special insight into the best way to coerce compliance when all cooperative efforts had failed. From our detached vantage point, we can hardly judge as well as he which coercive sanctions or combination thereof was most likely to work quickly and least disruptively. Because the Court's *ex post* rationalization of what Judge Sand should have done fails to do justice either in the facts of this case or the art of judging, I must dissent.

. . . In light of the limited scope of the principle of legislative independence underlying the immu-

nity doctrine, the Court's desire to avoid "perversion of the normal legislative process" by preserving the "sort of calculus in which legislators engage regularly" . . . is misguided. The *result* of the councilmembers' "calculus" is preordained, and the only relevant question is how the court can best encourage—or if necessary coerce—compliance. There is no independent value at this point to replicating a familiar decisionmaking process; certainly there is none so overwhelming as to justify stripping the District Court of a coercive weapon it quite reasonably perceived to be necessary under the circumstances.

Moreover, even if the Court's characterization of personal fines against legislators as "perverse" were persuasive, it would still represent a myopic view of the relevant remedial inquiry. To the extent that equitable limits on federal courts' remedial power are designed to protect against unnecessary judicial intrusion into state or local affairs, it was obviously appropriate for Judge Sand to have considered the fact that the city's accrual of fines would have quickly disrupted every aspect of the daily operation of local government. . . . Particularly when these broader effects are considered, the Court's pronouncement that fining the city is categorically less intrusive than fining the legislators personally is untenable.

. . . The key question here, therefore, is whether Judge Sand abused his discretion when he decided not to rely on sanctions against the city alone but also to apply coercive pressure to the recalcitrant councilmembers on an individual basis. Given the city council's consistent defiance and the delicate political situation in Yonkers, Judge Sand was justifiably uncertain as to whether city sanctions alone would coerce compliance at all and, if so, whether they would do so promptly; the longer the delay in compliance, the more likely that city services would be curtailed drastically and that both budgetary constraints and growing racial tensions would undermine the long-term efficacy of the remedial decree. Under these conditions, Judge Sand's decision to supplement the city sanctions with personal fines was surely a sensible approach. The Court's contrary judgment rests on its refusal to take the fierceness of the councilmembers' defiance seriously, a refusal blind to the scourge of racial politics in Yonkers and dismissive of Judge Sand's wisdom borne of his superior vantage point.

McCLESKEY V. KEMP
481 U.S. 279 (1987)

Warren McCleskey, a black man, was convicted of armed robbery of a furniture store and the killing of a white police officer during the course of the

robbery in 1978. He was sentenced to death. After unsuccessful attempts at seeking postconviction relief in state courts, McCleskey sought habeas corpus relief in federal court. His petition claimed that the Georgia capital sentencing process was administered in a racially discriminatory manner, in violation of the Eighth and Fourteenth Amendments. McCleskey offered a sophisticated statistical study performed by Professors David C. Baldus, Charles Pulaski, and George Woodworth (the Baldus study), examining more than 2,000 murder cases that occurred in Georgia during the 1970s. After taking into account 230 variables in explaining the disparities in the imposition of the death sentence in Georgia on the basis of the race of the murder victim and the race of the defendant, the Baldus study found that black defendants who kill white victims have the greatest likelihood of receiving the death penalty. The district court rejected McCleskey's Fourteenth Amendment claim and his reliance on the Baldus study. The court of appeals affirmed the district court's denial of McCleskey's writ of habeas corpus. *Vote: 5-4.*

* * *

JUSTICE POWELL delivered the opinion of the Court.

This case presents the question whether a complex statistical study that indicates a risk that racial considerations enter into capital sentencing determinations proves that petitioner McCleskey's capital sentence is unconstitutional under the Eighth or Fourteenth Amendment.

. . . McCleskey's first claim is that the Georgia capital punishment statute violates the Equal Protection Clause of the Fourteenth Amendment. He argues that race has infected the administration of Georgia's statute in two ways: persons who murder whites are more likely to be sentenced to death than persons who murder blacks, and black murderers are more likely to be sentenced to death than white murderers. As a black defendant who killed a white victim, McCleskey claims that the Baldus study demonstrates that he was discriminated against because of his race and because of the race of his victim. In its broadest form, McCleskey's claim of discrimination extends to every actor in the Georgia capital sentencing process, from the prosecutor who sought the death penalty and the jury that imposed the sentence, to the State itself that enacted the capital punishment statute and allows it to remain in effect despite its allegedly discriminatory application. We agree with the Court of Appeals, and every other court that has considered such a challenge, that this claim must fail.

Our analysis begins with the basic principle that a defendant who alleges an equal protection violation has the burden of proving "the existence of purposeful discrimination." *Whitus v. Georgia,* 385 U.S. 545, 550 (1967). A corollary to this principle is that a criminal defendant must prove that the purposeful discrimination "had a discriminatory effect" on him. *Wayte v. United States,* 470 U.S. 598, 608 (1985). Thus, to prevail under the Equal Protection Clause, McCleskey must prove that the decisionmakers in *his* case acted with discriminatory purpose. He offers no evidence specific to his own case that would support an inference that racial considerations played a part in his sentence. Instead, he relies solely on the Baldus study. McCleskey argues that the Baldus study compels an inference that his sentence rests on purposeful discrimination. McCleskey's claim that these statistics are sufficient proof of discrimination, without regard to the facts of a particular case, would extend to all capital cases in Georgia, at least where the victim was white and the defendant is black.

. . . McCleskey's statistical proffer must be viewed in the context of his challenge. McCleskey challenges decisions at the heart of the State's criminal justice system. . . . Implementation of these laws necessarily requires discretionary judgments. Because discretion is essential to the criminal justice process, we would demand exceptionally clear proof before we would infer that the discretion has been abused. The unique nature of the decisions at issue in this case also counsels against adopting such an inference from the disparities indicated by the Baldus study. Accordingly, we hold that the Baldus study is clearly insufficient to support an inference that any of the decisionmakers in McCleskey's case acted with discriminatory purpose.

McCleskey also suggests that the Baldus study proves that the State as a whole has acted with a discriminatory purpose. He appears to argue that the State has violated the Equal Protection Clause by adopting the capital punishment statute and allowing it to remain in force despite its allegedly discriminatory application. . . . For this claim to prevail, McCleskey would have to prove that the Georgia Legislature enacted or maintained the death penalty statute *because of* an anticipated racially discriminatory effect. In *Gregg v. Georgia* [428 U.S. 153 (1976)] . . . this Court found that the Georgia capital sentencing system could operate in a fair and neutral manner. There was no evidence then, and there is none now, that the Georgia Legislature enacted the capital punishment statute to further a racially discriminatory purpose.

Nor has McCleskey demonstrated that the legislature maintains the capital punishment statute because of the racially disproportionate impact suggested by the Baldus study. As legislatures necessarily have wide discretion in the choice of criminal laws and penalties, and as there were legitimate reasons for the Georgia Legislature to adopt and maintain capital punishment, . . . we will not infer a discriminatory purpose on the part of the State of Georgia. Accordingly, we reject McCleskey's equal protection claims.

McCleskey also argues that the Baldus study demonstrates that the Georgia capital sentencing system violates the Eighth Amendment. We begin our analysis of this claim by reviewing the restrictions on death sentences established by our prior decisions under that Amendment.

. . . In sum, our decisions since *Furman* [*v. Georgia,* 408 U.S. 238 (1972)] have identified a constitutionally permissible range of discretion in imposing the death penalty. First, there is a required threshold below which the death penalty cannot be imposed. In this context, the State must establish rational criteria that narrow the decisionmaker's judgment as to whether the circumstances of a particular defendant's case meet the threshold. Moreover, a societal consensus that the death penalty is disproportionate to a particular offense prevents a State from imposing the death penalty for that offense. Second, States cannot limit the sentencer's consideration of any relevant circumstance that could cause it to decline to impose the penalty. In this respect, the State cannot channel the sentencer's discretion, but must allow it to consider any relevant information offered by the defendant.

In light of our precedents under the Eighth Amendment, McCleskey cannot argue successfully that his sentence is "disproportionate to the crime in the traditional sense." See *Pulley v. Harris,* 465 U.S. 37, 43 (1984). He does not deny that he committed a murder in the course of a planned robbery, a crime for which this Court has determined that the death penalty constitutionally may be imposed. . . . His disproportionality claim "is of a different sort." . . . McCleskey argues that the sentence in his case is disproportionate to the sentences in other murder cases.

On the one hand, he cannot base a constitutional claim on an argument that his case differs from other cases in which defendants *did* receive the death penalty. On automatic appeal, the Georgia Supreme Court found that McCleskey's death sentence was not disproportionate to other death sentences imposed in the State. . . . The court supported this conclusion with an appendix containing citations to 13 cases involving generally similar murders. . . . Moreover, where the statutory procedures adequately channel the sentencer's discretion, such proportionality review is not constitutionally required. . . .

On the other hand, absent a showing that the Georgia capital punishment system operates in an arbitrary and capricious manner, McCleskey cannot prove a constitutional violation by demonstrating that other defendants who may be similarly situated did *not* receive the death penalty. . . .

Because McCleskey's sentence was imposed under Georgia sentencing procedures that focus discretion "on the particularized nature of the crime and the particularized characteristics of the individual defendant," . . . we lawfully may presume that

McCleskey's death sentence was not "wantonly and freakishly" imposed . . . and thus that the sentence is not disproportionate within any recognized meaning under the Eighth Amendment.

Although our decision in *Gregg* as to the facial validity of the Georgia capital punishment statute appears to foreclose McCleskey's disproportionality argument, he further contends that the Georgia capital punishment system is arbitrary and capricious in *application,* and therefore his sentence is excessive, because racial considerations may influence capital sentencing decisions in Georgia. We now address this claim.

To evaluate McCleskey's challenge, we must examine exactly what the Baldus study may show. Even Professor Baldus does not contend that his statistics *prove* that race enters into any capital sentencing decision or that race was a factor in McCleskey's particular case. Statistics at most may show only a likelihood that a particular factor entered into some decisions. There is, of course, some risk of racial prejudice influencing a jury's decision in a criminal case. There are similar risks that other kinds of prejudice will influence other criminal trials. . . . The question "is at what point that risk becomes constitutionally unacceptable." . . . McCleskey asks us to accept the likelihood allegedly shown by the Baldus study as the constitutional measure of an unacceptable risk of racial prejudice influencing capital sentencing decisions. This we decline to do.

. . . McCleskey's argument that the Constitution condemns the discretion allowed decisionmakers in the Georgia capital sentencing system is antithetical to the fundamental role of discretion in our criminal justice system. Discretion in the criminal justice system offers substantial benefits to the criminal defendant. Not only can a jury decline to impose the death sentence, it can decline to convict or choose to convict of a lesser offense. Whereas decisions against a defendant's interest may be reversed by the trial judge or on appeal, these discretionary exercises of leniency are final and unreviewable. Similarly, the capacity of prosecutorial discretion to provide individualized justice is "firmly entrenched in American law." . . .

At most, the Baldus study indicates a discrepancy that appears to correlate with race. Apparent disparities in sentencing are an inevitable part of our criminal justice system. The discrepancy indicated by the Baldus study is "a far cry from the major systemic defects identified in *Furman*." . . . As this Court has recognized, any mode for determining guilt or punishment "has its weaknesses and the potential for misuse." . . . Despite these imperfections, our consistent rule has been that constitutional guarantees are met when "the mode [for determining guilt or punishment] itself has been surrounded with safeguards to make it as fair as possible." . . . Where the discretion that is fundamental to our criminal process is involved, we decline to assume that what is unexplained is invidious. In light of the safeguards designed to minimize racial bias in the process, the fundamental value of jury trial in our criminal justice system, and the benefits that discretion provides to criminal defendants, we hold that the Baldus study does not demonstrate a constitutionally significant risk of racial bias affecting the Georgia capital sentencing process.

Two additional concerns inform our decision in this case. First, McCleskey's claim, taken to its logical conclusion, throws into serious question the principles that underlie our entire criminal justice system. The Eighth Amendment is not limited in application to capital punishment, but applies to all penalties. . . . Thus, if we accepted McCleskey's claim that racial bias has impermissibly tainted the capital sentencing decision, we could soon be faced with similar claims as to other types of penalty. Moreover, the claim that his sentence rests on the irrelevant factor of race easily could be extended to apply to claims based on unexplained discrepancies that correlate to membership in other minority groups, and even to gender. Similarly, since McCleskey's claim relates to the race of his victim, other claims could apply with equally logical force to statistical disparities that correlate with the race or sex of other actors in the criminal justice system, such as defense attorneys or judges. Also, there is no logical reason that such a claim need be limited to racial or sexual bias. If arbitrary and capricious punishment is the touchstone under the Eighth Amendment, such a claim could—at least in theory—be based upon any arbitrary variable, such as the defendant's facial characteristics, or the physical attractiveness of the defendant or the victim, that some statistical study indicates may be influential in jury decisionmaking. As these examples illustrate, there is no limiting principle to the type of challenge brought by McCleskey. The Constitution does not require that a State eliminate any demonstrable disparity that correlates with a potentially irrelevant factor in order to operate a criminal justice system that includes capital punishment. . . .

Second, McCleskey's arguments are best presented to the legislative bodies. It is not the responsibility—or indeed even the right—of this Court to determine the appropriate punishment for particular crimes. It is the legislatures, the elected representatives of the people, that are "constituted to respond to the will and consequently the moral values of the people." . . . Despite McCleskey's wide-ranging arguments that basically challenge the validity of capital punishment in our multiracial society, the only question before us is whether in this case . . . the law of Georgia was properly applied. . . .

Accordingly, we affirm the judgment of the Court of Appeals for the Eleventh Circuit.

It is so ordered.

* * *

JUSTICE BRENNAN, with whom JUSTICE MARSHALL joins, and with whom JUSTICE BLACKMUN and JUSTICE STEVENS join in all but Part I, dissenting.

. . . At some point in this case, Warren McCleskey doubtless asked his lawyer whether a jury was likely to sentence him to die. A candid reply to this question would have been disturbing. First, counsel would have to tell McCleskey that few of the details of the crime or of McCleskey's past criminal conduct were more important than the fact that his victim was white. . . . Furthermore, counsel would feel bound to tell McCleskey that defendants charged with killing white victims in Georgia are 4.3 times as likely to be sentenced to death as defendants charged with killing blacks. . . . In addition, frankness would compel the disclosure that it was more likely than not that the race of McCleskey's victim would determine whether he received a death sentence: 6 of every 11 defendants convicted of killing a white person would not have received the death penalty if their victims had been black, . . . while among defendants with aggravating and mitigating factors comparable to McCleskey's, 20 of every 34 would not have been sentenced to die if their victims had been black. . . . Finally, the assessment would not be complete without the information that cases involving black defendants and white victims are more likely to result in a death sentence than cases featuring any other racial combination of defendant and victim. . . . The story could be told in a variety of ways, but McCleskey could not fail to grasp its essential narrative line: there was a significant chance that race would play a prominent role in determining if he lived or died.

. . . The majority thus misreads our Eighth Amendment jurisprudence in concluding that McCleskey has not demonstrated a degree of risk sufficient to raise constitutional concern. The determination of the significance of his evidence is at its core an exercise in human moral judgment, not a mechanical statistical analysis. It must first and foremost be informed by awareness of the fact that death is irrevocable, and that as a result "the qualitative difference of death from all other punishments requires a greater degree of scrutiny of the capital sentencing determination." . . . For this reason, we have demanded a uniquely high degree of rationality in imposing the death penalty. A capital sentencing system in which race more likely than not plays a role does not meet this standard. It is true that every nuance of decision cannot be statistically captured, nor can any individual judgment be plumbed with absolute certainty. Yet the fact that we must always act without the illumination of complete knowledge cannot induce paralysis when we confront what is literally an issue of life and death. Sentencing data, history, and experience all counsel that Georgia has provided insufficient assurance of the heightened rationality we have required in order to take a human life.

[The dissenting opinion of JUSTICE BLACK-MUN, with whom JUSTICE MARSHALL and JUS-TICE STEVENS join, and with whom JUSTICE BRENNAN joins in all but Part IV-B, is omitted.]

[The dissenting opinion of JUSTICE STEVENS, with whom JUSTICE BLACKMUN joins, is omitted.]

POWERS V. OHIO
499 U.S. 400 (1991)

* * *

Larry Joe Powers, a white man, was indicted in Franklin County, Ohio, on two counts of aggravated murder and one count of attempted aggravated murder. Each count also included a separate allegation that Powers had a firearm while committing the offense. Powers pleaded not guilty and invoked his right to a jury trial. During the jury selection process, Powers objected when the prosecutor exercised his first peremptory challenge to remove a black venireperson. Powers requested the trial court to compel the prosecutor to explain, on the record, his reasons for excluding a black person. The trial court denied the request and excused the juror. The state proceeded to use nine more peremptory challenges, six of which removed black venirepersons from the jury, and Powers renewed his objections, citing *Batson v. Kentucky* (1986). Powers's objections were overruled. The jury convicted Powers of murder, and he was sentenced to life imprisonment. Powers appealed his conviction, contending that (a) the prosecutor's discriminatory use of peremptories violated his Sixth Amendment guarantee of a fair cross section in his petit jury and the equal protection clause of the Fourteenth Amendment and (b) his own race was irrelevant to the right to object to the peremptories. The Ohio Court of Appeals affirmed the conviction, and the Ohio Supreme Court dismissed Powers's appeal on the ground that it presented no substantial constitutional question. In addition to the equal protection issue, the Supreme Court concluded that a criminal defendant has standing to raise the third-party equal protection claims of jurors excluded by the prosecution because of race. *Vote: 7-2.*

* * *

JUSTICE KENNEDY delivered the opinion of the Court.

. . . We returned to the problem of a prosecutor's discriminatory use of peremptory challenges in *Batson v. Kentucky* [476 U.S. 79 (1986)]. There, we considered a situation similar to the one before us today, but with one exception: Batson, the defendant who complained that black persons were being excluded from his petit jury, was himself black. During the *voir dire* examination of the venire for Batson's trial, the prosecutor used his peremptory challenges to strike all four black persons on the venire, resulting in a petit jury composed only of white persons. Batson's counsel moved without success to discharge the jury before it was impaneled on the ground that the prosecutor's removal of black venirepersons violated his rights under the Sixth and Fourteenth Amendments. Relying upon the Equal Protection Clause alone, we overruled *Swain* to the extent it foreclosed objections to the discriminatory use of peremptories in the course of a specific trial. . . . In *Batson* we held that a defendant can raise an equal protection challenge to the use of peremptories at his own trial by showing that the prosecutor used them for the purpose of excluding members of the defendant's race. . . .

The State contends that our holding in the case now before us must be limited to the circumstances prevailing in *Batson* and that in equal protection analysis the race of the objecting defendant constitutes a relevant precondition for a *Batson* challenge. Because Powers is white, the State argues, he cannot object to the exclusion of black prospective jurors. The limitation on a defendant's right to object conforms neither with our accepted rules of standing to raise a constitutional claim nor with the substantive guarantees of the Equal Protection Clause and the policies underlying federal statutory law.

In *Batson,* we spoke of the harm caused when a defendant is tried by a tribunal from which members of his own race have been excluded. But we did not limit our discussion in *Batson* to that one aspect of the harm caused by the violation. *Batson* "was designed to 'serve multiple ends,'" only one of which was to protect individual defendants from discrimination in the selection of jurors. . . . *Batson* recognized that a prosecutor's discriminatory use of peremptory challenges harms the excluded jurors and the community at large. . . .

. . . Discrimination in the jury selection process is the subject of a federal criminal prohibition, and has been since Congress enacted the Civil Rights Act of 1875. The prohibition has been codified at 18 U.S.C. § 243, which provides:

"No citizen possessing all other qualifications which are or may be prescribed by law shall be disqualified for service as grand or petit juror in any court of the United States, or of any State on account of race, color, or previous condition of servitude; and whoever, being an officer or other person charged with any duty in the selection or summoning of jurors, excludes or fails to summon any citizen for such cause, shall be fined not more than $5,000.

. . . In *Peters v. Kiff,* 407 U.S. 493 (1972), JUSTICE WHITE spoke of "the strong statutory policy of § 243, which reflects the central concern of the Fourteenth Amendment." . . . The Court permitted a white defendant to challenge the systematic exclusion of black persons from grand and petit juries. While *Peters* did not produce a single majority opinion, six of the Justices agreed that racial discrimination in the jury selection process cannot be tolerated and that the race of the defendant has no relevance to his or her standing to raise the claim. . . .

Racial discrimination in the selection of jurors in the context of an individual trial violates these same prohibitions. A State "may not draw up its jury lists pursuant to neutral procedures but then resort to discrimination at 'other stages in the selection process.' " . . . We so held in *Batson,* and reaffirmed that holding in *Holland* [*v. Illinois,* 493 U.S. 474 (1990)]. . . . In *Holland,* the Court held that a defendant could not rely on the Sixth Amendment to object to the exclusion of members of any distinctive group at the peremptory challenge stage. We noted that the peremptory challenge procedure has acceptance in our legal tradition. . . . On this reasoning we declined to permit an objection to the peremptory challenge of a juror on racial grounds as a Sixth Amendment matter. As the *Holland* Court made explicit, however, racial exclusion of prospective jurors violates the overriding command of the Equal Protection Clause, and "race-based exclusion is no more permissible at the individual petit jury state than at the venire stage." . . .

We hold that the Equal Protection Clause prohibits a prosecutor from using the State's peremptory challenges to exclude otherwise qualified and unbiased persons from the petit jury solely by reason of their race, a practice that forecloses a significant opportunity to participate in civic life. An individual juror does not have a right to sit on any particular petit jury, but he or she does possess the right not to be excluded from one on account of race.

It is suggested that no particular stigma or dishonor results if a prosecutor uses the raw fact of skin color to determine the objectivity or qualifications of a juror. We do not believe a victim of the classification would endorse this view; the assumption that no stigma or dishonor attaches contravenes accepted equal protection principles. Race cannot be a proxy for determining juror bias or competence. "A person's race simply is unrelated to

his fitness as a juror." . . . We may not accept as a defense to racial discrimination the very stereotype the law condemns.

We reject as well the view that race-based peremptory challenges survive equal protection scrutiny because members of all races are subject to like treatment, which is to say that white jurors are subject to the same risk of peremptory challenges based on race as are all other jurors. The suggestion that racial classifications may survive when visited upon all persons is no more authoritative today than the case which advanced the theorem, *Plessy v. Ferguson,* 163 U.S. 537 (1896). This idea has no place in our modern equal protection jurisprudence. It is axiomatic that racial classifications do not become legitimate on the assumption that all persons suffer them in equal degree. *Loving v. Virginia,* 388 U.S. 1 (1967).

. . . The judgment is reversed, and the case is remanded for further proceedings not inconsistent with our opinion.

It is so ordered.

* * *

JUSTICE SCALIA, with whom THE CHIEF JUSTICE [REHNQUIST] joins, dissenting.

Since in my view today's decision contradicts well established law in the area of equal protection and of standing, I respectfully dissent.

. . . Thus, both before and after *Batson,* and right down to the release of today's opinion, our jurisprudence contained neither a case holding, nor even a dictum suggesting, that a defendant could raise an equal protection challenge based upon the exclusion of a juror of another race; and our opinions contained a vast body of clear statement to the contrary. We had reaffirmed the point just last Term in *Holland.* . . . After quoting the language from *Batson* requiring the defendant to show that he is a member of the racial group alleged to have been removed from the jury, we contrasted the requirements for standing under the Fourteenth Amendment's Equal Protection Clause and the Sixth Amendment. . . .

. . . The Court's decision today is unprecedented in law, but not in approach. It is a reprise, so to speak, of *Miranda v. Arizona,* 384 U.S. 436 (1966), in that the Court uses its key to the jail-house door not to free the arguably innocent, but to threaten release upon the society of the unquestionably guilty unless law enforcement officers take certain steps that the Court newly announces to be required by law. It goes beyond *Miranda,* however, in that there, at least, the mandated steps related to the defendant's own rights, if not to his guilt. Here they relate to neither. The sum and substance of the Court's lengthy analysis is that, since a denial of equal protection to other people occurred at the defendant's trial, though it did not affect the fairness of that trial, the defendant must go free. Even if I agreed that the exercise of peremptory strikes constitutes unlawful discrimination (which I do not), I would not understand why the release of a convicted murderer who has not been harmed by those strikes is an appropriate remedy.

. . . Today's supposed blow against racism, while enormously self-satisfying, is unmeasured and misdirected. If for any reason the State is unable to reconvict Powers for the double murder at issue here, later victims may pay the price for our extravagance. Even if such a tragedy, in this or any case, never occurs, the prosecutorial efforts devoted to retrials will necessarily be withheld from other endeavors, as will the prosecutorial efforts devoted to meeting the innumerable *Powers* claims that defendants of all races can be relied upon to present—again with the result that crime goes unpunished and criminals go free.

R.A.V. v. CITY OF ST. PAUL, MINNESOTA
112 S.Ct. 2538 (1992)

During the early morning hours of June 21, 1990, Robert A. Viktora and other white teenagers burned a cross inside the fenced yard of a black family that lived across the street from the house where Viktora was staying. Although the cross-burning could have been punished under a number of Minnesota laws, the city charged Viktora (a juvenile at the time) with violating the St. Paul Bias-Motivated Crime Ordinance. The ordinance made it a misdemeanor to place on public or private property a symbol, object, appellation, characterization, or graffiti, including a burning cross or swastika, that is likely to arouse anger, alarm, or resentment on the basis of race, color, creed, religion, or gender. The trial court dismissed the charge on the grounds that the ordinance was overbroad and content-based, in violation of the First Amendment. The Minnesota Supreme Court reversed on the ground that the ordinance applied only to fighting words, which are not protected by the First Amendment. The court also concluded that the ordinance was not content based because it was narrowly tailored to serve a compelling governmental interest in protecting the community against bias-motivated threats to public safety and order. *Vote. 9-0.*

* * *

JUSTICE SCALIA delivered the opinion of the Court.

. . . In construing the St. Paul ordinance, we are bound by the construction given to it by the Minnesota court. . . . Accordingly, we accept the Minnesota Supreme Court's authoritative statement that the ordinance reaches only those expressions that constitute "fighting words" within the meaning of *Chaplinsky* [*v. New Hampshire,* 315 U.S. 568 (1942)]. Petitioner and his *amici* urge us to modify the scope of the *Chaplinsky* formulation, thereby invalidating the ordinance as "substantially overbroad." . . . We find it unnecessary to consider this issue. Assuming, *arguendo,* that all of the expression reached by the ordinance is proscribable under the "fighting words" doctrine, we nonetheless conclude that the ordinance is facially unconstitutional in that it prohibits otherwise permitted speech solely on the basis of the subjects the speech addresses.

The First Amendment generally prevents government from proscribing speech, see *e.g. Cantwell v. Connecticut,* 310 U.S. 296 (1940), or even expressive conduct, see, *e.g. Texas v. Johnson,* 491 U.S. 397 (1989) because of disapproval of the ideas expressed. Content-based regulations are presumptively invalid. *Simon & Schuster, Inc. v. Members of N.Y. State Crime Victims Bd.* [502 U.S. 105 (1991)]. . . . From 1791 to the present, however, our society, like other free but civilized societies, has permitted restrictions upon the content of speech in a few limited areas, which are "of such slight social value as a step to the truth that any benefit that may be derived from them is clearly outweighed by the social interest in order and morality." . . .

We have sometimes said that these categories of expression are "not within the area of constitutionally protected speech" . . . or that the "protection of the First Amendment does not extend" to them. . . . Such statements must be taken in context, however, and are no more literally true than is the occasionally repeated shorthand characterizing obscenity "as not being protected at all." . . . What they mean is that these areas of speech can, consistently with the First Amendment, be regulated *because of their constitutionally proscribable content* (obscenity, defamation, etc.)—not that they are categories of speech entirely invisible to the Constitution, so that they may be made the vehicles for content discrimination unrelated to their distinctively proscribable content. Thus, the government may proscribe libel; but it may not make the further content discrimination of proscribing *only* libel critical of the government. . . .

. . . In other words, the exclusion of "fighting words" from the scope of the First Amendment simply means that, for purposes of that Amendment, the unprotected features of the words are, despite their verbal character, essentially a "nonspeech" element of communication. Fighting words are thus analogous to a noisy sound truck: Each is, as Justice Frankfurter recognized, "a mode of speech," . . . both can be used to convey an idea; but neither has, in and of itself, a claim upon the First Amendment. As with the sound truck, however, so also with fighting words: The government may not regulate use based on hostility—or favoritism—towards the underlying message expressed. . . .

. . . Even the prohibition against content discrimination that we assert the First Amendment requires is not absolute. It applies differently in the context of proscribable speech than in the area of fully protected speech. The rationale of the general prohibition, after all, is that content discrimination "rais[es] the specter that the Government may effectively drive certain ideas or viewpoints from the marketplace." . . . But content discrimination among various instances of a class of proscribable speech often does not pose this threat.

When the basis for the content discrimination consists entirely of the very reason the entire class of speech at issue is proscribable, no significant danger of idea or viewpoint discrimination exists. Such a reason, having been adjudged neutral enough to support exclusion of the entire class of speech from First Amendment protection, is also neutral enough to form the basis of distinction within the class. To illustrate: A State might choose to prohibit only that obscenity which is the most patently offensive *in its prurience*—*i.e.*, that which involves the most lascivious displays of sexual activity. But it may not prohibit, for example, only that obscenity which includes offensive *political* messages. . . .

Another valid basis for according differential treatment to even a content-based subclass of proscribable speech is that the subclass happens to be associated with particular "secondary effects" of the speech, so that the regulation is "*justified* without reference to the content of the . . . speech." . . . A State could, for example, permit all obscene live performances except those involving minors. Moreover, since words can in some circumstances violate laws directed not against speech but against conduct (a law against treason, for example, is violated by telling the enemy the nation's defense secrets), a particular content-based subcategory of a proscribable class of speech can be swept up incidentally within the reach of a statute directed at conduct rather than speech. . . . Thus, for example, sexually derogatory "fighting words," among other words, may produce a violation of Title VII's general prohibition against sexual discrimination in employment practices. . . . Where the government does not target conduct on the basis of expressive content, acts are not shielded from regulation merely because they express a discriminatory idea or philosophy. . . . Applying these principles to the St. Paul ordinance, we conclude that, even as narrowly construed by the Minnesota Supreme Court, the ordinance is facially unconstitutional. Although the phrase in the ordinance, "arouses anger, alarm, or resentment in others," has been limited by the Minnesota Supreme Court's construction to reach only those symbols or displays that amount to "fighting words," the remaining, unmodified terms make clear that the ordinance applies only to "fighting words" that insult, or provoke violence, "on the basis of race, color, creed, religion or gender." Displays containing abusive invective, no matter how vicious or severe, are permissible unless they are addressed to one of the specified disfavored topics. Those who wish to use "fighting words" in connection with other ideas—to express hostility, for example, on the basis of political affiliation, union membership, or homosexuality—are not covered. The First Amendment does not permit St. Paul to impose special prohibitions on those speakers who express views on disfavored subjects. . . .

In its practical operation, moreover, the ordinance goes even beyond mere content discrimination, to actual viewpoint discrimination. Displays containing some words—odious racial epithets, for example—would be prohibited to proponents of all views. But "fighting words" that do not themselves invoke race, color, creed, religion, or gender—aspersions upon a person's mother, for example—would seemingly be usable *ad libitum* in the placards of those arguing *in favor* of racial, color, etc. tolerance and equality, but could not be used by that speaker's opponents. One could hold up a sign saying, for example, that all "anti-Catholic bigots" are misbegotten; but not that all "papists" are, for that would insult and provoke violence "on the basis of religion." St. Paul has no such authority to license one side of a debate to fight freestyle, while requiring the other to follow Marquis of Queensbury Rules.

What we have here, it must be emphasized, is not a prohibiting of fighting words that are directed at certain persons or groups (which would be *facially* valid if it met the requirements of the Equal Protection Clause); but rather, a prohibition of fighting words that contain (as the Minnesota Supreme Court repeatedly emphasized) messages of "bias-motivated" hatred in particular, as applied to this case, messages "based on virulent notions of racial supremacy." . . . One must wholeheartedly agree with the Minnesota Supreme Court that "[i]t is the responsibility, even the obligation, of diverse communities to confront such notions in whatever form they appear," . . . but the manner of that confrontation cannot consist of selective limitations upon speech. St. Paul's brief asserts that a general "fighting words" law would not meet the city's needs because only a content-specific measure can communicate to minority groups that the "group hatred" aspect of such speech "is not condoned by the majority." . . . The point of the First Amendment is that majority preferences must be expressed in some fashion other than silencing speech on the basis of its content.

. . . The content-based discrimination reflected in the St. Paul ordinance comes within neither any of the specific exceptions to the First Amendment prohibition we discussed earlier, nor within a more general exception for content discrimination that does not threaten censorship of ideas. It assuredly does not fall within the exception for content discrimination based on the very reasons why the particular speech at issue (here, fighting words) is proscribable. . . . St. Paul has not singled out an especially offensive mode of expression—it has not, for example, selected for prohibition only those fighting words that communicate ideas in a threatening (as opposed to a merely obnoxious) manner. Rather, it has proscribed fighting words of whatever manner that communicate messages of racial, gender, or religious intolerance. Selectivity of this sort creates the possibility that the city is seeking to handicap the expression of particular ideas. That possibility would alone be enough to render the ordinance presumptively invalid, but St. Paul's comments and concessions in this case elevate the possibility to a certainty.

. . . Finally, St. Paul and its *amici* defend the conclusion of the Minnesota Supreme Court that, even if the ordinance regulates expression based on hostility towards its protected ideological content, this discrimination is nonetheless justified because it is narrowly tailored to serve compelling state interests. Specifically, they assert that the ordinance helps to ensure the basic human rights of members of groups that have historically been subjected to discrimination, including the right of such group members to live in peace where they wish. We do not doubt that these interests are compelling, and that the ordinance can be said to promote them. But the "danger of censorship" presented by a facially content-based statute . . . requires that the weapon be employed only where it is *"necessary* to serve the asserted [compelling] interest." . . . The existence of adequate content-neutral alternatives thus "undercut[s] significantly" any defense of such a statute, . . . casting considerable doubt on the government's protestations that "the asserted justification is in fact an accurate description of the purpose and effect of the law." . . . The dispositive question in this case, therefore, is whether content discrimination is reasonably necessary to achieve St. Paul's compelling interests; it plainly is not. An ordinance not limited to the favored topics, for example, would have precisely the same beneficial effect. In fact the only interest distinctively served by the content limitation is that of displaying the city council's special hostility towards the particular biases thus singled out. That is precisely what the First Amendment forbids. The politicians of St. Paul are entitled to

express that hostility—but not through the means of imposing unique limitations upon speakers who (however benightedly) disagree.

Let there be no mistake about our belief that burning a cross in someone's front yard is reprehensible. But St. Paul has sufficient means at its disposal to prevent such behavior without adding the First Amendment to the fire.

The judgment of the Minnesota Supreme Court is reversed, and the case is remanded for proceedings not inconsistent with this opinion.

It is so ordered.

* * *

JUSTICE WHITE, with whom JUSTICE BLACKMUN and JUSTICE O'CONNOR join, and with whom JUSTICE STEVENS joins except as to Part I(A), concurring in the judgment.

I agree with the majority that the judgment of the Minnesota Supreme Court should be reversed. However, our agreement ends there.

This case could easily be decided within the contours of established First Amendment law by holding, as petitioner argues, that the St. Paul ordinance is fatally overbroad because it criminalizes not only unprotected expression but expression protected by the First Amendment. . . . Instead, "find[ing] it unnecessary" to consider the questions upon which we granted review, . . . the Court holds the ordinance facially unconstitutional on a ground that was never presented to the Minnesota Supreme Court, a ground that has not been briefed by the parties before this Court, a ground that requires serious departures from the teaching of prior cases and is inconsistent with the plurality opinion in *Burson v. Freeman,* 112 S.Ct. 1846 (1992), which was joined by two of the five Justices in the majority in the present case.

. . . I agree with petitioner that the ordinance is invalid on its face. Although the ordinance as construed reaches categories of speech that are constitutionally unprotected, it also criminalizes a substantial amount of expression that—however repugnant—is shielded by the First Amendment.

* * *

JUSTICE STEVENS, with whom JUSTICE WHITE and JUSTICE BLACKMUN join as to Part I, concurring in the judgment.

. . . Our First Amendment decisions have created a rough hierarchy in the constitutional protection of speech. Core political speech occupies the highest, most protected position; commercial speech and nonobscene, sexually explicit speech are regarded as a sort of second-class expression; obscenity and fighting words receive the least protection of all. Assuming that the Court is correct that this last class of speech is not wholly "unprotected," it certainly does not follow that fighting words and obscenity receive the *same* sort of protection afforded core political speech. Yet in ruling that proscribable speech cannot be regulated based on subject manner, the Court does just that. Perversely, this gives fighting words *greater* protection than is afforded commercial speech. If Congress can prohibit false advertising directed at airline passengers without also prohibiting false advertising directed at bus passengers and if a city can prohibit political advertisements in its buses while allowing other advertisements, it is ironic to hold that a city cannot regulate fighting words based on "race, color, creed, religion or gender" while leaving unregulated fighting words based on "union membership or homosexuality." . . . The Court today turns First Amend-

ment law on its head: Communication that was once entirely unprotected (and that still can be wholly proscribed) is now entitled to greater protection than commercial speech—and possibly greater protection than core political speech. . . .

. . . In sum, the central premise of the Court's ruling—that "[c]ontent-based regulations are presumptively invalid"—has simplistic appeal, but lacks support in our First Amendment jurisprudence. To make matters worse, the Court today extends this overstated claim to reach categories of hitherto unprotected speech and, in doing so, wreaks havoc in an area of settled law. Finally, although the Court recognizes exceptions to its new principle, those exceptions undermine its very conclusion that the St. Paul ordinance is unconstitutional. Stated directly, the majority's position cannot withstand scrutiny.

[The opinion of JUSTICE BLACKMUN, concurring in the judgment, is omitted.]

WISCONSIN V. MITCHELL
113 S.Ct. 2194 (1993)

On October 7, 1989, a group of young black men and boys, including Todd Mitchell, gathered at an apartment complex in Kenosha, Wisconsin, to discuss the movie *Mississippi Burning*. One scene in the movie portrayed a white man beating a young black boy who was praying. After the group moved outdoors, Mitchell asked them: "Do you all feel hyped up to move on some white people?" Shortly thereafter, a young white boy approached the group on the opposite side of the street. As the boy walked by, Mitchell stated, "You all want to fuck somebody up? There goes a white boy, go get him." The group severely beat the teenager, who was rendered unconscious and remained in a coma for four days. Mitchell was convicted of aggravated battery, which under Wisconsin law ordinarily carried a maximum sentence of two years' imprisonment. In the late 1980s, however, Wisconsin enacted a penalty-enhancement provision that enhanced the maximum penalty for an offense whenever the defendant intentionally selected the person against whom the crime is committed because of race, religion, color, disability, sexual orientation, national origin, or ancestry of that person. The trial court then sentenced Mitchell to four years in prison. Mitchell appealed his conviction and sentence on the ground that the Wisconsin penalty-enhancement provision violated his First Amendment rights. The Wisconsin court of appeals rejected Mitchell's challenge, but the Wisconsin Supreme Court reversed, holding that the statute violated the First Amendment directly by punishing what the legislature has deemed to be offensive thought. *Vote: 9-0.*

* * *

CHIEF JUSTICE REHNQUIST delivered the opinion of the Court.

Respondent Todd Mitchell's sentence for aggravated battery was enhanced because he intentionally selected his victim on account of the victim's race. The question presented in this case is whether this penalty enhancement is prohibited by the First and Fourteenth Amendments. We hold that it is not.

. . . Mitchell argues that we are bound by the Wisconsin Supreme Court's conclusion that the statute punishes bigoted thought and not conduct. There is no doubt that we are bound by a state court's construction of a state statute. . . . But here the Wisconsin Supreme Court did not, strictly speaking, construe the Wisconsin statute in the sense of defining the meaning of a particular statutory word or phrase. Rather, it merely characterized the "practical effect" of the statute for First Amendment purposes. . . . This assessment does not bind us. Once any ambiguities as to the meaning of the statute are resolved, we may form our own judgment as to its operative effect.

The State argues that the statute does not punish bigoted thought, as the Supreme Court of Wisconsin said, but instead punishes only conduct. While this argument is literally correct, it does not dispose of Mitchell's First Amendment challenge. To be sure, our cases reject the "view that an apparently limitless variety of conduct can be labeled 'speech' whenever the person engaging in the conduct intends thereby to express an idea." *United States v. O'Brien,* 391 U.S. 367, 376 (1968) . . . Thus, a physical assault is not by any stretch of the imagination expressive conduct protected by the First Amendment. See *Roberts v. United States Jaycees,* 468 U.S. 609, 628 (1984) ("[V]iolence or other types of potentially expressive activities that produce special harms distinct from their communicative impact . . . are entitled to no constitutional protection"); *NAACP v. Claiborne Hardware Co.,* 458 U.S. 886, 916 (1982) ("The First Amendment does not protect violence").

But the fact remains that under the Wisconsin statute the same criminal conduct may be more heavily punished if the victim is selected because of his race or other protected status than if no such motive obtained. Thus, although the statute punishes criminal conduct, it enhances the maximum penalty for conduct motivated by a discriminatory point of view more severely than the same conduct engaged in for some other reason or for no reason at all. Because the only reason for the enhancement is the defendant's discriminatory motive for selecting his victim, Mitchell argues (and the Wisconsin Supreme Court held) that the statute violates the First Amendment by punishing offenders' bigoted beliefs.

Traditionally, sentencing judges have considered a wide variety of factors in addition to evidence bearing on guilt in determining what sentence to impose on a convicted defendant. . . . The defendant's motive for committing the offense is one important factor. . . .

But it is equally true that a defendant's abstract beliefs, however obnoxious to most people, may not be taken into consideration by a sentencing judge. *Dawson v. Delaware* [503 U.S. 159 (1992)]. In *Dawson,* the State introduced evidence at a capital-sentencing hearing that the defendant was a member of a white supremacist prison gang. Because "the evidence proved nothing more than [the defendant's] abstract beliefs," we held that its admission violated the defendant's First Amendment rights. . . . Thus in *Barclay v. Florida,* 463, U.S. 939 (1983) . . . we allowed the sentencing judge to take into account the defendant's racial animus towards his victim. The evidence in that case showed that the defendant's membership in the Black Liberation Army and desire to provoke a "race war" were related to the murder of a white man for which he was convicted. . . . Because "the elements of racial hatred in [the] murder" were relevant to several aggravating factors, we held that the trial judge permissibly took this evidence into account in sentencing the defendant to death. . . .

Mitchell suggests that *Dawson* and *Barclay* are inappropriate because they did not involve application of a penalty-enhancement provision. But in *Barclay* we held that it was permissible for the sentencing court to consider the defendant's racial animus in determining whether he should be sentenced to death, surely the most severe "enhancement" of all. And the fact that the Wisconsin Legislature has decided, as a general matter, that bias-motivated offenses warrant greater maximum penalties across the board does not alter the result here. For the primary responsibility for fixing criminal penalties lies with the legislature.

Mitchell argues that the Wisconsin penalty-enhancement statute is invalid because it punishes the defendant's discriminatory motive, or reason, for acting. But motive plays the same role under the Wisconsin statute as it does under federal and state antidiscrimination laws, which we have previously upheld against constitutional challenge. . . . Title VII, for example, makes it unlawful for an employer to discriminate against an employee "*because of* such individuals' race, color, religion, sex, or national origin." . . . In *Hishon* [*v. King & Spalding,* 467 U.S. 69 (1984)], we rejected the argument that Title VII infringed employers' First Amendment rights. And more recently, in *R.A.V. v. St. Paul,* [112 S.Ct. 2538 (1992)], we cited Title VII (as well as 18 U.S.C. § 242 and 42 U.S. § § § 1981 and 1982) as an example of a permissible content-neutral regulation of conduct.

Nothing in our decision last Term in *R.A.V.* compels a different result here. That case involved a First Amendment challenge to a municipal ordinance prohibiting the use of " 'fighting words' that insult, or provoke violence, 'on the basis of race, color, creed, religion or gender.' " . . . Because the ordinance only proscribed a class of "fighting words" deemed particularly offensive by the city—*i.e.,* those "that contain . . . messages of 'bias-motivated' hatred," . . . we held that it violated the rule against content-based discrimination. . . . But whereas the ordinance struck down in *R.A.V.* was explicitly directed at expression (*i.e.,* "speech" or "messages," . . .) the statute in this case is aimed at conduct unprotected by the First Amendment.

Moreover, the Wisconsin statute singles out for enhancement bias-inspired conduct because this conduct is thought to inflict greater individual and societal harm. For example, according to the State and its *amici,* bias-motivated crimes are more likely to provoke retaliatory crimes, inflict distinct emotional harms on their victims, and incite community unrest. . . . The State's desire to redress these perceived harms provides an adequate explanation for its penalty-enhancement provision over and above mere disagreement with offenders' beliefs or biases. . . .

Finally, there remains to be considered Mitchell's argument that the Wisconsin statute is unconstitutionally overbroad because of its "chilling effect" on free speech. Mitchell argues (and the Wisconsin Supreme Court agreed) that the statute is "overbroad" because evidence of the defendant's prior speech or associations may be used to prove that the defendant intentionally selected his victim on account of the victim's protected status. Consequently, the argument goes, the statute impermissibly chills free expression with respect to such matters by those concerned about the possibility of enhanced sentences if they should in the future commit a criminal offense covered by the statute. We find no merit in this contention.

The sort of chill envisioned here is far more attenuated and unlikely than that contemplated in traditional "overbreadth" cases. We must conjure up a vision of a Wisconsin citizen suppressing his unpopular bigoted opinions for fear that if he later commits an offense covered by the statute, these opinions will be offered at trial to establish that he selected his victim on account of the victim's protected status, thus qualifying him for penalty-enhancement. To stay within the realm of rationality, we must surely put to one side minor misdemeanor offenses covered by the statute, such as negligent operation of a motor vehicle . . .; for it is difficult, if not impossible, to conceive of a situation where such offenses would be racially motivated. We are left, then, with the prospect of a citizen suppressing his bigoted beliefs for fear that evidence of such beliefs will be introduced against him at trial if he commits a more serious offense against person or property. This is simply too speculative a hypothesis to support Mitchell's overbreadth claim.

The First Amendment, moreover, does not prohibit the evidentiary use of speech to establish the elements of a crime or to prove motive or intent. Evidence of a defendant's previous declarations or statements is commonly admitted in criminal trials subject to evidentiary rules dealing with relevancy, reliability, and the like. Nearly half a century ago, in *Haupt v. United States,* 330 U.S. 631 (1947), we rejected a contention similar to that advanced by Mitchell here. Haupt was tried for the offense of treason, which, as defined by the Constitution (Art. III, § 3), may depend very much on proof of motive. To prove that the acts in question were committed out of "adherence to the enemy" rather than "parental solicitude," . . . the Government introduced evidence of conversations that had taken place long prior to the indictment, some of which consisted of statements showing Haupt's sympathy with Germany and Hitler and hostility towards the United States. We rejected Haupt's argument that this evidence was improperly admitted. . . .

For the foregoing reasons, we hold that Mitchell's First Amendment rights were not violated by the application of the Wisconsin penalty-enhancement provision in sentencing him. The judgment of the Supreme Court of Wisconsin is therefore reversed, and the case is remanded for further proceedings not inconsistent with this opinion.

It is so ordered.

UWM POST, INC. V. BOARD OF REGENTS OF THE UNIVERSITY OF WISCONSIN SYSTEM
774 F. Supp. 1163 (1991)

In 1988 the Board of Regents of the University of Wisconsin System adopted a plan designed to increase minority representation, multicultural understanding, and greater diversity throughout the University of Wisconsin's 26 campuses. The plan responded to concern over an increase in the incidents of discriminatory harassment. Several highly publicized incidents involving fraternities took place in 1987: A fraternity erected a large caricature of a black Fiji Islander at a party, a fight with racial overtones took place between members of two fraternities, and a fraternity held a slave auction at which pledges in blackface performed skits parroting black entertainers. On June 9, 1989, the board adopted the UW Rule, "Policy and Guidelines on Racist and Discriminatory Conduct," which prohibited students from directing discriminatory epithets at particular individuals with intent to demean them and create a hostile educational environment. Student plaintiffs filed suit in federal district court, alleging that the UW Rule violated their right to free speech. *Disposition: summary judgment for the plaintiffs.*

ORDER

WARREN, Senior District Judge.

On March 29, 1990, the UWM Post, Inc. and others ("plaintiffs") filed this action seeking that this Court enter a declaratory judgment that Wis.Admin. Code § UWS 17.-06(2) (the "UW Rule") on its face violates: (1) plaintiffs' right of free speech guaranteed by the First Amendment to the United States Constitution and by Article I, Section 3 of the Wisconsin Constitution and (2) plaintiffs' right to due process and equal protection of the laws guaranteed by the Fourteenth Amendment and by Article I, Section 1 of the Wisconsin Constitution. In addition, plaintiffs request that this Court: (1) enter a permanent injunction prohibiting the Board of Regents of the University of Wisconsin System (the "Board of Regents" or the "Board") and its agents and employees from enforcing the UW Rule; (2) order the Board of Regents to vacate the disciplinary action taken against plaintiff John Doe under the UW Rule and expunge from his files all records related to that action and (3) award plaintiffs their reasonable attorneys' fees and costs pursuant to 42 U.S.C. § 1988.

Now before the Court are the parties' cross motions for summary judgment.

I. BACKGROUND

B. The UW Rule
The UW rule provides:
UWS 17.06 Offenses defined. The university may discipline a student in nonacademic matters in the following situations. . . .

(2)(a) For racist or discriminatory comments, epithets or other expressive behavior directed at an individual or on separate occasions at different individuals, or for physical conduct, if such comments, epithets or other expressive behavior or physical conduct intentionally:
1. Demean the race, sex, religion, color, creed, disability, sexual orientation, national origin, ancestry or age of the individual or individuals; and
2. Create an intimidating, hostile or demeaning environment for education, university-related work, or other university-authorized activity.
  (b) Whether the intent required under par. (a) is present shall be determined by consideration of all relevant circumstances.
  (c) In order to illustrate the types of conduct which this subsection is designed to cover, the following examples are set forth. These examples are not meant to illustrate the only situations or types of conduct intended to be covered.
1. A student would be in violation if:
  a. He or she intentionally made demeaning remarks to an individual based on that person's ethnicity, such as name calling, racial slurs, or "jokes"; and
  b. His or her purpose in uttering the remarks was to make the educational environment hostile for the person to whom the demeaning remark was addressed.
2. A student would be in violation if:
  a. He or she intentionally placed visual or written material demeaning the race or sex of an individual in that person's university living quarters or work area; and
  b. His or her purpose was to make the educational environment hostile for the person in whose quarters or work area the material was placed.
3. A student would be in violation if he or she seriously damaged or destroyed private property of any member of the university community or guest because of that person's race, sex, religion, color, creed, disability, sexual orientation, national origin, ancestry or age.

4. A student would not be in violation if, during a class discussion, he or she expressed a derogatory opinion concerning a racial or ethnic group. There is no violation, since the student's remark was addressed to the class as a whole, not to a specific individual. Moreover, on the facts as stated there seems no evidence that the student's purpose was to create a hostile environment.

Wis.Admin.Code § UWS 17.06(2).

Thus, in order to be regulated under the UW Rule, a comment, epithet or other expressive behavior must:

(1) Be racist or discriminatory;
(2) Be directed at an individual;
(3) Demean the race, sex, religion, color, creed, disability, sexual orientation, national origin, ancestry or age of the individual addressed; and
(4) Create an intimidating, hostile or demeaning environment for education, university-related work, or other university-authorized activity.

II. DISCUSSION

Plaintiffs argue that this Court should strike down the UW Rule because it violates the overbreadth and vagueness doctrines.

. . . Plaintiffs argue that the UW Rule has overbreadth difficulties because it is a content-based rule which regulates a substantial amount of protected speech. . . .

Although the First Amendment generally protects speech from content-based regulation, it does not protect all speech. The Supreme Court has removed certain narrowly limited categories of speech from First Amendment protection. These categories of speech are considered to be of such slight social value that any benefit that may be derived from them is clearly outweighed by their costs to order and morality. *Chaplinsky v. New Hampshire,* 315 U.S. 568, 572 (1942). The categories include fighting words, obscenity, and, to a limited extent, libel. . . .

The Board of Regents argues that the UW Rule falls within the category of fighting words. In the alternative, the Board asserts that the balancing test set forth in *Chaplinsky* leaves the speech regulated by the UW Rule unprotected by the First Amendment. The Board also argues that the Court should find the UW Rule constitutional because its prohibition of discriminatory speech parallels Title VII law. Finally, the Board asserts that, even if the Court finds the rule, as written, unconstitutional, it may apply a narrowing construction which limits the rule's reach to unprotected speech.

. . . As stated above, in order to be regulated by the rule which the UW has adopted, a comment, epithet or other expressive behavior must:

(1) be racist or discriminatory;

(2) be directed at an individual;

(3) demean the race, sex, religion, color, creed, disability, sexual orientation, national origin, ancestry or age of the individual; and

(4) create an intimidating, hostile or demeaning environment for education, university-related work, or other university-authorized activity.

Since the elements of the UW Rule do not require that the regulated speech, by its very utterance, tend to incite violent reaction, the rule goes beyond the present scope of the fighting words doctrine.

... While the Board is correct that the language regulated by the UW Rule is likely to cause violent responses in many cases, the rule regulates discriminatory speech whether or not it is likely to provoke such a response. It is unlikely that all or nearly all demeaning, discriminatory comments, epithets or other expressive behavior which creates an intimidating, hostile or demeaning environment tends to provoke a violent response. Since the UW Rule covers a substantial number of situations where no breach of the peace is likely to result, the rule fails to meet the requirements of the fighting words doctrine.

... The Board of Regents next argues that the UW Rule is in harmony with the First Amendment because it only regulates speech with minimum social value and which has harmful effects. The Board asserts that this balancing approach is consistent with the Supreme Court's holding in *Chaplinsky*. In support of this assertion, the Board notes that while the *Chaplinsky* Court created a *per se* rule with respect to fighting words, it used a balancing approach to reach this result. . . .

... [I]t is evident that this Court may employ a balancing approach to determine the constitutionality of the UW rule only if it is content neutral. It is clear, however, that the UW Rule regulates speech based on its content. The rule disciplines students whose comments, epithets or other expressive behavior demeans their addressees' race, sex, religion, etc. *See* UW Rule § 2(a)(1). However, the rule leaves unregulated comments, epithets and other expressive behavior which affirms or does not address an individual's race, sex, religion, etc.

Since the UW Rule regulates speech based upon its content, it is not proper for this Court to apply a balancing test to determine the constitutionality of the rule. Moreover, this Court finds that, even under the balancing test proposed by the Board of Regents, the rule is unconstitutional.

... On the benefits side of its proposed balancing test, the Board of Regents argues that the discriminatory speech proscribed by the UW Rule has little or no social value since it does not serve as a "step to the truth." The Board states that the proscribed speech lacks social utility because it: (1) is not intended to inform or convince the listener; (2) is not likely to form any part of a dialogue or exchange of views; (3) does not provide an opportunity for reply; (4) constitutes a kind of verbal assault on the person to whom it is directed and (5) is likely to incite reaction.

The Board first asserts that the speech proscribed by the UW Rule is not intended to inform or convince its listener. The Court disagrees with this assertion. Most students punished under the rule are likely to have employed comments, epithets or other expressive behavior to inform their listeners of their racist or discriminatory views. In addition, nothing in the UW Rule prevents it from regulating speech which is intended to convince the listener of the speaker's discriminatory position. Accordingly, the rule may cover a substantial number of situations where students are attempting to convince their listeners of their positions.

Moreover, even if the UW Rule did not regulate speech intended to inform or convince the listener, the speech the rule inhibits would be protected for its expression of the speaker's emotions. The Supreme Court has held that the Constitution protects speech for its emotive function as well as its cognitive content. . . . Most, if not all, of the cases covered by the UW Rule are likely to involve speech which expresses the speaker's feelings regarding persons of a different race, sex, religion, etc.

The Board next asserts that the regulated speech lacks First Amendment value because it is unlikely to form any part of a dialogue or exchange of views and because it does not provide an opportunity for a reply. In *American Booksellers* [*Association, Inc. v. Hudnut,* 771 F.2d 323 (7th Cir. 1985)], the Seventh Circuit addressed and rejected these arguments. . . .

Thirdly, the Board states that the prohibited speech constitutes a kind of verbal assault on the addressee. However, the Supreme Court has already performed a balancing test with respect to speech which inflicts injury and has found it to be worthy of First Amendment protection. Accordingly, it would be improper for this Court to find the speech regulated by the UW Rule unprotected based upon its assaultive characteristics.

Finally, the Board argues that the prohibited discriminatory speech lacks First Amendment value because of its tendency to incite reaction. While the Board is correct that the discriminatory speech prohibited by the UW Rule may in many circumstances tend to incite violent reaction, the rule prohibits speech regardless of its tendency to do this. . . . The Supreme Court has clearly defined the category of speech which is unprotected due to its tendency to incite violent reaction. This category of speech is limited to speech which by its very utterance tends to incite an immediate breach of the peace. It would be improper for this Court to expand the Supreme Court's definition of fighting words to include speech which does and speech which does not tend to incite violent reaction.

. . . On the costs side of the balance, the Board of Regents asserts that speech regulated under the UW Rule inflicts great harm since it prevents the universities from meeting several "compelling interests": (1) increasing minority representation; (2) assuring equal educational opportunities; (3) preventing interruption of educational activities; and (4) preserving an orderly and safe campus environment. Each of these asserted compelling interests has substantial difficulties. Accordingly, the costs side, like the benefits side, of the Board's balancing equation fails to support the constitutionality of the UW Rule.

The Board's first asserted compelling interest is increasing minority representation to add to the diversity of the University of Wisconsin System campuses. Increasing diversity is "clearly a constitutionally permissible goal for an institution of higher education." *University of California Regents v. Bakke,* 438 U.S. 265, 311-312 (1978). However, the UW Rule does as much to hurt diversity on Wisconsin campuses as it does to help it. By establishing content-based restrictions on speech, the rule limits the diversity of ideas among students and thereby prevents the "robust exchange of ideas" which intellectually diverse campuses provide. . . .

The Board's second asserted compelling interest is the provision of equal educational opportunities in accordance with the Fourteenth Amendment. . . . However, the Board of Regents presents no evidence that it is not already providing education on equal terms. Any inequality in educational opportunities addressed by the UW Rule is due to the discriminatory activity of students, not University of Wisconsin System employees. Since students are generally not state actors, the Board's Fourteenth Amendment equal protection argument is inapplicable to this case.

The Board's third asserted compelling interest is preventing interruption of educational activities. In support of this assertion, the Board cites a series of Supreme Court cases which permit schools to control the activities of students which interfere with the opportunity of other students to obtain an education. *See Tinker v. Des Moines Indep. Community School Dist.,* [393 U.S. 503 (1969)] . . . *Healy v. James,* [408 U.S. 169 (1972)] . . . *Widmar v. Vincent,* [454 U.S. 263 (§ 1981)]. . . . However, these cases allow time, place and manner restrictions on speech, not restrictions based upon the speech's content. . . .

Moreover, the Board's argument under this asserted compelling interest is inconsistent with the limits of the fighting words doctrine. In its brief, the Board has argued that the UW Rule does not cover speech within the classroom. . . . Accordingly, it has been forced to argue that discriminatory speech interrupts educational opportunities because of its negative psychological effects on students. However, this argument is inconsistent with the fighting words doctrine which leaves protected words which inflict injury.

Finally, the Board asserts that it has a compelling interest in maintaining safety and order on its campuses. In support of this assertion, the Board again argues that speech regulated by the UW Rule is likely to provoke violent reaction. However, as stated above, a substantial portion of the speech regulated by the rule is not likely to provoke such a reaction. Accordingly, this Court must find that the Board's final proposed interest is not compelling.

Because the UW Rule fails under both the fighting words doctrine and the UW System's proposed balancing test, this Court must find the rule overbroad and therefore in violation of the First Amendment.

. . . The Board of Regents argues that this Court should find the UW Rule constitutional because its prohibition of discriminatory speech which creates a hostile environment has parallels in the employment setting. The Board notes that, under Title VII, an employer has a duty to take appropriate corrective action when it learns of pervasive illegal harassment. *See Meritor Savings Bank v. Vinson,* 477 U.S. 57, 72 (1986).

The Board correctly states Title VII law. However, its argument regarding Title VII law has at least three difficulties. First, Title VII addresses employment, not educational settings. Second, even if Title VII governed educational settings, the *Meritor* holding would not apply to this case. The *Meritor* Court held that courts should look to agency principles when determining whether an employer is to be held liable for its employee's actions. . . . Since employees may act as their employer's agents, agency law may hold an employer liable for its employee's actions. In contrast, agency theory would generally not hold a school liable for its students' actions since students normally are not agents of the school. Finally, even if the legal duties set forth in *Meritor* applied to this case, they would not make the UW Rule constitutional. Since Title VII is only a statute, it cannot supersede the requirements of the First Amendment.

. . . In our case, plaintiffs argue that the UW Rule is unconstitutionally vague for two reasons: (1) the phrase "discriminatory comments, epithets or other expressive behavior" and the term "demean" are unduly vague and (2) the rule does not make clear whether the prohibited speech must actually create a hostile educational environment or whether speaker must merely intend to create such an environment. Upon review, it appears that the phrase and term referred to by plaintiff are not unduly vague. However, the rule is ambiguous since it fails to make clear whether the speaker must actually create a hostile educational environment or if he must merely intend to do so.

III. CONCLUSION

... The problems of bigotry and discrimination sought to be addressed here are real and truly corrosive of the educational environment. But freedom of speech is almost absolute in our land and the only restriction the fighting words doctrine can abide is that based on the fear of violent reaction. Content-based prohibitions such as that in the UW Rule, however well intended, simply cannot survive the screening which our Constitution demands.

Based on the above, this Court GRANTS plaintiffs' motion for summary judgment and DENIES the Board of Regents' motion for summary judgment. Accordingly, this Court ORDERS: (1) that a declaratory judgment be entered that the UW Rule on its face violates the overbreadth doctrine and is unduly vague; (2) that the Board of Regents and its agents and employees are permanently enjoined from enforcing the UW Rule and (3) that the Board of Regents is required to vacate the disciplinary action taken against plaintiff John Doe under the UW Rule and to expunge from his file all records related to that action.

So ordered.

Suggested Readings

Baer, J. A. (1983). *Equality under the Constitution: Reclaiming the Fourteenth Amendment.* Ithaca, NY: Cornell University Press.

Baker, R. (1964). *Following the color line.* New York: Harper Torchbooks.

Bardolph, R. (1970). *The civil rights record.* New York: Thomas Y. Crowell.

Barker, L. J., & Barker, T. W., Jr. (1994). *Civil liberties and the Constitution: Cases and commentaries* (7th ed.). Englewood Cliffs, NJ: Prentice Hall.

Bass, J. (1981). *Unlikely heroes.* New York: Simon & Schuster.

Bell, D. (1987). *And we are not saved: The elusive quest for racial justice.* New York: Basic Books.

Bell, D. (1992a). *Faces at the bottom of the well: The permanence of racism.* New York: Basic Books.

Bell, D. (1992b). *Race, racism, and American law* (3rd ed.). Boston: Little, Brown.

Berry, M. F. (1994). *Black Americans, white law: A history of Constitutional racism in America.* New York: Penguin Books.

Bickel, A. (1955). The original understanding of the segregation decision. *Harvard Law Review, 69,* 1-65.

Binion, G. (1982). The disadvantaged before the Burger Court: The newest unequal protection. *Law and Policy Quarterly, 4,* 37-69.

Black, C. L., Jr. (1967). Foreword: State action, equal protection, and California's Proposition 14. *Harvard Law Review, 81,* 69-109.

Blaustein, A. P., & Ferguson, C. C. (1957). *Desegregation and the law.* New Brunswick, NJ: Rutgers University Press.

Brisbane, R. (1970). *The black vanguard: Origins of the Negro social revolution, 1900-1960.* Valley Forge, PA: Judson.

Bromley, D., & Longino, C. (1972). *White racism and black Americans.* Cambridge, MA: Schenkman.

Brudno, B. (1976). *Poverty, inequality, and the law.* St. Paul, MN: West.

Bullock, C. S., & Lamb, C. M. (1984). *Implementation of civil rights policy.* Belmont, CA: Brooks/Cole.

Bumiller, K. (1988). *The civil rights society: The social construction of victims.* Baltimore: Johns Hopkins University Press.

Carr, R. K. (1947). *Federal protection of civil rights.* Ithaca, NY: Cornell University Press.

Carter, S. L. (1991). *Reflections of an affirmative action baby.* New York: Basic Books.

Chafe, W. (1980). *Civilities and civil rights.* New York: Oxford University Press.

Crenshaw, K. W. (1988). Race, reform, and retrenchment: Transformation and legitimation in antidiscrimination law. *Harvard Law Review, 101,* 1331-1387.

Curtin, P. (1969). *The Atlantic slave trade: A census.* Madison: University of Wisconsin Press.

Davidson, C. (Ed.). (1984). *Minority vote dilution.* Washington, DC: Howard University Press.

Davis, M. D., & Clark, H. R. (1992). *Thurgood Marshall: Warrior at the bar, rebel on the bench.* New York: Birch Lane.

DuBois, W. E. B. (1903). *The souls of black folk.* Chicago: A. C. McClury.

Eastland, T., & Bennett, W. J. (1979). *Counting by race.* New York: Basic Books.

Eisenberg, T. (1981). *Civil rights.* Charlottesville, VA: Michie.

Fehrenbacher, D. E. (1978). *The* Dred Scott *case: Its significance in American law and politics.* New York: Oxford University Press.

Finch, M. (1981). *The NAACP: Its fight for justice.* Metuchen, NJ: Scarecrow.

Fiss, O. (1976). Groups and the equal protection clause. *Philosophy and Public Affairs, 5,* 107-177.

Fitt, A. (1977, October). In search of a just outcome. *Change,* pp. 22-25, 59.

Foner, P. (1950). *The life and writings of Frederick Douglass.* New York: International Publishers.

Franklin, J. H. (1974). *From slavery to freedom: A history of Negro Americans.* New York: Knopf.

Franklin, J. H. (1976). *Racial equality in America.* Chicago: University of Chicago Press.

Goodell, W. (1969). *The American slave code in theory and practice.* New York: New American Library.

Graham, H. D. (1990). *The civil rights era.* New York: Oxford University Press.

Greenberg, J. (1959). *Race relations and American law.* New York: Columbia University Press.

Greenberg, J. (1968). The Supreme Court, civil rights, and civil dissonance. *Yale Law Journal, 77,* 1520-1544.

Greenberg, J. (1994). *Crusaders in the courts: How a dedicated band of lawyers fought for the civil rights revolution.* New York: Basic Books.

Grotzins, M. (1949). *Americans betrayed: Politics and the Japanese evacuation.* Chicago: University of Chicago Press.

Hall, K. L. (Ed.). (1987). *Race relations and the law in American history.* New York: Garland.

Hamilton, C. V. (1973). *The bench and the ballot: Southern federal judges and black voters.* New York: Oxford University Press.

Harris, R. (1960). *The quest for equality.* Baton Rouge: Louisiana State University Press.

Higginbotham, A. L. (1973). Racism and the early American Academy legal process, 1619-1896. *Annals of the American Academy of Political and Social Science, 407,* 1-17.

Higginbotham, A. L. (1978). *In the matter of color.* New York: Oxford University Press.

Hill, H., & Jones, J. E., Jr. (Eds.). (1993). *Race in America: The struggle for equality.* Madison: University of Wisconsin Press.

Hochschild, J. L. (1984). *The new American dilemma.* New Haven, CT: Yale University Press.

Howard, J. (1971). Why we organize. *Journal of Public Law, 20,* 381-383.

Irons, P. (1990). *The courage of their convictions: Sixteen Americans who fought their way to the Supreme Court.* New York: Penguin.

Jordan, W. (1968). *White over black.* Chapel Hill: University of North Carolina Press.

Karst, K. L. (1989). *Belonging to America: Equal citizenship and the Constitution.* New Haven, CT: Yale University Press.

Kirp, D. L. (1983). *Just schools: The idea of racial equality in American education.* Berkeley: University of California Press.

Kluger, R. (1976). *Simple justice: The history of Brown v. Board of Education and black America's struggle for equality.* New York: Knopf.

Konvitz, M. R. (1961). *Century of civil rights.* New York: Columbia University Press.

Lawson, S. F. (1976). *Black ballots: Voting rights in the South, 1944-1969.* New York: Columbia University Press.

Levy, L. W., Karst, K. L., & Mahoney, D. J. (Eds.). (1989). *Civil rights and equality.* New York: Macmillan.

Lewison, P. (1959). *Race, class, and party: A history of Negro suffrage and white politics in the South.* New York: Grossett & Dunlap.

Matsuda, M. J., Lawrence, C. R., III, Delgado, R., & Crenshaw, K. W. (1993). *Words that wound: Critical race theory, assaultive speech, and the First Amendment.* Boulder, CO: Westview.

McCloskey, R. G. (1960). *The American Supreme Court.* Chicago: University of Chicago Press.

McNiel, G-R. (1983). *Groundwork: Charles Hamilton Huston and the struggle for civil rights.* Philadelphia: University of Pennsylvania Press.

Meier, A. (1963). *Negro thought in America, 1880-1915.* Ann Arbor: University of Michigan Press.

Miller, K. (1908). *Race adjustment: Essays on the Negro American.* New York: Neale.

Moreland, L. (1970). *White racism and the law.* New York: Merrill/Macmillan.

Myrdal, G. (1944). *An American dilemma: The Negro problem and modern democracy.* New York: Harper.

Nieman, D. G. (1991). *Promises to keep: African-Americans and the Constitutional order, 1776 to the present.* New York: Oxford University Press.

Orfield, G. (1978). *Must we bus? Segregated schools and national policy.* Washington, DC: Brookings Institution.

Peltason, J. W. (1961). *Fifty-eight lonely men: Southern federal judges and school desegregation.* New York: Harcourt, Brace & World.

Phillips, U. (1966). *American Negro slavery.* Baton Rouge: Louisiana State University Press.

President's Committee on Civil Rights. (1947). *To secure these rights.* Washington, DC: Government Printing Office.

Quarles, B. (1969). *The Negro in the making of America.* New York: Collier-McMillan.

Rosenberg, G. N. (1991). *The hollow hope: Can courts bring about social change?* Chicago: University of Chicago Press.

Rostow, E. V. (1949). The Japanese American cases: A disaster. *Yale Law Journal, 54,* 489-533.

Sindler, A. P. (1978). *Bakke, DeFunis, and minority admissions: The quest for equal opportunity.* New York: Longman.

Smith, R. (1977). The truth about the *Bakke* case. *Focus, 5,* 3.

Tushnet, M. V. (1981). *The American law of slavery, 1810-1860.* Princeton, NJ: Princeton University Press.

Tushnet, M. V. (1987). *The NAACP's legal strategy against segregated education, 1925-1950.* Chapel Hill: University of North Carolina Press.

Tushnet, M. V. (1994). *Making civil rights law: Thurgood Marshall and the Supreme Court, 1936-1961.* New York: Oxford University Press.

Walton, H., Jr. (1988). *When the marching stopped: The politics of civil rights regulatory agencies.* Albany: SUNY Press.

Westie, F. R. (1965). The American dilemma: An empirical test. *American Sociological Review, 30,* 527-538.

Whalen, C., & Whalen, B. (1985). *The longest debate: A legislative history of the 1964 Civil Rights Act.* Cabin John, MD: Seven Locks.

White, W. F. (1948). *A man called White.* New York: Viking.

Wilkerson, J. (1979). *Harvie. From* Brown *to* Bakke: *The Supreme Court and school integration, 1954-1978.* New York: Oxford University Press.

Wilson, T. B. (1965). *The Black Codes of the South.* Tuscaloosa: University of Alabama Press.

Woodward, C. V. (1974). *The strange career of Jim Crow* (3rd rev. ed.). New York: Oxford University Press.

Index

Abernathy, Ralph David, 131
Affirmative action:
    Burger Court and, 245-250
    Bush administration and, 376
    Clarence Thomas and, 393
    Rehnquist Court and, 268-272, 369, 372-376
    Title VII and, 248
American Civil Liberties Union (ACLU), 258, 377
Annexations, 236, 363-365
Anti-Semitism, 377
Apportionment schemes, 132-134, 228-231,
    237-238, 366-368. *See also* Voting rights
Arab Americans, 376-377
Asian Americans, 20, 77-79
Associations and clubs, 62-63, 65, 267-270
At-large electoral schemes, 229, 232-233,
    235-236, 365-366
Attorney's fees, 150, 376

Bakke, Allan, 247
Baines, Lloyd, 79
Ballot counting fraud, 64
Black, Hugo L., 58
Black Codes, 12
Blackmun, Harry A., 217, 358
Blockbusting, 251

Bork, Robert, 357
Boycotts, 131, 270-271
Bradley, Tom, 396, 402-404
Brandeis, Louis D., 58
Brennan, William J., Jr., 116, 358
Brewer, David, 20
Breyer, Stephen G., 358
Briseno, Theodore, 400
Broadcast licensing, 372
Brown, Henry, 20
Brown cases, 117-126
Burger, Warren E., 217, 356
Burger Court era, xxxiv, xxxvi, 217-272
    affirmative action, 245-250
    boycotts, 271
    death penalty, 257-262
    fair employment-related cases, 238-245
    fair housing cases, 250-257
    jury discrimination, 262-267
    private discrimination, 157-158, 267-270
    school desegregation remedies, 218-228
    vagrancy laws, 271-272
    voting rights, 228-238
Bush, George, 374, 376, 392-393
Busing, 219-221
Butler, Pierce, 58
Byrnes, James F., 59

California Constitution, 252
Capital punishment. *See* Death penalty
Cardozo, Benjamin N., 58
Carter, Jimmy, 220
Chase, Salmon P., 6, 13
Chase Court era, 13-17
Chicago Housing Authority, 254
Child custody, 161
Chinese Americans, 20, 79
Civil remedies for civil rights violations, 157-158
Civil Rights Act of 1866, 12, 153, 376-379
Civil Rights Act of 1875, 13, 19
Civil Rights Act of 1957, 131
Civil Rights Act of 1960, 131
Civil rights Act of 1964, xxxii
    affirmative action and, 248-249
    employment discrimination and, 239-241, 244-245
    private discrimination and, 267
    public accommodations discrimination and, 149-152
    Rehnquist court interpretations, 373-379
    termination of federal funding title, 126
    voting rights title, 132-133
Civil Rights Act of 1968, 153
Civil Rights Act of 1990 (vetoed), 374
Civil Rights Act of 1991, xxxv, 374-376
Civil rights movement, 131-137
    mass demonstrations, 146-149
    sit-ins and peaceful demonstrations, 139-146
Civil War, 10
Clark, Kenneth, 117, 122-124
Clarke, John H., 58
Cleveland, Grover, 20
Clinton, Bill, 358
Coerced confessions, 72-73
Compromise of 1877, 13
Confessions, coerced, 72-73
Congress of Racial Equality, 139
Constitutional Amendments. *See specific Amendments*
Coram nobis, 78
Counsel, right to, 69-71
Countywide voting requirements, 133
Cox, William Harold, 126
Criminal remedies for civil rights violations, 155-157
Cruel and unusual punishment, capital punishment as, 73, 257-260
Curfews, 77-78
Custody, 161

Davis, David, 13
Day, William, 21
Death penalty, 73, 257-262, 382-386. *See also* Jury discrimination
Declaration of Independence, 1-2
De facto segregation concept, 221
Deferential scrutiny, 77
De jure segregation concept, 221
Demonstrations. *See* Protest
Denny, Reginald, 401-403
Desegregation. *See* Public accommodations; School desegregation
Devanter, Willis Van, 57
Douglas, William O., 1, 58
Douglass, Frederick, 21, 138
Due process, xxxii, 11
    exclusionary zoning and, 255-256
    police brutality and, 72-73
    right to counsel, 69-71
    See also Fourteenth Amendment

Education:
    affirmative action, 246-247
    discriminatory private institutions, 226-228
    opportunities for Mexican Americans, 223, 226
    separate-but-equal doctrine, 26, 79-81
    social science evidence, 80-81
    See also School desegregation
Educational requirements, 240
Eisenhower, Dwight D., 116, 119-121
Emancipation Proclamation, 10, 11
Employment-related discrimination:
    affirmative action, 248-250, 368-369, 372-376
    associational rights and, 269
    Burger Court and, 238-245
    Civil Rights Act of 1866 and, 373-374, 376-377
    Civil Rights Act of 1991 and, 374-376
    racial harassment, 373-374
    Rehnquist Court and, 372-377
    standards of proof, 240
    Title VII and, 239-241, 244-245, 248-249, 376-379
    working conditions, 21
Enforcement Act of 1870, 13, 17, 19
Equal Employment Opportunity Commission (EEOC), 239
Equal protection, xxxii, 11
    affirmative action problems, 246-250
    jury selection and, 18-19, 70, 267
    See also Fourteenth Amendment
Extradition, 10

Fair Housing Act of 1968, xxxii, 66, 153, 154, 252, 255
Fair Housing Amendments Act of 1988, 379-382
Federal Communications Commission (FCC), 372
Federal criminal statutes (sections 241 and 242), 155-157
Federalist view of government, xxxiv
Federal Jury Selection and Service Act, 158
Field, Stephen J., 13-14
Fifteenth Amendment, xxxii, 11-12, 60
    Enforcement Act, 13, 17, 19
    state action doctrine, 25, 65
    Waite Court and, 17-18
    See also Voting rights
First Amendment rights:
    group libel laws and, 85
    hate speech versus, 388-392
Footnote 11, 122, 124
Ford, Gerald, 217
Fortas, Abe, 116
Fourteenth Amendment, xxxii, 11
    Brown decision and, 121, 124
    early interpretations, 16, 60
    jury selection and, 18-19
    state action doctrine, 138, 267-268
Frankfurter, Felix, 58
Fugitive Slave Act of 1793, 6
Fugitive Slave Act of 1850, 6, 9
Fuller, Melville W., 20
Fuller Court era, 20-27

Gates, Darryl, 396, 402-405
Gender-related discrimination. *See* Sex discrimination
Gerrymandering, 132, 229, 366-369. *See also* Apportionment schemes
Ginsburg, Ruth Bader, 358
Goldberg, Arthur J., 116
Grandfather clause, 60-61
Green, Malice, 402-403
Group libel laws, 84-85
Guinier, Lani, 366

Habeus corpus petitions, 261, 384
Harassment, 373-374
Harding, Warren G., 58
Harlan, John Marshall, 24
Harlan, John Marshall, II, 116
Harrison, Benjamin, 20
Hasidic Jewish community, 237-238

Hastie, William H., 79
Hate crimes, 385-389
Hate speech, 386-392
    First Amendment rights and, 388-392
    group libel laws, 84-85
Higginbotham, A. Leon, Jr., 153, 396-397
Higher education, 79-81, 361-362
Hill, Anita, 394-396
Hiring practices. *See* Employment-related discrimination
Hispanics, 223, 226, 238
Holmes, Oliver Wendell, 21
Homosexuals, 387-388
Hoover, Herbert, 58
Housing and Urban Development (HUD), 254
Housing discrimination, 66-69, 152-153
    Burger Court and, 250-257
    Rehnquist Court and, 377-380
    standing to sue, 252-254
    Warren Court and, 152-153
Houston, Charles H., 79
Hughes, Charles Evans, 57, 58
Hughes Court era, 58-59, 63-64, 70-71

Insurance redlining, 379-382
Integration. *See* Public accommodations; School desegregation
Intelligence tests, 127
Internment cases, 78
Interracial sexual relationships, 19, 160-161
Interstate commerce and travel, 23, 81, 83, 138, 149-150

Jackson, Andrew, 5
Jackson, Don, 404
Jackson, Howell, 21
Jackson, Robert H., 59, 357
Japanese Americans, 77-78
Jaycees, 270
Jefferson, Thomas, 2
Jewish communities, 237-238
Jim Crow laws, 21-24, 59-60. *See also* Separate-but-equal doctrine
Johnson, Lyndon, 116, 246
Judicial elections, 363-366
Jury discrimination, 70-72
    Burger Court and, 262-267
    civil cases, 385-386
    Fourteenth Amendment interpretations, 18-19
    Fuller Court decisions, 24-25

Hughes Court and, 70-71
Rehnquist Court and, 385-386
Warren Court and, 158-159

Kaiser Aluminum Company, 248
Kennedy, Anthony M., 358
Kennedy, John F., 64, 116, 126, 246
King, Martin Luther, Jr., 131, 138
King, Rodney, 397-403
    and beating of, 397-405
    and civil rights trial, 399-402
    police brutality toward, 403-406
Klanwatch, 387
Koon, Stacey, 400-401
Ku Klux Klan Act of 1871, 13
Kunstler, William, 127

Law enforcement abuses, 72-73, 155-156, 401-405
    coerced confessions, 72
    Rodney King case, 395-401
    vagrancy laws, 271-272
Layoff plans, 249,
    250
Lawrence, Charles R., III, 391-392
Legislative redistricting, 362, 366-369
Lemar, Joseph R., 57
Lending discrimination, 251, 382
Lincoln, Abraham, 10, 13
Literacy tests, 133, 134-135
Lurton, Horace, 21, 57
Lynching, 69

Mandatory death penalty, 260-261
Marshall, John, 3
Marshall, Thurgood, xxxi, 6, 79, 116, 358, 392-393
Marshall Court era, 3-5
Mass demonstrations, 146-149
McKenna, Joseph, 21
McKinley, William, 21
McReynolds, James C., 58
Meese, Edwin, 356
Mexican Americans, 223, 226, 229, 263-265, 238
Military necessity, 78
Miller, Antoine, 399-400
Miller, Reginald, 403-404
Miller, Samuel F., 13
Minority vote dilution, 132-134, 228-238, 366-368
Miscegenation laws, 19, 160-161
Missouri Compromise, 8

Mixed-race marriages, 160-161
Moody, William, 21
Multi-member districts, 228-229, 233, 237, 363-366
Murphy, Frank, 58

National Association for the Advancement of Colored People (NAACP), 57, 64-65, 361, 382
    boycott-related litigation, 271
    Brown case, 117
    death penalty litigation, 258
    higher education and, 361-362
    housing cases, 66
    insurance redlining lawsuit, 382
    opposition to Clarence Thomas appointment, 394
    state attacks on, 128-130
    voting rights cases, 61
National security, 77-78
Nineteenth Amendment, 17
Nixon, Richard, 217, 219
Northwest Ordinance of 1787, 7

O'Connor, Sandra Day, 356

Palmeiri, Dennis, 404
Pannell, Derwin, 403
Parker, John J., 58
Parks, Rosa, 131
Pattern or practice suits, Title VII discrimination, 241
Peckham, Rufus, 20
Peonage Act of 1867, 27
Peremptory challenge, 159, 267, 385-386
Philadelphia Plan, 239
Picketing and mass demonstrations, 146-149
Pitney, Mahlon, 57
Police brutality, 72-73, 395-405. See also Law enforcement abuses
Political party membership, 62-63, 65
Poll tax, 63-64, 135
Powell, Adam Clayton, 132
Powell, Laurence, 400-401
Powell, Lewis F., 357
Primary elections, 61-65
Private schools, 226-228
Promotion practices. See Employment-related discrimination
Property tax, 359

Protest, 131
    boycotts, 131, 270-271
    mass demonstrations, 146-149
    rioting, 69, 72, 85, 148-149, 397, 400, 404
    sit-ins and peaceful demonstrations, 139-146
Public accommodations, 18, 83-84, 138-139
    Civil Rights Act of 1964, 149-152
    private discrimination applications, 268
    sit-ins and demonstrations, 139-146
    Warren Court and, 138-139, 149-152
Public housing, 252, 254, 380-382

Quota systems, 246, 368-373. See also
    Affirmative action

Radio broadcast licensing, 372
Rational basis test, 77
Reagan administration, 356-358
Redistricting, 362, 366-368. See also
    Apportionment schemes
Redlining, 251, 379-382
Reed, Stanley F., 58
Referendums, 252
Rehnquist, William H., 217, 356-357, 394
Rehnquist Court era, xxxiv-xxxv, xxxvi-xxxvii,
    355-405
    affirmative action, 268-272
    death penalty, 383-384
    employment discrimination, 372-377
    hate crimes, 387-389
    hate speech, 387-392
    housing discrimination, 379-382
    jury discrimination, 385-386
    school desegregation, 359-362
    voting rights, xxxv, 362-369
Residence requirements, 226
Restrictive Covenants, 66-69
Reverse discrimination, 246-248, 369, 374. See
    also Affirmative action
Right to counsel, 69-71
Riordan, Richard, 400
Rioting, 69, 72, 85, 148-149, 397, 400, 404
Roberts, Owen J., 58
Roosevelt, Franklin Delano, 58, 246
Roosevelt, Theodore, 21
Rotary Club, 270
Rutledge, Wiley B., 59

Sanford, Edward T., 58
Scalia, Antonin, 357
School desegregation:

Burger Court remedies, 218-228
busing remedies, 219-221
Fourteenth Amendment justification, 121, 124
in the North and West, 221-223
private institutions, 226-228
public colleges and universities, 361-362
Rehnquist Court and, 359-362
resistance and post-Brown litigation, 125-128
social science evidence, 80-81, 121-125
tax-exempt status and, 227-228
temporary remedies, 360
Warren Court and the Brown cases, 117-126
Scottsboro case, 69-71
Segregation, 59-60
    de jure/de facto distinction, 221
    interstate travel, 81, 83
    social science evidence, 80-81
    transportation legislation, 21-24
    See also Public accommodations; School
        desegregation; Separate-but-equal doctrine
Seniority systems, 244-245, 249, 250, 373
Separate-but-equal doctrine, 18, 21-26
    Brown decision and, 121
    public schools and, 26, 79-81
    Truman administration and, 117
Sex discrimination, 16-17, 63-64
    association membership restrictions, 270
    Title VII lawsuits, 373
    wage gap, 239
Shiras, George, 21
Sit-ins and peaceful demonstrations, 139-146
Sixth Amendment, 385-386
Slavery, 1-10
    Constitutional references, 1-2
    fugitive slave laws, 2, 6-7
    peonage system, 27
    prewar contracts, 16
    prohibited by Thirteenth Amendment, 11
    slave trade cases, 3-6
Social science evidence, 80-81, 121-125
Solicitor General, 356
Souter, David H., 358
Southern Christian Leadership Conference
    (SCLC), 131, 394
Southern Manifesto, 125-128
Speech plus issues, 146
State action doctrine, 65, 138, 267-268
Stevens, John Paul, 217
Stewart, Potter, 116
Stone Court era, 59, 77-78, 83
Stone, Harlan Fiske, 59
Sutherland, George, 58
Swayne, Noah H., 13
Swimming facility segregation, 138-139, 268

Taft, William Howard, 21, 57, 58
Taft Court era, 58, 62, 66, 79
Taney, Roger Brooke, 5
Taney Court era, 5-10
Tax-exempt status, 227-228
Television broadcast licensing, 372
Testing, 127, 240
Thirteenth Amendment, 10-11, 26-27
Thomas, Clarence, 358, 368-369, 393-397
Three-Fifths Compromise, 2
Transportation-related segregation, 21-24, 81, 83, 138
Truman, Harry S, 117
Twenty-Fourth Amendment, 135
Tyler, John, 7

Underground railroad, 6
United States Commission on Civil Rights, 355-356
United States Department of Housing and Urban Development (HUD), 254

Vagrancy laws, 271-272
Vinson, Frederick M., 59
Vinson Court era, 59, 65, 79-80, 85
Voir dire examination, 71, 265-266
Voting rights, xxxii, 11-12, 60-66
ballot counting fraud, 64
Burger Court and, 228-238
Civil Rights Act of 1964, 132-133
discriminatory intent standards, 232-233
Fuller Court decisions, 25-26
judicial elections, 363
legislative redistricting, 362, 366-368
literacy tests, 133, 134-135
minority vote dilution, 132-134, 228-238, 366-368
poll taxes, 63-64, 135
primary elections, 61-65
Rehnquist Court and, 362-368
Warren Court and, 131-137
women and, 16-17, 63-64

See also Fifteenth Amendment
Voting Rights Act of 1965, xxxii, 133-135, 228, 234-238, 363-366
1975 extension, 238
1982 Amendments, 233-234, 362

Wage disparities, 239
Waite, Morrison R., 17 Waite Court era, 17-20
Warren, Earl, xxvii, 85, 115-116
Warren Court era, xxxiv, xxxvi, 115-161
desegregation of public accommodations, 138-139, 149-152
housing discrimination, 152-153
jury discrimination, 158-159
mass demonstrations, 146-149
NAACP litigation, 128-130
peaceful demonstrations, 139-146
private infringements of civil rights, 155-157
school desegregation, 117-128
voting rights, 131-137
Washington, Booker T., 21
Waters, Maxine, 400
Watson, Henry, 399
Waugh, Oleatha, 401
West, E. Gordon, 126
White, Byron R., 116, 358
White, Edward D., 20, 57
White Court, 61
Whittaker, Charles, 116
Williams, Damian, 399-400, 404
Wills and trusts, 159-160
Wilmot Proviso, 8
Wilson, Woodrow, 58
Wind, Timothy, 400
Women's rights. *See* Sex discrimination
Working conditions, 21

Young, Coleman, 402-403

Zoning ordinances, 66, 251, 253, 254-256

Table of Cases

Ableman v. Booth, 62 U.S. (21 How.) 506 (1859),   9

Adams v. Richardson, 356 F. Supp. 1159 (1972); aff'd per curiam, 480 F.2d 1159 (1973),   361

Adderley v. Florida, 385 U.S. 39 (1966),   147

ADICKES V. S. H. KRESS & CO., 398 U.S. 144 (1970),   158, **206**

Akins v. Texas, 325 U.S. 398 (1945),   75

Albemarle Paper Co. v. Moody, 422 U.S. 405 (1975),   241

Aldridge v. United States, 238 U.S. 308 (1931),   71

Alexander v. Holmes County Board of Education, 396 U.S. 19 (1969),   218

Alexander v. Louisiana, 405 U.S. 625 (1972),   263

Allen v. State Board of Elections, 393 U.S. 544 (1969),   135

Allen v. Wright, 468 U.S. 737 (1984),   227

American Family Mutual Insurance Co. v. N.A.A.C.P., 978 F.2d 287; cert. denied, 111 S.Ct. 2335 (1993),   379

American Tobacco Company v. Patterson, 456 U.S. 63 (1982),   245

Anderson v. Martin, 375 U.S. 399 (1964),   132

The Antelope, 23 U.S. (10 Wheat.) 66 (1825),   3

Arlington Heights v. Metropolitan Housing Development Corp., 429 U.S. 252 (1977),   254

Arnold v. North Carolina, 376 U.S. 773 (1964),   158

Uppercase indicates excerpted cases. First page number indicates the beginning of in-text discussion cases. Second page number, in bold, indicates beginning of case excerpt.

Astroline Communications Company Limited Partnership v. Shurberg Broadcasting of Hartford, Inc., 497 U.S. 547 (1990), 369

Austin Independent School District v. United States, 429 U.S. 990 (1976), 225

Avent v. North Carolina, 373 U.S. 375 (1963), 141

Avery v. Georgia, 345 U.S. 559 (1953), 71

BAILEY V. ALABAMA, 219 U.S. 219 (1911), 27, **54**

Baker v. Carr, 369 U.S. 186 (1962), 116

Barefoot v. Estelle, 463 U.S. 880 (1983), 261

Barr v. City of Columbia, 378 U.S. 146 (1964), 145

Barrows v. Jackson, 346 U.S. 249 (1953), 68

Bartels v. Iowa, 262 U.S. 404 (1923), 76

Bates v. Little Rock, 361 U.S. 516 (1964), 129

BATSON V. KENTUCKY, 476 U.S. 79 (1986), 267, **346**

Bazemore v. Friday, 478 U.S. 385 (1986), 268

BEAUHARNAIS V. ILLINOIS, 343 U.S. 250 (1952) 85, **110**

Beck v. Alabama, 447 U.S. 625 (1980), 259

Beer v. United States, 425 U.S. 130 (1976), 237

Bell v. Maryland, 378 U.S. 226 (1964), 141

Belton v. Gebhart, 87 A.2d 862 (1952), 162

Benjamin v. Tyler, 273 U.S. 668 (1927), 68

BEREA COLLEGE V. COMMONWEALTH OF KENTUCKY, 211 U.S. 45 (1908), 26, **53**

Blyew v. United States, 80 U.S. (13 Wall.) 581 (1872), 14

Board of Directors of Rotary International v. Rotary Club of Duarte, 481 U.S. 537 (1987), 270

BOARD OF EDUCATION OF OKLAHOMA CITY PUBLIC SCHOOLS V. DOWELL, 498 U.S. 237 (1991), 360, **412**

Board of Trustees of University of North Carolina v. Frazier, 350 U.S. 979 (1956), 118

BOB JONES UNIVERSITY V. UNITED STATES, 461 U.S. 574 (1983), 227, **287**

Bob-Lo Excursion Co. v. Michigan, 333 U.S. 28 (1948), 83

BOLLING V. SHARPE, 347 U.S. 497 (1954), 125, **166**

Bouie v. City of Columbia, 378 U.S. 347 (1964), 146

BOYNTON V. VIRGINIA, 364 U.S. 454 (1960), 138, **176**

Bradwell v. The State of Illinois, 83 U.S. (16 Wall.) 130 (1873), 16

Breedlove v. Suttles, 302 U.S. 277 (1937), 63

Briggs v. Elliott, 98 F. Supp. 529 (1951), 122

Briggs v. Elliott, 103 F. Supp. 920 (1952), 125

Briscoe v. Bell, 432 U.S. 404 (1977), 238

Brown v. Board of Education, 345 U.S. 972 (1953), 120

BROWN V. BOARD OF EDUCATION (Brown I), 347 U.S. 483 (1954), 121, **164**

BROWN V. BOARD OF EDUCATION (Brown II), 349 U.S. 294 (1955), 125, **164**

Brown v. Louisiana, 383 U.S. 131 (1966),   146

Brown v. Mississippi, 297 U.S. 278 (1936),   72

Brown v. State of Mississippi, 6 Race Relations Law Reporter, 780 (1961),   163

BUCHANAN v. WARLEY, 245 U.S. 60 (1917),   66, **91**

Burns v. Richardson, 384 U.S. 73 (1966),   135

BURTON v. WILMINGTON PARKING AUTHORITY, 365 U.S. 715 (1961),   138, **179**

Cameron v. Johnson, 390 U.S. 611 (1968),   148

Carter v. Jury Commission of Greene County, 396 U.S. 320 (1970),   262

Carter v. Texas, 177 U.S. 442 (1900),   24

Carter v. West Feliciana Parish School Board, 396 U.S. 290 (1970),   224

Cassell v. Texas, 339 U.S. 282 (1950),   75

Castaneda v. Partida, 430 U.S. 482 (1977),   263

Chambers v. Florida, 309 U.S. 227 (1940),   72

Chesapeake & Ohio Railway Company v. Kentucky, 179 U.S. 388 (1900),   22

Chiles v. Chesapeake & Ohio Railway Company, 218 U.S. 71 (1910),   23

Chisom v. Roemer, 501 U.S. 380 (1991),   364

City of Eastlake v. Forest City Enterprises, Inc., 426 U.S. 668 (1976),   252

CITY OF MOBILE v. BOLDEN, 446 U.S. 55 (1980),   232, **291**

City of Petersburg v. United States, 410 U.S. 962 (1973),   236

City of Pleasant Grove v. United States, 479 U.S. 462 (1987),   363

City of Port Arthur v. United States, 459 U.S. 159 (1982),   231

CITY OF RICHMOND v. J. A. CROSON CO., 488 U.S. 469 (1989),   372, **430**

City of Richmond v. Deans, 281 U.S. 704 (1930),   68

City of Richmond v. United States, 422 U.S. 358 (1975),   236

City of Rome v. United States, 466 U.S. 156 (1980),   236

CIVIL RIGHTS CASES, 109 U.S. 3 (1883),   19, **46**

Clark v. Roemer, 500 U.S. 646 (1991),   364

Clyatt v. United States, 197 U.S. 207 (1905),   27

Coker v. Georgia, 433 U.S. 584 (1977),   261

Columbus Board of Education v. Penick, 443 U.S. 449 (1979),   222

Commonwealth of Pennsylvania v. Brown, 392 F.2d 120, cert. denied,
   391 U.S. 921 (1968),   159

Connor v. Finch, 431 U.S. 407 (1977),   237

Connor v. Johnson, 402 U.S. 690 (1971),   237

Cooley v. Board of Wardens of Port of Philadelphia, 53 U.S. (12 How.) 229 (1851),   83

Cooper v. Aaron, 385 U.S. 1 (1958),   126

Corrigan v. Buckley, 271 U.S. 323 (1926),   66

COX v. LOUISIANA (Cox I), 379 U.S. 536 (1965),   147, **188**

COX v. LOUISIANA (Cox II), 379 U.S. 559 (1965),   147, **190**

Crawford v. Board of Education of the City of Los Angeles, 458 U.S. 527 (1982),   220
Cumming v. Richmond County Board of Education, 175 U.S. 528 (1899),   26

Daniel v. Louisiana, 420 U.S. 1 (1975),   264
Daniel v. Paul, 395 U.S. 298 (1969),   151
Davis v. Board of School Commissioners of Mobile County, 402 U.S. 33 (1971),   224
Davis v. County School Board of Prince Edward County, 103 F. Supp. 337 (1952),   125
Dawson v. Delaware, 503 U.S. 159 (1992),   381
Dayton Board of Education v. Brinkman (Dayton I), 433 U.S. 406 (1977),   222
Dayton Board of Education v. Brinkman (Dayton II), 443 U.S. 526 (1979),   222
DeFunis v. Odegaard, 416 U.S. 312 (1974),   246
De Jonge v. Oregon, 299 U.S. 353 (1937),   76
Derrington v. Plummer, 240 F.2d 922 (1957); cert. denied sub nom.,
    Casey v. Plummer, 353 U.S. 924 (1957),   140
District of Columbia v. John R. Thompson Co., Inc., 346 U.S. 100 (1953),   84
Doe v. University of Michigan, 721 F. Supp. 852 (1989),   391
Dougherty County Board of Education v. White, 439 U.S. 32 (1978),   235
Dowell v. Board of Education of Oklahoma City Public Schools, 396 U.S. 269 (1969),   224
DRED SCOTT V. SANDFORD, 60 U.S. (19 How.) 393 (1857),   8, **31**

Edmonson v. Leesville Concrete Company, Inc., 500 U.S. 614 (1991),   385
EDWARDS V. SOUTH CAROLINA, 372 U.S. 229 (1963),   146, **186**
EEOC v. Arabian American Oil Company, 499 U.S. 244 (1991),   371
Emporium Capwell Co. v. Western Addition Community Organization, 420 U.S. 50 (1975),   242
Enmund v. Florida, 458 U.S. 782 (1982),   259
Eubanks v. Louisiana, 356 U.S. 584 (1958),   158
Evans v. Abney, 396 U.S. 435 (1970),   160
EVANS V. NEWTON, 382 U.S. 296 (1966),   160, **212**
Ex parte Gordon, 66 U.S. (1 Black) 503 (1861),   5
Ex parte Virginia, 100 U.S. (10 Otto) 339 (1880),   18
Ex parte Yarbrough, 110 U.S. 651 (1884),   19

Farrington v. Tokushige, 273 U.S. 284 (1927),   7
Fazzio Real Estate Co., Inc. v. Adams, 396 F.2d 146 (1968),   151
Feiner v. New York, 340 U.S. 315 (1951),   148
Firefighters v. Cleveland, 478 U.S. 501 (1986),   249
Firefighters v. Stotts, 467 U.S. 561 (1984),   249
Fisher v. Hurst, 333 U.S. 147 (1948),   79
Fiske v. Kansas, 274 U.S. 380 (1927),   76
Florida ex rel. Hawkins v. Board of Control of Florida, 347 U.S. 971 (1954),   118
Ford v. Georgia, 498 U.S. 411 (1991),   383

Ford v. Wainwright, 477 U.S. 399 (1986),   262

Fortson v. Dorsey, 379 U.S. 4 (1965),   133

Francis College v. Al-Khazraji, 481 U.S. 604 (1987),   379

Franks v. Bowman Transportation Co., Inc., 424 U.S. 747 (1976),   245

FREEMAN V. PITTS, 112 S.Ct. 1430 (1992),   361, **414**

FULLILOVE V. KLUTZNICK, 448 U.S. 448 (1980),   248, **320**

FURMAN V. GEORGIA, 408 U.S. 238 (1972),   259, **338**

Furnco Construction Corp. v. Waters, 438 U.S. 567 (1978),   243

GARNER V. LOUISIANA, 368 U.S. 157 (1961),   139, **181**

Gaston County, North Carolina v. United States, 395 U.S. 285 (1969),   135

Gayle v. Browder, 352 U.S. 903 (1956),   140

Georgia v. McCollum, 112 S.Ct. 2348 (1992),   386

Georgia v. United States, 411 U.S. 526 (1973),   227

Gibson v. Florida Legislative Investigation Committee, 372 U.S. 539 (1963),   129

Gideon v. Wainwright, 372 U.S. 335 (1963),   116

Giles v. Harris, 189 U.S. 475 (1903),   25

Gilmore v. City of Montgomery, Alabama, 417 U.S. 556 (1974),   227

Gitlow v. New York, 268 U.S. 652 (1925),   76

Gladstone, Realtors v. Village of Bellwood, 441 U.S. 91 (1979),   253

Gober v. City of Birmingham, 373 U.S. 374 (1963),   141

Goldsboro Christian Schools, Inc. v. United States, 461 U.S. 574 (1983),   227

GOMILLION V. LIGHTFOOT, 364 U.S. 339 (1960),   132, **172**

Gong Lum v. Rice, 275 U.S. 78 (1927),   79

Goss v. Board of Education, 373 U.S. 683 (1963),   127

GREEN V. COUNTY SCHOOL BOARD OF NEW KENT COUNTY,
   391 U.S. 430 (1968),   128, **168**

Gregg v. Georgia, 428 U.S. 153 (1976),   260

Gregory v. City of Chicago, 394 U.S. 111 (1969),   148

GRIFFIN V. BRECKENRIDGE, 403 U.S. 88 (1971),   157, **204**

Griffin v. Maryland, 378 U.S. 130 (1964),   145

Griffin v. Prince Edward County School Board, 377 U.S. 218 (1964),   127

GRIGGS V. DUKE POWER CO., 401 U.S. 424 (1971),   240, **304**

Grosjean v. American Press Co., 297 U.S. 233 (1936),   76

Groves v. Slaughter, 40 U.S. (15 Pet.) 449 (1841),   5

GROVEY V. TOWNSEND, 295 U.S. 45 (1935),   63, **87**

Growe v. Emison, 113 S.Ct. 1075 (1993),   364

Guinn v. United States, 238 U.S. 347 (1915),   60

Hale v. Kentucky, 303 U.S. 613 (1938),   70

HALL v. DeCUIR, 95 U.S. 485 (1878),   18, **40**

Hamm v. South Carolina, 409 U.S. 524 (1973),   265

Hamilton v. Alabama, 376 U.S. 650 (1964),   155

HAMM v. CITY OF ROCK HILL, 379 U.S. 306 (1964),   145, **184**

Harper v. Virginia Board of Elections, 383 U.S. 663 (1966),   135

Harrison v. NAACP, 360 U.S. 167 (1959),   128

Harry Roberts v. Louisiana, 431 U.S. 633 (1977),   261

HAVENS REALTY CORP. v. COLEMAN, 455 U.S. 363 (1982),   254, **330**

Hazelwood School District v. United States, 433 U.S. 299 (1977),   241

HEART OF ATLANTA MOTEL, INC. v. UNITED STATES, 379 U.S. 241 (1964),   149, **195**

Henderson v. United States, 339 U.S. 816 (1950),   83

Hernandez v. New York, 500 U.S. 352 (1991),   383

Herndon v. Lowry, 301 U.S. 242 (1937),   76

Herrera v. Collins, 113 S.Ct. 853 (1993),   384

Hill v. Texas, 316 U.S. 400 (1942),   71

Hills v. Gautreaux, 425 U.S. 284 (1976),   254

Hirabayashi v. United States, 320 U.S. 81 (1943),   77

Hishon v. King & Spalding, 467 U.S. 69 (1984),   269

Hobsen v. Hansen, 269 F. Supp. 401 (1967),   127

Hodges v. United States, 203 U.S. 1 (1906),   26

Holder v. Hall, 114 S.Ct. 2581 (1994),   368

Holland v. Illinois, 493 U.S. 474 (1990),   382

Hollins v. Oklahoma, 295 U.S. 394 (1935),   70

Holmes v. City of Atlanta, 350 U.S. 879 (1955),   140

Houston Lawyers' Association v. Attorney General of Texas, 501 U.S. 419 (1991),   364

HUNTER v. ERICKSON, 393 U.S. 385 (1969),   153, **200**

Hurd v. Hodge, 344 U.S. 24 (1948),   68

Independent Federation of Flight Attendants v. Zipes, 491 U.S. 754 (1989),   376

Iota Xi Chapter of Sigma Chi Fraternity v. George Mason University, 993 F.2d 386 (1993),   391

James v. Bowman, 190 U.S. 127 (1903),   25

James v. Valtierra, 402 U.S. 137 (1971),   252

Johnson v. DeGrandy, 114 S.Ct. 2647 (1994),   365

Johnson v. Railway Express Agency, 421 U.S. 454 (1975),   241

Johnson v. Virginia, 373 U.S. 61 (1963),   155

JONES v. ALFRED H. MAYER CO., 392 U.S. 409 (1968),   153, **197**

Jurek v. Texas, 428 U.S. 262 (1976),   260

Katzenbach v. McClung, 379 U.S. 294 (1964),   149

Katzenbach v. Morgan, 384 U.S. 641 (1966),   135
Keeney v. Tamayo-Reyes, 504 U.S. 1 (1992),   381
Kentucky v. Dennison, 65 U.S. (24 How.) 66 (1861),   10
KEYES V. SCHOOL DISTRICT NO. 1, DENVER, COLORADO, 413 U.S. 189 (1973),   221, **281**
Kolender v. Lawson, 461 U.S. 352 (1983)272
KOREMATSU V. UNITED STATES, 323 U.S. 214 (1944),   77, **100**

LaGrange v. Chouteau, 29 U.S. (4 Pet.) 287 (1830),   4
Landgraf v. USI Film Products, 114 S.Ct. 1483 (1994),   377
Lane v. Wilson, 307 U.S. 268 (1939),   61
Lassiter v. Northampton County Board of Elections, 360 U.S. 45 (1959),   134
Laufmann v. Oakley Building and Loan Company, 408 F. Supp. 489 (1976),   251
League of United Latin American Citizens v. Attorney General of Texas,
    111 S.Ct. 2376 (1991),   364
Lindsey v. Normet, 405 U.S. 56 (1972),   256
Lochner v. New York, 198 U.S. 45 (1905),   21
Lockett v. Ohio, 438 U.S. 586 (1978),   258
Lombard v. Louisiana, 373 U.S. 267 (1963),   139
Lorance v. AT&T Technologies, Inc., 490 U.S. 900 (1989),   374
Louisiana v. United States, 380 U.S. 145 (1965),   134
LOUISIANA EX REL. FRANCIS V. RESWEBER, 329 U.S. 459 (1947),   73, **98**
Louisiana ex rel. Gremillion v. NAACP, 366 U.S. 293 (1961),   129
Louisville, New Orleans & Texas Railway Co. v. Mississippi, 133 U.S. 587 (1890),   23
Love v. Griffith, 266 U.S. 32 (1924),   62
Lovell v. City of Griffin, 303 U.S. 444 (1938),   76
LOVING V. VIRGINIA, 388 U.S. 1 (1967),   161, **214**
Lucy v. Adams, 350 U.S. 1 (1955),   118
Lupper v. Arkansas, 379 U.S. 306 (1964),   145
Lyons v. Oklahoma, 322 U.S. 596 (1944),   73

Martin v. Texas, 200 U.S. 316 (1906),   24
Martin v. Wilks, 490 U.S. 755 (1989),   374
Martinez v. Bynum, 461 U.S. 321 (1983),   226
Mayor and City Council of Baltimore City v. Dawson, 350 U.S. 877 (1955),   140
McCabe v. Atchison, Topeka & Santa Fe Railway Company, 235 U.S. 151 (1914),   81
McCLESKEY V. KEMP, 481 U.S. 279 (1987),   382, **445**
McCleskey v. Zant, 499 U.S. 467 (1991),   384
McCulloch v. Maryland, 17 U.S. (4 Wheat.) 316 (1819),   76
McDaniel v. Barresi, 402 U.S. 39 (1971),   224
McDaniel v. Sanchez, 452 U.S. 130 (1981),   231

McDonald v. Santa Fe Trail Transportation Co., 427 U.S. 273 (1976), 241

McDonnell Douglas Corp. v. Green, 411 U.S. 792 (1973), 240

McGautha v. California, 402 U.S. 183 (1971), 259

McGhee v. Sipes, 334 U.S. 1 (1948), 66

McLaughlin v. Florida, 379 U.S. 184 (1964), 160

McLAURIN V. OKLAHOMA STATE REGENTS FOR HIGHER EDUCATION, 339 U.S. 637 (1950), 80, **105**

M'Cutchen v. Marshall, 33 U.S. (8 Pet.) 220 (1834), 3

MEMPHIS V. GREENE, 451 U.S. 100 (1981), 257, **335**

257, 335*Menard v. Aspasia,* 30 U.S. (5 Pet.) 505 (1831), 4

METRO BROADCASTING, INC. V. FCC, 497 U.S. 547 (1990), 372, **424**

Metropolitan County Board of Education of Nashville and Davidson County v. Kelley, 459 U.S. 1183 (1983), 220

Metropolitan School District v. Buckley, 429 U.S. 1068 (1977), 225

Meyer v. Nebraska, 262 U.S. 390 (1923), 76

MILLIKEN V. BRADLEY (Milliken I), 418 U.S. 717 (1974), 219, **277**

Milliken v. Bradley (Milliken II), 433 U.S. 267 (1977), 223

Minor v. Happersett, 88 U.S. (21 Wall.) 163 (1875), 16

Missouri v. Jenkins, 495 U.S. 33 (1990), 359

MISSOURI EX REL. GAINES V. CANADA, 305 U.S. 337 (1938), 79, **103**

MITCHELL V. UNITED STATES, 313 U.S. 80 (1941), 83, **107**

MOORE V. CITY OF EAST CLEVELAND, 431 U.S. 494 (1977), 255, **333**

Moore v. Dempsey, 261 U.S. 86 (1923), 72

Moore v. Illinois, 55 U.S. (14 How.) 13 (1852), 4

Moose Lodge No. 107 v. Irvis, 407 U.S. 163 (1972), 267

MORGAN V. VIRGINIA, 328 U.S. 373 (1946), 83, **108**

Muir v. Louisville Park Theatrical Association, 347 U.S. 971 (1954), 140

NAACP v. Alabama ex rel. Flowers, 377 U.S. 288 (1964), 124

NAACP V. ALABAMA EX REL. PATTERSON, 357 U.S. 449 (1958), 128, **169**

NAACP v. Button, 371 U.S. 415 (1963), 130

NAACP V. CLAIBORNE HARDWARE CO., 458 U.S. 886 (1982), 271, **350**

NAACP v. Overstreet, 384 U.S. 118 (1966), 130

Naim v. Naim, 197 Va. 80 (1955), 160

Neal v. Delaware, 103 U.S. (13 Otto) 370 (1880), 18

Near v. Minnesota ex rel. Olson, 283 U.S. 697 (1931), 76

Newberry v. United States, 256 U.S. 232 (1921), 61

Newman v. Piggie Park Enterprises, Inc., 390 U.S. 400 (1968), 150

New Orleans City Park Improvement Association v. Ditiege, 358 U.S. 54 (1958), 140

New York State Club Association, Inc. v. City of New York, 487 U.S. 1 (1988), 270

Nixon v. Condon, 286 U.S. 73 (1932),   62

NIXON v. HERNDON, 273 U.S. 536 (1927),   62, **86**

Norris v. Alabama, 294 U.S. 587 (1935),   70

North Carolina State Board of Education v. Swann, 402 U.S. 43 (1971),   224

Northeastern Florida Contractors v. Jacksonville,
    113 S.Ct. 2297 (1993),   371

Norwood v. Harrison, 413 U.S. 455 (1973),   227

Osborn v. Nicholson, 80 U.S. (13 Wall.) 654 (1872),   16

PACE v. ALABAMA, 106 U.S. 583 (1883),   19, **43**

Palmer v. Thompson, 403 U.S. 217 (1971),   138

Palmore v. Sidote, 466 U.S. 429 (1984),   161

Papachristou v. City of Jacksonville, 405 U.S. 156 (1972),   271

Pasadena City Board of Education v. Spangler, 427 U.S. 424 (1976),   221

PATTERSON v. McLEAN CREDIT UNION, 491 U.S. 164 (1989),   376, **440**

Patton v. Mississippi, 332 U.S. 463 (1947),   71

Payne v. Tennessee, 501 U.S. 808 (1991),   381

Pennsylvania v. Board of Directors of City Trusts of the City of Philadelphia,
    353 U.S. 230 (1957),   159

Perkins v. Matthews, 400 U.S. 379 (1971),   235

Peters v. Kiff, 407 U.S. 493 (1972),   263

Peterson v. City of Greenville, 373 U.S. 244 (1963),   139

Pierce v. Society of Sisters, 268 U.S. 510 (1925),   76

Pierre v. Louisiana, 306 U.S. 354 (1939),   71

PLESSY v. FERGUSON, 163 U.S. 537 (1896),   24, **50**

Plyler v. Doe, 457 U.S. 202 (1982),   223

POWELL v. ALABAMA, 287 U.S. 45 (1932),   69, **94**

POWERS v. OHIO, 499 U.S. 400 (1991),   385, **449**

PRESLEY v. ETOWAH COUNTY COMMISSION,
    502 U.S. 491 (1992),   336, **422**

Price Waterhouse v. Hopkins, 490 U.S. 228 (1989),   374

PRIGG v. THE COMMONWEALTH OF PENNSYLVANIA, 41 U.S. (16 Pet.) 539 (1842),   6, **28**

Proffitt v. Florida, 428 U.S. 242 (1976),   260

Pulley v. Harris, 465 U.S. 37 (1984),   262

Pullman-Standard v. Swint, 456 U.S. 273 (1982),   245

Queen v. Hepburn, 11 U.S. (7 Cranch) 290 (1813),   3

R.A.V. v. CITY OF ST. PAUL, MINNESOTA, 112 S.Ct. 2538 (1992),   388, **451**

Reed v. Reed, 404 U.S. 71 (1971),   17

REGENTS OF THE UNIVERSITY OF CALIFORNIA V. BAKKE, 438 U.S. 265 (1978), 247, **309**

Reitman v. Mulkey, 387 U.S. 369 (1967), 152

Reynolds v. Sims, 377 U.S. 533 (1964), 228

Ristaino v. Ross, 424 U.S. 589 (1976), 266

Rivers v. Roadway Express, Inc., 114 S.Ct. 1510 (1994), 377

Roberts v. United States Jaycees, 468 U.S. 609 (1984), 270

Robinson v. Florida, 378 U.S. 153 (1964), 146

Roe v. Wade, 410 U.S. 113 (1973), 394

Rogers v. Alabama, 192 U.S. 226 (1904), 22

Rogers v. Lodge, 458 U.S. 613 (1982), 232

Rosales-Lopez v. United States, 451 U.S. 182 (1981), 266

Rousseve v. Shape Spa for Health and Beauty, Inc., 516 F.2d 64 (1975), 151

RUNYON V. McCRARY, 427 U.S. 160 (1976), 226, **284**

St. Francis College v. Al-Khazraji, 481 U.S. 604 (1987), 377

St. Mary's Honor Center v. Hicks, 113 S.Ct. 2742 (1993), 377

San Antonio Independent School District v. Rodriguez, 411 U.S. 1 (1973), 223

Scott v. Negro Ben, 10 U.S. (6 Cranch) 3 (1810), 3

Scott v. Negro London, 7 U.S. (3 Cranch) 324 (1806), 3

SCREWS V. UNITED STATES, 325 U.S. 91 (1945), 73, **96**

Shaare Tefila Congregation v. Cobb, 481 U.S. 615 (1987), 379

SHAW V. RENO, 113 S.Ct. 2816 (1993), 367, **425**

Sheet Metal Workers v. EEOC, 478 U.S. 421 (1986), 249

SHELLEY V. KRAEMER, 334 U.S. 1 (1948), 66, **35**

Shelton v. Tucker, 364 U.S. 479 (1964), 130

Shuttlesworth v. City of Birmingham, 373 U.S. 262 (1963), 141

Sipuel v. Board of Regents of the University of Oklahoma, 332 U.S. 631 (1948), 79

SLAUGHTER-HOUSE CASES, 83 U.S. (16 Wall.) 36 (1873), 16, **35**

The Slavers, 69 U.S. 350 (2 Wall.) (1864), 5

SMITH V. ALLWRIGHT, 321 U.S. 649 (1944), 64, **89**

Smith v. Texas, 311 U.S. 128 (1940), 71

Smuck v. Hansen, 408 F.2d 175 (1969), 163

SOUTH CAROLINA V. KATZENBACH, 383 U.S. 301 (1966), 134, **173**

South Carolina State Highway Dept. v. Barnwell Brothers, 303 U.S. 177 (1938), 76

SPALLONE V. UNITED STATES, 493 U.S. 265 (1990), 380, **443**

Stanislaus Roberts v. Louisiana, 428 U.S. 325 (1976), 261

Stell v. Savannah-Chatham County Board of Education, 333 F.2d 55 (1964), 127

Strader v. Graham, 51 U.S. (10 How.) 82 (1851), 7

STRAUDER V. WEST VIRGINIA, 100 U.S. 303 (1880), 18, **42**

Street v. New York, 394 U.S. 576 (1969), 148

Stromberg v. California, 283 U.S. 359 (1931),   76

Sullivan v. Little Hunting Park, Inc., 396 U.S. 229 (1969),   153

SWAIN V. ALABAMA, 380 U.S. 202 (1965),   159, **210**

SWANN V. CHARLOTTE-MECKLENBURG BOARD OF EDUCATION,
   402 U.S. 1 (1971),   219, **274**

SWEATT V. PAINTER, 339 U.S. 629 (1950),   80, **106**

Tancil v. Woolls, 379 U.S. 19 (1964),   132

Taylor v. Louisiana, 370 U.S. 154 (1962),   142

Taylor v. Louisiana, 419 U.S. 522 (1975),   264

Teamsters v. United States, 431 U.S. 324 (1977),   244

Terry v. Adams, 345 U.S. 461 (1953),   65

Texas Department of Community Affairs v. Burdine, 450 U.S. 248 (1981),   240

Thomas v. Texas, 212 U.S. 278 (1909)23

THORNBURG V. GINGLES, 478 U.S. 30 (1986),   233, **295**

Tillman v. Wheaton-Haven Recreation Assn., Inc., 410 U.S. 431 (1973),   268

Tureaud v. Board of Supervisors of Louisiana State University, 347 U.S. 971 (1954),   118

Turner v. City of Memphis, 369 U.S. 350 (1962),   138

Turner v. Fouche, 396 U.S. 346 (1970),   264

Turner v. Murray, 476 U.S. 28 (1986),   265

UNITED JEWISH ORGANIZATIONS, INC. v. CAREY, 430 U.S. 144 (1977),   237, **301**

United States v. The Amistad, 40 U.S. (15 Pet.) 518 (1841),   5

United States v. Board of Commissioners of Sheffield, Alabama, 435 U.S. 110 (1978),   235

United States v. Carolene Products Co., 304 U.S. 144 (1938),   76

United States v. Classic, 313 U.S. 299 (1941),   64

United States v. Cruikshank, 92 U.S. (2 Otto) 542 (1876),   17

UNITED STATES V. FORDICE, 112 S.Ct. 2727 (1992),   361, **418**

United States v. Gooding, 25 U.S. (12 Wheat.) 460 (1827),   4

UNITED STATES V. GUEST, 383 U.S. 745 (1966),   155, **201**

UNITED STATES V. HARRIS, 106 U.S. 629 (1883),   19, **44**

United States v. Johnson, 390 U.S. 563 (1968),   156

United States v. Koon, 34 F.3d 1416 (1994),   401

United States v. Paradise, 480 U.S. 149 (1987),   369

United States v. Price, 383 U.S. 787 (1966),   155

UNITED STATES V. REESE, 92 U.S. (2 Otto) 214 (1876),   18, **38**

United States v. Reynolds, 235 U.S. 133 (1914),   27

United States Postal Service Board of Governors v. Aikens, 460 U.S. 711 (1983),   240

UNITED STEELWORKERS OF AMERICA V. WEBER, 443 U.S. 193 (1979),   248, **317**

University of Pennsylvania v. EEOC, 493 U.S. 182 (1990),   371

UWM POST, INC. v. BOARD OF REGENTS OF THE UNIVERSITY OF WISCONSIN SYSTEM, 774 F. Supp. 1163 (1991), 390, **456**

Virginia v. Rives, 100 U.S. (13 Otto) 313 (1880), 18
Virginia Board of Elections v. Hamm, 379 U.S. 19 (1964), 132
Voinovich v. Quilter, 113 S.Ct. 1149 (1993), 366

WALKER v. CITY OF BIRMINGHAM, 388 U.S. 307 (1967), 148, **192**
WARDS COVE PACKING CO., INC. v. ATONIO, 490 U.S. 642 (1989), 373, **437**
WARTH v. SELDIN, 422 U.S. 490 (1975), 253, **328**
WASHINGTON v. DAVIS, 426 U.S. 229 (1976), 240, **306**
Washington v. Seattle School District No. 1, 458 U.S. 457 (1982), 220
Watson v. City of Memphis, 373 U.S. 526 (1963), 141
Watson v. Fort Worth Bank and Trust, 487 U.S. 977 (1988), 370
West Coast Hotel Co. v. Parrish, 300 U.S. 379 (1937), 58
West Virginia University Hospitals v. Casey, 499 U.S. 83 (1991), 371
Wharton Jones v. John Van Zandt, 46 U.S. (5 How.) 215 (1847), 6
Whitcomb v. Chavis, 403 U.S. 124 (1971), 229
White v. Regester, 412 U.S. 755 (1973), 229
Whitney v. California, 274 U.S. 357 (1927), 76
Whitus v. Georgia, 385 U.S. 545 (1967), 158
Williams v. Mississippi, 170 U.S. 213 (1898), 24
WISCONSIN v. MITCHELL, 1135 S.Ct. 2194 (1993), 388, **454**
Wood v. Davis, 11 U.S. (7 Cranch) 271 (1812), 3
Woodson v. North Carolina, 428 U.S. 280 (1976), 260
Wright v. Council of Emporia, 407 U.S. 451 (1972), 219
Wright v. Georgia, 373 U.S. 284 (1963), 141
Wright v. Rockefeller, 376 U.S. 52 (1964), 132
Wright v. West, 112 S.Ct. 2482 (1992), 381
WYGANT v. JACKSON BOARD OF EDUCATION, 476 U.S. 267 (1986), 250, **324**

YICK WO v. HOPKINS, 118 U.S. 356 (1886), 20, **48**

Zimmer v. McKeithen, 485 F.2d 1297 (1973), 229

About the Authors

Abraham L. Davis is Professor of Political Science at Morehouse College in Atlanta, Georgia, where he teaches courses in constitutional law, civil liberties, and American government. He received his B.A. in political science from Morehouse College and his M. S. and Ph.D. degrees in political science from the University of Wisconsin and Ohio State University, respectively. He has been a Visiting Professor at Ohio Dominican College, Emory University, Texas Tech University, North Carolina A&T State University, and the University of Wisconsin at Madison. His books include *The Supreme Court and the Uses of Social Science Data* (1973) and *Blacks in the Federal Judiciary: Neutral Arbiters or Judicial Activists?* (1989). His articles have appeared in *Harvard BlackLetter Journal, Review of Black Political Economy, Journal of Negro History, Western Journal of Black Studies, Social Science Perspectives Journal,* and *National Political Science Review.*

Barbara Luck Graham is Associate Professor of Political Science at the University of Missouri in St. Louis, where she teaches courses in constitutional law, the judicial process, and American government. She received her B.A. in political science from Virginia State University and her Ph.D. in political science from Washington University in St. Louis. Some of her research projects have focused on Supreme Court policy making and civil rights, judicial selection and black representation on state courts, and the uses of legislative history by the Supreme Court. She has published articles in such publications as *Political Research Quarterly, American Politics Quarterly, Judicature,* and *National Political Science Review.*